ALAI Congress 2015/
Conference Proceedings
Congrès de l'ALAI 2015/
Actes de la Conférence

Silke von Lewinski (*Ed.*/*Éd.*)

Remuneration for the Use of Works
La Rémunération de l'Utilisation des Œuvres

Exclusivity vs. Other Approaches
Exclusivité c. autres approches

DE GRUYTER

ISBN 978-3-11-045001-9
e-ISBN 978-3-11-047819-8

Bibliografische Information der Deutschen Nationalbibliothek
Die Deutsche Nationalbibliothek verzeichnet diese Publikation in der Deutschen Nationalbibliografie; detaillierte bibliografische Daten sind im Internet über http://dnb.d-nb.de abrufbar.

Gedruckt mit Unterstützung des Förderungsfonds Wissenschaft der VG Wort.

Datenkonvertierung und Satz: jürgen ullrich typosatz, 86720 Nördlingen
Druck und Bindung: Hubert & Co. GmbH & Co. KG, Göttingen
♾ Gedruckt auf säurefreiem Papier
Printed in Germany

www.degruyter.com

Editor's Note

This book incorporates the proceedings of the International Congress of the International Literary and Artistic Association (ALAI) 2015 on the topic "Remuneration for the Use of Works – Exclusivity vs. Other Approaches", held in Bonn from June 18 to 19 and organized by the German ALAI group, ALAI Deutschland e.V. Most of the contributions have been kept as they were delivered in June 2015; only very few were updated, especially where the relevant topic was directly affected by a major new development.

Following the 2015 ALAI Congress in Bonn, the Executive Committee of ALAI, at its meeting in Rome on September 14, 2016, has unanimously adopted a resolution on the topic discussed in Bonn. This resolution, which is also available at the www.alai.org website, has been reprinted in Annex 2 of this volume.

Silke von Lewinski, 20 October 2016

Note de l'éditeur

Ce livre contient les actes du congrès international de l'Association Littéraire et Artistique Internationale (ALAI) 2015 sur "La rémunération de l'utilisation des œuvres – Exclusivité c. autres approches" – congrès tenu à Bonn du 18 au 19 Juin 2015 et organisé par le groupe allemand de l'ALAI, ALAI Deutschland e.V. La plupart des contributions ont été gardées comme elles étaient fournies en juin 2015; seulement très peu d'entre elles ont été mises à jour, en particulier quand le sujet était directement affecté par un nouveau développement majeur.

À la suite du congrès de Bonn de l'ALAI 2015, le Comité exécutif de l'ALAI, lors de sa réunion à Rome du 14 septembre 2016, a adopté à l'unanimité une résolution sur le sujet du congrès de Bonn. Cette résolution, qui est aussi disponible sur le site web www.alai.org, est reproduite dans l'annexe 2 de ce volume.

Silke von Lewinski, 20 Octobre 2016

Table of contents
Table des matières
Tabla de contenidos

Thursday, June 18: LEGAL MODELS TO ASSURE REMUNERATION FOR USE LES MODÈLES JURIDIQUES POUR GARANTIR UNE RÉMUNÉRATION DE L'UTILISATION MODELOS LEGALES PARA ASEGURAR LA REMUNERACIÓN POR USO

Session 1: Legal Models to Assure Remuneration for Use de lege lata Les modèles juridiques pour garantir une rémunération de l'utilisation de lege lata Modelos legales para aseguar una remuneración por el uso de lege lata

Session 2: Considerations de lege ferenda
Considérations de lege ferenda
Consideraciones de lege ferenda

Session 2: Challenges for the legislature and courts
Défis à relever par le legislateur et la jurisprudence
Retos para el legislador y los tribunales

Thursday, June 18:
LEGAL MODELS TO ASSURE REMUNERATION FOR USE

Jeudi 18 juin:
LES MODÈLES JURIDIQUES POUR GARANTIR UNE RÉMUNÉRATION DE L'UTILISATION

Jueves, 18 de junio:
MODELOS LEGALES PARA ASEGURAR LA REMUNERACIÓN POR USO

Victor Nabhan*

Discours d'ouverture-Opening speech

Meine Damen und Herren,
Guten Morgen

I only know a few words in German:

"Danke schön";

"Sehr gut";

and: "Genau", a most useful word.

I also know "Auf Wiedersehen". But perhaps it is a bit early for this!

So I am afraid I will have to continue in English and French. Schade!

14 years ago almost to the day, on the 11th of June 2001, Gerald Levin, the Chief Executive of AOL Time Warner, was asked about his company's vision. His answer consisted of one word:

"Subscriptions" he said. "Full stop".

When asked what kind of subscriptions he had in mind, he responded:

"Everything. Anything you want, You name it. Every movie, every written piece of paper, every piece of music will be delivered on demand".

At that time, not everyone agreed with Mr Levin's statement.

Looking back 14 years later, Mr Levin's predictions proved nevertheless to be prophetic.

Subscriptions are more than ever the name of the game. Delivery on demand is flourishing. And streaming is winning the day.

The new actors are called Spotify, Deezer, Rhapsody, Netflix. Not to forget Apple, which last week announced its new music offer. Apple, I mean, a giant sitting on a mountain of cash flow: not too long ago it had more operating cash in the bank than the US Treasury!

These developments sound like really good news for the investors: it means more revenues for them, more income. It's good for business.

But it's also good for the users: it means better access to a multiplicity of sources from which they can enjoy listening, watching, reading.

But what about the authors, the creators?

At ALAI, we do have this silly habit of caring for creators. We like authors. We loooove authors. I mean LOVE with capital letters. And perhaps for good reason.

Let me quote from Jean Michel Jarre:

> « Sans les créateurs, les sites de streaming n'existeraient pas. Il faut rappeler aux acteurs du Net que dans les smartphones, la partie smart, ce sont les créateurs! »

---

* President of ALAI; Professor at Nottingham University.

> "Without the creators, streaming sites would not even exist. One should remind the Net actors that in the smartphones, the smart part, it's the creators".

So what is there for the authors in today's practices? Are they getting their fair share?

Which raises another equally important question: in the context of the exploitation of their works on the web, which legal system or mechanism would best serve their interests? A remuneration right coupled with a legal licence? Traditional negotiation based on their exclusive rights? A mixture of both? Should there be only one system? I suspect these questions will be heavily debated during the coming 2 days. There will be no unanimity among the speakers. A good thing for a Congress!

We are gathered together in this lovely room to celebrate the German Copyright Act's 50th anniversary. In Bonn! Celebration implies a festive mood. And what better than French to express such mood: after all "la joie de vivre" is a French expression, nicht wahr? So I am left with no choice but to switch now to French!

Le fait de choisir Bonn comme lieu de ce Congrès n'est pas anodin. Evidemment c'était la capitale fédérale au moment où la loi a été adoptée. Mais mes recherches me portent à croire qu'il y avait des raisons encore plus subtiles qui ont motivé ce choix!

Dans une correspondance entre le peintre August Macke et un ami peintre de Munich, Franz Marc, Macke s'exprimait ainsi « Toi espagnol! Laisse-moi te raconter quelque chose très doucement: Cette ville de Bonn est une vraie ville de fonctionnaires et de retraités. Tout est très calme, sérieux, discret ».

Voilà donc qui annonce un Congrès studieux.

Mais il ne faut pas croire pour autant que Bonn est une ville où on s'ennuie. Bien au contraire, les dépliants nous disent aussi qu'elle a toujours été une ville multiculturelle, conviviale et chaleureuse, où il faisait bon vivre. A tel point que le Bavarois Clemens August, archevêque de profession, a reçu Casanova à Bonn! Yeah, yeah! Et Lola Montez a dansé sur les tables lors du premier festival Beethoven à Bonn.

Voilà qui promet aussi un Congrès convivial, voire même divertissant.

Enfin last, but not least, n'oublions pas qu'un des plus grands génies créateurs de tous les temps, Beethoven, est né à Bonn. N'est-ce pas là le lieu idéal pour réfléchir sur la protection des musiciens, gens de lettre, et autres créateurs?

Tout porte donc à croire que ces 2 prochaines journées seront sérieuses et qu'elles se dérouleront dans une ambiance conviviale. Puissent-elles être aussi inspirées par l'esprit créatif de Beethoven!

C'est sur ses mots que je déclare solennellement ouvert le Congrès de l'ALAI à Bonn.

Michele Woods*

WIPO Greetings and Introductory Remarks

Ladies and gentlemen, I bring greetings from the World Intellectual Property Organization and our Director General, Francis Gurry. My colleague Geidy Lung, who is also participating in this meeting, is known to many of you. I also see many distinguished WIPO alumni in the audience.

As we gather at this beautiful setting on the Rhine, WIPO wishes to congratulate the organizers for coordinating this important program on *making copyright and related rights work.* We also offer congratulations to our German colleagues for fifty years of successful operation of the German Copyright Act, which has evolved over that time to foster a strong, legal environment to nurture culture and the creative industries.

At WIPO and elsewhere in the multilateral system we can feel that copyright and related rights are under pressure from all sides, and are sometimes in danger of being shoved aside as an irrelevant inconvenience in the digital age.

That is why it is so important for organizations like ALAI, under the able guidance of Victor, Yves, and Jean, to continue its founding role as the protector of the rights of authors and creators.

We may come from different copyright traditions and have different views on how a balanced copyright and related rights system should evolve to meet the needs of the digital era and calls for economic development. But we share a common belief in the role of the copyright system and its importance as a positive force for the creation and expression of the fundamental roots of our culture and our humanity.

WIPO congratulates ALAI for ably carrying out this role. We look forward to this program as a notable example of ALAI's important work guarding the foundations of copyright and related rights.

* Director, WIPO Copyright Law Division.

Adolf Dietz*
Allocution de bienvenue

Madame la Directrice,
cher Victor Nabhan,
cher Reto Hilty,
chers anciens et nouveaux amis
Mesdames et Messieurs,

en tant que vétéran parmi les spécialistes allemands du droit d'auteur, je suis heureux de vous accueillir, avec à l'esprit cette pensée réconfortante que les sommités du droit d'auteur réunies ici, de toute évidence, ne considèrent pas encore le droit d'auteur comme une cause perdue.

Compte tenu de mon ancienneté, j'ai pu assister avec une pleine conscience scientifique à l'élaboration de la loi allemande de 1965 sur le droit d'auteur, et à sa promulgation, ici même à Bonn, dans notre ancienne et vénérable capitale fédérale. Doctorant chez Eugen Ulmer à l'époque, je m'étais alors penché sur le droit moral dans une perspective de droit comparé – une thématique qui devait m'accompagner, bon gré mal gré, tout au long de ma vie. Le fait qu'une réglementation pleinement adéquate du droit moral de l'auteur soit, pour la première fois, élaborée puis adoptée, a sans aucun doute exercé sur moi une incitation particulière à me consacrer à cette matière. Ce fut du reste une expérience extraordinaire de voir aboutir en 1965 des débats remontant aux années vingt du siècle dernier, autour de la modernisation devenue indispensable du droit d'auteur allemand.

On sait peut-être moins à quel point Eugen Ulmer influença la conception dogmatique de cette nouvelle loi allemande sur le droit d'auteur. Elle puise son origine dans un concept essentiel, appelé « monisme » avec une pertinence seulement relative, qui trouve son expression la plus évidente dans le caractère inaliénable du droit d'auteur considéré dans sa globalité. Eu égard notamment aux oppositions de plus en plus vives, qui se sont manifestées dernièrement, il serait donc nécessaire de trouver une autre appellation pour cette conception, et de la requalifier peut-être plus justement d'intégrale ou de synthétique, dans la mesure où elle réunit dans un dispositif unitaire toutes les prérogatives caractéristiques du droit d'auteur moderne.

Ce dernier point concerne directement les droits à rémunération, qui dominent l'agenda de ce congrès de l'ALAI. Même s'ils devaient évoluer vers un « fla-

* Ancien vice-président ALAI, ancient président du group allemand de l'ALAI, chercheur affilié à l'institut Max Planck pour l'innovation et la concurrence à Munich. A.Dietz@ip.mpg.de.
L'auteur remercie Mme Fabienne Michel pour la traduction de l'allemand en français.

trate » (une licence globale) ou vers une part virtuelle de celui-ci au profit des auteurs, ils font néanmoins partie de cette position juridique unitaire (économique, mais avec une tonalité de fond morale toutefois), qui est octroyée à l'auteur en vertu de la loi. Or justement, ce droit unitaire de forme mixte (« Recht von gemischter Gestalt ») selon une expression d'Ulmer, que l'on appelle le « droit d'auteur », n'a pas seulement un caractère exclusif. Ainsi s'effondrent ces arguments polémiques récurrents, selon lesquels le droit à rémunération pour la copie privée ou le droit à une rétribution proportionnelle dans le contexte du droit de suite, ne relèveraient plus du droit d'auteur, mais seraient une sorte de « levy » ou, pire encore, une taxe déguisée.

On doit aussi à l'influence d'Ulmer (dont l'institut universitaire qu'il dirigeait à l'époque, allait alors devenir, en partie tout au moins, le célèbre Institut Max Planck à Munich) l'idée géniale de reconnaître aux producteurs de films un droit voisin spécifique. Il devenait dès lors possible de préserver, dans le principe tout au moins, l'attribution, imposée par le droit constitutionnel, du droit d'auteur aux auteurs cinématographiques, en dépit d'ailleurs des présomptions de transfert au producteur prévues par la loi (cf. Ulmer, Lettre d'Allemagne, DdA 1965, p. 283 et suiv. et dès DdA 1953, p. 97 et suiv., p. 107 et suiv. et DdA 1954, p.108 et suiv.). Comme beaucoup d'autres, cette solution ancrée dans la loi allemande relative au droit d'auteur ferait son entrée sur la scène européenne par la suite.

Il en a été de même (ce qui est regrettable à mon sens) de la prorogation de la durée de protection des droits, qui sont passés de cinquante à soixante-dix ans *post mortem auctoris* – une évolution que l'on ne doit pas à l'influence d'Eugen Ulmer cette fois, même si elle fut finalement saluée par ce juriste. En raison d'une décision de dernière minute du comité juridique du Bundestag allemand, cette prolongation s'est substituée contre toute logique à l'option, initialement prévue, d'un concept discuté en Allemagne sous le nom de « Urhebernachfolgevergütung », et connu au plan international sous le nom de domaine public payant, qui portait l'empreinte des réflexions d'Heinrich Hubmann notamment.

La décision – fatale comme je le pense – du législateur allemand d'augmenter la durée habituelle de protection des droits, qui était de cinquante ans à l'époque, a également trouvé par la suite son prolongement dans le droit d'auteur européen harmonisé, et même au-delà. Une reconstitution pièce par pièce s'avère aujourd'hui nécessaire, avec des moyens de substitution comme la réglementation des œuvres orphelines ou la recherche d'une disposition plus libérale pour les exceptions.

Encore un mot sur le « contractual turn » ou, autrement dit, sur le droit des contrats d'auteur, une matière qui me tient également à cœur comme vous le savez peut-être. La loi de 1965 avait délibérément prévu une réglementation simplement sommaire car le législateur avait annoncé plein d'espoir que cet important pilier d'un système complet du droit d'auteur devait faire prochainement l'objet d'une loi indépendante. Mais il faudra ensuite attendre près de quarante ans pour que cette promesse du législateur soit à peu près honorée, avec l'adoption de la loi allemande du 22.3.2002 pour le renforcement de la position contractuelle des auteurs et des artistes-interprètes ou exécutants (« Gesetz zur Stärkung der vertraglichen Stellung von Urhebern und ausübenden Künstlern », traduction anglaise dans IIC 2002, 842). Cette loi puise sa source dans le concept de « rémunération équitable », que vous avez thématisé de façon également équitable aujourd'hui, et j'en suis ravi.

Vous savez sans doute que j'ai aussi participé, tout comme mes quatre amis et collègues Ulrich Loewenheim, Wilhelm Nordemann, Gerhard Schricker et Martin Vogel, à l'élaboration de ce dispositif audacieux du droit des contrats d'auteur. Aussi serez-vous probablement indulgent avec moi si j'éprouve encore à ce jour une pointe de fierté pour ce projet, même s'il a été un peu rogné et dilué, il est vrai, au cours de la procédure législative. Ce fut en effet un grand moment d'émotion, dans ma vie professionnelle, de pouvoir assister, le 25 janvier 2002, depuis la tribune visiteurs du Bundestag à Berlin, à l'adoption quasiment unanime de cette loi de réforme en deuxième et troisième lectures. Vous pouvez observer que les professeurs font eux aussi parfois l'expérience de la réussite.

Avec plus de dix années de recul, nous savons aujourd'hui que cette loi relative aux contrats, qui a été appliquée non sans succès pendant toute cette période, présentait pourtant quelques insuffisances, notamment dans le contexte de la procédure chronophage de mise en place de standards communs de rémunération par les associations d'auteurs d'un côté, et d'exploitants de l'autre. Sur ce point, le gouvernement de coalition actuel à Berlin a promis d'y apporter une rectification, promesse prévue à la section traitant du droit d'auteur dans le contrat de coalition de novembre 2013. Du reste, le contrat de coalition s'exprime d'une façon très générale en faveur d'un réajustement du droit d'auteur, pour tenir compte des exigences et des défis de l'âge numérique.

Ce dessein s'inscrit pleinement, je le pense, dans la lignée des objectifs que ce congrès de l'ALAI entend poursuivre avec son travail et ses débats visant l'évaluation des options possibles pour un droit d'auteur en phase avec l'avenir, bien au-delà du cadre de référence allemand. Je souhaite que nous ayons la main heureuse.

Reto Hilty*

Welcome Speech

Mr. President, ladies and gentlemen,

after these carefully chosen words addressed to you by the penultimate president of the German group of the ALAI, Adolf Dietz, I do not want to go on for too long but just briefly outline the intention behind the topic of our conference:

It is so to speak the other side of the coin that Adolf Dietz touched upon:

We basically want to investigate whether – and if so to what extent – we may learn from history, and in particular from the path the German legislature took 50 years ago.

What was established in this country in 1965 actually was the so called "liability approach", a term that only became common a few years later. This "liability approach" was and still can be seen as an alternative to the common "property approach" governing our IP regimes to a large degree.

This "liability approach" had (and still has) two tremendous advantages. First, certain uses of copyright-protected works – uses that formerly were prohibited, but nevertheless carried out, because the law was hardly enforceable in practice – such uses could be de-criminalized (to the benefit of the users concerned).

Second, beyond that (and even more important), a sophisticated compensation system was established, which generated substantial income; levies were collected by collective management organizations and ultimately distributed amongst the right holders.

Until today this "liability approach" retains a certain appeal; but the framework in which it applies has changed dramatically. In particular thanks to the digital revolution copyright industries have increasingly gained back their control over the use of copyright-protected works.

As a result, not only collective management organizations are now faced with new challenges. Beyond that, the relationship between creators (or performers) and the copyright industries needs to be reviewed under new (factual) conditions.

So far, however, the legal framework has been adapted only partly. Further steps might be advisable – but the crucial question is of course: steps in which direction?

---

* Director of the Max Planck Institute for Innovation and Competition, Munich, Full Professor (ad personam) at the University of Zurich and honorary Professor at the Ludwig Maximilians University, Munich.

To find an answer to this question is by no means trivial. If the main topic of our conference is "remuneration", we must be aware of matchless amounts of money at stake.

Not surprisingly, discussions about the future of copyright law are heavily influenced by conflicting interests. This is nothing extraordinary in legislative proceedings. However, we most probably will only make progress if all parties involved are sufficiently transparent and sincerely willing to achieve a fair balance between all interests concerned.

We – and when I say we, I mean the whole executive body of the German group that has been involved in the drafting of the program – we all very much hope that our conference will help to throw additional light on the different perspectives and that it may add a few new pieces to the complex puzzle of copyright law.

Before handing over to Thomas Dreier, the chair of our first panel, it is my duty and honor as the representative of the German group to express my sincere thanks to a few people – people without whom this conference could not be taking place.

First and foremost two "officials" of the German group deserve explicit mention.

This is on the one hand our Secretary General, Dr. Kaya Köklü, who literally acted as our "Jack of all trades". Although we worked together with a professional conference organizer (Eurokongress), he had to take care of countless and infinitesimal details, but also most vital issues – like e.g. the budgeting.

On the other hand, our Vice President, Dr. Silke von Lewinski, amongst other things had to assume two tough challenges:

Firstly, she had to find suitable speakers for the numerous topics during the two days. This was a particularly difficult task when it came to the search for those representatives from industry who will explain their business models (tomorrow morning).

Secondly, she smartly acted as contact person

- between a strong-willed national president who constantly developed new ideas on how to carry out such an international conference, on the one hand,
- and the "Comité exécutif" de l'ALAI, who preferred adhering to long-serving traditions and practices, on the other hand.

The outcome is something in between – and I very much hope that it will be satisfactory for everybody. Luckily it convinced at least those who are also indispensable for carrying out such a huge conference: our sponsors.

You find them listed in your documentation, and I will not read aloud all names. However, I would like to mention at least that the lion's share of our expenses is borne by all German collecting societies together, organized under the roof of the ZPÜ (Zentralstelle für private Überspielungsrechte).

One of them – the VG Bildkunst – is even so kind as to provide us with our evening program (including dinner) tonight.

Further, the Deutsche Forschungsgemeinschaft (the German Research Foundation) contributed substantially, and last but not least we received highly appreciated support from some important law firms and also from some publishing houses.

Session 1: Legal Models to Assure Remuneration for Use de lege lata

Les modèles juridiques pour garantir une rémunération de l'utilisation de lege lata

Modelos legales para aseguar una remuneración por el uso de lege lata

1. Exclusive Rights

Thomas Dreier*

1.1 Introduction

In copyright, exclusive rights are the fundamental tool allowing authors to control the dissemination and, in particular, to obtain appropriate remuneration for the use of their works. Therefore, this first part of Session 1 focuses on the role of exclusive rights in this regard. After the break, the second part of Session 1 will be devoted to the importance of remuneration rights.

Throughout the history of copyright, the extension of the exclusive rights to new technical modes of reproduction and communication – or, more precisely, the catching up with economic changes that resulted from the use of new dissemination technologies for the exploitation of copyrighted works – has always been a challenging task.

After broad coverage of uses was achieved with regard to analog exploitation, digital and networking technologies have again challenged the reach of exclusive rights. With the introduction of the making-available right in the WIPO Treaties of 1996 an attempt was made to close the gap yet again. But does that mean that all economically relevant use acts are now covered by an exclusive right? What about the different forms of linking, up- and downloading, and, last but not least, providing platform services? Of course, it is appropriate to leave the activity of most forms of mere linking outside of the realm of copyright's exclusivity. But the BestWater-decision of the CJEU (which applies the same rule to the embedding of someone else's copyrighted content in a user's website) gives rise to serious doubt. Perhaps even more important: although ISPs – and in particular platform providers such as Google's YouTube (to name only the most prominent) – today generate most of the income on the basis of the use of copyrighted material, they are not even addressed as players by copyright legislation. Rather, the legal liability of ISPs mostly results from legal rules outside of copyright law proper. Moreover, their liability is generally limited to injunctive relief, if it is not exempted altogether. It follows that platforms generally do not license for themselves in their own name, but at best only on behalf of their users.

Of course, problems of exclusivity in a digital and networked environment don't stop here. In some instances the possibilities to effectively enforce exclusive rights by obtaining injunctive relief and/or damages, are less strong in the

* Professor, Karlsruhe Institute of Technology (KIT), Head of the Institute for Information and Business Law (IIWR) and the Center for applied legal studies (ZAR) at the Karlsruhe Institute for Technology (KIT), Germany.

digital than in the analog world (because of the multiplicity of users and their anonymity). In some instances, however, the possibilities to effectively enforce exclusive rights are even stronger than in the analog world (due to the direct contact between right holders and end-users in which use conditions can be negotiated by contract or simply imposed upon the end-user by way of technical access and use restricting devices).

Another important question concerns the mechanisms for adequate remuneration of creators and performing artists vis-à-vis editors and media companies (in particular those which make use of a broad or even comprehensive repertoire). The exclusive right as such is silent on the issue of remuneration. Therefore, even in the analog world individual creators and performing artists often do not obtain adequate remuneration. So far, only some countries have tried to remedy this situation. Others leave the remuneration to the forces of the market, which often results in the stronger parties exploiting the weaker ones.

But whenever the granting of an exclusive right in the hands of individual creators and performers does not lead to an adequate sharing in the proceeds or at least the financial gains obtained from the exploitation of copyrighted subject matter, the exclusive right, it might be argued, has lost its raison d'être. In such circumstances, a claim for remuneration might indeed be the better tool in order to assure adequate remuneration for the use of copyrighted subject matter.

These two issues – scope and enforcement tools to assure remuneration as well as mechanisms to ensure adequate remuneration for creators and performers – will now be highlighted by Marshall Leaffer and Tristan Azzi. Marshall Leaffer is a Professor at the Indiana University Maurer School of Law, USA, and a longtime ALAI-Member. Tristan Azzi is Professor at the University Paris 1, Pantheon Sorbonne, France.

Mr. Leaffer, the floor is yours.

Marshall Leaffer*

1.2 General Report: Scope and enforcement tools to assure remuneration, part A of the questionnaire

INTRODUCTORY SUMMARY: In the internet environment, copyrighted works are used by dispersed, anonymous members of the public, under conditions of low visibility. In this environment, license agreements are difficult to conclude and recourse to litigation is impractical. How rights owners are remunerated in the digital age is the theme of our conference. My task here is to discuss the responses given to Part A of the questionnaire regarding the scope and enforcement of the exclusive rights under existing law. My colleagues in turn will discuss Parts B, C, and D, which cover different aspects of remuneration mechanisms.

This report is based on the responses from 20 countries. In the short time I have and for the purpose of clarity, I cannot provide a discussion in nuanced, intricate detail. My goal is to present the general tendencies revealed in the reports. For more nuance and perhaps accuracy one should access the individual national reports.[1]

Part A poses four questions (with subparts) on how each country's laws implemented the exclusive rights enjoyed by the copyright owner. I have placed in italics and bold the questions presented to the national groups of ALAI, followed by a general summary based on the national reports. As stated above, these short summaries, of course, are not intended to be exhaustive but are only to be used as a frame of reference in reading the national reports. These summaries are then followed by examples from the national reports.

Question one concerns how eight enumerated acts on the internet are treated by each country's law. I have broken down this question in three groupings. In "section I" of Question one I discuss hyperlinking, deep linking, and framing/embedding. In "section II", I discuss the acts of streaming, downloading, and uploading of works. In section III, I examine the "supply of a platform for 'user generated content' and "other novel forms of use on the internet".

---

* Professor, Indiana University, Maurer School of Law, USA.
1 For the national reports, see http://alai2015.org/en/national-reports.html.

I. First Question

How are the following acts covered by the copyright law of your country (statute and case law)?

i. Offering of hyperlinks to works
ii. Offering of deep links to works
iii. Framing/embedding of works
iv. Streaming of works
v. Download of works
vi. Upload of works
vii. Supply of a platform for 'user-generated content'
viii. Other novel forms of use on the internet

1. SUMMARY – HYPERLINKING, DEEP LINKING, FRAMING/EMBEDDING: The most interesting fact revealed in these reports is that, with the possible exception of Croatia, no country has addressed these acts of hyperlinking, deep-linking, and framing/embedding in their statutory law. As the Argentine Report (Barrenechea & Wegbrait) emphasizes:

> "The Argentine Intellectual Property Act[2] ... does not specifically regulate either the aspects contemplated in the question or any of the uses on the Internet of works or categories protected as neighboring rights. However, these uses are still covered because Section 2[3] of the Intellectual Property Act recognizes a broad and exclusive right to dispose of works, in whatever form and manner of exploitation. It is considered that this broad formulation covers the Internet."

It is surprising how little actual litigation we have had on this question given the importance of these typical uses of the internet. Another generalization: I found a slight consensus in the reports that hyperlinking, deep linking, and framing/embedding of works are legal absent other factors that would lead either to direct or to third party liability. As the Hungarian Report states: "offering hyperlinks, deep links, framing/embedding subject to certain conditions do not constitute a restricted act."

U.S law provides one solution. Under U.S. law, offering a hyperlink to a website that contains a copyrighted work does not constitute direct copyright infringement because hyperlinks do not themselves contain copyrighted works. However, under U.S. law, claims for third party liability, contributory or vicari-

2 Law #11,723.

3 Section 2. The right of ownership of a scientific, literary or artistic work shall include, for its author, the right to dispose of, publish, perform and publicly exhibit, alienate, translate, adapt or authorize the translation of, and reproduce the work in any form.

ous liability, are possible. Claims for secondary liability – for an action in contributory or vicarious liability – are available if a person offering a deep link is likely to have specific knowledge of the infringing work. Likewise, framing or embedding of works has been held not to constitute direct infringement where the work is not stored on an operator's own computer. There is the possibility of an action for unfair competition.

European law has achieved much the same result as the United States, but the resolution of the problem is more complicated and controversial as revealed in the reports. European reports specifically point out the effect of the jurisprudence of the CJEU in the Svensson and BestWater cases[4] in rendering the acts of linking, deeplinking, and framing/embedding as per se legal. The main bone of contention is not with the result of these two decisions but that Svensson and BestWater appear to conflict with some basic assumptions of the EU Information Society Directive where it is stated that no act of communication to the public can cause copyright exhaustion. The Italian Report reflects the controversy, stating that by requiring a new public or a new media as a requirement for finding infringement as a communication to the public, the court introduces the equivalent of exhaustion of the online communication right. Recall that the study approved by the ALAI Executive Committee in September 2014 maintains that the requirement conflicts with the rules of the WIPO treaties.[5] The ALAI study stated:

> While the CJEU in *Svensson* gave a correct and positive response to the basic question of whether hyperlinking is (interactive) making available/ communication – a position enunciated in the aforementioned statement of ALAI's Opinion of 15 September 2013 – the CJEU has in the very same decision, as to the question of whether that act concerns a communication to 'the public', confirmed a number of other recent decisions in which it introduced a problematic "new public" criterion, qualified by, *inter alia*, an equally problematic new "specific technical means" criterion.

I now turn to examples from the individual reports concerning the following acts:

i. Hyperlinking
ii. Offering deep links to works
iii. Framing/embedding of works

---

4 Cases C_466/12 ("Svensson") and C-348/13 ("BestWater").

5 The Hungarian report also criticizes the new public theory. For the ALAI critique see the Opinion adopted by the ALAI Executive Committee, at its 17 September 2014 session, on the "new public" theory, published at http://www.alai.org/en/assets/files/resolutions/2014-opinion-new-public.pdf and Dr Mihály J Ficsor, «Svensson: Honest attempt at establishing due balance concerning the use of hyperlinks – spoiled by the erroneous "new public" theory»; published at http://www.copyrightseesaw.net/archive/?sw_10_item=68. (both last accessed on April 6, 2015).

- United States: (Szewczyk & Besek): "Under U.S. law, offering a hyperlink to a website that contains a copyrighted work does not constitute direct copyright infringement because hyperlinks do not themselves contain copyrighted or protected derivative works." However, claims for third party liability, contributory or vicarious liability, are possible. Similarly, offering a deep link to works does not constitute direct infringement of copyright. Claims for secondary liability – for an action in contributory or vicarious liability – are available if a person offering a deep link is likely to have specific knowledge of the infringing work. Likewise, framing or embedding of works has been held not to constitute direct infringement where the work is not stored on an operator's own computer.
- United Kingdom: (Davies, Dimita, Edwards, Frabboni, Koempel, Suthersanen): "Offering a hyperlink to freely available content is not an infringement of section 20 of the Copyright, Designs and Patent Act." On the other hand, hyperlinks designed to circumvent pay-walls will infringe. "Nevertheless it is not clear whether the content must be freely available or authorised, even implicitly by the author/copyright owner." Guidelines state that the activity is not an infringement if the content has been published freely online with permission. According to the U.K. Report, the critical issue is whether the act of hyperlinking constitutes a communication to the public. The report indicates that for liability, some sort of knowledge and facilitation of infringement should be required. For offering deep links and for framing/embedding, infringement will not be found for the same reasons given above. But in the case of these two activities, moral rights concerns may be involved under the circumstances.
- Hungary: Offering hyperlinks, deep links, framing/embedding subject to certain conditions "does not constitute a restricted act". Like many of the reports, the Hungarian Report refers to the *Svensson* and *BestWate*r cases. Most of the reports that mentioned these two cases were generally favorable as the result but critical of the "new public" rationale in questioning the basis of the decision.
- Italy (Ercolani): The mere redirect to a different website by hyperlink is not an act of communication provided that the link is simply a referencing tool to external elements. The Italian report makes the distinction between hyperlinking and the acts of deep linking and framing/embedding: "On the basis of the interpretation of Italian law it could be assumed that a link constitutes a form of making available to the public when made in the form of a deep link or framing/embedding of works in such a way that the final user does not perceive the difference between works directly hosted in the website and works simply embedded or pulled from external sources. On the contrary, the case of mere redirect to a different web site by means of a hyperlink is not to be considered as an act of communication provided that the link is simply a referencing tool to external elements."

- Switzerland (Salvadé & Cherpillod): Simple hyperlinks without more are not actionable. Deep links are not actionable although there could be moral rights issues arising out of the particular circumstances. Framing and embedding is an actionable act of making available. Also these acts could be actionable under the integrity and paternity rights.
- Japan: The acts of hyperlinking, deeplinking, and framing/embedding involve the "right of making transmittable" under Japanese law.
- Finland (Oesch, Günther, Pihlajarinne): The Finnish report elaborated on the issue of framing/embedding.[6] Referring to *Svensson*, the Finish Copyright Council (2014:4) declared that offering a link to a picture on a non-commercial discussion page is legal "if the right holder had given his permission to use the picture freely on the Internet".[7]
- Canada: A number of countries such as Canada have not confronted the issue in either their copyright statutes or their case law.
- Greece (Kallinikou, Stavridou, Despotidou): Under Greek case law, hyperlinking can lead to liability under certain circumstances. The First Instance Court of Athens, in case 4042/2010, held that a radio broadcaster licensed by a collecting society to broadcast his radio program infringes copyright by placing on his website a hyperlink (interactive banner) enabling the transmission of his radio program on the Internet.
- Croatia (Jurić, Matanovac Furić, Katulić): Croatia is an exception to the general rule that most countries lack specific statutory provisions on hyperlinking. Article 19 of the Croatian Electronic Commerce Act provides: "The provider of services who by electronic links opens access to third information shall not be responsible for such information if: he does not know or could not know about the illegal activity of recipients or about the content of data in that information; [and] upon finding out about illegal activity or data removes or disables access to data."
- Belgium (Witmeur): The Belgian Report indicates that the collecting society SABAM wished to collect royalties for YouTube's embedded links in their website directed toward commercial websites. SABAM based its claim on the terms of its licensing agreements with YouTube which, as SABAM argues, are limited to communication to the public in the private sphere. YouTube understandably does not agree with SABAM's position.
- Netherlands (Kannekens, Sluiter, Salamanca, Eechoud): There is no provision for secondary liability or indirect copyright infringement in the Dutch

---

6 See expert opinion of the Finnish Copyright Council (2001:8 – framing of the articles).

7 See the Finnish Copyright Committee 2002:5 p. 2, and the Finnish Copyright Committee 2012:2 separate study by Taina Pihlajarinne about commercial linking especially in situations where new services are built for economic advantage based on automated linking.

Copyright Act. A plain (deep) hyperlink is not a communication to the public and does not directly infringe copyright. It can in some special cases still be considered an 'unlawful act' under general tort law (art 6:162 of the Dutch Civil Code, e.g., when a person systematically links to large amounts of unauthorized material and profits from it).[8]

- Austria (Walter): "The Austrian Copyright Act does not explicitly allude to these acts. In jurisprudence, the Supreme Court in 2011 held[9] that in case of hyperlinking there is no reproduction made in the user's computer and that hyperlinking is not to be regarded as an act of communication to the public. In doctrine, however, deep linking as well as framing is deemed to be communication to the public".

2. SUMMARY – STREAMING, DOWNLOADING, and UPLOADING: The second set of acts concerns the streaming, downloading and uploading of works. Absent consent of the copyright owner, these acts may infringe one or more of the exclusive rights. Clearly, streaming constitutes communication to the public as the reports universally indicate.[10] As for uploading the copyrighted material, most of the reports indicate that this act involves the rights of making available or of distribution. Downloading of works concerns the reproduction right. Some reports such as the Swiss (Salvade & Cherpillod) and Norwegian (Lund) refer to private use as a possible exception to the reproduction right for a downloaded work.[11] The downloading of works from the internet has caused excruciating headaches for the world copyright community. French law with the establishment of the HADOPI, described in detail in the French Report (Binctin), is a sui generis, albeit controversial, attempt to impose sanctions on those who have engaged in a pattern of illegal downloading.

I will now present examples from the national reports concerning the following acts:

iv. Streaming of works
v. Download of works
vi. Upload of works

---

8 Visser, D.J.G.,'Openbaar maken: Communication to the public', in: Hugenholtz, P.B., Quaedvlieg, A.A., Visser, D.J.G. (Eds.) *A century of Dutch Copyright Law*, Amstelveen: Uitgeverij deLex, 2012, p.225.

9 Supreme Court 20.9.2011 4 Ob 105/11m – "123people/Vorschaubilder/Thumbnails" MR 2011, 313 (*Michel Walter*) = ecolex 2012/29, 64 (*Axel Anderl*) = wbl 2012/38, 105 = RZ 2012/76, 123 (LS) = ÖBl 2012/45, 175 (*Manfred Büchele*).

10 The German report mentions section 19a UrhG (making available to the public); live streaming would be covered by section 20 UrhG (right of broadcasting).

11 The Swiss report indicates that art19 (1) lit. a LDA provides that the private use exception applies even if the source is illegal.

- Canada: Canadian case law[12] has ruled that streaming is considered a communication to the public but not a reproduction because the copies that are made by the streaming process are temporary by nature. By comparison, both uploading and downloading create permanent copies. Under U.S. law, the rights of performance, reproduction, and distribution are involved, leading to much the same result.
- UK (Davies, Dimita, Edwards, Frabboni, Koempel, Suthersanen): The U.K. Report makes the following points. Notwithstanding the lack of case law, downloading unauthorized content would infringe the reproduction right under section 17 CDPA. Since 2005, it has been clear that the uploading of a work (except for software) without authorisation infringes section 20 CDPA (section 20 concerns the right of communication to the public). Uploading software may infringe copyright as an act of public distribution under section 18 CDPA.[13]
- Norway (Lund): Streaming is covered by the making available right. Downloading of works involves the right of reproduction. Section 12 of the Norwegian Authors' Rights Act lists an exception for the reproduction for private use provided that the reproduction is made from a lawful rendering of the work, but "does not permit the making of "machine-readable" copies of computer programs nor "machine-readable" copies of "machine-readable" databases." Uploading of works is covered by the exclusive right of reproduction as well as making the copyright material available to the public.
- France (Binctin): As in other reports, streaming is considered as a communication to the public. As for downloading, which the French Report deems a communication to the public, and an act of reproduction, French law has established the Haute Autorité pour la diffusion des oeuvres et la protection des droits sur Internet (HADOPI). Starting in 2009, this sui generis authority was established to fight the growing battle against internet piracy. It has the authority to impose sanctions against those who have abused the downloading privilege. The actual workings of HADOPI are described in detail in the French Report.
- Austria (Walter): As to streaming, "the active making available of copyright subject matter by means of streaming is dependent upon the author's consent.[14] However the act of "reception" by the user is to be regarded as covered by the exception in favor of temporary, transient or incidental repro-

12 Entertainment Software Association v. Canadian Society of Authors, Composers, and Editors of Music (SOCAN), 2012 CSC 34 [ESA] and Rogers Communications, Inc. v. SOCAN, 2012 CSC 35.

13 Case C-128/11 UsedSoft GmbH v. Oracle International Corp.

14 Making available right under §18a (authors) respectively §71a (holders of related rights) of the Austrian Copyright Act.

duction under Article 5(1) of the InfoSoc-Directive. However, it is an open question whether this holds true in cases where such streams are made available illegitimately. In my opinion, also in this context, the legitimacy of the source is a prerequisite for the application of this exception, as this is the case in regards of private copying[15]."The Austrian Supreme Court inter alia marginally dealt with this question in its order for reference to the ECJ in the case „kino.to/UPC I".[16]

- Netherlands (Kannekens, Sluiter, Salamanca, Eechoud): "Uploading a copyright protected work is considered to be an act of 'openbaarmaking',[17] which without permission of the copyright holder, is an act of copyright infringement."[18]

  The Dutch Report states: "The downloading of a copyright protected work itself is an act of reproduction. In many cases downloads will not require permission as the private copying exception applies (thuiskopieuitzondering; art 16c DCA). The exception only applies to reproduction of (part of) a work that is made by a natural person without a direct or indirect commercial purpose and exclusively for his or her personal practice, use, or study.[19] A levy is due by manufacturers and importers of blank media/equipment (see Question C.1 below). It was controversial whether the Dutch private copying exception applied only to works copied from an authorized source, or also covered copies of unlawful sources; this matter is relevant for the way in which levies are administered. A reference was made to the ECJ, which judged on that: '*National legislation which makes no distinction between private copies made from lawful sources and those made from counterfeited or pirated sources cannot be tolerated.*'[20] Therefore, downloading from an illegal source no longer falls under private copy exemption. The Dutch government as a result had to review its longtime position that downloading from an illegal source is not illegal."

---

15 See ECJ 10.4.2014 C-435/12 – „ACI Adam/Thuiskopie" MR-Int 2014, 42 *(Michel Walter)* = EuZW 2014, 501 *(Carl C Müller/Sören Rößner)* = ZUM 2014, 573 *(Anne Lauber-Rönsberg)* = ecolex 2014/297, 727 *(LS) (Adolf Zeman)* = MMR 2014, 679 = ÖBl 2014, 232 *(Johannes Burgstaller/Mona Philomena Ladler).*

16 Supreme Court 11.5.2012 4 Ob 6/12d – MR 2012, 190 *(Michel Walter)* = ecolex 2012/291, 708 *(Axel Anderl)* = wbl 2012/180, 473 = GRUR Int 2012, 934.

17 The right of 'openbaarmaken', is a broad right which covers an array of acts such as public performance (public physically present), communication to the public (e.g. broadcasting), making available on demand and the right of distribution of physical copies, see Visser, D.J.G., 'Openbaar maken: Communication to the public', in: Hugenholtz, P.B., Quaedvlieg, A.A., Visser, D.J.G. (Eds.) *A century of Dutch Copyright Law*, Amstelveen: DeLex, 2012, p.225.

18 Court of Appeal The Hague 28 Jan 2014, JHG 2014/48 (*Brein/Ziggo XS4*ALL) para. 4.2.

19 Article 16c (1), Dutch Copyright Act.

20 European Court of Justice, 10 April 2014, C-435/12 (*ACI Adam BV e.a/Stichting de Thuiskopie*), para. 37.

3. SUMMARY – SUPPLY OF PLATFORMS, NOVEL FORMS OF USE ON THE INTERNET: The third grouping of the acts enumerated in question one concerns "the supply of user generated content" (UGC) and "other novel forms of use on the internet." Hardly surprising, most of the reports have much to say about UGC, which has been for some time the focus of copyright owners. The supplier of a platform communicates the copyrighted work to the public, performs an act of making available. Many reports referred to YouTube, without a doubt the biggest player in the field of UGC. Responses to other novel forms of use on the internet were sparse. The Italian Report (Ercolani) was an exception mentioning apps or applications providing access to copyrighted content that may raise the possibility of infringing acts under the same terms as what we have examined.

I will now present examples from the national reports concerning the following acts:

vii. Supply of platform for user generated content
viii. Other novel forms of use on the internet

- Germany (Pflüger): the mere supply of a platform for UGC is not an act covered by copyright. But it may trigger duties to verify the content.
- United States: (Szewczyk & Besek): platforms for UGC are exposed to copyright infringement but may benefit from the safe harbor for host service providers set out in section 512(c).
- Israel (Greenman): The supply of a platform for UGC is not of itself constrained by Israeli copyright law. Case law indicates that contributory copyright infringement can occur (i) when the supplier induces infringement or (ii) the platform does in fact serve for infringement in such volume as to constitute a non-legitimate forum.
- United Kingdom (Davies, Dimita, Edwards, Frabboni, Koempel, Suthersanen): In the case of infringing content, potential liabilities would include communication to the public, or reproduction or both. Platforms for "user generated content" are vulnerable to copyright infringement, but may often benefit from the safe harbor for host service providers.
- Italy (Ercolani): Case law shows some uncertainty in respect of UGC platforms. The Italian Report discusses *Mediaset v. Yahoo*, where the court ruled that Yahoo was liable for copyright infringement because Yahoo could not be deemed a "mere 'passive' hosting provider and, therefore, could not be exempted from liability by the EU E-commerce directive (Directive 2000/31/CE)". On appeal, the court reversed the holding that the right holder must specifically identify the illicit content before the hosting provider is liable to remove that content. The case will be decided by the Supreme Court.

II. Second Question

In cases in which there are practical obstacles to the conclusion of licensing agreements, in particular where multiple individual (end) users do not address right owners before using works (e.g., users uploading protected content on platforms like Youtube), are there particular clearing mechanisms? In particular, are license agreements possible and practiced with involved third parties, such as platforms, regarding the exploitation acts done by the actual users (e.g., license agreements with the platform operator rather than with the platform users [uploaders])?

SUMMARY of QUESTION TWO: Licensing of copyrighted works to end users has caused headaches for rights holders in the digital context. Effectuating a licensing regime that incorporates a disparate class of anonymous end users is hardly easy, often impossible, and provides a good example of market failure. Consequently, one might think that government regulation through legislation would provide the answer. None of the national reports, however, have indicated that clearing mechanisms have been included in their individual statutes.

The major advances have occurred in the private sector in two ways: by the use of digital technologies and agreements between CMOs and other organizations such as YouTube that supply information on the internet. The national reports have identified several methodologies for clearing content with content providers like YouTube when practical obstacles prevent licensing agreements with diverse, numerous, costly to find end users. Scanning systems have become increasingly proficient thanks to ever more powerful digital technologies as outlined the U.S. Report (Szewczyk & Besek) where YouTube uses a pre-clearance called Content ID and Audible Magic's set of Content Identification Databases. The UGC colossus, YouTube, was the focus of many reports in mentioning licensing agreements between YouTube and the collecting societies (U.K., PRS since 2013; Germany, GEMA, 2007; Egypt, SACERAU, 2011; Belgium, 2011; Croatia, 2014; Canada, SOCAN, 2007, and others) for remuneration for use of copyrighted works.

- United States: (Szewczyk & Besek): The United States Report points out two pre-clearance methods, one of which is used by YouTube, called Content ID. This method compares the content a user wants to upload to a list supplied by copyright owners, and blocks material identified on the "blacklist" from going onto the website in the first place. All videos uploaded to YouTube are scanned against a database of files that have been submitted to YouTube by content owners. Similarly, the U.S. report highlights Audible Magic's set of Content Identification Databases, such as their Advertising Database, Live TV Database, Motion Picture & Archived TV Database and

Music Database, in addition to other custom databases offering flexible multi-tiered pricing plans, to meet the needs of a varied set of customers.

- Italy (Ercolani): The Italian Report indicates that the only working mechanism in place with a UGC platform concerns agreements with YouTube. Here, Google has built up a business relationship with collecting societies and similar entities for the licensing of monetized music contents. Digital fingerprint technology is used to clear works. Publishing contracts with CMOs and notice and takedown procedures by content providers round out the other modalities used to clear rights. The situation outlined by the Italian report is similar to that found on this issue in other European countries.
- Hungary: The Hungarian Report points out that Hungary is one of the few countries of the world where the exclusive right of authors and performers to make works/fixed performances available to the public, in a way that the members of the public can choose the place and time of access individually, are exercised by way of extended collective administration.
- Japan: Similar to European countries, JASRAC, and other CMOs in Japan make licensing agreements with platform operators for all usages, including individual uploaders' content. The agreements apply to the usages of copyright songs on general services provided by YouTube, DWANGO, etc.
- Portugal: The Portuguese Report specifies the agreement that CMOs concluded with YouTube in 2014, elaborating on an intricate tariff system for the remuneration for use of content.

III. Third Question

1. If there is infringement of copyright, in particular of exclusive rights covering the acts listed under 1. above, and the direct infringer cannot be identified or addressed, does your law (including case law) provide for liability of intermediaries or others for infringement by third persons, namely:

i. for content providers
ii. for host providers
iii. for access providers
iv. for others

2. If so, under what conditions are they liable, and for what (in particular, damages, information on the direct infringer, information on the scope of infringement to estimate the amount of damage)?

SUMMARY of QUESTION THREE: The reports for Question Three indicate a consensus on the liability of intermediaries who are often placed in a delicate position in their activities of content providers, host providers and access providers. In general, content providers are the most often exposed to actions for direct infringement. As for host providers and access providers, variants of safe harbors and notice and takedown provisions are common. Other than to direct infringement, host and access providers are exposed to indirect liability. In general, European law is guided by two directives that have had dominant effect. For example, the Hungarian Report states that the relevant provisions of the Information Society Directive and the E-Commerce Directive 2000/31/EC, have been transposed into national law. As for remedies, the reports specify injunctive relief and damages (knowledge requirement). In a couple of instances (United States [Szewczyk & Besek]; Italy [Ercolani]), the service provider may be obligated to provide information about the infringing end user to permit the copyright owner to initiate an action for infringement.

- United States (Szewczyk & Besek): Content providers are directly liable for copyright infringement. Host providers can also be directly liable as well as contributorily liable, but section 512(c) of the U.S. Copyright Act provides a safe harbor if the service provider complies with the requirement of the statute.[21] Access providers are not liable for copyright infringement under the safe harbor of section 512(a) if they comply with the requirements of the statute. Similarly, search engines are not liable for copyright infringement under the safe harbor of section 512(d), if they comply with the requirements of the statute.

  "Failure to qualify for the safe harbor does not automatically mean that an ISP is an infringer." In a number of cases, "courts have held ISPs not liable for direct infringement, because their activities were non-volitional."[22] ISPs can, however, be secondarily liable, under contributory or vicarious liability. Available remedies include injunctions, actual and statutory damages. "Independently of the service provider's liability [...], the service provider may be compelled to provide information about the infringing end user in order to permit the copyright owner to initiate an action under section 512(h)." In practice, however, this measure is rarely used.

---

21 512(c) provides a safe harbor if the service provider (A) (i) does not have actual knowledge that the material or an activity using the material on the system or network is infringing; (ii) in the absence of such actual knowledge, is not aware of facts or circumstances from which infringing activity is apparent; or (iii) upon obtaining such knowledge or awareness, acts expeditiously to remove, or disable access to, the material; (B) does not receive a financial benefit directly attributable to the infringing activity, in a case in which the service provider has the right and ability to control such activity; and (C) upon notification of claimed infringement as described in paragraph (3), responds expeditiously to remove, or disable access to, the material that is claimed to be infringing or to be the subject of infringing activity.

22 See, e.g., Columbia Pictures Industries, Inc. v. Fung, 710 F.3d 1020 (9th Cir. 2013).

- Italy (Ercolani): In Italy, liability of internet intermediaries is limited to instances where they do not comply with the rules of Decree 70/2003, implementing the E-commerce Directive. Articles 14, 15, 16 and 17 of the Decree have transposed the provisions on safe harbors of the Directive for providers of conduit, caching services, and hosting services. In addition, these intermediaries have no obligation to monitor content.
  If internet intermediaries willfully do not comply with proper "take down notices", they are liable for damages. In addition, when required by judicial authority, they must provide information in their possession on the identity of the infringer as well as the name of the organization sponsoring the illicit activity.
- Germany (Pflüger): German law provides for the liability of intermediaries. Content providers are liable for infringing content. Host providers are liable for infringing content if the provider knows or should have known that the hosted work is infringing. "Access providers are not liable unless they initiate the data transmission, select the addressee, or select or change the transmitted data." Appropriate remedies consist of injunctive relief or removal of the infringing material. Damages are provided if the acts of infringement are intentional or negligent.
- Egypt (Omar Amine): The Egyptian Report indicates that the courts have not decided any cases concerning intermediaries. In addition, the Egyptian Intellectual Property Code does not specify the obligations of intermediaries. The liability of intermediaries and remedies are governed by the general doctrines of copyright law.
- Hungary: The Hungarian Report states that the relevant provisions of the Directive 2000/31/EC of the European Parliament and of the Council of 8 June 2000 on certain legal aspects of information society services, in particular electronic commerce, in the Internal Market ("E-Commerce Directive") have been transposed into national law by Act CVIII of 2001 on certain issues of electronic commerce services and information society services ("Ecommerce Act").[23] As for remedies, the Report specifies that hosting services and access providers are intermediary service providers that receive safe harbor protection. Remedies are limited to injunctive relief unless these intermediaries knew or should have known of the infringing activity.
- Argentina (Barrenechea & Wegbrait): The Argentine Report reveals that little case law exists on the liability of intermediaries. Lower courts, however, have had a tendency to limit intermediaries to indirect liability if they prove that they acted diligently when notified of the infringement. This is derived from Section 12 of the Argentine Copyright Act, which refers to the applica-

---

23 Act CVIII of 2001 on certain issues of electronic commerce services and information society services ("ECommerce Act").

tion of general law in all aspects not expressly contemplated in specific intellectual property provisions.[24]

Under Argentine law, the following elements are considered in establishing liability: the kind of activity carried out by the intermediary (automatic or merely technical activities, without content manipulation); the degree of knowledge (the so-called notice and takedown doctrine is analyzed); notice of the infringement (direct, administrative or court-ordered); scope of the infringing activity; benefit resulting from the infringing activity; etc.

- Croatia (Jurić, Matanovac Furić, Katulić): Under the Croatian Copyright and Related Rights Act, regarding damages, access providers will not be liable for infringement if the conditions stipulated in Article 16(1) of the Croatian Electronic Commerce Act (ECA) are met. An access provider must show that it did not (1) initiate the transfer of the content, (2) select the data of documents (content) that is the object of the transmission, (3) modify the content and (4) select the receiver of the transmission.

  Similarly, under Croatian law, "hosting providers enjoy limited liability under Article 18(1) of the ECA when they store information provided by a recipient of the service, on the condition that (1) the provider does not have or could not have had actual knowledge of an illegal activity of the recipient or of the content of information, and (2) the provider, upon obtaining such knowledge or awareness, acts expeditiously to remove or to disable access to the information. Furthermore, there is also a limited liability regime for linking activities established in Article 19 of the ECA."

IV. Fourth Question

Who has standing to sue for infringement of copyright among the following categories?

i. ***Author***
ii. ***Exclusive licensee***
iii. ***The non-exclusive licensee***
iv. ***Employer of the author***
v. ***CMO that manages the exclusive right***

SUMMARY of QUESTION FOUR: As general proposition, all the reports indicate that the author, and the assignee of rights have standing to sue. The consensus breaks down when considering the standing of the exclusive, non-exclusive licensee and the employer of the author. In some jurisdictions the exclusive

24 Section 12. Intellectual property shall be governed by the provisions of common law, subject to the conditions and limitations established in this Law.

licensee has standing to sue, as does the employer in the case of works made for hire (United States, UK); in others, standing for these entities is determined exclusively by contract and the consent of the rights holder (see Dutch Report, (Kannekens, Sluiter, Salamanca, Eechoud)). The Finnish Report (Oesch, Günther, Pihlajarinne) indicates another variation. In addition to the author, an exclusive licensee has standing to sue. In Finland, the situation is different for the non-exclusive licensee and the CMO. Here, standing to sue will depend on the contractual terms between these entities and the rights holder. The employer has standing only if rights to work have been assigned.

- United States (Szewczyk & Besek): "A creator's employer has standing to sue if the work is made for hire, because the employer in that instance will be the statutory author and copyright owner ab initio." The owner of an exclusive right (exclusive licensee) including a CMO that manages an exclusive right has standing to sue. Conversely, a non-exclusive licensee does not have standing to sue. The U.S. Report states: "A CMO that manages the exclusive right would have standing to sue, but not if the CMO has non-exclusive rights. CMOs in the US do not hold exclusive rights, so do not have independent authority to sue. Individual members of the CMO usually appear as the named plaintiffs, even though the CMO may be managing and financing the suit."
- Italy (Ercolani): Art 167 of the copyright law makes no explicit reference to licensees. The courts have consistently confirmed that the exclusive licensee has standing whereas the non-exclusive licensee does not. In the employment context, the economic rights for works created as part of the employee's contractual tasks are owned by the employer. CMOs also have standing to sue.
- United Kingdom (Davies, Dimita, Edwards, Frabboni, Koempel, Suthersanen): Unlike Italy and the United States, non-exclusive licensees are given standing to sue for certain infringements under Section 101A CDPA. Employers have standing "where the author was employed under a contract of service or made the work in the course of employment, subject to agreement to the contrary." CMOs have standing to enforce their member's rights by legal action.
- Germany (Pflüger): As in other jurisdictions, the author has standing unless he has transferred his exclusive rights to another but has standing to sue for moral rights. The holder of an exclusive right has standing to sue whereas a non-exclusive licensee has no standing to sue. The employer has standing to sue if he has an exclusive right to use the work. CMOs have standing to sue dependent on the exclusive rights they enjoy.
- Belgium (Witmeur): The copyright owner (author or assignee) has standing to bring an action for infringement. Both exclusive and non-exclusive licensees have standing to sue. Whether the employer has standing depends on his contractual rights.

- Norway (Lund): The author and exclusive licensee have standing to sue; a non-exclusive licensee does not. Employers have standing only if exclusive rights have been granted contractually. CMOs that manage an exclusive right have standing.
- Portugal: As in a number of other countries, licensees have no standing to sue unless provided for in the contract. The Portuguese report states that licensors act as guarantor of the licensed rights, and any potential challenge to the rights is to be governed by the copyright owner's intervention.
- France (Binctin): The owner of the exclusive license has standing in the case of a phonogram or videogram unless otherwise stipulated in the licensing agreement. Non-exclusive licensees have no standing. Employers who are given an exclusive right have standing to sue as well as CMOs for rights that they manage.
- Finland (Oesch, Günther, Pihlajarinne): The author, and exclusive licensee have standing to sue. For the non-exclusive licensee, the employer, and CMO, standing to sue is determined by the contractual relationship between these entities and the rights holder.
- Canada: In general, whoever owns a right by written assignment or license from the copyright owner has standing to sue.
- Mexico (Larrea and Schmidt): Standing to sue corresponds to the person or entity that is the holder of the patrimonial rights to bring an action for infringement.
- Greece (Kallinikou, Stavridou, Despotidou): Apart from primarily rights holders, the exclusive licensee has standing to sue for acts of infringement. According to Article 13 par. 3 of Greek Copyright Law N. 2121/93, in the absence of an agreement to the contrary, the other contracting parties shall be entitled in their own name to seek legal protection against illegal infringements by third parties of the rights he exercises. Collecting societies have standing to protect the rights in works and right holders. According to Article 55 par. 2 of Greek Copyright Law N. 2121/93, "a collecting society shall in all circumstances be entitled to initiate judicial or extrajudicial action in its own name and to exercise in full legitimacy all the rights transferred to it, or for which it holds power of attorney."
- Netherlands (Kannekens, Sluiter, Salamanca, Eechoud). "The general rule is that only the author or his successor in title (by transfer, inheritance, etc.) has standing to sue when enforcing copyright in civil procedures. They might also instruct a third party to sue on their behalf or grant permission to do so. CBOs enforce copyright because the author has transferred copyright or has granted authority to enforce. Art 27(1) DCA further states that 'notwithstanding the assignment of his copyright wholly or in part, the author shall retain the right to bring an action for damages against persons who infringe the copyright'. Art 27a (2) DCA provides that the author may claim

damages on behalf of a licensee. By law, a licensee has standing to sue only for damages and surrender of the profits, and only if he/she has the consent of the copyright owner (art 27a DCA)."

Marshall Leaffer*

1.2 Rapport général: Étendue et instruments de mise en œuvre pour garantir la remuneration, partie A du questionnaire

RESUME INTRODUCTIF : Dans l'environnement internet, les œuvres protégées sont utilisées par des particuliers anonymes et dispersés, dans des conditions de faible visibilité. Dans cet environnement, il s'avère difficile de conclure des accords de licence et peu pratique de recourir à des actions en justice. La question de savoir comment les titulaires de droits sont rémunérés à l'ère du numérique constitue le thème de notre congrès. La tâche qui m'a été confiée consiste à examiner les réponses apportées aux différents points de la partie A du questionnaire concernant l'étendue et la mise en œuvre des droits exclusifs en droit positif. Mes collègues analyseront à leur tour les réponses aux parties B, C et D portant sur des aspects différents des mécanismes de rémunération.

Le présent rapport s'appuie sur les réponses de vingt pays. Compte tenu du temps limité dont je dispose et dans un souci de clarté, il ne m'est pas possible dans le cadre de l'examen qui suit de fournir des détails complexes et nuancés. Mon but consiste à présenter les tendances générales qui ressortent des rapports nationaux. Pour obtenir une description plus nuancée et peut-être plus exacte, il convient de consulter ces différents rapports.[1]

Dans la partie A sont posées quatre séries de questions qui concernent la manière dont le droit national de chaque pays assure la mise en œuvre des droits exclusifs reconnus au titulaire du droit d'auteur. Après un rappel des termes des questions posées aux groupes nationaux de l'ALAI (en italiques et en gras), sont présentés des résumés généraux établis à partir des rapports nationaux. Comme déjà indiqué, ces brefs résumés ne visent évidemment pas à être exhaustifs mais sont destinés à servir uniquement de cadre de référence pour la lecture des rapports nationaux. Ces résumés sont suivis d'exemples tirés des rapports nationaux.

La première question porte sur la manière dont sont appréhendés par le droit de chaque pays les huit actes sur internet qui y sont énumérés. J'ai décomposé cette question en trois volets. Dans le premier volet sont traités les hyperliens, les liens profonds et la transclusion (cadrage) (I.). Le deuxième volet s'intéresse aux actes de *streaming*, de téléchargement descendant (*down-*

---

* Professeur, Université de l'Indiana, Maurer School of Law, États-Unis. Traduction de l'anglais par Margaret Platt-Hommel.

1 V. les rapports nationaux: http://alai2015.org/en/national-reports.html.

loading) et de téléchargement ascendant (*uploading*) d'œuvres (II.). Dans le troisième volet est examinée la fourniture d'une plateforme UGC pour les « contenus générés par les utilisateurs » ainsi que d'autres nouvelles utilisations sur internet.

I. Première question

Comment les actes suivants sont-ils couverts par le droit d'auteur dans votre pays (selon la loi et la jurisprudence) ?

i. Offre d'hyperliens à des œuvres
ii. Offre de liens profonds (deep links) à des œuvres
iii. Cadrage/transclusion (framing/embedding) d'œuvres
iv. Streaming d'œuvres
v. Téléchargement descendant (download) d'œuvres
vi. Téléchargement ascendant (upload) d'œuvres
vii. Fourniture d'une plateforme UGC pour les « contenus générés par les utilisateurs »
viii. Autres nouvelles utilisations sur internet

1. RESUME – HYPERLIENS, LIENS PROFONDS, CADRAGE/TRANSCLUSION :
Le fait le plus intéressant qui ressort de ces rapports est qu'aucun pays, à l'exception peut-être de la Croatie, n'a traité l'offre d'hyperliens, l'offre de liens profonds et la transclusion (cadrage) dans son droit écrit. Comme le souligne le rapport argentin (Barrenechea & Wegbrait) :

> « La loi argentine sur la propriété intellectuelle[2] ... ne traite expressément ni les aspects envisagés par la question ni les utilisations sur internet des œuvres ou des objets protégés par des droits voisins. Mais ces utilisations sont tout de même couvertes puisque l'article 2[3] de la loi sur la propriété intellectuelle consacre un droit exclusif étendu de disposer de l'œuvre et de l'exploiter sous quelque forme et de quelque manière que ce soit. Cette formulation large est considérée comme s'appliquant à Internet. »

Il est étonnant de constater le peu de litiges réels qu'il y a eu sur cette question compte tenu de l'importance de ces utilisations courantes sur internet. Autre généralisation : on trouve dans les rapports un faible consensus selon lequel la pose d'hyperliens et de liens profonds et la transclusion (cadrage) d'œuvres

2 Loi n° 11.723.

3 Article 2 : Le droit de propriété sur une œuvre scientifique, littéraire ou artistique, comprend, pour son auteur, le droit d'en disposer, de la publier, de l'exécuter, de la représenter et de l'exposer en public, de l'aliéner, de la traduire, de l'adapter ou d'en autoriser la traduction et de la reproduire sous quelque forme que ce soit.

sont licites en l'absence d'autres éléments qui entraîneraient une responsabilité directe ou indirecte. Comme le précise le rapport hongrois, « sous réserve de certaines conditions, ne constitue un acte soumis à l'autorisation du titulaire du droit d'auteur ni l'offre d'hyperliens ou de liens profonds ni la transclusion (cadrage) ».

Le droit des Etats-Unis fournit une solution. Selon le droit américain, un hyperlien vers un site internet qui contient une œuvre protégée ne constitue pas une violation directe du droit d'auteur puisque l'hyperlien ne contient pas lui-même une œuvre protégée. Mais, selon le droit américain, la responsabilité indirecte du lieur pour complicité de contrefaçon ou du fait d'autrui peut éventuellement être engagée. Une action en responsabilité indirecte – pour complicité ou du fait d'autrui – peut être intentée si la personne qui offre un lien profond a vraisemblablement connaissance du caractère contrefaisant de l'œuvre. De même, le cadrage ou la transclusion d'œuvres a été considéré comme ne constituant pas une violation directe lorsque l'œuvre n'est pas stockée sur le propre ordinateur de l'opérateur. Une action en concurrence déloyale est possible.

Le droit européen est parvenu à peu près au même résultat que les Etats-Unis, mais la résolution du problème s'avère plus compliquée et plus controversée comme le révèlent les rapports nationaux. Les rapports européens soulignent plus particulièrement l'incidence de la jurisprudence de la CJUE dans les affaires *Svensson* et *BestWater*[4] pour la reconnaissance de la licéité en soi des actes d'établissement de liens simples, de liens profonds et de transclusion (cadrage). Le principal sujet de discorde concerne non pas la solution dégagée dans ces deux affaires mais le fait que les arrêts *Svensson* et *BestWater* semblent contredire certains principes de base de la directive de l'UE sur la société de l'information, où il est affirmé qu'aucun acte de communication au public ne peut entraîner l'épuisement du droit d'auteur. Cette polémique est mise en évidence par le rapport italien qui indique que la Cour, en exigeant la présence d'un public nouveau ou d'un nouveau mode technique pour conclure à un acte de communication au public en violation du droit d'auteur, instaure l'équivalent de l'épuisement du droit de communication en ligne. Rappelons que l'étude approuvée par le Comité exécutif de l'ALAI en septembre 2014 affirme que cette exigence est en contradiction avec les règles des traités de l'OMPI.[5] Cette étude de l'ALAI déclare :

4 Affaires C-466/12 ("Svensson") et C-348/13 ("BestWater").

5 Le rapport hongrois critique également la théorie du «public nouveau». Pour la critique de l'ALAI, voir l'Avis sur le critère de «public nouveau» adopté par son Comité exécutif réuni le 17 septembre 2014 et publié à l'adresse: http://www.alai.org/assets/files/resolutions/2014-avis-public-nouveau.pdf; voir également Dr. Mihály J. Ficsor, «Svensson: Honest attempt at establishing due balance concerning the use of hyperlinks – spoiled by the erroneous ‹new public›

> En l'espèce [dans l'affaire *Svensson*], la CJUE, tout en répondant correctement par l'affirmative à la question fondamentale de savoir si la fourniture d'un hyperlien constitue une mise à disposition/communication (interactive) – à l'instar de la position exposée dans l'Avis précité de l'ALAI du 15 septembre 2013 –, a dans la même décision, s'agissant de la question de savoir si cet acte constitue une communication « au public », confirmé un certain nombre d'autres décisions récentes par lesquelles elle a introduit un critère problématique de « public nouveau », circonscrit entre autres par un nouveau critère, tout aussi problématique, de « mode technique spécifique ».

Venons-en maintenant à quelques exemples tirés des rapports nationaux concernant les actes suivants :

i. Offre d'hyperliens
ii. Offre de liens profonds vers des œuvres
iii. Transclusion (cadrage) d'œuvres

- Etats-Unis (Szewczyk & Besek) : Selon le droit américain, l'offre d'un hyperlien vers un site internet qui contient une œuvre protégée ne constitue pas une violation directe du droit d'auteur puisque l'hyperlien ne contient pas lui-même une œuvre protégée. Mais une action en responsabilité indirecte – pour complicité ou du fait d'autrui – peut éventuellement être intentée. L'offre d'un lien profond vers une œuvre ne constitue pas non plus une violation directe du droit d'auteur, mais une action en responsabilité indirecte – pour complicité ou du fait d'autrui – peut être intentée si la personne qui offre un lien profond a vraisemblablement connaissance du caractère contrefaisant de l'œuvre. De même, le cadrage ou la transclusion d'œuvres a été considéré comme ne constituant pas une violation directe lorsque l'œuvre n'est pas stockée sur le propre ordinateur de l'opérateur.
- Royaume-Uni (Davies, Dimita, Edwards, Frabboni, Koempel, Suthersanen) : L'offre d'un hyperlien vers des contenus librement accessibles n'enfreindra pas l'article 20 de la loi (*CDPA*). En revanche, il en ira différemment des hyperliens conçus pour contourner des péages. Mais il n'est pas clair si le contenu doit être librement accessible ou autorisé, même implicitement par l'auteur/l'ayant droit du copyright. Des lignes directrices précisent que l'activité n'est pas contrefaisante si le contenu a été publié librement en ligne avec l'autorisation du titulaire du droit.

  Selon le rapport du Royaume-Uni, la question cruciale est de savoir si la fourniture d'un hyperlien constitue un acte de communication au public. Le rapport indique qu'un élément de connaissance ou de facilitation de la violation serait nécessaire pour établir la responsabilité du lieur. Pour les mê-

---

theory»; publié à l'adresse: http://www.copyrightseesaw.net/archive/?sw_10_item=68 (tous deux consultés la dernière fois le 6 avril 2015).

mes raisons que celles indiquées plus haut, ne constituera une violation ni l'offre d'un lien profond ni la transclusion (cadrage). Mais le respect des droits moraux pourra éventuellement entrer en jeu dans le cas de ces deux activités.

- Hongrie : Sous réserve de certaines conditions, ne constitue un acte soumis à l'autorisation du titulaire du droit d'auteur ni l'offre d'hyperliens ou de liens profonds ni la transclusion (cadrage). Comme beaucoup d'autres rapports, le rapport hongrois évoque les affaires *Svensson* et *BestWater*. La plupart des rapports qui font état de ces deux affaires critiquent la logique du critère de « public nouveau » sous-tendant la décision, tout en approuvant en général la solution dégagée.
- Italie (Ercolani) : Le simple renvoi vers un autre site au moyen d'un hyperlien n'est pas un acte de communication pourvu que le lien ne constitue qu'un outil de référencement conduisant à des éléments externes. Le rapport italien distingue l'acte qui consiste à fournir un hyperlien de l'acte d'établissement d'un lien profond ou de l'acte de transclusion (cadrage). « Selon l'interprétation du droit italien, on peut supposer que l'acte de lier constitue une forme de mise à la disposition du public lorsqu'il prend la forme d'un lien profond ou de la transclusion (cadrage) d'œuvres de telle sorte que l'utilisateur final ne perçoit pas la différence entre les œuvres directement hébergées par le site et les œuvres simplement insérées ou tirées de sources externes. En revanche, ne doit pas être considéré comme un acte de communication l'acte de simple renvoi vers un autre site internet au moyen d'un hyperlien pourvu que le lien ne constitue qu'un outil de référencement conduisant à des éléments externes ».
- Suisse (Salvadé & Cherpillod) : Les hyperliens simples, sans plus, ne sont pas susceptibles de donner lieu à des actions en justice. Ne le sont pas non plus les liens profonds même si ces derniers pourraient soulever des questions de respect des droits moraux dans certains contextes. Les techniques de transclusion/cadrage d'œuvres peuvent faire l'objet d'actions en justice en tant qu'actes de mise à disposition. Ces actes pourraient également donner lieu à des actions en tant que portant atteinte au droit à l'intégrité et au droit à la paternité.
- Japon : La fourniture d'hyperliens et de liens profonds et les activités de transclusion (cadrage) sont des actes qui mettent en jeu le droit de mise à disposition (« *making transmittable* ») selon le droit japonais.
- Finlande (Oesch, Günther, Pihlajarinne) : Le rapport finlandais donne des précisions sur la question des techniques de transclusion/cadrage.[6] Le Conseil finlandais sur le droit d'auteur (*Finnish Copyright Council*), se fon-

6 Voir l'avis d'experts présenté par le Conseil finlandais sur le droit d'auteur (2001:8 – cadrage des articles).

dant sur l'arrêt *Svensson*, a déclaré (2014:4) que l'offre d'un lien vers une image sur une page de discussion sans but commercial est licite si l'ayant droit a autorisé la libre utilisation de son image sur internet.[7]

- Canada : Dans un certain nombre de pays dont le Canada, cette question n'est spécifiquement visée ni par la législation ni par la jurisprudence.
- Grèce (Kallinikou, Stavridou, Despotidou) : Selon la jurisprudence grecque, l'offre d'hyperliens peut entraîner la responsabilité du lieur dans certaines circonstances. Le tribunal de première instance d'Athènes, dans l'affaire 4042/2010, a estimé qu'un radiodiffuseur qui a été autorisé par une société de gestion à diffuser son programme radio porte atteinte au droit d'auteur en mettant sur son site un hyperlien (bannière interactive) permettant la transmission de son programme radio sur internet.
- Croatie (Juric, Matanovac Furic, Katulic) : La Croatie fait figure d'exception à la règle générale selon laquelle la plupart des pays n'ont pas de dispositions particulières sur l'établissement d'hyperliens. L'article 19 de la loi croate sur le commerce électronique prévoit : « Le fournisseur de services qui, au moyen de liens électroniques, donne accès à des informations tierces n'est pas responsable de ces informations si : il n'a pas connaissance ou ne pouvait pas avoir connaissance de l'activité illicite des destinataires ou du contenu de ces informations ; [et] dès qu'il a connaissance de cette activité illicite ou de ce contenu, il retire le contenu ou le rend inaccessible ».
- Belgique (Witmeur) : Le rapport belge indique que la société de gestion SABAM souhaitait percevoir des droits pour les liens intégrés (*embedded links*) vers des sites commerciaux au départ du site internet de YouTube. La SABAM s'appuyait sur les conditions des accords de licence qu'elle avait signés avec YouTube qui, selon la SABAM, ne visent que la communication au public dans une sphère privée. Cette position est évidemment contestée par YouTube.
- Pays-Bas (Kannekens, Sluiter, Salamanca, Eechoud) : Ne figure dans la loi néerlandaise sur le droit d'auteur aucune disposition qui prévoit une responsabilité secondaire en cas de contrefaçon ou qui prévoit la contrefaçon indirecte. La fourniture d'un simple hyperlien (profond) ne constitue pas une communication au public et ne porte pas directement atteinte au droit d'auteur. Dans certains cas particuliers, elle pourrait néanmoins être considérée comme un « acte illicite » selon la disposition en matière de respon-

7 Voir le Comité finlandais du droit d'auteur (*Finnish Copyright Committee*) 2002:5, p. 2 ainsi que l'étude distincte du Comité finlandais du droit d'auteur (2012:2) réalisée par Taina Pihlajarinne et portant sur les liens à caractère commercial notamment dans des situations où sont créés de nouveaux services qui recherchent un avantage économique grâce à des liens automatiques.

sabilité civile prévue à l'article 6:162 du Code civil néerlandais (notamment lorsqu'une personne établit systématiquement des liens vers une grande quantité de contenus non autorisés et qu'elle en tire un profit).[8]

- Autriche (Walter) : « La loi autrichienne sur le droit d'auteur ne vise pas spécifiquement ces actes. Sur le plan jurisprudentiel, la Cour suprême autrichienne a estimé en 2011[9] que dans le cas d'un hyperlien il n'y a aucune reproduction faite dans l'ordinateur de l'utilisateur et que l'établissement de l'hyperlien n'est pas à considérer comme un acte de communication au public. En revanche, la doctrine estime que l'établissement de liens profonds ainsi que la transclusion (cadrage) sont des actes de communication au public ».

2. RESUME – *STREAMING*, TELECHARGEMENT DESCENDANT et TELECHARGEMENT ASCENDANT : La deuxième série d'actes concerne la diffusion en *streaming*, le téléchargement descendant (*downloading*) et le téléchargement ascendant (*uploading*) d'œuvres. En l'absence de l'autorisation du titulaire du droit d'auteur, ces actes sont susceptibles de porter atteinte à un ou à plusieurs droits exclusifs. Le *streaming* constitue clairement une communication au public comme l'indiquent tous les rapports.[10] Quant à la mise en ligne (téléchargement ascendant) de contenus protégés, la plupart des rapports indiquent que cet acte met en jeu à la fois le droit de mise à disposition et le droit de distribution. Le téléchargement descendant d'œuvres relève du droit de reproduction. Certains rapports, comme les rapports suisse (Salvadé & Cherpillod) et norvégien (Lund), évoquent l'usage privé de l'œuvre téléchargée en tant qu'exception éventuelle au droit de reproduction.[11] Le téléchargement d'œuvres depuis internet a créé un terrible casse-tête pour la communauté mondiale du droit d'auteur. La législation française avec la mise en place de la Haute Autorité pour la diffusion des œuvres et la protection des droits sur Internet (HADOPI), décrite de façon détaillée dans le rapport français (Binctin), constitue une tentative *sui generis* mais controversée de sanctionner les habitués du téléchargement illicite.

---

8 Visser, D.J.G., «Openbaar maken: Communication to the public», *in*: Hugenholtz, P.B., Quaedvlieg, A.A., Visser, D.J.G. (dir.) *A century of Dutch Copyright Law*, Amstelveen: Uitgeverij deLex, 2012, p. 225.

9 Cour suprême, 20.9.2011, 4 Ob 105/11m – «123people/Vorschaubilder/Thumbnails» MR 2011, 313 (*Michel Walter*) = ecolex 2012/29, 64 (*Axel Anderl*) = wbl 2012/38, 105 = RZ 2012/76, 123 (LS) = ÖBl 2012/45, 175 (*Manfred Büchele*).

10 Le rapport allemand évoque l'article 19a UrhG (mise à la disposition du public) ; le *streaming* en direct serait couvert par l'article 20 UrhG (droit de radiodiffusion).

11 Le rapport suisse indique que l'article 19, al. 1, litt. a LDA prévoit que l'exception d'usage privé s'applique même si la source est illicite.

Présentons maintenant quelques exemples tirés des rapports nationaux concernant les actes suivants :

iv. Le *streaming* d'œuvres
v. Le téléchargement descendant d'œuvres
vi. Le téléchargement ascendant d'œuvres

- Canada : Selon la jurisprudence canadienne,[12] le *streaming* doit être considéré comme une communication au public mais pas comme une reproduction dans la mesure où les copies réalisées lors du processus de *streaming* ont un caractère temporaire. En revanche, le téléchargement descendant et le téléchargement ascendant créent des copies permanentes. Selon le droit des Etats-Unis, les droits de représentation, de reproduction et de distribution sont mis en jeu, ce qui aboutit plus ou moins au même résultat.
- Royaume-Uni (Davies, Dimita, Edwards, Frabboni, Koempel, Suthersanen) : malgré le manque de jurisprudence, le téléchargement de contenus non autorisés porterait atteinte au droit de reproduction prévu par l'article 17 CDPA. Depuis 2005, la mise en ligne d'œuvres protégées sauf les programmes d'ordinateur sans l'autorisation de l'ayant droit porte atteinte à l'article 20 CDPA (l'article 20 CDPA concerne le droit de communication au public). La mise en ligne des programmes d'ordinateur est susceptible de porter atteinte au droit d'auteur en tant qu'acte de distribution au public selon l'article 18 CDPA.[13]
- Norvège (Lund) : Le *streaming* relève du droit de mise à disposition. Le téléchargement descendant d'œuvres met en jeu le droit de reproduction. L'article 12 de la loi norvégienne sur le droit d'auteur prévoit une exception en cas de reproduction pour un usage privé à condition que la copie soit réalisée à partir d'une source licite, mais « la réalisation de copies « exploitables par une machine » de programmes d'ordinateurs et la réalisation de copies « exploitables par une machine » de bases de données sous une forme « exploitable par une machine » en sont exclues. » Le téléchargement ascendant d'œuvres relève du droit exclusif de reproduction ainsi que du droit de mise à la disposition du public d'œuvres protégées.
- France (Binctin) : Comme dans d'autres rapports, le *streaming* est considéré comme une communication au public. Quant au téléchargement descendant, le rapport français indique qu'il s'agit d'un acte de communication au public et d'un acte de reproduction. Le législateur français a mis en place la Haute Autorité pour la diffusion des œuvres et la protection des droits sur

12 Entertainment Software Association c/ Société canadienne des auteurs, compositeurs et éditeurs de musique (SOCAN), 2012 CSC 34 [ESA], et Rogers Communications, Inc. c/ SOCAN, 2012 CSC 35.

13 Affaire C-128/11, UsedSoft GmbH c/ Oracle International Corp.

Internet (HADOPI). Cette instance *sui generis* a été créée en 2009 pour lutter contre la contrefaçon sur internet. Elle est habilitée à imposer des sanctions à ceux qui effectuent des téléchargements en méconnaissance du droit d'auteur. Le fonctionnement de la HADOPI est décrit de façon détaillée dans le rapport français.

- Autriche (Walter) : Dans le cas du *streaming*, « la mise à disposition en *streaming* de contenus protégés est soumise à l'autorisation de l'auteur[14]. Mais l'acte de « réception » par l'utilisateur est à considérer comme étant couvert par l'exception relative aux reproductions provisoires qui sont transitoires ou accessoires selon l'article 5.1 de la directive sur la société de l'information. Reste ouverte toutefois la question de savoir si cela vaut également lorsque les flux sont mis à disposition illicitement. L'auteur du rapport estime que la licéité de la source est également une condition préalable à l'application de cette exception, comme c'est le cas pour la copie privée ».[15]
  La Cour suprême autrichienne a notamment abordé cette question de façon limitée dans les questions préjudicielles posées à la CJUE dans l'affaire « kino.to c/ UPC I ».[16]
- Pays-Bas (Kannekens, Sluiter, Salamanca, Eechoud) : « La mise en ligne d'une œuvre protégée est considérée comme un acte de « *openbaarmaking* »[17] qui, lorsqu'elle est effectuée sans l'autorisation du titulaire du droit d'auteur, porte atteinte à ce droit ».[18]
  Selon le rapport néerlandais : « Le téléchargement descendant d'une œuvre protégée par le droit d'auteur est un acte de reproduction. Dans de nombreux cas, les téléchargements ne nécessiteront aucune autorisation du fait de l'application de l'exception de copie privée (*thuiskopieuitzondering*, art 16c LDA néerlandaise). Cette exception s'applique uniquement à la reproduction d'une (partie d'une) œuvre effectuée par une personne physique à des fins non directement ou indirectement commerciales et exclusivement

---

14 Droit de mise à disposition prévu à l'article 18a (auteurs) et à l'article 71a (détenteurs de droits voisins) de la loi autrichienne sur le droit d'auteur.

15 Voir CJUE, 10.4.2014, C-435/12 – «ACI Adam/Thuiskopie» MR-Int 2014, 42 *(Michel Walter)* = EuZW 2014, 501 *(Carl C Müller/Sören Rößner)* = ZUM 2014, 573 *(Anne Lauber-Rönsberg)* = ecolex 2014/297, 727 *(LS) (Adolf Zeman)* = MMR 2014, 679 = ÖBl 2014, 232 *(Johannes Burgstaller/ Mona Philomena Ladler).*

16 Cour suprême, 11.5.2012, 4 Ob 6/12d – MR 2012, 190 *(Michel Walter)* = ecolex 2012/291, 708 *(Axel Anderl)* = wbl 2012/180, 473 = GRUR Int 2012, 934.

17 Le droit de «openbaarmaken» est un droit large qui couvre un éventail d'actes tels que la représentation/exécution publique (où le public est physiquement présent), la communication au public (par exemple, la radiodiffusion), la mise à disposition à la demande et la distribution d'exemplaires ou de copies physiques. Voir Visser, D.J.G., «Openbaar maken: Communication to the public», *in*: Hugenholtz, P.B., Quaedvlieg, A.A., Visser, D.J.G. (dir.) *A century of Dutch Copyright Law*, Amstelveen: DeLex, 2012, p. 225.

18 Cour d'appel de la Haye, 28 janv. 2014, JHG 2014/48 (*Brein/Ziggo XS4*ALL) point 4.2.

destinée à l'exercice, à l'étude ou à l'usage personnel de cette personne[19]. Une rémunération doit être versée par les fabricants et importateurs de dispositifs/supports vierges (voir la question C.1, *infra*). Une question controversée a été de savoir si l'exception de copie privée néerlandaise s'appliquait uniquement aux œuvres reproduites à partir d'une source autorisée ou si elle s'étendait également aux copies faites à partir d'une source illicite ; cette question est pertinente du point de vue de la gestion du système de rémunération. A cet égard, la CJUE, saisie d'une demande de décision préjudicielle, a déclaré : "*Or, ne saurait ainsi être tolérée une législation nationale qui ne fait aucune différence entre les copies privées réalisées à partir de sources licites et celles qui le sont à partir de sources contrefaites ou piratées.*"[20] Le téléchargement à partir d'une source illicite n'entre donc plus dans le cadre de l'exception de copie privée. Il en résulte que le gouvernement néerlandais a dû revoir sa position de longue date selon laquelle n'est pas illicite le téléchargement à partir d'une source illicite. »

3. RESUME – FOURNITURE DE PLATEFORMES, NOUVELLES UTILISATIONS SUR INTERNET : La troisième série d'actes énumérés dans le cadre de la première question concerne la fourniture de contenus générés par les utilisateurs (« *user-generated content* » – UGC) ainsi que « d'autres nouvelles utilisations sur internet ». Il n'est guère surprenant que la plupart des rapports aient beaucoup à dire sur l'UGC qui est depuis un certain temps dans la ligne de mire des titulaires de droits. Le fournisseur de la plateforme représente l'œuvre protégée, il exécute un acte de mise à la disposition du public. Nombreux sont les rapports qui citent le cas de YouTube qui est sans aucun doute l'acteur le plus important dans le domaine de l'UGC. Quant aux autres nouvelles utilisations sur internet, les réponses sont peu nombreuses. Le rapport italien (Ercolani) fait figure d'exception et évoque les applications, ou « applis », qui donnent accès à des contenus protégés et pourraient donc constituer des actes de contrefaçon dans les mêmes conditions que ceux précédemment examinés.

Présentons maintenant des exemples tirés des rapports nationaux concernant les actes suivants :

vii. Fourniture d'une plateforme UGC (*user-generated content*)
viii. Autres nouvelles utilisations sur internet

- Allemagne (Pflüger) : La simple fourniture d'une plateforme de contenus générés par les utilisateurs n'est pas un acte visé par le droit d'auteur. Mais elle peut donner lieu à une obligation de vérifier les contenus.

---

19 Article 16c 1) de la loi néerlandaise sur le droit d'auteur.
20 CJUE, 10 avril 2014, C-435/12 (*ACI Adam BV e.a c/ Stichting de Thuiskopie*), point 37.

- Etats-Unis (Szewczyk & Besek) : L'activité des plateformes UGC les expose à des violations du droit d'auteur mais elles peuvent bénéficier du régime de responsabilité allégée (*safe harbour*) prévu pour les fournisseurs de services d'hébergement par l'article 512 c) du *Copyright Act*.
- Israël (Greenman) : La fourniture d'une plateforme UGC n'est pas restreinte en tant que telle par la loi israélienne sur le droit d'auteur. La jurisprudence précise qu'il peut y avoir complicité de contrefaçon : i) lorsque le fournisseur incite à la contrefaçon, ou ii) lorsque la plateforme sert effectivement à des contrefaçons en si grand nombre qu'elle constitue un forum non légitime.
- Royaume-Uni (Davies, Dimita, Edwards, Frabboni, Koempel, Suthersanen) : En cas de contenus contrefaisants, les chefs de responsabilité pourraient éventuellement comprendre la communication au public ou la reproduction ou les deux. Les plateformes UGC sont vulnérables aux violations du droit d'auteur mais peuvent souvent bénéficier du régime de responsabilité allégée prévu pour les fournisseurs de services d'hébergement.
- Italie (Ercolani) : Il ressort de la jurisprudence quelque incertitude à l'égard des plateformes UGC. Le rapport italien évoque l'affaire *Mediaset c/ Yahoo* où le tribunal avait estimé que Yahoo était responsable des violations du droit d'auteur puisque Yahoo ne pouvait pas être considéré comme « un simple fournisseur d'hébergement passif et donc ne pouvait pas bénéficier d'une exonération de responsabilité en application de la directive de l'UE sur le commerce électronique (directive 2000/31/CE) ». Cette décision a été infirmée par la Cour d'appel qui a déclaré que le titulaire du droit d'auteur doit identifier précisément le contenu illicite avant que le fournisseur d'hébergement soit obligé de retirer le contenu. Cette affaire sera tranchée par la Cour suprême.

2. Deuxième question

Lorsque des obstacles pratiques empêchent la conclusion de contrats de licence, en particulier quand de multiples utilisateurs individuels (et finaux) ne s'adressent pas aux ayants droit avant d'utiliser les œuvres (par exemple, les utilisateurs ont mis en ligne des œuvres et des prestations protégées sur une plateforme comme YouTube), y-a-t-il des mécanismes particuliers pour liciter l'utilisation ("des mécanismes de clearing") ? Est-ce que, en particulier, des accords de licence sont possibles et pratiqués avec des parties tierces impliquées, telles que des plateformes, à propos d'actes d'exploitation commis par les réels utilisateurs de la plateforme (tels que les téléchargeurs/uploaders) ?

RESUME des réponses à la DEUXIEME QUESTION : Les titulaires de droits ont été confrontés à la difficulté d'octroyer aux utilisateurs finaux des licences d'utilisation des œuvres protégées dans l'environnement numérique. La mise en œuvre d'un régime de licences qui intègre une catégorie hétérogène d'utilisateurs finaux anonymes est loin d'être facile, souvent même impossible, et offre un bon exemple d'une défaillance du marché. On pourrait donc penser que la solution serait d'intervenir par voie législative. Mais aucun rapport national n'indique que des mécanismes de licitation sont prévus par leur loi nationale.

Des avancées majeures ont eu lieu dans le secteur privé sur deux plans : grâce au recours à des technologies numériques et par la conclusion d'accords entre les organismes de gestion collective (OGC) et d'autres organisations comme YouTube qui fournissent de contenu sur l'internet. Les rapports nationaux identifient plusieurs méthodologies de licitation des contenus avec des fournisseurs comme YouTube lorsque des difficultés pratiques font obstacle à la conclusion d'accords de licence avec des utilisateurs finaux très hétérogènes, très nombreux et dont la localisation coûte très cher. Les systèmes de balayage sont devenus de plus en plus performants grâce au développement de technologies numériques de plus en plus puissantes, comme l'indique le rapport des Etats-Unis (Szewczyk & Besek) qui évoque l'utilisation par YouTube d'un outil de licitation préalable appelé Content ID ainsi que la série de bases de données d'identification de contenus développée par Audible Magic. Le colosse de l'UGC, YouTube, a été cité par de nombreux rapports qui évoquent les accords de licence signés entre YouTube et les OGC (la PRS au Royaume-Uni depuis 2013; la GEMA en Allemagne depuis 2007; la SACERAU en Egypte depuis 2011; en Belgique depuis 2011; en Croatie depuis 2014; la SOCAN au Canada depuis 2007, et d'autres) aux termes desquels une rémunération est due pour l'exploitation des œuvres protégées.

- Etats-Unis (Szewczyk & Besek) : Le rapport des Etats-Unis fait état de deux méthodes de licitation préalable dont l'une, appelée Content ID, est utilisée par YouTube. Cet outil rapproche le contenu qu'un utilisateur souhaite mettre en ligne des données d'une liste fournie par les titulaires de droits et bloque les contenus identifiés sur la « liste noire » avant leur mise en ligne sur le site. Toutes les vidéos téléchargées sur YouTube sont comparées à une base de données de fichiers communiqués à YouTube par des titulaires de droits. De même, le rapport des Etats-Unis fait état de la série de bases de données d'identification de contenus d'Audible Magic, dont la base de données de la publicité, la base de données de la télévision en direct, la base de données des films cinématographiques et des émissions de télévision archivées et la base de données de la musique, en plus d'autres bases de données personnalisées proposant une tarification différenciée et souple pour répondre aux besoins d'un large éventail de clients.

- Italie (Ercolani) : Le rapport italien indique que le seul mécanisme opérationnel mis en place avec une plateforme UGC concerne les accords avec YouTube. Google a établi des relations d'affaires avec les sociétés de perception et des entités similaires pour l'exploitation sous licence des contenus musicaux monétisés. Une technologie d'empreintes numériques est utilisée pour l'autorisation des œuvres. Des contrats de licence avec les OGC et des procédures de notification et de retrait par les fournisseurs de contenu complètent les autres modalités de licitation. Dans d'autres pays européens on trouve à cet égard une situation similaire à celle exposée dans le rapport italien.
- Hongrie : Le rapport hongrois souligne que la Hongrie est l'un des rares pays du monde où le droit exclusif reconnu aux auteurs et aux artistes interprètes ou exécutants de mettre à la disposition du public des œuvres et des interprétations ou exécutions fixées de manière que chacun puisse y avoir accès de l'endroit et au moment qu'il choisit individuellement est exercé par voie de gestion collective étendue.
- Japon : A l'instar des pays européens, la JASRAC et d'autres OGC japonais concluent avec les exploitants de plateformes des accords de licence pour toutes les utilisations, y compris pour le contenu émanant des téléchargeurs/*uploaders*. Ces accords s'appliquent aux utilisations d'œuvres musicales protégées dans le cadre des services généraux fournis par YouTube, DWANGO, etc.
- Portugal : Le rapport portugais fait état des accords que les OGC ont conclus avec YouTube en 2014 et décrit le système tarifaire complexe qui fixe la rémunération due pour l'utilisation des contenus.

III. Troisième question

1. Lorsqu'il y a une contrefaçon de droit d'auteur, notamment de droits exclusifs couvrant les actes énoncés sous 1 ci-dessus, et que le contrefacteur direct ne peut pas être identifié ou contacté, votre droit (y compris la jurisprudence) prévoit il la responsabilité d'intermédiaires ou d'autres pour une contrefaçon commise par un tiers, c'est-à-dire :

i. pour les fournisseurs de contenu
ii. pour l'hébergeur
iii. pour le fournisseur d'accès
iv. pour d'autres ?

2. Dans ce cas, quelles sont les conditions de la responsabilité, et à quoi le tiers est-il tenu (notamment, à la réparation des dommages, ou à fournir des informations sur le contrefacteur direct ou des informations sur l'étendue de la violation afin d'estimer le préjudice) ?

RESUME des réponses à la TROISIEME QUESTION : Il ressort des rapports un consensus au sujet de la responsabilité des intermédiaires qui se trouvent souvent dans une situation délicate dans l'exercice de leur activité de fournisseurs de contenu, de fournisseurs d'hébergement et de fournisseurs d'accès. Les fournisseurs de contenu sont en général le plus souvent exposés à des actions en contrefaçon directe. Quant aux fournisseurs d'hébergement et d'accès, des déclinaisons du régime de limitation de responsabilité (« safe harbor ») sont courantes, de même que des dispositions en matière de notification et de retrait. En dehors de la contrefaçon directe, les fournisseurs d'hébergement et d'accès sont exposés à des actions en responsabilité indirecte. En général, le droit européen repose sur deux directives qui ont eu un effet dominant. Par exemple, le rapport hongrois indique que les dispositions pertinentes de la directive sur la société de l'information et de la directive 2000/31/CE sur le commerce électronique ont été transposées en droit interne. Quant aux mesures de redressement, les rapports citent les injonctions et les dommages et intérêts (condition de connaissance). Dans deux cas (Etats-Unis [Szewczyk & Besek] et Italie [Ercolani]), il est indiqué que le prestataire de services peut être soumis à une obligation de fournir des données sur l'utilisateur final contrevenant pour permettre au titulaire du droit d'auteur d'intenter une action en contrefaçon.

- Etats-Unis (Szewczyk & Besek) : Les fournisseurs de contenu sont directement responsables en cas de contrefaçon. Les hébergeurs peuvent également être tenus soit directement responsables soit indirectement responsables pour complicité de contrefaçon, mais l'article 512c) du *Copyright Act* des Etats-Unis prévoit une limitation de responsabilité (« *safe harbor* ») si le prestataire de services remplit les conditions requises par la loi.[21] Les fournisseurs d'accès ne sont pas responsables en cas contrefaçon s'ils remplissent les conditions d'exonération prévues par l'article 512a) de la loi. De même, les moteurs de recherche ne sont pas responsables en cas contrefaçon s'ils remplissent les conditions d'exonération prévues par l'article 512d) de la loi.

  « Le fait qu'un prestataire de services internet ne remplit pas les conditions d'exonération (« *safe harbor* ») ne signifie pas en soi qu'il est contrefac-

---

21 L'article 512c) prévoit un «*safe harbor*» si le fournisseur: A) i) n'a pas effectivement connaissance que le contenu, ou une activité qui utilise ce contenu sur le système ou le réseau, est illicite; ii) en l'absence d'une connaissance effective, n'a pas connaissance de faits ou de circonstances selon lesquels l'activité illicite est apparente; ou iii) dès qu'il en prend effectivement connaissance ou conscience, agit promptement pour retirer le contenu ou rendre impossible l'accès à ce contenu; B) ne retire aucun avantage économique directement attribuable à l'activité illicite, dans le cas où le fournisseur a le droit et le pouvoir de contrôler cette activité; et C) dès que la violation alléguée lui est notifiée dans les formes décrites au paragraphe 3), agit promptement pour retirer ou rendre inaccessible le contenu qui serait illicite ou qui ferait l'objet d'une activité illicite.

teur. » Dans un certain nombre de cas, « les tribunaux ont jugé que le prestataire de services en cause n'était pas responsable d'actes de contrefaçon directe dans la mesure où son activité ne révélait pas un comportement volontaire.[22] » Toutefois, les prestataires de services peuvent être tenus indirectement responsables pour complicité de contrefaçon ou du fait d'autrui. Parmi les mesures de redressement qui peuvent être ordonnées figurent les injonctions, l'indemnisation des dommages réels ainsi que des dommages et intérêts préétablis. « Indépendamment de la responsabilité du prestataire de services [...], celui-ci peut être soumis à une obligation de fournir des données sur l'utilisateur final contrevenant pour permettre au titulaire du droit d'auteur d'intenter une action en application de l'article 512 (h). » Mais cette mesure est rarement utilisée dans la pratique.

- Italie (Ercolani) : En Italie, la responsabilité des intermédiaires sur internet se limite aux cas où ils ne respectent pas les règles du décret 70/2003 transposant la directive sur le commerce électronique. Les articles 14, 15, 16 et 17 du décret transposent les dispositions de la directive qui limitent la responsabilité des fournisseurs de services de transport, de stockage (*cache*) et d'hébergement. Par ailleurs, ces intermédiaires n'ont aucune obligation de surveiller les contenus.
  Si l'intermédiaire choisit délibérément de ne pas réagir aux « notifications de retrait » adressées dans les formes, il engage sa responsabilité en dommages et intérêts. En outre, à la demande de l'autorité judiciaire, l'intermédiaire doit fournir les données dont il dispose concernant l'identité du contrefacteur ainsi que le nom de l'entité qui « parraine » l'activité illicite.
- Allemagne (Pflüger) : La loi allemande prévoit la responsabilité des intermédiaires. Les fournisseurs de contenu sont responsables des contenus illicites. Les fournisseurs d'hébergement sont responsables des contenus illicites s'ils savent ou auraient dû savoir que l'œuvre hébergée est illicite. « Les fournisseurs d'accès ne sont responsables que s'ils sont à l'origine de la transmission, s'ils sélectionnent le destinataire de la transmission ou s'ils sélectionnent ou modifient les données transmises. » Des mesures correctives sous forme d'injonction ou de retrait des contenus illicites sont possibles. Des dommages et intérêts peuvent être accordés si les actes de contrefaçon sont commis intentionnellement ou par négligence.
- Egypte (Omar Amine) : Le rapport égyptien indique qu'il n'y a pas de jurisprudence des tribunaux égyptiens relative à la responsabilité des intermédiaires. En outre, le Code égyptien de la propriété intellectuelle ne précise pas les obligations des intermédiaires. La responsabilité des intermédiaires et les moyens de recours relèvent des règles générales du droit d'auteur.

22 Voir, notamment, Columbia Pictures Industries, Inc. c/ Fung, 710 F.3d 1020 (9th Cir. 2013).

- Hongrie : Le rapport hongrois indique que les dispositions pertinentes de la Directive 2000/31/CE du Parlement européen et du Conseil du 8 juin 2000 relative à certains aspects juridiques des services de la société de l'information, et notamment du commerce électronique, dans le marché intérieur (« directive sur le commerce électronique ») ont été transposées en droit interne par la Loi CVIII de 2001 relative à certains aspects des services du commerce électronique et des services de la société de l'information (« loi sur le commerce électronique »).[23] Quant aux moyens de recours, le rapport précise que les fournisseurs d'hébergement et d'accès sont des fournisseurs de services intermédiaires qui bénéficient du régime de responsabilité allégée (« *safe harbor* »). Seules sont possibles des mesures de redressement par voie d'injonction, sauf si l'intermédiaire savait ou aurait dû savoir que l'activité était illicite.
- Argentine (Barrenechea & Wegbrait) : Le rapport argentin précise qu'il existe peu de jurisprudence sur la responsabilité des intermédiaires. Toutefois, les juridictions inférieures ont eu tendance à n'admettre que la responsabilité indirecte des intermédiaires s'ils ont pu prouver qu'ils ont agi avec diligence dès que la violation leur a été notifiée. Cette solution est tirée de l'article 12 de la loi argentine sur le droit d'auteur qui renvoie au droit commun pour tous les aspects non expressément visés par les dispositions spéciales relatives à la propriété intellectuelle.[24]
  Selon le droit argentin, sont pris en considération les éléments suivants pour établir la responsabilité : le type d'activité exercé par l'intermédiaire (opérations automatiques ou simplement techniques sans manipulation des contenus) ; le degré de connaissance (analyse de la doctrine dite de notification et de retrait) ; la notification de la violation (notification directe, administrative ou ordonnée par l'autorité judiciaire) ; l'étendue de l'activité illicite ; l'avantage tiré de l'activité illicite, etc.
- Croatie (Juric, Matanovac Furic, Katulic) : En ce qui concerne les dommages et intérêts, il ressort de la législation croate sur le droit d'auteur et les droits voisins que les fournisseurs d'accès ne seront pas responsables des actes de contrefaçon si les conditions prévues par l'article 16.1) de la loi croate sur le commerce électronique sont remplies. Le fournisseur d'accès doit démontrer : 1) qu'il n'est pas à l'origine de la transmission du contenu, 2) qu'il n'a pas sélectionné les données (contenu) faisant l'objet de la transmission, 3) qu'il n'a pas modifié le contenu et 4) qu'il n'a pas sélectionné le destinataire de la transmission.

---

23 Loi CVIII de 2001 relative à certains aspects des services du commerce électronique et des services de la société de l'information (« loi sur le commerce électronique »).

24 Article 12 : La propriété intellectuelle est régie par les dispositions du droit commun, sous réserve des conditions et limitations établies par la présente loi.

De même, il ressort de la législation croate que « les fournisseurs d'hébergement bénéficient d'une limitation de responsabilité en vertu de l'article 18.1) de la loi sur le commerce électronique lorsqu'ils stockent des informations fournies par un destinataire du service, à condition 1) que le fournisseur n'ait pas ou n'aurait pas pu avoir effectivement connaissance du caractère illicite de l'activité du destinataire du service ou du contenu des informations, et 2) que le fournisseur, dès qu'il prend connaissance ou conscience de ce caractère illicite, agisse promptement pour retirer les informations ou rendre l'accès à celles-ci impossible. Par ailleurs, certaines activités d'établissement de liens relèvent aussi d'un régime de limitation de responsabilité prévu par l'article 19 de la loi sur le commerce électronique. »

IV. Quatrième question

Dans ces cas de contrefaçon, qui peut ester en justice :
i. l'auteur
ii. le titulaire d'une licence exclusive
iii. le titulaire d'une licence non exclusive
iv. l'employeur de l'auteur
v. la société de gestion collective qui gère ce droit ?

RESUME des réponses à la QUATRIEME QUESTION : En tant que règle générale, les rapports indiquent que auteurs et cessionnaires de droits peuvent ester en justice. Mais le consensus s'effrite lorsqu'on examine la situation du titulaire d'une licence exclusive ou non exclusive et de l'employeur de l'auteur. Dans certains pays, le titulaire d'une licence exclusive a qualité pour ester en justice, tout comme l'employeur pour les œuvres créées dans le cadre d'un contrat de louage d'ouvrage ou de services (Etats-Unis, Royaume-Uni) ; dans d'autres pays, leur qualité pour agir dépend exclusivement des dispositions du contrat et de l'autorisation du titulaire du droit d'auteur. Voir le rapport néerlandais (Kannekens, Sluiter, Salamanca, Eechoud). Le rapport finlandais (Oesch, Günther, Pihlajarinne) indique une autre variante. En plus de l'auteur, le titulaire d'une licence exclusive a qualité pour agir. En Finlande, la situation du titulaire d'une licence non exclusive et de l'OGC est différente. Dans ces derniers cas, la qualité pour ester en justice dépendra des dispositions du contrat qu'ils ont conclu avec le titulaire du droit d'auteur. L'employeur est habilité à ester en justice uniquement si les droits en cause lui ont été cédés.

- Etats-Unis (Szewczyk & Besek) : « L'employeur du créateur a qualité pour ester en justice s'il s'agit d'une œuvre créée dans le cadre d'un contrat de louage d'ouvrage ou de services (*work made for hire*) puisque l'employeur, dans ce cas, est considéré par la loi comme étant l'auteur et le titulaire du droit d'auteur *ab initio.* » Le titulaire d'un droit exclusif (licencié exclusif) a qualité pour agir tout comme un OGC qui a la gestion d'un droit exclusif. En revanche, le titulaire d'une licence non exclusive n'a pas qualité pour agir. Le rapport des Etats-Unis précise : « Un OGC qui gère le droit exclusif serait habilitée à ester en justice, mais un OGC qui dispose uniquement de droits non exclusifs ne le serait pas. Aux Etats-Unis, les OGC ne détiennent pas de droits exclusifs et n'ont donc pas qualité pour ester en justice en leur nom propre. Le plus souvent, divers membres de l'OGC sont nommément désignés en tant que demandeurs, même si l'action est gérée et financée par l'OGC ».

- Italie (Ercolani) : L'article 167 de la loi sur le droit d'auteur ne mentionne pas explicitement les titulaires de licences. Il est de jurisprudence constante que le licencié exclusif a qualité pour ester en justice tandis que le licencié non exclusif ne l'a pas. S'agissant de l'emploi salarié, les droits patrimoniaux afférents aux œuvres créées dans le cadre des missions contractuelles du salarié appartiennent à l'employeur. Les OGC ont également qualité pour ester en justice.
- Royaume-Uni (Davies, Dimita, Edwards, Frabboni, Koempel, Suthersanen) : Contrairement à la situation en Italie et aux Etats-Unis, le titulaire d'une licence non exclusive peut agir en contrefaçon dans certains cas en vertu de l'article 101A du CDPA. L'employeur a qualité pour ester en justice lorsque l'auteur est engagé sous un contrat de louage de services ou s'il a créé l'œuvre dans le cadre de son emploi, sauf accord contraire. Les OGC sont habilités à agir en justice pour défendre les droits de leurs membres.
- Allemagne (Pflüger) : Comme dans d'autres pays, l'auteur a qualité sauf s'il a cédé ses droits exclusifs à autrui, auquel cas il peut néanmoins ester en justice pour défendre ses droits moraux. Le titulaire d'une licence exclusive a qualité pour ester en justice tandis que le titulaire d'une licence non exclusive ne l'a pas. L'employeur a qualité pour ester en justice s'il détient un droit exclusif d'exploitation de l'œuvre. La qualité pour agir des OGC dépend des droits exclusifs dont ils bénéficient.
- Belgique (Witmeur) : Le titulaire du droit d'auteur (auteur ou cessionnaire) a qualité pour agir en contrefaçon. Les licenciés exclusifs et non exclusifs peuvent ester en justice. La qualité de l'employeur pour ester en justice dépend des droits contractuels qu'il détient.
- Norvège (Lund) : L'auteur et le licencié exclusif ont qualité pour agir ; le titulaire d'une licence non exclusive ne l'a pas. L'employeur n'a qualité que si les droits exclusifs lui ont été accordés par contrat. Les OGC qui gèrent un droit exclusif ont qualité.
- Portugal : Comme c'est le cas dans un certain nombre d'autres pays, les licenciés n'ont qualité pour ester en justice que si le contrat le prévoit. Le rapport portugais indique que le concédant sert de garant des droits concédés et que toute contestation éventuelle des droits implique l'intervention du titulaire du droit d'auteur.

- France (Binctin) : Le titulaire d'une licence exclusive a qualité pour agir s'agissant du droit exclusif d'exploitation d'un phonogramme ou d'un vidéogramme, sauf stipulation contraire dans le contrat de licence. Le titulaire d'une licence non exclusive n'est pas recevable à agir. L'employeur qui bénéficie d'un droit exclusif peut ester en justice, comme le peuvent les OGC pour les droits dont elles ont la gestion.
- Finlande (Oesch, Günther, Pihlajarinne) : L'auteur et le licencié exclusif ont qualité pour agir. S'agissant du licencié non exclusif, de l'employeur et de l'OGC, c'est le contrat qui les lie au titulaire du droit d'auteur qui détermine cette qualité.
- Canada : En général, quiconque possède un droit acquis par cession ou concession consentie par écrit par le titulaire du droit d'auteur peut ester en justice.
- Mexique (Larrea & Schmidt) : A qualité pour ester en justice la personne physique ou morale qui est titulaire des droits patrimoniaux l'habilitant à agir en contrefaçon.
- Grèce (Kallinikou, Stavridou, Despotidou) : Outre le titulaire originaire des droits, le licencié exclusif a qualité pour agir en contrefaçon. Selon l'article 13, al. 3 de la loi grecque sur le droit d'auteur n° 2121/93, sauf accord contraire, l'autre partie contractante est habilitée à demander en son nom propre une protection juridique contre la violation par des tiers des droits dont elle a l'exercice. Les sociétés de gestion collective ont qualité pour défendre les droits d'auteur et les titulaires de ceux-ci. Selon l'article 55, al. 2 de la loi grecque sur le droit d'auteur n° 2121/93, « une société de gestion collective est habilitée dans tous les cas à mener en son nom propre des actions judiciaires et extrajudiciaires et à exercer en toute légitimité tous les droits qui lui ont été cédés ou pour lesquels elle dispose d'un mandat. »
- Pays-Bas (Kannekens, Sluiter, Salamanca, Eechoud) : « La règle générale prévoit que seul l'auteur ou son ayant droit (par cession, héritage ...) est recevable à agir en justice pour défendre le droit d'auteur dans les procédures civiles. L'auteur ou son ayant droit peut également donner mandat ou son consentement à un tiers pour agir en son nom. Un OGC est habilité à agir pour faire respecter le droit d'auteur puisque l'auteur lui a cédé ses droits ou lui a conféré le pouvoir de défendre ses droits. L'article 27.1) de la loi néerlandaise sur le droit d'auteur précise en outre que « nonobstant la cession totale ou partielle de son droit d'auteur, l'auteur conserve la faculté d'intenter une action en dommages et intérêts contre celui qui porte atteinte au droit d'auteur ». L'article 27a 2) de la LDA néerlandaise prévoit que l'auteur peut réclamer des dommages et intérêts pour le compte d'un licencié. Selon la loi, un licencié n'est recevable à agir qu'en dommages et intérêts et remise du gain et uniquement avec le consentement du titulaire du droit d'auteur (art 27a LDA). »

Marshall Leaffer*

1.2 Informe General: Ámbito y mecanismos de ejecution para asegurar la remuneración, Parte A del cuestionario

RESUMEN INTRODUCTORIO: En el entorno de internet, las obras protegidas por derechos de propiedad intelectual son utilizadas por miembros dispersos y anónimos del público, en condiciones de baja visibilidad. En este entorno, la celebración de contratos de licenciamiento resulta complicado, y el ejercicio de acciones judiciales, poco práctico. Nuestra conferencia tiene por objeto analizar cómo los titulares son remunerados en la era digital. Mi trabajo aquí consiste en examinar las respuestas recibidas a la Parte A del cuestionario sobre el alcance de los derechos exclusivos y su aplicación y cumplimiento, conforme a la legislación actual. Mis colegas a su vez debatirán las Partes B, C y D, que se centran en diferentes aspectos de los mecanismos de remuneración.

Este informe se basa en las respuestas obtenidas de 20 países. Teniendo en cuenta el poco tiempo del que dispongo y para mayor claridad, no puedo plantear un debate centrado en demasiados detalles. Mi objetivo consiste en presentar las tendencias generales que se desprenden de los informes. Para mayor detalle e incluso precisión, conviene consultar con cada uno de los informes nacionales.[1]

La Parte A formula cuatro preguntas (con subapartados) sobre la forma escogida por las legislaciones de cada país para implementar los derechos exclusivos reconocidos al titular de derechos de autor. He marcado en cursiva y negrita las preguntas formuladas a los grupos nacionales de ALAI, siguiendo a continuación un resumen general basado en los informes nacionales. Tal y como se ha advertido anteriormente, estos breves resúmenes, por supuesto, no pretenden ser exhaustivos, sino únicamente un marco de referencia tras la lectura de los informes nacionales. A continuación se incluyen algunos ejemplos que aparecen en los informes nacionales.

La Primera pregunta se centra en el tratamiento que da la legislación de cada país a las ocho actividades indicadas que se realizan a través de internet. He dividido esta pregunta en tres apartados. En la "sección I." de la Primera Pregunta, me centro en los hipervínculos, los enlaces profundos, y los marcos/enlaces ensamblados ("*framing/embedding*"). La "sección II." tiene por objeto los actos de streaming, de descargas y de subida o carga de obras. En la "sec-

---

* Profesor, Universidad de Indiana, Maurer School of Law, USA. Traducción del inglés para Cristina Perpiña-Robert.

1 V. los informes nacionales: http://alai2015.org/en/national-reports.html.

ción III.", se examina el suministro de una plataforma para 'contenidos generados por el usuario' y otros usos novedosos en Internet.

I. Primera Pregunta

¿Cómo regula el derecho de autor de su país (ley aplicable y jurisprudencia) los siguientes actos?

i. Establecimiento de hipervínculos a las obras
ii. Establecimiento de enlaces profundos a las obras
iii. Marcos/enlaces ensamblados
iv. Streaming de obras
v. Descarga de obras
vi. Subida o carga de obras
vii. Suministro de una plataforma para "contenidos generados por usuarios'
viii. Otros usos novedosos en Internet

1. RESUMEN – HIPERVÍNCULOS, ENLACES PROFUNDOS, MARCOS/ENLACES ENSAMBLADOS: El aspecto más interesante puesto de manifiesto en estos informes fue que, con la posible excepción de Croacia, ningún país ha abordado estos actos de utilización de hipervínculos, enlaces profundos y marcos/enlaces ensamblados en su legislación. Tal y como subraya el Informe de Argentina (Barrenechea & Wegbrait):

> "La Ley de Propiedad intelectual argentina[2] ... no regula de forma concreta los aspectos que se contienen en la pregunta, ni ninguno de los usos en Internet de las obras o categorías protegidas como derechos conexos. Aun así, dichos usos están protegidos ya que el Artículo 2[3] de la Ley de Propiedad intelectual reconoce un derecho amplio y exclusivo para disponer de las obras, de cualquier forma y por cualquier método de explotación. Se considera que esta amplia formulación cubre los usos que se efectúan a través de Internet."

Resultan sorprendentes los bajos índices de litigiosidad que existen sobre esta cuestión, teniendo en cuenta la importancia de estos usos tan habituales en internet. Otra generalización: los informes parecen levemente coincidir en el hecho de que la utilización de hipervínculos, enlaces profundos y marcos/enlaces en-

2 Ley nº 11.723.
3 Art2°. – El derecho de propiedad de una obra científica, literaria o artística, comprende para su autor la facultad de disponer de ella, de publicarla, de ejecutarla, de representarla, y exponerla en público, de enajenarla, de traducirla, de adaptarla o de autorizar su traducción y de reproducirla en cualquier forma.

samblados de obras es legal si no concurren otros factores que pudieran dar lugar a responsabilidad directa o de terceros. Como indica el Informe húngaro: "el establecimiento de hipervínculos, enlaces profundos o marcos/enlaces ensamblados, con sujeción a ciertas condiciones, no constituye un acto ilícito."

La legislación estadounidense ofrece una solución. Conforme a dicha legislación, el establecimiento de un hipervínculo a una página web que contenga una obra protegida por derechos de autor no constituye una vulneración directa de propiedad intelectual ya que los hipervínculos en sí no contienen obras protegidas. Sin embargo, conforme al derecho estadounidense, cabe ejercitar acciones por responsabilidad de terceros, o por responsabilidad indirecta u objetiva ("contributory o vicarious liability"). Estas acciones de responsabilidad secundaria – por responsabilidad indirecta u objetiva (contributory o vicarious liability") – pueden ejercitarse siempre que sea probable que la persona que ofrece el enlace profundo tenga conocimiento específico sobre el contenido ilícito. Se considera, del mismo modo, que la utilización de marcos o enlaces ensamblados de obras no constituye una infracción directa cuando la obra no se encuentra almacenada en el ordenador del enlazador. En estos casos, cabe ejercitar una acción de competencia desleal.

Las legislaciones europeas han conseguido en la práctica el mismo resultado que en Estados Unidos, pero la resolución del problema resulta más complicado y controvertido según se deduce de los informes. Los informes europeos citan en particular el efecto de la jurisprudencia del TJUE en los asuntos Svensson y BestWater[4], al considerar que los actos de enlazar, de utilizar enlaces profundos y marcos/enlaces ensamblados son, por sí mismos, lícitos. El principal elemento en discordia no es la conclusión de estas dos resoluciones, sino el hecho de que Svensson y BestWater parecen incompatibles con determinados principios básicos de la Directiva UE de la Sociedad de información, según la cual, ningún acto de comunicación al público puede agotarse. El Informe italiano refleja la controversia, indicando que al exigir la existencia de un público nuevo o un medio diferente como requisito para que exista una vulneración del derecho de comunicación al público, el tribunal introduce lo equivalente al agotamiento del derecho de comunicación al público en línea. Conviene recordar que el estudio aprobado por el Comité ejecutivo de ALAI en el mes de septiembre de 2014 mantiene que este requisito es incompatible con lo dispuesto en los Tratados de la OMPI.[5] El estudio de ALAI establece lo siguiente:

4 Asuntos C_466/12 ("Svensson") y C-348/13 ("BestWater").

5 El Informe húngaro también critica la teoría del público nuevo. Para la crítica de ALAI, véase la Opinión adoptada por el Comité ejecutivo de ALAI, en su sesión de 17 de septiembre de 2014, sobre la teoría del "Público nuevo", publicado en http://www.alai.org/en/assets/files/resolutions/2014-opinion-new-public.pdf y Dr Mihály J Ficsor «Svensson: Honest attempt at establishing due balance concerning the use of hyperlinks – spoiled by the erroneous "new pu-

Si bien en *Svensson* el TJUE respondió de forma correcta y afirmativa a la cuestión básica de si el establecimiento de hipervínculos constituye una puesta a disposición/comunicación (interactiva), postura enunciada en el citado dictamen de ALAI de 15 de septiembre de 2013, en la misma resolución, y por lo que respecta a la cuestión de si dicho acto constituye una comunicación «al público», confirmó una serie de resoluciones recientes donde introdujo un criterio problemático de «público nuevo», circunscrito, entre otros, por un criterio, igualmente problemático, de "medio técnico específico".

Ofrezco a continuación ejemplos de los informes individuales sobre los siguientes actos:

i. Hipervínculos
ii. Establecimiento de enlaces profundos a las obras
iii. Marcos/enlaces ensamblados de obras

- Estados Unidos: (Szewczyk & Besek): Conforme a la legislación estadounidense, el establecimiento de un hipervínculo a una página web que contiene una obra protegida no constituye una vulneración directa de la propiedad intelectual ya que los hipervínculos en sí no contienen obras protegidas. Sin embargo, cabe ejercitar acciones por responsabilidad de terceros, o por responsabilidad indirecta u objetiva ("contributory o vicarious liability"). De forma semejant, el establecimiento de un enlace profundo no constituye una vulneración directa de propiedad intelectual. Cabe ejercitar acciones por responsabilidad de terceros, o por responsabilidad indirecta u objetiva ("contributory or vicarious liability") cuando es probable que la persona que establece el enlace profundo tenga conocimiento específico sobre el contenido ilícito. Se considera, del mismo modo, que el establecimiento de enlaces enmarcados o ensamblados de obras no constituye una infracción directa cuando la obra no se encuentra almacenada en el ordenador del enlazador.
- Reino Unido: (Davies, Dimita, Edwards, Frabboni, Koempel, Suthersanen): El establecimiento de un hipervínculo a un contenido puesto libremente a disposición del público, no constituye una infracción del artículo 20 de la Ley de Copyright. Sin embargo, los hipervínculos diseñados para eludir barreras o muros de pago sí que lo infringen. Pero no resulta claro si debe tratarse de un contenido libremente accesible o autorizado, aun implícitamente por el autor o titular del derecho de copyright. Las directrices indican que la actividad no es infractora si el contenido es publicado libremente en línea con autorización.

  Según el Informe del Reino Unido, la cuestión esencial consiste en determinar si el acto de establecer hipervínculos constituye una comunicación al

blic" theory»; publicados en http://www.copyrightseesaw.net/archive/?sw_10_item=68 ambos visitados en fecha 6 de abril de 2015).

público. El informe establece que para que exista responsabilidad, debe exigirse algún tipo de conocimiento y de facilitación de la infracción. En el caso de enlaces profundos y de marcos/enlaces ensamblados, no existirá infracción por las mismas razones indicadas anteriormente. Pero en ambos casos, pueden verse afectados los derechos morales.

- Hungría: El establecimiento de hipervínculos, enlaces profundos y marcos/enlaces ensamblados, con sujeción a determinadas condiciones, no está sujeto a restriccìon alguna. Como muchos otros, el Informe húngaro cita los asuntos *Svensson* y *BestWater*. La mayoría de los informes que citan estos dos asuntos apoyaban el resultado, pero criticaban el razonamiento basado en el "público nuevo" al cuestionar la argumentación de las resoluciones.
- Italia (Ercolani): El mero redireccionamiento a otra página web mediante un hipervínculo no constituye un acto de comunicación, siempre que el enlace sea únicamente una herramienta de remisión a elementos externos. El Informe italiano distingue entre los hipervínculos y el establecimiento de enlaces profundos y marcos/enlaces ensamblados: "Sobre la base de la interpretación de la ley italiana, cabe sostener que un enlace constituye una forma de puesta a disposición del público cuando se ofrece en forma de enlace profundo o de marco/enlace ensamblado de obras, de tal manera que el usuario final no percibe la diferencia entre las obras directamente almacenadas en la página web y aquellas que simplemente han sido integradas o extraidas de fuentes externas. Por el contrario, el mero redireccionamiento a una página web distinta mediante un hipervínculo, no debe considerarse un acto de comunicación, siempre que el enlace sea únicamente una herramienta de remisión a elementos externos."
- Suiza (Salvadé & Cherpillod): No cabe dirigirse sin más contra simples hipervínculos. Tampoco cabe dirigirse contra enlaces profundos, aunque pueden verse afectados los derechos morales en determinadas circunstancias. Las técnicas de utilización de marcos y de enlaces ensamblados constituyen una *mise à disposition* contra las que cabe dirigirse. También cabe ejercitar acciones por vulneración de los derechos de integridad y paternidad en estos casos.
- Japón: Los actos de establecimiento de hipervínculos, enlaces profundos, y marcos/enlaces ensamblados afectan al "derecho de transmisión" conforme a la legislación japonesa.
- Finlandia (Oesch, Günther, Pihlajarinne): El Informe finlandés expone el problema de los marcos o enlaces ensamblados.[6] Refiriéndose a *Svensson*, el Consejo finlandés de Derechos de autor (2014:4) declaró que el estableci-

6 Véase la Opinión de expertos del Consejo finlandés de Derechos de autor (2001:8 – enmarcado de los artículos).

miento de un enlace a una fotografía en una página de debate no comercial, es lícito si el titular ha permitido utilizar la fotografía libremente en Internet.[7]

- Canadá: Algunos países, como Canadá, no han abordado el problema en su legislación sobre propiedad intelectual, ni en la jurisprudencia.
- Grecia (Kallinikou, Stavridou, Despotidou): Conforme a la jurisprudencia griega, los hipervínculos pueden dar lugar a responsabilidad en determinados casos. El Tribunal de Primera instancia de Atenas, en el asunto 4042/2010, mantuvo que una emisora de radio que había sido licenciada por una entidad de gestión para la emisión de su programa de radio, había cometido una infracción de los derechos de autor al colocar en su página web un hipervínculo (un banner interactivo) que permitía la transmisión de su programa de radio a través de Internet.
- Croacia (Jurić, Matanovac Furić, Katulić): Croacia constituye una excepción a la regla general de que la mayoría de los países carecen de una legislación específica sobre los hipervínculos. El artículo 19 de la Ley croata de comercio electrónico establece: "El proveedor de servicios que mediante enlaces electrónicos da acceso a información de terceros, no será responsable de dicha información si: no tuviese conocimiento, ni pudiese tenerlo, sobre la actividad ilícita de los destinatarios o sobre el contenido de los datos en dicha información; [y] suprime o bloquea el acceso a los datos en cuanto tuviese conocimiento de la actividad o de los datos ilícitos."
- Bélgica (Witmeur): El Informe belga explica que la sociedad de gestión SABAM intentó recaudar derechos por los enlaces ensamblados de YouTube situados en su página web que se dirigiían a páginas comerciales. SABAM basó su reclamación en los términos de sus licencias con YouTube, que según esta entidad de gestión, únicamente se limitan a la comunicación al púbico dentro del ámbito privado. Lógicamente, la posición de YouTube no coincide con la de SABAM.
- Países Bajos (Kannekens, Sluiter, Salamanca, Eechoud). No existe ninguna disposición sobre responsabilidad secundaria o por infracción indirecta de derechos de autor en la Ley de Derechos de Autor holandesa. Un hipervínculo sencillo (profundo) no constituye una comunicación al público y no infringe derechos de autor de forma directa. Puede en algunos casos considerarse un "acto ilícito" conforme al derecho general de responsabilidad civil, art 6:162 del Código civil holandés (por ej., cuando una persona enlaza de

7 Véase el Consejo finlandés de Derechos de autor 2002:5 pág. 2, y el estudio independiente del Consejo finlandés de Derechos de autor 2012:2 por Taina Pihlajarinne sobre enlaces comerciales, especialmente en situaciones en las que los nuevos servicios son creados con ventajas económicas al basarse en enlaces automáticos.

forma sistemática a grandes cantidades de material no autorizado y obtiene beneficios por ello).[8]

- Austria (Walter): La Ley de propiedad intelectual austriaca no se refiere de forma expresa a estos actos. En cuanto a la jurisprudencia, el Tribunal Supremo mantuvo en 2011[9], que en el caso de hipervínculos, no se realiza ninguna reproducción en el ordenador del usuario y los hipervínculos no deben considerarse un acto de comunicación al público. La doctrina, sin embargo, considera que tanto los enlaces profundos, como los marcos, son actos de comunicación al público.

2. RESUMEN – STREAMING, DESCARGAS Y SUBIDA O CARGA DE OBRAS: El segundo tipo de actos tiene por objeto las actividades de streaming, descarga y subida o carga de obras. A falta de consentimiento del titular de derechos, estos actos pueden infringir uno o más derechos exclusivos. Claramente, la actividad de streaming constituye un acto de comunicación al público según se reconoce de forma generalizada en los informes.[10] En cuanto a la subida o carga de material protegido por derechos de autor, la mayoría de los informes coinciden en que este acto afecta tanto al derecho de puesta a disposición, como al derecho de reproducción. La descarga de obras afecta al derecho de reproducción. Algunos informes, como el suizo (Salvade & Cherpillod) y el noruego (Lund), mencionan el uso privado como posible excepción al derecho de reproducción en el caso de una obra descargada.[11] La descarga de obras a través de Internet ha dado varios quebraderos de cabeza a la comunidad mundial de propiedad intelectual. La legislación francesa, con la constitución de la HADOPI, descrita en detalle en el Informe francés (Binctin), supone un intento sui generis, aunque controvertido, para imponer sanciones a aquellos que se han dedicado a un patrón de descargas ilícitas.

Presentaré a continuación ejemplos obtenidos de los informes nacionales sobre los siguientes actos:

iv. Streaming de obras
v. Descarga de obras
vi. Carga o subida de obras

---

8 Visser, D.J.G.,'Openbaar maken: Communication to the public', en: Hugenholtz, P.B., Quaedvlieg, A.A., Visser, D.J.G. (Eds.) *A century of Dutch Copyright Law*, Amstelveen: Uitgeverij deLex, 2012, pág.225.

9 Tribunal Supremo 20.9.2011 4 Ob 105/11m – „123people/Vorschaubilder/Thumbnails" MR 2011, 313 (Michel Walter) = ecolex 2012/29, 64 (Axel Anderl) = wbl 2012/38, 105 = RZ 2012/76, 123 (LS) = ÖBl 2012/45, 175 (Manfred Büchele).

10 El informe alemán cita el artículo 19a UrgH (puesta a disposición del público), estando la actividad de streaming en vivo cubierta por el artículo 20 UrhG (derecho de radiodifusión).

11 El Informe suizo considera que el art19 al. 1 litt. a LDA establece que la excepción de uso privado es de aplicación incluso si la fuente es ilegal.

- Canadá: La jurisprudencia canadiense[12] ha establecido que el streaming debe considerarse una comunicación al público, pero no una reproducción, ya que las copias realizadas durante el proceso de streaming son por su propia naturaleza temporales. En comparación, tanto la carga como la descarga, dan lugar a copias permanentes. Conforme al derecho estadounidense, estos actos afectan a los derechos de comunicación, reproducción y distribución, lo que conduce prácticamente al mismo resultado.
- Reino Unido (Davies, Dimita, Edwards, Frabboni, Koempel, Suthersanen): Pese a la ausencia de jurisprudencia, la descarga de contenido no autorizado vulneraría el derecho de reproducción en base al artículo 17 de la Ley de Propiedad intelectual (CDPA). Desde 2005, resulta evidente que subir o cargar una obra (salvo programas de ordenador) sin autorización, infringe el artículo 20 de la CDPA (el artículo 20 de la CDPA afecta el derecho de comunicación al público). La carga de programas de ordenador puede infringir los derechos de propiedad intelectual al considerarse un acto de distribución al público en base al artículo 18 de la CDPA.[13]
- Noruega (Lund): La actividad de streaming está cubierta por el derecho de puesta a disposición. La descarga de obras afecta al derecho de reproducción. El artículo 12 de la ley de derechos de autor noruega incluye una excepción en el caso de reproducciones para uso privado, siempre que la reproducción se realice a partir de un ofrecimiento legal de la obra. Sin embargo, la ley "no permite la realización de copias "legibles por máquina" de programas de ordenador ni de copias "legibles por máquina" de bases de datos." La carga de obras está cubierta por los derechos exclusivos de reproducción y de puesta a disposición del público de material protegido.
- Francia (Binctin): Al igual que el resto de los informes, la actividad de streaming se considera una comunicación al público. Con motivo de la descarga, considerada un acto de comunicación al público por el Informe francés, así como un acto de reproducción, la ley francesa constituyó la *Haute Authorité pour la diffusion des oeuvres et la protection des droits sur Internet* (HADOPI). Comenzado a actuar en 2009, este organismo sui generis fue creado para llevar a cabo la batalla creciente contra la piratería en internet. Tiene la capacidad de aplicar sanciones a aquellos que han abusado del privilegio de la descarga. El Informe francés describe en detalle el funcionamiento actual de la HADOPI.
- Austria (Walter): "la puesta a disposición activa de contenido protegido por propiedad intelectual mediante la técnica de streaming requiere el consen-

---

12 Entertainment Software Association contra Canadian Society of Authors, Composers, and Editors of Music (SOCAN), 2012 CSC 34 [ESA] y Rogers Communications, Inc. contra SOCAN, 2012 CSC 35.

13 Asunto C-128/11 UsedSoft GmbH contra Oracle International Corp.

timiento del autor.[14] Sin embargo, la "recepción" por el usuario debe considerarse cubierta por la excepción de actos de reproducción temporales, transitorias o incidentales en base al artículo 5(1) de la Directiva de la Sociedad de la información. Sin embargo, la cuestión acerca de si esto sigue siendo válido cuando dichos streams se facilitan de forma ilícita, sigue abierta. En mi opinión, también en este contexto, la legitimidad de la fuente es un requisito previo para beneficiarse de esta excepción, al igual que en el caso de la copia privada."[15] El Tribunal Supremo austriaco abordó esta cuestión, entre otras, de forma marginal en el planteamiento de su cuestión preliminar ante el TJE en el asunto „kino.to/UPC I".[16]

- Países Bajos (Kannekens, Sluiter, Salamanca, Eechoud): "La carga de una obra protegida por derechos de autor debe considerarse un acto de 'openbaarmaking',[17] que constituye una infracción al derecho de autor si se realiza sin autorización del titular de derechos."[18]

  Según el Informe holandés: "La descarga en sí de una obra protegida por derechos de autor constituye un acto de reproducción. En muchos supuestos, las descargas no requieren autorización ya que sería de aplicación la excepción de copia privada (thuiskopieuitzondering; art 16c DCA). La excepción únicamente beneficia a la reproducción de (una parte de) una obra que se realiza por una persona física sin interés comercial directo o indirecto, y exclusivamente para su práctica, uso o estudio personal.[19] Los fabricantes e importadores de soportes/grabadoras vírgenes deben pagar un canon (véase Pregunta C.1 más adelante). No es cuestión pacífica si la excepción holandesa de copia probada se aplica únicamente a las copias realizadas a partir de de fuentes autorizadas, o si también beneficia a las copias obtenidas de fuentes ilícitas; esta cuestión es importante para la de-

---

14 Derecho de puesta a disposición previsto en §18a (autores) y §71a (titulares de derechos afines), respectivamente de la Ley de propiedad intelectual austriaca.

15 Véase TJE 10.4.2014 C-435/12 – "ACI Adam/Thuiskopie" MR-Int 2014, 42 (Michel Walter) = EuZW 2014, 501 (Carl C Müller/Sören Rößner) = ZUM 2014, 573 (Anne Lauber-Rönsberg) = ecolex 2014/297, 727 (LS) (Adolf Zeman) = MMR 2014, 679 = ÖBl 2014, 232 (Johannes Burgstaller/Mona Philomena Ladler).

16 Tribunal Supremo 11.5.2012 4 Ob 6/12d – MR 2012, 190 (Michel Walter) = ecolex 2012/291, 708 (Axel Anderl) = wbl 2012/180, 473 = GRUR Int 2012, 934.

17 El derecho de 'openbaarmaken', es un derecho amplio que cubre toda una serie de actos como la ejecución pública (con público físicamente presente), la comunicación al público (por ej. radiodifusión), la puesta a disposición a demanda y el derecho de distribución de copias físicas. Véase Visser, D.J.G., 'Openbaar maken: Communication to the public', en: Hugenholtz, P.B., Quaedvlieg, A.A., Visser, D.J.G. (Eds.) A century of Dutch Copyright Law, Amstelveen: DeLex, 2012, p.225.

18 Tribunal de Apelaciones de La Haya 28 de enero de 2014, JHG 2014/48 (Brein/Ziggo XS4ALL) para. 4.2.

19 Artículo 16c (1) de la Ley de Propiedad intelectual holandesa.

terminación de la forma de administración de los cánones. La cuestión prejudicial plantea lo siguiente: '*No se puede tolerar una norma nacional que no establece ninguna diferencia entre las copias privadas realizadas a partir de fuentes lícitas y aquellas que se realizan a partir de fuentes falsificadas o piratas.*'[20] Por lo tanto, la descarga a partir de una fuente ilícita ya no puede beneficiarse de la excepción de copia privada. El gobierno holandés tuvo que revisar la posición mantenida desde hacía tiempo según la cual, la descarga realizada a partir de una fuente ilícita no era ilegal."

3. RESUMEN – SUMINISTRO DE PLATAFORMAS, USOS NOVEDOSOS EN INTERNET: El tercer grupo de actos que se incluye en la primera pregunta tiene por objeto "el suministro de contenido generado por usuarios" y "otros usos novedosos en Internet." De forma poco sorprendente, la mayoría de los informes tenían mucho que decir acerca del contenido generado por usuarios (UGC), un fenómeno que ha sido el objetivo de titulares de derechos de propiedad intelectual desde hace tiempo. El proveedor de una plataforma realiza una comunicación pública de la obra, llevando a cabo un acto de puesta a disposición del público. Muchos informes citan la plataforma YouTube, sin duda la más importante en el ámbito del UGC. Las respuestas a otros usos novedosos en Internet fueron más escasas. El Informe italiano (Ercolani) constituye la excepción, mencionando apps o aplicaciones que dan acceso a contenidos protegidos, un tipo de uso que puede dar lugar a la posibilidad de que consituya una actividad ilícita conforme a los mismos términos que hemos examinado.

Presento a continuación los ejemplos de los informes nacionales sobre los siguientes actos:

vii. Suministro de plataformas para contenidos generados por el usuario
viii. Otros usos novedosos en Internet

- Alemania (Pflüger): el mero suministro de una plataforma para los contenidos generados por el usuario no constituye un acto protegido por derechos de propiedad intelectual. Pero esta actividad puede imponer el deber de comprobar el contenido.
- Estados Unidos: (Szewczyk & Besek): las plataformas para contenidos generados por el usuario son susceptibles de infringir derechos de propiedad intelectual, pero pueden beneficiarse del puerto seguro del proveedor de alojamiento que se establece en el artículo 512(c).
- Israel (Greenman): La provisión de una plataforma para el UGC no se considera una actividad restringida por sí misma conforme a la ley de propiedad intelectual de Israel. La jurisprudencia establece que puede dar lugar a una

20 Tribunal de Justicia europeo 10 de abril de 2014, C-435/12 (ACI Adam BV e.a/Stichting de Thuiskopie), párrafo 37.

infracción indirecta de propiedad intelectual (i) cuando el proveedor es el inductor de la infracción, o (ii) cuando la plataforma facilita en la práctica tal volumen de infracción que pueda considerarse un foro ilegítimo.

- Reino Unido (Davies, Dimita, Edwards, Frabboni, Koempel, Suthersanen): En el caso de contenido ilícito, puede existir potencial responsabilidad por los actos de comunicación al público, de reproducción, o ambos. Las plataformas destinadas para "contenidos generados por el usuario" son susceptibles de infringir derechos de propiedad intelectual, pero pueden beneficiarse a menudo de la excepción que existe para los proveedores de alojamiento.
- Italia (Ercolani): La jurisprudencia no es uniforme en el caso de plataformas UGC. El Informe italiano analiza el asunto *Mediaset v. Yahoo*, en el que el tribunal consideró que Yahoo era responsable de una infracción de propiedad intelectual al no poder considerarse un "mero proveedor de alojamiento pasivo, y por tanto no poder beneficiarse de la excepción de responsabilidad establecida en la Directiva de la UE de Comercio electrónico (Directiva 2000/31/CE)". En la apelación, el Tribunal revocó la sentencia de instancia, entendiendo que el titular de derecho debía identificar de forma específica el contenido ilícito antes de poder obligar al proveedor de alojamiento a eliminar el contenido. El asunto será finalmente resuelto por el Tribunal Supremo

II. Segunda Pregunta

En aquellos supuestos en los que existen obstáculos en la práctica para la celebración de contratos de licenciamiento, en concreto, cuando múltiples usuarios (finales) individuales no se dirigen a los titulares de derechos antes de utilizar las obras (por ej., usuarios que suben o cargan contenido protegido en plataformas como YouTube), ¿existen mecanismos concretos de autorización o licenciamiento de derechos? En particular, ¿es posible celebrar contratos de licenciamiento con terceros intervinientes, como las plataformas, en relación con los actos de explotación llevados a cabo por los usuarios finales (así, contratos de licenciamiento con el operador de la plataforma, en vez de con los usuarios de la plataforma ["uploaders"])?

RESUMEN de la SEGUNDA PREGUNTA: El licenciamiento de obras protegidas a los usuarios finales ha causado auténticos quebraderos de cabeza a los titulares de derechos en el entorno digital. El establecimiento de un régimen de licenciamiento que integre a una grupo disperso de usuarios finales anónimos es complicado, incluso muchas veces imposible, y constituye un buen ejemplo de las deficiencias del mercado. Por consiguiente, cabe pensar en la intervención pública a través de su regulación como una posible solución. Sin embargo, ninguno de los informes nacionales menciona la adopción de mecanismos de licenciamiento en sus legislaciones nacionales.

Los principales avances se han producido en el sector privado de dos maneras: mediante el uso de tecnologías digitales y por la conclusión de acuerdos entre las EEGG y los otras organizaciones como YouTube, que suministran información a través de Internet. Los informes nacionales han identificado diversas metodologías para la obtención de licencias o permisos con proveedores de contenidos como YouTube, cuando existen obstáculos en la práctica que impiden el licenciamiento directo con un grupo diverso y numeroso de usuarios finales que sean difíciles de localizar. Los sistemas de escaneo se están perfeccionando gracias a las cada vez más poderosas tecnologías digitales, tal y como se subraya en el Informe de EE.UU. (Szewczyk & Besek), citando el sistema de prelicenciamiento de YouTube denominado Content ID y el conjunto de Bases de Datos de Contenidos de Audible Magic. El coloso UGC, YouTube, ha sido el centro de interés de varios informes al mencionarse los contratos de licenciamiento entre YouTube y las sociedades de gestión (Reino Unido, PRS desde 2013; Alemania, GEMA, 2007; Egipto, SACERAU, 2011; Bélgica, 2011; Croacia, 2014; Canadá, SOCAN, 2007, y otros) para la remuneración por el uso de obras protegidas por derechos de autor.

- Estados Unidos: (Szewczyk & Besek): El Informe de Estados Unidos señala dos métodos de "pre-licenciamiento", siendo uno el utilizado por YouTube, denominado Content ID. Este método cruza el contenido que el usuario desea subir, con una lista facilitada por los titulares de derechos, bloqueando el material identificado en la "lista negra" de forma que no puede introducirse en la página desde el principio. Todos los videos que se suben a YouTube son escaneados y cruzados con una base de datos de archivos facilitados a YouTube por los titulares de contenidos. De forma parecida, el informe de EE.UU. señala el conjunto de Bases de Datos de Identificación de Contenidos de Audio Magic, incluyendo la Base de Datos de Publicidad, la Base de Datos de TV en vivo, la Base de Datos de Películas cinematográficas y TV en archivo y la Base de Datos de Música, además de otras soluciones personalizadas que ofrecen planes flexibles con distintos niveles de tarificación, para satisfacer las necesidades de un conjunto variado de clientes.
- Italia (Ercolani): El Informe italiano señala que el único mecanismo en vigor con una plataforma UGC se limita a los acuerdos con YouTube. En este punto, Google ha construido una relación comercial con las sociedades de gestión y entidades similares para el licenciamiento de contenidos musicales monetizados. Se utiliza la tecnología de huella digital para licenciar las obras. Los contratos editoriales con las EEGG y los procedimientos de notificación y retirada por parte de los proveedores de contenidos son otros sistemas que sirven para regularizar la utilización de los derechos. La situa-

ción expuesta en el Informe italiano es similar a la descrita sobre el particular en otros países europeos.

- Hungría: El Informe húngaro señala que es uno de los pocos países del mundo en el que el derecho exclusivo de los autores y artistas de poner las obras/interpretaciones fijadas a disposición del público, de forma que los miembros del público puedan elegir el lugar y el momento de acceso de forma individual, se ejercita a través de un sistema de administración colectiva ampliada.
- Japón: De forma similar a los países europeos, JASRAC, junto con otras EEGG's, suscribe contratos de licenciamiento con operadores de plataformas para todo tipo de usos, incluyendo los contenidos subidos por los usuarios de forma individual. Los acuerdos son de aplicación a los usos de obras protegidas por derechos de autor en servicios generales prestados por YouTube, DWANGO, etc.
- Portugal: El Informe portugués describe el acuerdo de las EEGG's con YouTube en 2014, que elabora un sistema tarifario complejo para la remuneración por el uso del contenido.

III. Tercera Pregunta

1. Si se produce una infracción de derechos de autor, en concreto de los derechos exclusivos que se ven afectados por los actos indicados en el anterior apartado 1., y el infractor directo no puede ser identificado ni localizado, ¿establece su ordenamiento jurídico (incluyendo la jurisprudencia) la responsabilidad de los intermediarios u otros intervinientes por las infracciones cometidas por terceros, concretamente, responsabilidad:

i. de los proveedores de contenidos
ii. de los proveedores de alojamiento
iii. de los proveedores de acceso
iv. de terceros intervinientes?

2. En caso afirmativo, ¿en qué condiciones son considerados responsables, y con qué alcance (en concreto, el infractor directo, información sobre el alcance de la infracción para calcular el importe de los daños y perjuicios)?

RESUMEN de la TERCERA PREGUNTA: Existe consenso entre las respuestas a la Tercera Pregunta contenidas en los informes respecto de la responsabilidad de los intermediarios que a menudo se encuentran en una situación delicada en su actividad como proveedores de contenidos, proveedores de alojamiento y proveedores de acceso. En general, los proveedores de contenidos son contra los que con mayor frecuencia se dirigen las acciones de responsabilidad directa.

En cuanto a los proveedores de alojamiento y de acceso, a menudo se utilizan variantes de puertos seguros y de sistemas de notificación y retirada. Aparte de responsabilidad directa, los proveedores de alojamiento y de acceso pueden ser considerados responsables indirectos. En general, el Derecho comunitario se basa en dos directivas que han tenido un efecto dominante. Por ejemplo, el Informe húngaro establece que las disposiciones pertinentes de la Directiva de Sociedad de Información 2000/31/EC y de la Directiva de Comercio electrónico han sido traspuestas al Derecho nacional. En cuanto a las posibles acciones y medidas, el informe se refiere a las medidas de cese y las acciones de daños y perjuicios (con el requisito de conocimiento). En algunas instancias (Estados Unidos [Szewczyk & Besek]; Italia [Ercolani]), el prestador de servicios puede estar obligado a suministrar información sobre el usuario final infractor para permitir que el titular de derechos puede ejercitar una acción de daños y perjuicios.

- Estados Unidos (Szewczyk & Besek): Los proveedores de contenidos son responsables directos de la infracción de propiedad intelectual. Los proveedores de alojamiento pueden también considerarse responsables directos e indirectos, aunque el articulo512(c) de la Ley de Copyright de Estados Unidos establece un puerto seguro si el prestador de servicios cumple con los requisitos legales.[21] Los proveedores de acceso no son responsables por las infracciones de propiedad intelectual en base a la excepción de puerto seguro del artículo 512(a) si cumplen con los requisitos de la ley. De forma similar, los motores de búsqueda no se considerarán responsables por las infracciones de propiedad intelectual en base a la excepción de puerto seguro del artículo 512(d) si cumplen con los requerimientos de la ley.
  "El no poder beneficiarse de la excepción de puerto seguro no significa que de manera automática el ISP sea considerado un infractor." En varios casos, "los tribunales han considerado que los ISPs no son responsables en calidad de infractores directos, al entender que su actividad no era voluntaria."[22] Pueden, no obstante, ser considerados responsables secundarios,

21 El art512(c) establece un puerto seguro si el prestador de servicios (A) (i) no tiene conocimiento efectivo de que el contenido, o la actividad basada en la utilización del contenido en el sistema o la red, es ilícito; (ii) en ausencia de dicho conocimiento efectivo, no ser consciente de hechos o circunstancias que revelen que la actividad infractora es aparente; o (iii) en cuanto obtuviese dicho conocimiento, actuase rápidamente para suprimir o impedir acceso al contenido; (B) no obtiene un beneficio económico directamente vinculado a la actividad ilícita, en un supuesto en el que el prestador de servicios tiene el derecho y la facultad de controlar dicha actividad; y (C) al recibir una notificación sobre una supuesta infracción según se describe en el apartado (3), responde rápidamente para suprimir o impedir el acceso al contenido supuestamente ilícito o que sea objeto de la actividad ilícita.

22 Véase, por ej., Columbia Pictures Industries, Inc. contra Fung, 710 F.3d 1020 (9th Cir. 2013).

conforme al régimen de responsabilidad indirecta o secundaria ("contributory o vicarious liability"). En estos casos, cabe ejercitar medidas cautelares y acciones por daños efectivamente causados e indemnizaciones establecidas en la ley *("actual and statutory damages")*. "Con independencia de la responsabilidad del prestador de servicios [...], éste puede verse obligado a suministrar información sobre el usuario final infractor para permitir que el titular de derechos pueda ejercitar acciones en base al artículo 512(h)." Sin embargo, esta medida no suele utilizarse.

- Italia (Ercolani): En Italia, la responsabilidad de los intermediarios de internet se limita a los supuestos en los que no cumplen con lo dispuesto en el Decreto 70/2003, de implementación de la Directiva de comercio electrónico. Los artículos 14, 15, 16 y 17 del Decreto trasponen las disposiciones sobre puertos seguros de la Directiva para prestadores de servicios de mera transmisión, servicios caché y servicios de alojamiento. Además, estos intermediarios no tienen obligación alguna de monitorizar el contenido.

  Si los intermediarios de internet no cumplen voluntariamente con las "notificaciones y retiradas," responden por daños y perjuicios. Además, cuando son requeridos judicialmente, deben facilitar la información que esté en su posesión sobre la identificación del infractor, además del nombre de la organización que promociona la actividad ilícita.
- Alemania (Pflüger): La ley alemana establece la responsabilidad de los intermediarios. Los proveedores de contenidos son responsables del contenido ilícito. Los proveedores de alojamiento son responsables del contenido ilícito que alojan si conocen o debieran de haber conocido que la obra alojada es ilícita. "Los proveedores de acceso no responden a menos que inicien la transmisión de datos, seleccionen al destinatario, o seleccionen o modifiquen los datos que se transmiten." Entre las medidas y recursos disponibles, se encuentran las medidas cautelares o de cese y la supresión del contenido infractor. Cabe exigir daños y perjuicios si los actos infractores son intencionales o negligentes.
- Egipto (Omar Amine): El Informe egipcio señala que no existe jurisprudencia sobre la figura de los intermediarios. Además, el Código egipcio de propiedad intelectual no especifica las obligaciones de los intermediarios. La responsabilidad de los intermediarios y las medidas posibles se rigen por la doctrina general del derecho de propiedad intelectual.
- Hungría: El Informe húngaro afirma que las disposiciones pertinentes de la Directiva 2000/31/CE del Parlamento Europeo y del Consejo, de 8 de junio de 2000, relativa a determinados aspectos jurídicos de los servicios de la sociedad de la información, en particular el comercio electrónico en el mercado interior (Directiva sobre el comercio electrónico) se traspuestos al derecho nacional mediante la Ley CVIII de 2001 sobre determinadas cuestio-

nes relacionadas con servicios de comercio electrónico y de la sociedad de información ("Ley de Comercio electrónico").[23] En cuanto a los recursos disponibles, el Informe especifica que los proveedores de alojamiento y de acceso son prestadores de servicios de intermediación que se benefician de la protección de los puertos seguros. Cabe ejercitar acciones de cese a menos que estos intermediarios tuviesen conocimiento o debiesen haber tenido conocimiento sobre la infracción.

- Argentina (Barrenechea & Wegbrait): Según el Informe argentino, existe poca jurisprudencia sobre la responsabilidad de los intermediarios. No obstante, los juzgados y tribunales de primera instancia suenen limitarla a una responsabilidad indirecta si se acredita que éstos actuaron de manera diligente al recibir la notificación de la infracción. Esto se basa en la Artículo 12 de la Ley de Propiedad intelectual de Argentina que se remite a las disposiciones del derecho común para todo lo que no se regule de manera específica en las disposiciones sobre propiedad intelectual.[24]

  Según la ley argentina, la atribución de responsabilidad se basa en la concurrencia de los siguientes factores: el tipo de actividad llevada a cabo por el intermediario (actividades automáticas o meramente técnicas, sin alteración del contenido); el grado de conocimiento (se analiza la denominada doctrina de notificación y retirada); la notificación de la infracción (directa, administrativa o por vía judicial); el alcance de la actividad infractora; el beneficio derivado de la actividad infractora; etc.
- Croacia (Jurić, Matanovac Furić, Katulić): Conforme a la Ley de Derechos de autor y derechos afines de Croacia, en relación con los daños y perjuicios, los proveedores de acceso no son considerados responsables si cumplen los requisitos establecidos en el Artículo 16(1) de la Ley croata de Comercio electrónico. Los proveedores de acceso deben acreditar que (1) no iniciaron la transmisión del contenido, (2) no seleccionaron los datos (el contenido) que son objeto de la transmisión, (3) no modificaron el contenido, y (4) no seleccionaron al destinatario de la transmisión.

  De manera similar, conforme a la ley croata, "los proveedores de alojamiento pueden beneficiarse de un régimen de responsabilidad limitada en base al Artículo 18(1) de la ECA cuando almacenan información facilitada por el destinatario del servicio, con la condición de que (1) el prestador no tuviese, o no pudiese haber tenido, conocimiento efectivo sobre la actividad ilícita del destinatario, ni sobre el contenido de la información, y (2) el prestador, al obtener dicho conocimiento, actuase rápidamente para suprimir la in-

---

23 Ley CVIII de 2001 sobre determinadas cuestiones relacionadas con servicios de comercio electrónico y de la sociedad de información ("Ley de Comercio electrónico").

24 Section 12. Intellectual property shall be governed by the provisions of common law, subject to the conditions and limitations established in this Law.

formación o impedir acceder a la misma. Existe además un régimen de responsabilidad limitada para actividades de enlazamiento conforme a lo dispuesto en el Artículo 19 de la ECA."

IV. Cuarta Pregunta

¿Quién tiene legitimación para ejercitar acciones por infracción de derechos de propiedad intelectual de entre las siguientes categorías?
i. El Autor
ii. El Licenciatario en exclusiva
iii. El Empresario
iv. La Sociedad de gestión que administra el derecho exclusivo

RESUMEN de la CUARTA PREGUNTA: Como norma general, los informes señalan que tanto el autor, como el cesionario de los derechos, tienen legitimación activa. Las diferencias empiezan al referirse al licenciatario en exclusiva o en no exclusive y el empresario. El algunos ordenamientos juridícos, el licenciatario en exclusiva tiene legitimación activa, al igual que el empresario en el caso de obras por encargo ("*works made for hire*") (Estados Unidos, Reino Unido); en otras jurisdicciones, la legitimación de estas personas depende exclusivamente de lo establecido en el contrato y del consentimiento del titular de derechos. Véase el Informe de Países Bajos, (Kannekens, Sluiter, Salamanca, Eechoud). El Informe de Finlandia (Oesch, Günther, Pihlajarinnne) añade otra variación: además del autor, el licenciatario en exclusiva está legitimado para demandar. En Finlandia, la situación difiere en el caso del licenciatario en no exclusiva y la sociedad de gestión. En este país, la legitimación activa depende de las condiciones contractuales acordadas entre estas entidades y el titular de derechos. El empresario solo está legitimado si le han sido cedidos los derechos de la obra.

- Estados Unidos (Szewczyk & Besek): "El empresario tiene legitimación activa si se trata de una obra por encargo, ya que en este supuesto el empresario es considerado por ley, autor y titular de los derechos de autor *ab initio.*" El titular de un derecho exclusivo (licenciatario en exclusiva), incluyendo la sociedad de gestión que administra los derechos exclusivos, está legitimado. Por el contrario, el licenciatario en no exclusiva no puede ejercitar acciones legales. El Informe de EE.UU. establece: "Si la sociedad de gestión administra el derecho exclusivo, está legitimada para ejercitar acciones judiciales, pero no en el caso de la sociedad de gestión que administre derechos en no exclusiva. Las sociedades de gestión en Estados Unidos no tienen derechos exclusivos, por lo que no tienen facultad independiente para demandar. Los miembros individuales de la sociedad de gestión suelen aparecer como los demandantes, a pesar de que la sociedad de gestión dirija y financie el procedimiento judicial."

- Italia (Ercolani): El art 167 de la Ley de propiedad intelectual no se refiere de forma expresa a los licenciatarios. Los tribunales han confirmado de forma constante que el licenciatario en exclusiva está legitimado activamente, mientras que el licenciatario en no exclusiva no tiene legitimación. En el caso de un contrato de trabajo, los derechos patrimoniales de las obras creadas como parte de las obligaciones de trabajo del empleado pertenecen al empresario. Las sociedades de gestión también están legitimadas para ejercitar acciones judiciales.
- Reino Unido (Davies, Dimita, Edwards, Frabboni, Koempel, Suthersanen): A diferencia de Italia y Estados Unidos, los licenciatarios en no exclusiva tienen legitimación para ejercitar acciones judiciales en el caso de determinadas infracciones en base al artículo 101A CDPA. Los empresarios tienen legitimación activa cuando el autor fue contratado mediante un contrato de servicios o si creó la obra en el curso de su relación laboral, si bien cabe acuerdo en contrario. Las sociedades de gestión pueden exigir el cumplimiento de los derechos de sus miembros mediante el ejercicio de acciones judiciales.
- Alemania (Pflüger): Igual que en otras jurisdicciones, el autor tiene legitimación, a menos que haya transferido sus derechos exclusivos a un tercero, aunque siempre puede ejercitar acciones judiciales en defensa de sus derechos morales. El titular de un derecho exclusivo puede demandar, frente al licenciatario en no exclusiva. El empresario puede demandar si es titular del derecho exclusivo sobre la obra. En el caso de las sociedades de gestión, depende de los derechos exclusivos que tengan.
- Bélgica (Witmeur): el titular del derecho de autor (autor o cesionario) puede ejercitar acciones judiciales de reclamación de daños y perjuicios. Tanto los licenciatarios en exclusiva, como en no exclusiva, pueden demandar. En el caso del empresario, depende de sus derechos contractuales.
- Noruega (Lund): El autor y licenciatario exclusiva pueden demandar, a diferencia del licenciatario en no exclusiva. Los empresarios tienen legitimación únicamente si se les han transferido por contrato los derechos exclusivos. Las sociedades de gestión están legitimadas si administran un derecho exclusivo.
- Portugal: Al igual que en algunos otros países, los licenciatarios no pueden demandar a menos que así se especifique en el contrato. El Informe portugués aclara que los licenciantes actúan como garantes de los derechos licenciados, de forma que cualquier disputa sobre los derechos debe contar con la intervención del titular de los derechos de autor.
- Francia (Binctin): El titular de una licencia en exclusiva tiene legitimación en el caso de fonogramas o videogramas, a menos que se establezca lo contrario en el contrato el contrato de licencia. Los licenciatarios en no exclusi-

va no tienen legitimación activa. Los empresarios que reciben un derecho exclusivo pueden demandar, al igual que las sociedades de gestión, respecto de los derechos que administran.

- Finlandia (Oesch, Günther, Pihlajarinne): El autor y el licenciatario en exclusiva pueden demandar. En el caso del licenciatario en no exclusiva, el empresario y la sociedad de gestión, la legitimación activa depende de la relación contractual entre estas entidades y el titular de derechos.
- Canadá: En general, cualquier titular derivado por cesión por escrito o licencia del titular del derecho tiene legitimación activa para ejercitar acciones judiciales.
- México (Larrea and Schmidt): La legitimación para ejercitar acciones en caso de infracción depende de la persona o entidad que sea titular de los derechos patrimoniales.
- Grecia (Kallinikou, Stavridou, Despotidou): Aparte de los titulares de derechos originarios, el licenciatario en exclusiva puede ejercitar acciones judiciales en caso de infracción. Conforme al Artículo 13, apartado 3 de la Ley nº 2121/93 de Propiedad intelectual, a falta de acuerdo en contrario, las demás partes contractuales podrán ejercitar acciones legales en su propio nombre en el caso de infracciones de los derechos que ejercitan por parte de terceros. Las sociedades de gestión están legitimadas para proteger los derechos de las obras y a los titulares de derechos. Según el Artículo 55, apartado 2 de la Ley nº 2121/93 de Propiedad intelectual, "las sociedades de gestión tienen siempre legitimación para ejercitar acciones judiciales o extrajudiciales en su propio nombre, y para ejercitar con plenas facultades todos los derechos que les han sido transferidos, o los derechos para los que estén apoderado."
- Países Bajos (Kannekens, Sluiter, Salamanca, Eechoud): "La norma general es que únicamente el autor o su causahabiente (ya sea por cesión o transmisión mortis causa, etc.) están legitimados para ejercitar acciones civiles. Pueden también dar instrucciones a un tercero para que demande en su nombre o facultarles a estos efectos. CBOs exigen el cumplimiento de los derechos de autor, porque el autor se los ha trasferido o porque les ha facultado para ejercitar acciones. El art 27(1) DCA añade además que 'sin perjuicio de la cesión total o parcial de sus derechos, el autor conserva el derecho a ejercitar acciones por daños y perjuicios contra las personas que infrinjan sus derechos'. El art 27a (2) DCA establece que el autor puede exigir daños y perjuicios en nombre de un licenciatario. Legalmente, el licenciatario únicamente puede reclamar daños y perjuicio o rendición de cuentas, y sólo con el consentimiento del titular de los derechos de autor (art 27a DCA)."

Tristan Azzi*

1.3 Rapport général : Mécanismes destinés à garantir une rémunération appropriée aux créateurs et artistes-interprètes

La nature du droit d'auteur et des droits voisins paraît aujourd'hui acquise. La propriété littéraire et artistique est, comme son nom l'indique, une forme particulière de propriété. Pareille qualification est consacrée, entre autres, par le préambule de la directive européenne du 22 mai 2001 sur l'harmonisation de certains aspects du droit d'auteur et des droits voisins dans la société de l'information[1] et par la Charte des droits fondamentaux de l'Union européenne[2]. La Cour européenne des droits de l'homme[3] ainsi que plusieurs juges constitutionnels nationaux[4] la retiennent également. Il en résulte, en raisonnant à partir du droit d'auteur[5], qu'à l'image de n'importe quel propriétaire, le créateur d'une œuvre de l'esprit doit en principe se voir octroyer les trois prérogatives classiquement attachées au droit de propriété : l'*usus*, l'*abusus* et le *fructus*. La corrélation des deux dernières signifie que l'auteur a tout loisir pour autoriser par contrat une personne à exploiter son œuvre en lui cédant ou en lui concédant ses droits (*abusus*) et qu'il peut, en contrepartie, exiger une rémunération (*fructus*).

Avant d'envisager les mécanismes destinés à garantir qu'une telle rémunération soit appropriée, deux précisions s'imposent. D'une part, précisément parce qu'il a la qualité de propriétaire, l'auteur devrait pouvoir renoncer à percevoir une rétribution à l'occasion de l'exploitation de son œuvre. En ce sens, certaines lois nationales reconnaissent expressément la validité des contrats

---

* Professeur à l'Ecole de droit de la Sorbonne, Université Paris I Panthéon-Sorbonne, France.

1 Considérants 3 et 9.

2 Art 17. Pour une application, v. CJUE, 9 févr. 2012, aff. C-277/10, *Martin Luksan*, points 68 et s., *D.* 2012. 2841, obs. P. Sirinelli; *RTD com.* 2012. 318, obs. F. Pollaud-Dulian; *RTD eur.* 2012. 964, obs. E. Treppoz; *Propr. intell.* 2012. 425 et 434, obs. V.-L. Benabou; *CCE* 2012, comm. 37, obs. C. Caron.

3 CEDH, 29 janv. 2008, *Balan c/ Moldavie*: *Propr. intell.* 2008. 338, obs. J.-M. Bruguière; *Comm. com. électr.* 2008, comm. 76, obs. C. Caron; *RTD com.* 2008. 732, obs. F. Pollaud-Dulian.

4 V. par ex. les références citées dans le rapport allemand. V. aussi en France, Cons. const., 27 juill. 2006, *Loi DADVSI*: *Propr. intell.* 2006. 240, chron. V.-L. Benabou; *D.* 2006. 2157, chron. C. Castets-Renard; *Com. com. électr.* 2006, comm. 140, obs. C. Caron; *RTD com.* 2006. 779, obs. F. Pollaud-Dulian; *Propr. intell.* 2007. 193, obs. M. Vivant; Cons. const., 10 juin 2009, *Loi HADOPI.*

5 La plupart des développements qui composent le présent rapport général valent également pour les artistes-interprètes. Quelques différences de traitement existant entre ces derniers et les auteurs seront cependant présentées *infra*, p. 77.

d'exploitation conclus à titre gratuit ou du moins de certains d'entre eux. Ainsi, la loi allemande autorise l'auteur à concéder gratuitement un droit d'exploitation non exclusif au public, ce qui correspond à l'hypothèse d'une licence libre[6]. Quant à la loi française, elle admet plus généralement que le droit de représentation et le droit de reproduction sont cessibles à titre gratuit[7]. D'autre part, lorsque le contrat est passé à titre onéreux, rien n'interdit que l'auteur accepte de recevoir, en échange des autorisations qu'il accorde, une contrepartie non monétaire. Par exemple, si un créateur apporte en société son monopole d'exploitation, il obtiendra en retour des parts sociales. Dans un registre différent, il n'est pas rare que l'auteur d'un ouvrage scientifique se contente de céder ses droits à un éditeur moyennant simplement quelques exemplaires du livre réalisé.

Il apparaît néanmoins que les contrats d'exploitation sont le plus souvent conclus à titre onéreux et en échange d'une rémunération au sens strict, c'est-à-dire d'une rétribution en argent. La question se pose alors de savoir si l'auteur dispose de moyens juridiques pour obtenir une rémunération satisfaisante, au regard notamment des conditions dans lesquelles son œuvre est exploitée. C'est en vain que l'on cherchera la réponse à cette question dans les conventions internationales relatives à la propriété littéraire et artistique, celles-ci ne traitant que très accessoirement des contrats d'exploitation[8]. Quant aux directives européennes, elles se contentent pour certaines d'indiquer, généralement dans leur préambule, que les titulaires de droits doivent recevoir une « rémunération appropriée »[9], mais sans en préciser, à quelques exceptions près[10], les modalités.

---

6 §32 (3), 3e phrase, UrhG.

7 Art L. 122-7 CPI. V. aussi l'art. L. 122-7-1 CPI, proche du §32 (3), 3e phrase, UrhG préc., qui prévoit que « l'auteur est libre de mettre ses œuvres gratuitement à la disposition du public (...) ».

8 Indiquons simplement que certains instruments internationaux généraux prévoient le droit pour chacun de bénéficier de « la protection des intérêts moraux et matériels découlant de toute production (...) littéraire ou artistique dont il est l'auteur » (art 27, §2, de la Déclaration universelle des droits de l'Homme et 15, §1, c, du Pacte international relatif aux droits économiques, sociaux et culturels).

9 V. le considérant 25 de la directive du 27 sept. 1993 relative à la coordination de certaines règles du droit d'auteur et des droits voisins du droit d'auteur applicables à la radiodiffusion par satellite et à la retransmission par câble, et le considérant 10 de la directive du 22 mai 2001 sur l'harmonisation de certains aspects du droit d'auteur et des droits voisins dans la société de l'information. V. aussi, mais cette fois-ci dans le dispositif de la directive, l'art 16, §2, de la directive du 26 févr. 2014 concernant la gestion collective du droit d'auteur et des droits voisins et l'octroi de licences multiterritoriales de droits sur des œuvres musicales en vue de leur utilisation en ligne dans le marché intérieur.

10 V. le considérant 17 de la directive du 27 sept. 1993 préc. qui énonce, à propos des diffusions par satellite, que « au moment de déterminer la rémunération correspondant aux droits qui ont été acquis, les intéressés doivent prendre en compte tous les paramètres de l'émission, tels que l'audience effective, l'audience potentielle et la version linguistique ». V. aussi, mais peu éclairant, le considérant n° 10 de la directive du 22 mai 2001, lequel pose que la rémunéra-

Afin d'identifier les mécanismes visant à garantir aux auteurs le bénéfice effectif d'une telle rémunération, il convient donc de se tourner vers les droits nationaux. Il ressort de la lecture des vingt-deux rapports nationaux reçus que ces mécanismes sont nombreux et variés. Afin de les décrire, on raisonnera en deux temps, en envisageant d'abord ceux qui sont susceptibles de jouer lors de la formation du contrat (I), puis ceux qui ont vocation à intervenir au cours de l'exécution de celui-ci (II).

I. La formation du contrat

La consultation des rapports nationaux permet de classer les différents systèmes juridiques en trois catégories, en fonction de la protection qu'ils accordent à l'auteur au moment de la formation du contrat. On trouve dans la première catégorie les pays qui ne prévoient pas de règles spécifiques en ce qui concerne la détermination de la rémunération, lesquels semblent donc conférer, au premier abord du moins, une entière liberté aux parties (1.). Appartiennent à la deuxième catégorie les Etats qui assurent à l'auteur le bénéfice d'une rémunération équitable (2.). Enfin, relèvent de la troisième catégorie les pays qui lui garantissent une rémunération proportionnelle aux résultats de l'exploitation (3.).

1. Les systèmes juridiques consacrant un principe de liberté en matière de rémunération

Certains pays sont très attachés à l'autonomie de la volonté et à la liberté contractuelle, y compris en droit de la propriété littéraire et artistique. Suivant cette approche libérale, il importe peu que les auteurs soient souvent en position de faiblesse par rapport aux exploitants avec lesquels ils contractent : un tel déséquilibre ne saurait justifier qu'ils bénéficient d'un traitement de faveur. Aussi bien la détermination de la rémunération repose-t-elle en principe, dans ces pays, sur le libre jeu de la négociation contractuelle. Les lois sur la propriété

---

tion doit «permettre un rendement satisfaisant de l'investissement». V. aussi le dispositif de rémunération supplémentaire mis en place au profit des artistes-interprètes par la directive du 27 sept. 2011 modifiant la directive du 12 déc. 2006 relative à la durée de protection du droit d'auteur et de certains droits voisins. Sur ce dispositif, v. *infra*, p. 77. V. encore l'art16, §2, de la directive du 26 févr. 2014 préc., qui énonce, à propos de la gestion collective, que «les tarifs appliqués pour les droits exclusifs et les droits à rémunération sont raisonnables, au regard, entre autres, de la valeur économique de l'utilisation des droits négociés, compte tenu de la nature et de l'ampleur de l'utilisation des œuvres et autres objets, ainsi qu'au regard de la valeur économique du service fourni par l'organisme de gestion collective. Les organismes de gestion collective informent l'utilisateur concerné des critères utilisés pour fixer ces tarifs».

littéraire et artistique des Etats concernés ne renferment donc pas de disposition spéciale permettant aux auteurs de revendiquer une rémunération appropriée au moment de la formation du contrat. Appartiennent à cette première catégorie les droits américain, anglais, argentin, autrichien, israélien[11], japonais, norvégien, suisse et, semble-t-il, italien. En attendant une réforme présentée comme imminente, le droit néerlandais relève lui aussi de cette première catégorie[12].

À bien y regarder cependant, même dans ces systèmes, la liberté des parties est rarement totale. Deux séries de mécanismes sont en effet susceptibles d'empêcher les exploitants d'imposer aux créateurs des rémunérations trop faibles.

En premier lieu, à défaut de règles prévues par la législation spéciale sur la propriété littéraire et artistique, il est généralement possible d'avoir recours au droit commun des contrats. Le rapport suisse évoque, par exemple, la faculté offerte à un auteur, qui aurait accepté un contrat financièrement défavorable à la suite d'une erreur ou d'un dol, d'en demander la nullité. Le rapport anglais, quant à lui, consacre d'importants développements à l'application par les tribunaux, en matière de contrats d'exploitation du droit d'auteur, de la doctrine de *restraint of trade* de *common law*, qui permet de lutter contre les contrats par trop désavantageux. La possibilité qu'ont les juges d'appliquer, à défaut de règles spéciales, les techniques issues de la théorie générale des contrats ressort également des rapports américain, autrichien et norvégien.

En second lieu, pour ce qui est spécifiquement de la gestion collective, certains pays ont adopté des règles assez strictes sur la fixation et le contrôle des tarifs pratiqués par les sociétés de perception et de répartition. Tel est le cas, notamment, de la Suisse[13].

2. Les systèmes juridiques consacrant un principe d'équité en matière de rémunération

La protection des créateurs peut sembler mieux assurée lorsque la législation spéciale sur la propriété littéraire et artistique comporte des règles relatives à la détermination de la rémunération. Certaines lois nationales exigent qu'une telle rémunération soit « équitable ». Appartiennent à ce deuxième groupe les droits allemand, croate et finlandais. Le projet de loi sur les contrats d'exploitation du

---

11 Excepté pour ce qui est du contrat d'édition : v. *infra*, p. 77.

12 Une loi spécifique sur les contrats d'exploitation du droit d'auteur est, en effet, en cours d'adoption aux Pays-Bas. Il en résulte que le droit néerlandais devrait basculer prochainement dans la deuxième catégorie.

13 Comp. sur ce point la directive du 26 févr. 2014 préc., ainsi que les rapports belge et hongrois.

droit d'auteur en cours d'adoption aux Pays-Bas devrait prochainement permettre au droit néerlandais de rejoindre ce groupe.

Toute la question consiste à savoir ce qu'il faut entendre par rémunération « équitable ». Le rapport allemand est à cet égard très riche. Aussi nous servira-t-il d'illustration[14]. Le droit allemand accorde un rôle important à la négociation collective, laquelle fait en quelque sorte présumer le caractère équitable de la rémunération et, partant, la légitimité de son mode de fixation : pour parodier une formule française célèbre, en Allemagne, « qui dit collectif dit juste »[15]. Ainsi, la rémunération des auteurs est réputée équitable lorsqu'elle découle d'une convention collective. A défaut de convention collective, la rémunération est considérée comme équitable lorsqu'elle résulte de l'application d'autres « règles communes de rémunération ». De telles règles sont le fruit, dans chaque secteur d'activité, d'une concertation entre, d'une part, les organismes représentant les auteurs et, d'autre part, les exploitants. Cependant, selon les rapporteurs allemands, le mécanisme, institué par la loi du 22 mars 2002, ne produit guère de résultats probants pour l'heure. Enfin, hors des conventions collectives et des règles communes de rémunération, une rémunération doit être considérée comme équitable lorsqu'elle répond aux critères posés par la loi. Celle-ci invite à tenir compte de ce qui est considéré comme usuel et loyal dans les relations commerciales au moment de la conclusion du contrat, mais aussi de la nature et de l'étendue de l'autorisation donnée, en particulier de sa durée et de son époque, ainsi que, plus généralement, de toutes les circonstances. La doctrine et les juges allemands ont tendance à se plaindre du manque de précision de ces critères. En outre, comparé aux systèmes juridiques relevant à la troisième catégorie que nous examinerons dans quelques instants, le droit allemand conduit à des solutions plus souples[16] : pour que la rémunération soit qualifiée d'équitable, les tribunaux allemands n'exigent pas qu'elle soit proportionnelle aux recettes provenant de l'exploitation de l'œuvre ; elle peut certes l'être, mais elle est également susceptible de prendre la forme d'un forfait ; il est aussi possible de mélanger les deux formules.

Ajoutons que, dans les systèmes exigeant une rémunération équitable, l'existence d'une disposition en ce sens dans la loi sur la propriété littéraire et

14 §32 et 36 UrhG. Précisons qu'une réforme du droit contractuel d'auteur allemand est actuellement à l'étude.

15 Selon la formule du philosophe français Alfred Fouillée (1838–1912), «qui dit contractuel dit juste». L'apparition de contrats inégalitaires, comme le contrat de travail ou le contrat de consommation, a largement remis en cause ce postulat.

16 V. plus généralement, renfermant de nombreux éléments de comparaison entre les systèmes allemand et français, A. Lucas-Schloetter, «Le droit contractuel d'auteur allemand depuis la réforme du 22 mars 2002», *Propr. intell.* 2005. 403, et du même auteur, «Lettre d'Allemagne – qu'y a-t-il dans la "deuxième corbeille"? La loi allemande du 26 octobre 2007 relative au droit d'auteur dans la société de l'information», *Propr. intell.* 2008. 308.

artistique n'interdit pas d'avoir recours dans certains cas au droit commun des contrats. Ce dernier peut en effet intervenir en complément de la protection offerte par le droit spécial. Les rapports allemand, croate et finlandais insistent sur ce point. Pour ne prendre qu'un exemple, en Finlande, les règles relatives à la rémunération figurant dans la loi sur le droit d'auteur ne s'appliquent qu'aux contrats d'exploitation auxquels le titulaire initial du monopole intellectuel est partie. Les transferts subséquents sont soumis à des règles certes équivalentes, mais issues du droit commun.

3. Les systèmes juridiques consacrant un principe de proportionnalité en matière de rémunération

La solution la plus protectrice de l'auteur, à tout le moins en théorie, consiste à lui accorder une rémunération proportionnelle aux recettes provenant de l'exploitation[17]. L'auteur est ainsi assuré d'être associé aux produits générés par l'utilisation de son œuvre. Cela l'empêche de surcroît d'abandonner définitivement ses droits pour une somme forfaitaire dérisoire. Plusieurs pays ont consacré un tel mécanisme. On pense notamment à l'Algérie[18], à la Belgique, à l'Egypte, à l'Espagne, à la France, à la Grèce ou encore à la Hongrie.

La vigueur du principe de rémunération proportionnelle varie en réalité d'un Etat à l'autre. Il convient à cet égard de prendre en compte divers facteurs.

Tout d'abord, alors que dans plusieurs systèmes juridiques l'exigence vaut normalement pour tous les contrats d'exploitation du droit d'auteur, dans d'autres elle ne concerne que certains contrats particuliers. En Espagne[19] et en France[20], par exemple, la règle a une portée générale, tandis qu'en Belgique son application se limite, aux termes de la loi, aux contrats de production audiovisuelle et d'édition[21].

Les règles relatives à l'assiette et au taux de la rémunération sont également assez hétérogènes. On se contentera, pour illustrer le propos, d'examiner les secondes. Le plus souvent, la détermination du taux de la rémunération proportionnelle est laissée à la discrétion des parties. Le risque est alors que l'exploitant profite de sa position de force pour imposer à l'auteur un taux très faible et donc très désavantageux. En pareil cas, le droit commun des contrats peut, à nouveau, prendre utilement le relai du droit spécial pour conférer à

17 Notons toutefois que le forfait peut s'avérer plus avantageux dans certains cas, en particulier lorsque le volume d'exploitation est faible.

18 Le contenu du droit algérien est évoqué dans le rapport égyptien.

19 Art 46.1 de la loi sur la propriété intellectuelle espagnole.

20 Art L. 131-4 CPI.

21 Art XI. 183, §2, et XI. 196, §2, du Code de droit économique.

l'auteur une protection efficace. On se réfèrera en ce sens aux rapports espagnol et grec, le second évoquant l'hypothèse d'une annulation du contrat pour contrariété aux bonnes mœurs. Le droit commun est également susceptible de s'appliquer lorsque, plus radicalement, le contrat ne prévoit pas le taux de la rémunération. La jurisprudence française en offre une intéressante illustration : afin d'annuler une convention de cession du droit d'auteur qui se contentait de prévoir un pourcentage « à débattre », le Tribunal de grande instance de Paris a considéré, entre autres motifs, que ladite convention, dépourvue de prix et de cause, violait les « principes généraux du droit civil »[22]. Afin d'éviter toute difficulté, on pourrait concevoir que le taux de la rémunération – ou du moins un taux minimum – soit imposé par la loi. Toutefois, sans doute parce qu'elle constitue une réelle entorse à la liberté contractuelle, cette solution n'est consacrée qu'assez exceptionnellement[23]. Parmi les rares lois nationales à l'avoir admise en droit d'auteur, on peut citer la loi grecque, qui en réserve cependant l'application à certains contrats nommés : contrat d'édition, contrat de radiodiffusion, contrat de représentation théâtrale, contrat de composition de musique de film, contrat de cession de droits conclu par un photographe[24]. Un taux de rémunération est aussi prévu par la loi israélienne, mais uniquement en matière d'édition littéraire. La solution existe également au Portugal, où elle se présente sous la forme d'une disposition supplétive inscrite dans les règles standard applicables au contrat d'édition. Enfin, on la retrouve ponctuellement en droit de l'Union européenne, mais cette fois-ci dans le domaine des droits voisins. La directive du 27 septembre 2011 prolongeant la durée de certains droits voisins prévoit ainsi, à propos des exploitations d'interprétations ayant lieu durant les vingt années supplémentaires de protection qu'elle accorde[25], que le producteur doit verser aux artistes-interprètes 20 % des recettes qu'il perçoit en contrepartie desdites exploitations[26].

Une autre question consiste d'ailleurs à savoir si, plus généralement, la règle de rémunération proportionnelle dont bénéficient les auteurs couvre aussi

22 TGI Paris, 9 mai 1990, *RIDA* janv. 1991, n° 147, p. 355 : le tribunal vise plus précisément, en sus des dispositions de la loi du 11 mars 1957 sur la propriété littéraire et artistique, les art 1108, 1131 et 1583 du Code civil, qui ont respectivement trait aux conditions générales de validité des contrats (consentement, capacité, objet, cause), à la cause (existence et licéité) et aux exigences propres au contrat de vente (accord sur la chose et le prix).

23 Les taux de rémunération fixés par les lois nationales concernent généralement les droits à rémunération, mais non les droits exclusifs susceptibles d'être cédés ou concédés. Or le présent rapport ne porte que sur ces derniers.

24 Art 33 et s. de la loi grecque sur le droit d'auteur.

25 La directive fait passer la durée de protection des droits voisins en matière sonore (droits des artistes-interprètes et des producteurs de phonogrammes) de cinquante à soixante-dix ans.

26 Sur la transposition de ce dispositif, v. les rapports allemand, espagnol, français, grec et italien.

les contrats conclus par les artistes-interprètes. Dans plusieurs systèmes juridiques étudiés, une réponse positive est apportée à cette question. Il en va ainsi en Belgique, en Grèce – selon la doctrine majoritaire du moins – et en Hongrie. Le droit français fait exception : si l'on met de côté la nouvelle règle prévue par la directive européenne évoquée à l'instant, la loi française n'impose pas que les rémunérations perçues par les artistes-interprètes soient proportionnelles aux recettes d'exploitation. Le forfait semble donc autorisé.

Par ailleurs, pour en revenir au droit d'auteur, alors que, selon certains droits nationaux, la règle de la rémunération proportionnelle est, sous réserve des exceptions prévues par la loi, impérative, selon d'autres, elle n'est que supplétive, en sorte que les parties ont la faculté d'y déroger d'un commun accord. Plus précisément, la rémunération proportionnelle est impérative en France et en Algérie. Elle est, en revanche, supplétive en Belgique[27], en Egypte[28] et en Hongrie[29]. Il y a fort à craindre, dans ce second cas, que la clause contraire se développe au point de devenir une clause de style et que, en pratique, la rémunération forfaitaire supplante la rémunération proportionnelle. Ce risque est clairement exposé dans le rapport hongrois.

En outre, les lois nationales ont institué des exceptions au principe de rémunération proportionnelle. Une rémunération forfaitaire est ainsi autorisée dans certains cas, plus ou moins nombreux selon le système considéré, notamment lorsqu'il est impossible ou excessivement complexe de mettre en place une rémunération proportionnelle. On citera en guise d'illustration le rapport français[30] : en France, le contrat peut stipuler un forfait dans plusieurs hypothèses, par exemple lorsque le taux de consultation de l'œuvre par le public n'est pas connu ou encore lorsque les frais de calcul et de contrôle d'une rémunération proportionnelle seraient trop élevés par rapport au montant de celle-ci. Cependant, dans les cas où le forfait est autorisé, si ce dernier s'avère trop faible, le juge dispose du pouvoir de le réviser[31]. La protection de l'auteur est donc, là encore, au cœur du dispositif.

Il faut ajouter que les pays qui consacrent la règle de la rémunération proportionnelle imposent parfois, en complément, une obligation de ventilation des redevances au sein du contrat. Une rémunération distincte doit alors être prévue pour chaque mode d'exploitation. Cette règle, qui relève toute autant de la forme que du fond, a une portée générale en Belgique[32]. Elle ne s'applique, en revanche, qu'à certains contrats en France (contrat de production audiovisuelle

27 Art XI. 183, §2, et XI. 196, §2, du Code de droit économique.

28 Art 150 du Code égyptien de la propriété intellectuelle.

29 Art 16(4) de la loi hongroise sur le droit d'auteur.

30 Art L. 131-4 et L. 132-6 CPI. Rappr. art 46.2 de la loi espagnole sur le droit d'auteur et art 65 de l'ordonnance algérienne du 19 juill. 2003 relative au droit d'auteur et aux droits voisins.

31 Art L. 131-5 CPI.

32 Art XI. 167, §1er, du Code de droit économique.

et contrat de commande pour la publicité[33]) et en Grèce (contrat de production audiovisuelle uniquement[34]).

En conclusion, le principe de rémunération proportionnelle semble le mieux à même de permettre aux auteurs de bénéficier d'une rémunération appropriée. Sa longévité dans des pays comme la France, où il est inscrit dans la loi depuis plus d'un demi-siècle[35], est un signe d'efficacité. Celle-ci n'est cependant pas totale comme nous le verrons en conclusion. Notons pour l'heure que, afin que le mécanisme joue de manière satisfaisante, il faut que les auteurs puissent avoir connaissance du volume exact de l'exploitation de leurs œuvres et des recettes correspondantes. Or, comme le relève le rapport belge, leurs cocontractants ne leur communiquent pas toujours des informations fiables.

II. L'exécution du contrat

Les questions de rémunération peuvent être à l'origine de trois évènements affectant l'exécution du contrat. Seront examinées la possibilité d'une simple adaptation de celui-ci (1.), puis l'éventualité de sa révision (2.) et, enfin, l'hypothèse consistant plus radicalement en sa disparition (3.).

1. L'adaptation du contrat

Les changements de circonstances qui peuvent apparaître en cours d'exécution du contrat, et singulièrement les évolutions technologiques, sont susceptibles d'avoir une incidence sur la rémunération de l'auteur et sur son caractère (in)approprié. Deux mécanismes peuvent alors permettre l'adaptation du contrat.

Le premier est un mécanisme d'anticipation de nature conventionnelle, qui relève en réalité tout autant de la formation que de l'exécution du contrat. Afin d'en comprendre la teneur, il convient d'avoir à l'esprit que plusieurs systèmes juridiques consacrent, plus ou moins formellement, un principe d'interprétation stricte des contrats d'auteur. Il en résulte qu'un contrat conçu en contemplation des seules formes d'exploitation existant au jour de sa conclusion n'autorise normalement pas l'exploitant à reproduire et à communiquer l'œuvre au public au moyen de formes apparues postérieurement. C'est ainsi, en particulier, que

---

33 Art L. 132-25 et L. 132-31 CPI.

34 Art 34 de la loi grecque sur le droit d'auteur.

35 L'exigence de rémunération proportionnelle a été instituée par la loi du 11 mars 1957. La jurisprudence considère qu'elle ne s'applique pas aux contrats conclus antérieurement: Civ. 1re, 30 oct. 1967, *JCP* 1968. II. 15530, obs. P. Level.

certains contrats passés à l'époque du tout analogique ont été dépourvus d'effets dans l'environnement numérique. Les parties ont-elles la possibilité de contourner cette solution stricte en anticipant les évolutions technologiques dans le contrat lui-même ? Certaines lois nationales les y autorisent. En France, par exemple, l'auteur peut céder ses droits pour des exploitations sous une forme non prévue et non prévisible à la date de conclusion du contrat[36]. Cependant, une telle clause doit respecter des conditions strictes. Elle doit être expresse et stipuler une participation corrélative aux profits d'exploitation. L'auteur est ainsi assuré de percevoir une rémunération appropriée pour ce type d'utilisations. Un dispositif comparable existe désormais en droit allemand[37]. D'autres pays se montrent au contraire assez hostiles à ces clauses d'adaptation. Ainsi, en Belgique, elles sont en principe nulles, excepté lorsque l'œuvre est créée en exécution d'un contrat de travail, d'un statut ou d'un contrat de commande[38].

Le second mécanisme permettant l'adaptation des contrats réside dans une éventuelle obligation de renégociation. Semblable obligation peut d'abord résulter de la volonté des parties : la validité et les effets de la clause de renégociation seront alors appréciés au regard du droit commun des contrats. Mais une telle obligation peut également découler de la loi. La solution est pour l'heure assez peu répandue. Elle vient toutefois d'être consacrée par le législateur français au sujet du contrat d'édition de livre sous forme numérique. Issu de l'ordonnance du 12 novembre 2014 modifiant les dispositions du Code de la propriété intellectuelle relatives au contrat d'édition, le nouvel article L. 132-17-7 du Code énonce que « le contrat d'édition comporte une clause de réexamen des conditions économiques de la cession des droits d'exploitation du livre sous une forme numérique ». La raison d'être de ce nouveau mécanisme tient aux incertitudes liées au développement du marché du livre numérique. Il s'agit de permettre à chacune des parties – auteur mais aussi éditeur – de réclamer une renégociation de la rémunération prévue dans le contrat en fonction des évolutions du marché.

2. La révision du contrat

L'hypothèse de travail est différente de la précédente. Le changement apparu en cours d'exécution du contrat provient cette fois-ci du succès rencontré par

36 Art L. 131-6 CPI.
37 § 31a et 32c UrhG issus de la loi du 26 oct. 2007 relative au droit d'auteur dans la société de l'information. A la différence du droit français, le droit allemand prévoit un droit de révocation au profit de l'auteur.
38 Art XI. 167, § 1er et 3, du Code de droit économique.

l'œuvre. L'éventualité d'un tel succès n'a pas été envisagée initialement dans le contrat, de sorte que la rémunération qui y est stipulée peut apparaître injustement basse. Il s'agit donc de faire face à une situation imprévue de « *best seller* », pour reprendre l'expression utilisée dans le questionnaire auquel ont répondu les rapporteurs nationaux. Plus précisément, il convient de se demander si l'auteur est en droit de réclamer – le cas échéant devant un juge – la révision du contrat, de façon à ce que sa rémunération soit modifiée à la hausse.

Nombre de lois nationales sur le droit d'auteur admettent une telle possibilité de révision. On peut citer en ce sens les lois algérienne, allemande, belge, croate, espagnole, finlandaise, française, égyptienne, hongroise et portugaise, auxquelles il faudra sans doute ajouter bientôt la loi néerlandaise, actuellement en cours de révision. Les conditions d'exercice de cette prérogative sont cependant assez variables d'un pays à l'autre. Tantôt celle-ci porte sur tous les contrats d'auteur, quelle que soit leur nature, tantôt sur certains d'entre eux uniquement. Ainsi, en Espagne[39] et en France[40], elle est générale, alors qu'en Belgique, la révision n'est possible que pour les contrats d'édition et de représentation[41]. En outre, selon certaines lois nationales, telle la loi allemande, la rémunération peut être révisée quelle que soit sa nature, proportionnelle ou forfaitaire[42]. D'autres lois nationales, à l'image des lois belge et française, n'admettent la révision qu'en cas de forfait[43]. Des disparités assez nettes doivent également être constatées en ce qui concerne l'appréciation du déséquilibre autorisant la révision du contrat : les lois allemande et belge, par exemple, posent comme condition l'existence d'une disproportion manifeste entre la rémunération initialement convenue et les recettes tirées de l'exploitation[44], tandis que la loi française exige que l'auteur ait subi un préjudice de plus de sept douzièmes[45]. Ajoutons que, dans certains pays, les dispositions nationales autorisant la révision du contrat, quelle que soit leur teneur, s'appliquent semble-t-il assez rarement. Du moins est-ce qui ressort de la lecture du rapport belge, qui explique ce faible succès par l'imprécision des relevés d'exploitation fournis par les exploitants aux auteurs, lesquels ne disposent donc pas d'éléments suffisants pour invoquer une augmentation de leur rémunération.

Lorsque la possibilité d'obtenir la révision du contrat n'est pas prévue spécialement par la loi sur le droit d'auteur, elle est susceptible de découler,

---

39 Art 47 de la loi espagnole sur le droit d'auteur.

40 Art L. 131-5 CPI.

41 Art XI. 196, § 2, et XI. 202 du Code de droit économique.

42 § 32a UrhG.

43 Toutefois, en présence d'une rémunération proportionnelle dont l'assiette ou le taux seraient trop faibles ou incertains, il est possible d'avoir recours à des mécanismes issus du droit commun des contrats. Sur ce point, v. *supra* p. 77.

44 § 32a UrhG.

45 Art L. 131-5 CPI.

comme en Grèce, en Norvège, en Suisse et, en attendant la réforme évoquée plus haut, aux Pays-Bas, du droit commun des contrats. Une révision judiciaire n'est toutefois envisageable que dans les pays qui ont consacré, sous une forme ou une autre, la théorie de l'imprévision.

3. La disparition du contrat

L'auteur est en droit d'exiger l'exécution des diverses obligations que le contrat met à la charge de l'exploitant. A défaut d'exécution, il lui est possible de mettre fin au contrat et d'engager la responsabilité de son partenaire. Il peut en aller ainsi lorsque ce dernier ne lui a tout simplement pas versé la rémunération prévue par le contrat. Mais la solution est également applicable en cas de violation d'autres obligations, et notamment d'obligations liées à cette obligation de rémunération. On songe, d'une part, à l'obligation de rendre des comptes édictée par certains droits nationaux. Ainsi, dans des pays comme la Belgique, l'Espagne ou la France, celle-ci est prévue à propos du contrat d'édition, du contrat de production audiovisuelle et du contrat de représentation[46]. On pense, d'autre part, à l'obligation d'exploitation qui existe, par exemple, en droit belge[47] et en droit français[48] : associée à une rémunération proportionnelle, une telle obligation assure en principe à l'auteur le bénéfice de redevances effectives. Sa violation – *i.e.* le fait pour le cocontractant de l'auteur de ne pas chercher sérieusement à exploiter l'œuvre – est une cause d'anéantissement du contrat.

Dans certains systèmes juridiques, le contrat peut également prendre fin lorsqu'il n'est plus productif, alors même que l'exploitant s'est conformé à ses obligations. Citons en ce sens les nouvelles dispositions de la loi française qui accordent aux deux parties à un contrat d'édition de livre – auteur et éditeur – la possibilité de résilier le contrat si, pendant deux années consécutives au-delà d'un délai de quatre ans après la publication de l'œuvre, les états de comptes ne font apparaître aucune rémunération[49].

On évoquera pour finir la loi américaine sur le droit d'auteur, qui accorde aux créateurs un droit de résiliation assez spécifique auquel ils ne peuvent renoncer[50]. Ce droit leur permet de mettre fin, sans justification particulière, aux

---

46 Art XI. 183, §2, XI. 198 et XI. 202 du Code de droit économique belge, art 64, 78 et 90 de la loi espagnole sur le droit d'auteur et art L. 132-13, L. 132-17-3, L. 132-28 et L. 132-21 du CPI français. Rappelons qu'en Belgique, le contrat de représentation ne fait pas partie des contrats pour lesquels la rémunération doit nécessairement être proportionnelle.

47 Art XI. 167, §1er, du Code de droit économique.

48 Art L. 132-12 et L. 132-27 CPI, à propos respectivement des contrats d'édition et de production audiovisuelle.

49 Art L. 132-17-4 CPI.

50 Section 203 et 304(c) U.S. Copyright Act.

contrats qui les lient aux exploitants. Les auteurs peuvent notamment se servir de cette faculté s'ils ne sont pas satisfaits des redevances qui leur sont versées. Il s'agit de l'unique protection qui leur est offerte aux Etats-Unis afin d'obtenir une rémunération appropriée, hors droit commun toutefois[51]. Les conditions d'exercice de cette prérogative sont en outre assez strictes. Tout d'abord, la résiliation est impossible lorsque l'œuvre est un *work made for hire*, c'est-à-dire une œuvre de commande ou une œuvre créée par un salarié. Ensuite, la demande de résiliation ne peut intervenir qu'à partir de la trente-cinquième année qui suit la publication et uniquement durant cinq ans. Enfin, il faut que l'auteur respecte un préavis, ainsi que différentes formalités. Selon le rapport américain, ces nombreuses conditions ne facilitent pas la mise en œuvre du dispositif.

* * *

Pour conclure, il apparaît que plusieurs mécanismes, variables d'un système juridique à l'autre, devraient permettre aux auteurs et aux artistes-interprètes, liés par contrats à des exploitants, d'obtenir une rémunération appropriée. De tels mécanismes sont issus tantôt du droit de la propriété littéraire et artistique, tantôt du droit commun des contrats, celui-ci ayant vocation à compléter utilement la législation spéciale et à combler ses éventuelles lacunes. Cependant, l'efficacité de ces mécanismes, y compris de ceux qui sont censés être les plus protecteurs, n'est pas pleinement acquise. Les créateurs se plaignent souvent du faible montant des redevances qu'ils perçoivent et leur mécontentement n'a fait que s'accentuer avec le développement des exploitations en ligne[52]. Pour autant, il est assez rare qu'ils portent leurs revendications devant les tribunaux. Une première explication tient peut-être au caractère strict et, par suite, dissuasif des conditions de mise en œuvre de certaines des règles étudiées dans le présent rapport. Le coût d'un éventuel procès peut aussi décourager les titulaires de droits[53]. Toutefois, une autre raison, plus fondamentale, nous semble être à l'origine de leur inertie. Agir en justice revient, d'une certaine manière, à déclarer la guerre aux exploitants[54], de sorte que les auteurs et les interprètes qui font ce choix risquent d'avoir ensuite toutes les peines à retrouver du travail. Le pragmatisme l'emporte ainsi sur l'application des règles de droit.

---

51 V. *supra* p. 75.

52 Font naturellement exception les auteurs et artistes-interprètes qui ont acquis suffisamment de notoriété pour se retrouver en position de force lorsqu'ils négocient des contrats avec des exploitants. Il s'agit toutefois de cas assez rares.

53 Le remède peut alors consister à prévoir des hypothèses de résiliation de plein droit des contrats d'exploitation, sans recours au juge. V. not. en ce sens les dispositions de la loi française en matière de contrat d'édition.

54 V. à cet égard la suggestion des rapporteurs allemands qui proposent de dépersonnaliser les procédures en ouvrant davantage les actions en justice aux associations d'artistes.

Tristan Azzi*

1.3 General report: Mechanisms to ensure adequate remuneration for creators and performers

There appears to be no doubt today as to the nature of authors' rights/copyright and related rights. Literary and artistic property is, as its name indicates, a particular form of property. This classification is enshrined, *inter alia*, in the preamble to the European Directive of 22 May 2001 on the harmonisation of certain aspects of copyright and related rights in the information society[1] and in the Charter of Fundamental Rights of the European Union.[2] It is also accepted by the European Court of Human Rights[3] and by several national constitutional courts.[4] To reason from the perspective of authors' rights,[5] it follows that, like any owner of property, the creator of a work of authorship must in principle be granted the three prerogatives traditionally attached to the property right: *usus*, *abusus* and *fructus*. The correlation between the last two prerogatives means that an author may freely authorise others by contract to exploit his works by assigning or licensing his rights (*abusus*) to them and that he may require remuneration (*fructus*) in return for doing so.

Two points should be made before we consider the mechanisms designed to ensure that such remuneration is adequate. First, precisely because authors have the status of owners, they ought to be able to waive payment of remuneration for the exploitation of their works. To this effect, some national laws expressly accept the validity of exploitation contracts that are concluded for free,

---

* Professor of Law at the University of Paris I Panthéon-Sorbonne, France.
Translation from French by Margaret Platt-Hommel.

1 Recitals 3 and 9.

2 Art 17. For an application, see CJEU, 9 Feb. 2012, case C-277/10, *Martin Luksan*, §68 and following, *D.* 2012. 2841, obs. P. Sirinelli; *RTD com.* 2012. 318, obs. F. Pollaud-Dulian; *RTD eur.* 2012. 964, obs. E. Treppoz; *Propr. intell.* 2012. 425 et 434, obs. V.-L. Benabou; *CCE* 2012, comm. 37, obs. C. Caron.

3 ECtHR, 29 Jan. 2008, *Balan v Moldova*: *Propr. intell.* 2008, 338, obs. J.-M. Bruguière; *Comm. com. électr.* 2008, comm. 76, obs. C. Caron; *RTD com.* 2008, 732, obs. F. Pollaud-Dulian.

4 See, for example, the references cited in the German report. See also in France, Cons. const. [Constitutional Council], 27 July 2006, *"DADVSI" law*: *Propr. intell.* 2006, 240, chron. V.-L. Benabou; *D.* 2006, 2157, chron. C. Castets-Renard; *Com. com. électr.* 2006, comm. 140, obs. C. Caron; *RTD com.* 2006, 779, obs. F. Pollaud-Dulian; *Propr. intell.* 2007, 193, obs. M. Vivant; Cons. const., 10 June 2009, *"HADOPI" law*.

5 Much of the discussion in this general report also holds for performers. However, some differences in treatment existing between performers and authors are presented *infra*, p. 90 [no. 11].

or at least some such contracts. For example, the German law allows authors to grant a non-exclusive exploitation right to the public free of charge, corresponding to the case of a free licence.[6] In French law, there is a more general acceptance that the communication right (*«droit de représentation»*) and the reproduction right are assignable for free.[7] Moreover, when a contract is concluded for consideration, there is nothing to prevent authors from agreeing to receive non-monetary consideration in exchange for the authorisations granted by them. If, for example, a creator assigns his or her exploitation monopoly to a company, the creator will obtain shares in return. On a different note, it is not uncommon for authors of scientific works to assign their rights to a publisher merely for a few copies of the published book.

Nevertheless, exploitation contracts are usually concluded for consideration in the form of remuneration in the strict sense, i.e. monetary payment. The question then arises as to whether authors have legal means at their disposal to obtain satisfactory remuneration, particularly in the light of the conditions under which their works are exploited. No answer to this question can be found in the international conventions on literary and artistic property because they deal with exploitation contracts only to a very limited extent.[8] As to the European directives, it is merely stated in some of them, usually in the preamble, that rightholders should receive "appropriate remuneration"[9] but without specifying – barring a few exceptions[10] – how this is to be achieved. Therefore, it is necessary

6 §32(3), 3rd sentence, UrhG.

7 ArtL. 122-7 Intellectual Property Code (IPC). See also art L. 122-7-1 IPC, similar to §32(3), 3rd sentence, UrhG mentioned above, providing that "authors shall be free to make their works available to the public without charge [...]".

8 It should just be indicated that some general international instruments provide that everyone has the right "to the protection of the moral and material interests resulting from any [...] literary or artistic production of which he is the author" (art27, §2 of the Universal Declaration of Human Rights and art15, §1(c) of the International Covenant on Economic, Social and Cultural Rights).

9 See recital 25 in the preamble to the Directive of 27 September 1993 on the coordination of certain rules concerning copyright and rights related to copyright applicable to satellite broadcasting and cable retransmission, and recital 10 in the preamble to the Directive of 22 May 2001 on the harmonisation of certain aspects of copyright and related rights in the information society ("an appropriate reward"). See also, but this time in the enacting terms of the Directive, art 16(2) of the Directive of 26 February 2014 on collective management of copyright and related rights and multi-territorial licensing of rights in musical works for online use in the internal market.

10 See recital 17 in the preamble to the abovementioned Directive of 27 September 1993 which states, in connection with satellite broadcasts, that, "in arriving at the amount of the payment to be made for the rights acquired, the parties should take account of all aspects of the broadcast, such as the actual audience, the potential audience and the language version". See also, but offering little guidance, recital 10 in the preamble to the Directive of 22 May 2001 stating that the reward should "provide the opportunity for satisfactory returns on this investment". See also the supplementary remuneration mechanism introduced for the benefit of performers

to turn to national laws to identify the mechanisms designed to ensure that authors really do enjoy such remuneration. On reading the twenty-two national reports that were received, it emerges that the mechanisms are many and varied. To describe them, a two-step approach will be adopted. Those mechanisms that are liable to come into play when the contract is formed will be considered in the first place (I.), then those that are intended to apply in the course of the performance of the contract (II.).

I. Formation of the Contract

In the light of the national reports, it is possible to classify the various legal systems into three categories based on the protection afforded to authors when the contract is formed. In the first category are countries that do not lay down any specific rules on the subject of determining the remuneration and thus seem, at least at first sight, to give the parties complete freedom (1.). Belonging to the second category are countries that require authors to receive equitable remuneration (2.). Lastly, the third category covers those countries that guarantee authors remuneration that is proportional to the results of the work's exploitation (3.).

1. The Legal Systems establishing a Principle of Freedom in the Matter of Remuneration

Some countries are deeply attached to the principles of freedom of choice and contractual freedom, including in literary and artistic property law. According to this liberal approach, it does not matter whether authors are often in a weak position in relation to the parties with whom they enter into contracts for their exploitation rights: this imbalance is no justification for granting them preferential treatment. Therefore, in these countries, remuneration is determined, in principle, through the free play of contractual bargaining. As a result, the literary and artistic property laws of the countries in question do not include any special provisions to enable authors to claim adequate remuneration when the

---

in the Directive of 27 September 2011 amending the Directive of 12 December 2006 on the term of protection of copyright and certain related rights. On this mechanism, see *infra*, p. 90. See again art16(2) of the abovementioned Directive of 26February 2014 which states, with regard to collective management, that "[t]ariffs for exclusive rights and rights to remuneration shall be reasonable in relation to, *inter alia*, the economic value of the use of the rights in trade, taking into account the nature and scope of the use of the work and other subject-matter, as well as in relation to the economic value of the service provided by the collective management organisation. Collective management organisations shall inform the user concerned of the criteria used for the setting of those tariffs".

contract is formed. The Argentine, Austrian, Israeli,[11] Japanese, Norwegian, Swiss, UK, US and, it would seem, Italian laws belong to this first category. Pending a legislative reform that is reported to be imminent, Dutch law also falls into this first category.[12]

However, on closer scrutiny, the parties rarely have total freedom even in these systems. Indeed, two sets of mechanisms may prevent exploitation businesses from making creators accept excessively low remuneration.

Firstly, in the absence of rules in the special legislation on literary and artistic property, it is usually possible to turn to the general principles of contract law. The Swiss report mentions, for example, that an author who accepted a financially unfavourable contract following a mistake or misrepresentation could apply for it to be declared void. The UK report, for its part, details how the common law doctrine of restraint of trade, which provides a remedy against grossly unfair contracts, has been applied to copyright exploitation contracts by the courts. The ability of the courts, in the absence of special rules, to apply techniques stemming from the general theory of contracts also emerges in the Austrian, Norwegian and USA reports.

Secondly, with regard to the specific case of collective management, some countries have adopted fairly strict rules on the setting and monitoring of the tariffs applied by collecting societies. This is the case, notably, in Switzerland.[13]

2. The Legal Systems establishing a Principle of Equity in the Matter of Remuneration

Better protection for creators may seem to be afforded when the special legislation on literary and artistic property includes rules relating to the remuneration's determination. Some national laws require the remuneration to be "equitable". The Croatian, Finnish and German laws belong to this second group. The legislative bill on copyright exploitation contracts in the final stages of adoption in the Netherlands should soon enable Dutch law to be added to this group.

The big question is what is meant by "equitable" remuneration. As the German report is very detailed in this regard, German law will be used as an illustration here.[14] German law assigns an important role to collective bargaining, from which the equitable character of the remuneration, and thus the legitimacy

11 Except in connection with publishing contracts: see *infra*, p. 90.

12 Indeed, a specific law on copyright exploitation contracts is in the process of being adopted in the Netherlands. As a result, Dutch law should soon switch to the second category.

13 Compare, in this regard, the abovementioned Directive of 26 February 2014 and the Belgian and Hungarian reports.

14 §§32 and 36 UrhG. Note that a reform of German copyright contract law is currently under consideration.

of the method of fixing it, can be presumed in a way: to parody a famous French maxim, in Germany "whatever is collective is fair".[15] Therefore, authors' remuneration is deemed to be equitable when it stems from a collective agreement. Where no collective agreement exists, the remuneration is considered equitable if it is the result of the application of other "common remuneration rules". Such rules are the fruit of discussions, in each sector of activity, between the organisations representing authors, on the one hand, and exploitation businesses, on the other. However, according to the authors of the German report, the mechanism introduced by the Law of 22 March 2002 has not produced conclusive results so far. Lastly, apart from the cases of collective agreements and common remuneration rules, remuneration is to be considered equitable when it meets the criteria laid down in the law. The latter requires account to be taken of what is viewed as customary and fair in business relations at the time of the contract's conclusion as well as the nature and extent of the authorisation granted for exploitation, particularly the duration and time of exploitation, and more generally all the circumstances. German commentators and judges tend to complain about the vagueness of these criteria. Also, in comparison with the third category of legal systems that we shall consider in a moment, German law leads to more flexible solutions:[16] the German courts do not require the remuneration to be proportional to the revenue from the work's exploitation for it to be deemed equitable. While it certainly can be proportional, it may also take the form of a lump sum; it is also possible to have a combination of the two methods.

It should be added that, in the systems that require equitable remuneration, the existence of a provision to that effect in the literary and artistic property law does not prevent the general principles of contract law from being applied in some cases. Indeed, general contract law may supplement the protection afforded by the special law. The Croatian, Finnish and German reports stress this point. To take just one example, in Finland, the remuneration rules laid down in the copyright law apply only to those exploitation contracts concluded with the original rightholder. Subsequent transfers are subject to equivalent rules but under the general law.

---

15 Based on the phrase of the French philosopher Alfred Fouillée (1838–1912) "whatever is contractual is fair". The emergence of unequal contracts, like employment contracts or consumer contracts, has seriously undermined this premise.

16 See, generally, with numerous points of comparison between the German and French systems, A. Lucas-Schloetter, "Le droit contractuel d'auteur allemand depuis la réforme du 22 mars 2002", *Propr. intell.* 2005, 403, and, by the same author, "Lettre d'Allemagne – qu'y a-t-il dans la 'deuxième corbeille'? La loi allemande du 26 octobre 2007 relative au droit d'auteur dans la société de l'information", *Propr. intell.* 2008, 308.

3. The Legal Systems establishing a Principle of Proportionality in the Matter of Remuneration

The most protective solution for authors, at least in theory, is to grant them remuneration that is proportional to, or a percentage of, the revenue from exploitation.[17] In this way, authors are guaranteed a share of the income generated by the use of their works. In addition, it prevents them from giving up their rights for good in return for a paltry lump sum. Several countries have established such a mechanism, including Algeria,[18] Belgium, Egypt, France, Greece, Hungary and Spain, among others.

In actual fact, the forcefulness of the proportional remuneration principle varies from country to country. Several factors should be taken into account in this regard.

To begin with, in several legal systems, the requirement normally applies to all copyright exploitation contracts, whereas, in others, it concerns only certain specific contracts. In Spain[19] and France,[20] for example, the rule is of general scope, whereas, in Belgium, its application is limited under the law to publishing and audiovisual production contracts.[21]

The rules concerning the remuneration base and its rate are also fairly diverse. To illustrate this point, it is enough to consider the rates. In most cases, it is left to the parties to determine the rate of the proportional remuneration. The risk then is that the exploiting party will take advantage of its stronger bargaining position to force the author to accept a very low and thus highly disadvantageous rate. In this event, general contract law may again usefully supplement the special law by stepping in to secure the author effective protection. Reference can be made in this regard to the Spanish and Greek reports, the latter mentioning the eventuality of the contract's annulment for being contrary to good morals. The general law may also apply in the more radical case where the contract does not provide for the rate of remuneration. French case law offers an interesting illustration of such a case: to set aside an agreement for the assignment of an author's rights which merely provided for a "negotiable" percentage, the *Tribunal de grande instance de Paris* held, among other grounds, that the agreement, with no price and no cause, violated the "general principles of civil law".[22] To avoid any difficulty, it would be conceivable for the rate of remunera-

17 It should be noted, however, that lump-sum remuneration may prove to be more advantageous in certain cases, particularly when the volume of exploitation is low.

18 The substance of the Algerian law is mentioned in the Egyptian report.

19 Art 46.1 of the Spanish Intellectual Property Law.

20 Art L. 131-4 IPC.

21 Arts. XI. 183, §2, and XI. 196, §2, of the Code of Economic Law.

22 TGI Paris, 9 May 1990, *RIDA* Jan. 1991, no. 147, p. 355: in addition to the provisions of the Law of 11 March 1957 on literary and artistic property, the Court referred specifically to articles

tion – or at least a minimum rate – to be laid down by law. However, doubtless because it constitutes a real encroachment on contractual freedom, this solution is adopted only fairly exceptionally.[23] Reference can be made to the Greek law as one of the few national laws to have accepted it in the field of literary and artistic property, although it restricts its application to certain designated contracts: print publishing contracts, broadcasting contracts, theatrical performance contracts, contracts for the musical accompaniment of films and contracts concluded by photographers for the assignment of rights.[24] A rate of remuneration is also laid down in the Israeli law but only in the field of literary publishing contracts. The solution likewise exists in Portugal where it takes the form of a default provision in the standard rules on publishing contracts. Lastly, it is to be found occasionally in European Union law, but this time in the field of related rights. The Directive of 27 September 2011 extending the term of protection of certain related rights provides, for example, in connection with the exploitation of performances during the additional twenty-year period of protection granted by it,[25] that the producer must pay the performers 20% of the revenue that it receives for such exploitation.[26]

Moreover, another question is whether, more generally, the proportional remuneration rule benefiting authors also covers contracts concluded by performers. An affirmative answer is given to this question in several legal systems studied here. This is the case in Belgium, in Greece – at least according to the leading opinion – and in Hungary. French law is an exception: leaving aside the new rule established by the abovementioned European directive, French law does not require the remuneration received by performers to be proportional to the exploitation revenue. Therefore, a flat fee appears to be permitted.

Again, to return to authors' rights, while proportional remuneration is the mandatory rule in some national laws, subject to the exceptions provided for in the law, it is only a default rule in others and so the parties are able to depart from it by mutual agreement. Specifically, proportional remuneration is mandatory in France and Algeria. On the other hand, it is a default rule in Belgium,[27]

1108, 1131 and 1583 of the Civil Code concerning respectively the general conditions governing the validity of contracts (consent, capacity, object, and cause), the cause (existence and lawfulness) and particular requirements of sales contracts (agreement on the thing and the price).

23 The rates of remuneration set by national laws are usually for rights to remuneration rather than exclusive rights that may be assigned or licensed. This report covers only exclusive rights.

24 Art33 *et seq.* of the Greek Copyright Law.

25 The Directive extends the term of protection of related rights in the audio sector (rights of performers and producers of phonograms) from fifty to seventy years.

26 On the implementation of this mechanism, see the French, German, Greek, Italian and Spanish reports.

27 Arts. XI. 183, §2, and XI. 196, §2, of the Code of Economic Law.

Egypt[28] and Hungary.[29] In the second case, there is every reason to fear that clauses to the contrary will develop, to the point of becoming standard, and that proportional remuneration will be supplanted by lump-sum remuneration in practice. This risk is highlighted in the Hungarian report.

In addition, national laws have established exceptions to the principle of proportional remuneration. For example, lump-sum remuneration is permitted in certain cases, the number of which varies depending on the system involved, particularly where it is impossible or excessively complicated to introduce proportional remuneration. The French report can be cited as an illustration:[30] in France, contracts may provide for a lump sum in several situations including, for example, when the number of times the work is consulted by the public is not known or when the costs of calculating and monitoring proportional remuneration would be too high in relation to the amount of the remuneration. However, in those cases where a lump sum is permitted, the courts have the power to revise it if it proves to be too low.[31] So the author's protection is again at the heart of the mechanism.

It should be added that the countries which have established the rule of proportional remuneration sometimes also impose an obligation to break down the royalties within the contract. Separate remuneration must then be allocated for each method of exploitation. This rule, which is a matter of both form and substance, is of general scope in Belgium.[32] On the other hand, it applies only to certain contracts in France (audiovisual production contracts and commissioning contracts for advertising[33]) and in Greece (exclusively audiovisual production contracts[34]).

In conclusion, the principle of proportional remuneration seems best able to ensure that authors receive adequate remuneration. Its long existence in countries like France, where it has been enshrined in the law for over half a century,[35] is a sign that it is effective. Nevertheless, it is not entirely so, as we shall see in the conclusion. It can be noted at this stage that, for the mechanism to apply satisfactorily, authors need to be able to know the exact extent of the exploitation of their works and the corresponding revenue. However, as the Bel-

28 Art 150 of the Egyptian Intellectual Property Code.

29 Art 16(4) of the Hungarian Copyright Act.

30 Arts. L. 131-4 and L. 132-6 IPC. Comp. art 46.2 of the Spanish Intellectual Property Law and art 65 of the Algerian Ordinance of 19 July 2003 on copyright and related rights.

31 Art L. 131-5 IPC.

32 Art XI. 167, §1, of the Code of Economic Law.

33 Arts. L. 132-25 and L. 132-31 IPC.

34 Art 34 of the Greek Copyright Law.

35 The requirement of proportional remuneration was introduced by the Law of 11 March 1957. Case law considers that it does not apply to contracts concluded before then: Cass. 1st Civ., 30 Oct. 1967, *JCP* 1968. II. 15530, obs. P. Level.

gian report indicates, they do not always receive reliable information from their contractual partners.

II. Performance of the Contract

Remuneration issues may give rise to three events affecting the performance of a contract. We shall examine the possibility of a simple adaptation of the contract (1), then the eventuality of its revision (2) and, lastly, the more radical scenario of its disappearance (3).

1. The Contract's Adaptation

Changes of circumstances that may occur during the contract's performance, and particularly technological developments, can have an impact on the author's remuneration and its (in)adequacy. Two mechanisms may then enable the contract to be adapted.

The first is an anticipatory mechanism in contracts and actually concerns as much the contract's formation as its performance. To understand what this mechanism involves, it should be remembered that several legal systems establish – more or less explicitly – a principle of the strict interpretation of authors' contracts. It follows that a contract concluded with only the forms of exploitation existing at the time of its conclusion in mind does not normally entitle the exploiting party to reproduce the work and communicate it to the public by means of forms of exploitation that emerged later. In particular, that is why certain contracts concluded in the all-analogue age were unenforceable in the digital environment. Are the parties able to get round this strict result by anticipating technological developments in the contract itself? Some national laws allow it. In France, for example, authors may assign their rights for exploitation in a form that was not foreseen and was not foreseeable at the date of the contract's conclusion.[36] However, such a clause must comply with strict conditions. It must be express and provide for a corresponding share of the profits from exploitation. Authors are thus guaranteed to receive adequate remuneration for the type of use in question. A comparable mechanism now exists in German law.[37] Other countries, however, take a rather hostile view of such adaptation clauses. For example, in Belgium, they are null and void in principle, except

36 Art L. 131-6 IPC.

37 §§ 31a and 32c UrhG stemming from the Law of 26 Oct. 2007 on copyright in the information society. Unlike French law, German law affords authors a right of revocation.

where the work is created under an employment contract, employment regulations or a commissioning contract.[38]

The second mechanism through which contracts may be adapted takes the form of a possible obligation to renegotiate the contract. In the first place, such an obligation may follow from the intention of the parties, in which case the validity and effects of the renegotiation clause will be assessed in the light of general contract law. However, the obligation may also derive from the law. This solution is not very common for now. But it has just been adopted by the French legislator in connection with publishing contracts for books in digital form. Stemming from the Ordinance of 12 November 2014 amending the provisions of the Intellectual Property Code dealing with publishing contracts, the new article L. 132-17-7 of the Code states that "the publishing contract shall include a clause for reviewing the financial conditions of the assignment of the rights for the exploitation of the book in digital form". The reason for this new mechanism lies in the uncertainty regarding the development of the digital book market. The aim is to enable each of the parties – not only the author but also the publisher – to ask for the remuneration laid down in the contract to be renegotiated in the light of market developments.

2. The Contract's Revision

The working hypothesis is different from the previous one. This time, the change occurring in the course of the performance of the contract is due to the success achieved by the work. As the eventuality of such success was not initially contemplated in the contract, the remuneration stipulated in it may appear unfairly low. Therefore, the idea is to deal with an unforeseen "bestseller" situation, as it is termed in the questionnaire to which the national reports replied. Specifically, the question is whether the author is entitled to demand the contract's revision – in court if necessary – to increase the remuneration agreed in it.

A number of national literary and artistic property laws accept such a possibility of revising the contract. Examples include the Algerian, Belgian, Croatian, Egyptian, Finnish, French, German, Hungarian, Portuguese and Spanish laws, to which the Dutch law, which is currently being amended, should doubtless be added soon. Nevertheless, the conditions under which this right may be exercised vary somewhat from one country to another. In some cases, it covers all copyright contracts, whatever their nature, in others only some of them. For example, in Spain[39] and France,[40] it is a general right, whereas, in Belgium, revi-

38 Art XI. 167, §§1 and 3, of the Code of Economic Law.
39 Art 47 of the Spanish Intellectual Property Law.
40 Art L. 131-5 IPC.

sion is possible only for publishing and communication contracts (*"contrats de représentation")*.[41] Moreover, in some national laws, like the German one, the remuneration may be revised whatever its nature, proportional or lump-sum.[42] Other national laws, like the Belgian and French ones, accept revision only in the case of lump-sum remuneration.[43] Fairly clear disparities must also be found in the assessment of the imbalance giving rise to the revision of the contract: the German and Belgian laws, for example, make revision conditional upon the existence of a marked disproportion between the remuneration as initially agreed and the revenue derived from the work's exploitation,[44] whereas the French law requires the author to have suffered a prejudice of over seven-twelfths.[45] It should be added that, in some countries, the national provisions of whatever kind permitting the revision of contracts seem to apply fairly rarely in practice. At least this is what emerges on reading the Belgian report which puts this lack of success down to the vagueness of the reports on the exploitation of works that exploitation businesses send to authors who do not have sufficient information at their disposal to claim an increase in their remuneration.

Where the possibility of obtaining the contract's revision is not specifically mentioned in the literary and artistic property law, it may arise from general contract law, as in Greece, Norway, Switzerland and, pending the legislative reform mentioned earlier, the Netherlands. Nevertheless, judicial revision is a possible option only in countries that apply the doctrine of unforeseeability in one form or another.

3. The Contract's Disappearance

Authors are entitled to require that the various obligations incumbent on the exploiting party under the contract are actually performed, failing which they may terminate the contract and seek their contractual partner's liability. This may be the case when the contractual partner has simply failed to pay the author the remuneration stipulated in the contract. But the solution is also applicable if there is a breach of other contractual obligations, including in particular obligations related to the duty to pay remuneration. One example is the obligation to render accounts laid down in certain national laws. Thus, in countries like Belgium, France or Spain, this obligation is established for publishing con-

41 Arts. XI. 196, §2, and XI. 202 of the Code of Economic Law.

42 §32a UrhG.

43 However, in cases of proportional remuneration where the basis or the rate is too low or uncertain, it is possible to resort to mechanisms under general contract law. In this regard, see *supra*, p. 90.

44 §32a UrhG.

45 Art L. 131-5 IPC.

tracts, audiovisual production contracts and communication contracts *("contrats de representation")*.[46] Another is the duty to exploit the work which exists, for example, in Belgian law[47] and French law.[48] Combined with proportional remuneration, this duty ensures, in principle, that authors really will be paid royalties. Its breach – i.e. if the author's contractual partner does not make any serious effort to exploit the work – is a cause for terminating the contract.

In some legal systems, a contract may also be terminated if it has ceased to be productive, even though the exploiting party has complied with its obligations. Reference can be made in this regard to the new provisions of the French law granting the two parties to a publishing contract for books – author and publisher – the possibility of terminating the contract if the statements of accounts do not show any remuneration for two consecutive years following a period of four years after the work's publication.[49]

Lastly, we should mention the US Copyright Act which grants creators a fairly specific inalienable termination right.[50] This right enables them to bring their contracts with exploitation businesses to an end without any specific justification. Authors may exercise this right, for example, if they are not satisfied with the royalties paid to them. This is the only mechanism afforded to them in the United States to obtain adequate remuneration, barring the application of general principles of contract law.[51] In addition, the conditions governing the exercise of this right are fairly strict. Firstly, termination is impossible if the work in question is a work made for hire, i.e. a commissioned work or a work created by an employee. Secondly, termination can be requested only at the end of the thirty-fifth year following publication and only within a five-year period. Thirdly, the author must give prior notice and comply with various formalities. According to the USA report, these numerous conditions do not make it easy to implement the mechanism.

* * *

To conclude, it emerges that several mechanisms, which vary from one legal system to another, should enable authors and performers bound by contracts

46 Arts. XI. 183, §2, XI. 198 and XI. 202 of the Belgian Code of Economic Law, arts. 64, 78 and 90 of the Spanish Intellectual Property Law and arts. L. 132-13, L. 132-17-3, L. 132-28 and L. 132-21 of the French IPC. Note that, in Belgium, the communication contract is not one of the contracts for which the remuneration is required to be proportional.

47 Art XI. 167, §1 of the Code of Economic Law.

48 Arts. L. 132-12 and L. 132-27 IPC concerning publishing contracts and audiovisual production contracts respectively.

49 Art L. 132-17-4 IPC.

50 Sections 203 and 304(c) of the US Copyright Act.

51 See *supra* p. 88.

with exploitation businesses to obtain adequate remuneration. Such mechanisms sometimes have their basis in literary and artistic property law and sometimes in general contract law, which may serve as a useful supplement to the special law and fill any gaps in it. Nevertheless, these mechanisms, including the ones that are supposed to afford the most protection, are not totally effective in practice. Creators often complain about the low level of royalties that they receive and their dissatisfaction has increased further with the development of online exploitation.[52] Yet they rarely bring their claims before the courts. One explanation may have to do with the strict and thus dissuasive character of the conditions governing the application of some of the rules discussed in this report. The cost of a possible lawsuit may also discourage rightholders.[53] However, it seems to us that another more fundamental reason lies behind their passivity. Taking legal action amounts, to a certain extent, to a declaration of war on exploitation businesses[54] and, as a result, those authors and performers who choose to do so may well struggle to find work again afterwards. So pragmatism prevails over the application of the rules of law.

52 Of course, authors and performers who have gained sufficient prominence to be in a position of strength when they negotiate contracts with exploiting parties are exceptions. Nevertheless, these are fairly rare cases.

53 The remedy may then be to provide for possibilities of terminating exploitation contracts *ipso jure*, without applying to the courts. See notably along these lines the provisions of the French law on publishing contracts.

54 See in this regard the German report's suggestion of allowing legal proceedings to be instituted on a collective basis by opening them up more to artists' associations.

Tristan Azzi*

1.3 Informe general: Mecanismos destinados a garantizar una remuneración apropiada a los creadores y artistas-intérpretes

La naturaleza del derecho de Autor y de los derechos conexos parece hoy día ganada. La propiedad literaria y artística es, como su propio nombre indica, una forma particular de propiedad. Tan calificación fue establecida, entre otros, por el preámbulo de la directiva europea del 22 de mayo de 2001, sobre la armonización de determinados aspectos de los derechos de autor y derechos afines a los derechos de autor en la sociedad de la información[1] y por la Carta de los Derechos fundamentales de la Unión Europea[2]. El Tribunal Europeo de los Derechos Humanos[3], así como diversos magistrados constitucionales nacionales[4] la adoptan igualmente. De todo esto resulta, basándonos en el derecho de autor[5], que a imagen y semejanza de cualquier propietario, al creador de una obra del espíritu, se le debe conceder las tres prerrogativas asociadas al derecho de propiedad: el usus, el abusus y el frutus. La correlación de las dos últimos significa que el autor goza de libertad para autorizar por contrato a una persona para que explote su obra, cediéndole o concediéndole sus derechos (abusus) y para que, exija, en contrapartida, una remuneración (frutus).

Antes de considerar los mecanismos destinados a garantizar que tal remuneración sea la apropiada, hay que precisar dos cosas. Por una parte, precisamente por su calidad de propietario, el autor debería poder renunciar a percibir

---

* Profesor de la Facultad de Derecho de la Universidad de París Panthéon-Sorbonne.
Traducción del francés por Mar Delgado.

1 Considerandos 3 y 9.

2 Art 17. Para una aplicación, TJEU, 9 Feb. 2012, caso C-277/10, *Martin Luksan*, §68 et sig., *D.* 2012. 2841, obs. P. Sirinelli; *RTD com.* 2012. 318, obs. F. Pollaud-Dulian; *RTD eur.* 2012. 964, obs. E. Treppoz; *Propr. intell.* 2012. 425 y 434, obs. V.-L. Benabou; *CCE* 2012, comm. 37, obs. C. Caron.

3 TEDH, 29 enero 2008, Balan c/Moldavie: Propr. intell. 2008. 338, obs. J.-M. Bruguière; Comm. com. électr. 2008, comm. 76, obs. C. Caron; RTD com. 2008. 732, obs. F. Pollaud-Dulian.

4 Por ej. las referencias citadas en el informe alemán. Ver también en Francia, Cons. const., 27 juill. 2006, Loi DADVSI: Propr. intell. 2006. 240, chron. V.-L. Benabou; D. 2006. 2157, chron. C. Castets-Renard; Com. com. électr. 2006, comm. 140, obs. C. Caron; RTD com. 2006. 779, obs. F. Pollaud-Dulian; Propr. intell. 2007. 193, obs. M. Vivant; Cons. const., 10 juin 2009, Loi HADOPI.

5 La mayoría de los desarrollos que componen el presente informe general vale igualmente para los artistas intérpretes. Las pocas diferencias de trato entre estos últimos y los autores, serán expuestas *infra*, p. 103.

retribución por la explotación de su obra. En ese sentido, ciertas leyes nacionales reconocen expresamente la validez de contratos de explotación a título gratuito o al menos de algunos de entre ellos. De este modo, la ley alemana autoriza al autor a conceder gratuitamente un derecho de explotación no exclusivo al público, lo que equivaldría a una licencia libre[6]. La ley francesa, por su parte, de modo más general, admite que el derecho de representación y el derecho de reproducción pueden ser cedidos a título gratuito[7] Por otro lado, una vez llevado el contrato a título oneroso, nada impide que el autor acepte recibir, a cambio de las autorizaciones acordadas, una contrapartida no monetaria. Por ejemplo, si un creador aporta a una sociedad su monopolio de explotación, recibirá su capital social. En otro ámbito, no es raro que el autor de una obra científica se conforme con ceder sus derechos a un editor, simplemente a cambio de algunos ejemplares del libro.

Sin embargo, lo más habitual es que los contratos de explotación sean establecidos a título oneroso y a cambio de una remuneración en el sentido estricto, es decir una retribución monetaria. La cuestión ahora es saber si el autor dispone de medios jurídicos para obtener una remuneración satisfactoria en relación, particularmente, a las condiciones en las que su obra está siendo explotada. En vano encontraremos respuesta a esta cuestión en las convenciones internacionales relativas a la propiedad literaria y artística ya que en ellas sólo se trata de modo accesorio el tema de los contratos de explotación[8]. En cuanto a las directivas europeas, se limitan a indicar, generalmente en el preámbulo que los titulares de derechos deben recibir una "remuneración adecuada"[9] , pero sin concretar, salvo alguna excepción[10], en qué modo. Para identificar los meca-

---

6 §32 (3), 3ᵉ phrase, UrhG.

7 Art L. 122-7 CPI. Vid. tambien el art. L. 122-7-1 CPI, cercano a §32 (3), frase 3, UrhG citado, que prevee que «el autor es libre de poner sus obras gratuitamente a la disposición del público(...) ».

8 Indiquemos simplemente que ciertos instrumentos internacionales generales preven el derecho para cada uno de beneficiar "la protección de los intereses morales y materiales que le correspondan por razón de las producciones (...) literarias o artísticas de que sea autor" (art27, §2, de la Declaración Universal de los derechos Humanos y 15, §1, c, del Pacto internacional sobre los derechos económicos, sociales y culturales.).

9 Ver el considerando 25 de la directiva de 27 de sept. 1993 sobre coordinación de determinadas disposiciones relativas a los derechos de autor y derechos afines a los derechos de autor en el ámbito de la radiodifusión via satélite y de la distribución por cable, y el considerando 10 de la directiva de 22 de mayo de 2001 sobre la armonización de determinados aspectos de los derechos de autor y derechos afines a los derechos de autor en la sociedad de la información. V. también, pero esta vez en el dispositivo de la directiva, el art16 §2, de la directiva de 26 de febrero de 2014 relativa a la gestión colectiva de los derechos de autor y derechos afines y a la concesión de licencias multiterritoriales de derechos sobre obras musicales para su utilización en línea en el mercado interior.

10 Ver el considerando de la directiva del 27 de sept 1993 citada, que enuncia, a propósito de la difusión por satélite que «con ocasión de la adquisición de los derechos y a efectos de pactar

nismos que velan por garantizar a los autores el beneficio efectivo de tal remuneración debemos fijarnos en las leyes nacionales. Lo que se extrae de la lectura de los 22 informes nacionales recibidos es que dichos mecanismos son numerosos y variados. Para describirlos los dividiré en dos grupos, primero los que pueden actuar durante la formación del contrato (I.), después, aquellos cuya vocación es intervenir en el curso de su ejecución (II.).

I. El establecimiento del contrato

La consulta de los informes nacionales nos permite clasificar los diferentes sistemas jurídicos en tres categorías, en función de la protección que proporcionan al autor en el momento del establecimiento del contrato. Dentro de la primera categoría, encontramos países que no prevén reglas específicas en lo que concierne a la determinación de la remuneración, parecen conferir en principio, total libertad a cada una de las partes (1.). Dentro de la segunda categoría, encontramos estados que aseguran al autor el beneficio de una justa remuneración (2.). Finalmente, dentro de la tercera categoría, están los países que garantizan una remuneración proporcional a los resultados de la explotación (3.).

1. Sistemas jurídicos que establecen un principio de libertad en materia de remuneración

Ciertos países están muy comprometidos con la autonomía de la voluntad y la libertad contractual, incluida la propiedad literaria y artística. De acuerdo a este planteamiento liberal, poco importa que los autores queden a menudo en una posición de debilidad en relación a los explotadores con los cuales establecen

---

la remuneración pertinente, las partes deberán tener en cuenta todos los elementos que caracterizan la emisión, tales como la audiencia real, la audiencia potencial y la versión linguística». V. también, aunque es poco esclarecedor, el considerando 10 de la directiva del 22 de mayo de 2001, que establece que la remuneración debe «ofrecer un rendimiento satisfactorio a tal inversión». V. también el dispositivo de remuneración suplementaria establecido para el beneficio de los artistas-intérpretes por la directiva de 27 de septiembre de 2011 por la que se modifica la Directiva 2006/116/CE relativa al plazo de protección del derecho de autor y de determinados derechos afines. Sobre este dispositivo, ver *infra* p. 103. Ver también el artículo 16 §2 de la directiva de 26 de febrero de 2014 citada, que enuncia a propósito de la gestión colectiva que «Las tarifas aplicadas a los derechos exclusivos y a los derechos a remuneración serán razonables en relación con, entre otros factores, el valor económico de la utilización de los derechos negociados, teniendo en cuenta la naturaleza y ámbito de uso de las obras y otras prestaciones, y el valor económico del servicio prestado por la entidad de gestión colectiva. Las entidades de gestión colectiva informarán al usuario de que se trate de los criterios utilizados para la fijación de esas tarifas».

contrato: un desequilibrio tal que más se asemeja a un trato de favor. De igual manera la determinación de la remuneración en dichos países, se basa en el libre juego de la negociación contractual. Las leyes sobre la propiedad literaria y artística en estos países no guardan ninguna disposición especial que permita a los autores reivindicar una remuneración adecuada en el momento del establecimiento de contrato. A esta primera categoría pertenece el derecho americano, inglés, argentino, austriaco, isrealí[11], japonés, noruego, suizo y, parece ser, el italiano. A la espera de una inminente reforma, el derecho holandés, se está apartando de esta categoría[12]. Hay que dejar claro, sin embargo, que en estos sistemas, la libertad de las partes muy pocas veces es total. Dos tipos de mecanismos son susceptibles de impedir a los explotadores imponer a los creadores condiciones demasiado desfavorables.

En primer lugar, a falta de reglas previstas por la legislación especializada en la propiedad literaria y artística, es posible generalmente recurrir al derecho común de contratos. El informe suizo hace referencia, por ejemplo, a la facultad que se ofrece a un autor que hubiera aceptado un contrato en condiciones financieramente desventajosas por un error o engaño, de pedir la nulidad del mismo. El informe inglés por su parte, dedica importantes desarrollos a la aplicación por los tribunales, en materia de contratos de explotación del derecho de autor, de la doctrina "restraint of trade" de *common law*, que permite luchar contra los contratos por abusivos. La posibilidad que tienen los jueces de aplicar, a falta de reglas especiales, las técnicas procedentes de la teoría general de contratos aparece igualmente en los informes americano, austriaco y noruego.

En segundo lugar, en lo que concierne específicamente a la gestión colectiva, ciertos países han adoptado reglas bastante estrictas sobre la fijación y el control de las tarifas practicadas por las sociedades de recaudación y reparto. Es claramente, el caso de Suiza[13].

2. Sistemas jurídicos que establecen un principio de justa remuneración

La protección de los creadores parece más asegurada cuando la legislación específica para la propiedad literaria y artística contiene reglas relativas a la determinación de la remuneración. Ciertas leyes nacionales exigen que la remune-

---

11 A excepción del contrato de edición: v *infra*, p. 103.

12 Una ley específica sobre los contratos de explotación del derecho de autor está en proceso de adoptarse en los Países Bajos. De este hecho resulta que el derecho holandés, se pasa próximamente a la segunda categoría.

13 Comp. sobre este punto la directiva de 26 de febrero 2014 citada, así como los informes belga y húngaro.

ración sea "justa". A este segundo grupo pertenecen el derecho alemán, croata y finlandés. El proyecto de ley sobre los contratos de explotación del derecho de autor a punto de ser adoptado en los Países Bajos debería próximamente adherirlo a este grupo.

La cuestión candente es saber qué se debe entender por remuneración "justa". El informe alemán es rico a este respecto y nos servirá de ilustración[14]. El derecho alemán concede un rol importante a la negociación colectiva, que hace suponer de alguna manera, el carácter justo de la remuneración y por lo tanto la legitimidad de su modo de fijación: por parodiar una fórmula francesa célebre en Alemania, "quien dice colectivo dice justo"[15]. De este modo, la remuneración de los autores adquiere reputación de justa siempre que proceda de la aplicación de otras "reglas comunes de remuneración". Dichas reglas son el fruto de la concertación entre los organismos que representan a los autores y los explotadores. Sin embrago, según los autores del informe alemán, el mecanismo instituido por la ley del 22 de marzo de 2002, no ha dado resultados comprobados por ahora. En fin, más allá de los convenios colectivos y de las reglas comunes de remuneración, una remuneración debe considerarse justa cuando responda a los criterios establecidos por la ley. Esto invita a tener en cuenta, no sólo lo que es considerado usual y leal en las relaciones comerciales en el momento de la conclusión del contrato, sino también la naturaleza, el alcance de la autorización dada y, en particular de su duración y su época y, en general, todas sus circunstancias. La doctrina y los jueces alemanes suelen quejarse de la falta de precisión en los criterios. Ciertamente, comparándolo con los sistemas jurídicos pertenecientes a la tercera categoría que pasaremos rápidamente a examinar, el derecho alemán conduce a soluciones más flexibles[16]: para que la remuneración sea considerada justa, los tribunales alemanes no exigen que sea proporcional a los ingresos resultantes de la explotación de la obra; pueden ciertamente serlo, pero es también susceptible de adoptar la fórmula de un "todo incluido"; también se da el caso de la mezcla de ambos.

Añadimos que, en los sistemas que exigen una remuneración justa, la existencia de una disposición de la ley sobre la propiedad literaria y artística, no

---

14 §§32 y 36 UrhG. Precisemos que una reforma del derecho contractual alemán se estudia actualmente.

15 Según la forma del filósofo francés Alfred Fouillé (1838–1912), "quien dice contractual, dice justo". La aparición de contratos poco igualitarios, como el de trabajo o el contrato de consumo, puso bastante en entredicho este postulado.

16 V. con una visión más general, incluyendo numerosos elementos de comparación entre los sistemas alemán y francés, A. Lucas-Schloetter, "Le droit contractuel d'auteur allemand depuis la réforme du 22 mars 2002» («El derecho contractual de autor alemán desde la reforma del 22de marzo de 2002 »), Propriété Intellectuelle 2005, 403, y del mismo autor, "Lettre d'Allemagne – qu'y a-t-il dans la "deuxième corbeille"? La loi allemande du 26 octobre 2007 relative au droit d'auteur dans la société de l'information" Propriété intellectuelle 2008, 308.

impide que se pueda recurrir al derecho común de contratos. Este último puede en efecto intervenir como complemento de la protección concedida por el derecho específico. Los informes alemán, croata y finlandés insisten sobre este punto. Por no tomar más que un ejemplo, en Finlandia, las reglas relativas a la remuneración, que figuran en la ley sobre el derecho de autor sólo se aplican a los contratos de explotación en los que el titular inicial del monopolio intelectual es parte del mismo. Las transferencias posteriores se someten a las reglas equivalentes pero del derecho común.

3. Los sistemas jurídicos que establecen un principio de proporcionalidad en materia de remuneración

La solución más protectora del autor, al menos en teoría, consiste en acordar una remuneración proporcional a los ingresos procedentes de la explotación[17]. El autor se asegura de ser asociado a los productos generados por la utilización de su obra. Esto le impide definitivamente abandonar sus derechos por una suma fija irrisoria. Varios países han establecido este mecanismo. Pensamos claramente en Argelia[18], Bélgica, Egipto, España, Francia, Grecia e incluso Hungría.

La fuerza del principio de remuneración proporcional varia en realidad de un estado a otro. A la vista de ello debemos tener en cuenta diversos factores.

En primer lugar, mientras que en muchos sistemas jurídicos, la exigencia es válida para todos los contratos de explotación del derecho de autor, en otros no afecta más que a ciertos contratos peculiares. En España[19] y en Francia[20], por ejemplo, la regla tiene carácter general, mientras que en Bélgica su aplicación se limita, según la ley, a los contratos de producción audiovisual y de edición[21].

Las reglas relativas a la base y coeficientes de la remuneración son igualmente bastante heterogéneas. Nos conformaremos, para ilustrar este propósito, con examinar las segundas. Lo más habitual es que la determinación de los porcentajes de remuneración proporcional se deje a la discreción de las partes. El riesgo está en que el explotador se aproveche de su posición para imponer al autor un porcentaje demasiado bajo y por consiguiente desventajoso. En tal caso, el derecho general de contratos puede de nuevo tomar el relevo del derecho específico a fin de conferir al autor una protección eficaz. Nos referiremos en este sentido al derecho español y griego, este último presenta la posibilidad de

---

17 Notemos sin embargo que el "todo incluido" puede ser más ventajoso en ciertos casos, en particular cuando el volumen de explotación es muy bajo.

18 El contenido del derecho argelino se menciona en el informe egipcio.

19 Art46.1 de la Ley de la propiedad intelectual española.

20 Art L. 131-4 CPI.

21 Art XI. 183, §2, et XI. 196, §2, del Código de derecho económico.

anulación del contrato por ser contrario a las buenas costumbres. El derecho general es susceptible también de aplicarse cuando, el contrato no prevé el porcentaje de remuneración. La jurisprudencia francesa ofrece un ilustrativo ejemplo: a fin de anular un convenio de cesión de derecho de autor que se limitaba a prever un porcentaje "a convenir", el Tribunal de gran instancia de París consideró, entre otros motivos, que dicho convenio desprovisto de precio y razón violaba los "principios generales del derecho civil"[22]. Para evitar mayores problemas, se debería concebir una tasa de remuneración, o al menos una tasa mínima, impuesta por ley. A pesar de todo, esta tasa mínima, por presentar un impedimento real a la libertad contractual, no se ha concretado más que excepcionalmente[23]. Entre las escasas leyes nacionales que la han admitido en el derecho de autor podemos citar la ley griega que, sin embargo reserva su aplicación a ciertos contratos: contrato de edición, contrato de radiodifusión, contrato de representación teatral, contrato de composición de banda sonora, contrato de cesión de derechos firmado por un fotógrafo[24]. La ley israelí prevé un porcentaje de remuneración pero sólo para los contratos de edición literaria. La solución existe también en Portugal y se presenta bajo la forma de disposición suplementaria, inscrita en las reglas de standard aplicables a los contratos de edición. Finalmente la encontramos puntualmente en el derecho comunitario, pero esta vez en el dominio de los derechos conexos. La directiva de 27 de septiembre de 2011, que prolonga la duración de ciertos derechos conexos prevé, en cuanto a las explotaciones que tengan lugar durante los veinte años suplementarios que acuerda[25], que el productor debe pagar a los artistas-intérpretes el 20% de los beneficios que perciba en contrapartida a la explotación[26].

Otra cuestión diferente es si, en general la regla de remuneración proporcional de la que se benefician los autores, cubre también los contratos establecidos por intérpretes-ejecutantes. En varios sistemas jurídicos examinados, la respuesta es positiva. Así ocurre en Bélgica, en Grecia-según la doctrina mayori-

---

22 TGI París, 9 de mayo 1990, RIDA enero 1991, nº 147, p. 335: el tribunal se refiere, más precisamente, además de las disposiciones de la ley de 11 de marzo 1957, sobre la propiedad literaria y artística, los art 1108, 1131 y 1583 del Código Civil, que se refieren a las condiciones generales de validez de los contratos (consentimiento, capacidad, objeto y causa), a la causa (existencia y legitimidad) y a las exigencias propias del contrato de venta (acuerdo sobre el objeto y precio).

23 Las tasas de remuneración fijadas por las leyes nacionales afectan generalmente a los derechos de remuneración pero no a los derechos exclusivos susceptibles de ser cedidos o concedidos. Es presente informe se refiere únicamente a estos últimos.

24 Art 33 y sig. de la ley griega del derecho de autor.

25 La directiva ha extendido de cincuenta a sesenta años la duración de la protección de los derechos conexos en materia sonora (derechos de los artistas-intérpretes y de los productores de fonogramas).

26 Sobre la transposición de este dispositivo, v. los informes alemán, español, francés, griego e italiano.

taria al menos- y en Hungría. El derecho francés es la excepción: dejando de lado la nueva regla prevista por la directiva europea, mencionada más arriba, la ley francesa sólo impone que las remuneraciones percibidas por los artistas-intérpretes sean proporcionales a los ingresos de explotación. El todo incluido parece autorizado.

Por otro lado, volviendo al derecho de autor, mientras que, según algunas leyes nacionales, la regla de la remuneración proporcional es, salvo excepciones dadas por la ley, imperativa, según otras, no es más que suplementaria, de modo que las partes tienen la facultad de derogarlas de común acuerdo. Concretamente, la remuneración proporcional es imperativa en Francia y Argelia. Sin embargo es suplementaria en Bélgica[27], en Egipto[28] y en Hungría[29]. Es lógico temer, en este segundo caso, que la cláusula contraria se desarrolle hasta el punto de convertirse en una cláusula de estilo y que al final, la remuneración basada en el todo incluido suplante a la remuneración proporcional. Este riesgo se ha planteado claramente en el informe húngaro.

Además de esto, las leyes nacionales han establecido excepciones al principio de remuneración proporcional. Una remuneración basada en el todo incluido se autoriza en ciertos casos, más o menos numerosos según el sistema que consideremos, en los casos en los que es imposible o excesivamente complejo poner en práctica una remuneración proporcional. Citaremos, a modo de ilustración el informe francés[30]: en Francia, el contrato puede estipular un todo incluido en diversas hipótesis, por ejemplo cuando la tasa de consulta de la obra por parte del público no se conozca o incluso cuando sean demasiado caros los gastos de cálculo y control para una remuneración proporcional en proporción a su suma. Sin embrago, en los casos en los que se autoriza el todo incluido, si este último fuera demasiado bajo, el juez puede someterlo a revisión[31]. La protección del autor, también en estos casos, queda inherente al dispositivo.

Hay que añadir que los países que establecen la regla de remuneración proporcional, imponen a veces, como complemento al contrato, una obligación de desglosamiento de las tarifas. Una remuneración diferente ha de ser prevista para cada modo de explotación. Esta regla que compete tanto a la forma como el fondo, se ha adoptado en Bélgica de modo generalizado[32]. En Francia sólo se aplica a ciertos contratos (contratos de producción audiovisual y contratos de

27 Art XI. 183, §2, et XI. 196, §2, del Código de derecho económico.

28 Art 150 del Código egipcio de propiedad intelectual.

29 Art 16(4) de la ley húngara sobre el derecho de autor.

30 Art L. 131-4 et L. 132-6 CPI. Rappr. art46.2 de la ley española sobre el derecho de autor y art65 de la ordenanza argelina de19 de julio de 2003 relativa al derecho de autor y a los derechos conexos.

31 Art L. 131-5 CPI.

32 Art XI. 167, §1er, Código de derecho económico.

encargo publicitario[33]) y, en Grecia, (contrato de producción audiovisual únicamente[34]).

En conclusión: el principio de remuneración proporcional parece la mejor opción para permitir a los autores beneficiarse de una remuneración apropiada. Su longevidad en países como Francia, en donde está inscrito en la ley desde hace medio siglo[35], es un signo de su eficacia. A pesar de todo, esta remuneración no llega a ser totalmente proporcional como veremos en la conclusión. Seamos conscientes de que, para que el mecanismo funcione adecuadamente, es necesario que los autores puedan tener acceso a saber cuál es el volumen exacto de la explotación de sus obras y de la recaudación correspondiente. En caso contrario, como relata el informe Belga, los contratantes no siempre proporcionan información fiable.

II. La ejecución del contrato

El tema de la remuneración puede dar lugar a tres escenarios que afecten a la ejecución del contrato. Examinaremos la posibilidad de una simple adaptación de este (1.), posibilidadde su revisión (2.) y, finalmente, la hipótesis más radical, de su disolución (3.).

1. La adaptación del contrato

Los cambios en las circunstancias que pueden aparecer en el curso de la ejecución del contrato, especialmente las medidas tecnológicas, son susceptibles de ejercer una incidencia sobre la remuneración del autor y de su carácter (in)apropiado. Dos mecanismos pueden permitir la adaptación del contrato.

El primero es un mecanismo de anticipación de naturaleza convencional, que rige en realidad tanto durante la formación del contrato como en su posterior ejecución. Con el fin de comprender su contenido, conviene tener en cuenta que muchos sistemas jurídicos establecen, más o menos formalmente, un principio de interpretación estricta de los contratos de autor. De ello resulta que un contrato concebido teniendo en cuenta las únicas formas de explotación existentes en el momento de su firma, no suele autorizar al explotador ni a reproducir ni a comunicar la obra al público por medio de las formas aparecidas po-

---

33 Art L. 132-25 et L. 132-31 CPI.

34 Art 34 de la ley griega sobre el derecho de autor.

35 La exigencia de una remuneración proporcional ha sido instituida por la ley del 11 de marzo 1957. La jurisprudencia considera que no se aplica a los contratos establecidos anteriormente. Civ. 1re, 30 oct. 1967, *JCP* 1968. II. 15530, obs. P. Level.

steriormente. De este modo, ciertos contratos realizados en la época analógica han quedado desprovistos de efecto en la era digital. ¿Tienen acaso las partes la posibilidad de dar la vuelta a esta resolución estricta anticipándose a la evolución tecnológica en el contrato mismo? Ciertas leyes nacionales lo autorizan. En Francia por ejemplo, el autor puede ceder sus derechos para una explotación bajo forma no prevista ni previsible a la fecha de firma del contrato[36]. Sin embargo dicha cláusula debe respetar condiciones estrictas. Debe expresamente estipular una participación correlativa a los beneficios de la explotación. De este modo el autor se asegura de percibir una remuneración apropiada al tipo de utilización. Un dispositivo parecido existe a partir de ahora en el derecho alemán[37]. Otros países se muestran, por el contrario, bastante hostiles a estas cláusulas de adaptación. Por ejemplo en Bélgica, son en principio nulos, excepto cuando la obra ha sido creada en ejecución de un contrato de trabajo, de un estatuto o por encargo[38].

El segundo mecanismo que permite la adaptación de los contratos se basa en una eventual obligación de renegociación. Tal obligación puede, en principio, resultar de la voluntad de las partes: la validez y los efectos de la cláusula de renegociación se extraerán a la vista del derecho común de contratos. Tal obligación puede igualmente venir de la ley aunque esta solución está por ahora poco extendida. Ha sido hace poco establecida por el legislador francés en relación al contrato de edición de libro digital. Resultante de la ordenanza del 12 de noviembre de 2014 que modifica las disposiciones del Código de la propiedad intelectual relativas al contrato de edición, el nuevo artículo L. 132-17-7 del Código enuncia que "el contrato de edición incluya una cláusula de reexamen de las condiciones económicas de la cesión de los derechos de explotación del libro digital". La razón de ser de ese nuevo mecanismo se apoya en la incertidumbre ligada al desarrollo del mercado del libro digital. Se trata de permitir a cada una de las partes – autor pero también editor- reclamar una renegociación de la remuneración, prevista en el contrato en función de las evoluciones del mercado.

2. La revisión del contrato

La hipótesis de trabajo es distinta de la precedente. EL cambio producido durante la ejecución del contrato proviene esta vez del éxito alcanzado por la obra. La

36 Art L. 131-6 CPI.

37 §§31a et 32c UrhG extraídos de la ley de 26 oct. 2007 relativa al derecho de autor en la sociedad de la información. A diferencia del derecho francés, el derecho alemán prevé el derecho de revocación en beneficio del autor.

38 Art XI. 167, §1er et 3, du Código de Derecho económico.

eventualidad de tal éxito no se contempló inicialmente en el contrato, de modo que la remuneración estipulada puede resultar injustamente baja. Se trata de hacer frente a una situación imprevista de "best seller", retomando la expresión utilizada en el cuestionario que se planteó a los autores de los informes nacionales. Más concretamente, conviene preguntarse si el autor está en su derecho de reclamar – si fuese necesario delante de un juez- la revisión del contrato, para modificar su remuneración a la alza.

Bastantes leyes nacionales sobre el derecho de autor admiten tal posibilidad de revisión. Podemos citar a este respecto la ley argelina, alemana, belga, croata, española, finlandesa, francesa, egipcia, húngara y portuguesa, a las cuales habrá que añadir muy pronto a la ley holandesa, actualmente en proceso de revisión. Las condiciones del ejercicio de esta prerrogativa varían, sin embargo de un país a otro. En unos casos se aplica a todos los contratos de autor, sea cual sea su naturaleza y en otros casos sólo a algunos de entre ellos. De este modo, en España[39] y Francia[40] es general, mientras que en Bélgica, la revisión sólo es posible en el caso de los contratos de edición y representación[41]. Por otro lado, según algunas leyes nacionales como es el caso de la ley alemana, la remuneración puede ser revisada ya sea su naturaleza – proporcional o una cantidad fija[42]. Otras leyes nacionales, como la belga y la francesa, sólo admiten revisión en caso de todo incluido[43]. Disparidades tan claras se dan igualmente en lo que concierne a la apreciación del desequilibrio que autoriza la revisión del contrato. Las leyes alemana y belga, por ejemplo, ponen como condición la existencia de una desproporción manifiesta entre la remuneración inicialmente convenida y los beneficios alcanzados por la explotación[44], mientras que la ley francesa exige que el autor haya sufrido un perjuicio de más de 7 doceavos[45]. Digamos que en ciertos países, las disposiciones nacionales que autorizan la revisión del contrato, sea cual sea su contenido, se aplican muy raramente. Al menos es lo que se extrae de la lectura del informe Belga, que explica este escaso éxito por la imprecisión de los informes que los explotadores ofrecen a los autores, los cuales se ven desprovistos de elementos suficientes para invocar un aumento de la remuneración.

Cuando la posibilidad de revisión del contrato no está contemplada expresamente por la ley de derecho de autor es susceptible de derivarse del derecho

39 Art 47 de la ley española sobre el derecho de autor.
40 Art L. 131-5 CPI.
41 Art XI. 196, §2, et XI. 202 del código de derecho económico.
42 §32a UrhG.
43 Sin embargo, ante una remuneración proporcional cuya base o porcentaje fueran demasiado bajos o inciertos es posible recurrir a mecanismos extraídos del derecho común de contratos. Sobre este punto v. *supra*, p. 103.
44 §32a UrhG.
45 Art L. 131-5 CPI.

general de contratos, tal como sucede en Grecia, Noruega, Suiza y, a la espera de la reforma antes mencionada, en los Países Bajos. Una revisión judicial no es, sin embargo abordable, más que en los países que han establecido de una forma u otra, la teoría de la imprevisión.

3. La disolución del contrato

El autor tiene derecho a exigir la ejecución de las diferentes obligaciones que el contrato obliga al explotador. A falta de dicha ejecución puede poner fin al contrato responsabilizando a la otra parte. Puede hacerlo también cuando este último simplemente no le haya abonado la remuneración prevista por el contrato. Pero la disolución es igualmente aplicable en caso de violación de otras obligaciones y más aún si son obligaciones relativas a la remuneración. Nos referimos por una parte a la obligación de rendir cuentas, dictada por ciertos sistemas jurídicos nacionales. En algunos países como Bélgica, España y Francia, dicha obligación está prevista a propósito del contrato de edición, del contrato de producción audiovisual y del contrato de representación[46]. Tenemos en mente, por otra parte, la obligación que existe en el derecho belga[47] y en el derecho francés[48]: tal obligación, asociada a una remuneración proporcional, asegura, en principio al autor el beneficio de ingresos efectivos. Su violación – i.e. el hecho de que el contratante del autor no se empeñe seriamente en la explotación de la obra – es causa de disolución del contrato.

En ciertos sistemas jurídicos, el contrato puede igualmente finalizarse cuando ya no sea productivo, aunque el explotador haya cumplido sus obligaciones. Citemos en este sentido, las nuevas disposiciones de la ley francesa que acuerdan a las dos partes en un contrato de edición de libros – autor y editor – la posibilidad de rescindir el contrato si durante dos años consecutivos, pasados cuatro años de la publicación de la obra, los estados de cuentas no reflejan remuneración alguna[49].

Nos referiremos, para terminar a la ley americana sobre derecho de autor, que concede a los creadores el derecho a rescindir el contrato bastante específico y de carácter irrenunciable[50]. Este derecho les permite poner sin, sin justifi-

46 Art XI. 183, §2, XI. 198 et XI. 202 del código de derecho económico belga, art64, 78 et 90 de la ley española sobre el derecho de autor y art L. 132-13, L. 132-17-3, L. 132-28 et L. 132-21 del CPI francés. Recordamos que en Bélgica, el contrato de representación no forma parte de los contratos cuya remuneración ha de ser proporcional.

47 Art XI. 167, §1er, del código de derecho económico.

48 Art L. 132-12 et L. 132-27 CPI, a propósito respectivamente de los contratos de edición y de producción audiovisual.

49 Art L. 132-17-4 CPI.

50 Sección 203 y 304(c) U.S. Copyright Act.

cación alguna, a los contratos que los atan a los explotadores. Los autores pueden evidentemente hacer uso de esta facultad si no están satisfechos de los ingresos que les son abonados. Se trata esta de la única protección que se les ofrece en Estados Unidos, afín de obtener una remuneración apropiada, fuera del derecho general[51]. Las condiciones para el ejercicio de esta prerrogativa son muy estrictas. Para empezar, la rescisión es imposible en el caso de que la obra sea un "*work made for hire*", es decir, una obra escrita por encargo o una obra creada por un asalariado. Por otro lado, la demanda de rescisión solo puede llevarse a cabo a partir de los 35 años siguientes a la publicación y durante un período de cinco. Finalmente es necesario que el autor realice un preaviso así como diversas formalidades. Según el informe americano, estas numerosas condiciones no facilitan la puesta en marcha del dispositivo.

A modo de conclusión, parece que diversos mecanismos que varían se un sistema jurídico a otro, deberían permitir a autores y artistas-intérpretes, ligados por contrato a explotadores, obtener una remuneración adecuada. Tales mecanismos provienen tanto del derecho de la propiedad literaria y artística como del derecho general de contratos, teniendo este último la vocación de completar adecuadamente la legislación específica y rellenar sus eventuales lagunas. Sin embargo la efectividad de dichos mecanismos, incluso de los que están concebidos como más protectores, no está del todo conseguida. Los creadores a menudo se quejan de los bajos ingresos que perciben y su descontento se ha acentuado desde el desarrollo de las explotaciones en línea[52]. A pesar de ello es raro que lleven sus reivindicaciones a los tribunales. Una primera explicación se basa en el carácter estricto y por consiguiente disuasivo de las condiciones para llevar a la práctica de algunas de las reglas estudiadas en el presente informe. Los costes de un eventual proceso pueden también desalentar a los titulares de derechos[53]. Sin embargo nos parece que el origen de esta inercia está en otra razón más fundamental. Actuar en justicia se convierte, de cierto modo en declarar la guerra a los explotadores[54], de modo que los autores y los intérpretes que toman esta decisión corren el riesgo de no volver a encontrar trabajo fácilmente. El pragmatismo vence sobre la aplicación de las reglas del derecho.

51 V. *supra*, p. 101.

52 Son excepción los autores y artistas intérpretes que han conseguido suficiente popularidad como para encontrarse en posición de fuerza para negociar con los explotadores. Se trata sin embargo de casos raros.

53 El remedio puede ser prever cláusulas de desistimiento de pleno derecho de los contratos de explotación sin tener que recurrir a un juez. V. en este sentido las disposiciones de la ley francesa en materia de contrato de edición.

54 V. en relación a esto la sugerencia de los autores del informe alemán que proponen que los procedimientos de actuar en justicia se hagan anónimamente desde las asociaciones de artistas.

2. Statutory remuneration rights

Pierre-Yves Gautier*

2.1 Introduction: Droits (légaux) à rémunération

Nous allons reprendre nos discussions et pouvons féliciter les organisateurs de cette session, car le programme est très homogène et progressif. Victor Nabhan nous a brossé l'évolution du droit d'auteur et des usages des œuvres, qui se produit avec la révolution numérique que certains avaient anticipée. Tristan Azzi tout à l'heure a rappelé à quel point le contrat, ce vieil instrument qui existe depuis l'antiquité, surtout le droit romain, avec les correctifs nécessaires, peut continuer à régir les relations entre les auteurs et leurs co-contractants immédiats, ainsi que toute la chaîne de contrats. Le producteur, l'éditeur, etc. vont aller eux-mêmes conclure des conventions avec des sous-exploitants.

La révolution technologique amène a se poser des questions plus radicales précisément sur le point de savoir si ces anciens outils juridiques dont nous disposons, avant même l'avènement du droit d'auteur, sont encore pertinents et si de nouveaux mécanismes légaux sans remettre pour l'instant en cause le droit de propriété incorporelle, ne devraient pas dans certains cas remplacer le droit exclusif par des systèmes de rémunération plus en moins impérative.

Avec d'autres partenaires, notamment les sociétés de gestion collectives qui font irruption dans le modèle de contrat individuel ; avec d'autres formes de rémunération et surtout d'autres formes de répartition car au fond la question est toujours la même et Victor Nabhan l'a rappelé également: il y a le travail d'un créateur ou d'un artiste – ce travail doit être rémunéré et comment le sera-t-il? Cela devient plus délicat.

C'est à toutes ces questions que nous devons répondre, avec ce mot que je voudrai rappeler, qui existe encore depuis les Romains et a été prononcé déjà ce matin: l'équité – la rémunération équitable, le taux juste et équitable etc. L'équité constitue une notion de justice, ce n'est pas seulement un mot (que les Politiques utilisent trop, pour son symbole, surtout) ; évidemment, un des risques de ces nouveaux systèmes de rémunération légales se multipliant, dont nous allons parler, c'est que l'équité ne soit pas forcément au rendez-vous pour les créateurs, dans la répartition individuelle et non pas les flux financiers collectifs.

Pour discuter de ces différents points, nous aurons deux spécialistes: Christophe Geiger et Tobias Holzmüller.

---

* Professeur de droit d'auteur et de droit civil à l'Université Paris II, Panthéon-Assas (France).

Christophe Geiger and Oleksandr Bulayenko*

2.2 General report: Scope and enforcement tools to ensure remuneration

Introduction

The purpose of the ALAI Congress was to reflect on available legal models to ensure remuneration for the use of copyright protected works. To this end, two main mechanisms have been identified, namely exclusive rights and statutory rights to remuneration. The contributors to the conference – and hence to this volume – have thus been invited to conduct a sort of audit of the existing "various mechanisms for achieving equitable remunerations". This general report focuses on statutory remuneration rights, their scope and enforcement tools to ensure remuneration.

It is not surprising that the topic of statutory remuneration rights was chosen for discussion on the occasion of the celebration of 50 years of the German Copyright Act. This Act, although clearly placing the author at the core of its provisions (the Act is entitled "Urheberrechtsgesetz", which could be translated by "Act on authors' rights"), includes no less than 9 limitations and exceptions that open up the possibility of a fair remuneration for the author,[1] alongside what the German report calls the "other rights of an author" such as the resale right, the rental and public lending rights, and the right resulting from cable retransmission.[2] Thus, it is probably not an accident that the German Federal Supreme Court in a remarked decision of 11 July 2002 justified the extension of the classical exception for press reviews to electronic press reviews, on the grounds of the protection of the author's interests in receiving remuneration.[3]

---

* Christophe Geiger is Professor of law, Director General and Director of Research Department of CEIPI, Affiliated Senior Researcher at the Max Planck Institute for Innovation and Competition in Munich (Germany) and Spangenberg Fellow at the Spangenberg Center for Law, Technology & the Arts, Case Western Reserve University School of Law in Cleveland (USA); Oleksandr Bulayenko is Researcher and PhD candidate at CEIPI. This chapter relies to a large extent on the responses to the questionnaire submitted for this ALAI Congress, with a special focus on Part C of the questionnaire "Questions in relation to statutory remuneration rights". The national reports cover legislation and practices in 22 countries (Argentina, Austria, Belgium, Canada, Croatia, Egypt, Finland, France, Greece, Germany, Hungary, Israel, Italy, Japan, Mexico, Netherlands, Norway, Portugal, Spain, Switzerland, UK and USA). They are available at: http://www.alai2015.org/en/national-reports.html (last visited October 2016).

1 National report Germany, pp. 15–16.

2 *Ibid.* p. 15.

3 The Court, referring to Article 49(1) of the Copyright Act (which provides for a statutory license for the use of articles as part of a press review), pointed out that a consequence of this

Before turning to the analysis of different national approaches to statutory remuneration rights (II.),[4] we will first briefly address some issues of terminology (I.).

I. Statutory remuneration rights: Issues of Terminology

One of the most delicate issues within the framework of this general report is certainly the question of terminology. In fact, the national reports sometimes used certain notions as if they were synonyms, although the various terms might have very different implications at legal level.

While for example, at first sight, the terms "statutory remuneration rights", "compulsory licenses", and related notions might seem to have uniform meaning, their comprehension is profoundly influenced by national legal traditions and languages. Understanding of the key-notions has an effect on the responses to the different parts of the questionnaire prepared by ALAI and filled out by 22 of its national groups. Indeed, there is no universally agreed legal definition of statutory remuneration rights. Furthermore, different terms are being used in legal scholarship to refer to mechanisms other than exclusive rights that provide for remuneration to rightholders, notably: "legal license", "compulsory license", "obligatory license", "non-voluntary license", "statutory license" and "limitation-based remuneration rights".[5] This proliferation of related terms and

---

provision is that a considerable part of the remuneration levied for the use of protected works with respect to press reviews is paid to the authors of the texts used. By contrast, if the exclusive right is upheld, the position of the author is generally not improved. Cf. decision of the German Federal Supreme Court ("Bundesgerichtshof"), 11 July 2002, "Electronic press reviews", 2002 *GRUR* 963. See also in this sense Adolf Dietz (2015), 'Protection of Creative People via Copyright – The Five Pillars of Modern Continental European Copyright Law (Authors' Rights Law)', *RIDA*, No. 243, p. 149: "[I]n many cases legal remuneration rights and levy systems, administered by collecting societies, paradoxically, appear to be more favourable to authors and performers than apparently stronger exclusive rights, individually managed and controlled by the right owner companies."

4 Relying to a large extent on the information submitted by the national reports.

5 Mihály Ficsor (2003), *Guide to the Copyright and Related Rights Treaties Administered by WIPO and Glossary of Copyright and Related Rights Terms*, WIPO Publication No. 891(E), pp. 277, 298 and 312, Andrew F. Christie (2011), 'Maximising permissible exceptions to intellectual property rights', in Annette Kur and Vytautas Mizaras (eds), *The Structure of Intellectual Property Law: Can One Size Fit All?*, Cheltenham, UK: Edward Elgar, p. 125, Christophe Geiger and Franciska Schönherr (2012), 'Defining the Scope of Protection of Copyright in the EU: The Need to Reconsider the Acquis regarding Limitations and Exceptions', in Tatiana-Eleni Synodinou (ed.), *Codification of European Copyright Law: Challenges and Perspectives*, Alphen aan den Rijn, The Netherlands: Kluwer Law, International, pp. 166–167; Christophe Geiger (2010),

differences in their understanding potentially leads to some incoherencies. This was demonstrated by answers to the same questions of the questionnaire by different national groups of ALAI. Even in the national reports from the EU/EEA member states, whose legislation transposing European Union norms into national legislation is harmonized to certain extent, some differences or doubts about the interpretation of the terms "statutory remuneration right" and "compulsory license" can be observed. For example, the Norwegian national report replies to the question on "compulsory licenses" by referring to "statutory licenses" and "extended collective licences";[6] the country report from the UK classified remuneration for certain uses of orphan works as "statutory remuneration"[7], while the country report from Portugal referred to the remuneration for the uses of orphan works as a "compulsory license", acknowledging that it can be also classified as a "legal license"[8]. Such terminological differences obscure the meaning and render a simple comparison a challenging task.

In addition, there is also a subtle difference in the perception of the statutory remuneration as either "compensations for caused harm" or as "remunerations for uses". Such, at first sight, insignificant nuance may play an important role in the national perception of non-exclusive mechanism for remuneration, their purpose and, hence, calculation of relevant amounts. Differences between languages and the copyright vocabulary also have an impact on the transposition of international texts into national legislation.[9]

Furthermore, the borderline between legal models for assuring remuneration through exclusive rights and the statutory remuneration rights is not always clear-cut when it comes to the mandatory collective management of exclusive rights. For example, some national reports referred to the mandatory exercise of the exclusive rights to reprography[10] through a collective management organisation (CMO) in the context of statutory remuneration rights, while

'Promoting Creativity through Copyright Limitations, Reflections on the Concept of Exclusivity in Copyright Law', *Vanderbilt Journal of Entertainment & Technology Law*, Vol. 12, Issue 3, pp. 515–548.

6 National report Norway, pp. 12–14.

7 National report UK, pp. 11–12.

8 National report Portugal, p. 8.

9 Christophe Geiger and Franciska Schönherr (2014), 'Limitations to copyright in the digital age', in Andrej Savin and Jan Trzaskowski (eds), *Research Handbook on EU Internet Law*, Cheltenham, UK/ Northampton, MA, USA: Edward Elgar, pp. 131–133.

10 National report France, pp. 14 and 22. Article L122-10 of the French Intellectual Property Code (CPI) provides for an automatic transfer of the exclusive right to reprography, upon publication of a work, to a CMO (currently to the *Centre français du droit d'exploitation du droit de copie (CFC)*) specially authorized to this end by the ministry in charge of culture. Philippe Masseron (2011), *Sociétés de perception et de répartition des droits : Centre français d'exploitation du droit de copie (CFC)*, Fasc. 1580 and Sylvie Nérisson (2013), *La gestion collective des droits des auteurs en France et en Allemagne : quelle légitimité ?*, Paris, France: IRJS, pp. 287, 313 and 314.

others explicitly exclude exclusive rights subject to mandatory collective management from the scope of the report[11].

Given different approaches that can be taken when defining the key notions and for the purpose of inclusiveness, this general report defines statutory remuneration rights as any statutory entitlements providing holders of copyright and/or related rights with a claim to remuneration without any possibility to control the use of copyrighted works or subject matter.[12] This definition covers remuneration rights defined as such by international or national norms ("remuneration rights *per se*"), remuneration rights created in the context of limitations or exceptions to exclusive rights ("limitation-based remuneration rights") and the integration of remuneration rights in the structure of exclusive rights (so called "residual remuneration rights"[13]).

II. National approaches to statutory remuneration rights

1. Brief overview

Various forms of statutory remuneration rights constitute an integral part of the copyright legislation in countries throughout the world. Submitted national reports differ in the depth in which they cover different remuneration rights and how they classify them, often describing some rights more in detail while leaving others aside. Nevertheless, the overall volume of information provided ap-

---

11 National report Hungary, pp. 11–12. National reports from the EU member states do not unanimously classify the case of mandatory exercise of exclusive rights to cable retransmission as a statutory remuneration right. In the EU, the mandatory collective management of an exclusive right to cable retransmission is provided by Article 9 of the Council Directive 93/83/EEC of 27 September 1993 on the coordination of certain rules concerning copyright and rights related to copyright applicable to satellite broadcasting and cable retransmission [1993] L 248/15.

12 The questions of moral rights and non-voluntary collective management of exclusive rights are being put aside, as there is a debate on whether the latter affects the nature of the exclusive rights.

13 Mihaly Ficsor (2010), 'Collective Management of Copyright and Related Rights from the Viewpoint of International Norms and the Acquis Communautaire', in Daniel J. Gervais (ed.), *Collective Management of Copyright and Related Rights*, 2nd edn., Alphen aan den Rijn, The Netherlands: Kluwer Law International, p. 42. Mihály Ficsor (2002), *Collective Management of Copyright and Related Rights*, WIPO Publication No. 855, pp. 23 ("'residual right' for individual creators 'surviving' the transfer of rights") and 139 ("'residual rights'; that is, rights to remuneration which are provided for (usually for authors and performers) in the case of transfer of certain exclusive rights (such as in the case of the right of rental under the Rental and Lending Directive of the European Community)."

pears sufficient to draw some general conclusions and to depict an overall situation.

All the countries covered by the responses to the questionnaire provide performers and producers of phonograms with a **remuneration right for communication to the public of commercial phonograms.**[14]

Most of the countries covered by the national reports have remuneration mechanisms in place for **resale** of original works of art, **private copying, lending** and **rental** of copies of protected subject matter.

More rare are remuneration schemes for **reproduction for persons with disabilities** (e.g., in Austria,[15] Germany,[16] the Netherlands[17] and Switzerland[18]), for use of **orphan works** (e.g., in Austria,[19] Germany[20] and the UK[21]), for **reproduction for the purpose of education and research** (e.g., in Croatia,[22] Germany[23] and the Netherlands[24]), for **making available of phonograms or audiovisual recordings** (e.g., Spain[25]), for digital **reproduction and making available of out-of-commerce books** (e.g., France[26]), as compensation for the

---

14 This widespread adoption of the remuneration right for communication to the public of commercial phonograms reflects the international obligations undertaken by states parties under the Rome Convention and the WPPT.

15 Article 42d of the Austrian Copyright Act. National report Austria, p. 8.

16 Article 45a of the German Copyright Act. National report Germany, pp. 15–16.

17 Article 15i of the Dutch Copyright Act. National report Netherlands, p. 11.

18 Article 24c of the Swiss Copyright Act. National report Switzerland, p. 5.

19 Article 56e of Austrian Copyright Act. National report Austria, p. 7.

20 Article 61b of the German Copyright Act. National report Germany, p. 16.

21 Article 10(2) of the Copyright and Rights in Performances (Licensing of Orphan Works) Regulations 2014 No. 2863. National report UK, pp. 11–12.

22 National report Croatia, p. 10.

23 Article 46 of the German Copyright Act. National report Germany, p. 15.

24 Article 16 of the Dutch Copyright Act. National report Netherlands, pp. 11–12.

25 Article 108.3 of Texto Refundido de la Ley de Propiedad Intelectual (TRLPI). National report Spain, pp. 35–36.

According to the national report, Spanish performers preferred to have a right to remuneration, which could not be transferred, instead of the transferable exclusive right to making available to the public. As this could not be achieved because of the obligation under Article 3 of the InforSoc Directive to introduce an exclusive right to making available, a residual right to equitable remuneration of performers was integrated in the exclusive right of making available provided by Article 108.1, which implements the aforementioned obligation under the InfoSoc Directive.

26 Articles L134-1–L134-9 of the CPI. National report France, pp. 22–24. Although the national report speaks of the French legislation on out-of-commerce books in the context of the right to remuneration, the French doctrine is not unanimous on this question. Since the enactment of the law facilitating digital use of out-of-commerce books, its legitimacy has been challenged (Loi n° 2012-287 relative à l'exploitation numérique des livres indisponibles du XXe siècle, *JORF n°0053*, 2 mars 2012). 28 February 2014 the French Constitutional Council (*Conseil constitutionnel*) established that the mechanism established by this law complied with the Constitution

legally presumed transfer **of a film author's principal economic rights** to the film producer (e.g., in the Netherlands[27]) or for the **public display of copies of works of art and of handicrafts that are in public ownership** (e.g., in Norway[28]).

It is important to observe that some countries, relying on their freedom under the international law, do not subject some of the above-mentioned uses to an obligation to remunerate rightholders qualifying them as unremunerated exceptions or limitations.[29] Hence, no payment is due to rightholders.

Some level of harmonization can be observed among the member states of the EU. Notably, the scope of the resale right seems to be provided in a relatively harmonious manner in the EU member states. Nevertheless, although some efforts were undertaken to harmonize copyright legislation of the member states for the sake of creating a single market, national legislations still diverge on the question of other remuneration rights (e.g., not all of the 28 member states provide for the right to remuneration for reproduction by means of reprography or for private copying).[30] This can partly be explained by the means chosen for achieving the harmonization (i.e., directives[31]) and the non-binding nature of

(C.C., 28 février 2014, M. Marc S. et autre, n° 2013-370 QPC). Following persistent opposition, 6 March 2015 the Council of State (*Conseil d'Etat*) decided to refer to the CJEU the question of whether the mechanism introduced by the law for use of out-of-commerce books implemented though a collective management organisation is compatible with the InfoSoc Directive (C.E., 6 mai 2015, n° 368208, M.S., Mme D., art. 2. Request for a preliminary ruling from the Conseil d'État (France) lodged on 19 June 2015 – Marc Soulier Sara Doke v Ministre de la Culture et de la Communication Premier ministre (Case C-301/15) OJ C 294/35, 7 September 2015). For comment, see Oleksandr Bulayenko (2016), 'Permissibility of Non-Voluntary Collective Management of Copyright under EU Law: The Case of the French Law on Out-of-Commerce Books', *JIPITEC*, Vol. 7, Issue 1, pp. 51–68. In its Opinion on the case delivered on 7 July 2016, the Advocate General Whatelet answered negatively (ECLI:EU:C:2016:536).

27 Article 45d of the Dutch Copyright Act. National report Netherlands, p. 12.

28 This remuneration is provided by the Act on Remuneration for the Display of Works of Art and Handicrafts, 1993-05-28-52. National report Norway, p. 10.

29 E.g., in France, Article L122-5(7) read in conjunction with Article L311-8(I)(3) of the CPI, provide for an exception or limitation for the benefit of persons with disabilities without making it subject to remuneration.

30 Cyprus, Ireland, Luxembourg, Malta and the UK do not provide for remuneration for private copying according to de Thuiskopie and WIPO (2016), *International Survey on Private Copying: Law and Practice 2015*, WIPO Publication No. 1037E/16, p. 3.

31 Article 288 of the TFEU states: "A directive shall be binding, as to the result to be achieved, upon each Member State to which it is addressed, but shall leave to the national authorities the choice of form and methods." For criticism of directives as tools for harmonisation see P. Bernt Hugenholtz (2013), 'The dynamics of harmonization of copyright at the European level', in Christophe Geiger (ed.), *Constructing European Intellectual Property: Achievements and New Perspectives*, Cheltenham, UK/ Northampton, MA, USA: Edward Elgar, pp. 274–275.

the exhaustive list of exceptions and limitations that member states may choose to introduce in their national copyright legislation.[32]

2. Scope of some remuneration rights

As it was already mentioned, all the countries covered by the report provide performers and producers of phonograms with a statutory remuneration right to receive remuneration for the **communication to the public of commercial phonograms**. However, the scope of this right can differ to a large extent from country to country, as the Rome Convention and the WPPT make it possible for contracting parties not to apply this right to remuneration or to apply it only partially by making a formal notification to this end.[33] For example, the USA, non-party to the Rome Convention but party to the WPPT[34], provides for this right only in respect of communication to the public by means of a digital audio transmission. An interesting borderline case was reported from Norway regarding an exclusion of supply of radio equipment in cars from the scope of the communication to the public[35]. A common feature of many remuneration rights is their unwaivable character[36] or limited alienability[37]. This feature of the remuneration rights differentiating them from the tradable exclusive rights is of-

32 Article 5 of the InfoSoc Directive.

33 Article 16 of the Rome Convention and Article 15(3) of the WPPT.

34 Article 15(3) of the WPPT provides for the possibility to limit the scope of the remuneration right by submitting a declaration for this purpose. The USA submitted the declaration taking advantage of this provision, available at: http://www.wipo.int/treaties/en/remarks.jsp?cnty_id=1279C (last visited October 2016).

35 National report Norway, p. 19 (it was a final decision in the case where a court of a lower instance reached an opposite view).

36 E.g., the resale right and the residual right to equitable remuneration for rental of phonograms and films are inalienable in all the EU member countries by virtue of Article 1 of the EU Resale Right Directive and Article 5 of the EU Rental and Lending Rights Directive, respectively. In the case Luksan, C-277/10 ECLI:EU:C:2012:65, the CJEU made the following observation: "Here, with regard to the right to the fair compensation payable to authors under the private copying exception, it does not follow from any provision of Directive 2001/29 that the European Union legislature envisaged the possibility of that right being waived by the person entitled to it." (para. 105). E.g., Article 63a of the German Copyright Act stipulates: "Statutory remuneration rights as provided in this Section may not be waived by the author in advance. They may be assigned in advance only to a collecting society, or together with the grant of the right of publication to the publisher, provided that the publisher lets them be managed by a collecting society which manages publishers' and authors' rights jointly."

37 E.g., in France alienability of the rights of performers to remuneration for communication to the public of commercial phonograms and for private copying was limited by the addition of Article L212-11 to the CPI on 7 July 2016 in order to protect performers' interests when they sign their contracts with publishers.

ten seen as a key element of the mechanism ensuring direct connection between generated revenues and remuneration to creators.[38]

The scope of the **resale right** seems not to differ much in the countries covered by the reports. Usually, its scope is confined to the sale by public auctions or through dealers, and some laws only trigger the remuneration right if there is an increase in value. As it was already noted, a rather high level of harmonization was achieved among the member states of the EU by virtue of the Resale Rights Directive.[39] In the EU and Egypt, the scope of the resale right encompasses in addition to the original works of art[40] also original copies.[41] At the same time, EU legislation excludes "original manuscripts of writers and composers" (to use the wording of the Berne Convention) from the scope of the resale right[42] and, uniquely, limits the maximum amount of royalty to be paid by the seller to 12.500 euros.[43]

A specific remuneration right for **private copying** is not explicitly provided by the international treaties and is introduced as a remunerated exception or limitation to the right to reproduction in cases when rightholders cannot practically exercise their exclusive right. This statutory mechanism creates a revenue stream for rightholders, who otherwise would not receive any remuneration for private copying of their works, through imposition of an obligation to pay on manufacturers, importers and/or retailers of equipment and/or devices used for private copying, as well as by economic operators making equipment available for private copying by individuals.[44]

---

38 Assistant General Secretary of the British Musician's Union stated the following in 2015 with regard to the right to equitable remuneration for the public performance and broadcast of recordings: "The equitable remuneration right has become the jewel in the crown of performers' rights because it is non-assignable under the law". Horace Trubridge (2015), 'Safeguarding the Income of Musicians', *WIPO Magazine*, Issue 2, p. 9.

39 For an overview of the implementation of the Directive in the member states, see Jens Gaster (2014), 'The Resale Right Directive', in Irini Stamatoudi and Paul Torremans (eds), *EU Copyright Law: A Commentary*, Cheltenham, UK/ Northampton, MA, USA: Edward Elgar, pp. 360–362.

40 As indicated in Article 14*ter* of the Berne Convention.

41 National report Egypt, p. 7 and Article 2(1) of the EU Resale Right Directive refers to "copies considered to be original works of art".

42 Ibid. Jens Gaster (2014), 'The Resale Right Directive', in Irini Stamatoudi and Paul Torremans (eds), *EU Copyright Law: A Commentary*, Cheltenham, UK/ Northampton, MA, USA: Edward Elgar, p. 367.

43 Article 4(1) of the Resale Right Directive. Establishment of a "ceiling" for remuneration is an uncommon tool for balancing interests of rightholders and others.

44 For a more detailed overview of different systems, see de Thuiskopie and WIPO (2016), *International Survey on Private Copying: Law and Practice 2015*, WIPO Publication No. 1037E/16 and IFRRO and WIPO (2015), *International Survey on Text and Image Copyright Levies: 2015 Edition*, WIPO Publication No. 1042E/16.

The contours of the private copying systems are similar in different countries. Uses need in general to be undertaken by a natural person[45] in a manner that is considered private and to be for non-commercial purpose.[46] The main aspects differentiating the scope of the right in different countries are the type of products on which the levies are imposed and the setting of tariffs.

In some countries copyright levies are applied to recording equipment and to media on which copyrighted works can be recorded (e.g., France,[47] Netherlands[48] and Portugal[49]), while in others only to blank media (e.g., in Canada and Denmark).[50] In Canada, only blank CDs are levied,[51] and in Israel private copying levies are due only for copying of works on tape,[52] thus excluding devices designed for use in a computer, such as hard discs and discs-on-key[53]. Nevertheless, the formalistic distinction between equipment and media does not convey a complete picture of national approaches to levied devices, since in some countries (e.g., France) multifunctional devices capable of recording (as one of their functional capabilities) qualify as "blank media" (e.g., TV sets with integrated memories and hard disks, TV decoders/ADSL boxes designed for the sole purpose of recording audiovisual broadcasts).[54]

---

45 There are some exceptions to this general approach, e.g., according to Article 19(1)c of the Swiss Copyright Act, private use is understood to mean the reproduction of copies of works within enterprises, public administrations, institutions, commissions and similar organisations for internal information or documentation purposes.

46 Legislation of some countries specifies that private copies in order to fall within the scope of the exception or limitation need to be made from a licit source (e.g., in France, according to Article L311-1 of the CPI).

47 Décision n° 15 du 14 décembre 2012 de la commission prévue à l'article L. 311-5 du code de la propriété intellectuelle.

48 National report Netherlands, pp. 10–11.

49 Decreto de Lei n.º 320/XII – Segunda alteração à Lei n.º 62/98, de 1 de setembro, que regula o disposto no artigo 82.º do Código do Direito de Autor e dos Direitos Conexos, sobre a compensação equitativa relativa à cópia privada, [DAR II série A Nº.89/XII/4 2015.03.05 (pág. 28–40)].

50 de Thuiskopie and WIPO (2016), *International Survey on Private Copying: Law and Practice 2015*, WIPO Publication No. 1037E/16, p. 7. The survey also observes that it is increasingly difficult to make a clear distinction between recording equipment and media due to technological convergences and emergence of multifunctional devices.

51 Tariff of Levies to Be Collected by the Canadian Private Copying Collective (CPCC) in 2015 on the Sale, in Canada, of Blank Audio Recording Media certified by the Copyright Board 13 December 2014. National report Canada, p. 8.

52 Article 3D of the Israeli Copyright Ordinance. National report Israel, pp. 6–7.

53 It seems to us that if a number of devices to which the levies are applied in Israel is not extended it will eventually completely lose its significance for rightholders as the technological evolution continues to change the way in which people access protected subject matter. On Israel, see also Afori, p. 282 ff. below in this volume.

54 de Thuiskopie and WIPO (2016), *International Survey on Private Copying: Law and Practice 2015*, WIPO Publication No. 1037E/16, pp. 7 and 77. Décision no. 15 du 14 décembre 2012 de la commission prévue à l'article L. 311-5 du code de la propriété intellectuelle.

Convergence of technologies and use of new media for private copying poses a challenge for the private copying levies. In an attempt to follow trends in consumer behavior, the number of levied devices tends to expand as well. A relatively recent idea is extension of the copyright levies to online storage services (e.g., "in the cloud").[55] France is the first country that has extended the private copying exception to some online storage services.[56]

It is interesting to observe that all the countries covered by the national reports that provide for remuneration for copying by means of reprography also provide for remuneration for private copying[57].

In the EU, there were attempts to establish a common approach to copyright levies[58] but so far they did not materialize in any concrete legislative actions. Meanwhile, the number of cases decided by the CJEU continues to increase, creating European jurisprudence interpreting some key notions pertaining to levies for private copying.[59]

---

55 European Commission, Communication from the Commission to the European Parliament, the Council, the European Economic and Social Committee and the Committee of the Regions, *Unleashing the Potential of Cloud Computing in Europe*, 27 September 2012, COM(2012) 529 final, p. 7 and European Parliament resolution on private copying levies (2013/2114(INI)) of 27 February 2014, P7_TA-PROV(2014)0179, paras. 29–30.

56 According to Article L. 311-4 of the CPI, as amended on 7 July 2016, the remuneration for private copying should be paid by providers of radio or television services or distributors of such services that provide a physical person with a remote access to a reproduction for private use of works of programmes of linear broadcasts, provided that such reproduction was requested by the physical person before or during the broadcasts.

57 E.g., in Hungary: Articles 20, 21 and 73(3) of the Hungarian Copyright Act. National report Hungary, p. 11. In France the right to reprography is an exclusive right subject to mandatory collective management (Article L122-10 of the CPI). André Lucas (2014), *Droits des Auteurs : Droits patrimoniaux : Droit de reproduction par reprographie (CPI, art. L. 122-10 à L. 122-12)*, JurisClasseur Propriété littéraire et artistique, Fasc. 1265, para. 6. National report France, p. 14. However, in the UK, the Copyright and Rights in Performance (Personal Copies for Private Use) Regulations 2014 (SI 2014/2361) made on 26 August 2014 were quashed 17 July 2015 by a court on demand of rightholders concerned (British Academy of Songwriters, Composers and Authors Musicians' Union & Ors, R v Secretary of State for Business, Innovation and Skills & Anor [2015] EWHC Admin 2041). Hence the private copying for research and private study in the UK permitted under an unremunerated exception or limitation enacted by the Regulations, which came into force on 1 October 2014, are now subject to an exclusive right to reproduction.

58 European Commission, *Follow-up to the European Parliament resolution on private copying levies*, 28 May 2014 (SP(2014)447), António Vitorino (2013), *Recommendations Resulting from the Mediation on Private Copying and Reprography Levies*, 31 January 2013, and European Commission, *A Single Market for Intellectual Property Rights Boosting creativity and innovation to provide economic growth, high quality jobs and first class products and services in Europe*, Communication from the Commission to the European Parliament, the Council, the European Economic and Social Committee and the Committee of the Regions, 24 May 2011, COM(2011) 287 final, pp. 12–13.

59 CJEU Judgments in Copydan Båndkopi, C-463/12, EU:C:2015:144, ACI Adam and Others, C-435/12, EU:C:2014:254, VG Wort, C-457/11, EU:C:2013:426, Amazon.com International Sales

Statutory remuneration for certain uses of **orphan works** may be established within the framework of the EU/EEA exception or limitation provided by the Orphan Works Directive. As it can be seen from the national reports, not all the member states have transposed the mechanism provided by the Directive into national law. In the context of the discussion on the scope, it is worth noting that the Directive's review clause (Article 10) obliges the European Commission to submit by 29 October 2015 a report concerning "the possible inclusion in the scope of application of this Directive of publishers and of works or other protected subject-matter not currently included in its scope, and in particular stand-alone photographs and other images." It appears that this revision target was missed as no report was released.

A rather particular case is the remuneration for use of works or subject-matter commonly not protected by copyright systems. The regime of the **"domaine public payant"**, serving to provide resources for funds supporting cultural activities, exists, for example, in Hungary[60] and Norway.[61] In the latter country, the payment is due for the use of phonograms which are in the public domain and/or with respect to which the national treatment does not apply. The right to claim remuneration for the use of works in the public domain is difficult to qualify as an exception or limitation to the exclusive rights, since there is no copyright protection, in the usual sense of the term, as provided by the international law.

Furthermore, in Norway, some remuneration is due to creators by virtue of **special agreements for remuneration** negotiated between organisations representing artists' interests and the government (similar to the agreements concluded by labour unions). Two of such agreements reported by the response to the questionnaire provide for:

- remuneration for performance of music at religious services, while such performance is covered by an exception and limitation;
- remuneration for the exhibit of works of visual art, handicraft and photographic art owned by artist.[62]

---

and Others, C-521/11, EU:C:2013:515, Luksan, C-277/10, EU:C:2012:65, Stichting de Thuiskopie, C-462/09, EU:C:2011:397 and Judgment in Padawan, C-467/08, EU:C:2010:620, Hewlett-Packard Belgium, C-572/13, EU:C:2015:750, EGEDA and Others, C-470/14, EU:C:2016:418, and Nokia Italia and Others, C-110/15, ECLI:EU:C:2016:717.

60 Article 100 of the Hungarian Copyright Act. This provision relates only to the resale of original works of art which are in the public domain. National report Hungary, pp. 10 and 12.

61 Act no. 4 of 14 December 1956 relating to a levy on the public presentation of recordings of performers' performances, as subsequently amended. National report Norway, pp. 10–11.

62 National report Norway, pp. 11–12.

3. Exercise of remuneration rights

International treaties usually do not explicitly deal with the question of exercise of rights to remuneration, leaving it to the discretion of contracting parties.[63]

In the vast majority of countries covered by the national reports, remuneration schemes are implemented using a **system of collective management of rights.**[64] Some EU instruments even explicitly refer to the possibility to exercise remuneration rights through CMOs (Article 6(2) of the Resale Right Directive[65] and Article 5(4) of the Rental and Lending Directive[66]). The recourse to the collective exercise of rights is often dictated by the practical difficulty of individual exercise of rights to remuneration.[67]

In some countries, all the remuneration rights are subjected to **mandatory collective management** (e.g., in Finland, Norway and Switzerland).[68] All the countries covered by the reports use this legal mechanism for management of at least one remuneration right (except Egypt, as it seems[69]). This legal mechanism

---

63 Sometimes they refer to the involvement of "competent authorities" in the tariff-setting (e.g., Article 11*bis*(2) and 13(1) of the Berne Convention) or other modalities, but in general contracting states enjoy a great freedom in determining the exercise of remuneration rights.

64 Some reports do not permit to state with certainty whether all the remuneration rights are managed collectively.

65 "Member States may provide for compulsory or optional collective management of the royalty ...". The UK made the exercise of the resale right through CMOs mandatory (Article 14 of the Artist's Resale Right Regulation 2006 No. 346; National report UK, p. 12) while in Austria, the resale right is the only remuneration right that is not subjected to mandatory collective management (Article 16b of Austrian Copyright Act; National report Austria, p. 8). CMOs managing resale rights are active in the majority of the European Economic Area countries, EVA, Members & Observers: http://www.evartists.org/en/members-observers.html (last visited October 2016).

66 "Member States may regulate whether and to what extent administration by collecting societies of the right to obtain an equitable remuneration [for the rental] may be imposed.". Sylvie Nérisson (2014), 'The Rental and Lending Rights Directive', in Irini Stamatoudi and Paul Torremans (eds), *EU Copyright Law: A Commentary*, Cheltenham, UK/ Northampton, MA, USA: Edward Elgar, p. 176.

67 Mihály Ficsor (2002), *Collective Management of Copyright and Related Rights*, WIPO Publication No. 855, pp. 137–138 and Tarja Koskinen-Olsson (2014), *Study on Collective Negotiation of Rights and Collective Management of Rights in the Audiovisual Sector*, WIPO Doc. No. CDIP/14/INF/2, p. 18.

68 National report Finland, p. 6, National report Norway, pp. 14–15 and National report Switzerland, p. 5.

69 It was reported that collective management of copyright is not well-developed in other domains than management of musical rights without explicitly indicating whether any remuneration right is managed collectively. National report Egypt, p. 9. For a concise overview of the mandatory collective management of remuneration rights in the EU member states see KEA European Affairs (2006), *The Collective Management of Rights in Europe: The Quest for Effi-*

of non-voluntary collective management permits to solve the issue of so-called "outsiders" – rightholders who are not members of CMOs. CMOs managing rights under legal assumptions enabling mandatory collective management are obliged to treat members and non-members equally. Furthermore, rules ensuring good governance of CMOs in cases of the aforementioned legally-supported model of collective management of rights are of particular importance.[70]

4. Control of tariffs and CMOs

There is a great variety of national approaches to the control of tariffs for remuneration rights and of CMOs managing them. Moreover, the exercise of different remuneration rights is often being regulated differently within the same country. As practically all the remuneration rights are managed collectively (many of them are subject to non-voluntary collective management), the control of CMOs may often be assimilated to the control of exercise of these rights.

In some countries there is **no special mechanism of control over tariff-setting** in the areas where they are not set by the government (e.g., in Greece[71]), while others established a general control over CMOs by a governmental body having authority in the domain (e.g., in Austria,[72] Finland[73] and in the Netherlands[74]) or by application of competition (antitrust) law (e.g., in Italy[75]).

Most of the countries covered by the national reports have **special rules establishing tariff-setting** procedures. The control or establishment of the tariffs is usually done through involvement of IP offices, state bodies operating in the domain of cultural policies or other organisations, which may be competent to approve freely negotiated tariffs or to determine them in case no agreement could be reached by negotiations (e.g., in Croatia[76], Hungary[77], Japan[78] and Swit-

ciency, conducted on request of the European Parliament's Committee on Legal Affairs, IP/C/JURI/ST/2005-90, pp. 83–91.

70 Christophe Geiger (2007), 'The Role of the Three-Step Test in the Adaptation of Copyright Law to the Information Society', *UNESCO e-Copyright Bulletin*, January-March 2007, p. 12.

71 National report Greece, p. 13.

72 In Austria, there is a general supervision of all the CMOs by a special authority *Aufsichtsbehörde für Verwertungsgesellschaften* with the Federal Ministry of Justice (*Bundesministerium für Justiz*). National report Austria, p. 10.

73 In Finland it is the Ministry of Education and Culture. National report Finland, p. 7.

74 Law established a Supervisory Board overseeing activities of all the CMOs. Wet toezicht en geschillenbeslechting collectieve beheersorganisaties auteurs- en naburige rechten, Stb. 2013/179. National report Netherlands, p. 16.

75 National report Italy, p. 11.

76 National report Croatia, pp. 13–14.

77 Article 92/H of the Hungarian Copyright Act. National report Hungary, pp. 9 and 15.

78 Article 69 of the Japanese Copyright Act. National report Japan, pp. 7–8.

zerland[79]). A few countries maintain permanent copyright tribunals for establishment of tariffs and/or solving disputes regarding the tariffs (e.g., Copyright Board of Canada,[80] Copyright Tribunal in the UK[81] and Copyright Royalty Board in the USA[82]).[83] Some of the countries that regulate the tariff-setting process and have state bodies with respective competences also subject CMOs to the restrictions of competition rules to counter possible abuses of a dominant position (e.g., in Germany[84] and Norway[85]).

There are also countries where **tariffs are set by law** (e.g., for private copying in Portugal[86] and Greece[87]) or **another normative act** of a state authority (e.g., tariffs for public lending and private copying are determined by Ministerial Decrees in the Netherlands[88]).

In some countries, there is **no legislation regulating activities of CMOs** (e.g., in Egypt and in most of the Arab countries, with exception to Djibouti, Lebanon, Morocco and Tunisia[89]). While the UK also belongs to the countries that do not have special regulations on collective management of remuneration rights, its CMOs have themselves developed a system of **norms for self-regulation** (e.g. through codes of conduct[90]), and the government retains the power to intervene.[91] In addition to national non-legislative instruments, such as codes

79 National report Switzerland, pp. 5–6.

80 National report Canada, p. 9. For analysis of functioning of the board see Daniel J. Gervais (2008), 'A Uniquely Canadian Institution: The Copyright Board of Canada', in Ysolde Gendreau (ed.), *An Emerging Intellectual Property Paradigm: Perspectives from Canada*, Cheltenham, UK: Edward Elgar, pp. 197–223.

81 Article 149 of the Copyright, Designs and Patents Act 1988 c. 48. National report UK, pp. 11–13.

82 The Copyright Royalty and Distribution Reform Act of 2004 (P.L. 108-419) 30 November 2004 and the Copyright Royalty Judges Program Technical Corrections Act (P.L. 109-303) 6 October 2006. National report USA, pp. 9–10.

83 For an overview of different models of copyright tribunals see Michael J. Freegard (1994), 'Quis Custodiet ? The role of copyright tribunals', *EIPR*, Vol. 16, No. 7, pp. 286–292.

84 Articles 13 and 18(2) of the Law on the Administration of Copyright and Neighboring Rights. Federal Cartel Authority should be acting in cooperation with the Patent and Trade Mark Office. National report Germany, p. 18.

85 National report Norway, pp. 18–19.

86 National report Portugal, p. 7.

87 National report Greece, p. 13.

88 National report Netherlands, p. 15.

89 National report Egypt, p. 9.

90 British Copyright Council's Principles of CMOs' Codes of Conduct of 25 May 2012. For an overview of British and other self-regulatory approaches, notably the Australian Code of Conduct for Copyright Collecting Societies, see BOP Consulting, Benedict Atkinson and Brian Fitzgerald (2012), *Collecting Societies Codes of Conduct*, Report commissioned by the Intellectual Property Office of the UK.

91 The Copyright (Regulation of Relevant Licensing Bodies) Regulations 2014 No. 898. National report UK, pp. 13–14. To date the government has not used its powers.

of conduct regulating activities of CMOs, there are also international rules established by associations of CMOs and rightholders.[92] CMOs wishing to adhere to these international organisations need to comply with the requirements of these instruments regardless of the existence of any specific norms in domestic legislation.

Comparably, a **strict system of supervisions and control** over activities of CMOs can be observed in some European countries. Belgium is a notable example, as two special bodies are charged with supervisions of different aspects of rights management, from collection of remuneration to its distribution.[93] The law imposes a ceiling of 15% on the management costs that can be deducted by CMOs from the amounts collected to cover operational expenses. Uniquely, one of the two bodies, which was recently established, is financed by a 0,2% deduction from the collections made by CMOs.[94]

Furthermore, most of the EEA countries are currently in the process of transposing into their national law provisions of the EU Collective Management Directive introducing numerous rules on good governance and transparency.[95] Being the longest, in terms of its volume, copyright instrument in the common market, it requires significant amendments to be introduced into national legislation of the member states. It is worth noting that some EU member states went a step further in certain aspects when transposing the instrument. For example, in April 2015 Portugal passed a law implementing the directive's provisions regarding control and accountability of CMOs. Some additional rules on the schedules and procedures for negotiation, establishment of tariffs and licensing were established.[96] CMOs operating in the EEA countries, regardless of national

---

92 CISAC Professional Rules for musical societies of 6 June 2014, SG13-0787R2, CISAC Professional Rules for dramatic, literary and audiovisual societies of 6 June 2013, SG13-0788, CISAC Professional Rules for graphic, plastic and photographic arts societies of 6 June 2013, SG13-0789, IFPI Code of Conduct for Music Industry Music Licensing Companies, January 2014 version, IFRRO Code of Conduct – Reproduction Rights Organisations, revised 20 September 2007.

93 *Service de régulation du droit d'auteur et des droits voisins* (Articles XI.274–XI.278 of the Belgian Code of Economic Law) and *Service de contrôle des sociétés de gestion des droits* (Articles XI.279–XI.283 of the Belgian Code of Economic Law).

94 National report Belgium, pp. 14–17.

95 Directive 2014/26/EU of the European Parliament and of the Council of 26 February 2014 on collective management of copyright and related rights and multi-territorial licensing of rights in musical works for online use in the internal market (Text with EEA relevance) [2014] OJ L 84/72. Transposition deadline is 10 April 2016 (Article 43). For comments, see Lucie Guibault (2014), 'Collective Rights Management Directive', in Irini Stamatoudi and Paul Torremans (eds), *EU Copyright Law: A Commentary*, Cheltenham, UK/ Northampton, MA, USA: Edward Elgar, pp. 696–795.

96 Law on Collective Management Organisations 26/2015 of 14 April 2015. National report Portugal, pp. 9–11.

regulations, are also subjected to the **supranational control** by the European Commission in the area of competition law.[97]

5. Who has to pay remuneration?

Payers of remuneration can be divided into three broad categories:
- **users** (e.g., in the case of communication to the public of commercial phonograms);
- **intermediaries** (e.g., importers, manufacturers and/or distributors in case of private copying, or organisations making available equipment enabling reproduction by means of reprography);
- **state budget** (e.g., remuneration for private copying in Finland,[98] Israel[99] and Spain[100]).

In general, it can be said that **tax payers** are the final payers of any remuneration rights that are paid by publicly-funded users (e.g., remuneration rights for public lending by public libraries are covered by transfers from the state budget in Austria,[101] Croatia[102] and Italy[103]). Among the countries covered by the reports,

---

97 E.g., European Commission Notice published pursuant to Article 27(4) of Council Regulation (EC) No 1/2003 in Cases COMP/C2/39152 – BUMA and COMP/C2/39151 SABAM (Santiago Agreement – COMP/C2/38126), OJ C 200/11, 17 August 2005 and European Commission Decision of 8 October 2002 (Case No COMP/C2/38.014 – IFPI 'Simulcasting'), OJ L 107/58, 30 April 2003.

98 Article 26a(1) of the Finish Copyright Act. National report Finland, p. 6. This mechanism of compensation from the state budget was established at the end of 2014 and entered in force 1 January 2015 by virtue of Laki tekijänoikeuslain muuttamisesta 19.12.2014/1171.

99 National report Israel, p. 5.

100 Articles 25(1) of the Spanish Law on Intellectual Property (Real decreto legislativo 1/1996, de 12 de abril, por el que se aprueba el texto refundido de la Ley de propiedad intelectual, regularizando, aclarando y armonizando las disposiciones legales vigentes sobre la materia, *BOE*, n. 97, 22 de abril 1996, pp. 14369–14396, as amended by Ley N° 21/2014, de 4 de noviembre, por la que se modifica el texto refundido de la Ley de Propiedad Intelectual, aprobado por Real Decreto Legislativo 1/1996, de 12 de abril, y la Ley 1/2000, de 7 de enero, de Enjuiciamiento Civil., BOE n. 268, pp. 90404–90439). National report Spain, pp. 31–32. The compliance of the payment of compensation for private copying to rightholders by means of annual public grants from the state budget with Article 5(2) of the InfoSoc Directive was challenged by the rightholders in front of the CJEU. On 9 June 2016 the court condemned the Spanish mechanism, see EGEDA and Others, C-470/14, EU:C:2016:418. On this case, see Garrote, p. 270 ff., below in this volume.

101 A lump sum payment by the Austrian government. National report Austria, p. 9: "should be paid by libraries, but in practice is paid by the State from the general Budget".

102 "[T]he Ministry of Culture, by means allocated from the public budget, supports libraries in their obligation to pay the remuneration". National report Croatia, p. 13.

103 National report Italy, p. 11.

Norway is the only country where remunerations for private copying, public lending as well as for the public display of copies of works of art and handicrafts are paid from public funds.[104]

6. Problems with asserting remuneration

Most of the national reports indicated that the **length of the tariff-setting process** (e.g., negotiations, dispute settlement) constitutes a significant problem for the assertion of remuneration rights. For example, in Switzerland, if parties to the negotiations fail to conclude an agreement, the Federal Arbitration Commission for Management of Copyright and Related Rights (*Commission arbitrale fédérale pour la gestion de droits d'auteur et de droits voisins*) has to intervene in order to establish them. The decision of the Commission can be appealed to the Federal Administrative Court (*Tribunal administratif fédéral*), and then to the Federal Court (*Tribunal fédéral*).[105] It is being reported that this process can take years. In general, many reports expressed dissatisfaction with the **length of court proceedings** regarding the collection of remuneration, establishment of tariffs and other related issues (e.g., in Argentina,[106] Austria[107] and Mexico[108]). **Incoherent court decisions** pose an additional problem in some jurisdictions (e.g., in Croatia[109]).

Almost all the reports, directly or indirectly, referred to a **strong opposition from those who need to pay** (e.g., manufacturers and importers of levied devices or their associations). **Conflicting interpretations** of some general provisions of legislation, in particular on the scope of statutory remuneration rights concerned, is an issue. Some observe that situations when users go out of business before paying any remuneration are common.[110] It was noted as well that the **time lapse** between the moment of collection of remuneration by CMOs and

---

104 National report Norway, p. 16. The "Norwegian system" of remuneration to creators through revenues generated by taxes and distributed by special funds, coexisting with a more traditional copyright legislation, was established around the middle of the XXth century, Birger Stuevold Lassen (1963), 'Collectivism and Individual Rights in Norwegian Copyright Law', *Scandinavian Studies in Law*, Vol. 7, p. 83 and Tarja Koskinen-Olsson (2010), 'Collective Management in Nordic Countries', in Daniel J. Gervais (ed.), *Collective Management of Copyright and Related Rights*, 2nd edn., Alphen aan den Rijn, The Netherlands: Kluwer Law International, p. 288.

105 National report Switzerland, pp. 5–6.

106 National report Argentina, p. 7.

107 National report Austria, p. 11.

108 National report Mexico, p. 7.

109 National report Croatia, p. 15.

110 National reports Croatia, p. 15 and USA, p. 10.

the moment of claim by rightholders creates some difficulties for distribution.[111] In some cases, amounts that need to be paid by users do not amount to the **costs of court litigation**, and so they remain uncollected (e.g., in Canada[112]).

Sometimes tariffs are established as percentages from users' revenue from the activities requiring payment of remuneration to rightholders and sometimes as fixed amounts (which are often referred as "minimum amounts").[113] When tariffs are established by a government body or by law, they have more legitimacy and there are fewer disputes about them. If tariffs in the form of fixed amounts are not updated with frequencies corresponding to countries' economic climate, they are more likely to become outdated than the tariffs established as a percentage from the revenue. In general, **tariffs set by law are** even more **difficult to amend** than the tariffs fixed by an administrative authority. For example, in Portugal, where the exact amounts to be paid for private copying are determined by law, the Private Copy Act extending the scope of the levy system to digital storage equipment had been in preparation and discussion for more than three years.[114]

With regard to the **unwaivable right to equitable remuneration for the rental**, it is reported that when this right is not managed by a CMO charged with its exercise, sometimes authors and performers do not receive any subsequent royalties in addition to an initial payment for the transfer of rights to rental.[115]

Payment of remuneration from the state budget (e.g. for private copying), while sparing rightholders or CMOs from complex relations with numerous debtors, has some drawbacks. For example, CMOs may need to set up tariffs within the limits set forth specifically for the purpose of remuneration (e.g., for public lending in Hungary[116]). In Spain, where the system of collection of private copying levies from intermediaries was replaced by funding from the state budget, the change was detrimental to the interests of creators and rightholders due to the **lack of public finances.**[117]

---

111 National report Finland, p. 7.
112 National report Canada, p. 9.
113 National report Argentina, p. 7.
114 National report Portugal, pp. 7–8. On the issue of determination of devices and media subject to levies, as well as tariffs, see IFRRO and WIPO (2014), *International Survey on Text and Image Copyright Levies 2014*, WIPO Publication No. 1042E, p. 16.
115 National report Netherlands, p. 11.
116 Article 23/A of the Hungarian Copyright Act. National report Hungary, pp. 10–11.
117 de Thuiskopie and WIPO (2016), *International Survey on Private Copying: Law and Practice 2015*, WIPO Publication No. 1037E/16, p. 14.

7. Solutions to the problems of remuneration

One of the common legislative provisions aiming at providing rightholders with the information necessary for assertion of their rights is the **obligation** for users or intermediaries **to report on the use**. In addition to this common provision, some countries provide CMOs with a **possibility to request necessary information** for the exercise of their function from customs or VAT tax authorities (e.g., in Belgium[118]). In Greece, if a CMO authorized to administer the remuneration for private copying has some doubts about the statements made by importers or manufacturers of levied equipment, it has a right to request a certified accountant to verify it.[119]

Another legislative tool used to address the problem of remuneration is the implementation of a right of rightholders to request users (through a court) to make a **deposit** for securing pending future obligations (e.g., in Hungary[120] and Finland[121]). In Japan, in case of use of copyrighted works under compulsory licenses, a deposit equivalent to an ordinary rate of royalties should be deposited with the Commissioner of the Agency for Cultural Affairs, which is fixing the rate.[122] In the Japanese example, the law provides for the obligation to make a deposit as a precondition for lawful use.

Legislation of many countries also provides CMOs with a competence to request **injunctions** to prohibit use of protected works or to ensure execution of court judgements (e.g., in Argentina[123], Finland[124], Mexico[125] and Norway[126]).

Dutch legislation gives CMOs and those who need to pay a possibility to settle disputes below 100.000 euros through **arbitration**. Decisions of an arbitration board are binding if parties do not submit their case to a court afterwards.[127]

In Belgium, where there are more than one CMO managing the resale right, the legislator imposed the creation of a **single platform** (*plateforme unique*) managed by the CMOs for streamlining the collection of remuneration.[128] CMOs

118 Article XI.230 of the Belgian Code of Economic Law. National report Belgium, p. 17.
119 National report Greece, p. 13.
120 National report Hungary, p. 14.
121 Article 54b of the Finish Copyright Act. National report Finland, p. 7.
122 Articles 67(1), 67*bis*, 68(1) and 69 of the Japanese Copyright Act. National report Japan, pp. 7–8.
123 National report Argentina, p. 8.
124 Article 54b of the Finish Copyright Act. National report Finland, p. 7.
125 National report Mexico, p. 7.
126 Article 38b of the Norwegian Copyright Act. National report Norway, p. 8.
127 Articles 3, 23 and 25 of Wet toezicht en geschillenbeslechting collectieve beheersorganisaties auteurs- en naburige rechten, Stb. 2013/179. National report Netherlands, p. 16.
128 Article XI.177 of the Belgian Code of Economic Law. Arrêté royal fixant les conditions et les modalités de gestion du droit de suite visée aux articles XI.177 et XI.178 du Code de droit

operating in other domains opted for the creation of **"umbrella" CMOs** on a voluntary basis. Indeed, in case of countries with multiple CMOs operating in the same area, the establishment of an "umbrella" organisation may indeed facilitate relations with users, reduce costs and avoid possible confusion on the side of users.[129]

CMOs managing rights to remuneration often represent their members as well as non-members. In order to ensure that there are sufficient resources left after distribution of remuneration to members, legislation may **oblige CMOs to reserve some sums for claims from outsiders.** In Belgium, the CMO managing remuneration rights for private copying (AUVIBEL) does it on a voluntary basis[130].

In order to avoid the issue of tariffs established by a legislative act becoming obsolete over time and at the same time to take advantage of the legitimacy of tariffs established by state authorities, in Canada, for example, the Copyright **Board defines tariffs for a period** from 1 to 5 years after which interested parties need to repeat the tariff-setting process.[131]

III. Conclusions

This chapter represents an attempt to make a concise overview of national approaches. The undertaking revealed some terminological difficulties related to the use of different terms for designating economic rights different from the exclusive rights. These difficulties seem to be associated with a somewhat dualist view of the international copyright system, as being composed of exclusive rights on one side and exceptions and limitations to them on the other side. This chapter presents a more nuanced perspective, where statutory remuneration rights are a category of entitlements to remuneration encompassing three broad categories: remuneration rights *per se* (economic rights distinct from exclusive rights and which are not exceptions or limitations), limitation-related remuneration rights (economic rights created to remunerate uses covered by exceptions or limitations to the exclusive rights) and "residual" remuneration rights (economic rights created within the scope of the exclusive rights by rendering the remuneration aspect of the rights unwaivable).

économique, 11 June 2015. National report Belgium, p. 11. A similar solution was applied to the collective management of the unwaivable right of authors and performers for remuneration for retransmission of audiovisual works by cable (Article XI.225).

129 Mihály Ficsor (2002), *Collective Management of Copyright and Related Rights*, WIPO Publication No. 855, p. 135.

130 National report Belgium, p. 10.

131 National report Canada, p. 9.

As we have seen, legal rights to remuneration exist in all the countries examined but have a different scope depending on the national laws and traditions, and their enforcement tools are more or less successful, mainly depending on the efficiency of the collective management organisation collecting the remuneration at national level. This is interesting for the initial question of the ALAI conference on the possible competition of legal mechanisms (exclusivity vs. other approaches) and on the model to be adopted. The solution cannot be found on dogmatic grounds but rather by analysing the efficacy of the model proposed in order to ensure the objectives ascribed to the legal provision. From this pragmatic point of view, there is obviously essential data that is lacking in all the reports, namely the amount of the payments received by the authors, i.e. how much the creators earn under different systems.[132] It is easy to predict that the replies will be very different depending on the authors concerned (depending for example on how successful they are and how much bargaining power they have to impose fair remunerations), which is another argument in favour of a diversity of models. There are certainly a number of studies on the remuneration generated by the limitation-based remuneration right to private coping, but these studies deserve to be completed, particularly in order to determine the exact amount of the sums distributed to the authors.[133] Obviously, it is important to refrain from any generalisation. First of all, the situation of the creators can be very diverse, and it is probably necessary to distinguish between the creators who receive a salary and for whom the additional remuneration amounts to a supplement – welcomed but certainly not essential for their creative activity – and those who depend on the system for their daily living. Secondly, another distinction should also probably be made based on the performance of the system of collective management set up at national level.[134] If the remuneration

---

132 It is paradoxical and, unfortunately, characteristic of many contemporary policy-relevant copyright debates where questions of remuneration for creators are discussed without numbers on remuneration received by creators.

133 According to de Thuiskopie and WIPO (2016), *International Survey on Private Copying: Law and Practice 2015*, WIPO Publication No. 1037E/16 covering data on private copying systems of over 25 countries, the "total revenue has increased over the years from 598 million euros in 2007 to an all-time high of 804 million euros in 2014", pp. 13–15 and 22. IFRRO and WIPO (2015), *International Survey on Text and Image Copyright Levies: 2015 Edition*, WIPO Publication No. 1042E/16 estimates that 179 million euros were collected from text and image copyright levies worldwide in 2014 (p. 5 and 24). See also Martin Kretschmer (2011), *Private Copying and Fair Compensation: An empirical study of copyright levies in Europe*, UK Intellectual Property Office, p. 7: "Following the Directive of 2001, total collection from levies on copying media and equipment in the EU tripled, from about €170m to more than €500m per annum. Levy schemes exist now in 22 out of 27 Member States (with only the UK, Ireland, Malta, Cyprus and Luxembourg remaining outside)."

134 For a notable economic attempt of assessment and comparison of efficiency of CMOs from different countries, see Fabrice Rochelandet (2003), 'Are Copyright Collecting Societies Effi-

rights are to be effective, there is a need for collective management organisations that work well. This conclusion might encourage legislatures to carry out empirical studies more frequently in the future to evaluate the economic impacts of the one or the other constellation.[135] But this then raises questions that are much more fundamental in the field of copyright: Does the system aim to protect *all* authors equally or only those who enjoy a significant commercial success? What function is to be accorded to the idea of redistributive justice within copyright law?[136] How can an efficient distinction be made within legislation between the protection of the investors and the protection of the creators? These are fascinating but complex questions, which would probably need another ALAI congress.

cient Organisations? An Evaluation of collective Administration of Copyright in Europe', in Wendy J. Gordon and Richard Watt (eds), *The Economics of Copyright: Developments in Research and Analysis*, Cheltenham, UK/ Northampton, MA, USA: Edward Elgar, pp. 176–197.

135 Pleading for more evidence based legislative action in the EU, see Christophe Geiger (2016), 'Moving out of the Economic Crisis: what Role and Shape for Intellectual Property Rights in the European Union?', in: Harri Kalimo and Max S. Jansson (eds.), *EU Economic Law in a Time of Crisis*, Cheltenham, UK/ Northampton, MA, USA: Edward Elgar, p. 135.

136 See on this issue Christophe Geiger (2013), 'The Social Function of Intellectual Property Rights, Or how Ethics can Influence the Shape and Use of IP law', in: Graeme B. Dinwoodie (ed.), *Methods and Perspectives in Intellectual Property*, Cheltenham, UK/ Northampton, MA, USA: Edward Elgar, pp. 153–176.

Christophe Geiger et Oleksandr Bulayenko*

2.2 Rapport général : Etendue des droits et instruments de mise en œuvre pour garantir l'effectivité de la rémunération

Introduction

Le congrès de l'ALAI avait pour objet de réfléchir aux modèles juridiques dont on dispose pour garantir une rémunération pour l'utilisation des œuvres protégées par le droit d'auteur. Deux principaux mécanismes pour y parvenir ont été identifiés, à savoir les droits exclusifs et les droits légaux à rémunération. Ainsi, les personnes qui sont intervenues au congrès – et ont donc contribué au présent volume – ont été invitées à dresser une sorte d'inventaire des « divers mécanismes qui existent pour assurer une rémunération équitable ». Le présent rapport général s'intéresse plus particulièrement aux droits légaux à rémunération, à l'étendue de ces droits et aux instruments de mise en œuvre pour garantir l'effectivité de la rémunération.

Il n'est pas étonnant qu'on ait choisi de discuter du thème des droits légaux à rémunération à l'occasion de la célébration des 50 ans de la loi allemande sur le droit d'auteur. Cette loi, tout en plaçant clairement l'auteur au centre de ses dispositions (la loi est intitulée « Urheberrechtsgesetz » que l'on peut traduire par « loi sur le droit d'auteur »), prévoit pas moins de 9 limitations et exceptions qui ouvrent la possibilité pour l'auteur d'obtenir une rémunération équitable[1], ainsi que certains droits que le rapport allemand dénomme « autres droits de l'auteur », tels que le droit de suite, les droits de location et de prêt public et le droit afférent à la retransmission par câble[2]. Par conséquent, il ne tient sans

---

* Christophe Geiger est Professeur de droit, Directeur Général et Directeur du Laboratoire de recherche du CEIPI, Chercheur senior affilié à l'Institut Max Planck pour l'innovation et la concurrence à Munich (Allemagne) et Spangenberg Fellow au Spangenberg Center for Law, Technology & the Arts, Case Western Reserve University School of Law, à Cleveland (Etats-Unis); Oleksandr Bulayenko est Chercheur et doctorant au CEIPI. Le présent chapitre s'appuie dans une large mesure sur les réponses apportées au questionnaire préparé en vue du présent congrès de l'ALAI, et plus particulièrement sur les réponses à la partie C du questionnaire « Questions à propos des droits légaux à rémunération ». Les rapports nationaux portent sur la législation et la pratique de 22 pays (Allemagne, Argentine, Autriche, Belgique, Canada, Croatie, Egypte, Espagne, Etats-Unis, Finlande, France, Grèce, Hongrie, Israël, Italie, Japon, Mexique, Norvège, Pays-Bas, Portugal, Royaume-Uni et Suisse). Ces rapports sont disponibles sur : http://www.alai2015.org/en/national-reports.html (dernière visite en octobre 2016). Traduction de l'anglais par Margaret Platt-Hommel.

1 Rapport national Allemagne, p. 15–16.

2 *Ibid.* p. 15.

doute pas du hasard que la Cour fédérale de justice allemande, dans une décision remarquée du 11 juillet 2002, ait justifié l'élargissement aux revues de presse électroniques de l'exception classique de revue de presse au nom de la protection de l'intérêt de l'auteur à obtenir une rémunération[3].

Avant d'entrer dans l'analyse des différentes approches nationales des droits légaux à rémunération (II.)[4], nous évoquerons d'abord quelques problèmes de terminologie (I.).

I. Droits légaux à rémunération : problèmes de terminologie

L'une des questions les plus délicates qui se posent dans le cadre du présent rapport général est certainement celle de la terminologie utilisée. En effet, les rapports nationaux emploient certaines notions comme synonymes, alors que les divers termes peuvent avoir une portée différente sur le plan juridique.

Si, par exemple, les notions de « droits légaux à rémunération », de « licences obligatoires » et d'autres notions apparentées semblent à première vue avoir un sens uniforme, la manière dont on les entend est profondément influencée par la langue et les traditions juridiques nationales. Le sens attribué aux notions-clés influe sur les réponses apportées aux différentes parties du questionnaire de l'ALAI par 22 de ses groupes nationaux. En effet, il n'existe aucune définition juridique universellement reconnue de la notion de droits légaux à rémunération. De plus, la doctrine emploie des termes différents pour désigner des mécanismes autres que les droits exclusifs qui assurent aux titulaires de droits une rémunération, dont notamment la « licence légale », la « licence obli-

---

3 La Cour, se référant à l'article 49.1 de la loi sur le droit d'auteur (qui prévoit une licence légale pour l'utilisation d'articles journalistiques dans le cadre d'une revue de presse), souligne que cette disposition a pour conséquence qu'une partie importante de la rémunération perçue en contrepartie de l'utilisation d'œuvres protégées dans le cadre de revues de presse est versée aux auteurs des textes utilisés. En revanche, si l'application du droit exclusif est maintenue, la situation de l'auteur n'est généralement pas améliorée. Cf. la décision de la Cour fédérale de justice allemande (« Bundesgerichtshof ») du 11 juillet 2002, « Revues de presse électroniques », 2002 GRUR 963. Voir également en ce sens, Adolf Dietz, « Protection des personnes créatives par le droit d'auteur – Les cinq piliers du droit d'auteur moderne de l'Europe continentale », RIDA n° 243, janv. 2015, p. 148 : « il apparaît bien souvent que les droits à rémunération et systèmes de redevance prévus par la loi et gérés par des sociétés de gestion collective sont paradoxalement plus favorables aux auteurs et aux artistes interprètes ou exécutants que des droits exclusifs plus forts qui font l'objet d'une gestion individuelle sous le contrôle des entreprises détentrices des droits. »

4 En s'appuyant dans une large mesure sur les informations fournies par les rapports nationaux.

gatoire », la « licence non volontaire » et les « droits à rémunération liés à des limitations ou exceptions »[5]. Cette prolifération de termes apparentés et les différences de compréhension auxquelles ils donnent lieu peuvent mener à certaines incohérences. En témoignent les réponses des différents groupes nationaux de l'ALAI aux mêmes questions posées dans le questionnaire. Certaines divergences ou des doutes concernant l'interprétation des notions de « droit légal à rémunération » et de « licence obligatoire » s'observent même dans les rapports nationaux provenant d'Etats membres de l'UE/EEE dont la législation qui transpose les normes de l'Union européenne dans l'ordre juridique interne est harmonisée dans une certaine mesure. Ainsi, le rapport national norvégien répond à la question sur les « licences obligatoires » en évoquant les « licences légales » et les « licences collectives étendues »[6] ; le rapport national du Royaume-Uni qualifie de « rémunération légale » celle prévue pour certaines utilisations des œuvres orphelines[7], tandis que le rapport national portugais désigne sous le nom de « licence obligatoire » la rémunération pour l'utilisation des œuvres orphelines tout en reconnaissant qu'elle peut également être qualifiée de « licence légale »[8]. Ces différences terminologiques obscurcissent le sens et rendent délicate une simple comparaison.

On constate également une différence subtile de perception de la rémunération légale, considérée soit comme l'« indemnisation du préjudice causé », soit comme une « rémunération pour l'utilisation ». Cette nuance à première vue insignifiante peut jouer un rôle important dans la perception nationale des régimes de rémunération et de la finalité de ceux-ci, et influer donc sur le calcul des montants concernés. Les différences de langue et les variations terminologiques ont également une incidence sur la transposition des textes internationaux en droit interne[9].

---

5 Mihály Ficsor (2003), *Guide sur le droit d'auteur et les droits connexes administrés par l'OMPI et glossaire du droit d'auteur et des droits connexes*, Publication OMPI N° 891(F), p. 288, 295 et 314, Andrew F. Christie (2011), « Maximising permissible exceptions to intellectual property rights », *in* Annette Kur et Vytautas Mizaras (dir.), *The Structure of Intellectual Property Law: Can One Size Fit All?*, Cheltenham, Royaume-Uni : Edward Elgar, p. 125 ; Christophe Geiger et Franciska Schönherr (2012), « Defining the Scope of Protection of Copyright in the EU: The Need to Reconsider the Acquis regarding Limitations and Exceptions », *in* Tatiana-Eleni Synodinou (dir.), *Codification of European Copyright Law: Challenges and Perspectives*, Alphen aan den Rijn, Pays-Bas : Kluwer Law, International, p. 166–167 ; Christophe Geiger (2010), « Promoting Creativity through Copyright Limitations, Reflections on the Concept of Exclusivity in Copyright Law », *Vanderbilt Journal of Entertainment & Technology Law*, Vol. 12, n° 3, p. 515–548.

6 Rapport national Norvège, p. 12–14.

7 Rapport national Royaume-Uni, p. 11–12.

8 Rapport national Portugal, p. 8.

9 Christophe Geiger et Franciska Schönherr (2014), « Limitations to copyright in the digital age », *in* Andrej Savin et Jan Trzaskowski (dir.), *Research Handbook on EU Internet Law*, Cheltenham, Royaume-Uni/ Northampton, MA, Etats-Unis : Edward Elgar, p. 131–133.

En outre, la démarcation entre les modèles juridiques qui assurent une rémunération par le biais des droits exclusifs, d'une part, et les droits légaux à rémunération, d'autre part, n'est pas toujours nette lorsque les droits exclusifs font l'objet d'une gestion collective obligatoire. Par exemple, certains rapports nationaux font état, dans le contexte des droits légaux à rémunération, de l'exercice obligatoire du droit exclusif de reprographie[10] par un organisme de gestion collective (OGC), tandis que d'autres excluent explicitement du champ du rapport les droits exclusifs soumis à un régime de gestion collective obligatoire[11].

Compte tenu des approches différentes qui peuvent être retenues pour la définition des notions-clés et dans un souci d'inclusivité, le présent rapport général définit les droits légaux à rémunération comme étant tous les droits pécuniaires qui assurent aux titulaires du droit d'auteur et/ou des droits voisins le droit d'obtenir une rémunération non assorti de la possibilité de contrôler l'utilisation des œuvres ou autres objets protégés[12]. Cette définition englobe les droits à rémunération définis comme tels par les normes internationales ou nationales (« droits à rémunération proprement dits »), les droits à rémunération créés dans le cadre des limitations ou exceptions aux droits exclusifs (« droits à rémunération liés à des limitations/exceptions ») et les droits à rémunération intégrés dans le régime des droits exclusifs (« droits à rémunération inaliénables »[13] dits résiduels).

---

10 Rapport national France, p. 14 et 22. L'article L. 122-10 du Code de la propriété intellectuelle (CPI) français prévoit que la publication d'une œuvre emporte cession du droit de reproduction par reprographie à un OGC (actuellement au Centre français d'exploitation du droit de copie (CFC)) agréé à cet effet par le ministre chargé de la culture. Philippe Masseron (2011), *Sociétés de perception et de répartition des droits : Centre français d'exploitation du droit de copie (CFC)*, fasc. 1580, et Sylvie Nérisson (2013), *La gestion collective des droits des auteurs en France et en Allemagne : quelle légitimité ?*, Paris, France: IRJS, p. 287, 313 et 314.

11 Rapport national Hongrie, p. 11–12. Le cas de l'exercice obligatoire du droit exclusif de retransmission par câble n'est pas unanimement qualifié de droit légal à rémunération par les rapports nationaux des Etats membres de l'UE. Au sein de l'UE, la gestion collective obligatoire du droit exclusif d'autoriser la retransmission par câble est prévue par l'article 9 de la Directive 93/83/CEE du Conseil du 27 septembre 1993 relative à la coordination de certaines règles du droit d'auteur et des droits voisins du droit d'auteur applicables à la radiodiffusion par satellite et à la retransmission par câble [1993] L 248/15.

12 Il est fait abstraction des questions liées au droit moral et à la gestion collective obligatoire de droits exclusifs dans la mesure où fait débat la question de savoir si cette dernière a une incidence sur la nature des droits exclusifs.

13 Mihály Ficsor (2010), « Collective Management of Copyright and Related Rights from the Viewpoint of International Norms and the Acquis Communautaire », *in* Daniel J. Gervais (dir.), *Collective Management of Copyright and Related Rights*, 2e éd., Alphen aan den Rijn, Pays-Bas : Kluwer Law International, p. 42. Mihály Ficsor (2002), *La gestion collective du droit d'auteur et des droits connexes*, Publication OMPI N° 855, p. 25 (droit inaliénable en faveur des créateurs individuels qui "subsisterait" après la cession des autres droits) et 144 (« droits dont les titulai-

II. Approches nationales des droits légaux à rémunération

1. Bref aperçu

Des droits légaux à rémunération sous diverses formes font partie intégrante de la législation sur le droit d'auteur des pays du monde entier. Les rapports nationaux reçus diffèrent quant à l'ampleur de leur traitement des divers droits à rémunération et quant à la manière dont ils les classent, certains droits étant souvent décrits de façon plus détaillée que d'autres qui sont plutôt laissés de côté. Quoi qu'il en soit, le volume global des informations fournies semble suffisant pour en tirer quelques conclusions générales et dresser un tableau d'ensemble de la situation.

Tous les pays visés par les réponses au questionnaire prévoient pour les artistes interprètes ou exécutants et les producteurs de phonogrammes un **droit à rémunération au titre de la communication au public des phonogrammes du commerce**[14].

La plupart des pays faisant l'objet des rapports nationaux ont mis en place des mécanismes de rémunération pour la revente d'œuvres d'art originales (droit de suite), la **copie privée** et le **prêt** et la **location** d'exemplaires d'œuvres ou d'objets protégés.

Plus rares sont les systèmes de rémunération pour la **reproduction au bénéfice de personnes affectées d'un handicap** (p. ex. en Autriche[15], en Allemagne[16], aux Pays-Bas[17] et en Suisse[18]), pour l'utilisation d'**œuvres orphelines** (p. ex. en Autriche[19], en Allemagne[20] et au Royaume-Uni[21]), pour la **reproduc-**

---

res ne peuvent se dépouiller (“*residual rights*”), c'est-à-dire les droits à rémunération prévus (habituellement en faveur des auteurs et des artistes interprètes ou exécutants) en cas de transfert de certains droits exclusifs (c'est le cas notamment du droit de location défini dans la directive de la Communauté européenne relative au droit de location et de prêt) »).

14 L'adoption généralisée du droit à rémunération au titre de la communication au public des phonogrammes du commerce reflète les obligations internationales souscrites par les Etats parties à la Convention de Rome et au traité WPPT.

15 Article 42d de la loi autrichienne sur le droit d'auteur. Rapport national Autriche, p. 8.

16 Article 45a de la loi allemande sur le droit d'auteur. Rapport national Allemagne, p. 15–16.

17 Article 15i de la loi néerlandaise sur le droit d'auteur. Rapport national Pays-Bas, p. 11.

18 Article 24c de la loi suisse sur le droit d'auteur. Rapport national Suisse, p. 5.

19 Article 56e de la loi autrichienne sur le droit d'auteur. Rapport national Autriche, p. 7.

20 Article 61b de la loi allemande sur le droit d'auteur. Rapport national Allemagne, p. 16.

21 Article 10.2 du règlement relatif aux œuvres orphelines : *Copyright and Rights in Performances (Licensing of Orphan Works) Regulations 2014 No. 2863*. Rapport national Royaume-Uni, p. 11–12.

tion à des fins d'enseignement ou de recherche (p. ex. en Croatie[22], en Allemagne[23] et aux Pays-Bas[24]), pour la **mise à disposition de phonogrammes ou d'enregistrements audiovisuelles** (p. ex. en Espagne[25]), pour la **reproduction et la mise à disposition sous forme numérique de livres indisponibles dans le commerce** (p. ex. en France[26]), en contrepartie de la présomption de cession légale des **principaux droits patrimoniaux de l'auteur du film** en faveur du producteur du film (p. ex. aux Pays-Bas[27]) ou au titre de l'**exposition publique d'exemplaires d'œuvres d'art ou d'artisanat d'art qui sont de propriété publique** (p. ex. en Norvège[28]).

Il importe de relever que certains pays, en s'appuyant sur leur liberté au regard du droit international, ne subordonnent pas à une obligation de rémunérer les ayants droit certaines des exploitations susmentionnées, qualifiées alors

---

22 Rapport national Croatie, p. 10.

23 Article 46 de la loi allemande sur le droit d'auteur. Rapport national Allemagne, p. 15.

24 Article 16 de la loi néerlandaise sur le droit d'auteur. Rapport national Pays-Bas, p. 11–12.

25 Article 108.3 du *Texto Refundido de la Ley de Propiedad Intelectual* (TRLPI). Rapport national Espagne, p. 35–36. Selon le rapport national, les artistes interprètes espagnols auraient préféré avoir un droit à rémunération incessible au lieu d'un droit exclusif cessible d'autoriser la mise à la disposition du public. Cette possibilité étant exclue du fait de l'obligation de prévoir un droit exclusif de mise à disposition imposé par l'article 3 de la directive sur le droit d'auteur, un droit inaliénable pour les artistes interprètes d'obtenir une rémunération équitable a été intégré dans le droit exclusif de mise à disposition par l'article 108.1 qui transpose l'obligation susmentionnée prévue par la directive sur le droit d'auteur.

26 Articles L. 134-1 à L. 134-9 du CPI. Rapport national France, p. 22–24. Le rapport national évoque la législation française sur les livres indisponibles dans le contexte du droit à rémunération. Toutefois, la doctrine française n'est pas unanime à cet égard. Depuis la promulgation de la loi facilitant l'exploitation sous forme numérique des œuvres indisponibles dans le commerce, la légitimité de ce texte est contestée (Loi n° 2012-287 relative à l'exploitation numérique des livres indisponibles du XXe siècle, *JORF n° 0053*, 2 mars 2012). Le 28 février 2014, le Conseil constitutionnel français a statué que le régime mis en place par cette loi est conforme à la Constitution (C.C., 28 février 2014, M. Marc S. et autre, n° 2013-370 QPC). Le 6 mars 2015, à la suite de l'opposition persistante, le Conseil d'Etat a décidé de poser à la CJUE la question de savoir si le régime de gestion collective institué par la loi pour l'exploitation des œuvres indisponibles est compatible avec la directive sur la société de l'information (C.E., 6 mai 2015, n° 368208, M. S., Mme D., art. 2. Demande de décision préjudicielle présentée par le Conseil d'Etat (France) le 19 juin 2015 – Marc Soulier, Sara Doke/ Ministre de la Culture et de la Communication, Premier ministre (affaire C-301/15) JO C 294/35, 7 septembre 2015). Pour un commentaire, voir Oleksandr Bulayenko (2016), « Permissibility of Non-Voluntary Collective Management of Copyright under EU Law: The Case of the French Law on Out-of-Commerce Books », *JIPITEC*, Vol. 7, N° 1, p. 51–68. Dans ses conclusions présentées le 7 juillet 2016, l'Avocat général Whatelet a répondu par la négative (ECLI:EU:C:2016:536).

27 Article 45d de la loi néerlandaise sur le droit d'auteur. Rapport national Pays-Bas, p. 12.

28 Cette rémunération est prévue par la loi relative à la rémunération pour l'exposition des œuvres d'art et d'artisanat d'art, 1993-05-28-52. Rapport national Norvège, p. 10.

d'exceptions ou de limitations non-rémunérées[29]. Dans ce cas, aucun paiement n'est dû aux ayants droit.

Un certain niveau d'harmonisation peut être observé parmi les Etats membres de l'UE. Notamment, le champ d'application du droit de suite semble être prévu de manière relativement harmonieuse au sein des Etats membres de l'UE. Cela dit, malgré les efforts déployés pour harmoniser la législation sur le droit d'auteur des Etats membres dans le but de créer un marché unique, on constate encore des divergences entre les législations nationales s'agissant d'autres droits à rémunération (p. ex. les 28 Etats membres ne prévoient pas tous un droit à rémunération au titre de la reproduction par reprographie ou de la copie privée[30]). Cela s'explique en partie par le moyen retenu pour réaliser cette harmonisation (c'est-à-dire des directives[31]) et par le caractère facultatif de la liste limitative des exceptions et limitations que les Etats membres peuvent prévoir dans leur législation nationale sur le droit d'auteur[32].

2. Champ d'application de certains droits à rémunération

Comme déjà indiqué, tous les pays faisant l'objet des rapports prévoient pour les artistes interprètes ou exécutants et les producteurs de phonogrammes un droit légal à rémunération au titre de la **communication au public des phonogrammes du commerce**. Mais le champ d'application de ce droit peut fortement varier d'un pays à l'autre puisque la Convention de Rome et le traité WPPT permettent aux parties contractantes de ne pas appliquer ce droit à rémunération ou de ne l'appliquer que partiellement en déposant une notification à cet effet[33]. Ainsi, les Etats-Unis, qui sont parties au traité

29 Par exemple, en France, l'article L. 122-5, 7° CPI lu conjointement avec l'article L. 311-8, I, 3° prévoit une exception/limitation en faveur des personnes souffrant d'un handicap sans l'assortir d'une rémunération.

30 Chypre, l'Irlande, le Luxembourg, Malte et le Royaume-Uni n'ont pas de système de rémunération pour copie privée selon l'inventaire de la Stichting de Thuiskopie et de l'OMPI (2016), *International Survey on Private Copying: Law and Practice 2015*, WIPO Publication No. 1037E/16, p. 3.

31 L'article 288 du TFUE énonce : « La directive lie tout Etat membre destinataire quant au résultat à atteindre, tout en laissant aux instances nationales la compétence quant à la forme et aux moyens. » Pour une analyse critique des directives en tant qu'outils d'harmonisation, voir P. Bernt Hugenholtz (2013), « The dynamics of harmonization of copyright at the European level », *in* Christophe Geiger (dir.), *Constructing European Intellectual Property: Achievements and New Perspectives*, Cheltenham, Royaume-Uni/ Northampton, MA, Etats-Unis : Edward Elgar, p. 274–275.

32 Article 5 de la directive sur la société de l'information.

33 Article 16 de la Convention de Rome et article 15.3 du traité WPPT.

WPPT[34] mais pas à la Convention de Rome, prévoient ce droit uniquement en cas de communication au public par voie de transmission audionumérique. Le rapport norvégien fait état d'un cas limite intéressant qui concerne l'exclusion du champ de la communication au public des autoradios fournis dans les voitures de location[35]. De nombreux droits à rémunération ont pour caractéristique commune que la loi édicte l'impossibilité d'y renoncer[36] ou limite la possibilité de les aliéner[37]. Cette caractéristique des droits à rémunération, qui les distingue d'autres droits exclusifs cessibles, est souvent considérée comme un élément clef du mécanisme qui assure un lien direct entre les revenus générés et la rémunération versée aux créateurs[38].

Le champ d'application du **droit de suite** semble ne pas présenter beaucoup de différences dans les pays faisant l'objet des rapports. Son champ d'application est généralement limité aux reventes intervenant dans le cadre d'enchères publiques ou par l'intermédiaire de commerçants, et certaines lois prévoient que le droit à rémunération est déclenché uniquement en cas de plus-value. Comme cela a déjà été signalé, la directive relative au droit de suite a

---

34 L'article 15.3 WPPT prévoit la possibilité de limiter le champ d'application du droit à rémunération en déposant une notification en ce sens. Les Etats-Unis ont déposé une déclaration faisant usage de cette possibilité, accessible sur : http://www.wipo.int/treaties/en/remarks.jsp?cnty_id=1279C (dernière visite en octobre 2016).

35 Rapport national Norvège, p. 19 (il s'agissait d'une décision définitive dans une affaire où la juridiction inférieure s'était prononcée en sens inverse).

36 Par exemple, dans tous les Etats membres de l'UE, le droit de suite et le droit (résiduel) de percevoir une rémunération équitable au titre de la location de phonogrammes et de films sont des droits inaliénables auquel il ne peut être renoncé respectivement en vertu de l'article 1er de la directive européenne relative au droit de suite et de l'article 5 de la directive européenne relative au droit de location et de prêt. Dans l'affaire *Luksan*, C-277/10 ECLI:EU:C:2012:65, la CJUE fait l'observation suivante : « En l'espèce, s'agissant du droit à la compensation équitable due aux auteurs au titre de l'exception de copie privée, il ne résulte d'aucune disposition de la directive 2001/29 que le législateur de l'Union ait envisagé la possibilité, pour le bénéficiaire de ce droit, d'y renoncer. » (point 105). Par exemple, l'article 63a de la loi allemande sur le droit d'auteur stipule : « L'auteur ne peut pas renoncer par avance aux droits légaux à rémunération prévus par le présent chapitre. Ils peuvent être cédés par avance uniquement à une société de perception ou, conjointement avec la concession du droit d'édition, uniquement à l'éditeur, à condition que l'éditeur les fasse gérer par une société de perception qui assure la gestion conjointe des droits des éditeurs et des auteurs ».

37 Par exemple, en France, l'aliénabilité des droits à rémunération des artistes interprètes au titre de la communication au public des phonogrammes du commerce et au titre de la copie privée a été limitée par l'article L. 212-11 inséré dans le CPI le 7 juillet 2016 afin de protéger les intérêts des artistes interprètes lorsqu'ils signent des contrats avec les éditeurs.

38 Le Secrétaire général adjoint du Syndicat des musiciens britanniques a dit en 2015 à propos du droit de percevoir une rémunération équitable au titre de la radiodiffusion/diffusion publique des enregistrements : « le droit à une rémunération équitable s'est peu à peu transformé en un véritable joyau, la loi prévoyant expressément qu'il ne peut être cédé ». Horace Trubridge, « Préserver les revenus des musiciens », Magazine de l'OMPI, n° 2/2015, p. 9.

permis de réaliser un niveau assez élevé d'harmonisation au sein des Etats membres de l'UE[39]. Dans l'Union européenne et en Egypte sont visés par le droit de suite non seulement les œuvres d'art originales[40] mais également les exemplaires originaux[41]. En revanche, la législation de l'UE exclut du champ du droit de suite les « manuscrits originaux des écrivains et compositeurs » (selon les termes de la Convention de Berne)[42] et se démarque en limitant à 12 500 euros le montant maximal du droit susceptible d'être versé par le vendeur[43].

Le droit à rémunération pour **copie privée** n'est pas expressément prévu par les traités internationaux et est institué dans le cadre d'une limitation ou exception au droit de reproduction assortie d'une rémunération compensatoire lorsque les titulaires de droits se trouvent dans l'impossibilité pratique d'exercer leur droit exclusif. Ce mécanisme légal crée une source de revenus pour les titulaires de droits – qui à défaut ne percevraient aucune rémunération en contrepartie de la copie privée de leurs œuvres – en assujettissant à l'obligation de verser une redevance les fabricants, importateurs et/ou détaillants des appareils et/ou supports utilisés pour réaliser des copies privées ainsi que les acteurs économiques qui mettent à disposition des appareils permettant aux particuliers de réaliser des copies privées[44].

Les contours des systèmes de copie privée sont similaires dans les différents pays. L'utilisation doit généralement être effectuée par une personne physique[45], d'une manière considérée comme étant privée et à des fins non-commerciales[46].

---

39 Pour un aperçu de la transposition de la directive par les Etats membres, voir Jens Gaster (2014), « The Resale Right Directive », *in* Irini Stamatoudi et Paul Torremans (dir.), *EU Copyright Law: A Commentary*, Cheltenham, Royaume-Uni/ Northampton, MA, Etats-Unis : Edward Elgar, p. 360–362.

40 Comme l'indique l'article 14*ter* de la Convention de Berne.

41 Rapport national Egypte, p. 7 ; et l'article 2.1 de la directive de l'UE relative au droit de suite parle d'« exemplaires considérés comme œuvres d'art originales ».

42 Ibid. Jens Gaster (2014), « The Resale Right Directive », *in* Irini Stamatoudi et Paul Torremans (dir.), *EU Copyright Law: A Commentary*, Cheltenham, Royaume-Uni/ Northampton, MA, Etats-Unis : Edward Elgar, p. 367.

43 Article 4.1 de la directive relative au droit de suite. Le « plafonnement » de la rémunération constitue un outil peu habituel pour concilier les intérêts des ayants droit et des tiers.

44 Pour un aperçu plus détaillé des différents systèmes, voir les enquêtes de la Stichting de Thuiskopie et de l'OMPI (2016), *International Survey on Private Copying: Law and Practice 2015*, WIPO Publication No. 1037E/16, et de l'IFRRO et de l'OMPI (2015), *International Survey on Text and Image Copyright Levies: 2015 Edition*, WIPO Publication No. 1042E/16.

45 Cette approche générale fait l'objet de certaines exceptions ; par exemple, selon l'article 19.1.c de la loi suisse sur le droit d'auteur, on entend par usage privé la reproduction d'exemplaires d'œuvres au sein des entreprises, administrations publiques, institutions, commissions et organismes analogues, à des fins d'information interne ou de documentation.

46 La législation de certains pays précise que les copies privées qui entrent dans le champ de l'exception ou de la limitation doivent être réalisées à partir d'une source licite (p. ex. en France, selon l'article L. 311-1 CPI).

Les principales différences qui existent dans les divers pays quant aux caractéristiques de ce droit concernent les produits soumis à la redevance et les modalités de fixation des tarifs.

Dans certains pays, la rémunération pour copie privée est prélevée sur les appareils et supports d'enregistrement (p. ex. en France[47], aux Pays-Bas[48] et au Portugal[49]), tandis que, dans d'autres pays, elle est prélevée uniquement sur les supports vierges (p. ex. au Canada et au Danemark)[50]. Au Canada, la rémunération n'est perçue que sur les CD vierges[51] et en Israël la redevance pour copie privée n'est due que pour la reproduction d'œuvres sur bande[52], à l'exclusion donc des dispositifs destinés à être utilisés avec un ordinateur, tels que les disques durs et les clés USB[53]. Cela dit, la distinction formaliste entre appareils et supports ne donne pas une image complète des différentes approches nationales des produits soumis à la rémunération car, dans certains pays (p. ex. la France), sont considérés comme des « supports vierges » les dispositifs multifonctionnels susceptibles (parmi d'autres fonctions) d'être utilisés pour faire des enregistrements (p. ex. des téléviseurs avec mémoire intégrée et disque dur, ou des décodeurs TV/box ADSL destinés uniquement à l'enregistrement des émissions audiovisuelles)[54].

La convergence des technologies et l'utilisation de nouveaux moyens d'enregistrement privé présentent un défi pour les systèmes de rémunération

---

47 Décision n° 15 du 14 décembre 2012 de la commission prévue à l'article L. 311-5 du Code de la propriété intellectuelle.

48 Rapport national Pays-Bas, p. 10–11.

49 *Decreto de Lei n.º 320/XII – Segunda alteração à Lei n.º 62/98, de 1 de setembro, que regula o disposto no artigo 82.º do Código do Direito de Autor e dos Direitos Conexos, sobre a compensação equitativa relativa à cópia privada*, [DAR II série A Nº.89/XII/4 2015.03.05 (p. 28–40)].

50 Enquête de la Stichting de Thuiskopie et de l'OMPI (2016), *International Survey on Private Copying: Law and Practice 2015*, WIPO Publication No. 1037E/16, p. 7. L'enquête précise également qu'il devient de plus en plus difficile d'établir une nette distinction entre les appareils d'enregistrement et les supports en raison de la convergence des technologies et de l'apparition de dispositifs multifonctionnels.

51 Tarif des redevances à percevoir par la Société canadienne de perception de la copie privée (SCPCP) en 2015 sur la vente, au Canada, de supports audio vierges, homologué par la Commission du droit d'auteur le 13 décembre 2014. Rapport national Canada, p. 8.

52 Article 3D de l'Ordonnance israélienne sur le droit d'auteur. Rapport national Israël, p. 6–7.

53 Il nous semble qu'à défaut d'élargir les catégories de dispositifs assujettis à la redevance en Israël, celle-ci finira par perdre toute sa signification pour les titulaires de droits, au fur et à mesure que l'évolution technique modifie la manière dont les gens accèdent aux œuvres et objets protégés. Sur la situation en Israël, voir également T. Afori, plus loin dans le présent volume.

54 Enquête de la Stichting de Thuiskopie et de l'OMPI (2016), *International Survey on Private Copying: Law and Practice 2015*, WIPO Publication No. 1037E/16, p. 7 et 77. Décision n° 15 du 14 décembre 2012 de la commission prévue à l'article L. 311-5 du Code de la propriété intellectuelle.

pour copie privée. Pour essayer de suivre les évolutions dans le comportement des consommateurs, le nombre de dispositifs soumis à la rémunération tend également à augmenter. Une idée relativement récente envisage d'étendre l'application de la rémunération aux services de stockage en ligne (notamment « en nuage »)[55]. La France est le premier pays à avoir élargi l'exception de copie privée à certains services de stockage en ligne[56].

Il est intéressant de relever que tous les pays faisant l'objet des rapports nationaux qui prévoient une rémunération au titre de la reproduction par reprographie prévoient également une rémunération au titre de la copie privée[57].

Au sein de l'UE, des tentatives ont été faites pour définir une approche commune relative aux prélèvements pratiqués dans le domaine du droit d'auteur[58] mais, à ce jour, elles ne se sont pas concrétisées par des actions législatives. Entretemps, le nombre d'affaires décidées par la CJUE n'a cessé d'augmenter,

---

55 Commission européenne, Communication de la Commission au Parlement européen, au Conseil, au Comité économique et social européen et au Comité des régions, Exploiter le potentiel de l'informatique en nuage en Europe, 27 septembre 2012, COM (2012) 529 final, p. 7, et Résolution du Parlement européen sur les redevances pour copie privée (2013/2114(INI)) du 27 février 2014, P7_TA-PROV(2014)0179, points 29–30.

56 Selon l'article L. 311-4 CPI, modifié le 7 juillet 2016, la rémunération pour copie privée doit également être versée par l'éditeur d'un service de radio ou de télévision, ou le distributeur d'un tel service, qui fournit à une personne physique, par voie d'accès à distance, la reproduction à usage privé d'œuvres à partir d'un programme diffusé de manière linéaire, sous réserve que cette reproduction soit demandée par cette personne physique avant la diffusion du programme ou au cours de celle-ci.

57 Par exemple, en Hongrie : articles 20, 21 et 73.3 de la loi hongroise sur le droit d'auteur. Rapport national Hongrie, p. 11. En France, le droit de reprographie est un droit exclusif soumis à un régime de gestion collective obligatoire (article L. 122-10 CPI). André Lucas (2014), *Droits des Auteurs : Droits patrimoniaux : Droit de reproduction par reprographie (CPI, art. L. 122-10 à L. 122-12)*, JurisClasseur Propriété littéraire et artistique, fasc. 1265, para. 6. Rapport national France, p. 14. Mais, au Royaume-Uni, le règlement relatif aux copies personnelles à usage privé, *Copyright and Rights in Performances (Personal Copies for Private Use) Regulations 2014* (SI 2014/2361) du 26 août 2014 a été annulé le 17 juillet 2015 par un juge à la demande des titulaires de droits concernés (British Academy of Songwriters, Composers and Authors, Musicians' Union & Ors, R v Secretary of State for Business, Innovation and Skills & Another [2015] EWHC Admin 2041). Par conséquent, la copie privée à des fins de recherche et d'étude privée autorisée au Royaume-Uni en vertu d'une exception/limitation sans rémunération prévue par ce règlement et entrée en vigueur le 1er octobre 2014 est soumise désormais au droit exclusif de reproduction.

58 Commission européenne, Suites données à la résolution du Parlement européen sur les redevances pour copie privée, 28 mai 2014 (SP(2014)447), António Vitorino (2013), *Recommendations Resulting from the Mediation on Private Copying and Reprography Levies*, 31 janvier 2013, et Commission européenne, Vers un marché unique des droits de propriété intellectuelle – Doper la créativité et l'innovation pour permettre à l'Europe de créer de la croissance économique, des emplois de qualité et des produits et services de premier choix, Communication de la Commission au Parlement européen, au Conseil, au Comité économique et social européen et au Comité des régions, 24 mai 2011, COM(2011) 287 final, p. 15–16.

créant ainsi une jurisprudence européenne qui interprète certaines notions clés liées aux redevances pour copie privée[59].

La rémunération légale pour certaines utilisations des **œuvres orphelines** peut être prévue dans le cadre de l'exception/limitation de l'UE/EEE établie par la directive sur les œuvres orphelines. Comme cela ressort des rapports nationaux, les Etats membres n'ont pas tous transposé dans leur droit interne le mécanisme prévu par la directive. Dans le cadre de l'examen du champ d'application du dispositif, il convient de noter que la clause de réexamen prévue par la directive (article 10) fait obligation à la Commission européenne de soumettre au plus tard le 29 octobre 2015 un rapport « sur l'inclusion éventuelle, dans le champ d'application de la présente directive, des éditeurs et d'œuvres ou autres objets protégés qui n'en font pas actuellement partie, et en particulier des photographies et autres images qui existent en tant qu'œuvres indépendantes ». Il apparaît que le délai fixé pour ce réexamen n'a pas été respecté car aucun rapport n'a été publié.

Un cas assez particulier concerne la rémunération pour l'utilisation d'œuvres ou d'objets qui ne sont pas normalement protégés par le droit d'auteur. Le régime du « **domaine public payant** », qui sert à alimenter des fonds de soutien aux activités culturelles, existe notamment en Hongrie[60] et en Norvège[61]. Dans ce dernier pays, la rémunération est due pour l'utilisation de phonogrammes qui sont dans le domaine public et/ou auxquels ne s'applique pas le traitement national. Le droit de demander une rémunération pour l'utilisation des œuvres du domaine public peut difficilement être qualifié d'exception ou de limitation aux droits exclusifs dans la mesure où aucune protection du droit d'auteur, au sens habituel du terme, n'est prévue par le droit international.

De plus, en Norvège, une rémunération est due aux créateurs en vertu des **conventions spéciales de rémunération** négociées entre les organisations représentant les intérêts des artistes et le gouvernement (de nature similaire aux conventions conclues par les organisations syndicales). Deux conventions dont fait état la réponse au questionnaire prévoient respectivement :

---

59 Arrêts de la CJUE dans les affaires Copydan Båndkopi, C-463/12, EU:C:2015:144, ACI Adam e.a., C-435/12, EU:C:2014:254, VG Wort, C-457/11, EU:C:2013:426, Amazon.com International Sales e.a., C-521/11, EU:C:2013:515, Luksan, C-277/10, EU:C:2012:65, Stichting de Thuiskopie, C-462/09, EU:C:2011:397, Padawan, C-467/08, EU:C:2010:620, et dernièrement Hewlett-Packard Belgique, C-572/13, EU:C:2015:750, EGEDA e.a., C-470/14, EU:C:2016:418, et Nokia Italia e.a., C-110/15, ECLI:EU:C:2016:717.

60 Article 100 de la loi hongroise sur le droit d'auteur. Cette disposition vise uniquement la revente d'œuvres d'art originales qui sont dans le domaine public. Rapport national Hongrie, p. 10 et 12.

61 Loi n° 4 du 14 décembre 1956 relative à la redevance pour la diffusion publique d'enregistrements des interprétations ou exécutions d'artistes interprètes ou exécutants, telle que modifiée par la suite. Rapport national Norvège, p. 10–11.

- le versement d'une rémunération au titre de l'exécution d'œuvres musicales lors des services religieux, laquelle fait l'objet d'une exception/limitation ;
- le versement d'une rémunération au titre de l'exposition d'œuvres d'art graphique, plastique ou photographique ou d'artisanat d'art dont l'artiste est propriétaire[62].

3. Exercice des droits à rémunération

En général, les traités internationaux ne traitent pas explicitement de la question de l'exercice des droits à rémunération et laissent cette question à la discrétion des parties contractantes[63].

La vaste majorité des pays couverts par les rapports nationaux ont recours à des **systèmes de gestion collective** pour assurer la mise en œuvre effective des droits à rémunération[64]. Certains textes de l'UE prévoient même explicitement la possibilité de confier l'exercice des droits à rémunération à des organismes de gestion collective (art. 6.2 de la directive relative au droit de suite[65] et art. 5.4 de la directive relative au droit de location et de prêt[66]). Le recours à la gestion collective des droits est souvent dicté par la difficulté pratique de l'exercice individuel des droits à rémunération[67].

62 Rapport national Norvège, p. 11–12.

63 Les traités parlent parfois de l'intervention de « l'autorité compétente » dans la définition des tarifs (p. ex. les articles 11*bis*.2 et 13.1 de la Convention de Berne) ou d'autres modalités, mais les Etats contractants jouissent en général d'une grande liberté pour décider des conditions d'exercice des droits à rémunération.

64 Certains rapports ne permettent pas d'affirmer avec certitude que tous les droits à rémunération font l'objet d'une gestion collective.

65 « Les Etats membres peuvent prévoir la gestion collective obligatoire ou facultative du droit... ». Le Royaume-Uni a prévu l'exercice obligatoire du droit de suite par des OGC (art. 14 du règlement de 2006 sur le droit de suite, *Artist's Resale Right Regulation 2006 No. 346* ; rapport national Royaume-Uni, p. 12), tandis qu'en Autriche, le droit de suite est le seul droit à rémunération qui n'est pas soumis à un régime de gestion collective obligatoire (art. 16b de la loi autrichienne sur le droit d'auteur ; rapport national Autriche, p. 8). Des OGC qui assurent la gestion du droit de suite sont actifs dans la majorité des pays de l'Espace économique européen, EVA, Members & Observers: http://www.evartists.org/en/members-observers.html (dernière visite en octobre 2016).

66 « Les Etats membres peuvent réglementer la question de savoir si, et dans quelle mesure, la gestion par les sociétés de gestion collective du droit d'obtenir une rémunération équitable [pour la location] peut être imposée ». Sylvie Nérisson (2014), « The Rental and Lending Rights Directive », *in* Irini Stamatoudi et Paul Torremans (dir.), *EU Copyright Law: A Commentary*, Cheltenham, Royaume-Uni/ Northampton, MA, Etats-Unis : Edward Elgar, p. 176.

67 Mihály Ficsor (2002), *Gestion collective du droit d'auteur et des droits voisins/Collective Management of Copyright and Related Rights*, Publication OMPI n° 855, p. 137–138, et Tarja

Dans certains pays, tous les droits à rémunération sont soumis à la **gestion collective obligatoire** (p. ex. en Finlande, en Norvège et en Suisse)[68]. Tous les pays visés par les rapports ont recours à ce mécanisme légal pour la gestion d'au moins un droit à rémunération (sauf l'Egypte, semble-t-il[69]). Ce mécanisme de gestion collective non volontaire permet de résoudre le problème des personnes « extérieures », c'est-à-dire des titulaires de droits non membres d'un organisme de gestion collective. Les OGC qui gèrent des droits en application d'une présomption légale permettant la gestion collective obligatoire sont obligés d'accorder aux membres et aux non-membres un traitement égal. Ajoutons que des règles destinées à assurer la bonne gouvernance des OGC revêtent une importance particulière dans le cas des régimes de gestion collective obligatoire[70].

4. Contrôle des tarifs et des organismes de gestion collective

Les approches nationales retenues pour le contrôle des tarifs afférents aux droits à rémunération et des OGC qui les gèrent sont d'une grande diversité. De plus, l'exercice des droits à rémunération est souvent encadré de manière différente selon les droits au sein d'un même pays. Comme pratiquement tous les droits à rémunération font l'objet d'une gestion collective (et, pour beaucoup d'entre eux, d'une gestion collective obligatoire), le contrôle des OGC peut souvent être assimilé au contrôle de l'exercice de ces droits.

Dans certains pays, il n'existe **aucun mécanisme particulier de contrôle des tarifs** dans les cas où ils ne sont pas fixés par le gouvernement (p. ex. en Grèce[71]), alors que dans d'autres pays a été mis en place un contrôle général des OGC assuré soit par un organe gouvernemental compétent dans le domaine visé

Koskinen-Olsson (2014), *Study on Collective Negotiation of Rights and Collective Management of Rights in the Audiovisual Sector*, Doc. OMPI n° CDIP/14/INF/2, p. 18.

68 Rapport national Finlande, p. 6. Rapport national Norvège, p. 14–15, et rapport national Suisse, p. 5.

69 Le rapport précise que la gestion collective du droit d'auteur n'est pas très développée dans des domaines autres que celui des droits musicaux, sans indiquer explicitement si des droits à rémunération sont gérés collectivement. Rapport national Egypte, p. 9. Pour un bref aperçu de la gestion collective obligatoire des droits à rémunération dans les Etats membres de l'UE, voir KEA European Affairs (2006), *La gestion collective des droits en Europe : La quête de l'efficacité*, étude menée à la demande de la Commission des affaires juridiques du Parlement européen, IP/C/JURI/ST/2005-90, p. 88–96.

70 Christophe Geiger (2007), « Le rôle du test des trois étapes dans l'adaptation du droit d'auteur à la société de l'information »/« The Role of the Three-Step Test in the Adaptation of Copyright Law to the Information Society », *e-Bulletin du droit d'auteur/e-Copyright Bulletin*, UNESCO, janv.–mars 2007, p. 12.

71 Rapport national Grèce, p. 13.

(p. ex. en Autriche[72], en Finlande[73] et aux Pays-Bas[74]), soit par application du droit de la concurrence (législation antitrust) (p. ex. en Italie[75]).

La plupart des pays faisant l'objet des rapports nationaux prévoient des **règles particulières établissant des procédures de fixation des tarifs**. Le contrôle ou la définition des tarifs est généralement assuré par l'entremise des Offices de la propriété intellectuelle, des organes d'Etat intervenant dans le domaine de la politique culturelle ou d'autres organismes ayant compétence pour approuver les tarifs librement négociés ou pour les fixer si aucun accord n'a pu être conclu par voie de négociation (p. ex. en Croatie[76], en Hongrie[77], au Japon[78] et en Suisse[79]). Quelques pays disposent de tribunaux permanents du droit d'auteur compétents pour fixer les tarifs et/ou pour régler les différends relatifs aux tarifs (p. ex. la Commission du droit d'auteur du Canada[80], le *Copyright Tribunal* du Royaume-Uni[81] et le *Copyright Royalty Board* des Etats-Unis[82])[83]. Parmi les pays qui encadrent la procédure de définition des tarifs et qui disposent d'organes d'Etat compétents en la matière, certains soumettent également les OGC aux restrictions imposées par les règles de concurrence afin de prévenir d'éventuels abus de position dominante (p. ex. en Allemagne[84] et en Norvège[85]).

---

72 En Autriche, un contrôle général des OGC est assuré par une autorité spéciale (*Aufsichtsbehörde für Verwertungsgesellschaften*) avec le ministère fédéral de la justice (*Bundesministerium für Justiz*). Rapport national Autriche, p. 10.

73 Il s'agit du ministère de l'éducation et de la culture en Finlande. Rapport national Finlande, p. 7.

74 Une loi a créé une commission de surveillance qui contrôle l'activité de tous les OGC : *Wet toezicht en geschillenbeslechting collectieve beheersorganisaties auteurs- en naburige rechten*, Stb. 2013/179. Rapport national Pays-Bas, p. 16.

75 Rapport national Italie, p. 11.

76 Rapport national Croatie, p. 13–14.

77 Article 92/H de la loi hongroise sur le droit d'auteur. Rapport national Hongrie, p. 9 et 15.

78 Article 69 de la loi japonaise sur le droit d'auteur. Rapport national Japon, p. 7–8.

79 Rapport national Suisse, p. 5–6.

80 Rapport national Canada, p. 9. Pour une analyse du fonctionnement de la Commission, voir Daniel J. Gervais (2008), « A Uniquely Canadian Institution: The Copyright Board of Canada », *in* Ysolde Gendreau (dir.), *An Emerging Intellectual Property Paradigm: Perspectives from Canada*, Cheltenham, Royaume-Uni : Edward Elgar, p. 197–223.

81 Article 149 du *Copyright, Designs and Patents Act 1988* c. 48. Rapport national Royaume-Uni, p. 11–13.

82 Le *Copyright Royalty and Distribution Reform Act* de 2004 (P.L. 108-419), 30 novembre 2004, et le *Copyright Royalty Judges Program Technical Corrections Act* (P.L. 109-303), 6 octobre 2006. Rapport national Etats-Unis, p. 9–10.

83 Pour un aperçu des différents modèles, voir Michael J. Freegard (1994), « Quis Custodiet ? The role of copyright tribunals », *EIPR*, vol. 16, n° 7, p. 286–292.

84 Articles 13 et 18.2 de la loi sur la gestion du droit d'auteur et des droits voisins. L'Office fédéral des cartels doit agir en accord avec l'Office des brevets et des marques. Rapport national Allemagne, p. 18.

85 Rapport national Norvège, p. 18–19.

Dans d'autres pays encore, les **tarifs sont fixés par la loi** (p. ex. pour la copie privée au Portugal[86] et en Grèce[87]) ou par un **autre acte normatif** d'une autorité étatique (p. ex. les tarifs pour le prêt public et la copie privée sont définis par des décrets ministériels aux Pays-Bas[88]).

Certains pays ne disposent d'**aucun encadrement législatif des activités des OGC** (p. ex. en Egypte et dans la plupart des pays arabes à l'exception de Djibouti, du Liban, du Maroc et de la Tunisie[89]). Même si le Royaume-Uni fait également partie des pays qui n'ont pas de réglementation spécifique de la gestion collective des droits à rémunération, les OGC de ce pays ont eux-mêmes élaboré un système de **normes d'autoréglementation** (p. ex. sous forme de codes de conduite[90]) et le gouvernement conserve le pouvoir d'intervenir[91]. En plus des instruments non législatifs nationaux tels que les codes de conduite régissant l'activité des OGC, il existe également des règles internationales établies par des associations d'OGC ou d'ayants droit[92]. Les OGC qui souhaitent adhérer à ces organisations internationales doivent se conformer aux prescriptions de ces instruments, et ce indépendamment de l'existence de normes particulières prévues par la législation nationale.

Comparativement, l'existence d'un **système strict de surveillance et de contrôle** des activités des OGC peut être observée dans certains pays européens. La Belgique en offre un exemple notable puisque deux instances spéciales sont chargées de la surveillance des divers aspects de la gestion collective, allant de la perception de la rémunération jusqu'à sa répartition[93]. La loi plafonne à 15% le taux maximal que les OGC peuvent retenir sur les droits perçus pour couvrir

---

86 Rapport national Portugal, p. 7.

87 Rapport national Grèce, p. 13.

88 Rapport national Pays-Bas, p. 15.

89 Rapport national Egypte, p. 9.

90 *Principles of CMOs' Codes of Conduct* du 25 mai 2012 élaborés par le British Copyright Council. Pour un aperçu de l'approche britannique et d'autres approches fondées sur l'autoréglementation, notamment le code de conduite australien pour les sociétés de gestion collective, voir BOP Consulting, Benedict Atkinson et Brian Fitzgerald (2012), *Collecting Societies Codes of Conduct*, Rapport établi à la demande de l'Office de la propriété intellectuelle du Royaume-Uni.

91 *Copyright (Regulation of Relevant Licensing Bodies) Regulations 2014, No. 898.* Rapport national Royaume-Uni, p. 13–14. A ce jour, le gouvernement n'a pas usé de ses pouvoirs.

92 Règles professionnelles de la CISAC applicables aux sociétés musicales du 6 juin 2014, SG13-0787R2, Règles professionnelles de la CISAC applicables aux sociétés dramatiques, littéraires et audiovisuelles du 6 juin 2013, SG13-0788, Règles professionnelles de la CISAC applicables aux sociétés des arts graphiques, plastiques et photographiques du 6 juin 2013, SG13-0789, IFPI Code of Conduct for Music Industry Music Licensing Companies, version de janvier 2014, IFRRO Code of Conduct – Reproduction Rights Organisations, révisé le 20 septembre 2007.

93 Service de régulation du droit d'auteur et des droits voisins (articles XI.274–XI.278 du Code de droit économique belge) et Service de contrôle des sociétés de gestion des droits (articles XI.279–XI.283 du Code de droit économique belge).

leurs frais de gestion. Le plus récent des deux services constitue un cas unique en étant financé par un prélèvement de 0,2% sur le chiffre d'affaires des OGC[94].

Par ailleurs, la plupart des pays de l'EEE sont actuellement en train de transposer dans leur droit national les dispositions de la directive de l'UE sur la gestion collective qui institue de nombreuses règles de bonne gouvernance et de transparence[95]. Dans la mesure où il s'agit de l'instrument le plus volumineux sur le droit d'auteur dans le marché commun, cette directive nécessite d'apporter d'importantes modifications à la législation nationale des différents Etats membres. Il est intéressant de constater que certains Etats membres de l'UE sont allés encore plus loin sur certains aspects lors de la transposition de cet instrument. Ainsi, en avril 2015, lorsque le Portugal a adopté une loi destinée à mettre en œuvre les dispositions de la directive relatives au contrôle et à la responsabilité des OGC, y ont été ajoutées certaines règles supplémentaires portant sur les calendriers et les procédures de négociation, la définition des tarifs et l'octroi des licences[96]. Indépendamment de la réglementation nationale, les OGC qui exercent leur activité dans un pays de l'EEE sont également soumis **au contrôle supranational** de la Commission européenne dans le domaine du droit de la concurrence[97].

5. Qui doit payer la rémunération ?

Ceux qui doivent payer la rémunération peuvent être classés en trois grandes catégories :

- **Utilisateurs** (p. ex. dans le cas de la communication au public de phonogrammes du commerce) ;

---

94 Rapport national Belgique, p. 14–17.

95 Directive 2014/26/UE du Parlement européen et du Conseil du 26 février 2014 concernant la gestion collective du droit d'auteur et des droits voisins et l'octroi de licences multiterritoriales de droits sur des œuvres musicales en vue de leur utilisation en ligne dans le marché intérieur (Texte présentant de l'intérêt pour l'EEE) [2014] JO L 84/72. Date limite de transposition : 10 avril 2016 (article 43). Pour un commentaire, voir Lucie Guibault (2014), « Collective Rights Management Directive », *in* Irini Stamatoudi et Paul Torremans (dir.), *EU Copyright Law: A Commentary*, Cheltenham, Royaume-Uni/ Northampton, MA, Etats-Unis : Edward Elgar, p. 696–795.

96 Loi 26/2015 du14 avril 2015 relative aux organismes de gestion collective. Rapport national Portugal, p. 9–11.

97 Par exemple, la Communication de la Commission européenne publiée conformément à l'article 27.4 du Règlement (CE) n° 1/2003 du Conseil dans les affaires COMP/C2/39152 – BUMA et COMP/C2/39151 – SABAM (accord de Santiago – COMP/C2/38126), JO C 200/11, 17 août 2005, et décision de la Commission européenne du 8 octobre 2002 (affaire n° COMP/C2/38.014 – IFPI « Simulcasting »), JO L 107/58, 30 avril 2003.

- **Intermédiaires** (p. ex. les importateurs, fabricants et/ou distributeurs dans le cas de la copie privée, ou les entités qui mettent à disposition des appareils permettant la reproduction par reprographie) ;
- **Budget de l'état** (p. ex. la rémunération pour copie privée en Finlande[98], en Israël[99] et en Espagne[100]).

D'une manière générale, on peut dire que les **contribuables** sont ceux qui paient en bout de ligne les rémunérations versées par les institutions utilisatrices financées par des fonds publics (p. ex. la rémunération pour le prêt public est assurée par des transferts à partir du budget de l'état en Autriche[101], en Croatie[102] et en Italie[103]). Parmi les pays faisant l'objet des rapports, seule la Norvège rémunère sur les fonds publics à la fois la copie privée, le prêt public et aussi l'exposition publique d'exemplaires d'œuvres d'art et d'artisanat d'art[104].

---

98 Article 26a.1 de la loi finlandaise sur le droit d'auteur. Rapport national Finlande, p. 6. Ce mécanisme de compensation financée sur le budget de l'Etat a été mis en place fin 2014 et est entré en vigueur le 1er janvier 2015 en vertu de la *Laki tekijänoikeuslain muuttamisesta* 19.12.2014/1171.

99 Rapport national Israël, p. 5.

100 Article 25.1 de la loi espagnole sur la propriété intellectuelle (*Real decreto legislativo 1/1996, de 12 de abril, por el que se aprueba el texto refundido de la Ley de propiedad intelectual, regularizando, aclarando y armonizando las disposiciones legales vigentes sobre la materia, BOE, n. 97, 22 de abril 1996*, p. 14369–14396, modifiée par la *Ley N° 21/2014, de 4 de noviembre, por la que se modifica el texto refundido de la Ley de Propiedad Intelectual, aprobado por Real Decreto Legislativo 1/1996, de 12 de abril, y la Ley 1/2000, de 7 de enero, de Enjuiciamiento Civil., BOE n. 268, p. 90404–90439*). Rapport national Espagne, p. 31–32. La compatibilité avec l'article 5.2 de la directive sur la société de l'information du système selon lequel la compensation pour copie privée est versée aux ayants droit au moyen d'une allocation annuelle du budget de l'Etat a été contestée par les ayants droit devant la CJUE. Dans son arrêt du 9 juin 2016, la Cour a condamné le mécanisme espagnol, voir EGEDA e.a., C-470/14, EU:C:2016:418. Sur cette affaire, voir I. Garrote, plus loin dans le présent volume.

101 Une somme forfaitaire payée par le gouvernement autrichien. Rapport national Autriche, p. 9 : elle « devrait être acquittée par les bibliothèques mais, dans la pratique, elle est versée par l'Etat sur le budget général ».

102 « Le ministère de la culture, par des ressources allouées sur le budget public, aide les bibliothèques à remplir leur obligation de verser la rémunération ». Rapport national Croatie, p. 13.

103 Rapport national Italie, p. 11.

104 Rapport national Norvège, p. 16. Le « système norvégien » de rémunération des créateurs par des revenus de taxation répartis par des fonds spéciaux, qui coexiste avec la législation plus traditionnelle en matière de droit d'auteur, a été mis en place vers le milieu du XXème siècle, Birger Stuevold Lassen (1963), « Collectivism and Individual Rights in Norwegian Copyright Law », *Scandinavian Studies in Law*, vol. 7, p. 83, et Tarja Koskinen-Olsson (2010), « Collective Management in Nordic Countries », *in* Daniel J. Gervais (dir.), *Collective Management of Copyright and Related Rights*, 2ème éd., Alphen aan den Rijn, Pays-Bas : Kluwer Law International, p. 288.

6. Problèmes pour faire valoir les droits à rémunération

La plupart des rapports nationaux indiquent que la **longueur de la procédure de fixation des tarifs** (p. ex. négociations, règlement des différends) constitue un problème important pour faire valoir les droits à rémunération. Ainsi, en Suisse, si les parties aux négociations ne parviennent pas à un accord, la Commission arbitrale fédérale pour la gestion de droits d'auteur et de droits voisins doit intervenir pour les définir. La décision de la Commission arbitrale peut faire l'objet d'un recours devant le Tribunal administratif fédéral puis devant le Tribunal fédéral[105]. On rapporte que ce processus peut prendre des années. En général, les rapports sont nombreux à exprimer une insatisfaction à l'égard de la **lenteur des procédures judiciaires** portant sur la perception de la rémunération, la définition des tarifs et d'autres questions connexes (p. ex. en Argentine[106], en Autriche[107] et au Mexique[108]). Des **décisions judiciaires incohérentes** posent un problème supplémentaire dans certains pays (p. ex. en Croatie[109]).

Presque tous les rapports mentionnent directement ou indirectement la **forte opposition des redevables** (p. ex. les fabricants et importateurs de dispositifs assujettis à la redevance ou leurs associations). Les **interprétations divergentes** de certaines dispositions générales de la loi, s'agissant notamment du champ d'application des droits légaux à rémunération, sont une source de problèmes. Certains rapports relèvent que des situations où l'utilisateur cesse son activité avant d'avoir versé une quelconque rémunération sont fréquentes[110]. Il est précisé également que le **décalage** entre le moment où la rémunération est perçue par l'OGC et le moment où elle est réclamée par l'ayant droit peut créer des problèmes de répartition[111]. Dans certains cas, les montants dus par l'utilisateur sont moindres que les **frais d'une procédure judiciaire** et restent donc impayés (p. ex. au Canada[112]).

Les tarifs sont parfois fixés proportionnellement aux revenus que l'utilisateur tire de l'activité donnant lieu à l'obligation de verser une rémunération aux titulaires de droits et parfois fixés forfaitairement (souvent désignés comme des « montants minimaux »)[113]. Lorsque les tarifs sont établis par un organe gouvernemental ou par la loi, ils ont une plus grande légitimité et soulèvent moins de contestations. Les tarifs fixés forfaitairement, s'ils ne sont pas revalorisés avec

---

105 Rapport national Suisse, p. 5–6.
106 Rapport national Argentine, p. 7.
107 Rapport national Autriche, p. 11.
108 Rapport national Mexique, p. 7.
109 Rapport national Croatie, p. 15.
110 Rapports nationaux Croatie, p. 15, et Etats-Unis, p. 10.
111 Rapport national Finlande, p. 7.
112 Rapport national Canada, p. 9.
113 Rapport national Argentine, p. 7.

une fréquence qui suit l'évolution de la conjoncture économique du pays, risquent davantage de devenir obsolètes que les tarifs qui sont fixés sous forme de pourcentage des revenus. En général, les **tarifs fixés par la loi** sont encore plus **difficiles à modifier** que ceux fixés par une autorité administrative. Ainsi, au Portugal où les montants précis dus pour la copie privée sont définis par la loi, il a fallu plus de trois ans pour achever la préparation et l'examen du texte devenu la loi sur la copie privée qui élargit le champ d'application du système de rémunération aux dispositifs de stockage numérique[114].

En ce qui concerne le **droit à une rémunération équitable auquel il ne peut être renoncé au titre de la location**, il a été rapporté que lorsque ce droit n'est pas géré par un OGC chargé d'en assurer l'exercice, il arrive parfois que les auteurs et artistes interprètes ne reçoivent plus de rémunération après un premier paiement en contrepartie de la cession du droit de location[115].

Une rémunération payée sur le budget de l'état (p. ex. pour la copie privée), tout en épargnant aux titulaires de droits ou aux OGC des relations complexes avec de nombreux débiteurs, présente des inconvénients. Ainsi, les OGC peuvent être obligés de définir des tarifs dans les limites fixées expressément pour cette rémunération (p. ex. le prêt public en Hongrie[116]). En Espagne, où la perception de la rémunération pour copie privée auprès des intermédiaires a été remplacée par son financement sur le budget général de l'Etat, le changement de système a été préjudiciable aux intérêts des créateurs et autres ayants droit en raison du **manque de fonds publics**[117].

7. Solutions aux problèmes liés au recouvrement de la rémunération

Au nombre des dispositions législatives qui ont pour objet la communication aux titulaires de droits des informations nécessaires pour faire valoir leurs droits figure souvent l'obligation faite aux utilisateurs et aux intermédiaires de **déclarer les utilisations**. En plus de cette **obligation** courante, certains pays prévoient que les OGC **peuvent obtenir les renseignements nécessaires** à l'exercice de leur mission auprès de l'administration des douanes ou de

114 Rapport national Portugal, p. 7–8. Sur la question de la définition des appareils et supports assujettis à la redevance et des tarifs appliqués, voir l'enquête de l'IFRRO et de l'OMPI (2014), *International Survey on Text and Image Copyright Levies 2014*, WIPO Publication No. 1042E, p. 16.

115 Rapport national Pays-Bas, p. 11.

116 Article 23/A de la loi hongroise sur le droit d'auteur. Rapport national Hongrie, p. 10–11.

117 Enquête de la Stichting de Thuiskopie et de l'OMPI (2016), *International Survey on Private Copying: Law and Practice 2015*, WIPO Publication No. 1037E/16, p. 14.

l'administration de la TVA (p. ex. en Belgique[118]). En Grèce, si un OGC chargé de la gestion de la rémunération pour copie privée a des doutes à propos des déclarations fournies par des importateurs ou fabricants des dispositifs assujettis à la rémunération, il a le droit de demander à un comptable agréé de les vérifier[119].

Un autre outil législatif utilisé pour parer au problème du recouvrement de la rémunération consiste à accorder aux titulaires de droits la faculté d'exiger des utilisateurs (par l'intermédiaire d'un juge) un **dépôt de sécurité** pour garantir des obligations futures (p. ex. en Hongrie[120] et en Finlande[121]). Au Japon, lors de l'exploitation d'œuvres protégées dans le cadre d'une licence obligatoire, un montant égal au taux normal de rémunération doit être déposé auprès du Commissaire de l'Agence des affaires culturelles qui fixe le taux[122]. Dans cet exemple japonais, c'est la loi qui prévoit l'obligation de procéder à un dépôt de sécurité comme condition préalable à une exploitation licite.

La législation de nombreux pays prévoit également que les OGC ont qualité pour demander une **injonction** en vue de faire cesser l'utilisation d'œuvres protégées ou de faire exécuter un jugement (p. ex. en Argentine[123], en Finlande[124], au Mexique[125] et en Norvège[126]).

La législation néerlandaise accorde aux OGC et à ceux qui doivent payer la possibilité de soumettre à l'**arbitrage** les litiges d'un montant inférieur à 100.000 euros. Les décisions arbitrales s'imposent aux parties si l'affaire n'est pas portée ensuite devant la justice[127].

En Belgique où le droit de suite est géré par plusieurs OGC, le législateur a imposé la création d'une **plateforme unique** administrée par les OGC pour rationaliser la perception de la rémunération[128]. Les OGC qui exercent leur activité dans d'autres domaines ont choisi volontairement de créer des **sociétés « cou-**

118 Article XI.230 du Code de droit économique belge. Rapport national Belgique, p. 17.
119 Rapport national Grèce, p. 13.
120 Rapport national Hongrie, p. 14.
121 Article 54b de la loi finlandaise sur le droit d'auteur. Rapport national Finlande, p. 7.
122 Articles 67.1, 67*bis*, 68.1 et 69 de la loi japonaise sur le droit d'auteur. Rapport national Japon, p. 7–8.
123 Rapport national Argentine, p. 8.
124 Article 54b de la loi finlandaise sur le droit d'auteur. Rapport national Finlande, p. 7.
125 Rapport national Mexique, p. 7.
126 Article 38b de la loi norvégienne sur le droit d'auteur. Rapport national Norvège, p. 8.
127 Articles 3, 23 et 25 de la *Wet toezicht en geschillenbeslechting collectieve beheersorganisaties auteurs- en naburige rechten*, Stb. 2013/179. Rapport national Pays-Bas, p. 16.
128 Article XI.177 du Code de droit économique belge. Arrêté royal fixant les conditions et les modalités de gestion du droit de suite visée aux articles XI.177 et XI.178 du Code de droit économique, 11 juin 2015. Rapport national Belgique, p. 11. Une solution semblable a été retenue pour la gestion collective du droit à rémunération reconnu aux auteurs et aux artistes interprètes ou exécutants et auquel ils ne peuvent pas renoncer au titre de la retransmission par câble des œuvres audiovisuelles (art. XI.225).

poles ». Dans le cas des pays où il existe une pluralité d'OGC dans le même domaine, la mise en place d'une structure de regroupement peut en effet faciliter les relations avec les utilisateurs et éviter le risque de confusion chez les utilisateurs tout en réduisant les coûts[129].

Les OGC qui gèrent des droits à rémunération représentent souvent non seulement leurs propres membres mais également des non-membres. Pour veiller à ce que suffisamment de ressources soient conservées après la répartition de la rémunération aux membres, le législateur peut **obliger les OGC à mettre en réserve une certaine somme en cas de réclamation de la part d'ayants droit non membres.** En Belgique, l'OGC qui gère le droit à rémunération pour copie privée (AUVIBEL) prévoit une telle réserve sur une base volontaire[130].

Pour éviter le problème de l'obsolescence progressive des tarifs fixés par un texte législatif tout en bénéficiant de la légitimité des tarifs établis par une autorité étatique, au Canada, par exemple, la Commission du droit d'auteur **définit les tarifs pour une période** de 1 à 5 ans à l'issue de laquelle les parties intéressées doivent recommencer le processus d'homologation[131].

III. Conclusions

Le présent chapitre tente de faire la synthèse des diverses approches nationales. Cette entreprise a mis en évidence quelques difficultés terminologiques liées à l'emploi de termes différents pour désigner des droits patrimoniaux distincts des droits exclusifs. Ces difficultés semblent se rapporter à une conception plutôt dualiste du système international du droit d'auteur, considéré comme étant composé d'un côté des droits exclusifs et de l'autre des limitations et exceptions à ces droits. Le présent chapitre présente une optique plus nuancée, selon laquelle les droits légaux à rémunération constituent une catégorie de droits pécuniaires se répartissant en trois grands groupes : les droits à rémunération proprement dits (des droits patrimoniaux distincts des droits exclusifs mais qui ne constituent pas des exceptions ou limitations), les droits à rémunération liés à des limitations/exceptions (des droits patrimoniaux créés pour rémunérer des utilisations faisant l'objet de limitations ou d'exceptions aux droits exclusifs) et les droits à rémunération « résiduels » (des droits patrimoniaux créés dans le cadre des droits exclusifs en imposant l'impossibilité de renoncer à l'aspect pécuniaire des droits).

---

129 Mihály Ficsor (2002), *Gestion collective du droit d'auteur et des droits voisins/Collective Management of Copyright and Related Rights*, Publication OMPI n° 855, p. 135.

130 Rapport national Belgique, p. 10.

131 Rapport national Canada, p. 9.

Comme nous l'avons vu, des droits légaux à rémunération existent dans tous les pays examinés mais leur champ d'application peut être différent selon les lois et traditions nationales, et les instruments de mise en œuvre de ces droits peuvent être plus ou moins réussis, surtout selon l'efficacité de l'organisme de gestion collective qui perçoit la rémunération au niveau national. Ce constat est intéressant pour l'analyse de la question initiale du congrès de l'ALAI concernant la concurrence éventuelle entre les différents mécanismes juridiques (exclusivité c. autres approches) et le modèle à adopter. Ce n'est pas en s'appuyant sur des fondements dogmatiques qu'on peut y apporter une réponse mais en analysant l'efficacité du modèle proposé pour déterminer si les objectifs de la disposition légale sont réalisés. De ce point de vue pragmatique, il y a évidemment une donnée essentielle qui est absente dans tous les rapports, à savoir le montant effectivement versé aux auteurs, c'est-à-dire combien les créateurs gagnent selon les systèmes[132]. On peut facilement prédire que les réponses seraient très différentes en fonction des auteurs considérés (p. ex. selon leur degré de succès et leur pouvoir de négocier une juste rémunération). Ce qui est un argument de plus en faveur d'une diversité de modèles. Un certain nombre d'études ont certes été réalisées sur la rémunération générée par le droit à rémunération liée à l'exception de copie privée, mais ces études mériteraient d'être complétées, notamment pour déterminer le montant exact réparti aux auteurs[133]. Il est évidemment important d'éviter toute généralisation. D'une part, la situation des créateurs entre eux peut être très diverse et il est sans doute nécessaire de distinguer les créateurs salariés pour qui cette rémunération constitue un supplément de revenu – bienvenu mais certainement pas indispensable à leur activité de création – des créateurs qui comptent sur le système pour vivre. D'autre part, il convient sans doute de faire une autre distinction en fonction de

132 C'est un élément paradoxal et malheureusement caractéristique de bon nombre de débats sur le droit d'auteur qui abordent des questions politiques d'actualité relatives à la rémunération des créateurs sans chiffrer la rémunération qu'ils perçoivent.

133 Selon l'enquête de la Stichting de Thuiskopie et de l'OMPI (2016), *International Survey on Private Copying: Law and Practice 2015*, WIPO Publication No. 1037E/16, qui présente des données relatives aux systèmes de copie privée de plus de 25 pays, « le montant total des revenus est passé au fil des ans de 598 millions d'euros en 2007 à son niveau record de 804 millions d'euros en 2014 », p. 13–15 et 22. Selon l'enquête de l'IFRRO et de l'OMPI (2015), *International Survey on Text and Image Copyright Levies: 2015 Edition*, WIPO Publication No. 1042E/16, il est estimé que le montant de la rémunération perçue dans le monde au titre du droit d'auteur sur les œuvres textuelles et visuelles s'est élevé à 179 millions d'euros en 2014 (p. 5 et 24). Voir également Martin Kretschmer (2011), *Private Copying and Fair Compensation: An empirical study of copyright levies in Europe*, UK Intellectual Property Office, p. 7 : « A la suite de la directive de 2001, le montant total des redevances perçues sur les supports et appareils d'enregistrement dans l'UE a triplé, passant d'environ 170 M€ à plus de 500 M€ par an. Des systèmes de redevance existent désormais dans 22 des 27 Etats membres (seuls le Royaume-Uni, l'Irlande, Malte, Chypre et le Luxembourg restent en dehors) ».

l'efficacité du système de gestion collective mis en place au niveau national[134]. Si l'on veut assurer l'effectivité des droits à rémunération, il faut qu'il y ait des organismes de gestion collective qui fonctionnent bien. Cette conclusion encouragera peut-être les législateurs à mener plus souvent à l'avenir des études empiriques pour évaluer l'impact économique des différentes configurations[135]. Mais se poseront alors des questions beaucoup plus fondamentales dans le domaine du droit d'auteur : Le système vise-t-il à protéger *tous* les auteurs de façon égale ou uniquement ceux qui jouissent d'un important succès commercial ? Quelle fonction doit être accordée à la notion de justice redistributive dans le domaine du droit d'auteur[136] ? Comment opérer une distinction efficace dans la législation entre la protection des investisseurs et la protection des créateurs ? Ce sont des questions fascinantes mais complexes, dont l'examen nécessiterait sans doute un autre congrès de l'ALAI.

134 Pour une tentative économique notable d'évaluation et de comparaison de l'efficacité des OGC de divers pays, voir Fabrice Rochelandet (2003), « Are Copyright Collecting Societies Efficient Organisations? An Evaluation of collective Administration of Copyright in Europe », *in* Wendy J. Gordon et Richard Watt (dir.), *The Economics of Copyright: Developments in Research and Analysis*, Cheltenham, Royaume-Uni / Northampton, MA, Etats-Unis : Edward Elgar, p. 176–197.

135 Voir, plaidant pour davantage d'actions législatives fondées sur des données concrètes dans l'UE, Christophe Geiger (2016), « Moving out of the Economic Crisis: what Role and Shape for Intellectual Property Rights in the European Union? », *in* Harri Kalimo et Max S. Jansson (dir.), *EU Economic Law in a Time of Crisis*, Cheltenham, Royaume-Uni / Northampton, MA, Etats-Unis : Edward Elgar, p. 135.

136 Voir sur cette question Christophe Geiger (2013), « The Social Function of Intellectual Property Rights, Or how Ethics can Influence the Shape and Use of IP Law », *in* Graeme B. Dinwoodie (dir.), *Methods and Perspectives in Intellectual Property*, Cheltenham, Royaume-Uni/ Northampton, MA, Etats-Unis : Edward Elgar, p. 153–176.

Christophe Geiger y Oleksandr Bulayenko*

2.2 Informe general: Ámbito y mecanismos de ejecución para asegurar la remuneración

Introducción

El Congreso de ALAI tuvo por objeto reflexionar acerca de los modelos jurídicos existentes para asegurar el pago de la remuneración por el uso de obras protegidas por derechos de autor. Con esta finalidad, se identificaron dos mecanismos, es decir, los derechos exclusivos y los derechos de remuneración establecidos en la ley ("*statutory rights to remuneration*"). De esta manera, se ha invitado a las personas que participaron en la conferencia – y que, por lo tanto, han contribuido en este volumen– a realizar una especie de auditoría de los « diversos mecanismos existentes para obtener la consecución de una remuneración equitativa ». Este informe general tiene por objeto los derechos de remuneración establecidos en la ley, su ambito y mecanismos de ejecución para asegurar la remuneración.

No debe sorprender la elección de este tema sobre los derechos de remuneración establecidos en la ley para su debate con motivo de la celebración de los 50 años de la Ley de Propiedad intelectual alemana. Esta Ley, a pesar de centrarse claramente en el autor (la Ley se titula "Urheberrechtsgesetz", que puede traducirse como "Ley sobre derechos del autor"), incluye nada menos que 9 limitaciones y excepciones que se establecen con la posibilidad de remuneración justa para el autor,[1] junto con lo que el Informe alemán denomina

---

* Christophe Geiger es Catedrático de Derecho, Director General y Director del Departamento de Investigación de CEIPI, Investigador Superior Afiliado del Max Planck Institute for Innovation and Competition en Múnich (Alemania) y Spangenberg Fellow en el Spangenberg Center for Law, Technology & the Arts, Case Western Reserve University School of Law en Cleveland (EE.UU); Oleksandr Bulayenko es Investigador y está realizando su doctorado en CEIPI. Este capítulo se basa fundamentalmente en las respuestas recibidas al cuestionario enviado para este Congreso de ALAI, centrándose especialmente en la Parte C del cuestionario "*Questions in relation to statutory remuneration rights*". Los informes nacionales abarcan el ordenamiento jurídico y la práctica de 22 países (Alemania, Argentina, Austria, Bélgica, Canadá, Croacia, Egipto, España, Estados Unidos, Finlandia, Francia, Grecia, Hungría, Israel, Italia, Japón, México, Noruega, Países Bajos, Portugal, Reino Unido y Suiza). Están disponibles en: http://www.alai2015.org/en/national-reports.html (página visitada por última vez en enero de 2016). Traducción del inglés por Cristina Perpiña-Robert.

1 Informe nacional de Alemania, págs. 15–16.

los "otros de-rechos de autor", tales como el derecho de participación, los derechos de alquiler y préstamo y el derecho de retransmisión por cable.[2] Por consiguiente, no es casualidad que el Tribunal Supremo alemán, en una destacada sentencia de 11 de Julio de 2002, justificase la extensión de la excepción tradicional para resúmenes de prensa a los resúmenes de prensa digitales, basándose en la protección del interés del autor a recibir una remuneración.[3]

Antes de entrar en los análisis de los distintos planteamientos nacionales en relación con los derechos de remuneración establecidos obligatorios o establecidos en la ley ["*statutory remuneration rights*"] (II.),[4] abordaremos en primer lugar algunos problemas de terminología (I.).

I. Derechos de remuneración establecidos en la ley/obligatorios ("*Statutory remuneration rights*"): Problemas de terminología

Sin duda, una de las cuestiones más delicadas dentro del marco de este informe general es la terminología. De hecho, los informes nacionales utilizaban a veces determinadas expresiones como si fuesen sinónimos, a pesar de que estas pudiesen tener consecuencias muy diferentes en el ámbito jurídico.

Mientras que, por ejemplo, a primera vista, conceptos como "derechos de remuneración establecidos en la ley/obligatorios" ["*statutory remuneration rights*"], "licencias obligatorias" ["*compulsory licenses*"] y algunos términos similares pudiesen parecer tener el mismo significado, su interpretación está

2 *Ibid.* p. 15.

3 El Tribunal, citando el artículo 49(1) de la Ley de Propiedad intelectual (que establece una licencia obligatoria por el uso de artículos que son parte de los resúmenes de prensa), subrayó que una consecuencia de esta disposición es que, una parte considerable de la remuneración sobre la que se aplica el canon por el uso de obras protegidas en relación con resúmenes de prensa, se paga a los autores de los textos utilizados. En cambio, si se mantiene el derecho exclusivo, normalmente no se mejora la posición del autor. Cf. sentencia del Tribunal Supremo alemán ("Bundesgerichtshof"), de 11 de julio de 2002, "Resúmenes de prensa digitales", 2002 *GRUR* 963. Véase también en este sentido, Adolf Dietz (2015), 'Protection of Creative People via Copyright – The Five Pillars of Modern Continental European Copyright Law (Authors' Rights Law)', *RIDA*, No. 243, p. 149: "[E]n muchos supuestos, los derechos legales de remuneración y los sistemas de cánones, administrados por entidades de gestión, paradójicamente, parecen más beneficiosos para los autores y artistas que los derechos exclusivos supuestamente más fuertes, gestionados de manera individual y controlados por las empresas de los titulares de derechos."

4 Basándonos en gran medida en la información aportada por los informes nacionales.

fuertemente condicionada por las tradiciones jurídicas y por el idioma. La comprensión de los conceptos clave tiene efectos sobre las respuestas a las distintas partes del cuestionario elaborado por ALAI y cumplimentado por 22 de sus grupos nacionales. En efecto, no existe una definición comúnmente aceptada de los "*derechos de remuneración establecidos en la ley/obligatorios*". Es más, se utilizan distintas expresiones por parte de la doctrina para referirse a mecanismos distintos de los derechos exclusivos que sirven para remunerar a los titulares de derechos, en particular: "licencia legal" ["*legal license*" o "*statutory license*"], "licencia obligatoria ["*compulsory license*" u "*obligatory license*"], "licencia no voluntaria" ["*non-voluntary license*"], y "derechos de remuneración basados en excepciones o limitaciones" ["*limitation-based remuneration rights*"].[5] Esta proliferación de términos relacionados, y su diferente interpretación, pueden potencialmente ocasionar ciertas incoherencias. Esto es evidente a la vista de las respuestas a las mismas preguntas del cuestionario por distintos grupos nacionales de ALAI. Incluso en los informes nacionales de países europeos, cuyas leyes de transposición del ordenamiento jurídico comunitario están, en cierta medida, armonizadas, cabe observar ciertas diferencias o dudas sobre la interpretación de los términos "derechos de remuneración establecidos en la ley/obligatorios" ["statutory remuneration right"] y "licencias obligatorias" ["compulsory license"]. Por ejemplo, el informe nacional noruego contesta a la pregunta sobre "licencias obligatorias" ["compulsory licenses"] refiriéndose a "licencias obligatorias" ["statutory licenses"] y "licencias colectivas ampliadas" ["extended collective licences"];[6] el informe del Reno Unido clasifica la remuneración por determinados usos de obras huérfanas como una "remuneración establecida legalmente u obligatoria" ["*statutory remuneration*"][7], mientras que el informe portugués se refiere a la remuneración en el caso de obras huérfanas como una "licencia obligatoria" ["*compulsory license*"], reconociendo que también puede clasificarse como "licencia legal" ["*legal license*"][8]. Dichas diferen-

5 Mihály Ficsor (2003), *Guide to the Copyright and Related Rights Treaties Administered by WIPO and Glossary of Copyright and Related Rights Terms*, Publicación de la OMPI Nº 891(E), págs. 277, 298 y 312, Andrew F. Christie (2011), 'Maximising permissible exceptions to intellectual property rights', en Annette Kur and Vytautas Mizaras (eds), *The Structure of Intellectual Property Law: Can One Size Fit All?*, Cheltenham, UK: Edward Elgar, p. 125, Christophe Geiger and Franciska Schönherr (2012), 'Defining the Scope of Protection of Copyright in the EU: The Need to Reconsider the Acquis regarding Limitations and Exceptions', en Tatiana-Eleni Synodinou (ed.), *Codification of European Copyright Law: Challenges and Perspectives*, Alphen aan den Rijn, The Netherlands: Kluwer Law, International, págs. 166–167. Christophe Geiger (2010), 'Promoting Creativity through Copyright Limitations, Reflections on the Concept of Exclusivity in Copyright Law', *Vanderbilt Journal of Entertainment & Technology Law*, Vol. 12, Issue 3, págs. 515–548.

6 Informe nacional de Noruega, págs. 12–14.

7 Informe nacional del Reino Unido, págs. 11–12.

8 Informe nacional de Portugal, p. 8.

cias terminológicas oscurecen el significado, convirtiendo una mera comparación en un reto complicado.

Además, existe una sutil diferencia en la percepción del derecho de remuneración establecidos en la ley u obligatorio como una “compensación por el daño causado” o como una “remuneración por el uso”. Dicho detalle, a primera vista insignificante, puede tener un papel importante en la percepción nacional del mecanismo de remuneración no basado en la exclusividad, en su finalidad, y por ello, en el cálculo de los derechos en cuestión. Las diferencias entre idiomas y el vocabulario de derechos de autor influyen además en la transposición de los textos internacionales a los ordenamientos nacionales[9].

A mayor abundamiento, no siempre está claro el límite entre los modelos jurídicos que garantizan la remuneración a través de derechos exclusivos, y los derechos de remuneración establecidos en la ley/obligatorios, cuando se trata de derechos de gestión colectiva obligatoria de derechos exclusivos. Por ejemplo, algunos informes nacionales se refieren al ejercicio obligatorio de los derechos exclusivos de reprografía[10] a través de una entidad de gestión colectiva (EGC) en el ámbito de los derechos de remuneración establecidos en la ley u obligatorios, mientras que otros informes expresamente excluyen los derechos exclusivos que son de gestión colectiva obligatoria del ámbito de este informe[11].

Teniendo en cuenta los distintos planteamientos que pueden adoptarse a la hora de definir los conceptos clave y para poder abarcar todos los posibles supuestos, el presente informe define los derechos de remuneración establecidos en la ley/obligatorios (“*statutory remuneration rights”)* como cualquier derecho reconocido en la ley que atribuya a los titulares de derechos de autor o de dere-

9 Christophe Geiger y Franciska Schönherr (2014), ‘Limitations to copyright in the digital age’, en Andrej Savin y Jan Trzaskowski (eds), Research Handbook on EU Internet Law, Cheltenham, UK/ Northampton, MA, USA: Edward Elgar, págs. 131–133.

10 Informe nacional de Francia, págs. 14 y 22. El artículo L122-10 del Código de Propiedad Intelectual francés (CPI) establece un sistema de transmisión automática del derecho exclusivo de reprografía a una EGC, en el momento de la publicación de la obra (en la actualidad al *Centre français du droit d'exploitation du droit de copie (CFC)*), especialmente autorizada para estos fines por el Ministerio de cultura. Philippe Masseron (2011), *Sociétés de perception et de répartition des droits : Centre français d'exploitation du droit de copie (CFC)*, Fasc. 1580 y Sylvie Nérisson (2013), *La gestion collective des droits des auteurs en France et en Allemagne : quelle légitimité ?*, Paris, Francia: IRJS, págs. 287, 313 y 314.

11 Informe nacional de Hungría, págs. 11–12. Los informes nacionales de los Estados miembros de la UE no clasifican de forma unánime el supuesto de la gestión colectiva obligatoria del derecho exclusivo de retransmisión por cable como un derecho de remuneración obligatorio. En la UE, la gestión colectiva obligatoria del derecho exclusivo de retransmisión por cable se establece en el artículo 9 de la Directiva 93/83/CEE del Consejo, de 27 de septiembre de 1993, sobre coordinación de determinadas disposiciones relativas a los derechos de autor y derechos afines a los derechos de autor en el ámbito de la radiodifusión vía satélite y de la distribución por cable [1993] L 248/15.

chos afines una remuneración, sin posibilidad alguna de ejercitar un control sobre la utilización de la obra o de la prestación protegida[12]. Esta definición cubre los derechos de remuneración definidos de esta forma por los ordenamientos jurídicos internacionales o nacionales ("derechos de remuneración *per se*"), los derechos de remuneración creados en el contexto de las limitaciones o excepciones a los derechos exclusivos ("derechos de remuneración basados en excepciones o limitaciones") y la integración de los derechos de remuneración en la estructura de los derechos exclusivos (los denominados "derechos de remuneración residuales"[13]).

II. Planteamientos nacionales en relación con los derechos de remuneración establecidos en la ley u obligatorios

1. Resumen

Distintos modelos de derechos de remuneración establecidos en la ley/obligatorios forman parte integrante del derecho de propiedad intelectual en países de todo el mundo. Los informes nacionales presentados difieren en cuanto al alcance de la regulación de los derechos de remuneración, y a su clasificación, a menudo describiendo algunos derechos en detalle, dejando otros al margen. No obstante, el volumen general de la información facilitada parece suficiente para extraer algunas conclusiones generales y para describir una situación general.

Todos los países que se incluyen en las respuestas al cuestionario atribuyen a los artistas y productores un **derecho de remuneración por la comunicación pública de fonogramas comerciales.**[14]

12 Se está dejando al margen las cuestiones acerca de los derechos morales y la gestión colectiva no voluntaria de los derechos exclusivos, debido a la existencia de un debate acerca de si esto último afecta a la naturaleza de los derechos exclusivos.

13 Mihaly Ficsor (2010), 'Collective Management of Copyright and Related Rights from the Viewpoint of International Norms and the Acquis Communautaire', en Daniel J. Gervais (ed.), Collective Management of Copyright and Related Rights, 2° edición, Alphen aan den Rijn, The Netherlands: Kluwer Law International, pág. 42. Mihály Ficsor (2002), Collective Management of Copyright and Related Rights, Publicación de la OMPI N° 855, págs. 23 ("'derecho residual' para creadores individuales 'que sobreviven' a la transmisión de derechos") y 139 ("'derechos residuales'; esto es, derechos a una remuneración que se establecen (normalmente a favor de autores y artistas) en el caso de transmisión de determinados derechos exclusivos (tales como en el caso del derecho de alquiler, de conformidad con la Directiva de Alquiler y Préstamo de la Comunidad europea)."

14 Este reconocimiento generalizado del derecho de remuneración por la comunicación pública de fonogramas comerciales refleja las obligaciones internacionales asumidas por los Es-

La mayoría de los países descritos en los informes nacionales disponen de mecanismos de remuneración en el caso de **reventa** de obras de arte originales (derecho de participación), **copia privada**, **préstamo** y **alquiler** de copias de obras y prestaciones protegidas.

Menos habituales resultan los sistemas de remuneración en el caso de **reproducciones realizadas por personas con discapacidad** (por ej., en Austria,[15] Alemania,[16] Países Bajos[17] y Suiza[18]), por el uso de **obras huérfanas** (por ej., en Austria,[19] Alemania[20] y el Reino Unido[21] y), **reproducciones con fines educativos o de investigación** (por ej., en Croacia,[22] Alemania[23] y los Países Bajos[24]), por **la puesta a disposición de fonogramas o grabaciones audiovisuales** (por ej., España[25]), por la **reproducción digital y la puesta a disposición de libros fuera de comercio** (por ej., Francia[26]), como compensación en el caso

---

tados parte en base a la Convención de Roma y el Tratado de la OMPI sobre Interpretación o Ejecución y Fonogramas (WPPT).

15 Artículo 42d de la Ley de Propiedad intelectual austriaca. Informe nacional de Austria, p. 8.

16 Artículo 45a de la Ley de Propiedad intelectual alemana. Informe nacional de Alemania, págs. 15–16.

17 Artículo 15i de la Ley de Propiedad intelectual holandesa. Informe nacional de los Países Bajos, p. 11.

18 Artículo 24c de la Ley de Propiedad intelectual suiza. Informe nacional de Suiza, p. 5.

19 Artículo 56e de la Ley de Propiedad intelectual austriaca. Informe nacional de Austria, p. 7.

20 Artículo 61b de la Ley de Propiedad intelectual alemana. Informe nacional de Alemania, p. 16.

21 Artículo 10(2) del Reglamento 2014 N° 2863 Copyright and Rights in Performances (Licenciamiento de Obras Huérfanas). Informe nacional del Reino Unido, págs. 11–12.

22 Informe nacional de Croacia, p. 10.

23 Artículo 46 de la Ley de Propiedad intelectual alemana. Informe nacional de Alemania, p. 15.

24 Artículo 16 de la Ley de Propiedad intelectual holandesa. Informe nacional de los Países Bajos, págs. 11–12.

25 Artículo 108.3 del Texto Refundido de la Ley de Propiedad Intelectual (TRLPI). Informe nacional de España, págs. 35–36.
Según el informe nacional, los artistas españoles prefirieron disponer un derecho de remuneración, que no es transmisible, en vez de un derecho exclusivo transmisible de puesta a disposición del público. Como esta solución no era posible debido a la obligación del Artículo 3 de la Directiva de la Sociedad de Información de introducir un derecho exclusivo de puesta a disposición, se integró un derecho residual de remuneración equitativa de los artistas intérpretes y ejecutantes en el derecho exclusivo de puesta a disposición reconocido en el Artículo 108.1, que implementa la obligación citada conforme a la Directiva de la Sociedad de Información.

26 Artículos L134-1–L134-9 del CPI. Informe nacional de Francia, págs. 22–24. Aunque el informe nacional se refiere a la legislación francesa sobre obras fuera de comercio en el contexto del derecho de remuneración, la doctrina francesa está dividida en este punto. Desde la promulgación de la ley que facilita el uso digital de libros que estén fuera de comercio, su legitimidad ha sido cuestionada (Loi n° 2012-287 relative à l'exploitation numérique des livres indisponibles du XXe siècle, *JORF n°0053*, 2 mars 2012). El 28 de febrero de 2014, el Consejo constitucional francés (*Conseil constitutionnel*) reconoció que el mecanismo establecido por es-de la presunción legal de cesión de los **derechos económicos principales del autor de una obra cinematográfica** al productor audiovisual (por ej., en los Países Bajos[27]) o para la **exhibición pública de copias de obras de arte y artesanía que sean de titularidad pública** (por ej., en Noruega[28]).

Conviene tener en cuenta que algunos países, basándose en la libertad que le confiere el derecho internacional, no establecen en algunos de los usos mencionados una obligación de remunerar a los titulares de derechos, clasificando dichos usos como excepciones o limitaciones sin remuneración.[29] Por lo tanto, en estos supuestos, no se debe genera ninguna obligación de pago a los titulares de derechos.

Cabe observar cierto nivel de armonización entre los Estados miembros de la UE. En particular, el derecho de participación parece estar reconocido de forma relativamente armonizada en los estados miembros de la UE. No obstante, aunque se han realizado esfuerzos para armonizar la regulación sobre los derechos de propiedad intelectual en los estados miembros con la finalidad de creación de un Mercado único, los ordenamientos juridicos nacionales siguen estableciendo diferencias en relación con otros derechos de remuneración (por ej., no todos los 28 estados miembros establecen un derecho de remuneración en el caso de reproducción por medio de reprografía o por copia privada).[30] Esto puede deberse en parte, al instrumento utilizado para lograr la armonización

---

ta ley era compatible con la Constitución (C.C., 28 février 2014, M. Marc S. et autre, n° 2013-370 QPC). Tras una persistente oposición, el 6 de marzo de 2015, el Consejo de Estado (*Conseil d'Etat*) decidió plantear ante el TJUE la cuestión acerca de si el sistema introducido por la ley para el uso de libros que estén fuera de comercio implementado a través de una entidad de gestión colectiva, es compatible con la Directiva de la Sociedad de Información (C.E., 6 mai 2015, n°368208, M.S., Mme D., art. 2. Planteamiento de cuestión prejudicial por el Conseil d'État (Francia) registrado el 19 de junio 2015 – Marc Soulier Sara Doke v Ministre de la Culture et de la Communication Premier minister (Asunto C-301/15) DO C 294/35, 7 de septiembre de 2015). Para comentarios, véase Oleksandr Bulayenko (2016), 'Permissibility of Non-Voluntary Collective Management of Copyright under EU Law: The Case of the French Law on Out-of-Commerce Books', JIPITEC, Vol. 7, Issue 1, págs. 51–68. En su Opinión publicada el 7 de julio de 2016, el Abogado General Whatelet contestó de forma negativa (ECLI:EU:C:2016:536).

27 Artículo 45 de la Ley de Propiedad intelectual holandesa. Informe nacional de los Países Bajos, p. 12.

28 Esta remuneración se establece en la Ley de Remuneración por la Exhibición de Obras de arte y Artesanía, 1993-05-28-52. Informe nacional de Noruega, p. 10.

29 Por ej., en Francia, el Artículo L122-5(7) en relación con el Artículo L311-8(I)(3) de la CPI, establece una excepción o limitación en beneficio de las personas con discapacidad sin estar sujeta a remuneración alguna.

30 Chipre, Irlanda, Luxemburgo, Malta y el Reino Unido no tienen remuneración por copia privada según se establece en el Informe de Thuiskopie y la OMPI (2016), *International Survey on Private Copying: Law and Practice 2015*, Pulicación de la OMPI N° 1037E/16, p. 3.

(esto es, una directiva[31]) y al carácter no vinculante de la lista cerrada de excepciones y limitaciones que los estados miembros pueden elegir para su transposición a sus ordenamientos jurídicos nacionales.[32]

2. Ámbito de aplicación de algunos derechos de remuneración

Tal y como se ha indicado anteriormente, todos los países que se incluyen en los informes reconocen un derecho de remuneración obligatorio en beneficio de los artistas y productores de fonogramas por la **comunicación al público de fonogramas comerciales.** No obstante, el alcance de este derecho puede diferir mucho de un país a otro, ya que la Convención de Roma y el Tratado de la OMPI sobre Interpretación o Ejecución y Fonogramas (WPPT) permiten a las partes contratantes no aplicar este derecho de remuneración, o aplicarlo sólo parcialmente, si depositan una notificación formal a estos efectos.[33] Por ejemplo, Estados Unidos, que no es parte de la Convención de Roma, pero sí del WPPT[34], reconoce este derecho, pero únicamente en relación con la comunicación al público mediante una transmisión digital sonora. El informe de Noruega describe un caso límite, en relación con la exclusión del suministro del equipo de radio en automóviles del ámbito de la comunicación al público[35]. Una característica común de varios derechos de remuneración es su carácter irrenunciable[36] o de transmisión limita-

---

31 El artículo 288 del TFUE establece: "La directiva obligará al Estado miembro destinatario en cuanto al resultado que deba conseguirse, dejando, sin embargo, a las autoridades nacionales la elección de la forma y de los medios." Para conocer las críticas a las directivas como herramienta de armonización, véase P. Bernt Hugenholtz (2013), 'The dynamics of harmonization of copyright at the European level', en Christophe Geiger (ed.), *Constructing European Intellectual Property: Achievements and New Perspectives*, Cheltenham, UK/ Northampton, MA, USA: Edward Elgar, págs. 274–275.

32 Artículo 5 de la Directiva de la Sociedad de Información.

33 Artículo 16 de la Convención de Roma y Artículo 15(3) del WPPT.

34 El artículo 15(3) del WPPT permite limitar el alcance del derecho de remuneración depositando una declaración con esta finalidad. Estados Unidos depositó la declaración aprovechándose de esta disposición, disponible en: http://www.wipo.int/treaties/en/remarks.jsp?cnty_id=1279C (visitado por última vez en octubre de 2016).

35 Informe nacional de Noruega, p. 19 (se trata de una sentencia firme en un caso en el que el tribunal inferior había resuelto lo contrario).

36 Por ej., el derecho de participación y el derecho residual a una remuneración equitativa por el alquiler de fonogramas y películas son intransmisibles en todos los Estados miembros de la UE, en base a lo dispuesto en el artículo 1 de la Directiva relativa al derecho de participación y el artículo 5 de la Directiva de Alquiler y Préstamo, respectivamente. En el asunto Luksan, C-277/10 ECLI:EU:C:2012:65, el TJUE hizo la siguiente observación: "En el presente caso, en relación con el derecho a la compensación equitativa debida a los autores en virtud de la excepción de copia privada, no resulta de ninguna disposición de la Directiva 2001/29 que el legislador de la Unión haya previsto la posibilidad de que el beneficiario de tal derecho renuncie a

da.[37] Este aspecto de los derechos de remuneración, que los distingue de los derechos exclusivos objeto de negociación o comercialización, suele considerarse un elemento clave del sistema, al asegurar una vinculación directa entre los ingresos generados y la remuneración para los creadores.[38]

El ámbito del **derecho de participación** no parece tener muchas diferencias en los países objeto de los informes. Normalmente, su objeto se circunscribe a la reventa mediante subastas públicas o a traves de marchantes, y algunos ordenamientos jurídicos únicamente reconocen el derecho si se produce un incremento de valor. Como se ha indicado anteriormente, se alcanzó un alto grado de armonización entre los estados miembros de la UE mediante la Directiva del derecho de participación.[39] En la UE y en Egipto, el ámbito del derecho de participación incluye, además de las obras de arte originales,[40] también las copias o ejemplares originales.[41] Al mismo tiempo, el Derecho comunitario excluye "los manuscritos originales de escritores y compositores" (por utilizar la terminología del Convenio de Berna) del ámbito del derecho de participación[42] y, singularmente, limita a 12.500 euros el importe máximo de derechos que debe pagar el vendedor.[43]

éste." (párrafo 105). Por ej., el artículo 63a de la Ley de Propiedad intelectual alemana establece: "Los derechos de remuneración establecidos en esta Sección no pueden ser objeto de renuncia por el autor de forma anticipada. Pueden ser transmitidos de forma anticipada únicamente a una sociedad de gestión, o junto con la cesión del derecho de publicación, al editor, siempre que el editor permita que sean administrados por una sociedad de gestión que administra los derechos de autor y de editor de forma conjunta."

37 Por ej., en Francia, se limitó la transmisibilidad de los derechos de los artistas a una remuneración por la comunicación al público de los fonogramas comerciales y por copia privada, mediante la introducción del artículo L212-11 al CPI el 7 de julio de 2016 con el fin de proteger los intereses de los artistas cuando firman contratos con los editores.

38 El Secretario General adjunto de la Unión de Músicos británicos ("*British Musician's Union*") declaró lo siguiente en relación con el derecho de remuneración equitativa por la comunicación al público y radiodifusión de grabaciones: "El derecho de remuneración equitativa se ha convertido en la joya de la corona de los derechos de los artistas ya que es intransmisible por ley". Horace Trubridge (2015), 'Safeguarding the Income of Musicians', *WIPO Magazine*, Issue 2, p. 9.

39 Para un estudio sobre la implementación de la Directiva en los estados miembros, véase Jens Gaster (2014), 'The Resale Right Directive', en Irini Stamatoudi y Paul Torremans (eds), *EU Copyright Law: A Commentary*, Cheltenham, UK/ Northampton, MA, USA: Edward Elgar, págs. 360–362.

40 Como se indica en el Artículo 14*ter* del Convenio de Berna.

41 Informe nacional de Egipto, p. 7 y el Artículo 2(1) de la Directiva de la UE del derecho de participación se refiere a "ejemplares considerados como obras de arte originales".

42 Ibid. Jens Gaster (2014), 'The Resale Right Directive', en Irini Stamatoudi y Paul Torremans (eds), *EU Copyright Law: A Commentary*, Cheltenham, UK/ Northampton, MA, USA: Edward Elgar, p. 367.

43 Artículo 4(1) de la Directiva sobre el derecho de participación. El establecimiento de un "techo" para la remuneración no suele ser una herramienta utilizada con frecuencia para equilibrar los intereses de los titulares de derechos y los usuarios.

Los tratados internacionales no reconocen expresamente un derecho específico de remuneración por **copia privada,** sino que suele introducirse como una excepción o limitación sujeta a remuneración en aquellos supuestos en los que los titulares de derechos no pueden ejercitar en la práctica su derecho exclusivo. Este mecanismo legal crea un flujo de ingresos para los titulares de derechos, quienes de otro modo, no percibirían ninguna remuneración por la realización de copias privadas de sus obras, mediante el establecimiento de una obligación de pago por parte de fabricantes, importadores y/o distribuidores de equipos o soportes utilizados para la realización de copias privadas, así como de operadores económicos que ponen los equipos a disposición del público para la realización de copias privadas por parte de personas físicas.[44]

Los límites en los sistemas de copia privada son similares en los distintos países. Las copias deben realizarse por lo general por personas físicas[45] de una forma que se considere privada y con fines no comerciales.[46] Las principales diferencias entre los distintos países se basan en el tipo de productos que pueden ser objeto de gravamen y la fijación de las tarifas.

En algunos países, el canon se aplica sobre equipos de grabación y dispositivos en los que pueden grabarse las obras protegidas (por ej., Francia,[47] Países Bajos[48] y Portugal[49]), mientras que en otros sólo sobre soportes vírgenes (por ej., en Canadá y Dinamarca).[50] En Canadá, solo se gravan los CDs vírgenes,[51] mien-

---

44 Para una vision general más detallada de los distintos sistemas, véase de Thuiskopie and WIPO (2016), *International Survey on Private Copying: Law and Practice 2015*, Publicación de la OMPI N° 1037E/16, e IFRRO y la OMPI (2016) (2015), *International Survey on Text and Image Copyright Levies*: *Edición* 2015, Publicación de la OMPI n° 1042E/16

45 Existen algunas excepciones a este planteamiento general, por ej., de conformidad con el artículo 19(1)c de la Ley de Propiedad intelectual suiza, se entiende por uso privado, la reproducción de copias de obras dentro de las empresas, administraciones públicas, instituciones, comisiones y organizaciones similares para fines de información interna o de documentación.

46 Algunos ordenamientos especifican que para que las copias privadas entren dentro del ámbito de la excepción o limitación, deben proceder de una fuente lícita (en este sentido, en Francia, conforme a lo dispuesto en el Artículo L311-1 del CPI).

47 Décision n° 15 du 14 décembre 2012 de la commission prévue à l'artículo L. 311-5 du code de la propriété intellectuelle.

48 Informe nacional de los Países Bajos, págs. 10–11.

49 Decreto de Lei n.° 320/XII – Segunda alteração à Lei n.° 62/98, de 1 de setembro, que regula o disposto no artigo 82.° do Código do Direito de Autor e dos Direitos Conexos, sobre a compensação equitativa relativa à cópia privada, [DAR II série A N°.89/XII/4 2015.03.05 (pág. 28–40)].

50 de Thuiskopie y la OMPI (2016), *International Survey on Private Copying: Law and Practice 2015*, Publicación de la OMPI N° 1037E/16, p. 7. El informe también señala que resulta cada vez más difícil distinguir claramente entre equipos de grabación y dispositivos, debido a la convergencia tecnológica y la aparición de dispositivos multifunción.

51 Tarifa del Canon que debe recaudarse por el Colectivo de copia privada de Canadá (CPCC) en 2015 por la Venta en Canadá, de Soportes audio vírgenes certificado por el Copyright Board el 13 de diciembre de 2014. Informe nacional de Canadá, p. 8.

tras que en Israel únicamente se devengan derechos en el caso de copias de obras en cintas,[52] excluyendo de esta manera los dispositivos diseñados para su utilización en ordenadores, como discos duros y memorias USB (discs-on-key)[53]. De todos modos, la distinción formal entre equipos y dispositivos no refleja una imagen completa de los planteamientos nacionales en relación con los medios sujetos a copia privada, ya que en algunos países (por ej., France) los dispositivos multifunción aptos para la grabación (como una de sus capacidades funcionales) se clasifican como "soportes/dispositivos vírgenes" (por ej., televisores con memorias integradas y discos duros, decodificadores/cajas ADSL diseñados únicamente con el fin de grabar radiodifusiones audiovisuales).[54]

La convergencia de tecnologías y la utilización de nuevos medios para la copia privada plantean un reto para el sistema de cánones por copia privada. En un intento por seguir los hábitos en el comportamiento de los consumidores, el número de dispositivos gravados suele también expandirse. Otra idea relativamente reciente es la extensión a servicios de almacenamiento en línea (por ej., "en la nube").[55] Francia es el primer país que ha extendido la excepción de copia privada a los servicios de almacenamiento en línea.[56]

Resulta interesante observar que todos los países objeto de los informes nacionales que establecen una remuneración en el caso de copia mediante la reprografía, también reconocen un derecho de remuneración por copia privada[57].

---

52 Artículo 3D de la Ordenanza israelí de Derechos de autor. Informe nacional de Israel, págs. 6–7.

53 Nos parece que si el número de dispositivos gravados en Israel no se amplía, terminará perdiendo todo su significado para los titulaires de directos, teniendo en cuenta el cambio constante en la evolución tecnológica de la forma en la que las personas acceden a material protegido. Sobre Israel, véase también Afori, p. 282 ff. más adelante en este volumen.

54 de Thuiskopie y OMPI (2016), *International Survey on Private Copying: Law and Practice 2015*, Publicación de la OMPI, n° 1037E/14, págs. 7 y 77. Décision no. 15 du 14 décembre 2012 de la commission prévue à l'artículo L. 311-5 du code de la propriété intellectuelle.

55 Comisión europea, Comunicación de la Comisión al Parlamento europeo, al Consejo, al Comité económico y social europeo y al Comité de Regiones, *Unleashing the Potential of Cloud Computing in Europe*, 27 de septiembre de 2012, COM(2012) 529 final, p. 7 y la Resolución del Parlamento europeo sobre derechos de copia privada (2013/2114(INI)) de 27 de febrero de 2014, P7_TA-PROV(2014)0179, paras. 29–30.

56 Según el artículo L. 311-4 del CPI, versión actualizada a 7 de Julio de 2016, la remuneración por copia privada debe ser abonada por los proveedores de servicios de radio o televisión, o para los distribuidores de dichos servicios que proporcionen a las personas físicas un acceso remoto a la reproducción para el uso privado de obras de programas de radiodifusiones lineales, siempre que dicha reproducción hubiese sido solicitada por la persona física antes o durante la radiodifusión.

57 E.g., en Hungary: Artículos 20, 21 y 73(3) de laLey de propiedad intelectual húngara. Informe nacional de Hungría, p. 11. En Francia, el derecho a la reprografia es un derecho exclusivo de gestión colectiva obligatoria (Artículo L122-10 del CPI). André Lucas (2014), *Droits des Auteurs : Droits patrimoniaux : Droit de reproduction par reprographie (CPI, art. L. 122-10 à L. 122-*

En la UE, existieron intentos para establecer un planteamiento común en relación con los derechos de copia privada[58], pero hasta la fecha no se ha podido materializar con ninguna acción legislativa concreta. Mientras tanto, aumenta el número de asuntos resueltos por el TJUE, creando jurisprudencia comunitaria para la interpretación de algunos conceptos clave relacionados con la copia privada.[59]

Cabe establecer una remuneración legal para ciertos usos de **obras huérfanas** dentro del marco de la excepción o limitación de la UE/EEE prevista en la Directiva de Obras huérfanas. Según se deduce de los informes nacionales, no todos los estados miembros han traspuesto el mecanismo previsto en la Directiva a sus ordenamientos jurídicos. En contexto del análisis de su alcance, cabe señalar que la cláusula de reexamen de la Directiva (Artículo 10) obliga a la Comisión europea a presentar antes del 29 de octubre de 2015 un informe sobre "la posible inclusión dentro del ámbito de aplicación de la presente Directiva de editores y obras u otras prestaciones protegidas que actualmente no estén englobados en su ámbito de aplicación, en particular, fotografías y otras imágenes independientes." Parece que no se ha cumplido este plazo de reexamen, ya que no se ha publicado ningún informe.

Un caso especial lo constituye la remuneración por el uso de obras o prestaciones que no suelen estar protegidos por los sistemas de propiedad intelectual. El régimen del **"domaine public payant"**, que pretende obtener recursos para fondos de apoyo a las actividades culturales, existe, por ejemplo, en Hungría[60] y Noruega.[61] En este último país, el pago es debido por el uso de fonogramas que

12), JurisClasseur Propriété littéraire et artistique, Fasc. 1265, para. 6. Informe nacional de Francia, p. 14.

58 Comisión Europea, *Follow-up to the European Parliament resolution on private copying levies*, 28 May 2014 (SP(2014)447), António Vitorino (2013), *Recommendations Resulting from the Mediation on Private Copying and Reprography Levies*, 31 de enero de 2013, y Comisión europea, *A Single Market for Intellectual Property Rights Boosting creativity and innovation to provide economic growth, high quality jobs and first class products and services in Europe*, Comunicación de la Comisión al Parlamento europeo al Consejo, al Comité europeo económico y social y al Comité de las regiones, 24 de mayo de 2011, COM(2011) 287 final, págs. 12–13.

59 Sentencias del TJUE en los asuntos Copydan Båndkopi, C-463/12, EU:C:2015:144, ACI Adam y otros, C-435/12, EU:C:2014:254, VG Wort, C-457/11, EU:C:2013:426, Amazon.com International Sales y otros, C-521/11, EU:C:2013:515, Luksan, C-277/10, EU:C:2012:65, Stichting de Thuiskopie, C-462/09, EU:C:2011:397 y Sentencia Padawan, C-467/08, EU:C:2010:620, así como los asuntos pendientes Hewlett-Packard Belgium, C-572/13 y EGEDA y Otros, Asunto C-470/14. EU:C:2016:418, y Nokia Italia y Otros, C-110/15, ECLI:EU:C:2016:717.

60 Artículo 100 de la Ley de Propiedad intelectual húngara. Esta disposición se refiere únicamente a la reventa de obras de arte originales que estén en dominio público. Informe nacional de Hungría, págs. 10 y 12.

61 Ley n° 4 de 14 de diciembre de 1956 sobre el derecho de remuneración por la presentación pública de grabaciones de interpretaciones de artistas, en su versión actualizada. Informe nacional de Noruega, págs. 10–11.

estén en dominio público o a los que no les sea de aplicación el trato nacional. Resulta difícil clasificar el derecho de remuneración por el uso de las obras en dominio público como una excepción o limitación a los derechos exclusivos, ya que no existe ninguna protección basada en la propiedad intelectual, en el sentido habitual de su palabra, según se reconoce por el Derecho internacional.

Además, en Noruega, los creadores tienen derecho a cierta compensación en virtud de **acuerdos especiales de remuneración** negociados entre las organizaciones que representan los intereses de los artistas y el gobierno (similares a los convenios colectivos laborales). Dos de estos acuerdos sobre los que se informa en la respuesta al cuestionario reconocen:

- Una remuneración por la comunicación pública de música en servicios religiosos, mientras dicha comunicación sea objeto de una excepción o limitación;
- Una remuneración por la exhibición de obras de arte visual, artesanía o arte fotográfico que pertenezca al artista.[62]

3. Ejercicio de los derechos de remuneración

Los tratados internacionales no suelen abordar de forma expresa la cuestión acerca del ejercicio de los derechos de remuneración, dejándolo al arbitrio de las partes contratantes.[63]

En una amplia mayoría de países descritos en los informes nacionales, los esquemas de remuneración se implementan recurriendo a la **gestión colectiva de derechos.**[64] Algunos instrumentos de la UE incluso admiten expresamente la posibilidad de ejercitar los derechos de remuneración a través de las entidades de gestión colectiva (EEGG) (Artículo 6(2) de la Directiva sobre el derecho de participación[65] y Artículo 5(4) de la Directiva de alquiler y présta-

62 Informe nacional de Noruega, págs. 11–12.

63 En ocasiones se refieren a la intervención de las "autoridades competentes" en la determinación de tarifas (por ej., Artículos 11*bis* (2) y 13(1) del Convenio de Berna) o a otras modalidades, pero en líneas generales, los estados contratantes disfrutan de una gran libertad a la hora de determinar el ejercicio de los derechos de remuneración.

64 Algunos informes no permiten afirmar con rotundidad si todos los derechos de derechos de remuneración se gestionan de manera colectiva.

65 "Los Estados miembros podrán prever la gestión colectiva opcional u obligatoria del derecho ...". El Reino Unido hizo obligatorio el ejercicio del derecho de participación a través de las EEGG (Artículo 14 del Reglamento sobre el Derecho de participación del artista de 2006 No. 346; Informe nacional del Reino Unido, p. 12), mientras que en Austria, el derecho de participación es el único derecho de remuneración que no es de gestión colectiva obligatoria (Artículo 16b de la Ley de propiedad intelectual austriaca; Informe nacional de Austria, p. 8). Las EEGG que gestionan el derecho de participación están activas en la mayoría de los países de

mo[66]). Suele acudirse a la gestión colectiva debido a la dificultad práctica del ejercicio individual de los derechos de remuneración.[67]

En algunos países, todos los derechos de remuneración son objeto de **gestión colectiva obligatoria** (por ej., en Finlandia, Noruega y Suiza).[68] Todos los países de los informes utilizan este mecanismo legal para la gestión de al menos un derecho de remuneración (salvo Egipto, al parecer[69]). Este mecanismo legal de gestión colectiva no voluntaria permite solucionar el problema de los denominados "terceros/externos" – titulares de derechos que no son miembros de EEGG. Las EEGG que gestionan derechos en base a las presunciones legales que permiten los sistemas de gestión colectiva obligatoria o ampliada, están obligadas a dar el mismo trato a socios y no socios. Además, son especialmente importantes las reglas que garantizan el buen gobierno de las EEGG en los modelos anteriormente indicados basados legalmente en la gestión colectiva de derechos.[70]

4. Control de tarifas y de las EEGG

Existe una enorme variedad de planteamientos en los distintos países en relación con el control de tarifas de los derechos de remuneración y de las EEGG que los gestionan. Es más, el ejercicio de los distintos derechos de remuneración suele regularse de forma diferente dentro de un mismo país. Dado que

---

Espacio Económico Europeo, EVA, Miembros y Observadores: http://www.evartists.org/en/members-observers.html (vistado por última vez en octubre de 2016).

66 "Los Estados miembros podrán establecer la obligatoriedad total o parcial de la gestión a través de entidades de gestión colectiva del derecho a obtener una remuneración equitativa" Sylvie Nérisson (2014), 'The Rental and Lending Rights Directive', en Irini Stamatoudi and Paul Torremans (eds), *EU Copyright Law: A Commentary*, Cheltenham, UK/ Northampton, MA, USA: Edward Elgar, p. 176.

67 Mihály Ficsor (2002), *Collective Management of Copyright and Related Rights*, OMPI Publicación n° 855, págs. 137–138 y Tarja Koskinen-Olsson (2014), *Study on Collective Negotiation of Rights and Collective Management of Rights in the Audiovisual Sector*, OMPI Doc. Nº CDIP/14/INF/2, p. 18.

68 Informe nacional de Finlandia, p. 6, Informe nacional de Noruega, págs. 14–15 e Informe nacional de Suiza, p. 5.

69 Se informa que la gestión colectiva de los derechos de propiedad intelectual no está bien desarrollada en otros ámbitos, distintos de la música, sin afirmar expresamente si algún derecho de remuneración se gestiona de forma colectiva o no. Informe nacional de Egipto, p. 9. Para una visión concisa de la gestión colectiva obligatoria de los derechos de remuneración en los estados miembros de la UE, véase KEA European Affairs (2006), *The Collective Management of Rights in Europe: The Quest for Efficiency*, elaborado por encargo del Comisión de Asuntos Jurídicos del Parlamento Europeo, IP/C/JURI/ST/2005-90, págs. 83–91.

70 Christophe Geiger (2007), 'The Role of the Three-Step Test in the Adaptation of Copyright Law to the Information Society', *UNESCO e-Copyright Bulletin*, Enero-Marzo 2007, p. 12.

prácticamente todos los derechos de remuneración se gestionan colectivamente (estando muchos sujetos a una gestión colectiva no voluntaria), a menudo se asimila el control de las EEGG, al control del ejercicio de estos derechos.

En algunos países, **no existe ningún mecanismo especial de control de la fijación de tarifas** en aquellos ámbitos en los que no se determinen por el gobierno (por ej., en Grecia[71]), mientras que otros países imponen un control general sobre las EEGG por una autoridad pública con competencias en su ámbito (por ej., en Austria,[72] Finlandia[73] y en los Países Bajos[74]) o por la aplicación de la normativa de defensa de la competencia (por ej., en Italia[75]).

La mayoría de los países a los que se refieren los informes nacionales tienen **reglas especiales de establecimiento de procedimientos de determinación de tarifas.** El control o el establecimiento de tarifas suele hacerse mediante la intervención de oficinas de propiedad intelectual, de entidades estatales que operen en el ámbito de las políticas culturales o de otras organizaciones que pueden tener competencias de aprobación de tarifas libremente negociadas o para su fijación en caso de no alcanzarse un acuerdo mediante la negociación (por ej., en Croacia[76], Hungría[77], Japón[78] y Suiza[79]). Algunos países mantienen tribunales permanentes de propiedad intelectual para la determinación de tarifas, o para la resolución de conflictos sobre tarifas (por ej., Copyright Board de Canadá,[80] Copyright Tribunal en el Reino Unido[81] y Copyright Royalty Board en

---

71 Informe nacional de Grecia, p. 13.

72 En Austria, existe una supervision general de todas las EEGG por una autoridad especial, *Aufsichtsbehörde für Verwertungsgesellschaften* del Ministeio Federal de Justicia (*Bundesministerium für Justiz*). Informe nacional de Austria, p. 10.

73 En Finlandia, corresponde al Ministerio de Educación y Cultura. Informe nacional de Finlandia, p. 7.

74 La ley constituyó un Comité de supervision Law para controlar las actividades de todas las EEGG. Wet toezicht en geschillenbeslechting collectieve beheersorganisaties auteurs- en naburige rechten, Stb. 2013/179. Informe nacional Países Bajos, p. 16.

75 Informe nacional de Italia, p. 11.

76 Informe nacional de Croacia, págs. 13–14.

77 Artículo 92/H de la Ley de Propiedad intelectual de Hungría. Informe nacional de Hungría, págs. 9 and 15.

78 Artículo 69 de la Ley de Propiedad intelectual japonesa. Informe nacional de Japón, págs. 7–8.

79 Informe nacional de Suiza, págs. 5–6.

80 Informe nacional de Canadá, p. 9. Para un análisis del funcionamiento del Board, véase Daniel J. Gervais (2008), 'A Uniquely Canadian Institution: The Copyright Board of Canada', en Ysolde Gendreau (ed.), *An Emerging Intellectual Property Paradigm: Perspectives from Canada*, Cheltenham, UK: Edward Elgar, págs. 197–223.

81 Artículo 149 de la Copyright, Designs and Patents Act 1988 c. 48. Informe nacional del Reino Unido, págs. 11–13.

los EE.UU[82]).[83] Algunos países que regulan el proceso de determinación de tarifas y disponen de organismos públicos con sus respectivas competencias también imponen a las EEGG prohibiciones establecidas por las normas de competencia para impedir posibles abusos de posición dominante (por ej., en Alemania[84] y en Noruega[85]).

En otros países, **las tarifas se determinan por la ley** (por ej., ara copia privada en Portugal[86] y Grecia[87]) o por **otra norma** estatal (por ej., las tarifas de préstamo público y de copia privada se determinan mediante Decreto ministerial en los Países Bajos[88]).

En algunos países, **no existe ninguna normativa que regule la actividad de las EEGG** (por ej., en Egipto y en la mayoría de los países árabes, con la excepción de Djibouti, Líbano, Marruecos y Túnez[89]). Mientras que el Reino Unido también pertenece a los países sin una regulación especial sobre la gestión colectiva de los derechos de remuneración, sus EEGG por su cuenta han desarrollado un sistema de **normas de auto-regulación** (por ej. a través de códigos de conducta[90]), manteniendo el gobierno la facultad de intervención.[91] Además de instrumentos nacionales no legislativos, tales como los códigos de conducta que regulan la actividad de las EEGG, existen también reglas internacionales establecidas por asociaciones de EEGG y titulares de derechos.[92] Las EEGG que de-

---

82 Copyright Royalty and Distribution Reform Act of 2004 (P.L. 108-419) 30 de noviembre de 2004 y Copyright Royalty Judges Program Technical Corrections Act (P.L. 109-303) 6 de octubre de 2006. Informe nacional de Estados Unidos, págs. 9–10.

83 Para una vision general de los distintos modelos de tribunales de Propiedad intelectual, véase Michael J. Freegard (1994), 'Quis Custodiet ? The role of copyright tribunals', *EIPR*, Vol. 16, No. 7, págs. 286–292.

84 Artículos 13 y 18(2) de la Ley sobre la Administración de los derechos de autor y derechos afines. La Autoridad Federal de Competencia debería actuar en colaboración con la Oficina de Patentes y Marcas. Informe nacional de Alemania, p. 18.

85 Informe nacional de Noruega, págs. 18–19.

86 Informe nacional de Portugal, p. 7.

87 Informe nacional de Grecia, p. 13.

88 Informe nacional de los Países Bajos, p. 15.

89 Informe nacional de Egipto, p. 9.

90 Los Principios del British Copyright Council de los Códigos de conducta de las EEGG de 25 de mayo de 2012. Para un repaso del sistema británico y de otros sistemas de auto-regulación, especialmente el Código de conducta australiano de las Entidades de gestión clectiva de derechos de autor, véase BOP Consulting, Benedict Atkinson y Brian Fitzgerald (2012), *Collecting Societies Codes of Conduct*, un Informe encargado por la Oficina de Propiedad intelectual del Reino Unido.

91 The Copyright (Regulation of Relevant Licensing Bodies) Regulations 2014 No. 898. Informe nacional del Reino Unido, págs. 13–14. Hasta la fecha, el gobierno aún no ha ejercitado sus facultades.

92 Las Reglas profesionales de la CISAC para sociedades musicales de 6 de junio de 2014, SG13-0787R2, las Reglas profesionales de la CISAC para sociedades de derechos dramáticos,

seen adherirse a estas organizaciones internacionales deben cumplir con los requisitos de estos instrumentos, independientemente de la existencia o no de normas concretas en la legislación nacional.

De manera similar, existe un **sistema estricto de supervisión y control** sobre las actividades de las EEGG en determinados países europeos. Bélgica es un ejemplo notable, ya que dos entidades especiales están encargadas de la supervisión de distintos aspectos de la gestión de derechos, desde la recaudación de la remuneración, hasta su distribución.[93] La ley establece un máximo 15% de costes de gestión que pueden ser deducidos por la entidad de gestión de las cantidades recaudadas para cubrir los gastos de funcionamiento. Singularmente, una de las dos entidades, recientemente constituida, se financia con una deducción de un 0,2% de la recaudación de las EEGG.[94]

A mayor abundamiento, la mayoría de los países del EEE se encuentran en estos momentos en el proceso de transposición en sus ordenamientos jurídicos de la Directiva de la UE de Gestión colectiva, que introduce numerosas reglas de buena gobernanza y transparencia.[95] Siendo el instrumento más voluminoso sobre propiedad intelectual en el Mercado único, requiere la introducción de modificaciones significativas en los ordenamientos jurídicos de los estados miembros. Conviene subrayar que algunos estados miembros de la UE fueron más allá en determinados aspectos al transponer la Directiva. Por ejemplo, Portugal aprobó en abril de 2015 una ley de transposición de las disposiciones de la Directiva sobre el control y las obligaciones de rendición de cuentas de las EEGG. También se establecieron determinadas reglas sobre plazos y procedimientos de negociación, determinación de tarifas y licenciamiento[96]. Las EEGG que operan en los países del EEE, con independencia de su ordenamiento jurí-

---

literarios y audiovisuales de 6 de junio de 2013, SG13-0788, las Reglas profesionales de la CISAC para sociedades de artes gráficas, plásticas y fotográficas de 6 de junio de 2013, SG13-0789, el Código de Conducta de la IFPI para Sociedades de Licenciamiento de música de la Industria musical, versión de enero de 2014, Código de Conducta de IFRRO – Entidades de Derechos de reproducción, revisado el 20 de septiembre de 2007.

93 *Service de régulation du droit d'auteur et des droits voisins* (Artículos XI.274–XI.278 del Código belga de Derecho económico) y *Service de contrôle des sociétés de gestion des droits* (Artículos XI.279–XI.283 del Código belga de Derecho económico).

94 Informe nacional de Bélgica, págs. 14–17.

95 Directiva 2014/26/U del Parlamento Europeo y del Consejo de 26 de febrero de 2014 relativa a la gestión colectiva de los derechos de autor y derechos afines y a la concesión de licencias multiterritoriales de derechos sobre obras musicales para su utilización en línea en el mercado interior [2014] OJ L 84/72. La fecha límite de transposición es el 10 de abril de 2016 (Artículo 43). Para comentarios, véase Lucie Guibault (2014), 'Collective Rights Management Directive', en Irini Stamatoudi y Paul Torremans (eds), *EU Copyright Law: A Commentary*, Cheltenham, UK/ Northampton, MA, USA: Edward Elgar, págs. 696–795.

96 Ley sobre las Organizaciones de gestión colectiva 26/2015 de 14 de abril de 2015. Informe nacional de Portugal, págs. 9–11.

dico nacional, están también sometidas al **control supranacional** de la Comisión europea en el ámbito del derecho de competencia.[97]

5. ¿Quién debe pagar la remuneración?

Los deudores de la remuneración pueden dividirse en las siguientes tres amplias categorías:

- **usuarios** (por ej., en el caso de comunicación al público de fonogramas comerciales);
- **intermediarios** (por ej., importadores, fabricantes y/o distribuidores en el caso de copia privada, u organizaciones que ponen a disposición equipos que facilitan la reproducción mediante la reprografía);
- **presupuesto del estado** (por ej., remuneración para la copia privada en Finlandia,[98] Israel[99] y España[100]).

En general, puede afirmarse que los **contribuyentes** son los deudores finales de cualquier derecho de remuneración que sea abonado por usuarios financiados públicamente (por ej., los derechos de remuneración por préstamo público a bibliotecas públicas se financian con las transferencias del presupuesto estatal en

97 Por ej., Comunicación de la Comisión, en base al Artículo 27(4) del Reglamento del Consejo (CE) No 1/2003 en los Asuntos COMP/C2/39152 – BUMA y COMP/C2/39151 SABAM (Acuerdo de Santiago– COMP/C2/38126), OJ C 200/11, 17 de agosto de 2005 y Decisión de la Comisión europea de 8 de octubre de 2002 (Asunto COMP/C2/38.014 – IFPI 'Simulcasting'), DO L 107/58, 30 de abril de 2003.

98 Artículo 26a(1) de la Ley de propiedad intelectual finlandesa. Informe nacional de Finlandia, p. 6. Este mecanismo de compensación basado en un presupuesto estatal se estableció al finales de 2014 y entró en vigor el 1 de enero de 2015 en virtud de Laki tekijänoikeuslain muuttamisesta 19.12.2014/1171.

99 Informe nacional de Israel, p. 5.

100 Artículo 25(1) de la Ley española de propiedad intelectual (Real decreto legislativo 1/1996, de 12 de abril, por el que se aprueba el texto refundido de la Ley de propiedad intelectual, regularizando, aclarando y armonizando las disposiciones legales vigentes sobre la materia, *BOE,* n. 97, 22 de abril 1996, págs. 14369–14396, modificada por la Ley N° 21/2014, de 4 de noviembre, por la que se modifica el texto refundido de la Ley de Propiedad Intelectual, aprobado por Real Decreto Legislativo 1/1996, de 12 de abril, y la Ley 1/2000, de 7 de enero, de Enjuiciamiento Civil., BOE n. 268, págs. 90404–90439). Informe nacional de España, págs. 31–32. Los titulares de derechos cuestionaron la compatibilidad del sistema de pago de la compensación por copia privada mediante su financiación a cargo de las partidas públicas anuales derivadas de los presupuestos generales del estado con el Artículo 5(2) de la Directiva de la Sociedad de Información. El 9 de junio de 2016, el tribunal condenó el mecanismo español, véase EGEDA y Otros, C-470/14, EU:C:2016:418. Sobre este asunto, véase Garrote, p. 270 ff., más adelante en este volumen.

Austria,[101] Croacia[102] e Italia[103]). Entre los países a los que se refieren los informes, Noruega es el único ejemplo que financia la copia privada, los préstamos públicos y la exhibición pública de copias de obras y artesanía con el presupuesto del estado.[104]

6. Problemas para la cuantificación de la remuneración

La mayoría de los informes nacionales informan que la **larga duración del proceso de determinación de tarifas** (por ej., las negociaciones y la resolución de conflictos) constituye un grave problema para poder exigir el cumplimiento de los derechos de remuneración. Por ejemplo, en Suiza, si las partes en la negociación no alcanzan un acuerdo, la Comisión arbitral federal para la gestión de los derechos de autor y derechos vecinos (*Commission arbitrale fédérale pour la gestion de droits d'auteur et de droits voisins*) debe intervenir para su determinación. La decisión de la Comisión puede ser recurrida ante el Tribunal administrativo federal (*Tribunal administratif fédéral*), y después ante el Tribunal Federal (*Tribunal fédéral*).[105] Se indica que este proceso puede durar años. Por lo general, muchos informes expresaron su insatisfacción con la **duración de los procedimientos judiciales** sobre la recaudación de la remuneración, la determinación de las tarifas y otros asuntos relacionados (por ej., en Argentina,[106] Austria[107] y México[108]). La existencia de **resoluciones judiciales incoherentes** plantea un problema adicional en algunos ordenamientos (por ej., en Croacia[109]).

---

101 Un pago a tanto alzado por el gobierno austriaco. Informe nacional de Austria, p. 9: "debe abonarse por las bibliotecas, pero en la práctica se financia por el Estado a través del Presupuesto."

102 "El Ministerio de Cultura, mediante partidas del presupuesto estatal, apoya a las bibliotecas con respecto a su obligación de pago de la remuneración". Informe nacional de Croacia, p. 13.

103 Informe nacional de Italia, p. 11.

104 Informe nacional de Noruega, p. 16. El "sistema noruego" de remuneración a los creadores a través de los ingresos generados por los impuestos y distribuidos mediante fondos especiales, que coexiste con una legislación sobre propiedad intelectual más tradicional, fue establecido a mediados del siglo XX, Birger Stuevold Lassen (1963), 'Collectivism and Individual Rights in Norwegian Copyright Law', *Scandinavian Studies in Law*, Vol. 7, p. 83 y Tarja Koskinen-Olsson (2010), 'Collective Management in Nordic Countries', en Daniel J. Gervais (ed.), *Collective Management of Copyright and Related Rights*, 2º ed., Alphen aan den Rijn, The Netherlands: Kluwer Law International, p. 288.

105 Informe nacional de Suiza, págs. 5–6.

106 Informe nacional de Argentina, p. 7.

107 Informe nacional de Austria, p. 11.

108 Informe nacional de México, p. 7.

109 Informe nacional de Croacia, p. 15.

Casi todos los informes, directa o indirectamente, se refieren a la **fuerte oposición de los que deben pagar** (por ej., fabricantes e importadores de dispositivos gravados o sus asociaciones). También es un problema la existencia de **interpretaciones contradictorias** en algunas disposiciones legales, en concreto, sobre el ámbito de derechos de remuneración afectados. Algunos informes afirman que es habitual que los usuarios abandonan el negocio antes de pagar ninguna remuneración.[110] Se informa además acerca de los problemas de reparto ocasionados por el **periodo de tiempo** que transcurre entre el momento del cobro de la remuneración por la entidad de gestión, y el de su reclamación por los titulares de derechos.[111] El algunos casos, los importes debidos por los usuarios no alcanzan las **costas judiciales**, y por lo tanto, quedan sin recaudarse (por ej., en Canadá[112]).

A veces, las tarifas se establecen como un porcentaje de los ingresos de los usuarios por las actividades sujetas al pago de una remuneración a los titulares de derechos, y en otras, como cantidades fijas (a veces consideradas "importes mínimos").[113] Si las tarifas son establecidas por una autoridad pública o por la ley, tienen mayor legitimidad y existe menor conflictividad. Si las tarifas son a tanto alzado, y no se actualizan conforme a la situación económica del país, es probable que resulten anticuadas si se comparan con las tarifas basadas en un porcentaje de los ingresos. En general, las **tarifas fijadas por ley son** incluso más **difíciles de corregir** que las tarifas fijadas por una autoridad pública. Por ejemplo, en Portugal, donde la determinación exacta del importe que debe pagarse en concepto de copia privada se fija legalmente, la Ley de Copia Privada que amplía el ámbito de la copia privada a los equipos de almacenamiento digital, lleva elaborándose y debatiéndose durante más de tres años.[114]

En cuanto al **derecho irrenunciable de remuneración equitativa por el alquiler**, se informa que cuando este derecho no se administra por una entidad de gestión, a veces los autores y artistas no reciben ningún derecho adicional distinto del pago inicial por la cesión de los derechos.[115]

El pago de la remuneración a cargo del presupuesto estatal (por ej. para la copia privada), a pesar de ahorrar a los titulares de derechos y a las EEGG relaciones complicadas con numerosos deudores, tiene algunos inconvenientes. Por ejemplo, las EEGG pueden tener que establecer tarifas dentro de los límites

110 Informes nacionales de Croacia, p. 15 y EE.UU, p. 10.
111 Informe nacional de Finlandia, p. 7.
112 Informe nacional de Canadá, p. 9.
113 Informe nacional de Argentina, p. 7.
114 Informe nacional de Portugal, págs. 7–8. Para conocer acerca de la determinación de los equipos y dispositivos sujetos a canon, así como las tarifas, véase IFRRO y OMPI (2014), *International Survey on Text and Image Copyright Levies 2014*, Publicación de la OMPI Nº 1042E, p. 16.
115 Informe nacional de los Países Bajos, p. 11.

específicamente establecidos para los fines de la remuneración (por ej., en el caso del préstamo público en Hungría[116]). En España, donde se sustituyó el sistema de cobro de los cánones de copia privada por parte de los intermediarios, por un sistema de financiación a cargo de los presupuestos estatales, el cambio fue perjudicial para los intereses de los creadores y titulares de derechos debido a la **falta de recursos públicos.**[117]

7. Soluciones a los problemas de remuneración

Es habitual establecer por vía legal la **obligación** de los usuarios o intermediarios **de informar sobre los usos**, para facilitar a los titulares de derechos la información necesaria para permitir el cumplimiento de sus derechos. Además de esta norma común, algunos países atribuyen a las EEGG la **facultad de requerir la información necesaria** para el ejercicio de sus funciones a las autoridades de aduanas o tributarias responsables del IVA (por ej., en Bélgica[118]). En Grecia, si una entidad de gestión legitimada para la administración del derecho de remuneración por copia privada tiene dudas acerca de las liquidaciones efectuadas por los importadores o fabricantes de equipos sujetos a gravamen, tiene derecho a exigir que un censor jurado de cuentas las verifique.[119]

Otra herramienta legal utilizada para resolver el problema de la remuneración, es el reconocimiento de la facultad de los titulares de derechos de requerir a los usuarios (judicialmente) que realicen un **depósito** en garantía de las obligaciones futuras pendientes (por ej., en Hungría[120] y Finlandia[121]). En Japón, en caso de uso de obras protegidas bajo un sistema de licencias obligatorias, se debe depositar una cantidad igual a la tarifa ordinaria de derechos ante el Comisario de la Agencia de Asuntos Culturales, que determina la cuantía de la tarifa.[122] En el ejemplo japonés, la ley exige que se realice el depósito como condición previa para el uso lícito.

---

116 Artículo 23/A de la Ley de Propiedad intelectual de Hungría. Informe nacional de Hungría, págs. 10–11.

117 de Thuiskopie y OMPI (2016), *International Survey on Private Copying: Law and Practice 2015*, Publicación de la OMPI Nº 1037E/16, p. 14.

118 Artículo XI.230 del Código belga de Derecho económico. Informe nacional de Bélgica, p. 17.

119 Informe nacional de Grecia, p. 13.

120 Informe nacional de Hungría, p. 14.

121 Artículo 54b de la Ley de Propiedad intelectual finlandesa. Informe nacional de Finlandia, p. 7.

122 Artículos 67(1), 67*bis*, 68(1) y 69 de la Ley de Propiedad intelectual japonesa. Informe nacional de Japón, págs. 7–8.

Varios ordenamientos jurídicos atribuyen a las EEGG facultades para solicitar como **medidas cautelares,** la prohibición de utilización de las obras protegidas, o medidas de garantía de ejecución de las resoluciones judiciales (por ej., en Argentina[123], Finlandia[124], México[125] y Noruega[126]).

La ley holandesa permite a las EEGG y los deudores la posibilidad de someter los conflictos inferiores a 100.000 euros a **arbitraje**. Los laudos arbitrales son vinculantes si las partes no acuden posteriormente a la vía judicial.[127]

En Bélgica, con más de una entidad de gestión administrando el derecho de participación, el legislador impuso la creación de una **plataforma única** (*plateforme unique*) dirigida por las EEGG para canalizar la recaudación de la remuneración.[128] Las EEGG que operan en otros ámbitos optaron por la creación de forma voluntaria de una **entidad de gestión "paraguas"**. En efecto, en aquellos países con múltiples EEGG que intervienen en el mismo ámbito, la creación de una organización "paraguas" puede efectivamente facilitar las relaciones con los usuarios, reducir los costes y evitar posibles confusiones por parte de los usuarios.[129]

Las EEGG que administran derechos de remuneración a menudo representan, además de a sus propios socios, a no socios. Para garantizar que hay recursos suficientes después de la distribución de los derechos de remuneración a sus socios, la ley puede **obligar a las EEGG a reservar fondos para las reclamaciones de terceros**. En Bélgica, la entidad de gestión que administra los derechos de remuneración de copia privada (AUVIBEL) lo hace de forma voluntaria[130].

Para evitar el problema de que las tarifas fijadas por ley se queden obsoletas en el tiempo y poder aprovecharse al mismo tiempo de la mayor legitimidad de las tarifas establecidas por una autoridad pública, en Canadá, por ejemplo, el **Copyright Board establece las tarifas durante un plazo de** 1 a 5 años, trans-

---

123 Informe nacional de Argentina, p. 8.
124 Artículo 54b de la Ley de Propiedad intelectual finlandesa. Informe nacional de Finlandia, p. 7.
125 Informe nacional de México, p. 7.
126 Artículo 38b de la Ley de Propiedad intelectual noruega. Informe nacional de Noruega, p. 8.
127 Artículos 3, 23 y 25 de Wet toezicht en geschillenbeslechting collectieve beheersorganisaties auteurs- en naburige rechten, Stb. 2013/179. Informe nacional de los Países Bajos, p. 16.
128 Artículo XI.177 del Código belga de Derecho económico. Arrêté royal fixant les conditions et les modalités de gestion du droit de suite visée aux artículos XI.177 et XI.178 du Code de droit économique, 11 de junio de 2015. Informe nacional de Bélgica, p. 11. Se utilizó una solución similar en el caso de la gestión colectiva del derecho irrenunciable de los autores y artistas de retransmisión de obras audiovisuales por cable (Artículo XI.225).
129 Mihály Ficsor (2002), *Collective Management of Copyright and Related Rights*, Publicación de la OMPI Nº 855, p. 135.
130 Informe nacional de Bélgica, p. 10.

currido el cual, las partes interesadas deben repetir el procedimiento de determinación de taifas.[131]

III. Conclusiones

Este capítulo pretende realizar un breve repaso de los sistemas nacionales. El trabajo reveló algunas dificultades terminológicas por el uso de distintos términos para designar a los derechos económicos que no son derechos exclusivos. Estas dificultades parecen basarse en una visión algo dualista del sistema internacional de derechos de autor, compuesto por derechos exclusivos de una parte, y sus excepciones y limitaciones por otra. Este capítulo parte de una visión más matizada, en la que los derechos de remuneración estabecidos por la ley se sitúan en la categoría de derechos (entitlements) a recibir una remuneración englobando tres amplias categorías: los derechos de remuneración *per se* (derechos económicos distintos a los derechos exclusivos que no son excepciones ni limitaciones), los derechos de remuneración relacionados con las limitaciones (derechos económicos creados para remunerar los usos que se benefician de una excepción o limitación al derecho exclusivo) y los derechos de remuneración "residuales" (derechos económicos creados dentro del ámbito de los derechos exclusivos, al establecer el carácter irrenunciable de la remuneración).

Como se ha podido observar, el derecho legal a una remuneración existe en todos los países examinados, pero tiene un alcance diferente dependiendo del ordenamiento jurídico nacional y de la costumbre, mientras que los mecanismos para garantizar su cumplimiento tienen mayor o menor éxito, dependiendo fundamentalmente de la eficiencia de la entidad de gestión colectiva que recaude la remuneración a nivel nacional. Esto resulta interesante en el contexto de la pregunta inicial de la conferencia de ALAI sobre el concurso de diferentes mecanismos legales (exclusividad frente a otros enfoques) y sobre el modelo que debe adoptarse. La solución no puede basarse en cuestiones dogmáticas, sino que debe ser el resultado una vez analizada la eficacia del modelo propuesto a la hora de garantizar los objetivos de la disposición legal. Desde este punto de vista pragmático, resulta evidente la falta de datos esenciales en todos los informes, concretamente las cantidades recibidas por los autores, es decir, cuánto ganan los creadores en cada uno de los distintos sistemas.[132] Parece evidente que las respuestas serán muy distintas, dependiendo de los autores afectados

131 Informe nacional de Canadá, p. 9.

132 Resulta paradójico, y desgraciadamente, característico de muchos debates actuales políticamente relevantes sobre propiedad intelectual en los que se discute acerca de cuestiones sobre la remuneración de los creadores, sin aportar cifras sobre las cantidades percibidas por dichos creadores por la citada remuneración.

(dependiendo, por ejemplo, de su nivel de éxito y de su poder de negociación a la hora de exigir una remuneración justa), otro argumento a favor de la diversidad de modelos. Existen en efecto diversos estudios sobre la remuneración generada por el derecho de remuneración basado en la limitación o excepción de copia privada, pero estos estudios deben completarse, en concreto, con la cuantificación del importe exacto distribuido a los autores.[133] Obviamente, conviene evitar todo tipo de generalización. En primer lugar, la situación de los autores puede ser muy distinta, y probablemente resulta necesario distinguir entre aquellos creadores que perciben un salario, para los que la remuneración adicional constituye un suplemento – bienvenido pero ciertamente no esencial para su actividad creativa– de aquellos otros que dependen del sistema para su vida diaria. En segundo lugar, debe probablemente también distinguirse teniendo en cuenta el grado de funcionamiento del sistema de gestión colectiva establecido a nivel nacional.[134] Si los derechos de remuneración tienen que ser efectivos, es necesaria la existencia de entidades de gestión colectiva que funcionen correctamente. Esta conclusión puede animar a las autoridades a realizar estudios empíricos con mayor frecuencia en el futuro para evaluar el impacto económico de una u otra opción.[135] Pero esto a su vez plantea otras preguntas que son mucho más fundamentales en el ámbito del derecho de autor: ¿Preten-

133 Según de Thuiskopie y OMPI (2016), *International Survey on Private Copying: Law and Practice 2015*, Publicación de la OMPI N° 1037E/16 que recopila los datos sobre sistemas de copia privada de más de 25 países, los "ingresos totales han aumentado durante los años, pasando de 598 millones de euros en 2007 a una cifra máxima de 804 millones de euros en 2014", págs. 13–15 y 22. IFRRO y la OMPI (2015), *International Survey on Text and Image Copyright Levies: 2015 Edition*, Publicación de la OMPI N° 1042E/16 estiman que se recaudaron 179 millones de euros de derechos procedentes de texto e imágen en todo el mundo en el año 2014 (pág. 5 y 24). Véase también Martin Kretschmer (2011), *Private Copying and Fair Compensation: An empirical study of copyright levies in Europe*, UK Intellectual Property Office, p. 7: "Tras la Directiva de 2001, la recaudación total de derechos de equipos y medios de realización de copias se triplicó en la UE, pasando de alrededor de 170m€ a más de 500m€ por año. Los sistemas basados en canon existen actualmente 22 de los 27 Estados miembros (con la excepción de Reino Unido, Malta, Chipre y Luxemburgo)."["*Following the Directive of 2001, total collection from levies on copying media and equipment in the EU tripled, from about €170m to more than €500m per annum. Levy schemes exist now in 22 out of 27 Member States (with only the UK, Ireland, Malta, Cyprus and Luxembourg remaining outside)*.]"

134 Para un intento económico notable de valorar y comparar la eficiencia de las EEGG de distintos países, véase Fabrice Rochelandet (2003), 'Are Copyright Collecting Societies Efficient Organisations? An Evaluation of collective Administration of Copyright in Europe', en Wendy J. Gordon and Richard Watt (eds), *The Economics of Copyright: Developments in Research and Analysis*, Cheltenham, UK/ Northampton, MA, USA: Edward Elgar, págs. 176–197.

135 Solicitando acciones legislativas en la UE basadas más en evidencias, véase Christophe Geiger (2016), 'Moving out of the Economic Crisis: what Role and Shape for Intellectual Property Rights in the European Union?', en: Harri Kalimo and Max S. Jansson (eds.), *EU Economic Law in a Time of Crisis*, Cheltenham, UK/ Northampton, MA, USA: Edward Elgar, p. 135.

de el sistema proteger a *todos* los autores de forma igual o sólo aquellos con un éxito comercial relevante? ¿Qué función debe atribuirse a la idea de la justicia redistributiva en el ámbito de los derechos de autor?[136] ¿Cómo puede hacerse una distinción eficiente en la ley entre la protección de los inversores y la de los creadores? Estas son preguntas fascinantes pero complejas, que probablemente requerirían otro congreso ALAI.

136 Véase sobre esta cuestión, Christophe Geiger (2013), 'The Social Function of Intellectual Property Rights, Or how Ethics can Influence the Shape and Use of IP law', en: Graeme B. Dinwoodie (ed.), *Methods and Perspectives in Intellectual Property*, Cheltenham, UK/ Northampton, MA, USA: Edward Elgar, págs. 153–176.

Tobias Holzmüller*

2.3 Rapport général : mécanismes visant à garantir une rémunération appropriée des auteurs et des artistes

I. Introduction

Le présent rapport aborde la question de savoir qui sont les bénéficiaires des recettes provenant des droits légaux à rémunération, et quels sont les mécanismes propres à assurer une participation équitable des auteurs et artistes interprètes ou exécutants aux revenus issus des droits légaux à rémunération.

Lorsque fut « inventé » en 1965 le droit légal à rémunération pour copie privée en Allemagne, il s'agissait de mettre en place une indemnisation appropriée des auteurs et des artistes interprètes ou exécutants pour compenser le manque à gagner que représentait pour eux la copie privée d'enregistrements sonores. Mais le monde était encore relativement simple à cette époque.

Aujourd'hui, la situation est bien plus nuancée. Comme l'atteste l'analyse comparative des rapports rédigés par les groupes nationaux de l'ALAI pour cette conférence[1], la grande majorité des systèmes juridiques passés en revue prévoit l'intéressement d'une pluralité d'ayants droit aux bénéfices issus de la rémunération légale. Auteurs, créateurs artistes interprètes ou exécutants, producteurs, éditeurs, organisateurs, organismes de radiodiffusion et groupements revendiquent une participation aux recettes.[2] On peut donc s'interroger sur les critères d'une juste répartition des sommes collectées avec la redevance pour copie privée ou d'autres droits légaux à rémunération.

---

* Dr. iur., Responsable du département juridique de la GEMA, Allemagne. Traduction de l'allemand par Fabienne Michel.

1 Disponible sous le lien http://www.alai2015.org/en/national-reports.html.

2 Cf. rapport France, p. 28, rapport Allemagne, p. 19 et s., rapport Italie, p. 11 et s., rapport Japon, p. 8 et s., Rapport Etats-Unis, p. 11.

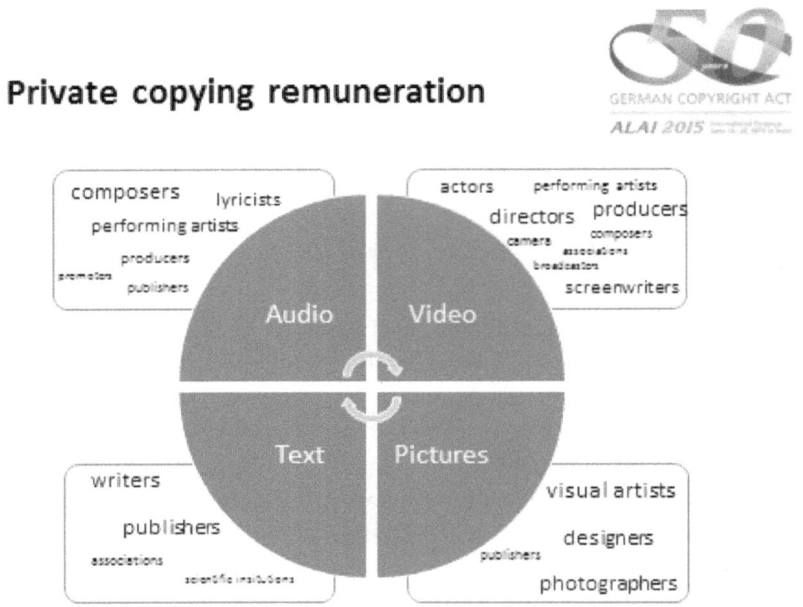

II. Classification sommaire des droits légaux à rémunération

Avant de nous pencher sur les différents mécanismes de répartition, une brève classification des droits légaux à rémunération s'avère intéressante ici. Même si la nature et l'étendue des droits légaux à rémunération varient beaucoup dans la comparaison internationale, il subsiste toutefois certains parallèles.

On distingue deux catégories de droits à rémunération:

Nous avons tout d'abord des droits à rémunération conçus a priori comme des droits légaux à rémunération en faveur de l'auteur ou de l'artiste interprète ou exécutant sans compensation des atteintes découlant de limitations. La rémunération pour le droit de location[3], que l'on trouve dans de nombreux systèmes juridiques, en est un example. En l'occurrence, un droit légal à rémunération est reconnu à l'auteur ou à l'artiste interprète ou exécutant. Cette prérogative est indépendante des droits exclusifs d'exploitation et vient s'ajouter au droit d'exploitation. L'objet de ce dispositif est d'assurer une participation équitable des auteurs et auxiliaires de la création aux recettes d'exploitation subséquentes. Le droit à rémunération doit rester attaché à

3 Cf. art. 78 al. 2 de la LDA hongroise, Sec. 93B de la Loi britannique sur le droit d'auteur, les dessins et modèles et les brevets/UK Copyright, Designs and Patents Act (CDPA) de 1988, ainsi que le § 27 al. 1 de la LDA allemande (UrhG).

l'auteur, et le préserver dans une certaine mesure d'un rachat, par l'exploitant, de la totalité des droits. Le droit de suite repose sur une motivation similaire : il doit garantir la participation de l'artiste aux revenues subséquents de l'exploitation de l'œuvre.[4] Il résulte aussi de cette visée qu'une renonciation anticipée ou un transfert anticipé dudit droit à rémunération est impossible, et que celui-ci ne peut être cédé qu'à des sociétés de gestion collective exclusivement[5].

La deuxième catégorie de droits à rémunération concerne la compensation d'atteintes découlant de limitations. Nous nous situons ici dans le contexte de la licence légale notamment. Une limitation représente une atteinte à un droit exclusif d'exploitation, sans l'obtention d'un consentement. Pour instaurer un équilibre entre les intérêts des auteurs et ceux des exploitants, un système de compensation légale est créé. La redevance pour copie privée[6], ainsi que les licences légales, largement répandues pour les organismes de radiodiffusion, les câblo-opérateurs[7] et la communication de phonogrammes pour les artistes-interprètes et exécutants et les producteurs de phonogrammes[8], en sont quelques exemples. Au cœur de ces règles se trouve non pas tant la protection de l'auteur dans la chaîne de l'exploitation de l'œuvre, mais bien plus l'indemnisation des ayants droit pour le préjudice économique subi dans le contexte du droit d'exploitation touché par la limitation. Le cercle des bénéficiaires potentiels s'en trouve donc élargi. Les obstacles systématiques, susceptibles d'entraver une cession ou une renonciation, tendent à être moins importants.

III. Répartition des recettes provenant de droits légaux à rémunération

La question de la distribution des sommes collectées entre les divers groupes d'ayants droit est soulevée en particulier par la deuxième catégorie de droits à rémunération évoquée ci-dessus. Il existe ici plusieurs mécanismes.

4 Par exemple §26 de la LDA allemande (UrhG), art L.122 du CPI français, UK Artist's Resale Right Regulations 2006/346, art 147 al.3 de la LDA égyptienne.

5 En Europe, voir par exemple l'art6 de la directive 2001/84/CE relative au droit de suite et l'art5 de la directive 2006/115/CE relative au droit de location.

6 Par exemple : art XI 229.234 CEL (Belgique), Section 81 de la LDA canadienne, art 20 de la LDA Suisse, art 30 al. 2, art 102 al. 1 de la LDA japonaise.

7 Par exemple : Sec. 111 US Copyright Act, art L. 132-20-1 du CPI français.

8 Par exemple : §78, al. 1, point 2 de la LDA allemande (UrhG).

1. Règle de partage fixée par la loi

Dans de nombreux États, la loi organise la répartition des revenus entre les différents ayants droit.

a) Pluralité d'ayants droit légaux

On trouve bien souvent des clés de répartition légales lorsque plusieurs groupes de droits et d'ayants droit sont concernés par une licence légale ou par une règle de rémunération. Par exemple, celles-ci peuvent s'appliquer dans le cas d'une coexistence de bénéficiaires de droits d'auteur et de titulaires de droits voisins.

GERMAN COPYRIGHT ACT
ALAI 2015

Private reproduction of sound recordings – legal splits

Country	Composers/Lyricists	Performers	Producers
SUI*	75,0%	12,5%	12,5%
GR	55,0%	25,0%	20,0%
F	50,0%	25,0%	25,0%
ITA	50,0%	25,0%	25,0%
HUN	45,0%	30,0%	25,0%
PT	40,0%	30,0%	30,0%
B	33,3%	33,3%	33,3%
NOR	33,3%	33,3%	33,3%

*assumption based on information in national report

Les exigences se limitent fréquemment ici à la définition d'une règle de partage entre les différents ayants droit au sein d'une catégorie d'objets, les phonogrammes par exemple.[9] La répartition entre plusieurs catégories d'objets, le film et les œuvres de musique dans le cadre de la copie privée par exemple, est généralement établie de façon empirique. Une réglementation spéciale s'applique en

9 Par exemple : rapport France, p. 26 ; rapport Italie, p. 12 ; rapport Hongrie , p. 14.

Suisse où même la convention collective prévoit une valorisation des droits d'auteur et des droits connexes dans un rapport de dix à trois.[10]

Des clés de répartition légales peuvent aussi pourvoir à un équilibre entre plusieurs bénéficiaires de droits voisins, par exemple entre le producteur de phonogrammes et les artistes interprètes ou exécutants dans le contexte de droits légaux à rémunération pour l'utilisation des phonogrammes. Dans les systèmes juridiques examinés, les taux de répartition oscillent entre 45% et 67% pour les artistes interprètes ou exécutants.[11] Ces deux dispositions légales visent le plus souvent à garantir une rémunération équitable des auteurs et des artistes interprètes ou exécutants, réputés être les parties faibles lors des négociations bilatérales avec les producteurs et les éditeurs. La portée de telles règles se révèle aussi dans la comparaison avec les pays ayant mis en place des clés de répartition non contraignantes, comme aux États-Unis par exemple (USA Sec. 114(g)(2) USCA), où les producteurs peuvent obtenir des artistes interprètes ou exécutants une cession de l'intégralité des recettes.

b) Distribution à des bénéficiaires qui ne sont pas des ayants droit légaux

Parfois, le législateur dispose aussi qu'une partie de la rémunération doit revenir à des organismes ou des personnes que la loi proprement dite n'a pas prévu de gratifier dans le contexte des droits concernés par la rémunération.

Il en est ainsi, tout d'abord, lorsqu'une fraction des sommes collectées est reversée légalement à des établissements sociaux et culturels, comme c'est le cas en France[12] où 25% des recettes sont affectées à des actions sociales ou culturelles, ou encore au Japon où 20% des recettes profitent à la protection juridique et à la diffusion.[13] La Cour de justice de l'UE admet cette règle, pour autant que ces établissements sociaux et culturels bénéficient effectivement auxdits ayants droit, et que les modalités de fonctionnement desdits établissements ne sont pas discriminatoires.[14]

Les choses se compliquent lorsque la loi impose l'intéressement de catégories de professions qui ne bénéficient pas d'un droit propre. La participation des éditeurs qui, dans bon nombre de systèmes juridiques, ne disposent pas d'un droit voisin spécifique, est l'exemple le plus remarquable. Cependant, dans de nombreux systèmes juridiques, la loi ordonne de façon explicite une participa-

---

10 Cf. art60 al. 2 de la LDA suisse.

11 A titre d'exemple: rapport Argentine p. 8 : 67% pour les artistes, contre 33 % pour les producteurs; rapport Grèce p. 15, rapport Pays-Bas p. 18 et rapport Norvège p. 21 50/50; rapport Etats-Unis p. 11 : 45%pour les artistes, 50% pour les producteurs, 5% pour des associations.

12 Rapport France, p. 25 et ss.

13 Rapport Japon, p. 8.

14 CJUE, aff. C-521/11, EU:C:2013:315; point 49 et s., *Amazon International Sales* par exemple.

tion des maisons d'édition aux recettes perçues au titre de la copie privée et de la reprographie, mais aussi du droit de prêt dans certains cas.

- Portugal, Grèce: copie privée 50% pour l'auteur, 50% pour l'éditeur (print)[15]
- Hongrie: reprographie 60% pour l'auteur, 40 % pour l'éditeur (print)[16]
- France: droit de prêt 50% pour l'auteur, 50% pour l'éditeur (print)[17]
- Belgique: 50% des recettes de la reprographie ou de la copie privée pour l'éditeur, 1/3 pour les producteurs (film/musique).[18]

A l'heure actuelle, le dispositif belge est l'objet d'une procédure préjudicielle devant la Cour de justice de l'UE. Selon la conception de GA Villalon, qu'il expose dans ses conclusions du 11 juin 2015, une telle disposition légale pour le domaine de la reprographie et de la copie privée est incompatible avec l'article 5, alinéa 2 de la directive 2001/29/CE, tout au moins tant qu'il n'est pas garanti que les sommes perçues par les éditeurs profitent aux auteurs[19]. En 2012, la CJUE avait déjà rendu un arrêt analogue à l'égard d'une présomption légale de cession en faveur de producteurs de films selon la législation autrichienne[20].

2. Distribution selon les plans de répartition des sociétés de gestion collective

a) Entre ayants droit légaux

Dans les États où aucune clé de répartition au titre d'une loi ou d'une réglementation n'a été prévue, les recettes provenant de droits légaux à rémunération sont distribuées entre les différents ayants droit selon les règles de répartition en vigueur au sein des sociétés de gestion collective concernées.[21] Ces organismes sont tenus de fixer des clés de répartition uniformes qui, en cas de doute, seront plus favorables aux auteurs et aux artistes interprètes ou exécutants que ne le seraient des clés de répartition négociées individuellement. Quelques sociétés de gestion collective admettent une libre négociation des clés de répartition, mais elles imposent alors des taux minimum à l'avantage des auteurs et des artistes interprètes ou exécutants.

15 Rapport Portugal, p. 11, rapport Grèce, p. 14.
16 Rapport Hongrie, p. 14.
17 Rapport France, p. 27.
18 Rapport Belgique, p. 19.
19 Désormais confirmé par la CJUE, 12.11.2015, aff. C-572/13 – *Hewlett-Packard Belgium SPRL./. Reprobel SPRL.*
20 CJUE, 09.2.2012, C-277/10 – *Martin Luksan ./. Petrus van der Let.*
21 Cf. par exemple rapport Allemagne p. 19 et s.; rapport Autriche, p. 12; rapport Grèce, p. 15.

En l'absence de dispositions légales spécifiques, les taux de répartition entre différentes sociétés de gestion collective sont définis par contrat entre lesdites sociétés.

b) Ayants droit indirects, droit dérivé ou cédé

Dans le cas d'une distribution par l'intermédiaire de sociétés de gestion collective, on peut se demander si (et dans quelles conditions le cas échéant) des personnes qui ne sont pas des ayants droit légaux peuvent bénéficier de la répartition de recettes provenant de droits légaux à rémunération. Cette fois encore, l'intéressement des éditeurs fournit un exemple majeur dans ce contexte.

Dans la plupart des sociétés de perception et de répartition de droits attachés aux œuvres de littérature et de musique, les plans de répartition prévoient une participation des éditeurs aux recettes provenant de certains droits légaux à rémunération, comme par exemple la copie privée, la reprographie, ou encore le droit de prêt.[22]

Ici encore, une distinction peut être établie entre les ayants droit indirects, qui peuvent recevoir des versements au titre de droits dérivés ou cédés, et les bénéficiaires dont les prétentions découlent juridiquement des plans de répartition des sociétés de gestion collective uniquement.

Plusieurs questions juridiques, dont la portée peut s'avérer considérable dans la pratique, n'ont pas encore été clarifiées. Ci-dessous quelques exemples.

- Une cession du droit légal à rémunération est-elle possible ?
- Une cession anticipée du droit à des versements au titre de revenus issus de rémunérations légales est-elle possible vis-à-vis de la société de gestion collective?
- L'accord collectif d'un plan de répartition fournit-il un fondement juridique suffisant pour la participation?
- Un accord individuel de participation, négocié dans le cadre du contrat d'édition, offre-t-il un fondement juridique suffisant?

Toutes ces questions étant toutefois l'objet de procédures judiciaires[23] en cours et n'ayant donc pas encore été tranchées, elles ne peuvent être épuisées dans le cadre du présent rapport, et cela d'autant moins qu'elles trouveront peut-être des réponses différentes selon les systèmes juridiques.

---

22 Les sociétés de gestion collective en France (rapport France, p. 29), en Allemagne (rapport Allemagne, p. 21), en Autriche (rapport Autriche, p. 12 et s.) et en Belgique en sont quelques exemples.

23 Cf. arrêt rendu le 17.10.2013 par la Cour d'appel OLG) de Munich – 6 U 2492/12 et jugement rendu le 13.5.2014 par le Tribunal de grande instance (LG) de Berlin – 16 O 75/13.

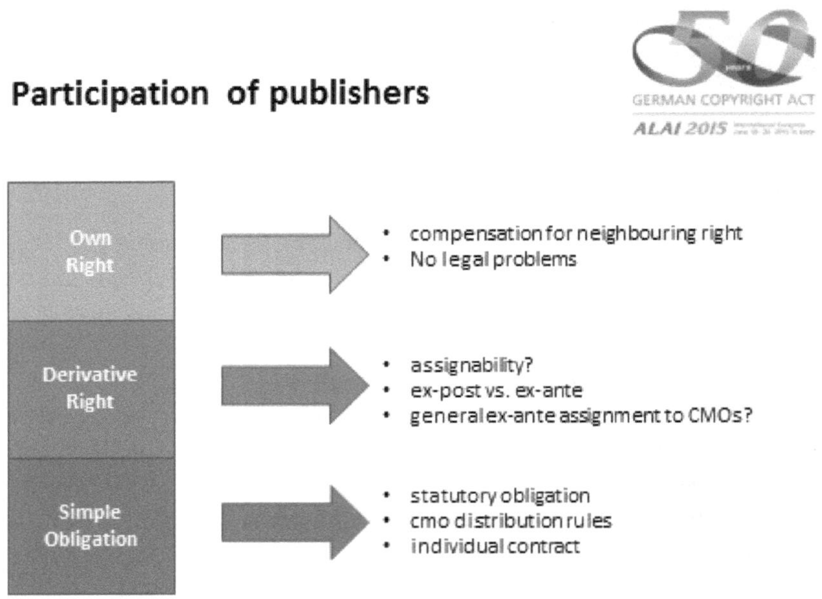

c) Contrôle des sociétés de gestion collective

Le contrôle des sociétés de perception et de répartition des droits présente des formes variées. Dans les quelques états où aucune surveillance spécifique n'est prévue, l'autonomie statutaire des sociétés de gestion collective est dans une large mesure illimitée.[24] Dans de nombreux pays en revanche, des règles prudentielles, appliquées par les tribunaux et les autorités, sont notamment consacrées entre autre à la question d'une distribution appropriée. Celles-ci peuvent énoncer des exigences concrètes pour la répartition[25] ou simplement envisager un «contrôle de l'équité ou de l'arbitraire».[26] Dans les États membres de l'UE tout au moins, la transposition de la directive 2014/26/UE donnera lieu prochainement à une harmonisation du contrôle et des obligations réglementaires. Cependant, des règles de partage légales seront toujours possibles.

24 Cf. rapport Argentine, p. 9, rapport Croatie, p. 16, rapport Mexique, p. 9.
25 Sur ces règles de partage légales, voir plus haut.
26 Voir par exemple l'interdiction de l'arbitraire, §7 de la loi allemande sur la gestion des droits d'auteur et des droits dits voisins (UrhWG) Les Antitrust Consent Decrees for ASCAP and BMI (rapport Etats-Unis, p. 12) contiennent des dispositions similaires.

IV. Conclusion

On constate finalement selon la thèse avancée ici l'existence de deux catégories de droits légaux à rémunération, qui ne suivent pas non plus les mêmes règles de répartition des sommes collectées.

Premièrement, les droit légaux à rémunération qui visent à garantir sans condition à l'auteur ou à l'artiste une participation équitable aux recettes provenant de l'exploitation de son œuvre. Cette prérogative vise à préserver l'auteur ou l'artiste d'un rachat de ses droits. S'agissant par conséquent d'un droit incessible,[27] il doit profiter au plan économique à l'auteur ou à l'artiste exclusivement, à défaut de quoi on s'exposerait à un risque de contournement. D'autres mécanismes légaux pour le renforcement de la position des auteurs ne sont ni habituels, ni nécessaires ici. En effet, toute intervention légale dans la répartition des recettes ne ferait qu'affaiblir les créateurs.

Deuxièmement, les droits légaux à rémunération qui sont destinés à compenser une atteinte découlant d'une limitation à un droit exclusif d'exploitation. Sur un plan économique, la compensation doit bénéficier au titulaire de ce droit exclusif. Le droit d'exploitation pouvant être transféré, le droit à rémunération peut l'être lui aussi, sauf si les dispositions nationales excluent explicitement ou limitent cette possibilité[28]. On le sait par expérience, en l'absence de mécanismes propres à garantir une rémunération équitable des auteurs et des auxiliaires de la création, les avantages économiques associés à ces droits à rémunération risquent de profiter aux exploitants avant tout.

Les mécanismes de protection en faveur des auteurs revêtent essentiellement les formes d'une interdiction de cession et de renonciation, d'une adhésion obligatoire à une société de gestion collective, et de clés de répartition fixées par la loi. Les clés de répartition légales, ou définies de façon collective au sein des sociétés de perception et de répartition des droits, peuvent compenser une inégalité de pouvoirs individuels, et contribuent à garantir une rémunération équitable des auteurs et des artistes interprètes ou exécutants. Dans le domaine des droits cédés ou dérivés, une clé de répartition uniforme peut empêcher une compétition autour de la cession, et prévenir des résultats aléatoires.

Des difficultés apparaissent lorsque la répartition, que celle-ci ait été fixée par la loi ou de façon collective, oblige les auteurs à partager les recettes avec des tiers, les éditeurs par exemple, qui ne disposent d'aucun droit couvert par la redevance obligatoire. Les règles de participation risquent alors de se retourner contre les ayants droit initiaux. Sur un plan juridique, quelques questions sont

---

27 Par exemple : le droit de suite en Allemagne, voir § 26, al. 3, UrhG.

28 Comme dans le droit allemand par exemple: § 63a UrhG.

ici sans réponse. La motivation sous-jacente à la règle de participation joue sans aucun doute un rôle prépondérant dans ce contexte, de même que la question de savoir dans quelle mesure le bénéficiaire peut dériver ses prérogatives de celles de l'ayant droit initial, dans le cadre d'accords contractuels par exemple.

Tobias Holzmüller*

2.3 General Report: Mechanisms to Ensure Adequate Remuneration for Authors and Performers

I. Introduction

This report addresses the following questions: who are the beneficiaries of the revenues from statutory remuneration rights and what mechanisms are there to ensure that authors and performers receive a fair share of the revenues from such remuneration rights?

When the statutory right to remuneration for private copying was "invented" in Germany in 1965, the aim was to introduce appropriate compensation for authors and performers to offset the loss of earnings that private copying of sound recordings represented for them. However, the world was still relatively simple at that time.

Today, the situation is far less straightforward. As emerges from a comparative analysis of the reports drawn up by the national groups of ALAI for this conference,[1] most of the legal systems reviewed in them grant several categories of rightholders a share in the revenues from the statutory remuneration system. Authors, performers, producers, publishers, promoters, broadcasting organisations and other groups claim a share of the income.[2] Therefore, the question of the criteria for a fair distribution of the monies collected through the private copying levy or other statutory rights to remuneration can be raised.

---

* Dr. iur., Head of the Legal Department of GEMA, Germany.
Translation from French by Margaret Platt-Hommel.

1 Available at http://www.alai2015.org/en/national-reports.html.

2 See Report France, p. 28; Report Germany, p. 19 f.; Report Italy, p. 11 f.; Report Japan, p. 8 f.; Report USA, p. 11.

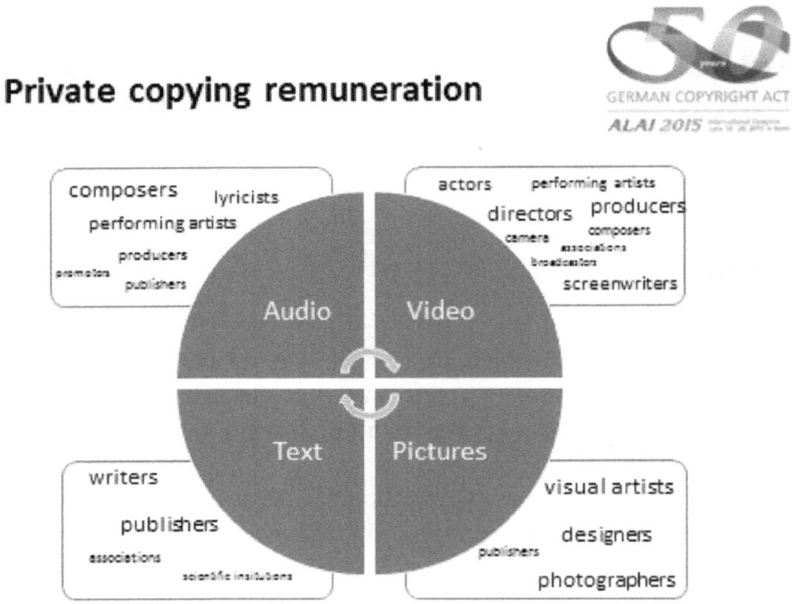

II. Summary classification of statutory remuneration rights

Before we consider the various distribution mechanisms, it is interesting to give a brief classification of the statutory remuneration rights here. Even though the nature and extent of the statutory remuneration rights vary considerably in the international comparison, some parallels nevertheless exist.

Two categories of remuneration rights can be identified:

Firstly, there are remuneration rights that are intended in principle to be statutory rights to remuneration in favour of authors or performers, without compensating for harm arising from limitations. An example is the remuneration for the rental right[3], to be found in many legal systems. In this case, a right to remuneration is granted to the author or the performer by law. This right is separate from the exclusive exploitation rights, and it is granted in addition to the exploitation right. The purpose of this mechanism is to ensure that authors and ancillary creative people receive a fair share of the subsequent exploitation revenues. The right to remuneration must be retained by authors, preserving them to an extent from a buy-out of all the rights by the exploiting party. The artist's resale right is based on a similar motivation: the resale right is to ensure

3 Cf. Art 78 (2) of the Hungarian Copyright Act, Sec. 93B of the UK Copyright, Designs and Patents Act 1988 (CDPA), § 27 (1) of the German Copyright Act (UrhG).

the artist's participation in the subsequent revenues from exploitation of the work.[4] It also follows from the aim of this mechanism that a prior waiver or prior transfer of the right to remuneration is impossible and that the right may only be assigned to collective management organisations.[5]

The second category of remuneration rights exists to compensate for the harm arising from limitations. In this case, the structural context is notably the application of a statutory licence (also known as a legal licence). A limitation represents a restriction on an exclusive exploitation right, without obtaining consent. To establish a balance between the interests of authors and the interests of users, a statutory compensation system is created. The private copying levy,[6] statutory licences that are in widespread use for broadcasting organisations and cable operators[7] and the communication of sound recordings for performers and phonogram producers[8] are some examples. The central aim of these rules is more to compensate rightholders for the economic harm suffered through the limitation's effect on the exploitation right than to guarantee the author's protection in the work's exploitation chain. The circle of potential beneficiaries is thus wider. The systematic barriers to prevent an assignment or waiver tend to be less important.

III. Distribution of the revenues from statutory remuneration rights

It is particularly the second category of remuneration rights referred to above which raises the question of the distribution of the collected monies between the various groups of rightholders. Several mechanisms exist here.

1. Rule of a split determined by the law

In many countries, the law organises the division of the revenue between the various groups of rightholders.

---

4 For example §26 of the German Copyright Act (UrhG), Art L.122-8 of the French CPI, UK Artist's Resale Right Regulations 2006/346, Art 147 (3) of the Egyptian IP-Law.

5 In Europe, see for example art 6 of Directive 2001/84/EC concerning the resale right and art 5 of Directive 2006/115/EC concerning the rental right.

6 For example Art XI.229–234 Belgian CEL, Sec. 81 Copyright Act of Canada, Art 20 Swiss Copyright Act (URG), Art 30(2), 102(1) Copyright Act of Japan.

7 For example, sec. 111 of the US Copyright Act; art L. 132-20-1 of the French CPI.

8 For example, §78, para. 1(2) of the German Copyright Act (UrhG).

a) Rightholders who are beneficiaries under the law

In many cases, distribution keys are laid down in the law when a statutory licence or remuneration rule concerns several categories of rights and rightholders. For example, they may apply in cases where owners of copyright and owners of related rights coexist.

Private reproduction of sound recordings – legal splits

Country	Composers/Lyricists	Performers	Producers
SUI*	75,0%	12,5%	12,5%
GR	55,0%	25,0%	20,0%
F	50,0%	25,0%	25,0%
ITA	50,0%	25,0%	25,0%
HUN	45,0%	30,0%	25,0%
PT	40,0%	30,0%	30,0%
B	33,3%	33,3%	33,3%
NOR	33,3%	33,3%	33,3%

*assumption based on information in national report

The requirements are often limited here to determining a split between the various groups of rightholders within a particular category of subject matter, for example sound recordings.[9] The distribution between several categories of works – films and music in the field of private copying for example – is established empirically in general. A special regulation applies in Switzerland where the collective agreement provides for percentage values between authors' rights and related rights in a ratio of ten to three.[10]

Statutory distribution keys may also ensure a balance between several holders of related rights, for example between producers of sound recordings and performers as regards remuneration rights for the use of sound recordings. In the legal systems discussed in the reports, the percentage share ranges from

9 For example Report France, p. 26; Report Italy, p. 12; Report Hungary, p. 14.
10 Cf. art 60(2) of the Swiss Copyright Act.

45% to 67% for performers.[11] These statutory provisions usually seek to guarantee fair remuneration for authors and performers who are considered to be the weak parties in bilateral negotiations with producers and publishers. The significance of such rules is also revealed in the comparison with countries that have instituted non-binding distribution keys, as in the United States for example (US Copyright Act, sec. 114(g)(2)), where producers may obtain an assignment of all the revenue from performers.

b) Distribution to rightholders who are not beneficiaries under the law

Sometimes the legislator also provides that part of the remuneration is payable to entities or persons whom the law itself did not institute as beneficiaries of the rights underlying the remuneration.

This is so, firstly, when the law requires part of the collected revenues to be allocated to social and cultural establishments, as is the case in France where 25% of the revenue must be used for social and cultural activities[12] and in Japan where 20% of the revenue benefits the legal protection of rights and the dissemination of works[13]. The Court of Justice of the European Union accepts this rule provided that such social and cultural establishments actually benefit the rightholders concerned and that the establishments do not operate in a discriminatory way.[14]

Things become more complicated when the law requires a share to be allocated to categories of professions that do not enjoy their own right. The participation of publishers who do not hold a specific related right in many legal systems is the most striking example. Yet in many legal systems, the law explicitly requires that publishing companies receive a share of the revenues collected for private copying and reprography as well as for the lending right in certain cases.

- Portugal, Greece: private copying, 50% for the author, 50% for the publisher (print)[15]
- Hungary: reprography, 60% for the author, 40% for the publisher (print)[16]
- France: lending right, 50% for the author, 50% for the publisher (print)[17]

---

11 For example: Report Argentina p. 8: 67% for performers and 33% for producers; Report Greece p. 15, Report Netherlands p. 18 and Report Norway p. 21 50/50; Report USA p. 11: 45% for performers, 50% for producers and 5% for associations.

12 Report France, p. 25 f.

13 Report Japan, p. 8.

14 CJEU, case C-521/11, EU:C:2013:315; para. 49 *et seq.*, *Amazon International Sales*, for example.

15 Report Portugal, p. 11; Report Greece, p. 14.

16 Report Hungary, p. 14.

- Belgium: 50% of the revenue from reprography or private copying for the publisher, 1/3 for producers (film/music).[18]

The Belgian mechanism is currently at issue in a case referred to the EU Court of Justice for a preliminary ruling. In the view of Advocate General Cruz Villalon, presented in his opinion of 11 June 2015, such a statutory provision in the field of reprography and private copying is incompatible with article 5(2) of Directive 2001/29/EC, at least as long as it is not guaranteed that the revenues received by publishers benefit authors.[19] In 2012, the CJEU had already ruled along similar lines in a case concerning a statutory presumption of transfer in favour of film producers under the Austrian law.[20]

2. Distribution based on collective management organisations' distribution schemes

a) Among rightholders who are beneficiaries under the law

In those countries where no split has been laid down by law or regulation, the revenues from statutory remuneration rights are shared between the various groups of rightholders in accordance with the distribution rules operating within the collective management organisations concerned.[21] These CMOs are required to set uniform distribution keys which, in case of doubt, will be more favourable to authors and performers than what individually negotiated distribution keys would be. Some collective management organisations accept freely negotiated distribution keys, but they then impose minimum rates in favour of authors and performers.

In the absence of specific statutory provisions, the distribution shares applicable between the various collective management organisations are determined between them by contract.

17 Report France, p. 27.
18 Report Belgium, p. 19.
19 Now confirmed by the CJEU, 12.11.2015, case C-572/13, *Hewlett-Packard Belgium SPRL v. Reprobel SCRL.*
20 CJEU, 9.2.2012, case C-277/10, *Martin Luksan v. Petrus van der Let.*
21 Cf. for example Report Germany, p. 19 f.; Report Austria p. 12; Report Greece, p. 15.

b) Indirect rightholders; derivative or assigned rights

Even where distribution is made through collective management organisations, the question arises as to whether (and, if so, on what conditions) persons who are not beneficiaries under the law may participate in the distribution of revenues from statutory remuneration rights. Again, the participation of publishers affords a major example of such a scenario.

Within most CMOs that collect and distribute royalties relating to literary and musical works, the distribution schemes provide for the participation of publishers in the revenues from certain statutory remuneration rights such as those, for example, from private copying, reprography or the lending right.[22]

Again, a distinction can be made here between indirect rightholders, who may receive payments for derivative or assigned rights, and beneficiaries whose legal claims stem exclusively from collective management organisations' distribution schemes.

Several legal issues, which may have significant implications in practice, have not yet been clarified. A few examples are listed below.

- Is an assignment of the statutory remuneration right possible?
- Is a prior assignment of the right to receive payments of the revenue from statutory remuneration rights possible vis-à-vis collective management organisations?
- Does a collective agreement on a distribution scheme afford a sufficient legal basis for the allocation of a share?
- Does an individual agreement on a share negotiated in a publishing contract offer a sufficient legal basis?

However, as all these questions are the subject of ongoing lawsuits[23] and thus have not been settled yet, they cannot be exhausted in this report, particularly as they may receive different answers in different legal systems.

---

22 The CMOs in France (Report France, p. 29), Germany (Report Germany, p. 21), Austria (Report Austria, p. 12 f.) and Belgium are some examples of such societies.

23 Cf. the decision rendered on 17.10.2013 by the Court of Appeal (OLG) of Munich, 6 U 2492/12, and the decision rendered on 13.5.2014 by the District Court (LG) of Berlin,16 O 75/13.

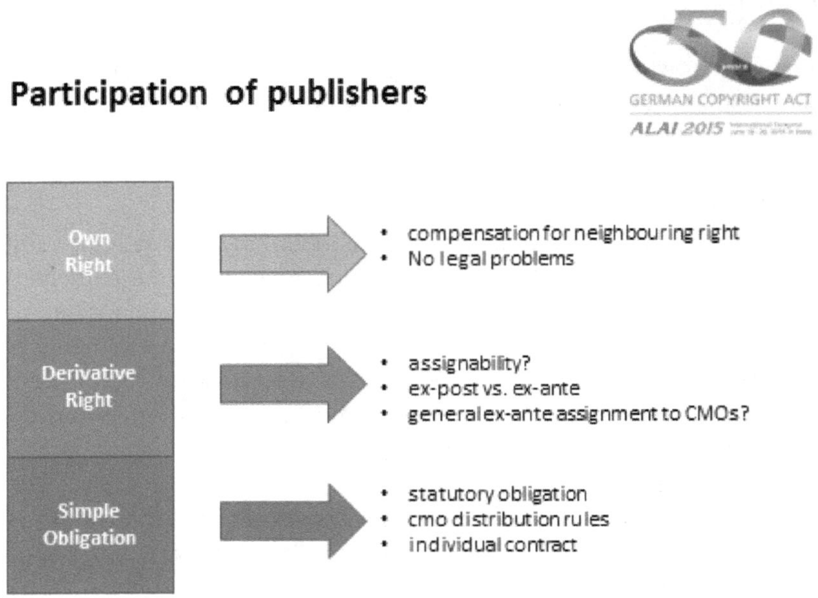

c) Supervision of collective management organisations

There are various forms of supervision of the societies that collect and distribute royalties. In the few countries where no specific supervision is provided for, the autonomy of collective management organisations under their bylaws is unlimited to a large extent.[24] In many countries, on the other hand, prudential rules that are applied by the courts and the authorities deal *inter alia* with the question of an appropriate split. Such rules may set out concrete requirements for the distribution[25] or may simply provide for monitoring to ensure "equitable or non-arbitrary" distribution.[26] At least in the EU Member States, the implementation of Directive 2014/26/EU will soon lead to a harmonisation of the supervision and regulatory obligations applicable in this field. However, statutory distribution rules will still be possible.

---

24 See Report Argentina, p. 9, Report Croatia, p. 16, Report Mexico, p. 9.

25 On the statutory rules concerning the shares, see *supra*.

26 See, for example, the rule prohibiting arbitrary distribution in §7 of the German law on the administration of authors' rights and related rights (UrhWahrnG). The Antitrust Consent Decrees for ASCAP and BMI (Report USA, p. 12) contain similar provisions.

IV. Conclusion

It can be noted in conclusion, based on the thesis advanced in this report, that two categories of statutory remuneration rights exist and that they are not subject to the same rules concerning the distribution of the collected revenues.

Firstly, the statutory rights to remuneration that seek to guarantee unconditionally that authors or performers receive a fair share of the revenues from the exploitation of their works. The aim of these rights is to protect authors or performers from any buy-out of their rights. As they are therefore non-transferable rights,[27] they must be exclusively for the economic benefit of authors or performers, failing which there would be a risk of circumvention. Other statutory mechanisms to strengthen the position of authors are neither common nor necessary here. Indeed, statutory intervention in the distribution of revenues would only weaken creators.

Secondly, statutory rights to remuneration that are intended to compensate for harm arising from a limitation of an exclusive exploitation right. Financially, the compensation must benefit the holder of that exclusive right. As the exploitation right may be transferred, so may the remuneration right unless national provisions explicitly exclude or limit that possibility.[28] As we know from experience, in the absence of mechanisms that will guarantee authors and ancillary creative people fair remuneration, there is a risk that the economic benefits linked to such remuneration rights will benefit primarily the parties exploiting their works.

The protection mechanisms in favour of authors basically take the form of the prohibition of transfers and waivers, compulsory collective management and percentage shares set by the law. Such distribution keys determined by statute or defined collectively within the CMOs responsible for collecting and distributing royalties may offset unequal individual bargaining powers and help to ensure that authors and performers receive fair remuneration. In the case of assigned or derivative rights in particular, a uniform distribution key may rule out competition around the assignment and prevent random results.

Difficulties arise when the distribution – whether set by statute or collectively – requires authors to share the revenue with third parties, for example publishers, who do not hold any right covered by the mandatory remuneration. The participation rules may then backfire on the initial rightholders. Some questions remain unanswered here at the legal level. The motivation behind the participation rule is undoubtedly a major factor in this context as is the extent to which the beneficiaries may derive their prerogatives from those of the initial rightholders under contractual agreements, for example.

---

27 For example, the artist's resale right in Germany, see §26(3) UrhG.

28 As in German law for example: §63a UrhG.

Tobias Holzmüller*

2.3 Informe General: Mecanismos con vistas a garantizar una remuneración adecuada para creadores e artistas intérpretes o ejecutantes

I. Introducción

El presente informe aborda la cuestión de saber quiénes son los beneficiarios de la recaudación de los derechos legales de remuneración y cuáles son los mecanismos más adecuados para asegurar un reparto equitativo entre autores y artistas intérpretes o ejecutantes de los ingresos provenientes de los derechos legales de remuneración.

Desde que se “inventó” en 1965 el derecho legal de remuneración por copia privada en Alemania, se ha tratado de establecer una indemnización apropiada para los autores, artistas intérpretes o ejecutantes que compensara el perjuicio que para ellos suponía la copia privada de fonogramas. Pero el mundo era demasiado simple en esta época.

Hoy en día, la situación conlleva bastantes más matices. Como atestigua el análisis comparativo de los informes redactados por los grupos nacionales de ALAI con ocasión de esta conferencia[1], la mayor parte de los sistemas jurídicos revisados prevé el interés de una pluralidad de derechohabientes beneficiarios de la remuneración legal. Autores, creadores, artista y ejecutantes, productores, organizadores, organismos de radiodifusión y asociaciones revindican una participación de los ingresos.[2] Nos plantearemos por consiguiente sobre los criterios de un justo reparto de las sumas recaudadas junto con el canon por copia privada y otros derechos de remuneración.

---

* Doctor en Derecho, Jefe de Servicios Jurídicos de GEMA, Alemania. Traducción del frances por Mar Delgado.

1 Disponible en el enlace http://www.alai2015.org/en/national-reports.html.

2 Informe Francés p. 28, Informe Alemán, p. 19 y siguientes, Informe Italiano p. 11 y siguientes, Informe Japón p.8 y siguientes, Informe USA p. 11.

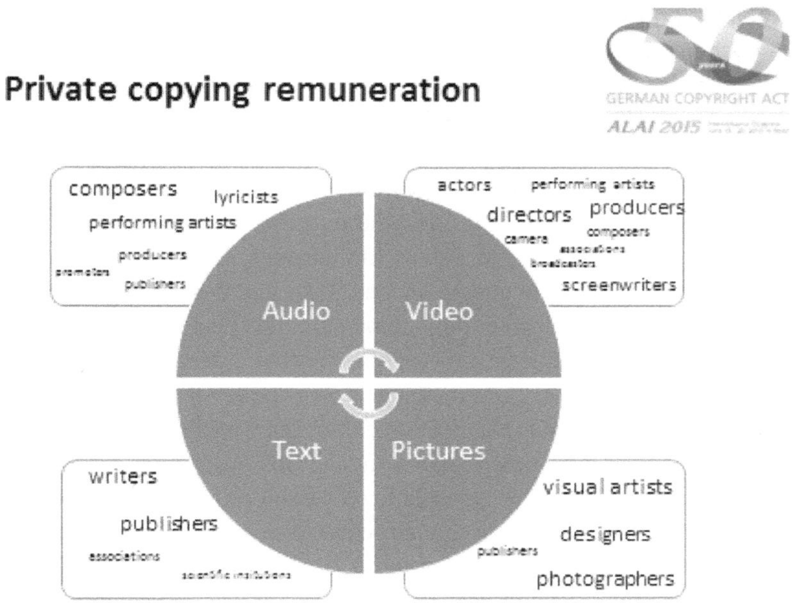

II. Clasificación sucinta de los derechos legales de remuneración

Antes de referirnos a los diferentes mecanismos de reparto, es interesante clasificar brevemente los derechos legales de remuneración. Aunque la naturaleza y la extensión de los derechos legales de remuneración varían mucho según los países, subsisten ciertos paralelismos.

Distinguimos dos categorías dentro de los derechos de remuneración:

Existen, en primer lugar, derechos de remuneración, concebidos a priori como derechos legales en favor del autor o del artista intérprete o ejecutante que no incluyen compensación alguna por el perjuicio resultante de las limitaciones. Ejemplo de ello es el derecho de participación o el derecho a la remuneración por alquiler,[3] que encontramos en numerosos sistemas jurídicos. En estos casos, un derecho legal de remuneración es reconocido al autor o al artista intérprete o ejecutante. Esta prerrogativa es independiente del derecho exclusivo de explotación y se suma en ocasiones a este. El objeto de este dispositivo es asegurar una participación equitativa de los autores y auxiliares de la creación de los ingresos de explotación subsecuentes. El derecho de remuneración debe

3 Cf. art78 al. 2 de la LDA húngara, Sec. 93B ley inglesa sobre derecho de autor, los diseños y modelos u esbozos/ UK Copyright, Designs and Patents Act (CDPA) 1988, § 27 al. 1 de la LDA alemana (UrhG).

quedar ligado al autor y protegerle, en cierta medida, de la adquisición de la totalidad de los derechos por parte de los explotadores. El derecho de participación se basa en un motivo similar: debe asegurar la participación del artista de los ingresos provenientes de la explotación de la obra.[4] Un resultado de este panorama es que la renuncia o transferencia anticipada de dicho derecho es imposible y sólo puede ser cedida a entidades de gestión colectiva.[5]

La segunda categoría de derechos de remuneración corresponde a la compensación de perjuicios resultantes de las limitaciones. En este contexto se puede hablar también de las licencias legales. Una limitación constituye un perjuicio a un derecho exclusivo de explotación, sin haber obtenido un consentimiento. A fin de establecer un equilibrio entre los intereses de los autores y de los explotadores, se crea un sistema de compensación legal. La remuneración por la copia privada,[6] así como las licencias legales, que han proliferado a favor de los organismos de radiodifusión, los operadores por cable,[7] y la comunicación de fonogramas, licencia legal establecidas para los autores, artistas intérpretes o ejecutantes y productores de fonogramas,[8] son ejemplos de ello. El objetivo de estas reglas no es tanto la protección del autor dentro de la cadena de explotación de la obra sino más bien la indemnización de los derechohabientes por el perjuicio económico sufrido durante la explotación afectada por la limitación. Por eso, el círculo de beneficiarios potenciales se amplía y los obstáculos susceptibles de impedir una cesión o renuncia pierden importancia.

III. El reparto de los ingresos resultantes del derecho legal de remuneración

Particularmente, en relación a la segunda categoría de derechos de remuneración nombrada previamente, es necesario plantearse la cuestión de cómo han de repartirse la sumas recolectadas entre los diversos tipos de derechohabientes. Existen diversos mecanismos.

4 Por ejemplo § 26 de la LDA alemana (UrhG), Art L.122 CPI francés, UK Artist's Resale Right Regulations 2006/346, Art 147 al.3 de la LDA egipcia.

5 En Europa, v. por ej. el art 6 de la directiva 2001/84/CE relativa al derecho de participación y el art 5 de la directiva 2006/115/CE relativa al derecho de alquiler.

6 Por ej.: art XI 229.234 CEL (Belgica), Seccion 81 LDA Canada, art 20 de la LDA suiza, art 30 al. 2, art 102 al. 1 de la LDA japonesa.

7 Por ej.: Sec. 111 US Copyright Act.

8 Por ej.: § 78, al. 1, punto 2 de la LDA alemana (UrhG).

1. Regla de reparto fijada por la ley

En numerosos estados, la ley organiza el reparto de ingresos entre los diferentes titulares de derechos.

a) Varios grupos de titulares legales de derechos

Encontramos frecuentemente normas de reparto legales cuando varios grupos de derechohabientes participan de una licencia legal o una regla de remuneración, un ejemplo de esto es la coexistencia entre beneficiarios de derechos de autor y titulares de derechos conexos.

Private reproduction of sound recordings – legal splits

GERMAN COPYRIGHT ACT
ALAI 2015

Country	Composers/Lyricists	Performers	Producers
SUI*	75,0%	12,5%	12,5%
GR	55,0%	25,0%	20,0%
F	50,0%	25,0%	25,0%
ITA	50,0%	25,0%	25,0%
HUN	45,0%	30,0%	25,0%
PT	40,0%	30,0%	30,0%
B	33,3%	33,3%	33,3%
NOR	33,3%	33,3%	33,3%

*assumption based on information in national report

En la mayoría de los casos las exigencias se limitan a fijar una regla de reparto entre los diferentes derechohabientes incluidos en una categoría de objetos, los fonogramas, por ejemplo.[9] El reparto entre varias categorías de objetos, como es el caso de las obras cinematográficas y las obras musicales, en el caso de la copia privada se establece generalmente de manera empírica. En Suiza se aplica un reglamento especial ya que un convenio colectivo establece un valor de los

9 Por ej. Informe francés, p. 26; Informe Italia, p. 12; Informe Hungría , p. 14.

derechos de autor frente a los derechos conexos en un porcentaje de diez à tres.[10]

Las claves de reparto legal pueden proporcionar equilibrio también entre varios beneficiarios de derechos conexos, por ejemplo, entre el productor de fonogramas y los artistas intérpretes o ejecutantes dentro del contexto del derecho legal a la remuneración por uso de fonogramas. En los sistemas jurídicos examinados, las tasas de reparto oscilan entre un 45% y 67% para los artistas intérpretes o ejecutantes.[11] Estas disposiciones legales tienen como objetivo garantizar una remuneración equitativa a los autores y los artistas intérpretes o ejecutantes ya que son la parte más débil en las negociaciones bilaterales con los productores y editores. La importancia de tales reglas se revela especialmente al comparar con los países que han establecidos reglas de reparto no vinculantes, como es el caso de Estados Unidos (USA Sec. 114(g)(2) USCA) donde los productores pueden obtener por parte de los artistas intérpretes o ejecutantes, la cesión de la totalidad de lo recaudado.

b) Distribución entre las personas no titulares legales de derechos

A veces, el legislador dispone también que una parte de la remuneración recaiga sobre organismos o personas que la ley no prevé como beneficiarios en el contexto de los derechos de remuneración. De este modo, un porcentaje de las sumas recaudadas puede emplearse en diferentes fines, en el caso de Francia,[12] donde el 25% de los ingresos se emplea en fines sociales y culturales, mientras que en Japón, el 20% de los ingresos se emplea en la protección jurídica y la difusión.[13] Il El tribunal de justicia de la UE admite esta regla, siempre que los fines sociales y culturales beneficien a dichos derechohabientes y que su modo de funcionamiento no sea discriminatorio.[14]

Las cosas se complican cuando la ley incluye entre los beneficiarios categorías profesionales que no son derechohabientes propiamente. Un ejemplo prominente es la participación de los editores, que en muchos sistemas jurídicos no tienen un derecho conexo propio pero, a pesar de ello, en numerosos sistemas jurídicos, la ley ordena de manera explícita que las editoriales participen de la recaudación por copia privada, por los derechos reprográficos y hasta por los del préstamo en algún caso:

---

10 Cf. art60 al. 2 de la LDA suiza.

11 Informe Argentino p. 8: 67% para los artistas, 33% para los productores; Informe griego p. 15, Informe Holandés p. 18 e Informe Noruego p. 21: 50/50; Informe USA p. 11: 45% para los artistas, 50% para los productores, 5% para las asociaciones.

12 Informe francés, p. 25 et sig.

13 Informe Japón p. 8.

14 TJUE, aff. C-521/11, EU:C:2013:315; punto 49 et s., *Amazon International Sales.*

- Portugal, Grecia: Copia privada 50 % para el autor, 50% para el editor (print)[15]
- Hungría: reprografía 60% para el autor, 40% para el editor (print)[16]
- Francia: préstamo 50% para el autor, 50% para el editor (print)[17]
- Bélgica: 50% de los ingresos por derechos reprográficos o de copia privada para el editor, 1/3 para el productor de cine o música.[18]

A día de hoy, el dispositivo belga está siendo objeto de un procedimiento prejudicial, ante el Tribunal de Justicia Europeo. Según la opinión de A.G. Villalon, expuesta en sus conclusiones del día 11 de junio de 2015, este tipo de disposiciones legales que afectan a la reprografía y a la copia privada son incompatibles con el artículo 5, párrafo 2 de la directiva 2001/29/CE, a menos que se garantice que las sumas percibidas por los editores reviertan sobre los autores.[19]

En 2012, el TJUE detuvo un juicio similar en cuanto a una presunción legal de cesión en favor de los productores cinematográficos, según la ley austriaca.[20]

2. Distribución según los planes de reparto de las sociedades de gestión colectiva

a) Entre titulares de derecho propiamente dichos

En los estados en los que no se han redactado reglas de reparto, los ingresos resultantes de los derechos legales de remuneración se distribuyen entre los diversos derechohabientes según las reglas establecidas por las entidades de gestión colectiva implicadas[21]. Estos organismos, se comprometen a fijar reglas de reparto uniformes que, en caso de duda, sean más favorables a los autores y a los artistas intérpretes o ejecutantes que las negociadas individualmente. Algunas entidades de gestión colectiva admiten libre negociación de las reglas de reparto imponiendo tasas mínimas que favorecen a los autores o los artistas intérpretes o ejecutantes.

En ausencia de disposiciones legales específicas, las tasas de reparto entre las diferentes entidades de gestión colectiva, son establecidas por contrato entre ellas.

---

15 Informe Portugal p. 11. Informe Grecia p. 14.
16 Informe Hungría p. 14.
17 Informe Francia p. 27.
18 Informe Bélgica p. 19.
19 Confirmado por TJUE, 12.11.2015, aff. C-572/13 – *Hewlett-Packard Belgium SPRL./.Reprobel SPRL.*
20 TJUE, 09.2.2012, C-277/10 – *Martin Luksan ./. Petrus van der Let.*
21 Infome Alemán p. 19 y sig., Informe Austriaco p. 12, Informe Griego p. 15.

b) Derechohabientes indirectos, derechos derivados o cedidos

En los casos en que las entidades de gestión se ocupan del reparto, podemos preguntarnos si es posible y en qué casos, personas que no son titulares de derecho propiamente dichos pueden beneficiarse del reparto de la recaudación de los ingresos del derecho de remuneración. El caso de los editores ofrece un buen ejemplo de ello.

En la mayor parte de las entidades que recaudan y reparten los derechos ligados a las obras literarias y musicales, los planes de reparto incluyen la participación de los editores de los ingresos fruto de ciertos derechos legales como el de copia privada, reprografía y préstamo.[22]

Aquí también podemos establecer una distinción entre los derechohabientes indirectos, que pueden recibir pagos a título de derechos derivados o cedidos y los beneficiarios cuyas pretensiones sólo derivan jurídicamente de los planes de reparto de las sociedades de gestión colectiva.

Varias cuestiones jurídicas cuyo alcance puede revelarse considerable en la práctica no han sido aún esclarecidas. He aquí algunos ejemplos:

- ¿Es posible la cesión del derecho de remuneración?
- ¿Es posible una cesión anticipada del derecho a percibir pagos provenientes del derecho de remuneración por parte de la entidad de gestión colectiva?
- ¿El acuerdo colectivo de un plan de reparto provee de fundamento jurídico suficiente para la participación?
- ¿Un acuerdo individual de participación, negociado dentro del marco de un contrato de edición ofrece fundamento jurídico suficiente?

Dichas cuestiones, aunque aún son objeto de procedimientos jurídicos[23] en curso que no se han resuelto, no pueden perderse de vista al esbozar este panorama y aún menos cuando puede que lleguen a resultados variados en los distintos sistemas jurídicos.

---

22 Hay algunos ejemplos por las sociedades de gestión colectiva en Francia (Informe Francia p. 29), en Alemania (Informe Alemania p. 21), en Austria (Informe Austria p. 12 y sig.) y en Bélgica.

23 Cf. Sentencia de 17.10.2013 Tribunal de apelación (OLG) de Múnich – 6 U 2492/12 y la sentencia de 13.5.2014 por el Tribunal de Gran Instancia (LG) de Berlin – 16 O 75/13.

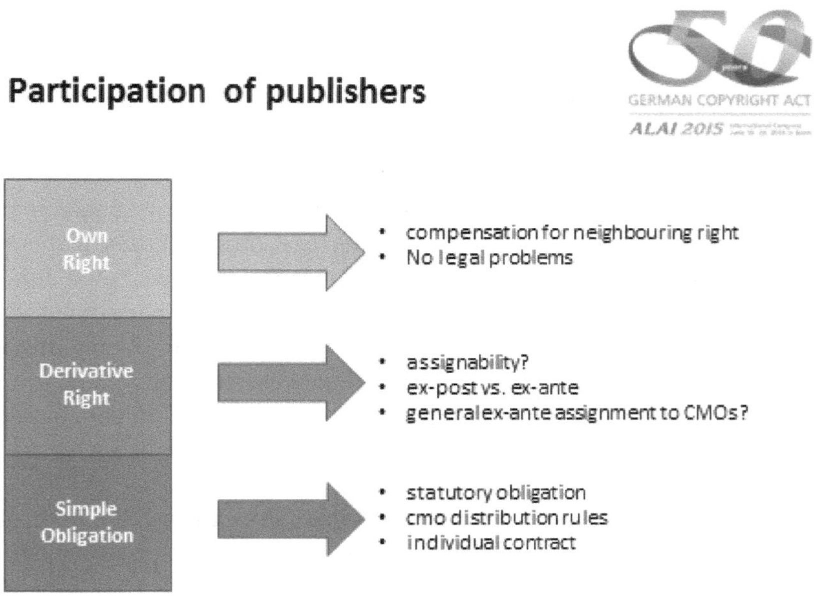

c) El control de las sociedades de gestión colectiva

El control de las sociedades de recaudación y reparto de derechos presenta formas variadas. En algunos estados no está establecido ningún control específico, y la autonomía estatutaria de las entidades de gestión colectiva es prácticamente ilimitada.[24] Por el contrario, en muchos países, las reglas de carácter prudencial, aplicadas por los tribunales y las autoridades, tienen como objeto, entre otros, establecer una distribución apropiada. Dichas reglas pueden establecer exigencias concretas para el reparto[25] o simplemente plantear un control que distinga entre lo apropiado y lo arbitrario.[26] Dentro de los estados miembros de la Unión Europea al menos, la transposición de la directiva 2014/26/UE dará lugar próximamente a una armonización del control y de las obligaciones reglamentarias. Sin embargo, reglas de reparto legal son todavía posibles.

24 Informe Argentino p. 9; Informe Croato, p. 16; Informe mexicano p. 9.

25 Sobre esas reglas de reparto ver arriba.

26 Ver por ejemplo la prohibición de lo arbitrario por parte de la Ley Alemana sobre la gestión de derechos de autor y derechos conexos (UrhWG). Los Antitrust Consent Decrees para ASCAP y BMI (Informe EE.UU., p. 12) contienen disposiciónes similares.

IV. Conclusión

Constatamos finalmente, según la tesis presentada aquí, que existen dos categorías de derechos legales de remuneración que no siguen las mismas reglas para el reparto de las sumas recaudadas.

En primer lugar, los derechos legales de remuneración que tienen como objeto garantizar incondicionalmente al autor o al artista de una participación equitativa de los ingresos provenientes de la explotación de su obra. Esta prerrogativa vela por proteger al autor o al artista de la recompra de sus derechos. A tratarse de un derecho intransferible[27] debe beneficiar al autor o al artista únicamente, en caso contrario habría riesgo de elusión. Por esa razón no son necesarios ni habituales otros mecanismos legales para reforzar la posición del autor. De hecho, cualquier intervención legal en el reparto de la recaudación no haría sino poner al autor en una posición más débil.

En segundo lugar están los derechos legales de remuneración destinados a compensar un perjuicio resultante de un límite del derecho exclusivo de explotación. En el plano económico, la compensación debe beneficiar el titular de ese derecho exclusivo. Como el derecho de explotación es un derecho transferible, se puede transferir también el derecho de remuneración (aunque algunas legislaciones lo excluyen de esa posibilidad).[28] Está más que demostrado que, en ausencia de mecanismos de protección destinados a garantizar una remuneración equitativa para los autores y los auxiliares de la creación, las ventajas económicas asociadas a estos derechos de remuneración, terminan beneficiando a los explotadores.

Los mecanismos de protección más habituales en favor de los autores son la prohibición de la cesión y la renuncia, la obligatoriedad de pertenecer a una sociedad de gestión colectiva y la fijación de reglas de reparto por parte de la ley. Las reglas de reparto establecidas por la ley o definidas de manera colectiva por las entidades de gestión pueden compensar el desequilibrio de poder individual y contribuyen a garantizar una remuneración equitativa de los autores y los artistas intérpretes o ejecutantes. En particular en el campo de los derechos transferidos o derivados, una regla de reparto previene la competencia alrededor de la cesión y prevenir resultados aleatorios.

El reparto siempre conlleva dificultades en los casos en que o por ley o por acuerdos colectivos el autor se ve obligado a compartir los ingresos con terceros que no son titulares del derechos propiamente dichos, como es el caso de los editores. En estos casos, las reglas de participación suelen volverse en contra de los derechohabientes iniciales. En el plano jurídico, varias cuestiones quedan

---

27 Por ejemplo de derecho de participación en Alemania, v. § 26, al. 3, UrhG.
28 Como en el derecho alemán § 63a UrhG.

sin respuesta. La motivación subyacente a la regla de participación juega un papel principal en esta panorama al igual que la cuestión de saber en qué medida el beneficiario puede acogerse a las prerrogativas del derechohabiente inicial, en el marco de acuerdos contractuales, por ejemplo.

Session 2: Considerations de lege ferenda
Considérations de lege ferenda
Consideraciones de lege ferenda

1. Could and should the approach of the German Copyright Act of 1965 (limitation and statutory remuneration right for private copy) be further developed?

Michel M. Walter*

1.1 Introduction

Ladies and Gentlemen,

We had already two very interesting sessions this morning focussing on models to assure authors fair remuneration for the use of their works on the grounds of exclusive rights or on the basis of statutory remuneration rights *de lege lata.* Thanks to all of you who participated in the presentation and analysis of such models and in the discussion. If I have understood the program's objective correctly, we are now expected to move on to the question of whether the system of limitation of exclusive rights in exchange for a statutory claim to an equitable remuneration should be further developed in the future. Without detaining you too long with introductory remarks, let me only mention the following.

First, I would like to remind you that the German copyright law of 1965 was one of the first legislations to limit the scope of exclusive rights on the one hand in granting financial claims to an equitable remuneration for the author on the other, in particular as regards private copying. Of course, in the period of 50 years, which elapsed since then, the technical circumstances have changed as well as users' practices. Nonetheless, in countries that have installed such remuneration systems, they operate quite well, in particular in cases, where private or in-house use is concerned, which could or should not be controlled by the right-holders, or in cases, where the exercise of exclusive rights could appear excessive. However, the further development of such remuneration systems and their adaptation to the digital age is one of the great challenges that must be coped with.

Second, as *Ferdinand Melichar* mentioned already this morning, some countries only provide for few and rather narrow exceptions or limitations to the author's exclusive reproduction right, e.g., regarding private use or use of works for research purposes. In such cases it is argued that no remuneration system would be necessary with respect to the limited concept of limitations (*de mini-*

* Dr. iur., Lawyer in Vienna; Hon. Prof. at the University of Vienna; Visiting Prof. at the Danube University Krems (Austria).

mis exception). However, the problem is that such narrowly worded limitations are widely disregarded in practice, which is why the damage suffered by authors is not even compensated from the economic perspective in such cases respectively countries. It appears to be worthwhile dealing with these inconveniences.

My third and last preliminary remark: In revisiting the existing systems of fair remuneration or compensation in general we should bear in mind that apart from the dichotomy of granting exclusive rights on the one hand or providing mere claims to an equitable remuneration on the other, there are intermediate solutions to be considered. For instance, one could, depending upon the case on issue, maintain exclusive rights along with their mandatory management by collecting societies (collective management organisations). Such system would combine the advantages of exclusive rights with the concerns of easy access to licenses. Furthermore, such systems could be complemented by the concept of extended licences assuring the acquisition of all necessary rights in contracting with one or a few CMOs only. Such intermediate solutions should be taken into consideration as well when discussing remuneration systems *de lege ferenda*.

Ysolde Gendreau*

1.2 Le régime allemand de copie privée comme modèle structurant du droit d'auteur

À l'occasion de ce congrès de l'ALAI qui a lieu en Allemagne pour célébrer le 50e anniversaire de la loi allemande sur le droit d'auteur de 1965, la question qui nous est posée est celle de savoir jusqu'à quel point l'approche que le législateur allemand a utilisée pour établir le régime de copie privée en 1965 pourrait, et même devrait, être reprise de nos jours. Il ne s'agit pas de se demander si le régime de copie privée qui a été adopté à cette époque doit être aujourd'hui maintenu : nous serions alors en présence d'une tout autre question qui, d'ailleurs, reflète des débats particulièrement nourris dans l'Union européenne.[1]

* Professeur, Université de Montréal, Québec, Canada.

1 A titre d'exemples, voir A. Christie, "Private copying licence and levy schemes: resolving the paradox of civilian and common law approaches" *in* D. Vaver & L. Bently, dirs., *Intellectual Property in the New Millennium – Essays in Honour of William R. Cornish*, Cambridge, Cambridge University Press, 2004, p. 248; A. Dietz, "Continuation of the Levy System for Private Copying also in the Digital Era in Germany", [2003] *A & M* 347; M. Ficsor, "Collective Management of Copyright and Related Rights in the Digital Networked Environment: Voluntary, Presumption-Based, Extended, Mandatory, Possible, Inevitable?" *in* D. Gervais, dir., *Collective Management of Copyright and Related Rights*, Alphen aan den Rijn, Kluwer Law International, 2006, p. 37, aux pp. 59–81; S. Dusollier & C. Ker, "Private copy levies and technical protection of copyright: the uneasy accommodation of two conflicting logics" *in* E.Derclaye, dir., *Research Handbook on the Future of EU Copyright*, Cheltenham, Edward Elgar, 2009, p. 349; K. More, *Les dérogations au droit d'auteur – L'exception de copie privée*, Rennes, Presses universitaires de Rennes, 2009; M. Kretschmer, *Private Copying and Fair Compensation: An empirical study of copyright levies in Europe*, Londres, Intellectual Property Office, 2011; A. Lucas, "Les dits et les non-dits de la copie privée", (2012) 43 *Propriétés intellectuelles* 232; F.Pollaud-Dulian, "L'exception de copie privée en France" *in* A. Lucas, P. Sirinelli, & A. Bensamoun, dirs., *Les exceptions au droit d'auteur – Etat des lieux et perspectives dans l'Union européenne*, Paris, Dalloz, 2012, p. 79; P.L.C. Torremans, "L'exception de copie privée au Royaume-Uni" *in* A. Lucas, P. Sirinelli, & A. Bensamoun, dirs., *Les exceptions au droit d'auteur – Etat des lieux et perspectives dans l'Union européenne*, Paris, Dalloz, 2012, p. 95; F. Castex, *Draft Report on Private Copying Levies*, European Parliament, Committee on Legal Affairs, 20 September 2013, 2013/2114 (INI); A. Vitorino, *Recommendations resulting from the mediation on private copying and reprography levies*, Bruxelles, 31 janvier 2013; A. Latreille, "La copie privée dans la jurisprudence de la CJUE", (2015) 55 *Propriétés intellectuelles* 165; *British Academy of Songwriters, Composers and Authors* v. *Secretary of State for Business, Innovation and Skills*, [2015] EWHC 1723 (Admin); K. Grisse & S. Koroch, "The British private copying exception and its compatibility with the Information Society Directive", (2015) 10 *J. I.P. Law & Practice* 562; J P. Quintais, "Private Copying and Downloading from Unlawful Sources", (2015) 46 *I.I.C.* 66; A. Lucas-Schloetter, "Les éditeurs peuvent-ils percevoir la rémunération pour copie privée?", (2015) 243 *R.I.D.A.* 3.

En fait, on cherche plutôt à savoir si l'on peut reprendre les caractéristiques du régime de copie privée qui a été créé en 1965 pour s'en servir dans l'élaboration de lois sur le droit d'auteur dans le monde d'aujourd'hui. Quelles sont ces caractéristiques? Elles sembleraient être au nombre de quatre. Ce régime repose d'abord sur un mécanisme de compensation « indirecte ». Par « indirecte », on veut ainsi créer une opposition avec une compensation directe qui, elle, repose sur l'exercice d'un droit exclusif. Ensuite, cette compensation indirecte est liée à l'existence d'une exception, à savoir l'exception de copie privée. Autre élément caractéristique : les calculs de la rémunération qui est perçue et ensuite versée aux ayants droits ne correspondent pas à une équation parfaite entre l'usage des œuvres protégées et le montant qui y est associé, mais repose plutôt sur une appréciation approximative. Finalement, la mise en œuvre de ce régime fait nécessairement appel à la gestion collective.

Pourquoi a-t-on créé un tel régime ? En fait, cette innovation dans la façon de concevoir le fonctionnement du droit d'auteur constitue une réponse à la reconnaissance de l'expansion des moyens de reproduction de masse.[2] À l'époque, on pressentait déjà la fulgurante expansion de la photocopie. Cinquante ans plus tard aujourd'hui, il faudrait s'adonner à de l'aveuglement volontaire pour ne pas reconnaître à quel point les moyens de reproduction, voire de communication de masse, continuent de vivre un essor prodigieux. Une réponse négative à la question posée par les organisateurs de ce congrès constituerait une négation de l'évolution de ces moyens dont une facette, la reprographie, a mené à la création de ce régime; mais elle signifierait aussi que le droit d'auteur continuerait de demeurer dans un univers bipolaire entre droits exclusifs et exceptions. Il ne s'agit certes pas de nier l'importance du caractère exclusif du droit d'auteur; mais la conséquence principale de cette summa divisio du droit d'auteur réside en une dépendance accrue sur l'exercice individuel du droit. Nous avons tous en mémoire les litiges très impopulaires qui ont été menés par les producteurs de phonogrammes contre des individus qui avaient téléchargé des enregistrements. On ne saurait poursuivre dans cette voie qui a beaucoup nui à l'image du droit d'auteur et, par le fait même, à sa légitimité aux yeux du public.

Reste donc l'autre possibilité : admettre que le modèle qu'a créé le régime allemand de copie privée de 1965 demeure pertinent. Cette réponse positive à la question ayant trait à la pertinence du régime allemand de copie privée dans l'aménagement du droit d'auteur contemporain ne saurait toutefois être émise sans quelques réserves, car on ne peut être aveugle aux difficultés qui accompagnent ce modèle. Il s'avère donc important de veiller à sa légitimité malgré les problèmes qu'il soulève. Nous verrons donc dans une première partie les pro-

---

2 Sur cette question, voir P.E. Geller, "Reprography and Other Processes of Mass Use", (1990) 38 *J. Copr. Soc'y* 21, (1992) 153 *R.I.D.A.* 3.

blèmes de perception que pose le régime de copie privée avant d'examiner, dans une seconde partie, les imperfections qui l'accompagnent.

I. La perception du régime de copie privée

Même s'il existe depuis 50 ans, le régime de copie privée souffre encore aujourd'hui d'un problème de perception : relève-t-il de l'univers des exceptions au droit d'auteur ou est-il un outil de gestion affirmative des droits? En fait, la question existentielle que soulève ce régime est celle du rôle de la rémunération dans l'univers des exceptions. Pour le spécialiste du droit d'auteur, la situation est relativement simple : une exception est une atteinte au caractère exclusif du droit d'auteur, qu'elle soit rémunérée ou non. Pour le public en général, cependant, exception rime avec gratuité. Lorsqu'une rémunération existe, l'activité visée ressortirait alors du domaine de l'exercice des droits et non d'une exception.

En fait, une confusion importante s'instaure entre les licences obligatoires de toutes sortes que permet le droit d'auteur et les exceptions. Il ne faut pas oublier, en effet, que le triple test de la Convention de Berne[3], de l'accord ADPIC[4], et des traités OMPI[5] est un outil d'évaluation des exceptions qui permet d'envisager une rémunération pour atténuer l'atteinte au caractère exclusif du droit. Il devient alors difficile de départager les champs d'application de ces deux techniques juridiques. Prenons ici deux exemples tirés du droit d'auteur canadien. Le premier vise la retransmission des œuvres par câble qui est encadrée par l'article 11*bis*, paragraphe 2 de la Convention de Berne. Le texte de cette disposition commence par énoncer que « il appartient aux législations des pays de l'Union de régler les conditions d'exercice des droits visés par l'alinéa 1 ... ». On parle donc ici d'exercice du droit d'auteur. Pourtant, dans la loi canadienne, le régime qui correspond à ces « conditions d'exercice des droits » est classé à l'article 31 de la loi, c'est-à-dire parmi les exceptions au droit d'auteur.[6] Cet article 31 contient en même temps un renvoi au mécanisme de gestion collective de la loi.[7] Autre exemple de la loi canadienne : le régime de copie privée qui ne vise

3 Convention de Berne, Art 9(2).

4 Accord ADPIC, art 13.

5 Traité de l'OMPI sur le droit d'auteur, art 10; Traité de l'OMPI sur les interprétations et exécutions et les phonogrammes, art 16 (2).

6 La Partie III de la loi, qui englobe les articles 27 à 33.2, s'intitule "Violation du droit d'auteur et des droits moraux, et cas d'exception".

7 L'alinéa 31 (2)d) exige que "dans le cas de la retransmission d'un signal éloigné, le retransmetteur [ait] acquitté les redevances et respecté les modalités fixées sous le régime de la présente loi". Ces modalités sont celles qui sont issues du processus prévu pour les "redevances pour les cas particuliers" aux articles 71 à 76.

que les œuvres musicales et les droits voisins afférents. Ce régime de copie privée, qui comporte une rémunération gérée collectivement, ne figure ni dans les parties de la loi consacrées aux droits exclusifs, les parties I et II, ni dans celle qui expose les exceptions aux droits, la partie III, mais plutôt dans une partie autonome, la partie VIII, qui est placée immédiatement avant les dispositions finales de la loi et juste après la partie VII qui contient les règles concernant la Commission du droit d'auteur et la gestion collective. Pourtant, tant dans le cas de la retransmission par câble que dans celui de la copie privée, le fonctionnement de la gestion collective repose sur les mêmes règles.[8]

On se trouve donc en présence d'une grande confusion des genres, car, d'un point de vue théorique, il devient difficile de savoir où on se loge. Est-on dans un univers de droits ou d'exceptions? Cette troisième voie entre les droits exclusifs et les exceptions que constitue le régime de copie privée, et qui a été identifiée par Ulmer[9], tend à s'imposer en tant que modèle autonome à l'intérieur du droit d'auteur. Cependant, à force d'emprunter des caractéristiques qui proviennent tant des droits que des exceptions, le régime de copie privée a de la difficulté à s'affirmer aujourd'hui comme un modèle structurant pour encadrer des activités qui seraient visées par la loi. Ajoutons aussi, pour complexifier la donne, que l'emprunt de caractéristiques provenant des droits et des exceptions entraîne l'emprunt des difficultés que vivent ces institutions avec d'autres éléments du droit d'auteur. On pense ici, par exemple, à la relation entre les prérogatives traditionnelles et le droit de mise à disposition des œuvres ou encore aux difficultés à concilier les exceptions avec les mesures techniques de protection.[10] Puisqu'il emprunte des deux composantes fondamentales du droit d'auteur, le régime de copie privée ne saurait être épargné des questions difficiles auxquelles elles sont confrontées. Il ne peut se présenter comme la solution miracle aux difficultés qu'engendre le droit d'auteur aujourd'hui.

Outre ces considérations d'ordre plutôt théorique qui nuisent, en même temps, à la perception que le public peut avoir de ce régime, le régime de copie privée est associé à une technique de mise en œuvre, à savoir la gestion collective, qui n'est pas sans présenter ses propres difficultés de légitimité.

II. Les imperfections du régime de copie privée

Les imperfections du régime de copie privée renvoient ici à l'impossibilité d'assurer une adéquation parfaite entre l'utilisation des œuvres, c'est-à-dire leur copie dans un contexte privé, avec la rémunération qui lui est associée. Au-

8 Comparer l'article 83 aux articles 71 à 76 de la loi.
9 E. Ulmer, *Urheber- und Verlagsrecht*, 3e éd., Berlin, Springer, 1980, p. 278.
10 Voir Dusollier & Ker, *supra*, note 1.

trement dit, on aborde ici une certaine obsession d'un régime juridique qui serait mis en œuvre avec perfection dans ses moindres détails. L'acceptation du régime de copie privée repose sur l'admission que la gestion collective qui doit l'accompagner crée une justice imparfaite, une « rough justice », qui est préférable à ne rien avoir du tout.[11] Pour faire fonctionner la gestion collective qui vient avec le régime de copie privée, il a fallu consentir à vivre avec des imprécisions quant à l'identification des supports visés, à l'identification des œuvres qui deviennent ainsi rémunérées, et même aussi à l'identification des auteurs qui finissent par toucher la rémunération.[12] Cette combinaison d'éléments incertains – qui peut être imparfaite dans les détails, mais acceptable d'un point de vue systémique – prête le flanc à une critique sur l'adéquation entre les utilisations visées et les rémunérations qui sont versées aux ayants droit.

Si un système de justice imparfaite qui passe par la gestion collective peut être mieux accepté lorsqu'il accompagne l'exercice de droits exclusifs – et là encore, il est loin d'échapper à toute critique –, un tel régime soulève encore davantage de difficultés quand il fait partie du fonctionnement des exceptions. En fait, on est de nouveau ici en présence d'un problème de perception du régime. Si l'imperfection de la gestion collective qui accompagne une exception pouvait être acceptée à l'époque des années 60, cette acceptation va beaucoup moins de soi aujourd'hui. Pourquoi en serait-il ainsi ? On peut avancer l'hypothèse que la montée du mouvement des « droits des utilisateurs » crée un climat où le pacte social antérieur, qui acceptait l'imprécision de la gestion collective, s'est rompu. La qualification des exceptions aux droits d'auteur en tant que *droits* des utilisateurs, qui ne peut que plaire à certains intervenants, est susceptible d'orienter le débat vers une micro-gestion du droit d'auteur lorsque ces « droits » sont confrontés à une gestion collective. Une affirmation très forte de ces « droits » des utilisateurs vient ici saper les bases de la gestion collective et de sa justice imparfaite. Deux exemples canadiens, c'est-à-dire provenant du pays où la Cour suprême a consacré les exceptions en tant que droits des utilisateurs[13], permettent d'illustrer ces propos.

---

11 Voir M. Ficsor, *Collective Management of Copyright and Related Rights*, Genève, OMPI, 2002, p. 91, para. 248, pp. 148–149, para. 41; Dietz, *supra*, note 1, à la p. 350.

12 Différents modèles nationaux sont d'ailleurs présentés dans Ficsor, *ibid.*, aux pp. 65–77.

13 *CCH Canadian Ltd.* v. *Law Society of Upper Canada*, 2004 CSC 13; [2004] 1 R.C.S. 339 est la décision en la matière à laquelle la jurisprudence subséquente fait référence lorsqu'il est question d'exceptions. La notion de "droits des utilisateurs" est beaucoup plus large au Canada que la compréhension qui semble avoir cours en Europe où elle est plus étroitement liée aux droits de l'homme. Voir C. Geiger, J. Griffiths, M. Senftleben, L. Bently, & R. Xalabarder, "Limitations and Exceptions as Key Elements of the Legal Framework for Copyright in the European Union – Opinion of the European Copyright Society on the Judgement of the CJEU in case C-201/13 *Deckmyn*", (2015) 46 *I.I.C.* 93, à la p. 98, où la décision à l'appui du concept de "droits des utilisateurs" est fondée sur l'interprétation d'un droit prévu par la Convention européenne des

La loi canadienne sur le droit d'auteur prévoit une rémunération équitable pour la reproduction et l'exécution de certaines émissions de télévision dans des contextes éducatifs.[14] Pour gérer ces droits, une société de gestion collective a été créée. Conformément à un mode de fonctionnement qui a cours en droit canadien, la société de gestion en question doit demander à la Commission du droit d'auteur de déterminer les tarifs des redevances qu'elle peut percevoir pour de telles utilisations.[15] Dans la foulée des amendements à la loi canadienne de 2012 et des décisions de la Cour suprême du Canada la même année, la société de gestion qui est autorisée à agir dans ces circonstances a choisi de se désister de sa demande de tarif en 2013, et pour les années suivantes, parce qu'elle considère que les montants qu'elle pouvait espérer toucher ne suffiraient même pas à compenser ses coûts de transaction. Ainsi, là où la loi prévoit une exception rémunérée, la seule d'ailleurs qui subsiste dans le milieu de l'éducation, l'exception est devenue, dans les faits, gratuite.[16]

Quel type de raisonnement permet d'arriver à une telle conclusion? La décision de la Commission du droit d'auteur canadienne du 22 mai 2015 en matière de reprographie par les gouvernements provinciaux et territoriaux nous en donne une idée.[17] Dans cette affaire, les actes de reprographie que l'on cherchait à tarifer étaient en concurrence avec l'exception d'utilisation équitable à des fins de recherche[18], tout comme la rémunération prévue en matière d'éducation dans l'affaire précédente était en concurrence avec la nouvelle exception d'utilisation équitable à des fins d'éducation.[19] Dans les deux cas, on peut constater que la présence d'une exception d'utilisation équitable dans le contexte idoine fait diminuer le montant des redevances qui peuvent être perçues. La décision de mai 2015 fournit des exemples d'éléments d'analyse intéressants. Ainsi, au lieu d'envisager les copies qui sont faites par les divers gouvernements d'une manière globale, la Commission a plutôt choisi de regarder la situation en fonction de chaque utilisateur ultime des œuvres en question, c'est-à-dire un fonctionnaire type. Ce fonctionnaire type ne ferait que quelques copies de quel-

---

droits de l'homme; il n'y est pas question que *toutes* les exceptions seraient des droits des utilisateurs.

14 *Loi sur le droit d'auteur*, L.R.C. 1985, ch. C-42, art29.7–29.9.

15 *Loi sur le droit d'auteur*, art71–76.

16 *Tarif des redevances à percevoir par la SCGDE des établissements d'enseignements, au Canada, pour la reproduction et l'exécution d'œuvres ou autres objets du droit d'auteur communiqués au public par télécommunication pour les années 2012 à 2016*, Décision de la Commission du droit d'auteur, 19 décembre 2013, http://www.cb-cda.gc.ca/decisions/2013/ercc-19122013.pdf.

17 *Tarif des redevances à percevoir par Access Copyright pour la reproduction, au Canada, d'œuvres de son répertoire [Gouvernements provinciaux et territoriaux – 2005–2014]*, Décision de la Commission du droit d'auteur, 22 mai 2015, http://www.cb-cda.gc.ca/decisions/2015/DEC-2015-03-22.pdf.

18 *Loi sur le droit d'auteur*, art29.

19 *Ibid.*

ques œuvres par année. De plus, la Commission remet en question les droits qui sont détenus par la société de gestion et lui reproche de ne pas être en mesure de faire la preuve d'un mandat explicite pour chaque œuvre qui serait copiée par un utilisateur. Au final, une telle approche analytique signifie que, alors qu'elle espérait obtenir deux millions et demi de dollars par année en redevances, la société de gestion n'a obtenu qu'entre quatorze mille et soixante mille dollars par année. Même en tenant compte du fait que le montant qui avait été initialement demandé pouvait ne représenter qu'un point de départ dans un contexte de négociation, on doit admettre que le résultat obtenu va nettement en-deçà des attentes même les plus pessimistes.

Que s'est-il passé? Dans un contexte pourtant ouvertement affiché de gestion collective, c'est plutôt à une micro-gestion du droit d'auteur que l'on a eu droit. Dans un univers qui accepte le fonctionnement approximatif, l'insistance sur les droits des utilisateurs en tant qu'individus a mené à la recherche d'une mise en œuvre individuelle du droit d'auteur qui refuse de reconnaître l'effet de masse de certains comportements. C'est parce que l'on a tenu à faire valoir des droits des utilisateurs, en l'occurrence une utilisation équitable à des fins de recherche, qui appartiennent à des individus et non à des collectivités que l'on a préféré nier la possibilité de rémunération que permet la gestion collective. Cette décision de la Commission du droit d'auteur, ainsi que le désistement de la société de gestion de droits éducatifs en 2013, illustre à point nommé les propos tenus par un économiste en 2012 sur les rapports entre l'utilisation équitable et l'économie de marché :

> The absence of market mechanisms, or the failure for such market mechanisms to emerge, may be the very consequence of a liberal interpretation of the fair dealing exception. Indeed, without property rights, the market cannot emerge. A broadened, liberal, and relatively unrestrictive interpretation of fair dealing could prevent the appropriate market from emerging and functioning efficiently, and this in turn would justify a broad, liberal, and relatively unrestrictive interpretation of fair dealing. This would all lead to a vicious circle that could be harmful to the production and dissemination of original works.[20]

L'auteur de ces propos ne pouvait pas exprimer plus justement les conséquences de l'émergence des exceptions en tant que droits des utilisateurs sur le développement des exceptions rémunérées comme la copie privée. Un régime de rémunération fondé sur la gestion collective comme celui que l'on trouve dans le contexte des licences obligatoires, tel celui qui a été instauré par le régime de copie privée de la loi allemande de 1965, pouvait fonctionner dans les années 60 parce que le pacte social que représente ce système acceptait la justice approximative (« rough justice ») qu'il créait. Si l'on s'en tient à l'expérience cana-

20 M. Boyer, "The Economics of Fair Use/Dealing: Copyright Protection in a Fair and Efficient Way", (2012) 9 *Rev. Ec. Research on Copyright Issues* 3, à la p. 35.

dienne récente, c'est-à-dire celle qui est en train d'émerger dans un pays de droits des utilisateurs et d'exception pour le contenu généré par les utilisateurs,[21] on peut considérer que ce pacte est en train de se rompre.

Dans un univers où la tyrannie du consumérisme[22] s'impose graduellement, on ne peut ignorer le modèle que représente le régime allemand de la copie privée si l'on veut que la loi sur le droit d'auteur continue de régir essentiellement des opérateurs commerciaux. Cependant, si l'on veut aller dans cette direction, cela signifie qu'il faut travailler à améliorer deux problèmes. Il faut d'abord chercher à mieux définir le statut juridique d'un tel régime parce que, dans l'état actuel du droit, son positionnement dans l'ensemble du système du droit d'auteur est équivoque. Par la même occasion, il est aussi nécessaire de mieux expliquer le fonctionnement de la gestion collective à laquelle un tel régime fait appel. En particulier, il faut démontrer que cette gestion collective, dans quelque contexte que ce soit, d'ailleurs, existe pour améliorer l'adéquation entre l'usage qui est fait des œuvres et les objets protégés par les droits voisins et la rémunération à laquelle correspond cet usage. Dans un monde où le seul exercice individuel du droit exclusif ne saurait réaliser la pleine mise en œuvre du droit, la gestion collective s'avère le meilleur outil pour combler les lacunes de cet exercice individuel. Le régime de copie privée de la loi allemande n'a jamais prétendu assurer une corrélation parfaite entre l'utilisation des œuvres et la rémunération des auteurs qui en découle; cependant, ce système est actuellement la meilleure voie que l'on connaisse pour tenter d'atteindre, dans un contexte d'utilisation massive des œuvres, une meilleure mise en œuvre de la loi sur le droit d'auteur. Voilà pourquoi, de nos jours, le régime de copie privée de la loi allemande demeure un modèle à considérer lorsque l'on s'interroge sur la forme que doit prendre le régime d'une composante du droit d'auteur.

---

21 *Loi sur le droit d'auteur*, art29.21.

22 Voir A. Strowel, "Licences non volontaires et socialisation du droit d'auteur: un danger ou une nécessité?" (1990–1991) 3 *C.P.I.* 161, surtout à la p. 179.

Richard Pfohl*

1.3 Exclusive vs. Remunerative Rights: The Third Way

In some ways I am ideally suited to address the themes of this year's Global Congress – albeit from a Canadian perspective. I represent the Canadian music industry's exclusive rights arm: as general counsel to Music Canada, which represents the major Canadian recording labels as well as some leading independent labels. I also represent its remunerative and collective arm: as general counsel to CONNECT Music Licensing, a collective of over 2000 Canadian labels.

In addressing the question before our panel, as well as the broader themes of the conference, I would like to propose a Third Way.

I. Private Copying Exceptions and Illegal Sources: The Canadian Experience

I will return to that broader theme in a minute, but first I want to address the specific question before our panel, namely: could and should the approach in the German private copying levy approach be further developed.

The caveat I wish to provide is this: should the private copying exception be further developed, then it must be subject to the limitations set out in the European Court of Justice's April 2014 **ACI Adam** decision.[1] That decision confirmed that the private copying exception does not apply to copies from illegitimate sources.

My concern here is the scope of the exception. I don't have a problem with applying the remuneration right broader, so long as it doesn't create an exception to the exclusive right of reproduction for copies from illegal sources.

The European Court of Justice found that applying the private copying exception to illegitimate sources would violate the three-step test. It would encourage the distribution of pirated works, which would inevitably reduce lawful transactions and consequently have an adverse effect on normal exploitation of those works. This, in turn, would unreasonably prejudice copyright holders.

The Canadian experience demonstrates that the ECJ got it right. In stark contrast to the ECJ, the Canadian Copyright Board noted in a 2004 decision its opinion that under Canadian law:

* General Counsel, Music Canada and CONNECT Music Licensing, Canada.

1 Case C-435/12, ACI Adam BV v. Stichting de Thuiskopie (E.C.J. Apr. 10, 2014).

> "The [private copying] regime does not address the source of the material copied. There is no requirement [under the private copying exception] that the source copy be a non-infringing copy. Hence, it is not relevant whether the source of the track is a pre-owned recording ... or a track downloaded from the Internet."[2]

In contrast to the ECJ, in my opinion, the Canadian Copyright Board got it wrong. Why do I think the Canadian tribunal got it wrong? Well, the violations of the three-step test that the ECJ anticipated if judicial tribunals legalize copies made from illegal sources is precisely what did happen in Canada.

Following the Canadian Copyright Board decision, people going on the internet to what they would think is an objective source, namely, the about.com website, found the following explanation:

"Unauthorized Downloading is Legal in Canada"

About.com

- About.com is an online neighborhood of hundreds of helpful experts, eager to share their wealth of knowledge with visitors... Founded in 1996, About.com was acquired in March 2005 by The New York Times Company (NYSE: NYT). Today, About.com is recognized as a top 15 content site and one of the largest producers of original content on the Web.
- Visits, August 2009: 75,987,213

"An explanation of torrents in Net for Beginners on About.com: "Warning for new users: while P2P file sharing technology is completely legal, many of the files traded through P2P are copyrighted. Unless you live in Canada where users are shielded from P2P lawsuits, then downloading P2P files may put you at risk for a civil lawsuit in any other country".

"**Even though Napster 1.0 has been shut down by American law, it is now legal to download free music if you are in Canada.** Millions of people upload and download billions of songs each week, without paying a cent, and as of March 2004, Canadians cannot be prosecuted for this file trading."

Illegal filesharing sites expressly noted that downloading infringing material is legal in Canada, as the following screen captures indicate:

2 Copyright Board of Canada, Private Copying 2003–2004, Dec. 12, 2003.

Torrent Portal

Similarly, a Canadian-based site intended to facilitate illegal filesharing by blocking IP addresses of rights holder organizations such as the RIAA or the MPAA from accessing files being shared was launched in Canada, with the following disclaimer:

"The theory behind *PeerGuardian* is to block 'bad' IP addresses from one's computer. If you can block the RIAA's or MPAA's IP addresses, you can share in relative safety."

-*Slyck.com*, PeerGuardian 2.0 Goes Beta, February 24, 2005

"**Important Technical and Legal Notes**: "no masking of your address is 100% foolproof. At the same time, remember that in **any other country outside of Canada**, downloading copyrighted movies and songs puts you at legal risk for copyright infringement prosecution. Hundreds of users in the USA and UK have been fined by the MPAA and RIAA for downloading files in the last three years. **Only in Canada is P2P file sharing tolerated legally**."

Some sites in fact touted their Canadian location as establishing an effective safe harbor, thus encouraging illegal filesharing not only in Canada, but worldwide, as the following screen capture indicates:

IWannaDownload

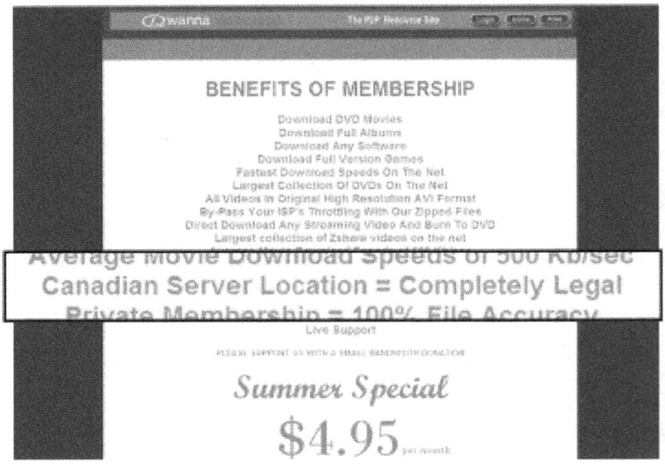

As a result of the perception that file sharing, or at least downloading, was legal in Canada, new music services were reluctant to launch in Canada. Meanwhile, commercial-scale piracy services flourished.

Our experience shows that the private copying regime has played an important role in the purpose for which it was conceived: filling a gap where licensing is impossible. But as the European Court of Justice recognized in **ACI Adam**, its use should be limited to gap filling, rather than competing with commercial marketplaces.

II. The Third Way: Licensing Exclusive Rights

Returning to the broader theme of this Congress, Remuneration for the Use of Works: Exclusivity vs. Other Approaches. What is to be done?

1. A True Dichotomy?

The Welcoming Statement for this Congress suggested a dichotomy:

> **"Current technical challenges make it seem more future-proof than ever to base the law not on rights to prohibit use [*i.e.*, exclusive rights] but on remuneration rights.** The "Digital Single Market" envisaged by the European Commission calls for a fully accessible network of content on the Internet; the unlimited exercise of exclusive rights contradicts this vision.
>
> "[P]articipants will examine the various mechanisms for achieving an equitable remuneration of right holders. Based on these mechanisms, the discussion will then focus on

> how to further develop the current system **so that copyright will act not to hamper development, but to promote it.**"[3]

There are a number of things I would agree with in this statement.

First, use of exclusive rights solely or primarily as an enforcement mechanism is not what economists would call an "efficient" approach.

Second, collective licensing can often be more efficient than individual licensing.

However, our experience challenges some of the assumptions of that dichotomy that associate exclusive rights solely with i) enforcement mechanisms and ii) individual rights holders, and remunerative rights with i) collective ii) licensing.

Our experience demonstrates:

- Exclusive rights are not a barrier to fully accessible networks of content.
- The most efficient means of licensing collectively is by exclusive rights. That allows bundling of rights and allows the marketplace to license uses rather than rights – that is, quickly and efficiently, with the least amount of artificial parsing of rights (e.g., determining the relative value of reproduction and communication rights).
- Furthermore, a system which bifurcates rights into exclusive and remunerative rights – as the Canadian system currently does – is in many ways the worst system. It guarantees that new services will sit on the sideline while tribunals attempt to value them – an exercise best and most efficiently handled by the marketplace.

I propose that the solution to such bifurcation of rights is not to abandon exclusive rights, but rather to embrace exclusive rights as a mechanism that enables the most flexibility for both collective and direct licensing.

2. Licensing Exclusive Rights vs. Remunerative Rights: The Canadian Experience

a) Responding to Technological Challenges

So, how are exclusive rights addressing *"current technological challenges"*?

From a consumer perspective, extremely well. Record companies have licensed over 40 million tracks and more than 400 digital music services worldwide, creating a € 5.1 billion digital business.

---

3 http://www.alai2015.org/en/home-welcome.html (emphasis added).

There is certainly a “value gap,” whereby digital music services invoke safe harbours, limitations on liability and shortcomings in notice-and-takedown regimes to present rights holders with a Hobson’s choice: accept low rates or have no effective recourse **or** compensation when infringing music is repeatedly reposted. To invoke Thomas Dreier’s eloquent metaphor from the earlier session, the fertilizer we have been using to nurture those trees we have so carefully cultivated – the ISPs and other intermediaries – is harming the ecosystem. But addressing these problems requires plugging loopholes to catch up with technological advances, not abandoning exclusive rights.

How are artists faring? Better than the recording industry. Both labels and the artists signed to them have seen their revenue decline in the past 5 years due to this value gap. But artists’ share of record industry revenues have actually increased over the past 5 years.

Six times out of seven, recording companies pay out more in royalties, advances to artists and investments in recording and marketing than they earn from a recording. But even with respect to the money that recording companies don’t pay out to existing artists, the amount of reinvestment in finding and developing new artists is, by objective standards, impressive. Viewing the recording industry’s investment in finding and developing new artists as a “research and development” (R&D) expense, the music industry invests more in R&D than industries traditionally viewed as R&D-intensive industries, as the following table shows:

How music’s global 15.6% A&R investment compare with other sectors’ R&D investment[4]

	Sector	Overall sector R&D intensity %
1	Music Industry	15.6
2	Pharmaceuticals and biology	14.4
3	Software and computer services	9.9
4	Technology hardware and equipment	7.9
5	Leisure goods	6.3
6	Aerospace and defence	4.5
7	Electronic and electrical equipment	4.3
8	Automobile and parts	4.2
9	Healthcare equipment and services	4.1
10	Industrial engineering	2.8
11	Chemicals	2.7

4 IFPI “Investing in Music: How Music Companies Discover, Develop & Promote Talent, 2014 (Source: Source: The 2013 EU Industrial R&D Investment Scoreboard. European Commission, JRC/DG RTD).

b) Remunerative Rights

How have collective remunerative rights addressed current technological challenges? In Canada, empirically, many Canadian artists would agree, frankly poorly.

Professor Ysolde Gendreau laid out some of the very significant challenges that we face now in Canada in trying to collectively license remunerative rights. In May 2014, The Canadian Copyright Board – the Canadian tribunal that is charged with certifying tariffs on remunerative rights – issued its decision in the Re:Sound Tariff 8 case. That decision set the rates that performers and makers receive for the communication right from semi- and non-interactive online music services.

Re:Sound, a "collective of collectives" that represents my organization, CONNECT Music Licensing, as well as other maker and performers' collectives, prepared for the decision by negotiating numerous commercial agreements with online music services. Re:Sound presented the negotiated agreements to the Canadian Copyright Board and asked them to certify what the marketplace had agreed to. The Board rejected the agreements negotiated by makers and performers and set rates at what it deemed "fair and equitable": approximately 10% of the marketplace rates negotiated by Re:Sound in its direct agreements with digital services.

And what did artists and performers think about the Canadian Copyright Board's decision of what their remunerative rights are worth? Social media exploded, as Canadian artists from the most established to the newest condemned the decision. Artist responses included the following:

Artist Responses on Twitter
Randy Bachman: #But I'm still ticked about Copyright Board disrespecting musicians. Their #Tariff8 decision is bad for all artists. That's the real story here. https://twitter.com/randysvinyltap/status/511641588947513344
Randy Bachman: #Tariff8 royalty rates an insult to & assault on music industry, sends message that the Board isn't taking care of business. #IStand4Music https://twitter.com/randysvinyltap/status/511605347971522560
Whiskey Jane: 4 million song plays to fill up a tour bus with gas...@BrettKissel Great article on Tariff 8 http://tinyurl.com/l457q47 #istand4music https://twitter.com/whiskeyjane/status/502143881748971520

Not only is a tribunal often a much worse rate setter than the marketplace, it is much slower.

Parties are required under Canadian law to submit proposed tariffs by March 31st of the year preceding which they will take effect. We then wait for at least nine months before a decision can, by law, take effect. But ironically, the Copyright Board takes so long to hear cases and issue rulings that the rates set are typically for periods of time that have already expired. Professor Jeremy DeBeer of the University of Ottawa undertook a survey of pending Canadian Copyright Board decisions, which produced the findings in the following table:

Canada's Copyright Tariff Setting Process: Average Time to Certify[5]
The average pending tariff has been outstanding for 5.3 years since filing
Certified tariffs took an average of 3.5 years to certify after filing
On average, tariffs are certified 2.2 years after the beginning of the year in which they become applicable, which is in effect a period of retroactivity
The average time from proposal filing to a hearing in those proceedings was just over 3 years. The average time from a hearing to tariff certification was almost 1.3 years

In the internet world in which our industry increasingly operates, you can imagine how outmoded and irrelevant tariffs often are by the time they're certified. The ensuing marketplace uncertainty makes new innovative services reluctant to launch in Canada. Because some of the rights are strictly remunerative, and consequently cannot be negotiated directly but must go through the statutory tribunal, the services and rights holders face years of uncertainty while the Copyright Board sorts out what some – but not all – of the rights are worth. Rights are bifurcated rather than bundled, so services are reluctant to do deals with anyone. Consumers, rights holders, and artists all suffer.

Finally, in certifying tariffs, the Canadian Copyright Board is constricted by what it is expressly authorized by statute to do. That means that much of the nuance in the Re:Sound agreements – setting different rates for services based on their level of interactivity or whether they agree to take reasonably available measures to prevent stream ripping – was stripped out of the tariff the Copyright Board certified for Tariff 8.

That's the remunerative rights side of the coin.

5 Source: Jeremy de Beer, Canada's Copyright Tariff Setting Process: An Empirical Review, 16 April 2015.

III. The Third Way

On the exclusive rights side, CONNECT Music Licensing can and does negotiate collective deals on behalf of our over 2000 rights holder members with music services, including new and innovative digital music services. We can include all the nuance the Copyright Board strips out. We can customize deals for specific services. And we can do it in a timely fashion.

For example, CONNECT licensed CBC Music, an online service and mobile app launched by Canada's national broadcaster, the Canadian Broadcasting Corporation, which contains a wide range of non-interactive and on-demand features, and features the first podcast service collectively licensed in Canada. This is just one of the innovative digital services that CONNECT has been able to license.

IV. Conclusion

This, then, I suggest is the Third Way: Use of exclusive rights not as an enforcement mechanism, but for both direct -- and collective – licensing. The following table compares the options of proceeding by licensing remunerative and by licensing exclusive rights:

REMUNERATIVE RIGHTS	EXCLUSIVE RIGHTS
License collectively	License individually or collectively (rights holders decide)
Tribunal determines pricing	Marketplace determines pricing
Rights bifurcated	Rights can be bundled
Statutory limitations on negotiable terms	Flexibility (no limitations)
Filed 9 months in advance; decided retroactively	Flexibility (immediate negotiation)

So to return to the Welcoming Statement to this Congress. The solution to current technological challenges is not to abandon exclusive rights in favor of remunerative rights. But rather, to reconceive exclusive rights not as a mere enforcement tool, but as a licensing tool. The Canadian experience empirically demonstrates that exclusive rights provide the flexibility to license rights both directly and collectively in a manner that optimizes returns to rights holders, flexibility and efficiency for service providers, and options for consumers in a rapidly evolving technological environment.

Paloma López*

1.4 The making available right for performers in Spain: a case of a statutory remuneration right managed by performers' collecting societies

The title of this panel leads us to ask whether a similar approach as the one set up for private copying by the German Copyright Act of 1965 could and should be further developed: in our view, a different legal approach should be established for other rights, especially regarding the making available right for performers.

I. The regulation of the making available for performers in Spain

The regulation of this right for performers in the Spanish Intellectual Property Act (as amended in 2006) is a reference for a diverse c approach:

- It is an **exclusive right** for audio and audiovisual performers included as a **special case of the right of communication to the public,** art 108.1 b).
- The right is **presumed by law to be assigned** to the producer, art 108.2.
- The law grants to the performer a **non-transferable remuneration right subject to compulsory management** through the performers' CMO, art 108.3.
- The equitable remuneration shall be **paid by anyone who makes it available to the public,** art 108.3. (users of phonograms published for commercial purposes and audiovisual recordings).

It is important to highlight that this model coexists with the right of communication to the public in the digital environment, which is another statutory remuneration right.

Both the making available right and the right of communication to the public are independent rights, compatible rights and cumulative rights.

* Head of International Legal Department, AIE.

II. Practical implementation of the making available right

Firstly, we have to identify the business models where works and other subject matter are made available to the public and/or communicated to the public. They refer to the audio and audiovisual areas.

In the audio area, we can make a distinction between music on demand without downloading (streaming/interactive webcasting) and music on demand with downloading. These cases fall under the making available right.

Also in the audio area, we find the use of automatic radio programming (webcasting), which is a case of digital communication to the public.

In respect of the practical implementation of the making available right, the following business models (audio) are mentioned:

- Communication to the Public on the Internet:
  - Automatic radio programming (webcasting):

- Making Available on Demand:
  - Music on demand without downloading (Streaming/interactive webcasting):

  - Music on demand with downloading:

In the audiovisual area, business models based on video on demand are covered by the making available right.

Other business models based on simulcasting/non interactive webcasting are covered by the right of communication to the public.

In respect of the practical implementation of the making available right, the following business models (audiovisual area) are mentioned:

- Communication to the Public on the Internet:
  - Simulcasting/non-interactive webcasting

- Making available on demand:
  - Video on demand:

Secondly, there are several key items to set up in the agreements:

In the audio field, the percentages are set up for each year, in conformity with a scale of implementation. For subscription services, the tariff is based on the application of a percentage of the revenues received by the user for its advertising and subscription activities in Spain.

As to the audiovisual environment, the tariff is based on the degree of use of audiovisual recordings depending also on the type of channel (Thematic TV channel and Generalist TV channel).

In order to be able to put each agreement in practice, AIE is provided with details on performances made available to the public and on the number of streams, on a quarterly basis. In addition to it, AIE is granted powers of verification.

How would a performers' CMO be able successfully to manage a statutory remuneration right for Internet uses?

From the experience of AIE, we find several necessary elements to set up an effective management of this right:

- Compulsory collective management;
- A strong capacity of negotiation granted by law, balanced with other stakeholders (producers);
- A supportive legal regulation of the right in case of legal actions against users;
- Information on the use of works and other subject matter furnished by users;
- A harmonized regulation of the statutory remuneration right for performers at EU level (it does not exist at the moment).

Why will this system be better for performers and why does an exclusive right without the additional remuneration right does not work for them?

1) If performers have only an exclusive right which is transferred to the producer, they will have a low remuneration and only for the main performers. Performers are against it, since they receive less than 4.6% of the exploitation revenues.
2) There is no remuneration for contents dated 70 years ago; in these cases, the link between the performer and the producer is lost (this is not an irrelevant question).
3) There is no remuneration for non-featured performers.

To sum up, a new legislation is necessary where the three categories of rightholders can manage their rights in a balanced way, without the rights of one of the categories prevailing over the others.
Conclusion, as to the question posed:

- A statutory remuneration right **can** be managed by a performers' CMO based on the pillars set out before.
- Setting up a strong remuneration right for performers according to the Spanish model will balance their position for the negotiation in the online environment, in respect of producers and users and will allow performers to secure the making available right that they are individually loosing. In this sense, the right **should** be granted to performers and be managed compulsorily by their CMOs.

I will conclude with a quotation from the Japanese writer and poet Ryunosuke Satoro, which serves to highlight how important it is for performers to have a collectively managed statutory remuneration right for Internet uses:

> "Individually, we are one drop. Together, we are an ocean" (1927–1982).

Thank you!

Rainald Ludewig*

1.5 Artenschutz für ein anachronistisches Rechtsinstitut – cui bono?

1. Es herrscht ein breiter gesellschaftlicher Konsens, dass gefährdete Arten im Zuge des Natur- und Umweltschutzes erhalten werden sollen. Fraglich ist, ob dieser Grundsatz auch für das Rechtsinstitut der Privatkopie uneingeschränkt gelten kann.
2. Die seit 50 Jahren erhobenen pauschalen Urheberrechtsvergütungen im Sinne der §§ 53, 54 ff. UrhG sind rechtsdogmatisch ein höchst eigenartiges Konstrukt. Weil man des eigentlichen Nutznießers praktisch nicht habhaft werden konnte, zog man einen allenfalls am Rande beteiligten Dritten heran, der den Nutznießer – den Verbraucher – sozusagen freikauft. Hierdurch sollte der Rechtsfrieden gesichert werden, der sonst durch massenhaft zu besorgende Urheberrechtsverstöße nachhaltig gestört worden wäre.
   Die Inanspruchnahme eines Dritten im Interesse hochrangiger Rechtsgüter lässt das Grundgesetz (GG) durchaus zu. Allerdings unterliegen solche Eingriffe strengen Voraussetzungen, vor allem im Hinblick auf den Grundsatz der Verhältnismäßigkeit und hier namentlich der Erforderlichkeit der Inanspruchnahme des Dritten.
   In der analogen Welt, für die die seit 1965 geltenden Vorschriften entwickelt wurden, konnte man diese Voraussetzungen mit guten Gründen als gegeben ansehen. Der Rechteinhaber hatte nach dem Verkauf des originalen Ton- oder Bildträgers bzw. der Ausstrahlung der Rundfunk- oder Fernsehsendung keine Möglichkeit mehr, eine Aufnahme oder Vervielfältigung durch den Verbraucher zu beeinflussen. So war es durchaus konsequent, Hersteller und ggfls. Einführer von Geräten, die zum privaten Kopieren urheberrechtlich geschützter Werke genutzt werden, heranzuziehen. Sie stellten die Geräte bereit, mit denen das Urheberrecht verletzt wurde und erzielten durch den Verkauf auch gewisse Erträge. Einen Teil dieser Erträge sollten daher die Rechteinhaber als Ausgleich dafür erhalten, dass ihre Eigentumsrechte nicht wirksam geschützt werden konnten. Da die Hersteller nach der Vorstellung des Gesetzgebers die Vergütung in ihren Abgabepreis einkalkulieren, zahlt idealerweise am Ende indirekt der tatsächliche Nutzer.

---

* Leiter Rechtsabteilung – Panasonic Marketing Europe GmbH. Note: Since this contribution was submitted at a very late stage, a translation was no longer possible, so that it is exceptionally published in German. Comme cette contribution a été soumise très tard, on ne pouvait plus la traduire, et l'a donc exceptionnellement publié en allemand.

Die EU-Richtlinie 2001/29/EG hat dies aufgenommen. Ausschließlich dann, wenn Urheber nicht in der Lage sind, die Werke von sich aus selbst zu schützen, soll der Verbraucher, der die Privatkopie erstellt, über eine Abgabe auf die Produkte, die eine private Kopie ermöglichen, belastet werden. Die frühere Justizministerin Zypries hat kurz und bündig zusammengefasst, wie die EU-Richtlinie auszulegen sei: *„Schützen, was man schützen kann. Vergüten, was man nicht schützen kann.“*[1].
Im Gegenzug müssen die Rechteinhaber die Erstellung von Privatkopien rechtlich dulden. Technische Schutzmaßnahmen zur Verhinderung von Privatkopien sind jedoch zulässig. Der Freikauf durch den Hersteller gibt dem Verbraucher also keinen Anspruch, von jedem Werk ohne gesonderte Berechnung eine oder mehrere Privatkopien herzustellen. Gelingt ihm die Kopie aus einer legalen Quelle ohne Durchbrechung oder Umgehung einer technischen Schutzmaßnahme, kann er allerdings sicher sein, vom Urheber oder Rechteinhaber nicht mehr belangt zu werden.
Die Geltendmachung der Vergütungsansprüche ist den Verwertungsgesellschaften zugewiesen. Sie nehmen auch die Verteilung vor und stellen hierfür Schlüssel auf. Ein nicht unbedeutender Teil der Einnahmen verbleibt ihnen als Mühewaltungsentgelt und Inkassoprovision. Damit sind sie neben Urheber, Hersteller und Verbraucher der vierte Beteiligte mit einem eigenen Interesse am Bestand der Privatkopieschranke und der Pauschalabgabe.

3. Seit Einführung der pauschalen Privatkopievergütung hat sich die Technologie grundlegend geändert. Das Nutzerverhalten und die Geschäftspraktiken der Rechteinhaber haben sich dieser Entwicklung umfassend angepasst. Dies hat drastische Konsequenzen für die Berechtigung der Inanspruchnahme des Drittstörers ebenso wie der Einschränkung des Urheberrechts durch die Zulassung der Privatkopie. Auch der Nutzen, den der Verbraucher hat, muss neu bewertet werden.
   a. Wer heute ein urheberrechtlich geschütztes Werk online bereitstellt, braucht nicht mehr resigniert zu dulden, dass damit Schindluder getrieben wird oder Mitbürger sich schamlos bedienen. Ihm steht eine breite Palette von Schutzmaßnahmen zur Verfügung. Er kann
      - den Zugang an Registrierung und Passwort knüpfen;
      - den Download im Umfang beschränken, also zum Lesen, zum Drucken, zum einmaligen oder mehrmaligen Speichern, zur uneingeschränkten Verwendung usw.
      - den Zugang oder Download entgeltlich oder unentgeltlich ermöglichen;
      - das Entgelt als Abonnementsgebühr oder pro Vorgang erheben und über Kreditkarte, Bankeinzug etc. kassieren.

1 Nach R. Sietmann, C't-Interview 16/2004, S. 158.

Entsprechende technische Systeme sind ausreichend vorhanden und etabliert. Es gibt – wie bei anderen Schutzgegenständen (z.B. Marken) auch – Firmen, die entsprechende Technologien und Überwachung von etwaigen Verletzungshandlungen anbieten. Entsprechender Schutz ist für jeden Urheber finanzierbar zu gestalten. Schon kleinste Fotos und Texte, wie sie z.B. im Bereich des Online-Handels für Artikelbeschreibungen eingesetzt werden, nutzen ganz selbstverständlich einen digitalen Schutz und steuern entsprechende Nutzungen.

Von diesen Möglichkeiten machen Rechteinhaber mittlerweile gern Gebrauch. Im Gegensatz zu früher sind heute digitale Werke weitgehend mit DRM-Systemen versehen. Der legale Handel mit kostenpflichtigen Downloads ist ein Multimilliardengeschäft mit vielen Millionen Verbrauchern als regelmäßigen Kunden.

Das digitale Fernsehen ermöglicht den Programmanbietern ebenfalls eine umfassende Kontrolle. Es lässt die Einflussnahme auf das Verhalten jedes einzelnen Nutzers zu. Kurioserweise beschweren sich Verbraucher bei den Herstellern und nicht beim Programmanbieter, dass man beim Abspielen der digitalen Kopie einer Fernsehsendung die mit aufgezeichneten Werbeblöcke nicht überspringen kann.

Der Rechteinhaber ist also in der Lage mittels moderner Technologien die Nutzungen nicht nur zu lizensieren, sondern auch zu steuern. Er kann mittels digitaler Technologie dafür sorgen, dass der Verbraucher nur eine bestimmte Anzahl Kopien machen kann. Natürlich kann er auch über den Preis der Originallizenz eine Kompensation für eventuelle Kopien geltend machen. Er könnte sogar für unterschiedliche Nutzungsmöglichkeiten unterschiedliche Preise verlangen.

Der Erfolg von Apple, Amazon und weiteren rund 70 Anbietern im Audio-Video-Bereich, aber auch Beck-Online und anderen zeigt, dass es nicht nur möglich ist, die richtigen Preise zu finden, sondern sie auch zu realisieren.

Vor diesem Hintergrund kann und muss der Urheber mehr Selbstverantwortung bekommen und selbst entscheiden können, welche Marketing-Strategien er verfolgen möchte, um seine Werke selbst zu vermarkten. Den Klagen mancher Künstler, Downloads und Streaming ihrer Werke würden von den Plattform-Providern nicht ausreichend honoriert, ist zu entgegnen, dass sie sich gegebenenfalls organisieren müssen, um sich durchzusetzen. Auch die Verwertungsgesellschaften wären eventuell geeignete Partner. Die Gerätehersteller können jedenfalls nicht für Einkommensdefizite aufkommen.

Es ist nicht nachvollziehbar, warum über Pauschal-Abgaben ausgerechnet die Hersteller der Technologie, die ihnen dies alles ermöglicht, für ein Zusatzeinkommen sorgen sollen. Eine derartige Subvention gibt es in keinem anderen Wirtschaftsbereich. Den Rechteinhabern sind die Technologien an die Hand gegeben. Es liegt an ihnen, sie zu nutzen. Unterlassen sie es, liegt kein unabwendbarer Nachteil vor, sondern schlicht eine Obliegenheitsverletzung. Die Berechtigung, den Hersteller als Drittstörer in Anspruch zu nehmen, weil das Eigentum anders nicht geschützt werden kann, ist in jedem Fall erloschen.

Viele Rechteinhaber stellen ihre Werke heute bewusst kostenlos zur Verfügung, etwa um ihren Bekanntheitsgrad zu steigern. Ein Download eines solchen Werks sollte nicht als pauschalvergütungspflichtige Privatkopie behandelt werden. Vielmehr ist es eine entgeltfreie Individuallizenz, deren Umfang der Rechteinhaber autonom festgelegt hat. Würde man die Hersteller trotzdem zur Kompensation heranziehen, läge eine Art Zwangssponsoring eines individuellen Marketingkonzepts vor. Selbst der Schutz der Kultur kann so etwas schwerlich rechtfertigen.

b. Für den Verbraucher ist das jetzige System der Pauschalabgabe nicht nachvollziehbar und führt zu Doppel- und Mehrfachvergütungen. So zahlt er zunächst einmal für einen Musikdownload. Ihm wird dann seitens der Contentanbieter eine Sicherungskopie empfohlen und hiermit vergütet er indirekt den Urheber durch die Abgabe auf die externe Festplatte noch einmal. Möchte der Verbraucher das online erworbene Werk aber auch auf anderen Endgeräten hören, so muss er, anders als bei der DVD, eine weitere Kopie erstellen, die eine weitere Pauschalvergütung begründet.

Trotz Mehrfachvergütung liegen Hinweise vor, dass im jetzigen System der pauschalen Vergütung auf Geräte und Speichermedien im Sinne der §§ 54ff. UrhG so viel Geld verlorengeht, dass der Urheber von jedem Euro lediglich weniger als die Hälfte erhält. Bei anderen Systemen, die eine Kompensation für die Privatkopie schaffen, erhält der Urheber hierbei über 80 Cent pro Euro[2]. Nimmt der Urheber zum Beispiel direkt beim Verkauf seines Werkes einen Aufschlag, erhält er vom Verbraucher, also dem, der tatsächlich die Möglichkeit der Privatkopie hat, unmittelbar eine Kompensation. Ein Aufschlag von 1–2,5% auf den Abgabepreis des Werks würde für eine angemessene Vergütung ausreichen[3].

Da die Privatkopievergütung für den Verbraucher in Deutschland häufig unsichtbar bleibt, erweckt dies vielfach den Eindruck, sie ermögliche dem Verbraucher kostenloses Kopieren und müsse daher erhalten bleiben. Zum einen ist dieser Eindruck falsch. Der Hersteller wird die

---

2 Ametic “Compensation for private copying – an economic analysis of alternative models”, Mai 2011.

3 Idem.

Vergütung nach Möglichkeit in seinen Abgabepreis einrechnen, Groß- und Einzelhandel handeln ebenso und schlagen noch ihre Marge auf. Der Verbraucher bezahlt die Illusion der Kostenfreiheit mit unnötig überhöhten, versteckten Kosten.
Zudem gibt es keine Rechtfertigung, über Geräte- und Speichermedienabgaben die Industrie zum Sponsor eines „Freibier-Internets" zu machen. Informationsfreiheit im Internet ist nicht gleichzusetzen mit Kostenfreiheit. Die französische Sprache ist hier präziser. Das Internet ist zwar „libre", aber nicht „gratuit". Insofern gilt dasselbe wie bei der Rundfunkfreiheit.

c. Somit verbleiben als letzte Nutznießer des anachronistischen Pauschalabgabensystems die Verwertungsgesellschaften. Sie halten stur am alten System fest, denn ihnen, nicht ihren Klienten, sichert es unverändert hohe Einnahmen. Dabei versäumen sie allerdings die Chancen, die ihnen eine Individuallizensierung bietet, denn eigentlich wären sie prädestiniert, ihre Klienten dabei zu unterstützen.

4. Nach allem ist es im wohlverstandenen Interesse aller Beteiligten, das komplizierte, aufwendige und ungerechte Vergütungssystem durch ein zeitgemäßes System der Individuallizenzen abzulösen. Die Schranke der Privatkopie könnte insoweit entfallen.
Ist dies wegen des Charakters der Quelle nicht möglich, etwa bei traditionellen Büchern oder analogen Tonträgern, wäre zu prüfen wie groß der Schaden der Rechteinhaber wirklich ist. Bei einem geringen Schaden, könnte die Kompensation laut EU-Richtlinie 2001/29/EG Erwägungsgrund 35 ganz entfallen.
Im Übrigen wäre es am wirtschaftlichsten und unkompliziertesten, eine Abgabe direkt beim Nutzer zu erheben. Hier bietet sich eine Erhebung pro Haushalt analog oder sogar in Verbindung mit dem Rundfunkbeitrag an. Würde man nur € 0,50 monatlich auf den Rundfunkbeitrag aufschlagen und diese den Urhebern zugutekommen lassen, erzielte man einen Jahresbetrag von über € 240 Millionen. Dies würde sämtliche einschlägigen Forderungen der Verwertungsgesellschaften abdecken. Den heutigen Reprographieeinnahmen entspräche ein Monatsbeitrag von nur € 0,20 je Haushalt. Eine politische Durchsetzung von derartigen Beträgen erscheint durchaus möglich. Dem Rechtsfrieden wäre ein Dienst erwiesen und der 6. Senat des OLG München könnte aufatmen.

2. How could contract law mechanisms be developed to improve economic protection of creators and performers?

Frank Gotzen*

2.1 Introduction

Meine sehr geehrten Damen und Herren, liebe Freunde,

At the 50th anniversary of the Copyright Act in Germany, it is a very good thing that the German group took the initiative of talking about the remuneration in the copyright world, and I realize from the discussions that were held before, that actually this is in line with the topic we are going to tackle now. Some time later on, we will have the opportunity to ask some questions. As for now, we shall have to look into the question of how to protect the artist and the author in a contractual relationship. The goal of our discussions is to see where we can find new evolutions. By saying that, we must be glad that things seem to happen not only in Germany, but also in France. Actually, the first speaker is going to talk about the most recent developments in France. It is my pleasure to give the floor right now to Pierre Sirinelli, professor at the University of Paris I.

* Emeritus professor at the KU Leuven (Belgium).

Pierre Sirinelli*

2.2 La rémunération de l'auteur dans la réforme française du contrat d'édition du 12 novembre 2014

La France a – en partie – modifié, il y a quelques mois[1] les règles relatives au contrat d'édition pourtant vieilles de moins de 60 ans et alors même que, originellement conçu en contemplation des œuvres littéraires, le *corpus* législatif antérieur avait été étendu par les juges – avec plus ou moins de bonheur – à d'autres secteurs (musique, logiciels, jeux vidéo, œuvres audiovisuelles, etc.).

La raison de cette évolution est sans contestation possible à rechercher dans le bouleversement des pratiques lié à la révolution numérique. De nouveaux modes d'exploitation apparaissent, de nouveaux modèles économiques se développent, de nouvelles figures contractuelles sont esquissées de sorte que les règles, le plus souvent d'ordre public, énoncées par le code de la propriété intellectuelle afin de protéger les auteurs, ne paraissaient plus pouvoir remplir leur office. Des discussions et des négociations ont été entamées entre auteurs et éditeurs mais les positions exprimées de part et d'autre ne se rejoignaient pas souvent tandis que les nouveaux contrats proposés ne paraissaient pas toujours équilibrés. En bref, pour les auteurs la liberté contractuelle paraissait un piège – au point d'exiger une évolution du cadre normatif – tandis que les éditeurs redoutaient de voir se dessiner les contours d'une nouvelle réglementation aussi contraignante que mal adaptée à une évolution inachevée et au dénouement encore inconnu.

Les créateurs revendiquaient depuis près de cinq ans une intervention législative dont la teneur serait assez simple. L'avenir étant incertain, il y avait lieu de se montrer prudent et de limiter les cessions : 1) une disposition légale viendrait exiger – à peine de nullité – un deuxième contrat, distinct du contrat prévoyant les modes d'exploitation classiques et notamment le papier, pour la cession des droits relatifs à l'édition numérique ; 2) la durée du transfert de droits opéré par ce deuxième contrat serait limitée par le législateur.

Les éditeurs, au contraire, entendaient pouvoir bénéficier d'une cession totale aussi bien s'agissant des droits que de la durée et cela afin de réaliser – pour le plus grand profit des deux parties – la meilleure exploitation possible de l'œuvre. Une politique éditoriale imprimée ou numérique a besoin de temps et

---

* Professeur, Université Paris 1 Panthéon-Sorbonne et Université Paris 11-Sceaux, France.

1 Ordonnance n°2014-1348 du 12 novembre 2014 modifiant les dispositions du code de la propriété intellectuelle relatives au contrat d'édition.

la persévérance est l'une des qualités de l'éditeur qui croit en ses auteurs parfois bien avant que les œuvres de ces derniers ne rencontrent le public.

Les pouvoirs publics, quant à eux, redoutaient qu'une intervention intempestive ne fige les situations au point d'enfermer les parties dans une construction obsolète au regard des évolutions à venir.

D'où la mise en place d'un lieu de négociation et de concertation destiné à permettre d'esquisser les contours de nouvelles règles, d'abord par la désignation d'une Commission spécialisée relative au contrat d'édition à l'heure du numérique au sein du Conseil supérieur de la propriété littéraire et artistique (CSPLA)[2] puis, toujours dans le but d'aboutir à un projet de loi consensuel portant modification du code de la propriété intellectuelle, par la création d'une Mission chargée de faire évoluer les règles pour le secteur du livre. Les négociations se sont alors ouvertes entre auteurs et éditeurs sous l'égide d'un médiateur (le signataire de ces lignes). A l'issue de nombreux mois de discussion, auteurs et éditeurs ont signé, le 21 mars 2013, l'accord-cadre (« l'Accord ») sur le contrat d'édition dans le secteur du livre qui a permis d'aboutir à la rédaction de règles nouvelles s'appliquant à l'ensemble du contrat d'édition mais aussi plus particulièrement à l'exploitation numérique et imprimée des livres. Le ministère en charge de la culture s'est immédiatement engagé à proposer une réforme du code la propriété intellectuelle traduisant les nouvelles règles issues de l'accord ce qui a été fait par le biais d'une ordonnance fondé sur l'article 28 de la Constitution, procédure rare mais réalisable tant les Parlementaires qui ont autorisé cette délégation étaient conscients que le corps de règles proposé avait recueilli, sous le contrôle du Ministère, l'assentiment unanime des négociateurs.[3]

Fort de ce consensus, la modification du Code de la propriété intellectuelle a été opérée par l'Ordonnance du 12 novembre 2014[4] et est entrée en vigueur le 1er décembre 2014.

Architecture de la Réforme – Le caractère consensuel de la réforme a permis d'une part, d'aboutir à une construction normative inédite reposant sur

---

2 La mission du CSPLA est de conseiller le ministre chargé de la culture en matière de propriété littéraire et artistique.

3 L'ordonnance poursuivait quatre objectifs :
- Etendre et adapter les dispositions générales relatives aux contrats d'édition à l'édition numérique ;
- Préciser les règles particulières applicables à l'édition d'un livre sous forme imprimée et sous forme numérique ;
- Organiser le renvoi, pour les modalités d'application de ces dispositions nouvelles, à des accords entre les organisations professionnelles représentatives du secteur du livre en vue de leur extension à l'ensemble des auteurs et éditeurs du secteur par arrêté du ministre chargé de la culture ;
- Préciser l'application dans le temps de ces dispositions.

4 L'Ordonnance n°2014-1348 du 12 novembre 2014 modifiant les dispositions du code de la propriété intellectuelle relatives au contrat d'édition.

l'articulation entre des dispositions, formellement, d'origine légale et des prescriptions contenues dans un accord professionnel. C'est dire que les solutions nouvelles – rédigées par les professionnels représentant les deux catégories d'acteurs : auteurs et éditeurs – ont été ventilées dans deux *corpus* normatifs à la fois liés et distincts.

La construction retenue est alors la suivante :

1) La loi pose les principes en renvoyant pour les « *modalités d'application* » à 2) un « *Accord* », signé par les auteurs (CPE) et les éditeurs (SNE) et également appelé « code des usages ».

Cet Accord est rendu obligatoire à l'ensemble des auteurs et éditeurs du secteur du livre par un arrêté (du 10 décembre 2014[5]) du ministre chargé de la culture. Son contenu est susceptible d'évoluer avec le temps. En effet dans le souci de permettre l'anticipation des évolutions induites par les technologies numériques, l'adaptation aux évolutions des usages professionnels ou pour régler toute difficulté née de l'application de cet Accord, l'arrêté du 10 décembre 2014 prévoit que les parties signataires engagent une discussion sur sa révision, sous l'égide du ministère chargé de la culture, tous les cinq ans à compter de sa signature. Les parties peuvent même conjointement convenir que ces discussions seront engagées dans un délai inférieur à cinq ans.[6]

L'Accord puise son autorité de la délégation expresse faite par le législateur à l'article L.132-17-8 du code de la propriété intellectuelle. L'ensemble constitue ainsi le nouveau statut de l'édition d'un livre. Il convient donc de lire le dispositif mis en place en tenant compte tant du donné légal que des dispositions de l'Accord auxquelles il est renvoyé. Dans le futur, à défaut d'Accord et afin d'assurer la cohérence du dispositif, les « *modalités d'application* » des dispositions du code de la propriété intellectuelle visées à l'article L.132-17-8 seraient adoptées par décret en Conseil d'État.

Souplesse et vigueur – Cette construction inédite visait donc à concilier, rapidement, vigueur et souplesse. La vigueur proviendrait de la place accordée à la loi et de la délégation formelle opérée par elle, sans risque d'incertitude quant au contenu de la norme. Le système nouveau se dégage de la pratique actuelle du Code de la propriété intellectuelle de renvoi aux simples usages[7], ce qui suppose des pratiques qui se dégagent peu à peu et dont le juge serait éventuellement le héraut. Dans la construction nouvelle, tout est déjà écrit (en concertation entre auteurs et éditeurs) et le juge ne peut écarter la solution à laquelle la loi renvoie. La souplesse, quant à elle, est le fruit de la facilité d'évolu-

5 Arrêté du 10 décembre 2014 portant extension de l'accord du 1er décembre 2014 entre le CPE et le SNE sur le contrat d'édition dans le secteur du livre.

6 Préambule de l'accord entre le CPE et le SNE sur le contrat d'édition dans le secteur du livre. Arrêté du 12 décembre 2014.

7 Pour exemple, le code des usages de littérature générale de 1981.

tion du deuxième *corpus* (renégociation d'un nouvel accord entre les parties sous l'égide du ministre de la Culture) sans avoir à solliciter à nouveau le législateur. En effet, il suffit d'un nouvel Accord.

C'est tout le régime du contrat d'édition de livres qui est ainsi revisité. Ce qui comprend bien naturellement, la question de la rémunération, point jugé comme absolument fondamental par les auteurs. Les règles mises en place en la matière s'articulent en deux axes : la réforme comprend des règles destinées à assurer le caractère juste de la rémunération due aux auteurs (I) ainsi que des règles destinées à assurer l'effectivité de cette rémunération juste (II).

I. Règles destinées à assurer le caractère juste de la rémunération due aux auteurs

Ces règles imposent dans les contrats des stipulations destinées à préserver les intérêts des auteurs. Cela passe par l'énoncé d'un certain nombre de principes (A) complétés par l'obligation d'insérer une clause de réexamen des conditions économiques du contrat (B).

1. Principes

Une fois énoncé le principe d'une rémunération proportionnelle, demeurait la difficulté de savoir sur quoi faire porter cette dernière.

Exigence d'une rémunération « juste et équitable » – Le contrat d'édition doit garantir à l'auteur une rémunération « *juste et équitable* » sur l'ensemble des recettes provenant de la commercialisation et de la diffusion d'un livre édité sous une forme numérique.

Rémunération proportionnelle – La rémunération proportionnelle est le principe et le recours au forfait l'exception.

Pour ce dernier, il est précisé que dans les cas prévus de recours à un forfait, celui-ci ne saurait être versé à l'auteur en contrepartie de la cession de l'ensemble de ses droits numériques et pour tous les modes d'exploitation numérique de l'ouvrage. Dans les cas de contributions à caractère accessoire ou non essentiel mentionnés au 4° de l'article L.131-4[8] CPI, une telle cession est possible.

8 La nature ou les conditions de l'exploitation rendent impossible l'application de la règle de la rémunération proportionnelle, soit que la contribution de l'auteur ne constitue pas l'un des éléments essentiels de la création intellectuelle de l'œuvre, soit que l'utilisation de l'œuvre ne présente qu'un caractère accessoire par rapport à l'objet exploité.

Le forfait ne peut être justifié que pour une opération déterminée et toute nouvelle opération permettant le recours à un forfait s'accompagne de sa renégociation.

Assiettes de la rémunération – Pour la vente à l'unité, la participation proportionnelle aux recettes au profit de l'auteur est calculée en fonction du prix public hors taxes (PPHT). Cette règle posée par la jurisprudence dans le cadre de la vente de livre imprimé est à présent expressément consacrée par la loi pour le livre numérique. Le taux de rémunération continue de relever, quant à lui, de la négociation individuelle entre l'auteur et l'éditeur.

Mais cette solution est loin d'épuiser la diversité des situations propres à l'univers numérique et les auteurs ont manifesté le souhait de voir la loi appréhender les nouveaux modèles (abonnements, bouquets, publicité, etc. ...) afin que des règles protectrices puissent être édictées. Ainsi, dans les cas où il n'y a pas de prix de vente à l'unité, la rémunération de l'auteur se fait sur la base du prix payé par le public au prorata des consultations et des téléchargements de l'œuvre. En cas d'impossibilité de reconstitution du prix public de vente, la rémunération de l'auteur est opérée à partir des recettes encaissées par l'éditeur au prorata des consultations et des téléchargements.

Dans les cas où le modèle économique mis en œuvre par l'éditeur repose en tout ou partie sur la publicité ou sur toutes recettes liées indirectement au livre, une rémunération est due à ce titre. Aucune clause du contrat ne peut exclure une source de revenu.

2. Clause de réexamen des conditions économiques du contrat

Il s'agit là d'une figure juridique totalement inhabituelle car le droit français repose plutôt sur l'intangibilité des contrats. Mais les dispositifs techniques et les modèles économiques étant extrêmement mouvants, un contrat « juste » au jour de sa formation ne le serait plus nécessairement quelques années plus tard, au cours de son exécution. Pour cette raison, le législateur a offert aux deux parties, sous certaines modalités, la possibilité de demander une renégociation du contrat.

Faculté de révision encadrée – Le réexamen des conditions économiques du contrat doit porter notamment sur l'adéquation de la rémunération de l'auteur, qu'elle soit proportionnelle ou forfaitaire, à l'évolution des modèles économiques de diffusion numérique de l'éditeur ou du secteur.

Cette solution tente de réaliser un équilibre entre sécurité contractuelle et caractère équitable de la rémunération. Afin de ne pas prendre le risque de trop fragiliser les conventions passées, le processus de renégociation – qui permet d'assurer le caractère « juste » de la rémunération – s'inscrit dans un processus légalement encadré, notamment en matière de délais. La possibilité de renégociation est plusieurs fois offerte aux deux parties suivant un agenda (voir le paragraphe suivant). Au-delà de ces occasions calibrées, la possibilité de renégociation est encore offerte en cas de modification substantielle de l'économie du secteur.

Afin que chacun puisse être conscient de cette possibilité de renégociation, le contrat d'édition doit comporter une clause de réexamen de plein droit des conditions économiques de la cession des droits d'exploitation numérique.

Procédure – L'auteur et l'éditeur peuvent chacun demander un réexamen au terme d'un premier délai de quatre ans à compter de la signature du contrat et cela pendant une durée de deux ans. Passé ce délai de six ans et pour une, nouvelle, durée de neuf ans, l'auteur et l'éditeur peuvent chacun introduire deux demandes de réexamen. Au-delà de cette période de quinze ans, la demande de réexamen n'est pas totalement épuisée mais est alors subordonnée à un cas de modification substantielle de l'économie du secteur entrainant un déséquilibre du contrat depuis sa signature ou sa dernière modification.

Dans tous les cas, l'autre partie au contrat dispose d'un délai maximum de trois mois pour faire droit à la demande de réexamen.

Effets – L'auteur et l'éditeur négocient de bonne foi les nouvelles conditions de rémunération de l'auteur. En cas de refus de réexamen ou de désaccord, l'une ou l'autre des parties peut saisir une commission de conciliation, composée à parité de représentants des auteurs et des éditeurs, dont l'avis est rendu dans les quatre mois suivant la saisine. La commission rend un avis qui ne lie pas les parties. La consultation de la commission n'est pas un préalable obligatoire à la saisine d'un juge.

II. Règles destinées à assurer l'effectivité du caractère juste de la rémunération due aux auteurs

Il ne suffit de poser des règles imposant le choix de la solution la plus intéressante possible pour les auteurs, il faut aussi imposer des obligations ou solutions permettant de rendre cette dernière bien réelle. Certaines étaient connues mais ont vu leur régime renforcé (A). Le législateur a, cependant, voulu aller plus loin jusqu'à créer une solution nouvelle qui permet une sortie aisée d'un contrat qui ne produit plus d'effet (B).

1. Le renforcement d'obligations classiques

L'auteur aura plus de chance de toucher une rémunération intéressante si son œuvre est bien exploitée. Tel est l'objet de l'obligation d'exploitation permanente et suivie (1). Mais il ne pourra vérifier la « sincérité » des sommes à lui versées que s'il est informé de la réalité de cette exploitation et de ses effets. C'est l'objet de la reddition de comptes (2). Ces obligations existaient déjà mais leur contour a été mieux cerné au point de faire peser des devoirs plus lourds sur les éditeurs. Le législateur a, en outre, imposé des sanctions plus efficaces dans l'hypothèse où ces obligations seraient méconnues.

a) Obligation d'exploitation permanente et suivie

Lorsque la rémunération est proportionnelle, l'importance des sommes dues est fonction, certes, du succès de l'œuvre mais aussi des efforts accomplis par l'éditeur pour communiquer l'œuvre au public.

Les principes généraux sont les mêmes que l'édition soit sous forme papier ou numérique. Mais certaines modalités peuvent varier suivant le type d'exploitation concernée.

Edition imprimée – Afin d'assurer l'exploitation permanente et suivie de l'édition imprimée de l'œuvre, l'éditeur est tenu d'assurer une « diffusion active » de l'ouvrage pour lui donner toutes ses chances de succès auprès du public. La loi dresse une liste d'actes devant être pris en considération pour savoir si l'obligation est respectée. Dans le respect de ces critères, un éditeur pourra cependant procéder à des impressions à la demande, il devra toutefois en informer l'auteur.

En cas de manquement, la résiliation de la cession des droits d'exploitation imprimée de l'œuvre a lieu de plein droit lorsque, sur mise en demeure de l'auteur lui impartissant un délai de six mois, l'éditeur n'a pas exécuté l'une de ses obligations. Cette résiliation n'a pas d'effet sur la partie distincte du contrat relative à l'exploitation numérique. Par ailleurs, la loi précise expressément que cette résiliation est sans effet sur les contrats d'adaptation audiovisuelle prévus à l'article L.131-3 du code de la propriété intellectuelle.

Forme numérique – En cas de communication du livre sous une forme numérique, l'éditeur est pareillement tenu d'assurer une exploitation permanente et suivie La réforme a entendu cerner dans le détail l'étendue de cette obligation car, dans la mesure où il est impossible de procéder au constat d'épuisement de l'édition numérique d'un livre, les rédacteurs de la réforme ont jugé nécessaire de définir objectivement les diligences éditoriales qui permettent d'assurer le respect de l'obligation d'exploitation permanente et suivie numérique. La liste est, naturellement, différente de celle donnée à propos de l'édition imprimée. Pour assurer une diffusion active de l'ouvrage et lui donner toutes ses chances de succès auprès du public, à compter de sa publication, l'éditeur est tenu :

- d'exploiter l'œuvre dans sa totalité sous une forme numérique ;
- de la présenter à son catalogue numérique ;

- de la rendre accessible dans un format technique exploitable en tenant compte des formats usuels du marché et de leur évolution et dans au moins un format non propriétaire ;
- de la rendre accessible à la vente dans un format numérique non propriétaire, sur un ou plusieurs sites en ligne, selon le modèle commercial en vigueur dans le secteur éditorial considéré. L'idée est de favoriser l'exploitation de l'œuvre dans un format interopérable.

Si l'éditeur manque à cette obligation, l'auteur peut résilier le contrat de plein droit lorsque, après une mise en demeure de l'auteur adressée par lettre recommandée avec demande d'avis de réception, l'éditeur ne satisfait pas dans un délai de six mois à compter de cette réception, aux obligations qui lui incombent à ce titre.

Cette résiliation n'a d'effet que sur la partie distincte du contrat d'édition relative à la cession des droits d'exploitation du livre sous une forme numérique. Par ailleurs, elle est sans effet sur les contrats d'adaptation audiovisuelle.

b) Obligation de reddition de comptes

L'obligation de reddition de comptes existait dans la loi française depuis 1957. Mais son efficacité prêtait à discussions. En effet, si l'article L.132-13 du code de la propriété intellectuelle prévoyait bien une obligation d'envoi des redditions, au moins une fois l'an, à la demande de l'auteur, aucune sanction n'était expressément prévue par ce texte et peu d'auteurs allaient jusqu'à saisir un tribunal pour voir constater un manquement à cette obligation.

Et cela alors même que cette obligation – qui permet indirectement de contrôler l'adéquation de la rémunération versée à l'auteur – est pourtant regardée comme fondamentale au point d'être présentée comme étant « de l'essence »[9] du contrat d'édition et au point d'être imposée par les tribunaux même pour une exploitation hors de France. Ceci explique que, lors de la négociation entre le CPE et le SNE, la question de la reddition des comptes était, pour les auteurs, l'un des thèmes de discussion les plus importants surtout au vu des différends assez fréquents à ce propos.[10]

---

9 A. Lucas, H.-J. Lucas et A. Lucas-Schloetter, *Traité de la propriété littéraire et artistique* : LexisNexis, 4e éd. 2012, §754.

10 En 2012, le 4ème baromètre sur les relations auteurs-éditeurs (SCAM/SGDL), relevait que «*l'absence de reddition des comptes ou la réception de redditions incomplètes ou incompréhensibles est un constat très largement partagé chez les auteurs. Moins de la moitié des auteurs reçoivent des redditions de comptes de la part de leurs éditeurs alors qu'elles sont obligatoires… Ceux qui les reçoivent ne les trouvent pas claires (49%) et/ou pas complètes (55%). Et pourtant, ils ne sont que 18 % à avoir réclamé à plusieurs reprises ces relevés de droits. Il reste difficile de mettre un éditeur en demeure de respecter la loi*».

Pour le secteur du livre, la réforme a permis de mieux préciser les contours de l'obligation de reddition de comptes, renforçant les devoirs pesant sur l'éditeur et offrant aux auteurs des possibilités de résiliation du contrat en cas d'inexécution de cette obligation.

Contenu de la reddition des comptes – Une reddition de comptes doit être établie par ouvrage, y compris dans le cas où l'éditeur exploite plusieurs ouvrages d'un même auteur, et ce pour l'ensemble des ventes réalisées, quel que soit le circuit de diffusion.

Lorsque le livre est édité sous une forme imprimé, l'état des comptes doit mentionner obligatoirement : le nombre d'exemplaires fabriqués en cours d'exercice, le nombre des exemplaires en stock en début et en fin d'exercice, le nombre des exemplaires vendus, le nombre des exemplaires hors droit et détruits au cours de l'exercice. Par ailleurs, dans les cas prévus à l'article L.132-6 du code de la propriété intellectuelle, les redditions de comptes indiquent le nombre d'exemplaires constituant le premier tirage.

Lorsque le livre est édité sous une forme numérique, l'état des comptes doit mentionner obligatoirement dans une partie spécifique : les revenus issus de la vente à l'unité et les revenus de chacun des autres modes d'exploitation du livre numérique qui doivent être spécifiquement identifiés par une ligne distincte, ainsi que l'assiette et le taux de rémunération.

Par ailleurs, l'état des comptes doit également mentionner obligatoirement : la liste des cessions de droits réalisés au cours de l'exercice, le montant des redevances correspondantes dues ou versées à l'auteur ainsi que les assiettes et le taux des différentes rémunérations prévues au contrat.

Envoi de la reddition des comptes – Dans le secteur du livre, l'éditeur est tenu, pour chaque ouvrage, d'adresser à l'auteur, au moins une fois l'an, ou de rendre disponible pour l'auteur sur un espace dédié une reddition des comptes complète, avec l'ensemble des mentions rappelées précédemment. La mise à disposition de la reddition des comptes sur un espace dédié par l'éditeur nécessite l'accord préalable de l'auteur et dans ce cas l'éditeur est tenu d'informer l'éditeur de la disponibilité de la reddition des comptes sur l'espace dédié.

L'envoi ou la mise à disposition des relevés de comptes doivent intervenir dans un délai maximum de six (6) mois à compter de la date d'arrêté des comptes prévue au contrat.

Sanctions de l'inexécution – Deux causes de résiliation du contrat ont été envisagées par le législateur : l'inexécution totale de l'obligation et le retard persistant dans l'exécution.

En cas de défaut d'exécution, c'est-à-dire lorsque l'éditeur n'a pas satisfait à son obligation selon les modalités et dans les délais précités, l'auteur dispose d'un délai de six mois pour mettre l'éditeur en demeure d'exécuter son obligation de reddition. Lorsque cette mise en demeure n'est pas suivie d'effet dans un délai de trois mois, le contrat est résilié de plein droit.

En cas de simple retard dans la reddition de comptes, l'auteur peut également obtenir la résiliation unilatérale du contrat de plein droit. Lorsque l'éditeur n'a satisfait, durant deux exercices successifs, à son obligation de reddition des comptes que sur mise en demeure de l'auteur, le contrat est résilié de plein droit dans les six mois qui suivent la seconde mise en demeure.

Dans ces deux cas, en raison du caractère essentiel et global de l'obligation de reddition des comptes qui porte à la fois sur l'exploitation imprimée et numérique du livre, la résiliation affecte l'ensemble du contrat d'édition.

2. Le constat du défaut d'activité économique

Cette solution est entièrement nouvelle et doit être comprise comme la conséquence des relations ouvertes et complètes existant entre un auteur et son éditeur. Ce dernier a demandé et obtenu une cession large, relative aussi bien aux ouvrages imprimés qu'à l'exploitation numérique mais lorsque cette construction contractuelle envisagée dans son ensemble ne produit en définitive plus aucun effet positif, il peut apparaître légitime de mettre fin au contrat sur la prise en considération objective de l'absence d'activité économique dans la vie d'un livre pendant une certaine durée, déduite d'une absence de revenus pendant cette période. Cette hypothèse est appelée « fin d'exploitation ». Les négociateurs l'appelaient, entre eux, la cause d'« *Electroencéphalogramme plat* ». Dans la mesure où cette solution offrant une facilité de sortie du contrat n'a pas pour objet de sanctionner un manquement par rapport à une obligation de l'une ou de l'autre des parties, la possibilité de résiliation est ouverte à l'auteur et à l'éditeur.

Principe – Le contrat d'édition prend fin à l'initiative de l'auteur ou de l'éditeur, si, pendant deux années consécutives au-delà d'un délai de quatre ans après la publication de l'œuvre, les états de comptes ne font apparaître de droits versés, ou crédités en compensation d'un à-valoir, au titre d'aucune des opérations suivantes :

« 1° Vente à l'unité du livre dans son intégralité sous une forme imprimée, à l'exception de la vente issue de systèmes de distribution réservés à des abonnés ou à des adhérents ;

« 2° Vente ou accès payant à l'unité du livre dans son intégralité sous une forme numérique ;

« 3° Consultation numérique payante du livre disponible dans son intégralité, pour les secteurs éditoriaux reposant essentiellement sur ce modèle de mise à disposition ;

« 4° Traductions intégrales du livre sous une forme imprimée ou sous une forme numérique.

Procédure – La résiliation est notifiée à l'autre partie par lettre recommandée avec demande d'avis de réception dans un délai de douze mois suivant la date limite d'envoi de l'état des comptes par l'éditeur ou de sa mise à disposition de l'auteur par un procédé de communication électronique. Le délai de préavis applicable à la résiliation est de trois mois. A l'expiration du délai de préavis, le contrat d'édition est résilié de plein droit. Dans ce cas, la résiliation porte sur l'ensemble du contrat d'édition.

Exception. Ces dispositions ne peuvent être mises en œuvre si l'œuvre est incluse en intégralité dans un recueil d'œuvres du même auteur ou d'auteurs différents, si l'auteur a donné son accord et si la vente à l'unité de ce recueil dans son intégralité, en version imprimée ou numérique, a donné lieu au versement ou au crédit de droits pendant la période considérée.

En conclusion, si l'objectif général du législateur a été d'offrir un cadre juridique équilibré et "sécurisé" à l'exploitation diversifiée des œuvres dans l'univers numérique, l'attention prêtée à l'auteur parait très importante s'agissant de toutes les règles qui concourent à l'attribution d'une rémunération juste. On observera cependant que le législateur n'a pas osé imposer son dirigisme jusqu'à intervenir sur le taux de la rémunération proportionnelle due. Seule l'assiette sur laquelle la rémunération est assise a fait l'objet de son attention au point d'entrer dans un certain nombre de précisions en fonction des modes économiques ou techniques de mise à disposition des livres.

Silke von Lewinski*

2.3 A model that may indeed help

Good afternoon, Ladies and Gentlemen!

The subtitle of this conference is, as we heard already this morning, "Exclusivity vs other Approaches", and by "other approaches" we usually mean statutory remuneration rights. To be frank, I do not really like this "either/or" opposition – I want it all. And in fact, I can present you with a model that offers both the exclusive right **and** a statutory remuneration right at the same time, for the same right owners (authors and performers) and for the same use – and this all in one package. Why should I offer that model as a solution for the challenges we talk about here? Simply because I want to make everybody happy. I have always wanted to make everybody happy, even a long time ago when I was asked to draft a proposal for the European Commission on a Directive on Rental Rights. At that time, some Member States of the then EEC had an exclusive right for rental; others, in particular Germany, had a statutory remuneration right for rental rather than an exclusive right. Both sides had good arguments for their approaches. So, for me as a young expert to the European Commission, the question seemed to be what would be the right choice: to propose an exclusive right or a remuneration right. However, the EEC Member States did not like the "either/or", and I still wanted to make everybody happy. "Everybody" meant, in particular, as regards interested parties, on the one hand, the producers, who favoured an exclusive right because they want to negotiate licences, they want to shape the market. And, on the other hand, it meant authors and performers who favoured – in particular in Germany, where this already existed – a statutory remuneration right administered by CMOs, because they thought they would receive more money for the uses than on the basis of an individual contract. So, I was desperately looking for a solution.

So I went out of my office into the adjacent park in Munich-Bogenhausen and let my thoughts flow, immersed in the search for a solution – and then it appeared, as shown on this slide:[1]

---

* Dr. iur., Max-Planck-Institute for Innovation and Competition, Germany; Adjunct Professor, Franklin Pierce Center for Intellectual Property, University of New Hampshire (USA) and Assistant Professor, University of Zagreb; Member of the Faculty of the Munich Intellectual Property Law Center (MIPLC) (Germany).

1 Text of Art 4 EC Rental Directive 92/100/EEC; Art 5 of the Directive as consolidated by Directive 2006/115/EC.

"Article 4 – Unwaivable right to equitable remuneration

1. Where an author or performer has transferred or assigned his rental right concerning a phonogram or an original or copy of a film to a phonogram or film producer, that author or performer shall retain the right to obtain an equitable remuneration for the rental.
2. The right to obtain an equitable remuneration for rental cannot be waived by authors or performers.
3. The administration of this right to obtain an equitable remuneration may be entrusted to collecting societies representing authors or performers.
4. Member States may regulate whether and to what extent administration by collecting societies of the right to obtain an equitable remuneration may be imposed, as well as the question from whom this remuneration may be claimed or collected."

This is Article 4 of the EEC Rental Right Directive of 1992, which was later renumbered Article 5 of the consolidated version of the Directive.[2] In a nutshell, its underlying concept is that, on the one hand, we have the regular exclusive right of the author who transfers it to the exploitation business – in this case, the phonogram producer or film producer. And upon such transfer, the law grants him a separate, unwaivable right to equitable remuneration for the rental.

For those of you who are more visual, I put the working mechanism of this article into the following form:

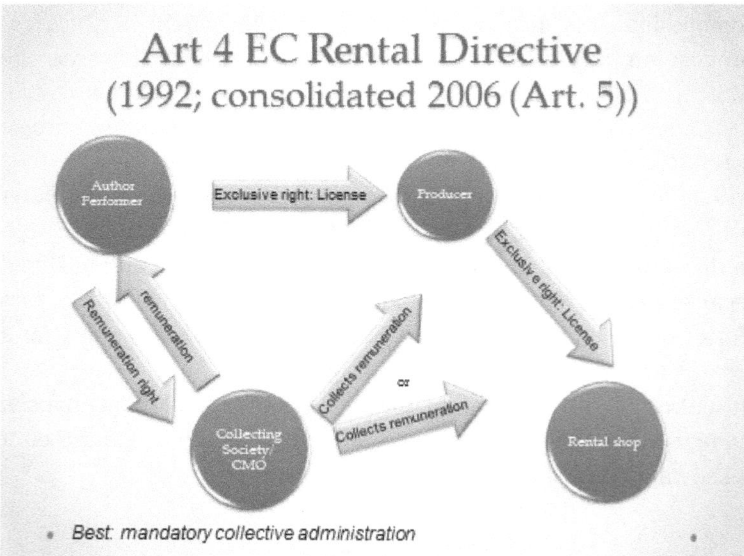

2 Consolidated version: Directive 2006/115/EC. On this provision and its background, see also, e.g., von Lewinski, Collectivism and its Role in the Frame of Individual Contracts, in: Jan Rosén (ed.): Individualism and Collectiveness In Intellectual Property Law, Cheltenham 2012, 117–127; von Lewinski, commentary on Art 4 Rental Directive 1992, in Walter/von Lewinski, European Copyright Law: A Commentary (Oxford 2010), 6.4.1 ff.

You have above on the left hand the author or performer with an exclusive right in the first place. He grants a licence to the producer, who is happy since he may shape the market through licensing. The producer then grants a licence to the rental shop, which is happy because it can do its rental business. Then, as you see again on the left side, the authors and performers are also happy since the law provides for them a separate remuneration right based on the law rather than on the contract, and they are even happier if this right is made subject to mandatory collective administration, since this is likely to strengthen their position as compared to their position in the individual contract. In this case, the author or performer transfers the remuneration right to the relevant CMO, which then collects the remuneration either from the producer or from the rental shop, depending on the choice made by the legislature. Regarding this choice, studies show that the second solution (claiming the remuneration from the rental shop) is the best one for authors and performers.[3] Under this solution, the CMO directly addresses the user, in this case the rental shop. Since we are talking here in Bonn about the future as well, one might think about applying this model to the making-available right – given in particular the news we have been hearing about Spotify. In this case, the CMO would directly claim remuneration from Spotify, which would have to pay to the CMO the authors' and performers' parts of the remuneration that would then go back, through the CMO, to the authors and performers.

The advantage of this solution is, of course, that authors and performers no longer have the problem that they need to negotiate the remuneration in the individual contractual relationship – and here I may refer back to what Tristan Azzi said this morning on "faire la guerre à son propre éditeur". So, here the authors do not need to fight against their own contractual partner, but the delicate problem of negotiating the remuneration is outsourced to the CMO. The CMO is principally in a more powerful position than the author alone since it negotiates for all authors collectively. Accordingly, there is a chance that more money will come back to the author.

For this model to work well, it is not only important that the remuneration right accompanying the exclusive right be based on the law rather than on contract, but also that this right be unwaivable. It is also essential that this right can be transferred only to a CMO for administration – in other words, that the law provides for mandatory collective administration. Otherwise, a producer might force the author or performer to transfer also the remuneration right to

---

3 This is the outcome of a study by AEPO/ARTIS, "Performers' Rights in International and European Legislation: Situation and Elements for Improvement", http://www.aepo-artis.org/usr/AEPO-ARTIS%20Studies/AEPO-ARTIS-study-on-performers-rights-1-December-2014-FINAL.pdf, – December 2014, p. 94 (see on that website also earlier versions, until June 2007, of the study).

him. Of course, I have to say that for a successful operation of this model in practice, you also need well-functioning CMOs. Overall, these are the elements that make this right a strong one for authors and performers.

It seems that at the time, I did succeed in convincing not only the European Commission but also the European Parliament and the Member States to take on this model. Although I have to say, as regards the Member States, I did have some trouble convincing the UK, due to something which again Tristan said this morning: in the UK, freedom of contract is really a sacrosanct principle. When I talked to the British delegates at that time, they looked shocked – they must have thought I was crazy when I proposed to intervene with the freedom of contract in favour of authors and performers through this model, which was supposed indirectly to remedy a typical contractual imbalance – but in the end the model found its place in the Directive.

And maybe this model could and should also be used beyond the field of rental rights, where it could serve as a solution to some of the current and new problems discussed here in Bonn regarding equitable remuneration for authors and performers. In fact, it has already been extended, for example in Germany, from the rental right to the cable retransmission right, where it works well.[4] And we have it in Spain for the making-available right – I think Paloma will talk about it.[5] Tomorrow we will have a chance to talk about it in the music flatrate context, and the SAA has claimed it for authors. Also, a very recent initiative by performers, the "fair internet for performers"[6] initiative, includes this model. And we will see tomorrow, maybe, from Maria of the European Commission, what they plan to do.

Thank you very much!

4 §20b(2) UrhG.

5 See P. López, p. 234 ff. below in this volume.

6 http://www.fair-internet.eu/wp-content/uploads/QA-2015-04-18-EN.pdf.

Sylvie Nérisson*

2.4 L'article 5.7 de la directive 2014/26/UE, une introduction diabolique du droit des contrats dans le droit d'auteur de l'Union européenne

Cette contribution a pour objet de mettre en évidence une anomalie au sein du droit d'auteur de l'Union européenne qui apparaît notamment dans la directive du 26 février 2014 « concernant la gestion collective du droit d'auteur et des droits voisins et l'octroi de licences multiterritoriales de droits sur des œuvres musicales en vue de leur utilisation en ligne dans le marché intérieur »[1] (« directive 2014/26) en son article 5.7 : depuis 10 ans, la Commission européenne ne parle plus que du groupe, indifférencié, des titulaires de droit, sans prêter attention à la situation particulière du titulaire originel des droits d'auteur[2].

Nous y voyons une anomalie diabolique car la lettre du 7e alinéa de l'article 5 de la directive 2014/26 est, à première lecture, *charmante*. Mais le charme réside dans l'étourdissement qu'il provoque : l'article 5 dans son ensemble consacre des libertés pour les titulaires de droit, et l'article 5.7 protège les titulaires de droit dans les contrats qu'ils concluent avec les sociétés de gestion collective. Or, comme dans l'ensemble des textes européens depuis une dizaine d'années, l'auteur a disparu et ne semble exister que du fait de la traduction de « *copyright* » par « droit d'*auteur* ». Le charme de l'article 5.7 est donc diabolique, car il ne protège pas ceux que le droit d'auteur et l'ALAI souhaitent protéger, les auteurs, et parce que la protection instituée désigne les organisations de gestion collective[3] comme les premières contre lesquelles le droit de l'Union protège des cocontractants dans le cadre du droit d'auteur.

Pour révéler l'anomalie et sa portée, nous allons présenter la protection introduite par l'article 5.7 (I), puis sa portée téléologique (II) en soulignant les

---

* Maître de conférences à l'IRDAP, Université de Bordeaux, chercheur affilié à l'institut Max Planck pour l'innovation et la concurrence, Munich.

1 Il n'est pas question ici de discuter de l'ensemble de la directive, ni du droit européen de la gestion collective. Sur ces deux aspects, nous renvoyons à nos travaux: «La directive 2014/26/EU du 26 février 2014 sur la gestion collective des droits d'auteur et des droits voisins: vol au-dessus de vaches sacrées intouchables», *Propriétés intellectuelles* n° 51, 2014, pp. 135–150 et notre thèse: *La gestion collective des droits des auteurs en France et en Allemagne : quelle légitimité?* IRJS éditions, 2013.

2 La jurisprudence de la CJUE tempère cette confusion, notamment dans le cadre de la question préjudicielle soulevée dans l'affaire *Hewlett Packard c. Reprobel*, aff. C-572/13.

3 Nous reprenons ici le terme de la directive, nous utiliserons par la suite l'expression courante en français de «*société* de gestion collective».

dangers de confondre auteurs et titulaires de droit et de désigner les sociétés de gestion collective comme les premiers cocontractants contre lesquels le droit d'auteur de l'UE protège le cédant de droit d'auteur.

I. La protection introduite par l'article 5.7 de la directive 2014/26

Selon l'article 5.7 :

> « Lorsqu'un titulaire de droits autorise un organisme de gestion collective à gérer ses droits, il donne son consentement spécifiquement pour chaque droit ou catégorie de droits ou type d'œuvres et autres objets qu'il autorise l'organisme de gestion collective à gérer.
> Ce consentement est constaté par écrit. »

Nous allons voir que l'exigence d'écrit et de mention spécifique est typique des contrats partisans qui protègent la partie réputée faible d'un contrat (A), puis que la portée de cette protection est très réduite par une phrase d'un considérant de la directive (B).

1. Des classiques de la protection de la partie faible d'un contrat

L'exigence d'écrit et de mention « spécifique » (on entend « expresse ») de l'objet d'un contrat est une figure classique des dispositions légales destinées à protéger une partie réputée faible dans un contrat. Elle se retrouve typiquement dans le droit de la consommation pour protéger le consommateur contre le professionnel, et dans le droit du travail pour protéger l'employé contre l'employeur. L'exigence d'écrit et l'interprétation stricte de la portée d'une licence de droit d'auteur caractérisent la plupart des dispositions nationales applicables aux contrats d'auteur[4] dans les pays d'Europe continentale.

L'idée sous-jacente est que, dans le respect de la liberté contractuelle, il convient de s'assurer que la partie non professionnelle d'un contrat est consciente de la portée du contrat auquel elle consent. Le charme du diable apparaît

4 Voir en ce sens les rapports sur les droits nationaux de la CEE puis de l'UE : A. Dietz, Le droit primaire des contrats d'auteur dans les états membres de la communauté européenne – situation législative et suggestions de réforme, Etudes secteur culturel, élaborée à la demande de la commission des communautés européennes, Luxembourg, 1981 ; S. Dusollier, C. Ker, M. Iglesias, Y. Smits, pour le parlement européen, www.europarl.europa.eu/meetdocs/2009_2014/documents/juri/dv/contractualarangements_/contractualarangements_en.pdf, Bruxelles, 2014.

ici : il promet la connaissance sous des traits séduisants et légitimes alors que dans la directive la confusion met en danger ceux, ou une partie de ceux, auxquels il semble s'adresser de manière bienveillante.

2. Une protection en grande partie neutralisée

Avant même de mesurer la portée de l'article 5.7 compte tenu de la vocation du droit d'auteur à protéger l'*auteur* contre ses cocontractants, la lecture attentive du dix-neuvième considérant de la directive atténue en grande partie la protection garantie par l'article 5. En effet, au sein des 3 alinéas et des 671 mots de ce considérable considérant, il convient de retenir à propos de l'article 5.7 que « l'obligation d'obtenir le consentement des titulaires de droits contenue dans l'autorisation à la gestion de chaque droit, catégorie de droits ou type d'œuvres et autre objet ne devrait pas empêcher les titulaires de droits d'accepter des modifications de cette autorisation proposées ultérieurement par accord tacite. »

L'admission de la modification tacite de la portée du contrat par lequel un titulaire de droit confie l'exercice de certains de ses droits d'auteur ou droits voisins à une société de gestion collective n'est certes pas totalement contradictoire avec les exigences de l'article 5.7. L'admission des modifications unilatérales et tacitement consenties ne concerne que les amendements au premier contrat conclu entre le titulaire de droit et la société de gestion collective, c'est le sens de l'adverbe « ultérieurement ». Mais cette phrase du dix-neuvième considérant limite donc la protection du titulaire de droit contre l'avidité (présupposée par l'article 5.7) de la société de gestion collective au premier contrat entre ces deux parties; libre ensuite à la société de gestion collective de se faire (con)céder tacitement des droits, étendant par là son champ de compétence et la portée de ce dont l'auteur se dépouille dans sa relation contractuelle avec la société de gestion collective.

Ainsi, l'assemblée générale d'une société de gestion collective peut décider d'étendre le champ de son activité aux droits numériques de ses membres, et assortir la décision de l'information des membres à propos de cet amendement au contrat de gestion[5]. L'extension vaudra sous réserve d'opposition expresse des membres dans un délai raisonnable. À défaut de réaction des membres, la société de gestion sera exclusivement compétente pour la gestion de ces droits. Cette réserve à la protection n'est pas exorbitante : elle est utile aux sociétés de gestion collective pour être réactive et soutenir leurs auteurs face à l'émergence de nouveaux modèles d'affaires.

5 Nous désignons par «contrat de gestion» le contrat par lequel un titulaire de droit charge une société de gestion collective de l'exercice de ses droits. Le droit allemand parle communément de *Wahrnehmungsvertrag*.

Nous y voyons toutefois un trait diabolique car cette limitation est cruciale et pourtant discrète au milieu d'un long alinéa, lui-même noyé dans la masse des 58 considérants de la directive.

II. Le sens de la protection garantie par l'article 5.7 de la directive 2014/26

L'article 5.7 nous semble diabolique car il protège indifféremment les auteurs et les cessionnaires, notamment commerciaux (A), contre les organismes à but non lucratif (art 1 a) ii) de la directive) que sont les sociétés de gestion collective (B) fondées par les *auteurs*[6] pour s'unir et ne pas laisser leur isolement les affaiblir dans leurs négociations avec les exploitants.

1. Les bénéficiaires de la protection : les titulaires de droit

L'article 5.7 ne protège ni les auteurs ni les artistes interprètes, ces créatifs trop contents de voir leurs œuvres et interprétations atteindre un public par le biais des licences accordées par les sociétés de gestion collective. L'article 5.7 protège les *titulaires de droit*, définis à l'article 3 c) de la directive comme toute personne détenant un droit d'auteur, un droit voisin, ou une quote-part des revenus provenant de ces droits, sans distinguer selon que ces titulaires le soient du fait de la loi ou d'un contrat d'exploitation.

La première disposition de « droit contractuel d'auteur » du droit de l'UE ne distingue donc pas entre, d'une part, les titulaires originels et, d'autre part, les cessionnaires et exploitants.

Le sens téléologique de la disposition est conséquemment que tous les titulaires de droit sont la partie faible du contrat entre eux et une société de gestion collective.

Il nous semble, ici comme ailleurs dans la directive et le droit européen, regrettable, pour ne pas dire dangereux, de ne pas distinguer, surtout dans le contexte contractuel, entre un auteur et son cessionnaire, puisqu'il est loin d'être exceptionnel que l'auteur, en principe une personne physique, se trouve face à une multinationale de l'édition.

6 V. J. Boncompain, *De Scribe à Hugo. La condition de l'auteur (1815–1870)*, Honoré Champion, coll. « Histoire du livre et des bibliothèques », 2014.

2. Le dangereux accapareur : la société de gestion collective

Le cocontractant contre lequel l'article 5.7 protège tous ces titulaires de droit est la société de gestion collective. L'article 3c n'exclut d'ailleurs qu'un seul type de « personne ou entité » dans sa définition des titulaires de droit : les sociétés de gestion collective elles-mêmes.

Certes, les sociétés de gestion collective ont, aujourd'hui, souvent une position monopolistique qui leur donne un ascendant notoire à l'égard de tous leurs cocontractants, y compris à l'égard d'exploitants. Ces exploitants sont admis parmi les membres des sociétés de gestion collective au nom de la symbiose entre auteurs et éditeurs, et pour une raison pratique : sans la présence des éditeurs dans les sociétés de gestion collective de l'écrit et de la musique, les utilisateurs devraient, pour être à même d'exploiter l'ensemble des œuvres des auteurs du répertoire sans courir le risque de contrefaire les droits d'éditeurs, s'adresser aussi à ces derniers pour s'assurer qu'aucune cession de droits antérieure à l'adhésion de l'auteur à la société de gestion collective ne limite la portée de la licence générale octroyée par la société de gestion collective. L'utilisateur devrait en effet obtenir le cas échéant une licence complémentaire. Une grande partie de l'utilité de l'intermédiation de la société de gestion collective, du point de vue de l'utilisateur, serait annihilée.

Si on tient compte des conditions à remplir pour adhérer à la plupart des sociétés de gestion collective, il y aura en effet généralement eu cession de droits de reproduction à un éditeur avant l'adhésion à une société de gestion collective, puisqu'une des conditions d'adhésion est l'exigence de publication d'un certain nombre d'ouvrages, d'articles ou de phonogrammes[7]. Il est donc nécessaire d'admettre les éditeurs au sein des sociétés de gestion collective. Mais une fois membre de la société de gestion, c'est à cette dernière que sont cédés les droits des œuvres créées par l'auteur après l'adhésion[8]. La titularité des éditeurs (voire leur rémunération) concernant des droits que la loi reconnaît aux auteurs et que ces derniers apportent aux sociétés de gestion collective n'est, pour le moins, pas systématiquement établie[9].

---

7 A ce propos v. notre thèse, précitée, points 50–51. Sur la participation des éditeurs aux distributions de redevances que la loi accorde a priori aux auteurs, v. A. Lucas-Schloetter, «Les éditeurs peuvent-ils percevoir la rémunération pour copie privée?», *RIDA* n° 243, janvier 2015, pp. 3–99; et l'arrêt de la Cour de justice de l'Union européenne dans l'affaire *Reprobel contre Hewlett Packard,* C 572/13, rendu le 12 novembre 2015.

8 Voir en ce sens l'arrêt du BGH rendu le 21 avril 2016 dans l'affaire *Vogel,* BGH IZR 198/13.

9 Sur cette question, v. l'affaire *Vogel* en Allemagne (Madame Lucas-Schloetter la présente dans son article précité, v. point 4), où les juges du fond ont en première instance et en appel estimé que la titularité des éditeurs sur les œuvres créées après l'adhésion du membre contestant la clé de répartition forfaitaire entre auteurs et éditeurs n'était pas établie (LG Munich 24 mai 2012, *Vogel c. VG Wort, MMR* 2012, p. 618 et OLG Munich 17 oct. 2013, *Verlegeranteil, GRUR*

Pour revenir à la position de la société de gestion collective à l'égard des cocontractants dont elle gère les droits, il convient de tenir compte aussi du fait que le monopole des sociétés de gestion collective est remis en cause, non seulement depuis longtemps parce que tout titulaire de droit de l'Union européenne peut confier ses droits à toute société de gestion collective établie dans l'UE, mais aussi par la mise en œuvre de la directive 2014/26. La conséquence en est que la partie faible du contrat entre un titulaire de droits et une société de gestion collective pourrait ne pas toujours être le titulaire de droit. Et ce, surtout, si on ne considère plus seulement des sociétés de gestion collective telles que la GEMA et la SACEM, mais aussi les sociétés de gestion collective des pays baltes ou scandinaves, autrement dit les « petites » sociétés de gestion collective.

Alors il est certain que la partie faible au contrat est la société de gestion collective quand elle contracte avec des multinationales de l'édition telles qu'Universal et Warner pour la musique ou Springer et Elsevier pour l'écrit.

Les dispositions du droit de l'UE à propos des contrats portant sur des droits d'auteur, à notre connaissance, ne concernaient avant 2014 que l'obligation de recourir à une société de gestion collective pour l'exercice de certains droits. Il s'agissait, d'une part, de droits à rémunération incessibles et à propos desquels les États membres pouvaient imposer la gestion collective obligatoire[10], afin d'assurer que les rémunérations atteignent les auteurs et, d'autre part, du droit de retransmission par câble intégrale et simultanée dont l'exercice doit être collectif pour éviter que chacun des auteurs et titulaires de droit voisins des multiples œuvres et émissions retransmises puissent s'opposer à une retransmission souhaitable dans le cadre du marché commun.

Jusqu'à la directive de 2014, le droit européen faisait donc intervenir les sociétés de gestion collective dans le droit contractuel d'auteur pour permettre une juste application du droit d'auteur : en assurant une rémunération des auteurs, et que l'exercice des droits exclusifs ne soit pas un obstacle à la diffusion des œuvres.

La position des sociétés de gestion collective aux côtés de l'auteur, *contre* le cessionnaire, se retrouve d'ailleurs ancrée dans les droits nationaux des États membres. Ainsi l'article L. 132-18 du Code français de la propriété intellectuelle (CPI) prévoit que la cession de droit sur des œuvres futures est valide quand le cessionnaire est une société de gestion collective, et exempte donc les sociétés

---

2014, p. 272). Le BGH (Cour de cassation allemande) a sursis à statuer en attendant la position de la CJUE dans l'affaire *Reprobel* précitée (BGH 18 déc. 2014, I ZR 198/13, v. www.vgwort.de/fileadmin/pdf/allgemeine_pdf/BGH_18.12.2014_Aktuelle_Information.pdf). L'arrêt est intervenu après la conférence de Bonn, BGH I ZR 198/13, le 21 avril 2016. Le BGH a suivi les juges du fond.

10 Voir la contribution de S. von Lewinski dans ce volume, p. 255 ff.

de gestion collective de la première des dispositions du CPI consacrée au droit contractuel d'auteur, la nullité de la « cession globale des œuvres futures » (art L 131-1 du CPI).

C'est aussi le cas du § 63a de la loi allemande sur le droit d'auteur (*UrhG*), qui établit que les droits à rémunération venant en compensation des limitations au droit exclusif ne peuvent faire l'objet d'une renonciation ni d'une cession, *sauf* au profit d'une société de gestion collective[11].

Pour conclure sur une note optimiste et saluer quelque chose dans cet article 5.7, il faut y voir l'ébauche d'un bel article à introduire dans le *corpus* des directives de l'UE sur le droit d'auteur, dans le cadre par exemple de la refonte annoncée de la directive sur le droit d'auteur dans la société de l'information. Il faudrait pour cela modifier les termes qui désignent les personnes à protéger et leurs cocontractants :

> « Lorsqu'un *auteur* ou un *artiste interprète* [les créatifs, selon les termes du Professeur Dietz] autorise un *tiers* à *exploiter* ses *œuvres* ou ses *interprétations*, il donne son consentement spécifiquement pour chaque droit ou œuvre et autres objets qu'il autorise *le tiers* à *exploiter*.
> Ce consentement est constaté par écrit. »

Il conviendra, dans le cadre de cette refonte, de ne pas oublier les sociétés de gestion collective, et le rôle qu'elles peuvent jouer, notamment pour les pratiques qui se développent en ligne, et peut-être par des systèmes d'autorisation tacite ou de présomption de cession. Les écueils à éviter alors seront ceux dans lesquels la loi française sur les livres indisponibles s'est échouée[12]. Mais c'est une autre histoire, et sera l'objet d'autres contributions.

---

11 Pour les non-germanophones, v. la traduction en anglais de la loi allemande sur le droit d'auteur : http://www.gesetze-im-internet.de/englisch_urhg/englisch_urhg.html.

12 Voir les conclusions de l'A.G. Wathelet présentée le 7 juillet 2016 (ECLI:EU:C:2016:536), en attendant la position de la CJUE, à propos de la question préjudicielle C 301/15, *Soulier et Doke*.

Rudolf Leška*

2.5 Contract law mechanisms from a practitioner's view

I will speak briefly about contract law mechanisms and, being an attorney, about some practical issues related to this.

As we all know, there is no international harmonization of copyright contract law, and fortunately, there's even no EU harmonization. Seeing the poor quality of the EU legislation, I hope it will remain so for a few years at least, although here and there, there are some provisions in the EU law that affect contract law, such as in the latest amendment to the Copyright Term Directive[1] (as an example – it is unclear whether the performer's right to additional remuneration is a statutory right or a contractual obligation) or the new Collective Rights Management Directive.[2] That being said, I truly believe we should not resort to the European Commission for solutions.

If we look into national reports and professor Azzi's general report, we can see some examples of solutions that are pretty much universally applicable at least in civil law jurisdictions besides the general law of contracts (*laesio enormis*, oppressive contracts etc.), namely:

I. the right to **fair (equitable) remuneration**, i.e. at the outset of the licence;
II. the right to **additional remuneration** (bestseller clause), i.e. once the paid remuneration becomes (significantly?) disproportionate to the licensee's proceeds;
III. the licensee's **obligation to use**, which has both monetary aspects (the author's royalties) and a moral aspect (the author's right to see his or her work disseminated) and the author's right to withdraw;
IV. **mandatory collective management** which is in fact still within the domain of contract law but involves interventions of a collective rights management organization (I will not speak about it here);
V. **administrative law** intervening in the agreement of the parties, for example by setting tariffs – I am not a fan of this approach as it brings into the system lobbying, politics, transactional costs etc. known to a Central European from the communist era. I felt the need to mention it however because

---

* President of ALAI Czech Republic, attorney (Czech Republic, Slovak Republic).

1 Directive 2011/77/EU of the European Parliament and of the Council of 27 September 2011 amending Directive 2006/116/EC on the term of protection of copyright and certain related rights.

2 Directive 2014/26/EU of the European Parliament and of the Council of 26 February 2014 on collective management of copyright and related rights and multi-territorial licensing of rights in musical works for online use in the internal market.

there are surprisingly many voices calling for more governmental regulation in copyright contract law.

If we generalize (and this is more or less true about authors as well as performers, although the situation of performers is more complex, e.g. regarding termination), what should such laws look like and how to improve them?

I. Such provisions should not be too casuistic, bureaucratic or difficult to apply. Here, I must say, I have some doubts with respect to the new French law presented by professor Sirinelli which seems to me too complicated, but we will see how it will work in practice.

II. The law must give enough guidance to courts on how to assess the fair amount of remuneration (factors), such as a combination of a lump sum fee and royalty (suggestion made by the German Supreme Court) while giving them enough room for case-to-case discretion. General cession of rights (if assignable) against lump sum payment should be subject to a particular scrutiny in case of doubts about the fair remuneration.

III. The parties must not be allowed to derogate from such rules. If the author can waive his right, then it is as if no such rule existed, because the licensees will usually incorporate a waiver into a contract. The same should apply to conflict-of-laws rules under which such contract laws should be interpreted as imperative norms within the meaning of the Rome I EU Regulation.

IV. Non-compliance with the law should not endanger the validity of the licence and thus the whole licence chain. As a side note – this was the solution of the 1965 Czechoslovak Copyright Act from the communist era which was valid until the 1990s. Under the act, which was very protective towards authors and required payment of a licence fee for each and every individual use of the work, any non-compliance with the rules led to nullity of the licence agreement with severe consequences also for innocent third parties. I prefer the German solution where the agreement remains valid and the author has a monetary claim against the licensee.

Currently, law of some countries provides one or more of the said instruments to balance the position of authors and producers, but often the law in action differs from the statutes. In my practical experience, these laws remain virtually non-litigated, and in the Czech Republic the law is completely dead. I know there has been *some* litigation in Germany (not that much if you take into account the size of the country) since the 2002 copyright reform which introduced some of the features named above and it is quite similar in many countries. There are some obvious reasons for it. You can build a reputation as a troublemaker in the small artistic community, which means you will not get another job. Another thing is that there is usually too little money involved to justify expensive litigation. Last but not least, in many countries the conditions e.g. for additional remuneration are too strict to be met by authors or performers. I have suggested some measures which could improve the situation and others can be discussed, such as author's termination right (proposed in Germany by the so called Cologne Draft[3] which goes too far in my opinion).

Finally, I would like to add one note. When talking about the author's contractual remuneration, we should not lose sight of the big picture – to ensure income for authors, we must ensure income for the industry through modern and enforced copyright in times when anti-copyright sentiments have for many become a religion.

3 Karl Nikolaus Peifer, Dieter Frey, Matthias Rudolph, Christopher Nohr, Benjamin Wahlen. Entwurf eines Gesetzes zur weiteren Stärkung der vertraglichen Stellung von Urhebern und zur besseren Durchsetzung einer angemessenen Vergütung („Kölner Entwurf").

3. Remuneration based on the national budget (examples: Spanish and Israeli private copy system) or alternative models: potential for development?

Gillian Davies*

3.1 Introduction

May I ask you all to take your seats as we are running a little bit late?

Good afternoon, ladies and gentlemen. I hope you are not too tired at this late stage of the day, because we are looking forward to a lively session, and I hope at the end there will be many interventions and questions from the floor.

I should introduce myself; there are many of you I do not know. My name is Gillian Davies. I am Chairman of BLACA, the UK national group of ALAI, and a barrister, practicing in intellectual property law in London. I am also a professor at the Centre for Commercial Law Studies (CCLS) at Queen Mary, University of London.

Now, our subject this afternoon is remuneration based on the national budget. This includes cases where the state has taken over paying for private copying royalties and also some alternative models for arranging remuneration for private copying. And I would like us to explore the potential for development of these new schemes. So, the panel will approach the subject in a broad sense covering not only the private copying systems in Spain and Israel, where the payment of the remuneration has been taken over by the State. We will also consider other methods of remuneration for private copying.

We have two speakers and two panelists in this session: four short presentations. As I said, I hope that we have time at the end to have a really good discussion. And in particular, we would welcome views at this stage on whether the state remuneration system is something that should be strongly opposed or whether there are circumstances in which we might consider it acceptable. So now I will introduce our first speaker. We are very pleased to have with us this afternoon, Ignacio Garrote, professor of civil law at the faculty of law at the Autonomous University of Madrid. He will explain the new Spanish system to us.

---

* Professor at the Centre for Commercial Law Studies (CCLS) at Queen Mary, University of London, chairman of UK group of ALAI (BLACA), Intellectual Property Barrister (UK).

Ignacio Garrote Fernández-Díez*

3.2 Spain is different: Los problemas de ajuste del sistema español con la Directiva 2001/29 en materia de compensación equitativa derivada de reproducciones para uso privado

I. Introducción

La cuestión de si el sistema de compensación por copia privada vigente en España desde el 1 de enero de 2012 era compatible con el Derecho de la Unión Europa fue objeto de debate en la doctrina desde el mismo momento de su entrada en vigor.

Dicha fecha marca un "giro copernicano" en el Derecho español, que pasó súbitamente de un sistema clásico de "canon" (cuya configuración se había actualizado y adaptado al entorno digital mediante la Ley 23/2006) al sistema actualmente vigente.

Ello se hizo mediante la regulación de la Disposición Adicional (D.A.) 10ª del Real Decreto-Ley 20/2011, que dispuso una novación subjetiva en la obligación que convierte en deudor al Estado, que hace frente a su obligación con una consignación en sus Presupuestos Generales.

El nuevo procedimiento de pago al que se refería la citada D.A. 10ª se estableció mediante Real Decreto 1657/2012, de 7 de septiembre, norma que señalaba en su artículo 3.1 que la cantidad adecuada para compensar el perjuicio causado a los titulares se debía determinar de manera anual mediante Orden del Ministerio de Educación Cultura y Deporte, Orden que debía elaborarse conforme al procedimiento contenido en el art 4 de la norma.

Dicho Real Decreto contenía distintos criterios objetivos para determinar el importe de la compensación (arts. 3.2., 3.3, 3.4), pero el Ministerio no podía sobrepasar en ningún caso "los límites presupuestarios establecidos para cada ejercicio [en la ley de Presupuestos Generales del Estado]".

---

* Professor, Universidad Autónoma de Madrid, Spain. El contenido de la presente publicación se corresponde, en lo fundamental, con mi intervención en el Congreso Internacional de la ALAI celebrado en Bonn el 18 de junio de 2015. Se ha introducido sin embargo una actualización específica con ocasión de la publicación de la sentencia del TJUE de 9.6.2016, que dio respuesta a algunas de las dudas que entonces nos planteábamos.

Esta cambio radical e inesperado en el sistema llevó a diversas entidades de gestión (EGEDA y otras) a impugnar el mencionado Real Decreto en vía contencioso-administrativa ante la Sala Tercera del Tribunal Supremo, que planteó mediante Auto de 10.9.2014 dos cuestiones prejudiciales al Tribunal de Justicia de la UE.

En la primera de ellas se preguntaba si el hecho de que la compensación sea abonada con cargo a los Presupuestos Generales del Estado es conforme con la interpretación que ha hecho el TJUE del mandato contenido en el art 5.2 b) de la Directiva 2001/29/CE, que obliga a que el importe de la compensación sea repercutido a los beneficiarios últimos del límite, los usuarios que hacen las copias para su uso privado.

En la segunda se preguntaba si la cuantía asignada en los Presupuestos en las distintas anualidades compensa realmente el daño sufrido por los derechohabientes como consecuencia de la existencia del límite en la legislación española, o si por el contrario es más bien una contraprestación mínima o simbólica.

El TJUE dio respuesta a las cuestiones planteadas mediante sentencia de 9.6.2016 (*caso EGEDA y otros*), aunque al responder en primer término que el sistema de determinación del deudor empleado en España no era compatible con el Derecho de la Unión, el Tribunal no entró a considerar si la cuantía que se desprende de la utilización de dicho sistema puede ser considerada mínima o simbólica.

Veamos ambas cuestiones por separado.

II. La incompatibilidad del sistema español de determinación del deudor con el Derecho de la Unión Europea

El hecho de que en España la compensación equitativa por copia privada se abonara con cargo a los Presupuestos Generales del Estado planteó desde un principio la duda de si resultaba *equitativo* (es decir, justo) que fueran los contribuyentes quienes se veían obligados de forma indirecta a reparar el daño, y no los beneficiarios del límite, que son quienes realizan copias para uso privado.

Dichas dudas provenían de la interpretación del concepto de "compensación equitativa" hecha por el Tribunal de Justicia en sus sentencias de 21.10.2010 (*caso Padawan*); 16.6.2011 (*caso Stichting*); 11.7.2012, (*caso Amazon*); 27.6.2013 (*caso VG Wort*); 10.4.2014 (*caso ACI Adam*) y 5.3.2015 (*caso Copydan*).

Así, en primer lugar, en la sentencia del *caso Padawan* el TJUE consideró que la utilización de un sistema de "canon" sobre soportes o equipos es admisible porque dicho canon se repercute en el precio final de los soportes o equipos, de modo que son los compradores de los mismos los auténticos "deudores indirectos de la compensación[1]".

Resulta por tanto injustificado que se considere como "deudores indirectos" a personas sin conexión alguna con la confección de copias privadas, como era el caso de las empresas y profesionales que adquirían equipos, aparatos y soportes materiales de grabación destinados manifiestamente a usos distintos de la confección de copias privadas[2]. Con ello el Derecho español no respetaba el requisito implícito en la Directiva comunitaria de que exista una "relación suficientemente estrecha" (en palabras de la Abogada General Trstenjak[3]) entre la realización de la copia privada por parte del usuario y la retribución compensatoria que se abona por ella.

Parecía claro por tanto que no hay una "relación suficientemente estrecha" entre la confección de las copias por parte de los usuarios privados y el pago de la compensación cuando el deudor designado por la Ley es el Estado, lo que de forma indirecta convierte en pagadores de la compensación a todos los contribuyentes, y no sólo a quienes realmente confeccionan reproducciones para uso privado.

Después, la jurisprudencia posterior del TJUE no hizo sino confirmar dicha idea. Así, en la sentencia del *caso Stichting* el Tribunal comienza señalando que los Estados miembros tienen en virtud del art 5.2 b) de la Directiva una obligación de compensar a los titulares si deciden incluir el límite de copia privada en su legislación a nacional, como han hecho países como España[4].

Pero dicha obligación es de resultado, correspondiendo a los Estados miembros elegir los instrumentos que consideren más adecuados para determinar cómo se debe llevar a cabo el resarcimiento de los titulares de derechos de propiedad intelectual. Sin embargo, el Tribunal de Justicia deja claro que la libertad que tienen los Estados en este ámbito no es absoluta, señalando que *en principio corresponde abonar la compensación al usuario final que realiza para su uso privado una reproducción de una obra o prestación protegida*[5].

El Tribunal admite que por motivos prácticos los Estados miembros pueden decidir que el "canon" no recaiga de forma directa sobre las personas físicas que hacen las copias, sino sobre quienes ponen a su disposición equipos, aparatos y soportes para confeccionarlas o almacenarlas. Pero esta determinación indirecta es admisible sólo si sistema utilizado por el Estado miembro permite re-

1 Vid. los párrafos 48 y 49 de la sentencia.
2 Vid. el párrafo 59 de la sentencia.
3 Vid. el párrafo 89 de las *Conclusiones del asunto C-467/08*, de 11 de mayo de 2010.
4 Vid. párrafo 22 de la sentencia.
5 El Tribunal de Justicia señale expresamente en el fallo que: "La Directiva 2001/29 (...) debe interpretarse en el sentido de que el usuario final que realiza a título privado la reproducción de una obra protegida debe, en principio, considerarse el deudor de la compensación equitativa prevista en dicho apartado 2, letra b)".

percutir el coste del canon en el precio del producto o servicio, porque, en este caso, también es en última instancia el usuario el que acaba abonando la compensación[6].

En el *caso Amazon* el TJUE insiste en que en principio la obligación de pago de la compensación corresponde al usuario que efectivamente reproduce para uso privado obras y prestaciones protegidas[7]. Reitera después el Tribunal que la designación de un deudor distinto sólo es admisible si dicho deudor puede repercutir el importe de la compensación en el precio de venta de los soportes, de modo que dicho precio se traslade hacia abajo en la cadena de consumo, hasta el usuario final, ya que son las personas que utilizan dichos aparatos y soportes quienes han de abonar el canon por copia privada[8].

Es conforme por tanto que el legislador nacional "suba" jurídicamente por la escalera de la distribución, siempre que haya un mecanismo económico de bajada hasta el consumidor final que permita incorporar el canon en el precio de venta del aparato o soporte. Y ello porque *"de este modo, en definitiva, el usuario privado que abona este precio soporta la carga de dicho canon*[9]", que es lo que garantiza que haya un *justo equilibrio* entre los intereses de los titulares del derecho de reproducción y los de los usuarios de equipos de reproducción y soportes de grabación.

En la sentencia del *caso VG Wort* el Tribunal se limita a reiterar su jurisprudencia en la materia, resaltando el hecho de que resulta posible cargar con un canon a quienes ponen en el mercado aparatos de reproducción porque "*dicho sistema permite a los deudores repercutir el canon sobre los usuarios privados y, en consecuencia, estos últimos asumirán la carga del canon por copia privada*[10]".

La sentencia del *caso ACI Adam* insiste de nuevo en la idea de que el usuario final es el que debe soportar el importe económico del canon, aunque añade[11] que no puede obligarse a que los usuarios que realizan copias privadas desde fuentes lícitas soporten el sobrecoste que tendrían que tener los equipos y soportes gravados con el canon si se admitiera también las copias realizadas desde fuentes ilícitas dentro del ámbito de la excepción[12]. Lo que, en esencia, vuelve a reiterar la idea de que no pueden "pagar justos por pecadores", no se puede obligar a unos usuarios a afrontar costes económicos por reproducciones de las que no se benefician otros.

En el *caso Copydan* se reitera la idea de que el sistema de "canon" sobre soportes o aparatos es admisible porque "En el marco de dicho sistema son, son

6 Vid. párrafo 28 de la sentencia.
7 Vid. párrafo 23 de la sentencia.
8 Vid. párrafo 24 de la sentencia.
9 Vid. párrafo 25 de la sentencia.
10 Vid. párrafo 76 de la sentencia.
11 Vid. párrafo 52 de la sentencia.
12 Vid. párrafo 56 de la sentencia.

las personas que disponen de tales equipos, aparatos o soportes quienes han de abonar el canon por copia privada[13]". Resulta por tanto imprescindible que haya una conexión suficiente entre quien realiza las copias para uso privado y quien paga la compensación,

En resumen, incluso antes de la sentencia del *caso EGEDA,* parecía claro que no era conforme con el Derecho comunitario que un Estado miembro asumiera la obligación de compensación mediante una asignación de los Presupuestos Generales del Estado, repercutiendo así el coste de la compensación equitativa mediante el sistema impositivo a todos los ciudadanos, y no sólo a las personas que realizan copias para uso privado de obras y prestaciones protegidas.

Y ello porque este sistema suponía la aplicación de un "canon" que grava de forma indiscriminada a todos los ciudadanos (incluyendo a los no residentes que abonen impuestos indirectos durante su estancia en el país), lo que en la práctica supone que el coste de la compensación no es afrontado de forma directa por quienes realizan las reproducciones amparadas por el límite (los usuarios privados), impidiendo así el *justo equilibrio* de intereses.

Dicha argumentación ha sido, en lo esencial, recogida por el TJUE en la sentencia del *caso EGEDA,* en la que el Tribunal comienza su argumentación señalando que en principio un Estado miembro puede decidir que la compensación se pague con cargo a los Presupuestos Generales del Estado. Sin embargo, el TJUE insiste de nuevo en que los obligados al pago sólo pueden ser quienes disfrutan del límite según el art 5.2 de la Directiva (las personas físicas), de manera que las personas jurídicas (que nunca pueden ser beneficiarias del límite) no deben soportar en última instancia la obligación de compensar un daño que por definición ellas no pueden causar.

El Tribunal admite que por motivos prácticos los Estados miembros decidan que el pago de la compensación no recaiga de forma directa sobre las personas físicas que hacen las copias, sino sobre quienes ponen a su disposición equipos, aparatos y soportes para confeccionarlas o almacenarlas, sean éstos personas físicas o jurídicas. Pero esta determinación indirecta es admisible sólo si el sistema utilizado por el Estado miembro permite repercutir el coste del canon en el precio del producto o servicio, porque en este caso, también es en última instancia el usuario el que acaba abonando la compensación.

Si falta ese mecanismo de traslación de la carga económica al consumidor el sistema no es compatible con el Derecho de la UE, puesto que "*las personas jurídicas no pueden, en ningún caso, ser el último término deudoras efectivas del mencionado gravamen*".

Y esta afirmación es válida según el TJUE no sólo para los sistemas de canon, también es aplicable a los sistemas en los que la compensación se abona

---

13 Vid. párrafo 23 de la sentencia.

con cargo a los Presupuestos Generales del Estado, dado que el concepto de "compensación equitativa" es un concepto autónomo de derecho de la UE que tiene que ser interpretado en toda la UE con independencia del mecanismo elegido por el Estado miembro para abonar dicha compensación. Y dado que Derecho español no admite la afectación de ingresos tributarios específicos al pago de la compensación, ésta se alimenta de la totalidad de los contribuyentes, incluyenda las personas jurídicas.

El sistema, con todo, podría ser válido si incluyera algún mecanismo de devolución o recuperación para las personas jurídicas o permitiera a éstas eximirse del pago. Al faltar dichos mecanismos, el sistema elegido por el legislador español de 2011 no es conforme con el art. 5.2b) de la Directiva 2001/29, ya que "*no garantiza que el coste de dicha compensación sólo sea sufragado en último término, por los usuarios de copias privadas*", como dice el Tribunal en la sentencia.

III. Compatibilidad de las cuantías fijadas mediante Orden Ministerial con el Derecho de la Unión europea

Como se ha avanzado ya, al entender que el sistema de determinación empleado en España no era compatible con el Derecho de la U.E., el Tribunal no entra a considerar si las cantidades finalmente repartidas a los titulares a partir del 1 de enero de 2012 son realmente suficientes para compensar el daño que sufren como consecuencia del límite de copia privada en nuestra legislación. Ello no significa sin embargo que dicha pregunta carezca de respuesta a la vista de la jurisprudencia del TJUE.

El punto de partida de nuestro análisis debe ser que (como ya se mencionó), en el sistema español el crédito presupuestario ha funcionado en la práctica como un techo insuperable para el importe de la compensación. De ahí que las tres Órdenes Ministeriales que han calculado la cuantía concreta de la compensación hasta el momento en España (para los ejercicios 2012 y 2013 y 2014) dijeran con toda claridad en su Exposición de Motivos que la determinación de la compensación debía tener en cuenta el carácter limitativo de los créditos para gastos consignado en los Presupuestos Generales[14].

Sin embargo, el art 25.1.II de la LPI (en la redacción de la Ley 21/2014) dice que este derecho tiene como objetivo "compensar los derechos de propiedad intelectual que se dejaran de percibir por razón del límite legal de copia priva-

14 Así lo señala Bercovitz Rodríguez-Cano, R., en VV.AA, *La reforma de la Ley de Propiedad Intelectual*, Tirant lo Blanch, Valencia, 2015, p. 66.

da[15]". Y hay que tener en cuenta que el legislador puede en cualquier momento establecer complementos a la cantidad originariamente prevista mediante los mecanismos de modificación presupuestaria para adecuarse al daño real.

Cabe concluir por tanto que esta vinculación entre daño y compensación debería existir en la Orden Ministerial que cada año determine su cuantía. De lo contrario, dicha orden no sólo sería nula por no cumplir lo previsto en los arts. 25.1, párrafo segundo y 25.3 LPI, también sería contraria al Derecho de la Unión por no ser "equitativa" (justa o adecuada para reparar el perjuicio causado por el límite), como requiere el art 5.2 b) de la Directiva 2001/29.

Con todo, para responder a la cuestión de si la cuantía asignada a los derechohabientes en España en concepto de compensación por copia privada desde el 1 de enero de 2012 es suficiente debemos distinguir cuidadosamente entre el momento anterior a la entrada en vigor de la Ley 21/2014 y el régimen posterior (vigente a partir del 1 de enero de 2015),

1. El régimen vigente hasta la Ley 21/2014

Los límites marcados en los Presupuestos Generales del Estado para sus respectivas anualidades fueron respetados en la cuantificación concreta realizada en las Órdenes Ministeriales ECD/2128/2013[16] (para el ejercicio 2012), ECD/2166/2014[17] (para el de 2013) y ECD 2226/2015[18] (para el ejercicio de 2014).

En la Orden ECD/2128/2013 dicho importe se fijó finalmente en 8.636.728 euros, de los que 3.636.728,09 correspondían a entregas a cuenta con cargo a los Presupuestos de 2012 y los cinco millones de euros restantes al importe exacto de la aplicación presupuestaria prevista para este concepto en la Ley 17/2012, de 27 de diciembre, de Presupuestos Generales del Estado para el año 2013.

Para el ejercicio de 2013 la Orden ECD/2116/2014 fijó el importe de la compensación en cinco millones de euros, que era exactamente lo consignado en la correspondiente aplicación presupuestaria de la Ley 22/2013, de 23 de diciembre, de Presupuestos Generales del Estado para el año 2014.

Para el ejercicio de 2014 la cantidad presupuestada en la Ley 36/2014, de 26 de diciembre, de Presupuestos Generales del Estado para el año 2015 fue de nuevo, de cinco millones de euros, que fue también la fijada como definitiva en la Orden ECD 2226/2015. Y esta cantidad se mantuvo también en la Ley de Presupuestos para 2016, que cubre la compensación equitativa del ejercicio 2015.

---

15 Se trata de algo que también se decía en la disposición adicional 10ª del Real Decreto-Ley 2011.

16 BOE de 16 de noviembre de 2013, núm. 275.

17 BOE de 20 de noviembre de 2014, núm. 281.

18 BOE de 26 de octubre de 2015, núm.0256.

A título comparativo cabe señalar que las previsiones de recaudación conforme al sistema anterior (canon digital sobre equipos y soportes) se elevaban a un importe que debía oscilar anualmente entre un mínimo de más de 110 millones de euros y un máximo posible de casi 118 millones (Orden PRE/1734/2008[19]). En la práctica, la recaudación conjunta correspondiente a las tres modalidades de reproducción durante el ejercicio de 2011 fue de 115 millones de euros[20]. El tránsito de un sistema a otro llevó aparejado por tanto una merma de casi cien millones de euros para los titulares entre los ejercicios de 2011 y 2012.

Tan extraordinaria diferencia hizo concluir a la doctrina española que o bien en el sistema anterior las cantidades anteriores eran tan exorbitantes que se estaba expoliando a los ciudadanos, empresas y Administraciones públicas que en última instancia soportaban el importe económico de la compensación, o bien la nueva cuantía suponía un expolio a los derechohabientes para no cargar en exceso las ya maltrechas arcas del Estado[21].

Pues bien, en mi opinión la respuesta a esta disyuntiva es clara: la estimación realizada por las Órdenes Ministeriales para los ejercicios de 2012, 2013 y 2014 no determinaron correctamente cuál fue el perjuicio realmente sufrido por los derechohabientes en las mencionadas anualidades. Y ello porque durante esos tres ejercicios se realizaron en España un número de copias para uso privado suficientes para concluir que el importe finalmente cobrado por los derechohabientes es mínimo o simbólico, y no compensa el daño efectivamente causado a los derechohabientes.

A esta conclusión no sólo se llega porque la cantidad del ejercicio de 2012 fuera poco más del 4% de la que correspondió al ejercicio anterior, o porque brillaran por su ausencia estudios empíricos que justifiquen de manera detallada cómo se han tenido en cuenta los "criterios objetivos" marcados por el Real Decreto 1657/2012 en el cálculo de la compensación para los ejercicios señalados.

Es que además falta un criterio de conexión suficiente entre el crédito presupuestario y la estimación de dicho daño en las sucesivas Leyes de Presupuestos Generales del Estado, que han fijado a tanto alzado la cuantía de cinco millones de euros. La cuantía no sólo es insuficiente, es también arbitraria.

---

19 Y ello porque en el apartado tercero de la mencionada Orden se establecía un proceso de revisión automática por parte de los Ministerios implicados en el supuesto de que las cantidades finalmente recaudadas en virtud de las declaraciones-liquidaciones presentadas por los distintos deudores entre el 1 de julio de 2008 y el 30 de junio de 2009 estuvieran, en el caso de la modalidad de libros y publicaciones asimiladas por debajo de 34.800.000 euros o por encima de 37.200.000 euros y, para las otras dos modalidades de reproducción, por debajo de 75.400.000 euros o por encima de 80.600.00 euro.

20 El dato lo apunta Bercovitz Rodríguez-Cano, R., en VV.AA, *La reforma de la Ley de Propiedad Intelectual,* cit., p. 66.

21 Vid. Bercovitz Rodríguez-Cano, R., en VV.AA, *La reforma de la Ley de Propiedad Intelectual,* cit., p. 64.

Y ello tiene la consecuencia de que (como señaló R. BERCOVITZ[22]) el Estado español no haya cumplido durante los ejercicios de 2012, 2013 y 2014 con la obligación de resultado a la que se refiere el art 5 2. b) de la Directiva 2011/29/CE según las sentencias del TJUE en los casos *Stichting, Amazon, VG Wort*, y, ahora, *EGEDA*.

El Estado tiene un amplio margen de discrecionalidad para establecer el mecanismo de compensación equitativa, pero no puede fijar importes que sean manifiestamente insuficientes para cumplir con su finalidad última, que es indemnizar a los titulares del derecho de reproducción por el daño causado por la existencia del límite en la legislación nacional[23].

Se trata ésta de una idea que el TJUE ya había apuntado en la sentencia de 30.6.2011 (*caso VEWA*) para el préstamo público contemplado en la Directiva 2006/115/CE[24]. En efecto, aunque puede ser discutible si la *remuneración* del art 6.1 de la Directiva 2006/115 por el préstamo es igual que la compensación equitativa por copia privada del art 5.2b) de la Directiva 2001/29 (como afirma el TJUE en esta sentencia[25]), la idea en ambos casos parece clara: se trata de compensar el perjuicio económico que sufren los derechohabientes como consecuencia del límite, perjuicio que no se resarce con una cantidad a todas luces insuficiente. De ahí que el importe de la remuneración "no puede ser puramente simbólico[26]".

Es por tanto incompatible con el Derecho de la Unión que el sistema elegido no alcance el *resultado* exigido por el art. 5.2b) de la Directiva, esto es, una compensación equitativa (justa) a los titulares de derechos de propiedad intelectual por las pérdidas que sufren como consecuencia del límite de copia privada, y el sistema vigente en España entre el 1 de enero de 2012 y el 31 de diciembre de 2014 no permite hablar de compensación realmente equitativa.

En la sentencia del caso EGEDA, como se mencionó, el Tribunal se limita a declarar la incompatibilidad del sistema establecido por la D.A. 10ª del Real Real Decreto-Ley 20/2001 y del Real Decreto 1657/2012 con el Derecho de la Unión. Lo que lleva lógicamente aparejada la nulidad del mismo. El nuevo sistema de

---

22 Vid. BERCOVITZ RODRÍGUEZ-CANO, R., en VV.AA, *La reforma de la Ley de Propiedad Intelectual*, cit., p. 67.

23 BERCOVITZ RODRIGUEZ-CANO, R., «Nuevas especificaciones sobre el canon de copia privada» *Revista Doctrinal Aranzadi Civil-Mercantil*, núm. 6/2013 (BIB 2013/1558, p. 3 de la versión online).

24 En la sentencia una sociedad de gestión de derechos de autor belga solicita la nulidad de un Real Decreto que establecía como remuneración por el préstamo o alquiler da Directiva 92/100 (codificada luego en la 2006/115) de un euro por año y persona inscrita en las instituciones donde se realiza dicho préstamo.

25 Vid. el párrafo 30 de la sentencia, que señala que en ambos el objetivo es indemnizar alas autores.

26 Vid. el párrafo 34 de la sentencia del caso VEWA.

determinación de la compensación tendrá que tener en cuenta por tanto no sólo una manera de determinación del deudor conforme con el Derecho comunitario, sino también, a mi juicio, una cuantía que compense realmente el daño causado, haciendo así a la compensación realmente "equitativa". De lo contrario el legislador español se expone a un nuevo problema de compatibilidad con el Derecho de la UE.

2. El ajuste de la Ley 21/2014

Ante las dudas que el sistema adoptado en 2011 por el legislador español había suscitado respecto de la suficiencia de la cuantía fijada para compensar efectivamente el daño sufrido por los derechohabientes, la Ley 21/2014 optó por estrechar de forma muy significativa la definición legal de "copia privada", introduciendo toda una serie de nuevas condiciones en los arts. 31.2 y 31.3 de la LPI.

La idea básica era por tanto muy sencilla: se trataba de reducir al máximo posible el número de copias que quedan dentro de la cobertura del límite, y que, en consecuencia, que deben ser objeto de compensación con cargo a los Presupuestos Generales del Estado. Ello serviría para justificar cuantías de muy escasa envergadura a partir del 1 de enero de 2015, momento en el que esta modificación entró en vigor. Así se desprende claramente de la Exposición de Motivos de la Ley 21/2014, que afirma expresamente que "Al dejar de quedar amparadas por el límite de copia privada, estas reproducciones, cuando carezcan de autorización, devienen ilícitas y no podrán ser objeto de la compensación equitativa".

En especial, el art 31.2b) LPI exige ahora que las reproducciones se hagan a partir del "acceso legal a una fuente lícita", requisito que ha sido objeto de interpretación auténtica por el legislador, que ha definido de forma taxativa los supuestos en los que cabe apreciara la existencia de dicho "acceso legal desde una fuente lícita". De ahí que todas las copias que no están específicamente contempladas en la Ley quedan fuera del límite y, por tanto, fuera del sistema de compensación (pues según la jurisprudencia del TJUE en los casos *ACI Adam*, *Copydan* y *Reprobel* la excepción de copia privada del art 5.2b) de la Directiva no es aplicable a las copias obtenidas a partir de una fuente ilícita).

Este hecho, unido al resto de modificaciones introducidas en el límite por la Ley 21/2014 provoca que a partir del 1 de enero de 2015 hayan quedado fuera del concepto de "copia privada" (entre otras posibles) las reproducciones realizadas por personas físicas o jurídicas para uso profesional o empresarial, las copias hechas con la asistencia comercial o profesional de terceros, las copias hechas a partir de obras prestadas o alquiladas, las realizadas a partir de ejemplares de segunda mano adquiridas a particulares, las copias hechas a partir de ejemplares ilícitos (por ejemplo, vendidos ilegalmente en la calle), las copias realizadas a partir de archivos descargados ilícitamente de la red o incluso de los archivos descargadas *de forma legal o lícita*, cuando el derechohabiente haya utilizado contrato o licencia para articular la transacción.

A ello se le debe añadir que la redacción actual del art 25.4 LPI ha determinado *ope legis* distintas categorías de reproducciones que no deben tenerse en cuenta a los efectos de determinar la cuantía de la compensación equitativa, incluso si en abstracto cumplieran con los requisitos de los arts. 31.2 y 31.3.

Y no debe olvidarse tampoco que el art 25.5 LPI señala que "No darán origen a una obligación de compensación aquellas situaciones en las que el perjuicio causado al titular del derecho de reproducción haya sido mínimo, que se determinarán reglamentariamente" El propio art 25.5 señala un ejemplo de estas situaciones (la copia de emisiones de radiotelevisión con finalidad de *time-shifting*), que es precisamente uno de los pocos supuestos en lo que aún había margen para aplicar el límite de copia privada con la nueva redacción de los arts. 31.2 y 31.3 LPI[27].

En resumen, la aplicación conjunta de los criterios enormemente restrictivos de los arts. 31.2 y 3 LPI en cuanto al límite, más las exclusiones de los arts. 25.4 y 25.5 hace más difícil seguir entendiendo que la compensación equitativa es mínima o meramente simbólica incluso si la cantidad fijada para el ejercicio de 2015 fuera similar a las de años anteriores. El número de copias privadas *legales* es tan exiguo que basta con una cantidad también exigua para compensar el daño.

No parece además que dicha conclusión se vea afectada en lo esencial por la sentencia del TJUE en el *caso EGEDA*. Y ello porque el hecho de que se fije *ex ante* una cantidad reducida en los Presupuestos Generales del Estado no es en sí misma incompatible con el Derecho europeo, siempre que dicha cantidad recaiga sobre las personas físicas que hacen las reproducciones privadas y que se pueda acomodar al daño efectivamente causado mediante los mecanismos habituales para el ajuste presupuestario[28]. Y debe tenerse en cuenta que la jurisprudencia del TJUE no ha proporcionado criterios que obliguen al legislador nacional a utilizar una metodología concreta para determinar dicho daño, existe una gran flexibilidad en este aspecto concreto[29].

Cabe concluir por tanto que si en España se adapta un nuevo sistema de determinación del deudor que resulte compatible con el Derecho de la Unión, el

---

27 Así lo señala BERCOVITZ RODRIGUEZ-CANO, R., en VV.AA., *La reforma de la Ley de Propiedad Intelectual*, cit., p. 87.

28 BERCOVITZ RODRÍGUEZ-CANO, R., en VV.AA, *La reforma de la Ley de Propiedad Intelectual*, cit., p. 72.

29 Se trata ésta de una cuestión sobre la que llamó la atención el Mediador nombrado por la UE en materia de copia privada y compensación equitativa (vid. las Recomendaciones de Antònio Vitorino de 31 de enero de 2013, p. 19, disponible en http://ec.europa.eu/internal_market/copyright/docs/levy_reform/130131_levies-vitorino-recommendations_en.pdf).

mero hecho de que la cuantía se determine *a priori* en los Presupuestos Generales del Estado y que ésta sea muy reducida no implica sin embargo que deba ser considerada no equitativa o injusta, dado el escaso número de copias privadas que se deben compensar en nuestro país a partir del 1 de enero de 2015.

Con todo, cabe plantearse si lo que se está produciendo es una situación de "piratería privada" tolerada *de facto* por el legislador, puesto que seguirá habiendo en nuestro país un número enorme de copias realizadas en el ámbito privado que, sin generar compensación alguna en la Ley para los titulares, tampoco son objeto de persecución por un entramado legal que deja *de facto* al margen de la acción judicial las conductas realizadas en el ámbito doméstico, tanto en el campo penal como en el civil.

De ahí que a partir del 1 de enero de 2015 existan en la práctica un número enorme de copias (en especial, descargadas desde la Red) que no son activamente combatidas por los poderes públicos, pero tampoco generan remuneración alguna para los titulares de derechos, que se limitan a sufrir las pérdidas que provocan.

Es posible que con ello el legislador español no sólo esté incumpliendo la jurisprudencia del TJUE sobre el art 5.2 b) de la Directiva, sino que tampoco se supere la "prueba de las tres etapas" del art 5.5 de la Directiva, por perjudicar injustificadamente los intereses legítimos de los titulares del derecho de reproducción.

Tamir Afori*

3.3 The Compensation Regime in Israel for Private Copying on Blank Cassettes

I. Statutory background

Israel's Copyright Act is relatively new, having been legislated in 2007; it repealed previous copyright legislation[1]. Notably, four sections of the previous copyright ordinance were left in force,[2] namely, regarding permitted private copying of works on "cassettes" and compensation paid by the government to authors and performers in connection to the permitted use.

These private copying sections that were legislated in 1996 permit recording and reproduction of works on cassettes, which are defined as devices "not intended for use with a computer". The compensation, according to the law, is calculated as 5% of the price of cassettes sold for private use in Israel, with the necessary data for calculation being prescribed by an intergovernmental committee. As will be further explained below, the compensation has stood at 1.25 million New Israeli Shekels (NIS)[3] per year based on data regarding analog tapes.

These four sections of 1996 remained in force during the 2007 discussions due to the issues they addressed, which were politically implausible to deal with. Removing these sections without properly handling the legislative gap would have presented serious controversies and would have caused delay in the modernizing of Israel's copyright legislation as a whole. The issues of private copying by itself and the compensation regime for private copying are controversial, to say the least, and even emotional at times; as a result, no consensus could have been reached. Thus, it was decided to leave these sections untouched and to deal with them separately at a later stage.

While the 1996 sections were left in force, a fair use section was introduced into the new Copyright Act. Although there was no explicit discussion in the

---

* Senior partner at Gilat, Bareket & Co. of the Reinhold Cohn Group (Israel).
This paper reflects the private opinion of its author. It does not reflect the position of any existing or previous clients of the author nor does it reflect any formal opinion of the government of Israel.

1 Namely, the Imperial Copyright Act of 1911 and the Copyright Ordinance, which was originally a British Mandate legislation intended to make specific amendments necessary in applying the 1911 Act to Palestine. The Ordinance later became the legal instrument by which Israeli legislatures made all amendments to copyright law, from the state's establishment in 1948 until the enactment of the new 2007 Act.

2 An unofficial translation of the relevant sections is attached as an annex to this paper.

3 Approximately 280,000 euros.

parliament committee hearings on the implications of fair use on private copying, it is reasonable to assume that at least some copying (recordings) made for "time shifting" and perhaps "format shifting" would be considered permissible, even if made on media not covered by the older analog private copying section.

In fact, the situation has not changed since 2007. No further changes were made to the law, despite repeated legal and political efforts made by performers' organizations to expand private copying to include digital media and along with it the compensation receivable by performers, which they want to collect directly from the market and not through the state's budget. The performers' efforts encountered strong resistance from both government ministries and copyright owners: owners of copyright (namely, phonogram and movie producers) disagree with expanding private copying to include digital media; authors of music do not support expanding private copying to digital media and express concerns regarding the implication on their rights; the Ministry of Finance disagrees with private taxation (as discussed below); and the Ministry of Justice does not seem to support the expansion of the private copying exception against the will of copyright owners and contrary to the previous adoption of the US doctrine of fair use.

Thus, a completely irrelevant and obsolete private copying exception for analog media is still on the books, and the government keeps providing copyright and performers' rights societies with compensation based on outdated data on analog tapes. In terms of market behavior, notwithstanding the very narrow definition of the analog private copying exception in the 1996 sections, the existence of a fair use clause is perceived to cover some typical private copying on digital media as well.

In this short paper I will not address the legal and political questions surrounding the scope of permitted private copying in Israel[4]. **The purpose of this paper is limited to exploring the compensation regime: Namely, what reasons were followed to justify choosing the state to provide the compensation? How does such a compensation regime operate? And what are the implications?**

II. The decision that the state shall provide compensation

When the idea of a blank tape levy was raised to public discussion by Israel's Ministry of Justice in the mid-90s, there was strong opposition from the Ministry

---

4 For example, why did the legislation include "analog only"? What function do the private copying sections, being alongside the fair use sections in the new Copyright Act, now serve?

of Finance. The following were the arguments against the collection of a levy by CMO's:

1. A blank tape levy should be considered a tax.[5] It is collected from the *entire* market and without particular examination as to the use made of the relevant media. When analog tapes were discussed in the mid-90s, many recording and copying activities at the time did not involve copyright or performers' rights at all; for example, recording and copying rabbis' lectures, which were then very popular, videotaping family events, etc. This persuasion is even better typified when discussing digital media. Digital media is used for copying and storing a wide variety of content objects, much of which has no connection at all to copyright or performers' rights. There is no way to directly connect the actual use to any levy collected, let alone allocate any collected sums to owners of the rights that were actually used. Under Israeli tax law, a private copying levy on digital media would likely be considered a tax.
2. Taxation should not be privatized. Collecting taxes is an expression of a state's power, and evasion of tax payment results in and involves criminal and civil remedies; such characteristics of state sovereignty should not be entrusted in the hands of private entities.
3. A separate and private collection system would be inefficient, especially when taking into consideration the amount estimated to be collected (not more than a few million NIS per year). Furthermore, a separate or new collection scheme opens up the door to future legal disputes,[6] which in turn only fuels inefficiency.
4. The main argument raised by the Ministry of Finance was that funds collected from the general public should bear no connection to the compensation distributed. Principles in managing the state budget discourage creating a tax intended for a singled-out purpose. Policy decisions on taxation are inherently autonomous from policy decisions on the allocation of tax money. That is, the allocation of tax funds, even if intended for certain purposes, should reflect no connection to the source of said tax funds; likewise, the collection of certain taxes should reflect no connection to how said taxes are ultimately utilized.

In brief, the train of thought in 1996 was: First, the government knows best how to collect taxes. Second, it neither wants nor needs to collect a few million NIS a

5 The possible definition of private copying levy as a tax is beyond the scope of this paper. In fact, Israeli courts have never dealt with the issue, as the political decision was not to impose any payment on the market and to have the state compensate the authors and performers. In Australia, when the issue was before court, it was held that a private copy levy was indeed a tax [Australian Tape Manufacturers Association Ltd v Commonwealth (1993) 176 CLR 480].

6 E.g. calculation of sums and so forth.

year in order to pay compensation to authors and performers. Third, where and how the government acquires funds should not be the concern of authors and performers.

With this line of reasoning in mind, the Knesset (Israel's legislature) approved the sections that prescribe the treasury for payment of compensation to authors and performers, without collection of any new levies or taxes for that purpose. The formula adopted as a basis to calculate compensation was 5% of the price (before VAT) of blank analog tapes sold in Israel.

One may wonder whether such rationale for paying compensation from the treasury would have held, had private copying been designated to include digital media and thus reflect greater sums of compensation; surely for the Ministry of Finance the same position would have stood its ground.

III. The compensation decision of 2001

According to the 1996 legislation, an inter-ministerial committee was to be convened in order to prescribe the data based on which the compensation would be calculated.[7] It took several years before this committee agreed on a way to do so.

In its 2001 decision, the committee explained that 100% of analog tapes in Israel were imported, either as a complete product (*cassettes* – film in plastic cartridge), or just film (the raw *tape*) to be cut to the relevant length and packaged in Israel with the plastic cartridge. Thus, importation data was sufficient to roughly calculate the number of tapes sold in Israel.

When importing into Israel, the importer is required to mark the category of goods, in accordance with detailed classification regulations. There were (at the time) specific classifications of *cassettes* and *tapes*; hence, gathering all information regarding such importation, including quantities and prices, was possible.

With this information in hand, the committee calculated the price of cassettes by way of adding the assumed regular profit margins to the cost of importation. This sum was then cross-checked with regular prices of cassettes in the market.

The calculated price was then multiplied by the quantity of cassettes imported into Israel for the year 2000. The result was then used as a basis for calculation of the compensation, i.e. 5% of the calculated result would be payable from the state budget, calculated to be 1.25 million NIS per year (around 280 thousand euros as per 2015 exchange rates).

This calculated sum of compensation has not undergone review since its inception, even though it was based on importation quantities and prices for the

7 The author was a member of this committee.

year 2000; and it is not entirely unreasonable to assume that today practically no blank analog tapes can be found in the market, or at least their number is negligible. Nevertheless, the compensation decision of 2001 still applies to date and the state keeps providing authors and performers' organizations the prescribed sum every year.

IV. Conclusions that may be drawn regarding the compensation regime

Since the government is providing the compensation, the government has an economic interest in the complicated substantive debate over private copying. One may argue that the government is in conflict of interests in this regard. Had the Israeli government not provided compensation in the first place, the public interest in having transparent permission to make certain private copies would have led to legislation along the lines of continental European countries, with a digital private copying regime and a blank digital media levy.

I personally do not share this view, and the legislative history in Israel clearly contradicts this view. I think that government involvement as a "payer" has had no effect on policy/legislative decisions with respect to the scope of private copying in Israel. Such conflict-of-interest arguments are seemingly baseless.

Even if private copying were broadened to cover digital media, the funds paid as a result would be insignificant when taken in relation to the state's budget.

In my opinion, policy decisions regarding private copying should be made, and in Israel are in fact made, on a professional basis. Considerations should include, *inter alia*: the property rights of the owners; the effect of such statutory permissions would have on enforcement[8]; the need to refrain from over-interfering with contractual relations[9]; the ability of the market to develop new business models[10]; and so forth.

Overly broad private copying exceptions do not properly serve the fundamental goals of copyright law. Creating a source of income for certain organizations – important as they are to the creative ecosystem – is not sufficient justifi-

---

8 Even if private copying only applied to copying from legitimate sources, it would still cause significant complications regarding the activity of intermediaries that might abuse the private copying regime to disguise pirate activity.

9 Relations between users and right owners of works as well as between right owners and individual authors.

10 For example, new business models relating to "cloud" computing, payments per access to works instead of per copy, etc.

cation to compromise these goals, and the question of whether payment comes from the state budget or from a separate tax collecting system is completely irrelevant to this point.

One may argue, counter to the hypothetical argument above regarding the government's conflict of interests, that the collecting of private copying levies by the organizations of authors and performers *itself* presents a conflict of interest. For a collecting society, such a source of income may very well be significant. Significant income might cause some organizations to support overly broad private copying legislation that is disadvantageous to the true interests of their members. Indeed, the Israeli association of authors ACUM tends to lobby against expanding permitted private copying to include the digital environment.

Are there any conclusions that can be drawn from the application of the Israeli private copying regime? In my opinion, Israel does not present a case for bad governmental management of private copying compensation. Indeed, genuine controversy over the scope of permitted uses persists; and at the current stage, the cautious position of the producers and the authors prevails over the position of the performers' organizations that demand broader permission to get larger compensation. Be that as it may, payment from the state's budget has nothing to do with that.

Annex

Existing private copying legislation[11]

3B. In sections 3C to 3F ...

"Royalty companies" – each of the following:

(1) An organization that represents a majority of copyright owners;
(2) An organization that represents a majority of owners of performers' rights;
(3) An organization that represents a majority of audio producers and an organization that represents a majority of audiovisual producers – jointly,

All of which were approved for purposes of this Law by the Minister of Education, Culture and Sport;

"recording" – preservation of a work by any means that makes it possible to see, hear or copy the work;

"cassette" – a device on which there is no recording and on which an audio or video recording can be recorded, except for a device which is intended for use with a computer;

---

11 Some definitions and parts of sections are irrelevant to the discussion and were omitted for the sake of brevity.

3C. Recording or copying a work on a cassette for non-commercial private and domestic use shall not be an infringement of copyright and performers' rights.

Payment to Owners of Copyright and Performers' Rights

3D. *(a)* The Government shall compensate the copyright owners and the owners of performers' rights for the loss of income and infringement of rights caused to them by the recording and copying for private and domestic use.

(b) The Government shall pay to the royalty companies every year an amount equal to 5% of the retail price without VAT of all cassettes sold in Israel for private and domestic use during the preceding year.

(c) The amount said in subsection *(b)* shall be divided equally between the three royalty companies enumerated in paragraphs (1), (2) and (3) of section 3B.

(d) A committee composed of a representative of the Minister of Justice, a representative of the Minister of Finance and a representative of the Minister of Education, Culture and Sport shall prescribe the data required for determination of the said amount.

3E. In the case of disagreement on the division of royalties, the Court shall decide the matter; to the Court hearings shall be summoned, in ways to be prescribed by regulations, representatives of the royalties companies, a representative of the Ministry of Education, Culture and Sport and the author or performer, in respect of whose royalties there is disagreement, as the case may be; the Court's decision shall bind all royalties companies and all holders of copyright and performers' rights, even if they were not parties to the proceeding before the Court.

Helga Tabuchi*

3.4 Compensation for Private Recording: Experiences in Japan and their Implications

I. Legislation on Compensation for Private Recording

The Japan Copyright Act permits reproduction for private use without the authorization of right holders.[1] The legislation also has provisions for compensation for private sound and visual recording on digital recording media by digital recording devices. The recording media and devices that are subject to compensation are specified by Cabinet Order.[2] Compensation is distributed to copyright owners, performers, and producers of phonograms.

---

* Associate Professor of Law, Faculty of International Social Sciences at Yokohama National University (Japan). She was previously Director of the Office for Promoting Works' Distribution, Copyright Division, Agency for Cultural Affairs.
This paper reflects the personal opinions of the author. It does not reflect any formal opinion of the government of Japan.

1 Copyright Act
(Reproduction for private use)
Article 30. (1) It shall be permissible for a user to himself reproduce a work forming the subject matter of copyright (hereinafter in this Subsection referred to as a "work") for personal use, family use, or other similar uses within a limited circle (hereinafter referred to as "private use")
(Limitations on neighboring rights)
Article 102. (1) The provisions of Article 30, paragraph (1) [...] shall apply *mutatis mutandis* to the exploitation of performances, phonograms, broadcasts, or wire diffusions which are the subject matter of neighboring rights.

2 Copyright Act
(Reproduction for private use)
Article 30. (2) Any person who, for the purpose of private use, makes sound or visual recording on a digital recording medium as specified by Cabinet Order by means of a digital recording machine as specified by Cabinet Order (excluding (a) machines having special efficiency generally not for private use but for business use, such as those for broadcasting, and (b) machines having sound or visual recording functions incidental to the primary functions, such as telephones with sound recording function) shall pay a reasonable amount of compensation to the copyright owners concerned.
(Limitations on neighboring rights)
Article 102. (1)
[...] the provision of Article 30, paragraph (2) [...] shall apply *mutatis mutandis* to the exploitation of performances or phonograms which are the subject matter of neighboring rights.

The compensation system for private sound and visual recording was introduced in 1992 in response to the development of inexpensive, high-quality, digital recording devices. It had been recognized that private recording with such devices would be prejudicial to the legitimate interests of right holders.

While those making private recording should pay compensation to right holders in principle, the right to claim compensation on behalf of right holders can only be exercised through the intermediary of an association established and designated for the purpose of exercising this right, when such an association exists.[3] A lump-sum compensation should be paid by purchasers of specified devices or media to the designated association.[4] In other words, payment of compensation by individual users to right holders is defined as a general rule, and lump-sum payment by purchasers of devices or media to the designated association is defined as an exception. The thinking behind this was that users

---

3 Copyright Act
(Exercise of the right to claim compensation for private recording)
Article 104bis. (1) Where there is an association, which is established for the purpose of exercising the right to claim compensation as mentioned in Article 30, paragraph (2) (including the case in which its application *mutatis mutandis* is provided for under the provisions of Article 102, paragraph (1); the same shall apply hereinafter in this Chapter.) (hereinafter in this Chapter referred to as "compensation for private recording") on behalf of the owners of such right (hereinafter in this Chapter referred to as "the owners of the right") and which is designated, with its consent, by the Commissioner of the Agency for Cultural Affairs as the only association throughout the country for each of the following two categories of compensation for private recording (hereinafter in this Chapter referred to as "the designated association"), the right to claim compensation for private recording shall be exercised exclusively through the intermediary of the designated association:
(i) compensation for sound recording made for the purpose of private use (excluding such sound recording as made exclusively with visual recording; hereinafter in this Chapter referred to as "private sound recording");
(ii) compensation for visual recording made for the purpose of private use (including such visual recording as made exclusively with sound recording; hereinafter in this Chapter referred to as "private visual recording").
(2) The designated association shall have the authority to deal, on behalf of the owners of the right and in its own name, with juridical and non-juridical matters in regard to the right to claim compensation for private recording.
4 Copyright Act
(Exceptional provisions for payment of compensation for private recording)
Article 104quater. (1) Any purchaser of a recording machine or a recording medium which is specified by Cabinet Order in accordance with the provision of Article 30, paragraph (2) (hereinafter in this Chapter referred to as "a specified recording machine" and "a specified recording medium", respectively) (limited to the initial purchasers of such retailed recording machines or media) shall pay, at the time of the purchase and on the claim by the designated association, a lump-sum compensation for private recording, the amount of which is fixed, for such recording machine and medium, respectively, in accordance with the provisions of Article 104sexies, paragraph (1).

should in principle be responsible for payment of compensation. It was also expected that development of digital rights management technologies might make such individual payment possible in the future. At the time of the legislation, however, a lump-sum payment of compensation, which was added to retail prices of specified media and devices, through the designated association, was the practical solution. Two associations were designated: the Society for Administration of Remuneration for Audio Home Recording (sarah) for sound recording, and the Society for the Administration of Remuneration for Video Home Recording (SARVH) for visual recording.

It should also be noted that, according to the Copyright Act, the compensation is to be paid by purchasers, not the manufacturers or importers, of specified devices and media. The manufacturers or importers are simply required to cooperate with the designated association in claiming and receiving compensation[5]. The interpretation of the nature of this obligation of manufacturers etc. to cooperate was one of the issues in question in the legal proceedings referred to in Section III of this paper.

II. Discussions on the Review of the Compensation System from 2006 to 2009

In specifying digital devices and media subject to compensation, the degree of their market penetration and use, as well as the existence and degree of use of technological rights protection measures (hereinafter referred to as "technological measures") have been considered. Having said this, many of the devices that are widely used for private recording are currently not specified by Cabinet Order.

In a process intended to specify which new devices should be subject to compensation in view of new market developments, it was decided to review the compensation system itself instead of simply expanding the scope of devices subject to compensation. The discussions started in 2006 and lasted three years. Due to wide differences in views among stakeholders, no agreement was reached. The Subcommittee on Private Recording of the Subdivision on Copyright of the Council for Cultural Affairs, which was the forum for these discus-

---

5 Copyright Act
(Cooperation by manufacturers and importers)
Article 104quinquies. When the designated association claims compensation for private recording in accordance with the provision of paragraph (1) of the preceding Article, any manufacturer or importer of specified recording machines or media shall cooperate with the designated association in claiming and receiving such compensation.

sions, consisted of representatives of right holders, manufacturers and consumers as well as academics. In particular, views differed greatly regarding the relationship between technological measures and the need for compensation. The relationship between visual recording made for time shifting and sound recording made for place shifting and the need for compensation for such recording was another issue with divided views.

III. Society for the Administration of Remuneration for Video Home Recording (SARVH) vs Toshiba

In November 2009, the Society for the Administration of Remuneration for Video Home Recording (SARVH) filed an action against Toshiba to claim compensation for DVD recorders that were not equipped with analog TV tuners.[6] In December 2011, the Intellectual Property High Court ruled that DVD recorders not equipped with analog TV tuners were not devices specified to be subject to compensation, and the case was dismissed. In November 2012, the Supreme Court of Japan turned down an appeal, and the ruling by the Intellectual Property High Court became final.

The outline of the ruling by the Intellectual Property High Court follows.

1. When manufacturers etc. violate the obligation to cooperate with the designated association (in this case, SARVH) in claiming and receiving compensation prescribed by the Copyright Act, depending on how the violation occurred, there could be cases in which they must compensate for damages suffered by the Association.
2. Devices that are subject to compensation for private recording are specified by Cabinet Order, i.e. in Article 1 paragraph (2) of the Order for Enforcement of the Copyright Act. It seems that at the time when the item (iii) of the said paragraph in question was added, questions, such as how its requirements should be interpreted when digital broadcast transmissions were directly recorded and when digital information, such as information on technological measures was embedded, were not discussed.[7] Therefore, item (iii) of

6 Terrestrial digital television broadcasting started in 2003 in limited areas in Japan, and until July 2011, there were both analog and digital broadcasts. In 2009, Toshiba started selling DVD recorders for digital broadcasting that were not equipped with analog TV tuners. In July 2011, the transition to terrestrial digital broadcasting was completed and analog broadcasting was terminated.

7 Item (iii) of paragraph (2) of Article 1 of the Order which specifies DVD recorders subject to compensation was added in 2000. Terrestrial digital broadcasting started in 2003 in limited areas in Japan, and until July 2011, there were both analog and digital broadcasts. In terrestrial

paragraph (2) of Article 1 of the Order does not include devices for DVD recording of digital broadcasts, and therefore, the device in question is not a specified device that is subject to compensation under current legislation.

3. To acknowledge that the defendant (Toshiba) had violated the obligation to cooperate with the designated Association, the device in question should be acknowledged to be a specified device. Since this was not the case, the defendant could not be held liable for compensation for damages resulting from a tortious act.[8]

IV. Current Situation

Because many devices that are widely used for private recording are not currently specified as devices subject to compensation,[9] the total amount of compensation received is declining.

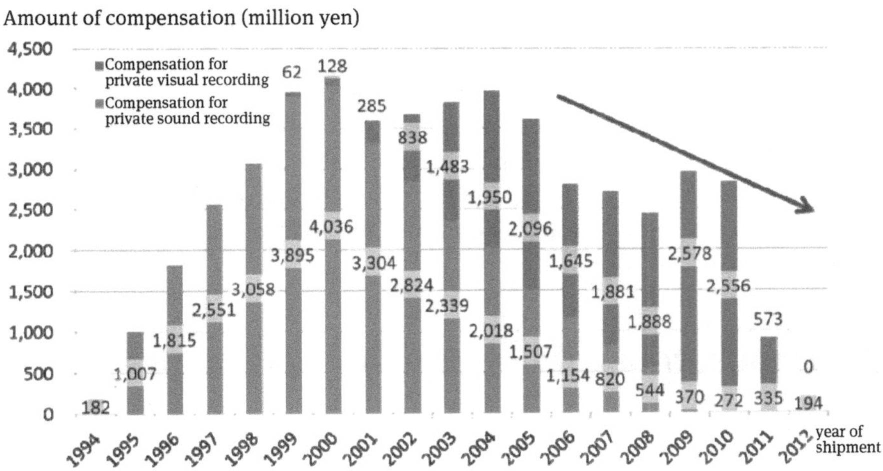

---

digital broadcasting, a technological right protection measure called "Dubbing 10" is used, allowing viewers to make as many as 10 copies of a digital TV broadcast. The defendant argued that, among other things, compensation was not necessary for recording of digital TV broadcasts because anticopying measures were used in the interests of right holders.

8 In the first trial at the Tokyo District Court, it was ruled that while a DVD recorder not equipped with an analog TV tuner was a specified device subject to compensation, the obligation of the manufacturers etc. to cooperate in claiming and receiving compensation was of an abstract nature and was not enforceable, and therefore, the defendant was not liable.

9 According to the 2014 Survey on Private Recording conducted by the Copyright Research Institute of the Copyright Research & Information Center (CRIC), 67.1% of respondents replied that they have used personal computers with optical media drive for digital sound recording or downloading, a rate higher than any other device. Yet, personal computers are not specified as devices that are subject to compensation.

For the fiscal year 2012, no compensation was made for private visual recording because no recorders equipped with an analog TV tuner were shipped. Due to these circumstances, SARVH was dissolved in March 2015. As for compensation for private reproduction of sound recordings, CD-R accounted for 53%, MD equipment accounted for 25%, and MDs accounted for 18% of compensation from devices and media shipped in the fiscal year 2012.

V. Discussions Resumed

In 2014, discussions concerning compensation for private recording resumed at the Subdivision on Copyright of the Council for Cultural Affairs. This was based on the Intellectual Property Strategic Program 2014, decided by the Intellectual Property Strategy Headquarters.[10]

In the Intellectual Property Strategic Program 2014, the Ministry of Education, Culture, Sports, Science and Technology (hereinafter referred to as "MEXT")[11] was requested, in order to promote creation and expansion of new businesses such as cloud services and other information services, to review the current limitations on copyright and related rights, and to consider ways and means to build effective licensing schemes. At the same time, MEXT and the Ministry of Economy, Trade and Industry were asked to review the compensation system for private recording and consider alternative schemes to replace the system, to ensure fair reward for creators. The Subdivision is continuing discussions to date.

VI. Implications of the Experiences in Japan

As noted in Section I of this article, the compensation system for private recording was introduced in 1992 in response to the development of inexpensive, high-quality, digital recording devices. The widespread practice of such private reproduction was considered to be prejudicial to the legitimate interests of right holders. It would be useful to examine whether the situation has changed in the past decades.

---

10 The Intellectual Property Strategy Headquarters was established in 2003 based on the "Intellectual Property Basic Act." It is responsible for formulation of the Intellectual Property Strategic Program. It plans, promotes and coordinates important intellectual property measures in cooperation with relevant government agencies. The Headquarters consists of the Prime Minister, all Cabinet Ministers, and experts.

11 The Agency for Cultural Affairs, which is responsible for policy on copyright, is affiliated with MEXT.

1. Use of technological measures

One of changes that occurred in the last years is the increase of use of technological measures to restrict copying. Those opposed to subjecting new types of devices to compensation argue that in cases in which technological measures are used to restrict copying, there is no need to compensate right holders. According to the current Japanese legislation, private copying is allowed, except when such copying is made by circumventing technological measures. If right holders release materials protected by copyright and related rights in the market with technological measures, copying made by circumventing such measures is no longer a permitted act under the limitation clauses of the Copyright Act.[12] Under the current framework, right holders receive compensation for legally permitted private recording. In a digital network environment, technological measures to restrict copying, combined with contractual arrangements, could be a means for right holders to enforce exclusive rights even in the private sphere. If such measures become prevalent, compensation for private copying would no longer be needed.

It should be noted however that private copying from physically distributed products such as CDs without any technological measures that restrict copying still occurs widely. In the Japanese market for recorded music, for example, physical format sales are very strong.[13] Compensation for private recording would still be relevant in such an environment. I should also note, however, that at the Subdivision on Copyright of the Council for Cultural Affairs, some have argued that a contractual agreement at the "upstream" of circulation could cover use at the "downstream" and therefore compensation would not be necessary. In other words, right holders might be able to be remunerated (or compensated) by initially including the price for subsequent private copies to be made when the protected material is offered for sale or rental to the public.

12 Copyright Act
(Reproduction for private use)
Article 30. (1) It shall be permissible for a user to himself reproduce a work forming the subject matter of copyright (hereinafter in this Subsection referred to as a "work") for personal use, family use or other similar uses within a limited circle (hereinafter referred to as "private use"), except in the case:
[...] (ii) where such reproduction is made by a person who knows that such reproduction becomes possible by the circumvention of technological protection measures or it ceases to cause obstruction, by such circumvention, to the results of acts deterred by such measures [...]
(Limitations on neighboring rights)
Article 102. (1) The provisions of Article 30, paragraph (1) [...] shall apply *mutatis mutandis* to the exploitation of performances, phonograms, broadcasts or wire diffusions which are the subject matter of neighboring rights.

13 According to the Recording Industry Association of Japan, physical media sales accounted for 87% of market sales and on-line distribution accounted for 13% of market sales in Japan.

Moreover, while compensation may not be necessary if copying is completely restricted, it may be necessary if copying is allowed to a certain extent. For example, in the case of terrestrial digital broadcasting in Japan, a technological measure called "Dubbing 10" is used, allowing viewers to make as many as 10 copies. If technological measures that are used reflect the contractually agreed scope of a license, it may not be necessary to further compensate right holders. This, however, may not be the case for free broadcasting. Therefore, the degree to which the intention of right holders is reflected in the technological measures may affect the need for compensation.

2. Rendering illegal the downloading of unauthorized recordings

In relation to the discussions on the revision of the compensation for private recording at the Subdivision on Copyright of the Council for Cultural Affairs between 2006 and 2009, the scope of the limitation for private use was also discussed, as the two issues are closely interrelated. As a result of these discussions, downloading of audio and video recordings illegally made available online without authorization was excluded from the scope of limitation for reproduction for private use and therefore became an unlawful act even if it is done for private use, by the amendment of the Copyright Act in 2009.[14]

3. Compensation system as opposed to exclusive rights

Some argue that the right to remuneration, including compensation systems such as private copying levies, as opposed to exclusive rights, might be better enforceable in a digital network environment. They suggest that, with increas-

14 Copyright Act
(Reproduction for private use)
Article 30. (1) It shall be permissible for a user to himself reproduce a work forming the subject matter of copyright (hereinafter in this Subsection referred to as a "work") for personal use, family use or other similar uses within a limited circle (hereinafter referred to as "private use"), except in the case:
[...] (iii) where a digital sound or visual recording is made by a person who knows that such recording is made upon reception of an interactive transmission which infringes copyright (including an interactive transmission which is made outside Japan and which would constitute an infringement of copyright if it were made in Japan);
Article 102. (1) The provisions of Article 30, paragraph (1) [...] shall apply *mutatis mutandis* to the exploitation of performances, phonograms, broadcasts or wire diffusions which are the subject matter of neighboring rights

ing difficulty to enforce exclusive rights in a digital network environment such as the Internet, some sort of levy system could be the answer to ensure that creators and creative industries can still gain monetary reward for the on-line use of the fruits of their creativity. The reward may be in the form of compensation for limiting their exclusive right of reproduction, or it may be in the form of a right to remuneration, to which an exclusive right is reduced. In either way, collective management plays an important role, in that individual management and enforcement of exclusive rights for mass use in a digital network environment is often difficult, if not impossible. Collective management can reduce transaction costs.

VII. Conclusion

It was difficult to adapt the scope of devices subject to compensation for private recording to new market developments in Japan, in part because the process for specifying new types of devices requires participation of, and agreement and/or compromise among, stakeholders including representatives of manufacturers and consumers. These difficulties may be similar to what some other countries face and indicate the general climate that surrounds the issue.

Having said so, a levy system may still be relevant for some forms of private reproduction at a time and in a situation where individual exercise of rights proves to be difficult. A compensation system in a form of levy may provide an interim or alternative solution to an exclusive right. At the same time, the cost benefit of installing such a mechanism, should also be carefully considered.

João Pedro Quintais*

3.5 Alternative compensation models for large-scale non-commercial online use of works

I. Introduction

This panel has so far discussed the private copying systems in Spain and Israel (based on the national budget), as well as the private copying system in Japan, as legal models that assure remuneration for use. *De lege ferenda*, this presentation will briefly discuss an alternative legal model to assure remuneration for non-commercial mass online use of works by individuals, covered by the exclusive rights of reproduction and communication to the public in Directive 2001/29/EC. In doing so, it will report on the results of an ongoing interdisciplinary research project on such alternative compensation systems ("ACS").

ACS intersect with the previously discussed models not only because they are often designed as an extension of the private copying system, but also as some proposals rely on remuneration based on the national budget. The study of ACS has both normative and empirical justifications. Currently, a significant number of individuals' online uses are restricted by copyright. Enforcement of these uses is either impossible (de facto or due to high transaction costs) or undesirable, as it might clash with fundamental rights: of individuals, such as freedom of expression and information online, privacy and protection of personal data; of online service providers, in what concerns freedom to conduct a business. Criminalization and strict enforcement alienate end-users – with file-sharers being among the best clients of the content industries – and diminish the respect for, and legitimacy of, copyright law. Furthermore, emerging online legal channels, like streaming platforms, are increasingly criticized by rights holders for their failure to provide adequate remuneration.[1]

---

* PhD Candidate, Institute for Information law (IViR), University of Amsterdam, Netherlands; j.p.quintais@uva.nl

1 For a list of scholarly literature on ACS, see *IViR Home/Research/Copyright in an Age of Access: Alternatives to Copyright Enforcement*, http://www.ivir.nl/onderzoek/acs and *ACS Literature*, http://acs-companion.tumblr.com/lit. On criticism to emerging online business models, see J.-J. Vallbé and others, 'Knocking on Heaven's Door. User Preferences on Digital Cultural Distribution' (2015) 1–2, 18, available at http://ssrn.com/abstract=2630519.

II. Alternative compensation systems

Simply put, ACS are legal mechanisms that forsake the need for direct authorization of end-user acts under the aforementioned rights (e.g. downloading, uploading, sharing, modifying), while simultaneously ensuring compensation to authors and performers (or all rights holders) of works included in the scheme. These mostly copyright-internal models entail a restriction to the scope or exercise of exclusive rights, but offer the assurance of remuneration. The previously unauthorized use becomes "permitted-but-paid".[2]

Since the early 2000s, legal and economics scholars, advocacy groups and political parties have come forward with ACS proposals under different labels: tax-and-royalty systems, *license globale*, content/culture flat-rate, creative contribution, file-sharing or broadband levies, sharing license, or alternative reward systems.[3] Legislative proposals of this type have been presented in the national parliaments of Portugal, France, Germany, Belgium and Italy; recently, a proposal to regulate online uses through a "radio" model was advanced by the Dutch consumer association.[4]

---

2 On the notion of "permitted-but-paid", see J. Ginsburg, 'Fair Use for Free or Permitted-But-Paid?' (2014) 28 Berkeley Technology Law Journal 1384. There is significant research on schemes external to copyright but with similar effects. An influential work is P. Aigrain, *Sharing – Culture and the Economy in the Digital Age* (Amsterdam University Press 2012). For convenience, "ACS" is adopted here as an umbrella term to refer also to those proposals.

3 For an overview of in this field, see *supra* note 1. Influential sources in legal scholarship are, e.g., N.W. Netanel, 'Impose a Noncommercial Use Levy to Allow Free Peer-to-Peer File Sharing' (2003) 17 Harvard Journal of Law & Technology 1; P. Eckersley, 'Virtual Markets for Virtual Goods: The Mirror Image of Digital Copyright?' (2004) 18 Harvard Journal of Law & Technology 85; W.W. Fisher, *Promises to Keep: Technology, Law, and the Future of Entertainment* (Stanford University Press 2004); S. Dusollier and C. Colin, 'Peer-to-Peer File Sharing and Copyright: What Could Be the Role of Collective Management?' (2011) 34 Columbia Journal of Law & the Arts 809; S. von Lewinski, 'Certain Legal Problems Related to the Making Available of Literary and Artistic Works and Other Protected Subject Matter Through Digital Networks' (2005) UNESCO E-Copyright Bulletin 1.

4 See Partido Comunista Português (Grupo Parlamentar), 'Projeto de Lei No. 228/XII/1.a: Regime Jurídico Da Partilha de Dados Informáticos' 1; L'ALLIANCE public.artistes, 'PRESS KIT. Downloading and Sharing Files on the Internet. An Alliance against Legal Proceedings. An Alliance for a Global Licence' 1; Caroline Colin, 'Etude the Faisabilite de Systemes de Licences Pour Les Echanges d'Oeuvres Sur Internet' (2011); Proposition de loi visant a adapter la perception du droit d'auteur a l'evolution technologique tout en preservant le droit a la vie privee des usagers d'Internet [Bill to Adjust Copyright Law to Technological Developments While Preserving Internet Users' Right to Privacy] (Sen. Benoit Hellings and Freya Piryns), Mar. 2, 2010, S.4–1686; Proposition de loi visant a adapter la perception du droit d'auteur a l'evolution technologique tout en preservant le droit a la vie privee des usagers d'Internet [Bill to Adjust Copyright Law to Technological Developments While Preserving Internet Users' Right to Privacy] (Sen. Jacky Morael and Frey Piryns), Dec. 9, 2010, S. 5-590; Beltrandi and others, 'CAMERA DEI

In the EU copyright field, recent interest in these models can be tied to judicial and institutional developments related to digital private copying. At the judicial level, two recent cases on private copying (*ACI Adam* and *Copydan*) raised the need to reconsider the private copying system in the digital environment, beyond a rekindling of the debate on phasing out levies.[5] Both cases provide a restrictive interpretation of the limitation that arguably fails to reach a fair balance of competing interests, with possible negative effects on the Internal Market.

In *ACI Adam*, the Court of Justice of the European Union (CJEU) excluded copies from *unlawful sources* (e.g. downloading films from unauthorized websites) from the scope of the private copying limitation. This judgement clarifies that a significant number of daily acts of Internet users qualify as infringing, and simultaneously disallows a type of private copying for which there was a strong economic case. In *Copydan*, the CJEU's ruling on the *use of third party devices for copying* – which it considered to be outside the scope of Directive 2001/29/EC – may have implications for the legal status of Cloud services that provide technical means for users to make or request their own copies, such as virtual storage spaces and online 'personal video recorders' for audiovisual works.[6]

At the institutional level, it is important to recognize the Commission's efforts to update and reform the private copying system,[7] as well as those of the EU Parliament. The latter, which in 2011 commissioned a study on content flatrates, passed in 2014 a Resolution recommending the examination of the possibility to levy Cloud services, a scenario which would approximate private copying to an ACS for certain digital reproductions.[8] Indeed, an early version of the

---

DEPUTATI N. 2963. PROPOSTA DI LEGGE – Modifiche Alla Legge 22 Aprile 1941, N. 633..." (presented 27 July 2007); Beltrandi and others, 'CAMERA DEI DEPUTATI N. 187. PROPOSTA DI LEGGE – Modifiche Alla Legge 22 Aprile 1941, N. 633..." (Presented 29 April 2008); Consumentenbond and others, 'Brief Consumentenbond, Mede Namens Ntb En FNV KIEM Aan Vaste Kamercommissie V&J Tbv AO Auteursrecht' (12 May 2014).

5 CJEU Case C-435/12 *ACI Adam BV and Others v. Stichting de Thuiskopie, Stichting Onderhandelingen Thuiskopie vergoeding* (10 April 2014), ECLI:EU:C:2014:254 [***ACI Adam***]; CJEU Case C-463/12 *Copydan Båndkopi v Nokia Danmark A/S* (5 March 2015), ECLI:EU:C:2015:144 [***Copydan***]. On phasing out of levies, see P.B. Hugenholtz, L. Guibault and S. van Geffen, 'The Future of Levies in a Digital Environment' (2003).

6 For a detailed analysis of *ACI Adam*, see J.P. Quintais, 'Private Copying and Downloading from Unlawful Sources' (2015) 46 IIC 66. For a case note on *Copydan*, see J.P. Quintais, 'Everything You Always Wanted to Know about Private Copying but Were Afraid to Ask (Case C-463/12 Copydan Båndkopi v Nokia Danmark A/S), Kluwer Copyright Blog, 16.03.2015.

7 See European Commission, 'Report on the Responses to the Public Consultation on the Review of the EU Copyright Rules' 1, 72–77; A. Vitorino, 'Recommendations Resulting from the Mediation on Private Copying and Reprography Levies' (2013).

8 On the study referred see A. Modot and others, 'The "Content Flat-Rate: A Solution to Illegal File-Sharing?' (2011). See also: European Parliament Resolution on private copying levies (2013/2114(INI)), adopted 11.2.2014; Report on private copying levies (2013/2114(INI)), 17.2.2014

draft resolution mentioned the need "to examine the possibility of legalizing works sharing for non-commercial purposes so as to guarantee consumers access to a wide variety of content and real choice in terms of cultural diversity".[9] In other words, it posited the need to examine the viability and feasibility of ACS.

III. Legal models and challenges

ACS can be implemented through different legal models imposing varying degrees of restriction on the nature or exercise of exclusive rights. It is beyond the scope of this short presentation to discuss the legal issues raised by these models. However, some general remarks are possible.

Among the most relevant schemes discussed in scholarship are voluntary collective licensing, extended collective licensing, mandatory collective management, legal (compulsory or statutory) licenses, and state-run remuneration, compensation or reward systems.[10]

These models are either offered as stand-alone solutions to regulate the acts in question or combined in myriad ways, for example to regulate different rights involved in mass online use of works by individuals. A common configuration is the extension of the private copying limitation to all acts of reproduction (irrespective of lawfulness of source) and the application of mandatory or extended collective licensing to the making available right. For the most part, this design is guided by concerns with legal compliance. Chief among those is the consideration that the application of a statutory license (and therefore an exception or limitation) to the online right of communication to the public is not admissible under the three-step test.[11]

Committee on Legal Affairs, Rapporteur: Françoise Castex [***Castex Report***], para. 30. The topic has been picked up by some scholars, but only tentatively. See, e.g., M. Senftleben, 'The International Three-Step Test. A Model Provision for EC Fair Use Legislation' (2010) 1 jipitec 67; Quintais, 'Private Copying and Downloading from Unlawful Sources', *supra* note 6.

9 *Castex Report*, *supra* note 8, para. 27. The suggestion was dropped in the final version of the document.

10 Generally identifying these models, see, e.g. von Lewinski, 'Certain Legal Problems Related to the Making Available of Literary and Artistic Works and Other Protected Subject Matter Through Digital Networks', *supra* note 3; C. Bernault and A. Lebois, 'Peer-to-Peer File Sharing and Literary and Artistic Property A Feasibility Study Regarding a System of Compensation for the Exchange of Works via the Internet' (2005); Colin, *supra* note 4; Dusollier and Colin, *supra* note 3.

11 See, e.g., A. Peukert, 'A Bipolar Copyright System for the Digital Network Environment' (2005) 28 Hastings Communications & Entertainment Law Journal 1; B. Rietjens, 'Copyright and the Three-Step Test: Are Broadband Levies Too Good to Be True?' (2006) 20 International Review of Law, Computers & Technology 323.

In addition, there is debate on the legal qualification of mandatory collective management. In particular, it is discussed whether this model goes beyond a restriction on the options of the exercise of the right and affects a change to its exclusive nature, transforming it into a compensated copyright limitation. The consequence is that, for the type of blanket license desired to implement an ACS, a model that does not qualify as an exception or limitation is not subject to the three-step test, but rather to the arguably less stringent requirements of collective rights management. Mandatory collective management, it is also said, would be better suited to address (substantive and territorial) fragmentation and participation problems typically attached to voluntary collective licensing.[12]

IV. The IViR research project

Since 2012 the Institute for Information Law (IViR) at the University of Amsterdam is conducting an interdisciplinary research project on the legal and socio-economic feasibility of ACS. The empirical research was based on *two surveys* conducted in November 2013 with a panel constituted by a representative sample of the Dutch population, aged over sixteen, including those with and without Internet. What follows is a brief description of the main results of the surveys. For a detailed explanation of the methodology and analysis of the data collected, I refer to the respective papers.[13] Importantly, neither of these papers

12 Representative examples of this debate can be found in S. von Lewinski, 'Mandatory Collective Administration of Exclusive Rights – A Case Study on Its Compatibility with International and EC Copyright Law' [2004] UNESCO E-Copyright Bulletin 1; von Lewinski, 'Certain Legal Problems Related to the Making Available of Literary and Artistic Works and Other Protected Subject Matter Through Digital Networks', *supra* note 3; M. Ficsor, 'Collective Management of Copyright and Related Rights Form the Viewpoint of International Norms and the Acquis Communautaire' in Daniel Gervais (ed), *Collective Management of Copyright and Related Rights* (2nd edn, Kluwer Law International 2010); C. Geiger, 'The Role of The Three-Step Test in the Adaptation of Copyright Law to the Information Society' [2007] UNESCO E-Copyright Bulletin 1; C. Geiger, 'Challenges for the Enforcement of Copyright in the Online World: Time for a New Approach' [2014] Max Planck Institute for Innovation and Competition Research Papers 1. For the ALAI's position, see ALAI, 'ALAI Resolution "Affirmation Droit Exclusif" (14 Janvier 2006)' (2006). Specific discussions on the legal nature of extended collective licensing can be found in T. Riis and J. Schovsbo, 'Extended Collective Licenses and the Nordic Experience: It's a Hybrid but Is It a Volvo or a Lemon?' (2010) 33 Columbia Journal of Law & the Arts 471; C. Rydning, *Extended Collective Licences – The Compatibility of the Nordic Solution with the International Conventions and EC Law* (Norwegian Research Center for Computers and Law 2010).
13 The papers in question are: Vallbé and others, *supra* note 1; C. Handke, B. Bodó and J.-J. Vallbé, 'Going Means Trouble and Staying Makes It Double: The Value of Licensing Recorded Music Online' [2015] Journal of Cultural Economics. For additional information on the project, see *supra* note 1.

addresses legal compliance issues, such as the compatibility of ACS with the three-step test.[14]

The *first survey* regarded individual media consumption habits for three types of content – music, audiovisual and books – in relation to different online and offline (lawful and unlawful) channels. In the *second survey* we conducted a discrete choice experiment, defining the ACS payment mechanism as a surcharge on the Internet subscription fee of households, and the functioning of the system under statutory regulation. In simple terms, different types of ACS were defined through a combination of *attributes* abstracted from legal analysis of existing proposals: *allowed uses* (downloading, sharing and modification), *subject matter* (music, audiovisual, and books), *catalogue completeness* (complete, partial, temporal restrictions), *monitoring* (anonymous or no monitoring), *distribution of revenues* (freedom of contract or minimum 50% for creators) and *price* (six 5-euro price points from € 5 to € 30).[15]

As this panel focuses on legal license models, it is appropriate to report the results of research as they apply to *mandatory* ACS, which would translate into a statutory license for the online rights of reproduction and communication to the public.

In a *first paper* we used the results of our research to examine whether such an ACS for recorded music would be welfare increasing. Our main findings were the following.[16]

– A well-designed ACS for recorded music makes users and rights holders better off, increasing their total welfare compared to the status quo even when the results are corrected for overestimation, in the best case scenario by about € 600 million.
– A € 1.74 surcharge on ISP subscription for all households with Internet connection would equal the entire revenues in the Dutch *physical and digital* market for recorded music in 2012, including all conventional purchases of recorded music of approximately € 144 million.[17]

---

14 Issues of compliance are addressed in my forthcoming book, based on my doctoral dissertation: João Pedro Quintais, *Copyright in the Age of Online Access. Alternative Compensation Systems in EU Copyright Law* (Working Title), Kluwer Information Law Series (Forthcoming, 2017).

15 For a more detailed explanation of the methodology, see ibid, *supra* note 13; Vallbé and others, *supra* note 1.

16 See Handke, Bodó and Vallbé, *supra* note 13.

17 *Revenues* are calculated resorting to industry statistics, such as IFPI, 'IFPI Digital Music Report 2013. Engine of a Digital World' (2013), which estimates rights holders revenues in the Dutch recorded music market at €143.6 million. The focus is on revenues rather than profits, due to the lack of reliable information on *costs*. Data on private copying levies collected in the Netherlands for recorded music were taken from WIPO, 'International Survey on Private Copying. Law & Practice 2013' (2013). The results assume the unlikely scenario that an ACS substi-

- Users' willingness to pay ("WTP") is € 9.25 per month for a mandatory ACS, despite low-risk associated with private copying from unauthorized sources (as the survey preceded *ACI Adam*) and widespread availability and use of online music subscription platforms.
- Results were calculated on the basis of a 100% substitution effect of the net revenues of rights holders identified above. Even if the measured € 9.25 price point overestimates WTP by a factor of three, the proposed ACS would improve the current revenues of the recorded music industry in the Dutch market.
- For *rights holders* in general, there will be economic advantages of monetizing previously unenforced and uncompensated uses, as well as savings in copyright enforcement. For *authors*, a mandatory claim of fair compensation (e.g. 50% of collected sums) would likely improve their current rights revenues.

In a *second paper* we studied whether the idea of an ACS enjoys public support in the Netherlands and attempted to identify how that support is structured. Our main findings were the following.[18]

- Nearly half (49%) of Dutch consumers do not use digital access channels to consume music, audiovisual content and books. This is mostly due to hold-out groups, characterized by older less educated people that do not consume culture online (29%) and older educated people who prefer print (but not e-) books (20%).
- Age is the dividing line for digital uses. Younger generations show "promiscuous" consumption patterns that include use of free/paid and legal/illegal channels. They can be divided into the following clusters: *occasional consumers* (28.88%), *digital consumers* (6.36%), and *pirates* (16.02%).
- *Occasional consumers* are infrequent and low intensity digital consumers, mostly focused on free sampling (complemented by purchase of physical copies).
- *Digital consumers* and *pirates* account for a disproportionate large share of the overall cultural consumption, and it is almost impossible to separate pirates from digital consumers. Indeed, *pirates are a subset of digital consumers*.
- There is substantial consumer support for ACS, especially among those already using legal access channels, namely pirates and digital consumers, but also occasional consumers. In fact, *increased usage of legal channels indicates increased inclination to support ACS, and higher WTP.*

---

tutes all current sales of recorded music (perfect substitution) and provides no cost-savings. See Handke, Bodó and Vallbé, *supra* note 13.

18 See Vallbé and others, *supra* note 1.

- The likely reason is discontent with the status quo. Possible sources of discontent are linked to the insufficiencies of current offers in what concerns *allowed uses/user rights* and *subject matter/types of content*. In essence, users want to be able to do more than *download* or *stream music*; they desire the freedom to share (make available) that extends to additional content, offered to them by unauthorized channels.

V. Concluding remarks

Enforcement alone is not a solution to digital piracy or to regulate unauthorized use of works by individuals. The emerging streaming model in the online environment is proving inadequate to compensate creators and other rights holders. ACS provide a different option to regulate and remunerate large-scale non-commercial uses through legal models that are internal to copyright and familiar to the European legal culture and tradition.

A mandatory ACS can be implemented through a statutory license for non-commercial online acts of reproduction and communication to the public by individuals. This system could be based on a compensated limitation for these uses, which would require articulation with existing compensated and uncompensated limitations in the Directive (temporary and transient copy, private copy, quotation, incidental inclusion, parody) and duly take into consideration *de minimis* uses. It would also require regulation of the relationship with the legal protection of technological measures (Article 6 Directive 2001/29/EC). The resulting fair compensation ought to require a mandatory and inalienable claim for creators, which would not only better align the system with the aims of copyright but also constitute a marked improvement over the status quo.

Naturally, where a ACS relies on a compensated limitation, it must pass the three-step test. For that, it is necessary that the limitation(s) have a strong non-economic motivation (here: freedom of expression and information, privacy and personal data, freedom to conduct a business for certain intermediaries), but also a careful delimitated of scope, so as to not conflict with the normal exploitation of works. To meet the conditions of the test, it is likely that a flexible interpretation of the same would have to be followed.[19] To be sure, some scholars

---

19 Along the lines suggested by C. Geiger, R. Hilty and J. Griffiths, 'Declaration A Balanced Interpretation Of The "Three-Step Test" In Copyright Law' (2008) 6 IIC 707; C. Geiger and F. Schönherr, 'Limitations to Copyright in the Digital Age', *Research Handbook on EU Internet Law* (Edward Elgar 2014); C. Geiger, D. Gervais and M. Senftleben, 'The Three-Step-Test Revisited: How to Use the Test's Flexibility in National Copyright Law' (2014) 29 American University International Law Review 581; M.Senftleben, 'How to Overcome the Normal Exploitation Obstacle : Opt-Out Formalities , Embargo Periods and the International Three-Step Test' (2014) 1 Berkeley Technology Law Journal Commentaries 1.

would argue that a statutory license of this type would indeed conflict with normal exploitation of works online.[20]

The IViR research project provides interesting empirical data to inform the political debate on this type of copyright reform, but also quantitative elements necessary for legal analysis. This is for example the case with the definition of normal exploitation, adequate compensation, and measurement of competing legitimate interests to be balanced in a proportionate manner. Chief among the findings are the willingness of users to pay for and participate in an ACS, its quantification and, using the case-study of recorded music, the realization that such a model holds the promise of being welfare increasing. It also illuminates the significant amount of remuneration rights holders and especially creators – due to their weakened bargaining position – have left on the 'virtual' table. In other words: the price of exclusivity.

20 On the obstacles raised by the second step of the test to ACS proposals based on statutory licensing, see, e.g., Dusollier and Colin, *supra* note 3, 829; Eckersley, *supra* note 3, 155–156; Peukert, *supra* note 11, 32, 43; Rietjens, *supra* note 11; Geiger, 'The Role of The Three-Step Test in the Adaptation of Copyright Law to the Information Society', *supra* note 12, 9; Colin, *supra* note 4, 51–55; Geiger and Schönherr, *supra* note 18, 135.

Friday, June 19:
BUSINESS MODELS TODAY AND OPTIONS FOR THE FUTURE

Vendredi 19 juin:
MODÈLES ÉCONOMIQUES AUJOURD’HUI ET DES OPTIONS POUR LE FUTUR

Viernes, 19 de junio:
MODELES DE NEGOCIO ACTUALES Y OPCIONES PARA EL FUTURO

Session 1: Examples for business models in the digital environment and their legal assessment
Exemples de modèles économiques dans l'environnement numérique et des options pour le futur
Ejemplos de modelos de negocio en el entorno digital y su evaluación legal

Stefanie Hubig*

Keynote

ALAI Congress Participants,
Ladies and gentlemen,

Thank you very much for your invitation. It is a great pleasure to speak to you today on copyright policy.

But let me begin by saying that the Federal Minister of Justice and Consumer Protection, Heiko Maas, sends his best regards. Unfortunately he is unable to attend himself, but will be following the results of your conference with keen interest – not least because copyright law is one of the main priorities of the current administration's legal policy programme.

I am very glad that ALAI's German national group took on the challenge of organising this Congress. It is fifty years since the German Copyright Act was introduced, making this an ideal occasion to hold the conference here in Bonn.

Looking at the programme you have put together, I have to congratulate you. With the topics selected for discussion, you are touching on some of the latest issues in copyright policymaking. Yesterday you focused on statutory remuneration rights and copyright contract law. You couldn't have chosen a more relevant topic. Only last week,[1] the Advocate General delivered his opinion to the European Court of Justice in the "Reprobel" case. We are very much looking forward to the decision of the ECJ. Furthermore, we will shortly be putting forward draft legislation that aims to reform copyright contract law – but I will come back to this in a moment.

Today's discussions will centre on current business models and the question of whether (and how) these models should be governed by law in future. Again, these issues are hugely relevant right now for copyright policymakers not just in Germany and Europe but worldwide. We have asked the Max Planck Institute in Munich to carry out research in this field so we can better evaluate the underlying empirical facts. This is another reason why we will be looking very closely at the results from this Congress, using your output to help inform our own policy decisions in future.

---

* Dr., State Secretary in the German Federal Ministry of Justice and Consumer Protection.

1 The Opinion by the Advocate General has been announced for 11 June 2015. Due to these proceedings, the German Federal Court of Justice has stayed proceedings in the Vogel case (regarding the distribution of revenues in *VG Wort*).

Ladies and gentlemen,
I would like to divide my talk into three parts:

- I will start by briefly looking back at how the 1965 German Copyright Act came into existence.
- In the second part, I will report on our current legislative projects in the field of copyright law.
- And in part three, I will address a number of issues that will be keeping us busy in this area over the next few years.

Ladies and gentlemen,
When we look back at the history of the 1965 German Copyright Act, many things strike us as rather familiar: attempts to reform copyright law have often involved bitter struggles. Of course the same could be said for many areas of legal policy – actual win-win situations in lawmaking are, unfortunately, very few and far between. Once a decision to change the status quo has been taken, the usual outcome is that some stakeholders benefit while others have to live with the negative consequences. But almost nowhere is the lobbying more intense, and the struggle more hard-fought, than in copyright law. And that was already the case fifty years ago.

Further evidence of the problem is visible in the duration of the reform process. After the Justice Ministry submitted its first official draft in 1954, the second draft did not appear until five years later. Another three years passed before the parliamentary process could be initiated after the government bill was submitted in 1962. All in all, it took eleven years to complete the reform! In the end, the Mediation Committee even had to be convened. (This committee is constitutionally obliged to mediate in conflicts between the Bundestag and the body representing the German federal states.) Further amendments were introduced at this stage too.

Ladies and gentlemen,
The 1965 German Copyright Act brought one fundamental change that was heavily disputed right up until the last minute, but was ultimately pushed through: this was the obligation to pay remuneration for private audio tape recordings. No doubt you are familiar with the background to this provision: several years previously, Germany's highest civil court – the Federal Court of Justice – had ruled that even private audio tape recordings of copyrighted works constituted an infringement of the author's exclusive rights. In other words, even if someone could afford to spend a month's wages on a tape recorder during the boom years of the West German economic miracle, they still had to purchase a licence from the collecting society, GEMA, before they were legally permitted to copy music from FM radio or vinyl records. This obviously did not work in practice: the new technology was available and was spreading on a

massive scale. Huge violations of individual privacy would have been necessary in order to enforce the exclusive rights in question. Lawmakers opted to make such copies legal – but to monetarise them at the same time. However, there was one further change: it was not the actual users themselves who were required to pay a flat-rate fee, but the manufacturers of the technology.

There are striking parallels here with the contemporary debate on the use of copyright-protected content: today we are once again facing the question of how to respond to the new usage possibilities that digitalisation and interconnectivity have opened up. All of us now carry personal copying and communication equipment around with us wherever we go: every smartphone with internet access is capable of reproducing and distributing content and making it available online. And where protected content is involved, this has a direct bearing on the most important utilisation and exploitation rights governed by copyright law. How do we wish to respond to this situation in future – by prohibiting or remunerating?

Ladies and gentlemen,
With our brief excursion into legal history complete, we are back in the present. I would like to quickly outline the projects we are currently working on at the Federal Ministry of Justice and Consumer Protection. The coalition agreement of December 2013 includes a whole series of detailed copyright policy measures to be implemented by the year 2017.

Our legislative project on collective rights management is one very topical example.

This week we have published draft legislation on collecting societies. This new law is intended to replace the Copyright Management Act which will also be fifty this year. With this act, we will be transposing the relevant EU Directive from 2014, which provides a common legal framework for collecting societies throughout the European Union for the first time. From the point of view of the collecting societies, not much will change in terms of fundamental principles, although certain specific areas will be heavily affected. This, I fear, is because the Directive has turned out to be rather too fond of detail. All of this now has to be accommodated within our national legislation – which is why we have decided to revamp the entire Act.

At the same time, we will be taking the opportunity to modernise the existing collection system for levies on equipment and storage media. This remuneration system was invented in Germany in 1965 and has been adopted by many other countries since then. However, the present situation is much less clear-cut than it was fifty years ago: In the average household, you will no longer find just one solitary tape recorder but at least one PC, possibly several tablets, a hard-drive recorder connected to a smart TV, half a dozen internet-capable telephones, and numerous USB flash drives. Under our present law, all of this hardware is subject to remuneration levies. Clearly this is another area where new systems of remuneration need to be considered in the medium term. But for the time being, the main priority is to tighten up the existing procedures so that the levies can be calculated more quickly. This helps both the creditors and debtors of copyright remuneration.

Ladies and gentlemen,

The second project on the agenda is a further reform of copyright contract law. Although the statutory right of creative artists to receive equitable remuneration has been enshrined in German copyright law since 2002, there are still problems involved with enforcing this right in practice. This is particularly true when freelance authors, artists or actors actually succeed in enforcing their rights. Because then, they face the risk of being blacklisted: no more follow-up contracts are awarded and their livelihood is threatened. We plan to submit a legislative draft on this matter before the summer break. The goal is to iron out shortcomings in the existing system and to strengthen collective legal instruments in particular, thereby allowing imbalances to be redressed in the negotiation of artists' contracts.

Furthermore, the Federal Government has declared its intention to introduce a blanket exception for education and research. The idea is to revise and reorganise the extremely complex individual provisions in German copyright law on exceptions and limitations. Researchers, students, librarians and school pupils are not experts in copyright law. In future, it will be easier for them to decide whether specific uses are permitted or not. We also need to explore how we can modernise licences. Many regulations still hark back to the "analogue" era – but education and research are becoming increasingly "digital". This points to a fundamental dilemma in the present regulatory framework: We have a flexible and open-ended list of exploitation rights, while at the same time we have a rigid and definitive list of exceptions and limitations. The emergence of new technologies and new forms of utilisation can upset the balance between exclusivity on the one hand and permitted use on the other. Again, we hope to submit a legislative draft on this legally challenging policy area this year.

Ladies and gentlemen,

The provisions on education and research – such as those concerning *text and data mining* – are also part of the EU agenda on copyright policy. Further concepts at the heart of the discussion in Brussels include *portability* and *territoriality* – in other words, the question of how to organise cross-border access to content. Questions of enforcement also figure prominently, of course, while the European Commission wishes to investigate the role of platforms that use copyrighted content. We are already in talks with the Commission, that is: we have been involved in the decision-making process in Brussels since day one. A regulatory proposal can be expected by the end of the year. This means it is now certain that the 2001 InfoSoc Directive will be revised, at least partially. High time indeed – the substance of the Directive is already two decades old. Back then, the *Internet of Things*, the social web, *YouTube* and *iPhones* were barely imaginable.

Ladies and gentlemen,
So that is the current legal policy agenda in Germany and the European Union. The aforementioned *Internet of Things* and the German concept of *Industry 4.0* bring me to the third part of my talk: I would now like to outline a few topics that will be featuring prominently in the debate about copyright law over the next few years.

Copyright law has long ceased to be an isolated legal field reserved for specialists. Thanks to digitalisation and interconnectivity, copyright issues have permeated many parts of our everyday lives:

- We are constantly surrounded by creative works such as text and music. The cultural industries have become an important part of our economy, and their turnover in Germany now runs to almost 64 billion euros a year, significantly more than the 40 billion euro turnover generated by the chemical industry.[2]
- Digitalisation and interconnectivity are driving two diametrically opposed trends. On the one hand, protected works are more vulnerable than ever before. You do not need a massive printing press to produce a perfect digital copy – a computer and an internet connection will do the job. On the other hand, the monitoring possibilities for rightholders are far more extensive than ever before. The software in my eBook reader knows which page of which text I was reading at what precise time.
- Production – and with this I mean both material production and the production of information – is already rooted in databases and software, and will become even more so in future. Both of these base technologies are regulated by copyright law. This means that much more is involved than just the "literary and artistic works" mentioned in the *Revised Berne Convention*.

It is not surprising, then, that copyright law is part of the German Federal Government's *Digital Agenda*. This corresponds with the *Digital Single Market* project at the EU level – copyright law is an integral element within the field of digital policymaking at the EU as well.

---

2 Commission of Experts for Research and Innovation (EFI), *Gutachten zur Forschung, Innovation und technologischer Leistungsfähigkeit Deutschlands* (Report on Research, Innovation and the Technological Capacity of Germany), Gutachten 2015, 2015, Berlin, http://www.e-fi.de/fileadmin/Gutachten_2015/EFI_Gutachten_2015.pdf p. 59.

Ladies and gentlemen,
Irrespective of this, it is important that we continue to regard copyright law not simply as an economic factor but as a part of cultural policy. Minister Maas and the French Cultural Minister Fleur Pellerin emphasised this in a recent Franco-German declaration on copyright law. To quote from the introduction: "*France and Germany underline the key role copyright law plays for fostering cultural diversity, creativity and innovation. Copyright law must continue to fulfil this task in our digital information and knowledge-based society.*"[3] In the upcoming reforms at the European level, we will thus be ensuring that copyright law is not just viewed in market-based terms, but that sufficient attention is also given to questions of cultural policy. After all, creative output is no ordinary kind of "product".

Ladies and gentlemen,
Copyright law is not just about protecting the interests of creative artists and those who exploit works commercially. It also regulates access to information. Thus, copyright law is also information law – even if the only explicit evidence of this in the German Copyright Act is currently to be found among the exceptions and limitations. Nevertheless, in a knowledge and information society, copyright law governs one of society's central eco-systems: who has access to knowledge, and at what price? Over the coming weeks and months, we will be focusing intensely on these questions – in connection both with our legislation on the education and research exception, and at the EU level.

Ladies and gentlemen,
These questions are not new. In December 1930, a company called *Photo Copie G.m.b.H.* (I hope the name says it all!) set up business in the reading room of the State Library in Berlin. The company's express copy service took between 30 and 60 minutes, and library users could even have copies delivered to their homes. For the first time, "analogue" photocopying made it possible to reproduce texts individually without having to copy them out by hand.

The real craze in America, of course, was microfilm. These new copying techniques helped fuel the dream of the universal library – an idea that runs right through from the Library of Alexandria to Google Books.

In her award-winning work *Autoren und Apparate*, the Swiss historian *Monika Domman* recounts the following observation by the American librarian *Robert Binkley* in January 1938:

3 *Urheberrecht – Gemeinsame deutsch-französische Erklärung, 31. März 2015* (Copyright – Joint German-French Declaration, 31 March 2015). See, in French: http://www.culturecommunication.gouv.fr/Presse/Communiques-de-presse/Fleur-Pellerin-et-Heiko-Maas-signent-a-Berlin-une-declaration-franco-allemande-sur-le-droit-d-auteur.

"The author of a scientific or learned article has an equitable right to have that article become available to all his colleagues in the field."[4] This argument is still being discussed today under the concept of *open access*. *Binkley* wanted the new technology to ensure the broadest possible access to knowledge – access to contemporary scientific journals in particular. Back then, most of the leading publications in the natural sciences and technical disciplines still came from Europe – the German-speaking countries included. Today the primary language of academia is English, and research organisations grumble about the pricing policies of *Reed Elsevier* and *Springer Science*. The protagonists may have changed – but ultimately the fault lines in the debate about access to information have remained the same. On the one side are the multinational media corporations, on the other are small academic publishers. The former bring out the world's leading science journals and the authors have to pay major sums for the opportunity to publish. The latter target a limited audience of specialists that is often largely confined to a single country. Should both be treated the same? And how do we deal with the fact that the academic community has ultimately chosen to submit to the dogma of *publish or perish* with the *Citation Index*? What can copyright law achieve here – and what is unrealistic?

Ladies and gentlemen,
In the historical context, many of today's fault lines are nothing new. In fact they are as old as the copyright system itself. Computerisation and the internet might have brought them more sharply into focus, but the structural foundations of such conflicts of interest have been in place for a long time. One-hundred years ago, the very music labels that are now claiming the exclusive right to exploit music online were fighting for compulsory licences to be able to access published sheet music. Back then, they were the "new economy". Meanwhile, the composers and music publishers tried in vain to defend *their* exclusive right, arguing above all that "canned music" would signal the demise of music culture as we know it. The complaints of today's established music labels don't sound all that different when it comes to platforms such as Facebook, YouTube and Spotify.

Copyright history has certainly taught us one thing: Fears that new technologies and new models of use and exploitation will somehow lead to cultural deterioration or decline, are a permanent feature of any fight for intellectual property. The printing press, the gramophone record, motion pictures with synchronised sound, radio, television: These inventions led to the disappearance of the monastic scribe of the middle ages, the village musician, and the live cinema orchestra. But at the same time, creative activity began to reach a larger

4 Dommann, *Autoren und Apparate, Die Geschichte des Copyrights im Medienwandel*, Frankfurt am Main, 1st edn. 2014, p. 165.

audience as more and more people gained better access to outstanding works of art and culture. The job of copyright cannot therefore be to protect the status quo. Instead, it should provide a level playing field that ensures fair competition between both new and existing business models. Seen in this light, copyright law is also competition law.

Ladies and gentlemen,
The challenges of the future will include striking a fair balance between contractual and statutory usage rights – in areas such as the utilisation of copyright-protected materials in education and research, for example. Here too, there are more questions than answers. Allow me to provide a few examples:

- When can users be reasonably expected to check whether a licence is available? A specialised librarian might be in the position to do so, but can the same also be expected of a lecturer at a music college who wants to add a few audio samples to the intranet repository for his seminar on classical modernity?
- Who verifies that the licence offered is appropriate? After all, one thing is clear: a statutory exception adopted by lawmakers in the public interest cannot be undermined by prohibitive pricing.
- How do we ensure due process here? At any rate, the practice so far – with exceptions being fought out in court battles over many years before even *some* amount of clarity is achieved – has not proven effective.

Ladies and gentlemen,
To conclude I would like to take another brief look at the past. ALAI is quite rightly proud that its founding father is Victor Hugo. As a great writer, he was France's social conscience, campaigning for justice and fighting against social suffering. And, he was one of the inspirers of international copyright protection. At the same time, the following passage from his opening address at the International Literary Congress in 1878 has gone down in history: I quote: *"The book, as a book, belongs to the author, but the thought belongs – the term is not too vast – to the human race. All minds have a right to it. If one of these two laws, the right of the author and the right of the human mind, were to be sacrificed, it would most certainly be the right of the author, because the public interest is our sole preoccupation and everyone, I tell you, everyone must come before us."*[5]

Luckily, we're not in a situation where we have to sacrifice either the rights of authors or the public interest. Indeed, we've seen many a heated debate in recent years between "copyright extremists" on the one hand and the "pirate" faction on the other. Maybe, however, now is the time for less agitated and ideo-

5 http://www.atramenta.net/lire/discours-douverture-du-congres-litteraire-international-de-1878/1923/1#oeuvre_page (there: p. 5).

logically motivated reforms. Conserving the status quo has no place on the agenda, nor does abolishing intellectual property rights. Scientists and academics, I believe, must support and encourage these efforts. I can only encourage you to play your part as well. We need your basic research, and your creative solutions. At the same time, I would ask for your understanding in case we should only be able to take up *some* of your proposals after the debate. After all, policymaking is the art of compromise.

Thank you very much for your attention. All the best for what I am sure will continue to be a productive conference!

Matthias Leistner*

Introduction

Thank you very much, Ms. Hubig, for that genuinely inspiring talk not only outlining the ambitious recent projects of the Ministry of Justice, but also widening the horizon and comparing today's challenges not only to the challenges of the 1965 German legislator, but even to the situation connected with the antique library of Alexandria, thus quite impressively illustrating the old saying by *Gerhard Schricker* that "the history of copyright law is a history of constant reactions to the challenges of technology." Thank you very much indeed!

Today's morning sessions will be governed by a motto along the lines of the famous German 20th century poet *Bertolt Brecht* who once coined the saying in a theatre piece: "Truth is concrete". Incidentally, there is a very interesting copyright issue behind that quote because actually it goes back to the 19th century philosopher *Friedrich Wilhelm Hegel*, and was later on used by *Lenin* as well. But it was only Bertolt Brecht who put it into a theatre piece and who is today widely associated with that saying. This inevitably leads to the provocant question: was the famous poet a copy kat? Be that as it may, this morning we want to deal with the specific analysis of concrete business models.

Which concrete questions will we ask in that context? Well, in all today's morning panels we will first ask how do certain business models work specifically in the digital arena? How do the specific revenue schemes work? What are the resulting revenue streams? Who profits to what extent and which part of the revenues reaches the actual authors? And we will then in each panel, secondly, have a closer look at the legal implications of certain business models.

In that general framework, we will first discuss business models of musical flatrates, such as offered by Spotify, Deezer and the like. These business models undoubtedly are a large success with the consumers, but they raise certain sensitive questions from the point of view of the artists. Where do the concrete revenues go, as regards the income from the paid premium offers, as well as regards the advertising gains from the free basic offers? How to deal with these business models in regard to future remuneration schemes (i.e. levies), which are at the moment connected to the storage media whereas in the streaming models the content isn't stored on the end users' devices at all? Against that background, an approach connecting the levies exclusively to blank storage media obviously tends to fail.

* Professor of Civil Law, Intellectual Property Law with Information Law and IT-Law, Ludwig-Maximilians-University, Munich, as well as Member of the Faculty of the Munich Intellectual Property Law Center (MIPLC) (Germany), and a guest professor for European Intellectual Property Law at the University of Xiamen (China).

We had invited people from Spotify and Deezer. Unfortunately, it was impossible to have them here, so we are particularly thankful to Mr. *Hernandez Pinzon* of the Spanish Sociedad des Artistas (Spanish Artists' Society), that he stepped in on short notice. And for reason of that short notice he will do both, he will present the business model as well as the legal issues behind it. Thank you very much, indeed, for this outstanding effort Mr. *Hernandez Pinzon!*

Secondly, we will discuss a specific licence offered by the U.S. Copyright Clearance Center (CCC) in association with the German VG Wort collecting society, i.e. the RightsDirect copyright clearance center. RightsDirect offers a tailor made licence for typical business digital users of copyright protected material which will be presented as a business model by *Fred Haber* of the CCC. Following up, Mr. *Robert Staats*, Chairman of VG Wort, will discuss the legal implications of the underlying licence.

Finally we will discuss business models of micro licensing, an approach also object of the European Commission's activities in the Licences for Europe Initiative where again, of course, the main question is of whether and to what extent the income from such microlicences really reaches the original authors. Also these models quite obviously raise legal questions with regard to the necessary regulation of the respective end-user licence agreements, either in consumer protection or in contract or competition law. With regard to that third part, we are happy to have *Olaf Wolters* with us, lawyer in Berlin and formerly working for the Fair Games Association, as well as *Ole Jani*, lawyer in Berlin and since long a friend of ALAI and known copyright law and policy expert in Germany.

The floor is yours, Mr. *Hernandez Pinzon*. Thank you very much again for stepping in on such short notice!

Alvaro Hernández-Pinzón*

1. Music Flatrates – Presentation and legal assessment

Muchos artistas han manifestado su descontento por las insignificantes cantidades que perciben de los servicios de música digital o, directamente, porque no perciben nada por la comunicación pública o la puesta a disposición de sus interpretaciones y actuaciones fijadas en los fonogramas que llevan a cabo estos servicios.

Podría traer varios ejemplos (los más conocidos los de Tailor Swift o Bette Midler), pero me quedo con el tweet que publicó Geoff Barrow, del grupo Portishead, el 13 de abril de 2015:

> "Thirty four millions of streams (are) one thousand seven hundred pounds. Thank you Apple, Youtube, Spotify, especially Universal Music Group for selling our music so cheaply".

I. Un modelo de negocio viejo en un entorno radicalmente nuevo

El consumo de contenidos ha cambiado radicalmente en el entorno digital, desde la aparición de Internet, los negocios tradicionales de las industrias de contenidos musicales y audiovisuales se ven abocados a la revolución o a la desaparición. Por el momento, los negocios de música online tienden a ser evoluciones del negocio tradicional, porque algunos de los agentes que participan en la cadena de valor de estos nuevos productos y servicios se resisten a adaptarse a la "revolución" del consumo.

Los primeros servicios (legales) que irrumpieron en el mercado, se limitaban a sustituir la copia física por la copia intangible; esto es, los modelos pasaban de actos de explotación del derecho de distribución *(artículo 6 TODA y artículo 8 TOIEF)* a actos de explotación del derecho de puesta a disposición *(artículo 8 TODA y artículos 10 y 14 TOIEF)*. La industria nos ofrecía ficheros de sonido (de alta calidad), en vez de a CDs, vinilos, DVD y las prehistóricas casetes; y accesos a páginas y aplicaciones web, en vez de a tiendas de discos y centros comerciales.

Servicios como iTunes, Google Play, Emusic o 7 Digital, nos ofrecían y, en algunos casos nos siguen ofreciendo, la posibilidad de comprar el mismo disco que

---

* Strategic Director of Collection and Legal Department AIE (Spanish Society of Performers), Spain.

antes guardábamos en una librería y escuchábamos en nuestro equipo HI-FI o walkman o discman, en un formato intangible, que permite meter toda nuestra discoteca en un bolsillo. Sin embargo, la industria (discográfica) no trasladó este cambio de dimensión y de hábito que, además, traía un sustancial ahorro en los costes de fabricación del formato físico, al precio que los compradores de la música pagaban por, además de disponer de la música, tener un soporte físico.

El problema de este modelo era (y es) que el mercado negro es un competidor muy fuerte, más en unos países (como el mío, España) que en otros, y ¿para qué pagar si puede obtener el mismo producto gratis?

Pero volviendo al negocio legal, el triunfador de este modelo fue Apple, con su iTunes, sin embargo el éxito no se debe, por lo menos sólo, a la venta de canciones, sino al aparato que las reproducía: el iPod.

En 2008, surgen los más exitosos servicios de música digital a través de streaming. En Francia nace DEEZER y en Suecia SPOTIFY. Estos servicios se adaptan a los nuevos hábitos de consumo: música portable, de calidad, variada e integrada en las redes sociales.

Parte de los consumidores con estos nuevos hábitos, se han acostumbrado al "gratis total", por lo que hay que recuperarlos para que vuelvan a apreciar el valor de la música y pagar por ella.

Estos servicios introducen el concepto *Freemium*, como modelo de negocio: «*Lo básico es gratis, los extras tienen un precio*». Así, los modelos que nos ocupan ofrecen música gratuita, modalidad que se financia a través de la publicidad, a los usuarios ocasionales por un servicio básico; y un servicio Premium a los usuarios que desean acceder al servicio sin limitaciones a cambio del pago de una cuota.

En estos modelos, la música pasa de ser un producto a ser un servicio.

II. Cadena de valor de los modelos de música digital y poder de negociación

Obviamente, una estructura de fuente de ingresos "vieja" no sirve en un modelo de negocio "nuevo"; si el consumo de música cambiaba con Spotify o Deezer, su modelo de ingresos debería cambiar igualmente. Para el cliente de Spotify o Deezer cambia, pero NO para los agentes que intervienen en la cadena de valor: desde la perspectiva del modelo de negocio todo ha cambiado, desde la perspectiva de los ingresos que generan hay que mantenerlo a toda costa.

Para la producción de la música y su comercialización en el nuevo mercado digital, la cadena de valor ha tenido que cambiar necesariamente: las actividades de fabricación y logística (de los soportes físicos) han desaparecido y en las actividades de marketing y promocionales el peso del productor como prescriptor de contenidos se ha reducido, tomando protagonismo el artista y el "consumidor" de música, sobre manera, en las redes sociales. No olvidemos que estos servicios (p.ej. Spotify) nos permiten compartir en Twitter o Facebook lo que estamos escuchando y hacer recomendaciones a nuestros amigos e incluso a desconocidos que compartan el gusto por un determinado tipo de música o artistas, a través de las listas de reproducción.

Pues bien, el reparto de valor entre los agentes que intervienen en el proceso de producción de la música apenas ha variado, es más, el productor es el que acapara la mayor parte de los ingresos (el 70%) cómo dice la propia Spotify[1] y, en el mejor de los casos, paga un pequeño royalty al artista, dependiendo de lo pactado en el contrato discográfico y el poder de negociación que tenga cada artista individualmente. En el caso de los jóvenes el poder de negociación es prácticamente nulo.

La entidad de gestión de derechos de los artistas franceses, ADAMI,[2] ha hecho un estudio entre 400 artistas principales, en el cual queda reflejado cómo se reparten entre los distintos participantes en los modelos de suscripción/Flat Rates, el importe (estándar) que abonan los usuarios de estos servicios:

De los 9,99 € que cuesta al mes la suscripción: 1,99 € corresponde a impuestos en general; 1 € a los autores y editores; 4,60 € a los productores de fonogramas; 1,90 € a la prestadora del servicio en streaming; y, finalmente, 0,46 € llega a los artistas.

La parte de los artistas, evidentemente, no llega a todos, sino que se reparte entre aquellos que tienen la capacidad de negociación suficiente para incluir algún royalty por este concepto en sus contratos.

III. Derechos y actos de explotación implicados en los servicios FLAT RATES

Estos servicios de tarifa plana/flat rates ofrecen a sus usuarios, principalmente, dos modalidades para escuchar música:

La primera, que fue el primer servicio que ofrecieron al público (en 2008), por el cual cada usuario (sea o no premium) disfruta de plena interactividad, es decir, selecciona de entre el conjunto de actuaciones musicales puestas a disposición del público por la Spotify, Deezer o Google Play, la concreta canción que

1 See, for example:
http://www.musicbusinessworldwide.com/10929203-streams-on-spotify-56329-35/
http://industriamusical.es/desmitificando-el-valor-de-los-pagos-por-reproducciones-de-los-servicios-de-streaming-spotify/.

2 See https://www.adami.fr/en/defending-performers-rights/the-sharing-of-proceeds-from-streaming.html.

desea escuchar en el momento que quiera. La diferencia entre la suscripción gratuita y la de pago, es que esta última permite disfrutar de la música sin "cortes"; mientras que, en la versión gratuita la escucha se ve interrumpida periódicamente por cuñas publicitarias.

La segunda modalidad, que se lanzó en el año 2010 bajo la denominación de "Spotify Radio" o "Deezer Radio", y que ya ofrecían webs como Last.fm, permite escuchar música pero con un grado de interactividad mínimo, puesto que el valor añadido que aporta este servicio es la similitud que presenta con una "radio musical", limitando la actividad del usuario a escoger un género musical o a un artista y, en base a la "inteligencia" de negocio desarrollada por las empresas explotadoras de estos servicios, emite actuaciones artísticas musicales no seleccionadas por el usuario, pero que son afines a la elección "temática" realizada por dicho usuario. En definitiva, en estos servicios denominados "Radio", son los prestadores del servicio quienes eligen qué va a escuchar el usuario y en qué momento va a hacerlo.

Desde un punto de vista jurídico, tiene gran relevancia ante el tipo de servicio que nos encontremos, ya que los derechos que se devengan a favor de los titulares de la obra, interpretación o ejecución, y grabación son diferentes y su régimen jurídico también.

En la primera modalidad, la de aquellos servicios que posibilitan al usuario acceder a una interpretación o fonograma concreto en el momento y lugar que elija, implica un acto de puesta a disposición, que devenga derechos de propiedad intelectual a favor de los autores *(artículo 8 TODA)*, de los artistas intérpretes o ejecutantes *(artículo 10 TOIEF)* y de los productores de fonogramas *(artículo 14 TOIEF)*. Como ya hemos visto, estos servicios realizan la puesta a disposición del público de fonogramas basados en el *streaming*, que permite al usuario acceder a un actuación artística concreta en el lugar y momento que elija sin necesidad de almacenar el contenido en el dispositivo desde el que accede al mismo.

En la segunda modalidad, las llamadas "radios" (tanto las que ofrecen esta modalidad únicamente como Last.fm, Rdio o Pandora, como las que la combinan con la "música a la carta" referida anteriormente entre ellas Spotify o Deezer), indudablemente nos encontramos ante actos de comunicación pública de fonogramas, puesto que su interactividad no permite al usuario elegir las actuaciones/fonogramas a los que acceder o no les permiten acceder en el momento que desean. En este caso nos encontramos ante un derecho reconocido en el Art 12 de la Convención de Roma, en el Art 15 del TOIEF y en el Art 8.2 de la Directiva 2006/115, que establecen a favor de los artistas intérpretes o ejecutantes y de los productores de fonogramas el derecho a una remuneración equitativa de quienes realicen tales actos de comunicación pública de fonogramas.

No obstante, esta diferencia conceptual y legal, en la práctica las entidades de gestión que tienen encomendadas la recaudación y administración de los derechos de remuneración de los artistas intérpretes o ejecutantes, están viendo como las licencias de uso que otorgan individualmente los productores de fonogramas a las empresas que explotan este tipo de servicios, incluyen todos los derechos de los artistas, cuando, obviamente, no ostentan la legitimación para ejercitar todos ellos; para ello tratan de asimilar todas las modalidades que se realizan por las plataformas de música y canalizarlas a través de la puesta a disposición, en donde el poder de negociación del productor es prácticamente omnímodo, condenando de esta forma a los artistas a poner su creatividad al servicio de grandes empresas sin obtener apenas rendimiento por su trabajo.

En conclusión, **el marco legal de los actos de explotación de derechos en los servicios de música online debe ser revisado para nivelar los desajustes en la retribución de cada derechohabiente que contribuye a la prestación de dichos servicios.** Para ello, debemos asegurarnos de:

Primero. – Que los artistas perciban los derechos que les corresponden por la comunicación pública de fonogramas, con el reparto 50/50 entre artistas y productores; como ocurre en EE.UU. con la comunicación pública digital y la gestión que lleva a cabo Sound Exchange.

Segundo. – Que se introduzca en la UE un derecho de remuneración adicional al exclusivo, siguiendo el modelo del Art 5 de la Directiva comunitaria 2006/115/EC (como en España).

2. CCC/RightsDirect and VG Wort

Frederic Haber*

2.1 Presentation of Voluntary Licensing: CCC/RightsDirect

I. Introduction to Voluntary Licensing: Getting to "Yes"

Copyright is essential in so many ways. But the key to its acceptance and survival in the 21st century is making copyright work. And making copyright work is about saying *yes*. That is, saying *yes* to content users who want an easy way to share published information while respecting copyright; and saying *yes* to copyright holders who want to control how their work can be used and at what cost.

Making copyright work is a concept built on understanding and compromise and it is driven by the customers, who, depending on the context, may be either the users or the rightsholders or both. Thus, making copyright work requires balance in a market where creators, publishers and users of copyrighted content co-exist; making copyright work requires understanding the limits of rightsholders' willingness to participate in a market and the limits of users' willingness to pay for the privilege of respecting copyright; and so making copyright work requires licensing.

My task today is to focus on one form of licensing in particular: voluntary non-exclusive collective licensing, which is, I think, uniquely designed to serve that concept of saying *yes*. Voluntary non-exclusive collective licenses are *sold* to both rightsholders and users, and are not imposed by law; that is, both rightsholders and users need to be convinced that the system offered is, for the rights involved, actually more efficient than individual one-to-one licensing and reduces the friction involved in all licensing. That is, this type of collective license is regulated by the market rather than by a specific legal regime – and so it requires a more commercial approach, including adopting technology, adapting to changes in rightsholders' and users' behavior, and adding rights and types of

---

* Vice President and General Counsel of Copyright Clearance Center, Inc. (Danvers, Massachusetts, USA). CCC and its subsidiary RightsDirect B.V. (Amsterdam, NL) provide collective repertory and individualized pay-per-use copyright licensing services, and rights and content management and workflow services and technology tools, to copyright rightsholders and users.

uses as necessary. At bottom, voluntary non-exclusive collective copyright licensing is about getting rightsholders to say *yes* to granting rights in exchange for receiving royalties, and getting users to say *yes* to lawfully acquiring the rights they need ... so that all of them can say *yes* to copyright.

II. How CCC Built Its Voluntary License

Voluntary licensing on a collective basis requires the entity who will manage the licenses to focus on practicality. And Copyright Clearance Center (CCC) has done this step by step over 30 years as a licensing agent for text reuse rights.

First. Since the early 1980s, shortly after its founding, CCC has chosen to devote particular focus on the market for internal use of text by businesses (while still continuing its other licensing services). Under fair use principles in the United States, the business market is where the law is most likely to insist that users must pay to use copyrighted materials, and, frankly, those are the users – frequently creators of substantial amounts of intellectual property themselves – who are most prepared to pay for the privilege of using others' intellectual property. So CCC has been selling licenses to businesses since that time – in the US marketplace, where there are no "requirements" that either rightsholders or users participate. What CCC has done is convince both of those groups that its multiple services, designed for different needs, take the friction out of copyright by making licenses convenient and useful.

Second. To serve the business market for text reuse rights, CCC recognized that the repertory that needed to be provided had to be the one that business users use – and that is science, technical and medical materials, trade press and general business periodicals, and the general press. And U.S. law provided CCC with no head start – without contracts, it had no rights to sell. So CCC spent years soliciting and signing contracts with rightsholders and with users, and continues to do so (both for its collective license for business and for its other licensing services). Today CCC has millions of those science, business and press works in its business license repertory for text, and millions of company employees covered by its collective license.

Third. CCC's collective license for business was built on compromise. Rightsholders grant rights for certain uses they might not otherwise allow, and they do so on a non-exclusive basis – and user companies accept certain restrictions they would otherwise hope to avoid. And this exchange helps preserve acceptance of a copyright licensing service, and of copyright itself in this context, by all parties.

Fourth. Based on close communication with buyers, CCC has evolved its standard repertory license to meet their needs. This has required a standard set of terms and conditions that smooth out the variations in the thousands of individual licenses that are available directly from rightsholders. On the other hand, users wanted more than the minimum amount of rights and CCC worked with rightsholders to get them. So, for example, CCC early on added the right to deliver copies to the government for regulatory purposes. Then, during the late 1990s, CCC adapted its original photocopy license to include digital uses. Digital demand grew steadily, and CCC signed thousands of new voluntary agreements, adding many millions of new rights and many millions of licensed users, over time.

Fifth. As the license was sold, CCC reached more and more companies with employees outside the U.S. and – with rightsholder consent – CCC expanded its standard license to cover these employees.

Sixth. Almost immediately thereafter, CCC started to receive requests from companies headquartered outside the U.S. which also wanted to buy the license, and so CCC set out to meet this need as well.

It quickly became clear that CCC had to develop closer relationships with these potential non-U.S. buyers for a business license and to obtain a better understanding of their needs. The buyers wanted both photocopy-based and digital-use rights, both at home and for their employees around the world, and they wanted rights covering both their internal networks and single devices in a device-neutral arrangement. So, in 2010, CCC established a subsidiary, based in Amsterdam, called RightsDirect. Both user-companies and content were crossing borders, and so CCC/RightsDirect and their licenses have done so too.

That said, CCC's approach has been to collaborate wherever possible to create a license that would meet this market demand. Thus, in Germany, we formed a partnership with the collecting society VG Wort. But Germany has a unique copyright environment that includes statutory licenses and a levy system. So we had to work together to find a way for a voluntary license and the German system to work together, and we succeeded. VG Wort and CCC/RightsDirect are now jointly offering digital copyright licenses on a collective basis to German companies and their global subsidiaries. Late in 2014, CCC announced a similar arrangement with the Japanese collecting society known as JAC, and the first combined JAC-CCC/RightsDirect licenses have now been issued to some major companies.

Seventh. Successful as its licenses have been, it became clear to CCC that it needed to offer more – and was well-placed to do so. CCC's license products are flexible solutions that support the principles of copyright, promote the work of content creators and simplify compliance for content users. But licensing by itself – in the digital world – is usually not enough if the point is to preserve, protect and promote copyright as a concept. So CCC uses technology to facilitate licensing and remove "speed bumps"; this allows rightsholders to more easily convey rights and allows content users to more readily understand what licensed rights they have to use content – both within their respective daily workflows. That is, the technology helps all parties say *yes* to copyright, and not just in the U.S.; the technology is being adapted to other markets and to languages other than English.

This decision to move in the direction of technology in order to support copyright had percolated for many years although licensing organizations had mostly steered clear of themselves offering technology beyond the most basic websites. But, in recent years, outside experts began to deliver hard evidence of the need to combine licenses and technology support.

Common sense and personal experience indicated that copyrighted material is read, distributed, cited, shared, and stored within companies every day. But that activity goes on behind companies' closed doors. In 2013 the information-industry research firm Outsell then validated and expanded on common sense by interviewing hundreds of professional employees located around the world about their behavior sharing copyrighted text-based materials and about their awareness of copyright. Outsell's report indicated that sharing in the workplace continues to increase, with business professionals sharing content with co-workers an average of 34 times per week, and that sharing involves more than 11 people per week, up from 7 people in 2007. Executives share copies of copyright works even more frequently . . . with an average of 15 people per week. And, while the majority of people interviewed reported that they share copyrighted works, 56% do not know their company's copyright policy or even if their company has a copyright policy. Outsell's report also made clear that many companies are uncomfortable with this relatively uncontrolled state of affairs.[1]

III. The Development of Technology Tools to Complement Licenses

With this knowledge, CCC set about to build on its initial technology tools for its customers in order to create more robust and more useful products and services. Different tools are needed by users and rightsholders to enable them to say *yes* to copyright, and both will be discussed below.

On the user side, CCC delivers tools, now collected under the RightFind brand, that alert end-users as to "how they can use the content in question" from wherever they are in their corporate network.

First, the RightFind suite of tools solves the user's problem of identifying what works and rights are covered by its CCC and RightsDirect licenses (including the licenses that RightsDirect administers on behalf of VG Wort and JAC), and also makes it possible for the end-user (i) to find the content within the

1 Outsell, Inc., Enterprise Information Access, Consumption and Use (2013).

company's systems if the employer has already purchased it or subscribed to it and (ii), if not, to buy the copy through a document delivery service.

The RightFind tools are embedded right in the end-user's workflow, put there in cooperation with the licensed company. And administrative tools allow the company to analyze what uses are being made, when additional purchases or subscriptions are necessary, and when additional copyright training may be needed. This takes a lot of the sting and inconvenience out of respecting copyright.

CCC has also expanded the RightFind suite recently by working with major publishers to make published content available to business users in convenient XML format. This enables companies to take full advantage of the text-mining tools (that they have built or bought elsewhere) while continuing to respect the copyrights of rightsholders.

On the rightsholder side, CCC provides technology to participating rightsholders as well. CCC's RightsCentral facility allows those rightsholders to see how their rights and works are being used by users participating in all of CCC's services, and allows the rightsholders to tailor and adjust their participation and their prices to fit the many markets CCC serves, and to say *yes* to more users. Participating rightsholders can download the usage information that RightsCentral makes available to them and combine it with their own business information to make informed choices about how to serve their own markets and their direct customers.

CCC has also built a suite of services, directed primarily to text publishers, under its RightsLink brand.

In the late 1990's – when text publishing was going digital – CCC saw that it could offer a new way for both rightsholders and users to say *yes* to copyright if it created a licensing tool that would take its skills from the collective licensing and rights management market, as well as its skills from its older pay-per-use online licensing market, and carry them to the individual websites where publishers make their content available. That tool was RightsLink for Permissions, which is a powerful transaction engine – an online pay-per-use licensing tool – that is essentially "attached" to digital content at the publisher's website and can go elsewhere with the content (for example, to distributors' websites) if the publisher wants it to. RightsLink is content neutral and, today, works with still and moving images as well as text, for publishers around the world. CCC's concept was that RightsLink would match micro-transactions with micro-licensing, and that high transaction costs involved in granting permissions and other licenses should never be the reason to say *no*; instead, CCC saw its role as facilitating new ways of saying *yes* in areas where the transaction costs would have otherwise been an obstacle.

RightsLink for Permissions allows visitors to publishers' websites to opt-in and self-serve – selecting the copyright license option that works best for them at that moment. They can instantly obtain a license to use the content they are viewing – because, instead of trying to determine whom to call, the license price and terms are conveniently laid out before them. At the same time, RightsLink delivers to publishers real-time data about what is being licensed from their own sites. RightsLink's capabilities have adapted as publishers have added hundreds of new types of uses that can be licensed – all based on user demand.

Here again, CCC found partners in Germany beyond publishers who have bought the service themselves. CCC is working with the Börsenverein to offer the tool through a central site to thousands of European publishers and booksellers.

Finally, in the past several years, CCC has expanded RightsLink into an efficient and effective workflow tool, called RightsLink for Open Access, that allows participating publishers to interact with authors and third-party funders – as well as with their own printers and website managers – in connection with the submission, acceptance and management of "open access" articles into science journals, a growing trend in the way that authors and publishers address copyright issues across the industry.

RightsLink is a strong and growing demonstration that rightsholders know that their business is about saying *yes* in various ways – and reserving the right to say *no* only where it is absolutely necessary. And the convenient transactions it enables invite users to say *yes* to copyright too.

IV. Conclusion

Licensing is a powerful tool for ensuring that both copyright holders and users of copyrighted material can say *yes* to copyright. And voluntary non-exclusive collective licensing is especially powerful. It is – it must be – driven by the market, in the sense of simultaneously serving both rightsholders and users and providing a bridge between them. And, for the same reason, it is regulated by the market – that is, by rightsholders' ability to choose to participate (or not) and their grant of non-exclusive mandates only, and by users' ability to evaluate it against alternative ways to comply with the law. It does not need special government regulation and receives no special government attention. Most importantly, it strengthens respect for, and voluntary compliance with, copyright as the mechanism most countries have created to ensure the growth of culture and knowledge through appropriate rewards to copyright holders.

Part of the operation of the market is its dictate that a successful licensing system will foster innovation – both in ways to expand the license system itself and in ways to build on that system, which today means by supplementing it with technology-driven tools for all participants. Failure to do so will either invite alternatives (which may or may not support the concept of copyright) or lead to stasis or collapse. In the context of text-based licensing, that imperative means that both rightsholders and CCC have had to, and must continue to, innovate to remain relevant, and that voluntary licensing – saying *yes* to copyright – is fundamental to a future where licensing is embedded in the workflow of both users and rightsholders, is made transparent through technology, continues to balance the needs of rightsholders and users, and strengthens copyright for the next generation to say *yes* too.

Robert Staats*

2.2 Legal Assessment – The VG WORT Digital Licence

I. VG WORT

VG WORT is a collective management organization governed by the Act on Administration of Copyright (UrhWG), and administers certain rights on behalf of over 400,000 authors and 10,000 publishers of literary works on a fiduciary basis. Those entitled to representation by VG WORT include writers, screenwriters, journalists, and scientific authors, as well as publishers of fiction, theatrical publishers and scientific publishers. Unlike the US based collective management organization Copyright Clearance Center (CCC), the core activity of VG WORT is the administration of statutory rights to remuneration under exceptions, especially claims to remuneration for legally permitted copying for purposes of one's private and own use (§§ 54, 54c Copyright Act – UrhG). The income from that source is substantially more than half of the total income of VG WORT, which was about 144 million Euro in 2014.

VG WORT, like all German collective management organizations, is subject to supervision by the German Patent and Trademark Office (DPMA).

II. Co-operation between CCC and VG WORT

1. Background of the licence

A few years ago various large German companies, especially in the pharmaceutical sector, expressed interest in being able to carry out certain digital uses within the company on the basis of a secure licence. The following factors were especially important:

- The companies wanted to be sure that they were complying with the law. They therefore needed a licence which clearly permitted the desired uses.

* Dr. jur., CEO of VG Wort, the German CMO for authors and publishers of textual works, vice-president of the Society of Audiovisual Authors (SAA) and a member of the Executive Committee of the European Group of the International Federation of Reproduction Rights Organizations (IFFRO).
The presentation was given in German. I would like to thanks Paul Greenwood for the translation into English.

While there were existing licences with various publishers, it was frequently unclear whether the relevant uses were really covered.

- The companies were interested in licences not only for Germany but also for subsidiaries in other countries.
- Access to the German repertoire was of interest for the companies, but not sufficient. A much more important requirement was to be able to use science, technical and medical (STM) works. The publishers for such works were often represented by CCC. CCC had been offering corresponding licences in the USA and world-wide for many years, and had a great deal of experience in this area.

The solution was to agree on co-operation between CCC and VG WORT, and to develop together a new licence, the VG WORT Digital Licence.

2. Structure of the licence

In concrete terms, the concept for the licence is as follows:

a) Works covered

The licence covers articles, or small parts of a work, which have been legally acquired. In concrete terms it therefore applies – similarly to many exceptions in Germany – to the use of articles, contributions to monographs, or extracts from books. It is possible to search an online database to determine whether the rights in the works concerned are represented by CCC or by VG WORT.

b) Types of use covered

The following types of use are covered by the licence:

- Digitisation of works not available from the rightholders in digital form.
- Storage of the work within the company (central hard discs, networks)
- Use and distribution of the work within the company.
- Digital transmission of the works to customers in individual cases ("responsive right")
- Distribution of the works in the context of obligations to report to authorities (e.g. application proceedings for medicines)

c) Territorial scope of the licence

The licence covers the companies themselves and their foreign subsidiaries.

d) Tariffs

The tariffs vary according to the sector and provide for a fixed payment per full-time employee.

e) Collection

The marketing of licences and collection of fees is carried out in Germany by the company Rights Direct, a subsidiary of CCC, in the name, and for the account, of VG WORT. The business is still being developed, but has already proved very successful. The main customers are from the pharmaceutical and chemical industries. But the aim is to extend the licences to other sectors as well. Licensing of public authorities is also feasible.

III. Legal Assessment

1. Agreement between CCC and VG WORT

The co-operation between CCC and VG WORT is based on an extension of the pre-existing bilateral agreement. Under that agreement CCC transferred the relevant rights for the rightholders it represented, including many STM publishers, to VG WORT. At the same time VG WORT amended its Contract of Representation, to enable it to acquire the same rights for the German repertoire. In this way both repertoires could be combined and offered from one source. This is the principal advantage of the agreement. The agreement also bridged the gap between collective rights administration in the USA, which uses an agency model for publishers, and collective rights administration in Germany, which is performed by the collective management organizations as trustees for authors and publishers.

2. Distinction between contractual and statutory licences

Fred Haber made it clear in his presentation that CCC's business in the USA involves contractual exploitation rights ("voluntary licensing"). In Germany the situation is very different, at least with the exception of GEMA. As already mentioned, VG WORT mainly administers statutory claims to remuneration on the basis of exceptions, so-called statutory licences. The two systems are quite different. This makes it necessary to tailor the Digital Licence for the relevant digital rights. Certain uses within companies, which must be licensed in the USA, are already covered by legal exceptions in Germany. This applies for example to print-outs of copyright protected works within companies: these are normally permitted in Germany as copies for one's other own use under § 53 paragraph 2, sentence 1, number 4 UrhG. The goal in Germany for the beginning was therefore merely to offer licences for uses which were not covered by these exceptions. In short: the Digital Licence begins where the exceptions stop. In this way conflict between remuneration on the basis of legal exceptions---in particular the equipment and storage media remuneration ("levies")--- was ruled out from the start. For the sake of completeness it should be mentioned that, according to the latest jurisprudence from the BGH and the CJEU, contractual licences covering the same ground as § 53 UrhG are without legal significance and have no effect on the equipment and storage media remuneration. It is especially important to note that the licence can cover uses by foreign subsidiaries; in contrast, national exceptions cannot cover uses in foreign countries.

3. Ensuring equitable remuneration

It may be presumed that uses within companies often take place without payment of remuneration. That is being changed by the new licence. This involves "Remuneration for the use of works" in the sense of this Congress. Under the distribution plan of VG WORT both authors and publishers participate in the remuneration. The new licence is therefore particularily advantageous for authors, since the publishers have most of the relevant rights. Incidentally, the authors also participate in the remuneration if the publisher is represented by CCC, but the author is represented by VG WORT. In summary, the licence is a good example of how it makes sense – especially from the point of view of authors – to have representation of both authors and publishers within a collective management organization.

IV. Summary

The VG WORT Digital Licence supplements the existing legal exceptions in Germany in a sensible way without making them superfluous. It gives access to both the VG WORT and CCC repertoires and ensures equitable remuneration for authors and publishers in this area.

3. "Micro Licensing" – Examples from the German Games Industry

Olaf Wolters*

3.1 Presentation

The games industry is a young industry and very business-model driven. Starting in the early 1970s with Arcarde Game Machines, where you put a coin in. Then we have faced the rise of home entertainment systems from Atari, CBS and Commodore. In the 1990s the industry had a boom-time with computer games and video consoles from Nintendo and SEGA. Between 2004 and 2014 the industry grew to a billion dollar industry with video games on Sony Playstation, Microsoft xbox and Nintendo Wii and DS. But a few years ago, starting in 2010, the whole situation for the industry changed again, when online and mobile gaming on smartphones became popular. This is to understand where the industry comes from and how the situation is with respect to business models and revenues.

I. Old business model: video games

The former business model was easy: It was comparable to the film industries' home entertainment market. Develop your product, store it on a data carrier and ship it to retailers. For box products the industry had a good price point between 60 or 70 Dollars per license/box and for Sony, Microsoft and Nintendo additional revenues for the hardware devices as well. In the past decade the industry was very much driven by games consoles.

II. Today: mobile and online games

Today the situation is slightly different. The mobile-sector is very much upcoming together with the online-sector. Now the industry is offering its games on smartphones or in online portals such as steam. In 2014, the games industry had a total revenue in Germany of 2.6 Billion Euros and additional 74 Million Euros for hardware-devices, mainly for video game-consoles like Playstation 4. The industry has generated revenues of 1.2 Billion Euros for game licenses at department

* Attorney-at-Law at Boehmert und Boehmert, Germany; former Managing Director of the German Games Association.

stores, mail order or by digital "distribution". This can be considered as the old business model.

III. New business model: micro transactions

But there are also very relevant revenues from new business models such as micro transactions. Within 2014, the games industry generated 477 Million Euros with micro transactions. Another 140 Million Euros are revenues from subscriptions for online games, such as World of Warcraft.

If we focus on micro-transactions it is very interesting how this market has developed in the past years. From the very beginning the smartphone market was divided into paid apps and free-to-play apps. The market for paid apps works with the old business model. Download your app for a certain fee and then you can use it completely for free.

The free-to-play business model is different. Download your game for free and pay for in-game-features and goods. These games are generating revenues by micro-transactions or in-game-advertising. In 2013 the overall revenue of mobile Apps in Germany was 104 Million Euros, which was divided in 39 Million Euros for downloads and 65 Million Euros for micro-transactions. The increase for app-distribution by download was plus 17 % and for macro-transactions it was a plus of 234 %. This is an on-going development as the gamers get used to these in-app-transactions and that is the business model driving the games industry.

IV. How micro transactions are working

And how does micro transaction really work? At the moment, the most successful apps in the app-stores are free-to-play games. Games like "Hayday", from Supercell. In Hayday you manage a small farm and you play together with millions of people from all over the world. This is a very special gaming experience as you interact online with other players. First of all you download Hayday for free and then you can play a couple of hours. But then it comes to micro-transaction as you like to boost your gaming experience by buying virtual goods for your farm via the app-store. And you can buy special game items, such as additional farm houses or animals. Furthermore, you can accelerate the gaming progress by buying time and resources. And it works. Millions of gamers are purchasing virtual goods with a worth of about 20 Million dollars every day within Hayday.

That is why the main focus within the game industry is on micro-transactions. This business model is very, very successful. That was briefly a games industry's view of micro-transactions and micro-licensing.

Ole Jani*

3.2 Legal Assessment

Good Morning! This provision – § 11 UrhG – is one of the key provisions of the German Copyright Act, which I have only here on the slide in German. And this is only about the relationship of the author to his work, and about the main goal of the copyright law to ensure a guarantee and an adequate reward for the use of the work. We find this concept in the Infosoc-Directive, in the recitals 10 and 11 of this Directive, where it is also applied to producers.

In short, the concept of copyright law is to give rightholders control over their copyright work or subject matter, and through this control enable them to monetize their work. In his seminal book "The Innovator's Dilemma", American economist Clayton M. Christensen has defined the principles of what he calls "Disruptive Innovation". In the digital world, industries are no longer challenged by competitors who enter existing markets with better products. Instead, new organizations that create entirely new products "disrupt" such established markets, because they satisfy other customer needs and have their advantages in entirely new features. An example related to copyright works is the digital "distribution" of music via download portals which has replaced the CD. Downloads are not per se better than a physical recording. In fact, due to data compression the sound quality of an mp3 file may be lower than the quality of a CD. But downloads have created a new market because of their ubiquity and the new devices on which they can be used. The step in the disruption of the music industry is streaming. And this process of disruption, which happens in all media industries, creates, of course, a huge challenge also for copyright law. Because copyright law ever since its early days has more than any other field of law been driven by technology. So, if the technology becomes the driving force behind the creation and the development of business models, it is inevitable that also copyright law must find ways to adapt to the specific needs created by such new technology. And the disruption that we are witnessing in the copyright industries has consequences for copyright law. And the question is whether these changes of copyright law, which are necessary in the digital world, can be incremental – or whether such changes must be "disruptive" as well.

Micro-licensing certainly is a good example for the changes that are currently happening in copyright law. And Olaf Wolters has given the example from the gaming industry. I think, to have a broader picture it is good to talk about micro licensing with regard to other fields of the media industries, because it goes far beyond gaming.

* Dr. iur., Partner at CMS Hasche Sigle, Germany; ole.jani@cms-hs.com.

Today, with respect to possible disruptions we see business models which set off classic business models. For example, consumers no longer ask for full music albums. Instead they satisfy their demand essentially with single track downloads. And streaming platforms enable consumers to listen to their preferred music on an "all-you-can-eat" basis, and consumers no longer even need to possess the music.

Coming backto the original concept of copyright law, which is about giving rightholders control over their work and enable them to monetize it: What are the implications of the digital revolution for this concept? What effect will disruptive innovation have on the control of copyright works? I believe, one of the key questions in the copyright debate is whether the law makers want to maintain this concept of control in the digital age. And if yes, what are the legal means to guarantee such control. Is it better to follow a license approach or to reduce the scope of rights by statutory exceptions and rather grant a statutory compensation instead?

As always in copyright law, we need a balance of interests. However, I believe that the future of copyright law essentially depends on the concept of the license. There are many good examples where it makes sense to have statutory compensation instead of an exclusive right. The private copy exemption is probably the best example. At present, such exceptions are – literally – the exception to the rule. If statutory exceptions prevailed over the exclusive right, this would turn things upside down.

Copyright law has to be discussed from an economic perspective and from a technological perspective. Today, more than ever, technology is driving the development of copyright law. But for the legal profession – for lawyers, for judges, and for law makers –, the question has always got to be who would benefit and who shall benefit from the provisions of copyright law. I believe that with a concept that would focus on compensation and turn the exclusive right into a fringe element of copyright law, the benefit would not be with the rightholders. Therefore I believe that in order to maintain control over copyright works, we must confirm the concept of the license and of the exclusive right for the future. And I further believe that because copyright law is essentially technology driven, the answers to the legal questions that are on the copyright agenda can to a large extent also be found in technology.

This means that in the debate about copyright law we have to consider the fact that consumers are no longer asking for ownership. They don't want to purchase in order to own a copy. Instead, they want to have access – anywhere, and any time. They want to have access only to what they really need, and they want to have easy access. In this situation, intermediaries those who distribute and curate copyright works are more important than ever before. In the online world, where practically every copyright work can be made available anywhere in the world, curation and selection is key. At the same time transactional costs have to go down. When people are no longer buying albums, and ask for single track downloads or individual music streams instead, or if people are no longer buying a video game anymore, but items within a game, the transactional cost compared to the total value of the consumer's use will become an issue.

In this environment and in this situation the concept of the micro license can help rightholders to address their audience, meet the new demands and still find ways to monetize their assets. The micro license can be the preferred tool for licensing in many fields, where the way people use copyright works, and the way intermediaries make their offerings is being disrupted by new forms of distribution and new products.

The good news is that copyright law is not a roadblock on the highway of digital innovation. Copyright law is not an outdated relic from the past. I believe that copyright law does not need to be fixed as some academics argue. Copyright will have to be modified and adapted to the new technologies. But copyright law as it is today offers many tools to create the legal framework for new businesses. Micro licensing is an example.

Thank you very much!

Jan Rosén*

Introduction

This morning session lays a focus on three different businesses models to learn about qualities and deficits of each one of them and to see whether there may be a common formula to follow, in spite of the vast and scattered landscape in which copyright contracts do operate. Those three areas are (i) open access in science publishing, (ii) Payment-based online access to newspapers and (iii) Free, advertisement-financed services.

This beautifully composed conference has already demonstrated that it is indeed very difficult to find a clear-cut solution (or maybe such solution is not at all desirable?) to conceptualize the content of copyright contracts for all types of contractual endeavours. Let me just briefly remind you of what Professor Pierre Sirinelli told us yesterday about certain recent amendments to the French Copyright Act concerning publishing contracts. Those new norms for that particular type of copyright contract are not meant to be a model for copyright contracts in general, but are designed for the very special case of text book publishing, the classical venue for copyright uses. Moreover, the conclusion from that example is that you'll even have difficulties in using a very specific element of it, such as norms for remuneration, if applied to another contractual context than the one it is designed for. With greatest interest we shall see how this panel contemplates these issues. Probably, also this session on business models will demonstrate the complexity of the market and how difficult it is to find suitable solutions acceptable to all parties, at least with pretentions to offer a general formula. Hopefully we'll also get to understand more about copyright management that is by all means successful. Maybe our expectations should more go in the direction of learning about successful market manners in specific areas, where respect for basic elements of authors' rights is well balanced with fair demands and wishes of contracting parties.

The first task for this session concerns open access in science publishing, which is indeed a very intriguing matter, demonstrating the expectations and needs of academia, authors' rights, publishers' rights, and those of the universities, scientific libraries in particular. Mr. Frank Sander is the first speaker, I'll introduce the others more carefully eventually, but let me just note that Mr Sander will be followed by Mr. Carlo Scollo Lavizzari, and that the topic on payment-based online access to newspapers will be introduced by Mr Rafael Sánchez Aristi and, finally, that the third topic, Free, advertisement-financed services, will be covered by Cedric Manara and Rafael Sikorski. Mr. Sander is the General Manager of the Max-Planck Digital Library since 2010, but by education he is a physicist and formerly a management consultant for a number of years before he joined the Max-Planck-Society.

* Emeritus Professor of Private Law, Stockholm University (Sweden).

4. Open Access in Science Publishing

Frank Sander*

4.1 Presentation – Open Access and Public Research

The situation of remuneration and rights of use in the application field of public research is discussed from a business and value chain perspective. We present the hypotheses that in the application field of public research the existence of *rights of use* is: a. often detrimental and b. largely unnecessary and unsuitable for the remuneration of the creatives *and* the information industry.

I. Special situation in the field of public research

Presented in a greatly simplified and overdrawn form, the following special features have to be taken into account in the field of public research:

The creatives have already been paid. They receive a salary, or later on a retirement pension, from their research institute. The few private research papers in the area of public research are often written for their marketing impact: the return then consists of the successful promotion of an idea, technology or personal reputation. Income from rights of use can normally only be earned by established figures, most of whom are already well paid in permanent positions.

Demand is inelastic. Unlike for literary publications, for example, no substitution is possible in science publications. Or in other words: Science publications feature essential facilities for research. In such a situation, strong rights of use can easily do damage to legitimate interests worthy of protection. For example, a rights holder may enforce the conclusion of contracts at extortionate prices, which ultimately means an unreasonable intervention in the injured party's wealth. Mostly, the injured party is the paying research organization, which in turn is typically financed by the general public or a private sponsor. In addition, the scientific user can be refused access to a scientific paper or be demanded a price that cannot be met in order to exclude the possibility of use, which ultimately means a restriction on freedom of research. For ordinary citizens, adequate research into an individual topic, e.g. a disease, using the methods of the digital age easily becomes unaffordable in a situation with restrictive usage rights (e.g. typical as of today: 30 articles opened at a price of € 30 per download), leading de facto to a restriction of recipient freedom.

---

* Director of the Max Planck Digital Library, sander@mpdl.mpg.de

Public research is to produce results freely accessible to the public. Two different business models are being used in parallel to achieve this goal: In the *intellectual property rights-based business model "subscription"*, the authors transfer exclusive rights of use to a publishing house. The publisher has to create a tradeable digital economic asset on this basis. As copying is easy, this can only be done in the digital world by creating an artificial shortage, which generates additional costs and is in conflict with the goal of free accessibility. In the *service business model "open access publishing"*, the publishing houses are paid directly for their publishing service. In most cases, the costs are borne by the corresponding author's research organization. The resulting publication is placed under an Open Access license (e.g. CC-BY), which guarantees everyone very extensive freedom of use. In addition, the publisher places the publication on the Internet in a freely downloadable form. This business model does not create any additional expenses for the creation of artificial shortages and complies with the "freely accessible" goal. Although there are today usage rights that make the subscription business model feasible and the subscription business model was historically predominating, the share of the open access publication model has constantly been increasing for some years.

Personal rights play a role. The prohibition of misrepresentation, the right to be named and the right of publication (in the sense of "whether to publish"), on the other hand, appear to make a significant contribution to securing the interaction of the creatives' motivation, personal rights and freedom to research.

II. Value chain structure

Value creation. A simplified representation of the value chain in public research with the "subscription" business model is shown in *Fig. 1 below*: Research organizations provide a research infrastructure. Researchers research, document – it is a common requirement for research data to have to be kept for 10 years – and write manuscripts. Other researchers review these manuscripts and further scientific discourse takes place in the course of general reception. This substantive work, the review and discourse, are supported by players in the information industry, normally publishers. This desirable and value-creating support includes: organizing the review, formatting, registration, web-based dissemination (hosting), marketing the publication, marketing the publication vehicle and promoting the formation of communities, as well as spreading the costs across the community of research organizations. The desired end product of "freely accessible scientific results" is at this stage of the value chain already readily available.

Digital asset creation. However, this readily available end product does not meet the requirements of an intellectual property rights-based, tradeable economic asset as required by the "subscription" business model. The information industry therefore adds a "value-destroying step" in which a massive restriction of use is introduced by restrictive licenses, authentication and authorization systems, credit card-based payment systems (paywalls) and in some cases also targeted technical barriers to use (Digital Rights Management or DRM systems). In addition, in this "value-destroying step" insecurity is introduced among scientific users, scientific organizations and the general public by way of incomplete or even wrong legal information, legal saber-rattling and commercial and legal complexity, with the effect that researchers no longer feel sure of their legal rights and freedoms. Likewise in the context of this step, distracting and cost-driving "dummy" services are performed, including lobbying for user-friendly legal systems and occasional disputes by way of warnings and in individual cases even legal disputes.

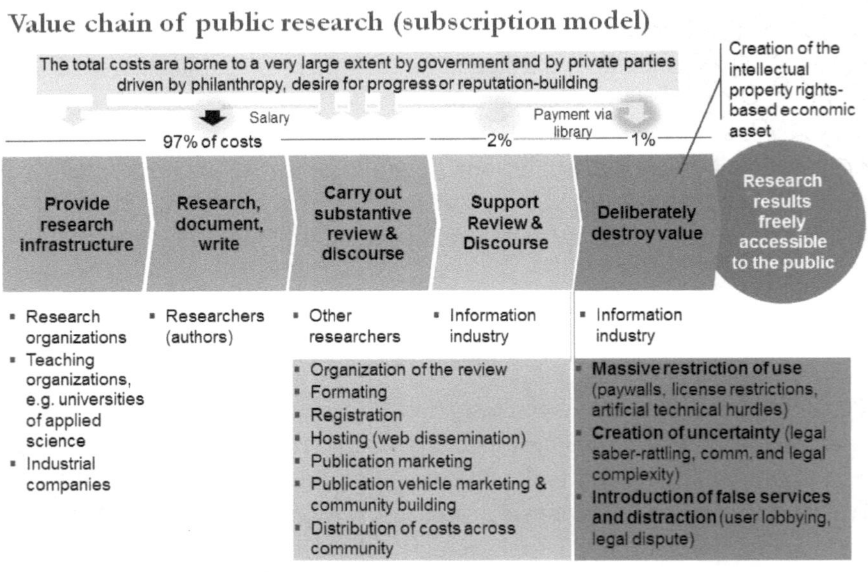

Fig. 1: Public research value chain for intellectual property rights-based business model "subscription". In order to create a tradeable economic asset on the basis of the right of use, value has to be deliberately destroyed from the point of view of the goal of "free access".

Cost. The total costs are distributed on average as follows across the different areas: 97% of the total costs arise in the value-creating steps of providing research infrastructure, researching-documenting-writing and reviewing & discourse. 3% of the total costs are incurred by the information industry. According to rough estimates, one third of this 3% is incurred by the step of deliberate value destruction. All costs of public research are typically borne by government sources, in some cases they are paid instead by private sponsors motivated by philanthropy, a desire for progress or their own reputation-building. The cash flow is handled in general by the research organizations in the form of salaries for the researchers and library expenditure for the information industry.

Service asset creation. The "open access publishing" service model does not contain the problematic step of value destruction. The desired service is paid for when the work is submitted, accepted for publication or published. It is then *unnecessary* to restrict access and use and to emphasize this by fostering insecurity, prosecution and other supporting measures in order to create a tradeable (digital) economic asset with a cash value by creating a shortage. *Fig.* 2 shows the value chain in this case.

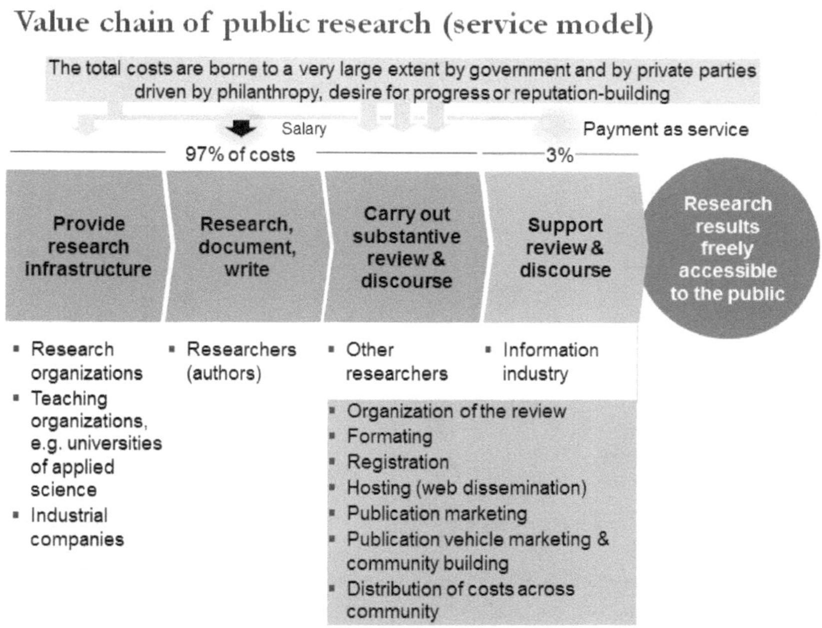

Fig. 2: Public research value chain for the service-based "open access publishing" business model. The service is paid for upon publication.

III. Development of the business models' market shares

Market share development up to now. If one then analyzes the development of the market shares of both business models for the total market of scientific journal articles, which has an annual turnover of approx. € 8 billion (2014), one finds (cf. *Fig. 3*) that the share published within the "open access publishing" service model compared to the total number of articles published per year (as a guideline, 2 million published articles in 2014) has risen from 1% in the year 2001 to 13% in the year 2014. In this period, there were essentially no obligations imposed to publish using this model, or only in exceptional cases. The increase is primarily due to the higher utility. In fact, it took place despite the fact that the budget provision and procurement processes for the purchase of the "open access publishing" service were not yet fully established in many research organizations.

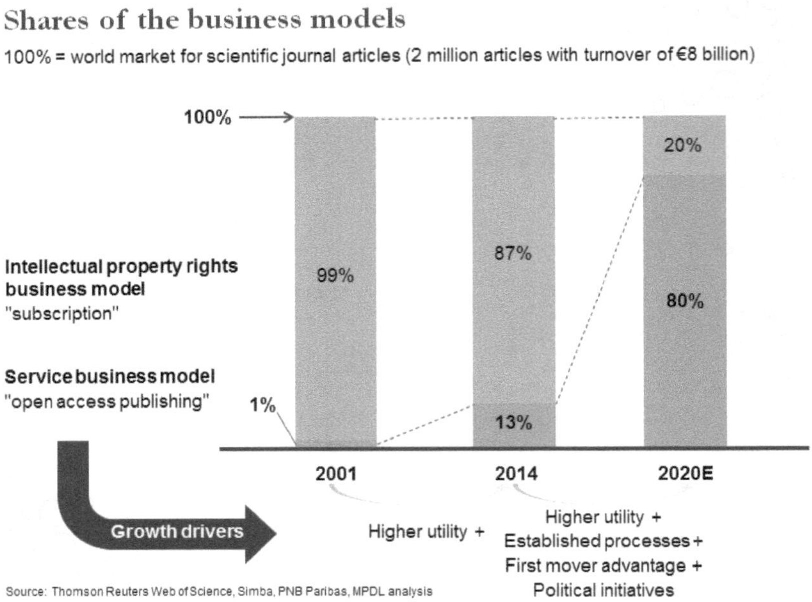

Fig. 3: Share of the business models a) intellectual property rights-based model "subscription", b) service-based model "open access publishing". An increasing shift in the shares towards the service model is to be observed. The estimate for 2020 shown assumes that the growth drivers stated will take full effect.

Considerations on the forecast of market share development. Since 2014, sponsors (e.g. the European Commission) have increasingly imposed obligations to make the results of the projects they support open access. They typically require choosing a journal where the articles may be used with few restrictions after a deferment period of typically 12 to 18 months (so-called "embargo period") if publishing is done under the subscription model, or simply by publishing via the open access publishing service model. It can be assumed that this has accelerated the growth of the service model's market share, particularly since many European countries have announced or already launched political initiatives to promote open access. Further acceleration is to be expected because the business model is now fully established in the processes of practically all research organizations and most researchers are familiar with it – neither of which criteria were the case in the period from 2001 to 2014. In addition, some publishers have realized that in a situation where journals from different publishers are competing for the manuscripts and favor of the same group of scientists, an advantage over competitors is obtained by the first mover. The advantage results from the higher utility of the "open access publishing" model's end product and is gained by switching journals from the subscription model to the open access publishing model. As a result, an accelerated conversion of established subscription journals to open access is to be expected at established publishers, which in turn will drive the growth of the open access publishing service model's market share. We therefore expect a faster and accelerating increase in the service model's market share in the next two to three years and consider a resulting market share of 80% in 2020 to be quite feasible.

IV. Hypotheses for further discussion

In view of the situation described above, a debate by the participants and panelists of the ALAI 2015 Congress on the following three hypotheses is suggested:

1. *Strong rights of use are often detrimental in the area of public research.* They should be granted sparingly. Examples of conceivable measures could be discontinuation of rights of use in public research at all, assigning transferable rights of use only in cases of truly unpaid authors, limitation by means of mandatory licenses as suggested in the essential facilities doctrine, creation of extensive secondary rights of use, very short deferment (embargo) periods, or increased licensing by the author to the general public (e.g. CC0 or CC-BY)[1].
2. Rights of use are, in the area of public research, largely unnecessary and unsuitable for the remuneration of creatives and(!) the information industry. The creatives' performance has already been paid for by other means. Only established creatives can earn any income at all. An existing proven means of remuneration for the information industry has been established for years in the form of the open access publishing service model – possible without any need to draw on rights of use. Remuneration by way of rights of use has to be regularly created completely artificially by the information industry's deliberately destroying value after the actual, desired service has been performed. This value destruction is undesirable, casts a questionable shadow on the information industry and takes place ultimately to the disadvantage of all concerned.

1 For a discussion of CC-BY, see C. Scollo Lavizzari, in this volume p. 351 ff.

3. Personal rights are essential for the orchestration of the interaction of the creatives' personal rights and motivation with freedom of research and recipient freedom in public research, irrespective of the above-mentioned challenges with regard to the rights of use. Prohibition of misrepresentation, the right to be named and the right of publication (in the sense of "whether" to publish) are areas that should be mentioned in particular here.

Carlo Scollo Lavizzari*

4.2 Legal Assessment

Thank you Chair and thank you all that I may talk to you today and may give a snapshot of how Open Access (OA) as a new business model is perceived at the moment. I am an attorney and mainly advise members of the STM association, some 120 publishers publishing in science, technology, engineering, medicine (STEM) on one hand, and social sciences, arts, and humanities (SSAH) on the other hand. Regarding the STEM/SSAH publishers who are not members of STM, I sometimes work with them too, a sort of a universe that represents maybe 300 to 400 different publishers in these fields who are very, very active in any case world-wide.

At this ALAI Congress, we just received by the previous speaker a very good outline of where open access is going. Let me say that for all small and large STM publishers, for-profit and not-for-profit alike, it is not a question of 'is OA good or is it bad', but it is totally beyond that question, the real question being: 'how do we make OA work?' What is interesting about open access for ALAI is that it is a **licensing system.** I think the outcome of the previous panel is that we need sound licensing mechanisms, and that is exactly what OA is. If it is to succeed, if one wants to get to a situation that scientists are happy to give their content away for free in the future up to 2020 (in my view a very ambiguous target), then those downstream licensing mechanisms must be sound. And I am afraid that the licenses currently propagated and used, the so-called creative commons (CC) licenses, mostly do not deliver and are a sleeping subprime crisis for the open access world. I may add that the CC licences, while they have a high visibility and name recognition as a brand, have not had a great penetration so far in absolute numbers of content available in any of the variants of OA.

Given that OA is a licensing regime, from the publisher's point of view, the situation, even as regards the whole work-flow, has not much changed when compared to the traditional subscription or other distribution licensing model. The economic reality remains the same, in that there is a 'publish or perish' situation: authors do want to be discovered and they make submissions to journals out of their free will (sometimes to what are known as "predatory publishers"), even though they can publish themselves. There is in fact the substitutability: there are many (certainly always more than one) journals in any scientific discipline. Thus, people can choose where and how they wish to publish and you would have an author-publisher agreement in almost all cases, exactly like under the traditional copyright publishing model. But the author-publisher agreement in OA will, of course, specify that the author and the pub-

* Lenz Caemmerer Attorneys, Basel,Switzerland.

lisher agree that the user will enjoy access at no cost. So, you need to cover this aspect in an author-publisher agreement for the obvious reason that if you do not do so and you then make the content available to users for free, you may be in breach of a number of laws on authors' contracts around the world.

The most difficult licensing questions arise for journals that offer both types of models for access to works, namely, subscription and individual access models for a fee and under open access licensing conditions, be they "gold" or "green", ie the types of OA that are currently being discussed most frequently. I think Dr. Frank Sander of the Max Planck Digital Library mainly referred to the gold model, which is – I would say – the dominant model, and I have no difficulty putting the gold model side by side with the copyright royalty-based licensing or subscription model. The green open access model is also known in the publishing circle as the 'nobody pays'-model; and, in fact, the green model is relying on the hope that subscription-financed journal or book sales are strong enough to cover access at no cost for the user in some version of the work after a so-called embargo period of one, two, or three years.

If we go to books, OA is not yet as mature as in the journal world. So, it is more complex to publish books under the OA model. I think university presses are in the lead, since they are often partly state-funded and have the necessary flexibility to run pilots, and they are getting there. I think that crowd funding is an exciting possible solution both to turn a subscription and copyright reliant work into open access content, what I call "azure open access" for books and journals. Azure OA by way of crowd funding has the potential to turn works with the consent of the author into open access works. But for books I can also imagine that even without crowd funding, after the advance that the author received has been repaid to the publisher, or the investment in the book by the publisher is recouped, that there can be a moment when you "flip" the book into either only digital or only in print OA. These models are quite exciting ones that are pursued in Germany; for instance, De Gruyter or O'Reilly are internationally well known publishers that have steamed ahead with this concept.

I would now like to come back to the legal-technical question of how to make open access licensing work. I alluded to the fact that right now the system relies on CC licenses, practically only for one reason: because they are there, they exist. As you can see on the slide, less than 80% of STEM/SSAH OA content is currently not governed by CC licences, so the penetration of CC licences is not that high at the moment, but it is the model that is pushed very heavily by the funders of research. In addition, if I go to the next slide, if CC are good marketers, I think there are three main advantages that they propose and that I have listed here:

(i) The first advantage is the "3-layer" approach (consisting of three layers), i.e., 1. the machine readability, 2. the human readability (=accessibility to humans not legally trained) through "icons", and 3. access to the "legalese" legal code, read only by lawyers, whom some may consider a subspecies of humans.

(ii) The second advantage is that the CC licences are "actionable". It is possible to have a robot interpret the CC labels and to resolve access to a document, or not, based on permissions granted in the CC licence. The licences facilitate linking and automated recognition and this, in turn, leads to greater proliferation of the CC licensing terms.

(iii) The third advantage is that they enjoy acceptance from funders of research and funders of OA publications.

Apart from the three "marketing" advantages above, the one big commercial advantage for the publishers is funder-acceptance: those publishers who go along with creative commons licenses know that they are accepted by the funders (the funders are paying the piper after all ...) who pay for a work to be available through OA. That is in fact the main advantage because the authors and many publishers are not that thrilled with CC and firmly believe that, in science, we can really do better (and should do better), if those who want to make OA work really want to make it work. ALAI is perhaps best-placed and could even develop better licenses that make this content available in a more seamless way than, in particular, the CC BY license. As you can see in this survey (conducted for a second time by Taylor & Francis), in both years a really big number of authors considered the CCBY as the least favored licence, and in fact, favored it even less than full copyright assignment (!), as you can also see from those questionnaires and their results that are available from the STM-website, if you want to drill down into how this survey has been constructed. So, coming back to what does not change in publishing: I think it is, as I said earlier in the panel, the fact that you still need a curator-organiser, a steward who makes sure the works reach the audience and remain available permanently. And maybe there is the dream by some that yes, you can do away with the publisher or the publisher's function, but I think that over time, the process of content organization, contextualization, and stewardship, which is the experience that publishers have gained within these 20 years of OA so far, is here to stay.

But the question is, does licensing really need to be this 'one size fits all'-option? I think, the funders mainly offered CC licences because it was there, it was there actually for other content types, not for the sciences; and since the funders did not trust the licenses developed by publishers, they opted to endorse the CC licences. So, it is due to a lack of trust that they said 'we need something else'. This 'something else', however, is not appropriate; often, authors are actually shocked by the true CCBY implications, especially if they later find other people who re-use their work for profit. They go to the publisher and complain that this should not happen, while under CCBY this is plainly legal. The author-scientists, however, wonder: "Why? I have donated my work to the community – now somebody else is selling it?!". Well, if you drill below the human-accessible icons of CC, you will read that this is exactly what CCBY says: "Welcome to the sharing economy – someone else will make the profit from your work". CCBY says that everyone else can make a commercial profit selling these works. So, authors are then disappointed, and I think that some of the statistics we saw earlier relate to this fundamental misunderstanding in the community. So, funders and publishers need to do a better job at taking the authors along with them and developing with them the licenses that are in fact appropriate rather than following a one-size–fits-all approach, e.g., for history and for other areas such as physics. Therefore, I think more work in making things happen in the right way is needed, and there is perhaps a role to play for many here in the ALAI Community. I may add that for publishers and their trade associations, the reliance on CC has been a mixed experience, in part because lobbying by CC now takes place, as was said by Dr. Frank Sander, and gets in the way as soon as countries consider legislation on types of access for data and text mining.

The FAQs of CC during the advocacy of, for instance, "Licences 4 Europe" changed significantly. Somebody said that text and data mining is now also included in the CC licences. So, I observed that often these FAQs are in truth "FAAs": Frequently Amended Answers to suit the needs of CC and whoever is able to influence it. For a licensing suite this is problematic, because not only is the "fine-print" of CC licences akin to a subprime mortgage legalese text (have you ever tried to read a cc licence rather than to look at the icon?), but also parties to a contract seem to have to consider extraneous materials such as FAQs/FAAs. However, legally this does not work. I cannot have a new set of FAAs on a website and thereby change, through a "collective will", howsoever identified, all the contracts that have already been concluded. This is against legal certainty and privity of contract and fairness – it would never be tolerated in a consumer contract. That is not how we traditionally think of sound licensing. So, that is a major problem that I see here.

I have listed a few other problems on my slides that have arisen in my practice for illustration rather than saying what is the problem and where should one go. Let me also say that I think this is just the tip of the iceberg of CC-related legal uncertainty and problems to come.

So what should be the test for a suitable OA licensing system? I would say it is the four criteria for a downstream open license: (i) First, it has to be flexible; that is the one good thing about CC. CC, at the same time allows licensing in ways other than through creative commons. Like any open source software, it is a **dual licensing model**. So, where the CC, when taking into account the subhuman text, does not suffice since it simply does not work, you may, as a publisher or as another rightholder, actually issue a second licence and make sure the use is permitted. For this purpose, STM has issued some "patches" on the

STM website for text and data mining. (ii) Secondly, the license has to be adaptable. I think this is where things are tricky with the CC license. I think it is described in a very unwieldy document and has come out of the era of 'P2P' file sharing; there are many clunky things in there that are hard to read and to make sense of. In addition, the CC license does not really look to work that well together with other licenses. Also because the OA licences are star-fish-like organized, they only are adaptable if publishers act as stewards and issue the CC licenses on behalf of authors. Otherwise a multitude of authors would for instance be unable to switch from a CC version 3 to a version 4. Likely there will be future versions. The adaptability is thus not built into the system and likely will lead to CC "orphans": legacy content stuck with an out-of-date CC licence no longer supported or not up-to-date for current usability.

The other two criteria are (iii) the enforceability and (iv) sustainability. Enforceability is key. It is maybe another weak point of CC and a reason that many OA works released under CC in my view stand to become "CC orphans" – similar to the copyright orphans. The CC licence does not state who is the "steward" to adapt licensing terms to the future – much of the content will be marooned in one or another version of CC and nobody can do anything against it. One big issue of enforceability is how moral rights are treated by CC. It is all very well to say that moral rights should be respected, but when you read the CC licences, you see that adaptation is completely permitted up front, i.e., the author has no say and permits any changes to any number of users for any number of contexts and purposes – that is a denial of moral rights in practice, and saying that moral rights are unaffected is a contradiction in terms. In my view, this renders the CC licences illegal and unenforceable in many countries.

It comes down to the lack of steward – moral rights should be respected but the licensing model should enable such respect rather than preventing it. Perhaps this could be achieved through an interest group on moral rights or an association that offers an open source licensing model, such as GNU. In this way the CC licences could be enforced and could stop people where they need to be stopped. Plagiarism is another example here. Moreover, with this I make a little teaser for a study I was asked to do by a group called the Publishers' Research Consortium, namely, to develop a guide of making open access licensing work. It is accessible over the web and those who want the slide later can have a copy of it (http://publishingresearchconsortium.com/index.php/prc-documents/prc-guides-1/53-prc-oa-licensing/file). My co-author and I developed ten recommendations which, for lack of time, we cannot really go into now, but I think that the question is not whether open access is good and bad; it just needs to be enabled properly. So the answer to the machine may be in the machine, but the answer to the answer remains "sound licensing".

Thank you for your attention!

5. Payment-based online access to newspapers

Patricia Riera Barsallo*

5.1 Presentation – Modelos de negocio de prensa digital

En primer lugar, agradecer a los organizadores que me hayan brindado la oportunidad de poder hacer hoy esta doble presentación.

Iniciaré la misma exponiendo algunos datos sobre los modelos de negocios que en España se están desarrollando alrededor de los contenidos periodísticos, y en concreto, subrayando las incertidumbres que el entorno digital está produciendo en dichos modelos.

Mi organización, CEDRO, es la entidad de gestión española que agrupa a autores y editores de obra texto. Entre nuestros socios, se encuentran los editores de prensa, y a partir de la reforma de la Ley de Propiedad Intelectual del año 2006, CEDRO gestiona la explotación de contenidos de prensa que realizan empresas de seguimiento de medios (conocidas también como empresas de clipping o media monitoring organizations MMOs) y también la reproducción y puesta a disposición posterior que realizan los clientes de estas empresas de clipping de los artículos de prensa contenidos en estos resúmenes. En este sentido, el modelo de autorizaciones que concede CEDRO es similar al de otros países tanto de nuestro entorno cercano (Reino Unido, Francia) como del más alejado (Australia).

Empezando por las autorizaciones que CEDRO concede a las empresas de clipping:

– En primer lugar, debo señalar que nuestra Ley de Propiedad Intelectual, en la modificación operada en el año 2006 del artículo 32.1, estableció un límite remunerado de carácter voluntario para los beneficiarios. Es decir, los editores tenían la posibilidad de escoger entre la remuneración equitativa por la elaboración de resúmenes de prensa realizado por empresas de seguimiento de medios u oponerse a dicho límite y por lo tanto este uso de artículos quedaría sometido al régimen general de derechos exclusivos. En la práctica es lo que han hecho. Cada editor establece la tarifa que desea percibir (en general, es un precio por artículo utilizado) y han dado un mandato a CEDRO para que otorgue en su nombre autorización a las empresas de clipping para la elaboración de resúmenes de prensa (cada empresa tendrá tantas autorizaciones como diarios utilice).

* Head of the CEDRO's Catalonia Office,Spain.

- Como ya habrán notado, estoy hablando en todo momento de los editores. Y es que en España los diarios tienen la consideración de obras colectivas y como tales es en el editor en quien recae la titularidad de los derechos. En consecuencia, son ellos los que mandatan a CEDRO, los que establecen la tarifa y los destinatarios de la recaudación que CEDRO obtiene de las autorizaciones (recaudación que se reparte en función de las declaraciones de artículos utilizados de cada diario que mensualmente nos reportan las empresas de seguimiento de medios).

Además de estas autorizaciones de reproducción para la elaboración de la llamada "primera copia", CEDRO concede a las empresas e instituciones usuarias de los resúmenes de prensa las licencias necesarias para la reutilización interna que realizan de los artículos contenidos en las revistas de prensa (diversas reproducciones, distribución o puesta a disposición en las intranets de las organizaciones, puesta a disposición de artículos en las web de las organizaciones o envío a sujetos externos a la organización). A través de estas licencias las empresas tienen acceso a todos los diarios y revistas del repertorio CEDRO y la remuneración se basa en una tarifa plana por empleado/año. La recaudación de estas licencias se reparte de nuevo entre los editores a partir de los datos que aportan las empresas que disponen de la licencia sobre los artículos utilizados.

Es evidente, que el modelo de negocio tanto del editor de prensa como de las empresas de seguimientos de medios se ha visto (y se está viendo) alterada por la evolución del entorno digital.

Para el editor, el debate oscila desde los replanteamientos sobre si dar en acceso abierto todos los contenidos de sus ediciones digitales o implantar sistemas mixtos en los que parte de dichos contenidos siguen siendo en abierto y gratuitos y otros de suscripción (o incluso, la posibilidad de que todo el contenido sea de suscripción – con la incertidumbre que planea sobre estos temas respecto a cómo convencer a unos usuarios criados en el concepto de que en Internet todo es y debe ser gratuito y con claras reticencias hacia los sistemas de pago –), pasando por la explotación individual de los contenidos de sus periódicos (sistemas de adquisición ya no de una suscripción completa al diario sino de secciones o incluso artículos sueltos), hasta la interacción con redes sociales como Facebook y similares en las que también se percibe un nicho de mercado para la explotación individualizada de sus contenidos.

Para las empresas de seguimiento de medios (y en lo que ello nos afecta, también a las entidades que gestionamos las autorizaciones que necesitan), el entorno digital también está siendo motivo, al menos en España, para el cuestionamiento y la aparición de nuevos debates. Algunos de estos nuevos debates serían los siguientes:

- Respecto al precio o tarifa a abonar por el uso de los contenidos de diarios digitales: existe la pretensión por parte de las empresas de clipping de abonar precios inferiores por los artículos publicados en las ediciones digitales de los diarios que los que abonan por las ediciones impresas. Su razonamiento se basa en la idea del supuesto menor coste que tiene para el editor la edición digital (ahorro en gastos de impresión, de distribución, principalmente). La argumentación a contrario consiste, por un lado, en cuestionar hasta qué punto esos ahorros de inversión deben afectar al ejercicio del derecho además de plantear el valor añadido que la edición digital presenta para este tipo de empresas (la actualización de los contenidos es continua, a diferencia de la edición en papel cuyos contenidos quedan estáticos en el tiempo una vez se han publicado)

- Respecto del origen de los contenidos de los que se nutren las empresas para realizar los resúmenes de prensa: podríamos decir que no sólo de prensa digital viven los resúmenes de prensa. El uso de blogs, contenidos provenientes de websites especializadas, redes sociales, abre nuevos retos en la gestión de las autorizaciones necesarias para realizar el uso (tanto para las entidades de gestión – ¿cómo identificar, localizar, gestionar un número creciente y disperso de titulares? – cómo para las empresas de clipping – la dispersión de titulares a los que solicitar autorización genera una gestión más costosa o la asunción de mayores riesgos si se decide utilizar los contenidos sin las autorizaciones pertinentes.)
- Respecto a los usos que realizan los usuarios finales de los artículos periodísticos contenidos en las revistas de prensa: se está extendiendo la tendencia a ofrecer al usuario no la consulta de la reproducción del artículo alojada en el servidor o plataforma de la empresa de seguimiento de medios, sino un link a la versión digital que de dicho artículo se puede encontrar en la web de cada diario. Aquí, y tras la doctrina Svensson, es evidente que cuando el diario tiene el contenido en abierto, no existe base jurídica que justifique la necesidad de otorgar autorización al usuario por el uso de dicho contenido. Pero el modelo se complica, con el ofrecimiento de herramientas por parte de las empresas de clipping para realizar copias en formato pdf de los artículos que el cliente está visualizando en línea y el posterior almacenamiento de dichas copias en la plataforma (la nube) de la empresa de clipping o en el servidor del propio cliente.
- Finalmente, y para acabar de complicar el panorama, desde finales del año pasado, con la última reforma de la Ley de Propiedad Intelectual operada en España por la Ley 21/2014, existe en mi país un nuevo límite, cuya redacción compleja daría para todo un congreso y del que sólo voy a apuntar sus contornos: conocida coloquialmente como "tasa Google" (en honor del que todo el mundo identificó como principal deudor), este nuevo límite (sujeto al pago de una compensación equitativa) gravaría a los llamados "*prestadores de servicios electrónicos de agregación de contenidos*" que pongan a disposición fragmentos no significativos de contenidos divulgados en (y cito

literalmente) "*en publicaciones periódicas o en sitios web de actualización periódica y que tengan una finalidad informativa, de creación de opinión pública o de entretenimiento*". El límite, no se sabe si consciente o inconscientemente, no cubre la reproducción.

Lo mejor que se puede decir de este límite es que es confuso. Si bien, parece que su intención era responder a las pretensiones de los editores de prensa de ser compensados por el daño ocasionado por el uso no autorizado de sus contenidos por parte de servicios como Google News, lo cierto es que de su redacción se desprende que no sólo los editores de prensa serían los beneficiarios del mismo (y a la literalidad del artículo me remito). Por otro lado, la reacción de Google ante la aparición de este nuevo límite fue cerrar el servicio de noticias en España sin esperar siquiera al inicio de contactos para la negociación que nos impone la LPI para fijar tarifa. Su marcha acabó generando más incertidumbre a un límite cuyo recorrido, tanto jurídico como práctico, es cuanto menos incierto.

En definitiva, el entorno digital y la tecnología están haciendo el papel que les corresponde: crear nuevos escenarios, generar nuevas oportunidades y plantear nuevos retos, tanto a creadores como a empresa usuarios a nivel jurídico y a nivel de modelos de negocios.

Con esto termino mi intervención, y procederé a la lectura de la presentación preparada por el profesor Sánchez Aristi.

Rafael Sánchez Aristi*

5.2 Legal Assessment

Desde el punto de vista de la propiedad intelectual, los periódicos que ofrecen acceso en línea a sus contenidos sobre la base de un pago, ponen en juego el derecho de "puesta a disposición del público" (art 3.1 Directiva 2001/29). Aunque en esto no se diferencian de los periódicos que ofrecen el acceso gratuito a sus contenidos,[1] ya que la caracterización jurídica de la actividad viene dada en ambos casos por el hecho de la accesibilidad en línea a los contenidos (por contraste con la distribución de ejemplares en soporte papel). En el ámbito de los derechos de autor, el carácter gratuito o no del acceso a los contenidos por parte del público no influye en la calificación de la actividad como un acto de explotación de uno u otro tipo.[2]

Sabemos que el medio –Internet– no proporciona *per se* la interactividad que permite hablar de "puesta a disposición del público",[3] pero el modo en que se comercializa un periódico en línea evoca esa modalidad de explotación. Ahora bien, no está claro si la puesta a disposición del público lo es de cada uno de los contenidos, del periódico como conjunto, o de ambos: ¿son las diferentes partes de un periódico "obras" en el sentido del artículo 3.1 Directiva 2001/29, o en todo caso éste se aplica con tal de que lo puesto a disposición del público sea una parte de una obra? ¿Puede estar puesta a disposición una parte de la obra sin que simultáneamente lo esté, a su vez, la obra como conjunto?

Si contemplamos el periódico digital en su exacta configuración en cada momento del día (antes de ser archivado –en su caso– en la hemeroteca), dada su prácticamente continua actualización, cabría decir de alguna manera que el periódico "está pasando", como un acontecimiento deportivo que sucede en vivo y que es objeto de retransmisión, por más que la secuencia cronológica sea más lenta en el primer caso que en el segundo.[4] Aunque convencionalmente podamos admitir que el periódico de las dos de la tarde es "el mismo" que el de las diez de la mañana, en rigor el contenido al que el internauta accede no coincide plenamente. La diferencia con un evento deportivo es que el destinatario no puede, ni tampoco pretende, disfrutar de la globalidad del periódico simul-

---

* Professor, Universidad Rey Juan Carlos, Madrid (Spain).

1 O de la parte de su actividad basada en el acceso libre: es raro que los periódicos de pago ofrezcan el 100% de sus contenidos cerrados, normalmente combinan la oferta de contenidos de pago con la de contenidos en abierto.

2 Análogamente, la calificación de la actividad de la prensa en papel, consistente en distribuir ejemplares impresos, no varía por el dato de que esa distribución se haga o no mediante precio.

3 Definida, como sabemos, por la posibilidad brindada a cada miembro del público de acceder a la obra en el momento y desde el lugar por él elegidos (art 3.1 Directiva 2001/29, art 8 WCT).

4 Al menos normalmente: la retransmisión televisiva de una partida de ajedrez no tiene por qué tener un ritmo más vivo que el de la actualización de un medio de prensa en línea.

táneamente. En cambio sí puede acceder, y sin duda eso es lo que busca como miembro del público, a las diferentes piezas o artículos del periódico. Es aquí pues donde se aprecia realmente el efecto de "puesta a disposición", de forma que aunque la obra sea realmente el periódico, la genuina puesta a disposición del público lo es de sus partes, sin que probablemente esa puesta a disposición se extienda al periódico, al menos hasta que la edición de cada día es archivada y queda disponible como un conjunto cerrado.[5]

Sea como fuere, la explotación en línea acentúa la percepción del periódico como un surtido de elementos separables, un repositorio o continente carente de entidad como obra superior a la mera suma de sus partes. El hecho de que los contenidos se sigan disponiendo en una forma que evoca la de las ediciones en papel es algo convencional, jurídicamente cada pieza ha pasado a funcionar como una unidad en sí misma. De hecho, el nuevo mercado que se abre para los contenidos de prensa no está concebido para el periódico como conjunto, sino para cada elemento del mismo.[6]

Esto tiene su trascendencia para la monetización de los contenidos, permitiendo llegar a acuerdos económicos *ad hoc* con cada articulista, en función de su audiencia. De hecho, la audiencia ya no es la del periódico como conjunto, sino la de cada uno de los articulistas por separado: el periodista, cada periodista, se dirige a su propio público.[7]

La parcelación del producto permite también aplicar una política de discriminación de precios en las relaciones con los lectores y usuarios: el periódico ya no cuesta lo mismo para todos los que lo adquieren: dependiendo de los contenidos que demande o disfrute, cada cliente pagará un precio diferente.

---

5 Esto podría tener alguna implicación si atendemos a la doctrina del Tribunal de Justicia de la Unión Europea (TJUE) en el caso C-More Entertainment AB v. Linus Sandberg (Sentencia de 26 de marzo de 2015 [asunto C-279/13]), donde el TJUE ha diferenciado entre retransmisión en vivo de un contenido, aunque sea por Internet [cuando no hay elección del "momento" para acceder a ese contenido porque éste acontece en vivo] y puesta a disposición del público propiamente dicha.

6 El propio negocio del *press-clipping* está basado en el despiece del periódico. Es como si los periódicos se armasen para a continuación ser fragmentados en una feroz labor de contra-edición. Las necesidades de los usuarios, al menos de los grandes usuarios, no pasan por la lectura íntegra del periódico como unidad, sino por la búsqueda de piezas sueltas, procedentes de diferentes periódicos, que versan sobre un determinado tópico.

7 Como ha dicho el director de *The Washington Post*, Martin Baron, en el Congreso Mundial de Medios de Comunicación celebrado en 2015 en Washington, los periodistas deben acceder a las estadísticas de audiencia de sus artículos y tienen que adquirir la responsabilidad de crear sus propias audiencias. Según explicó Baron, los reporteros del *Post* reciben datos sobre el número de lectores online de sus artículos, su ubicación y plataforma de acceso. Esos datos les permiten conocer mejor a sus lectores, analizar el impacto y aprender a promocionar sus historias en sus perfiles en las redes sociales. El periodista adquiere así una capacidad de promoción y análisis de audiencia que tradicionalmente recaía únicamente en los departamentos comerciales de los diarios y que, hasta la irrupción de Internet, era muy limitada dada la dificultad de conocer los hábitos de consumo de los lectores de las ediciones en papel de los diarios.

El hecho de que la explotación se realice en el entorno en línea facilita sin duda esa discriminación de precios. Como en definitiva favorece que las editoriales de prensa digital se comporten como comercializadores directos de sus productos en sus relaciones con los usuarios finales. A diferencia del editor de prensa tradicional, que ha de recurrir a intermediarios para comercializar sus producciones, y en particular para distribuirlas al por menor, el editor de prensa en línea puede operar como comercializador directo de los contenidos. En esto se asemeja menos a un editor de libros, un productor de cine o un productor discográfico, y más a un organismo de radiodifusión. De ahí que, como ocurre con los abonados de un servicio de televisión de pago, en el entorno en línea se hable más de usuarios o de suscriptores del periódico que de lectores o de compradores del mismo.

El "pago" puede adoptar a su vez, dependiendo del modelo de negocio, formas muy variadas: una suscripción periódica, un pago por ítems aislados o una mezcla de ambos. El periódico puede también ofrecer contenidos de pago, o bajo suscripción, y contenidos en abierto, los cuales pueden funcionar como un elemento de promoción. Se supone que el acceso de pago comportará prestaciones adicionales. Así, el usuario de pago podrá acceder a un servicio *premium*, con contenidos especiales (v. gr. entrevistas o reportajes en profundidad), o se le permitirá compartir el contenido, almacenarlo en la nube, imprimirlo más fácilmente, guardarlo en determinado formato o visualizarlo en diferentes dispositivos. También puede disfrutar de condiciones más ventajosas en las promociones lanzadas por el periódico (libros, discos, películas, viajes, equipamiento).

En su rol de comercializador al por menor de los contenidos, el editor es no sólo el que recibe el cobro del precio o de la suscripción, sino también el que decide la gama de usos que permite realizar, así como la implementación de medidas tecnológicas de protección para asegurarse el respeto a los usos permitidos. Siempre, a su vez, garantizando al usuario el disfrute de los límites que le beneficien, de acuerdo con lo dispuesto en el art 6.4 de la Directiva 2001/29.

En este sentido, la realización de copias permanentes por parte del usuario – descarga, impresión – sería en principio amparable en el límite de copia privada (artículo 5.2.b/ Directiva 2001/29). Sin embargo, la realización de las mismas en un entorno en línea y la aplicación de medidas tecnológicas de protección, permiten al editor restringir el número de reproducciones, e incluso impedir completamente la copia (artículo 6.4 de la Directiva 2001/29). No ocurre lo mismo con la visualización en pantalla o la copia caché web en el ordenador del usuario: de acuerdo con la doctrina del TJUE en el caso *Public Relations Consultants Association Ltd v. Newspaper Licensing Agency Ltd* (Sentencia de 5 de junio de 2014, asunto C-360/13), ambas constituyen reproducciones provisionales que caen bajo la excepción prevista en el art 5.1 de la Directiva 2001/29.

¿Cambiaría la calificación [copias privadas] de las descargas, por el hecho de que el editor permita al usuario almacenarlas "en la nube", en un servidor facilitado por el propio editor o por un tercero? Todo apunta a que no, si nos atenemos a la doctrina del TJUE en el caso VG Wort.[8] Aunque referida al límite del art 5.2.a) Directiva 2001/29, de ella se extrae que no importa el número de operaciones o la técnica utilizada en el proceso de reproducción (v. gr. uso combinado de un PC y un disco duro remoto), siempre que, las distintas etapas de ese proceso se desarrollen bajo el control de la misma persona y tengan por objeto reproducir la obra.[9] En la medida en que las reproducciones merezcan la consideración de copias privadas, serán susceptibles de ser remuneradas a través de la compensación equitativa. Ello con independencia de que hayan sido supuestamente hechas en el marco de la autorización del editor.[10]

Otro tipo de actos permitidos al usuario pueden afectar al derecho de puesta a disposición del público. Así, si se le faculta a compartir el contenido con terceros a través de una plataforma o red social.[11] Previsiblemente, ese tipo de permiso irá combinado con acuerdos entre el editor y los responsables de esas plataformas o redes, en virtud de los cuales el editor obtendrá un retorno económico proporcional al uso que se haga de sus contenidos dentro de la red o plataforma.

El hecho de que el editor sea el propio titular del producto que explota hace que pueda autorizar sin mayor inconveniente esas explotaciones adicionales de los contenidos. Lo mismo que si ofreciera al usuario un servicio de almacenamiento en el que quedase alojado automáticamente el historial de los ítems consultados por aquél. Cuando un periódico se distribuye en papel el editor no es responsable de lo que pueda hacer con su ejemplar el adquirente del mismo.

8 STJUE de 27 de junio de 2013, VG Wort v. Kyocera y otros (asuntos acumulados C-457/11a C-460/11).

9 También cabe recordar que en la Sentencia DR y TV Danmark A/S v. NCB, de 26 de abril de 2012 (asunto C-510/10), el TJUE ha establecido que incluso en un límite como el del art. 5.2.d) de la Directiva 2001/29, que exige realizar la actividad de referencia "por sus propios medios", esta expresión debe entenderse que incluye los medios de un tercero que actúe en nombre o bajo la responsabilidad del beneficiario del límite.

10 En el caso ACI-Adam c. Thuiskopie, resuelto por Sentencia de 10 de abril de 2014 (asunto C-435/12), el TJUE ha establecido que la excepción de copia privada (art. 5.2.b/ Directiva 2001/29) prohíbe a los titulares prevalerse de su derecho exclusivo de reproducción para autorizar la realización de copias privadas, en la medida en que son los Estados miembros y no los titulares quienes establecen la correspondiente excepción y autorizan, a efectos de la realización de tales copias, dicha utilización de contenidos protegidos.

11 Es dudoso el caso de la institución o compañía –persona jurídica– que elabora su propia reseña de prensa y, a continuación, la pone a disposición de sus usuarios, clientes y/o proveedores. ¿Conforman todos o algunos de esos círculos de personas un "público"? En caso afirmativo, ¿permite el límite de reseñas de prensa dar a las mismas un uso que implique ponerlas a disposición del público?

Pero si el editor presta servicios que implican realizar un uso más intensivo de los contenidos editados, ello debería traducirse en la remuneración de los que contribuyen a generar los contenidos. Esto puede tener implicaciones, sobre todo, en relación con contenidos provistos por terceros que no llegan a integrarse en el periódico en tanto obra colectiva (v. gr. colaboraciones literarias o económicas de firmas célebres).[12]

Pero los editores de prensa *online* no sólo nutren de modo directo el mercado minorista, sino que también alimentan algunos mercados mayoristas, propiciando así utilizaciones de segundo grado de sus contenidos por parte de usuarios comerciales. Un primer mercado mayorista, ya muy consolidado, es el de las empresas dedicadas al llamado *press-clipping*, que cada vez se sirven más de las ediciones digitales y no de las ediciones en papel de los periódicos. Como se sabe, estas empresas utilizan como *inputs* los diferentes artículos de prensa, con los cuales, tras un proceso de despiece, selección, clasificación y composición, generan un *output* –la reseña o índice de artículos– que es servido al cliente final. La actividad de *press-clipping* afecta, como mínimo, al derecho de reproducción, y en ocasiones también, dependiendo del modelo de negocio del *press-clipper*, al derecho de puesta a disposición del público (v. gr. si vuelca los ítems en un gran repositorio y los hace accesibles a sus clientes para que éstos, gracias a un sofisticado motor de búsqueda, se elaboren sus propios resúmenes de prensa). Es obvio, por tanto, que el operador de *press-clipping* deberá obtener una licencia de los editores de prensa y abonarles la correspondiente tarifa, con independencia de que los editores gestionen estas licencias por sí mismos o a través de entidades de gestión colectiva.

Un segundo –y más reciente– mercado mayorista para los medios de prensa es el de las plataformas y redes sociales. Los editores de prensa *online* están empezando a alcanzar acuerdos con Facebook y otros servicios similares, donde los contenidos no se difunden bajo la forma de una publicación entera, sino fragmentariamente, tratando de suministrar a cada cliente aquella información que más se le acomoda, en función de su perfil y de sus preferencias. Es un modelo de negocio a caballo entre el del editor de prensa y el de la empresa de *press-clipping*, ya que no se trata de atender peticiones explícitas del cliente sino de intuir o inferir cuáles son los contenidos que pueden interesarle. Por otro lado, iría dirigido más a usuarios particulares que a usuarios institucionales. También aquí se ponen en juego derechos de reproducción y puesta a disposición del público. El retorno económico del editor consistirá en compartir los in-

---

12 De hecho, cabe preguntarse hasta qué punto el periódico puede seguir siendo considerado una obra colectiva cuya titularidad se asigna de forma íntegra y originaria al editor, o si por el contrario la titularidad y transmisión de los derechos de todos y cada uno de los ítems que lo componen deben contratarse por separado (igual que si se tratase de colaboraciones externas). En el entorno digital, la diferenciación entre colaboradores internos y externos se desdibuja.

gresos (v. gr. por publicidad o por comercialización de *big data*) que obtenga el operador de la red social o plataforma.

Finalmente, debe observarse que la imposición de un pago sobre los contenidos servidos a los clientes minoristas puede bloquear la aparición de ciertos mercados mayoristas de artículos de prensa. Y es que el cargo de un precio o tarifa de suscripción implica una "medida de restricción de acceso" en el sentido de la Sentencia Svensson.[13] En ella el TJUE ha establecido que sólo cuando un contenido está puesto en Internet a disposición del público con consentimiento del titular y sin medidas de restricción de acceso, es lícito trazar un enlace a dicho contenido, por cuanto la puesta a disposición del público que el enlace implica no lo sería a un público nuevo. Si el contenido no es susceptible de libre consulta, por estar sujeto a una medida de restricción de acceso (p. ej. pago de un precio o suscripción), el enlace implicaría puesta a disposición de un público nuevo y no sería lícito sin los permisos adecuados. Cabe decir que la Sentencia Svensson ha delimitado un cierto mercado para la elaboración de "recopilaciones virtuales de prensa a base de enlaces". El modo que tienen los editores de prensa de impedir que, sobre la base de sus contenidos, un tercero pueda desarrollar libremente un negocio de tipo *press-clipping* en línea mediante enlaces, sería someter el acceso a sus contenidos a condiciones de pago o suscripción.

13 STJUE de 13 de febrero de 2014, Nils Svensson y otros v. Retriever Sverige AB (asunto C-466/12).

6. Free, advertisement-based services

Cédric Manara*

6.1 The example of remuneration on YouTube through Content ID

Google and YouTube offer a large variety of services of which the business models are very diverse. For example Google sells, rent or offers subscriptions to movies, music, books, newspapers, games, apps ...[1] and secures rights through partnerships or licenses. YouTube has recently launched Music Key,[2] a service which is distinct from the historical video sharing platform and allows subscribers to listen to music without ads, offline. Paid subscriptions to video channels also exist (some paid channels will show ads on their videos, and some won't).[3]

In addition to paid subscriptions, The YouTube Partner Programme allows creators to monetize content through merchandise[4] or advertisements.[5] With the former program, a creator can create links from a video to an approved external retail site (iTunes, for example), where she sells related merchandise. A creator who wants to enable video monetization[6] – note this is not a default option – can choose between several types of ads that may appear next to her videos: display ads, overlay ads, skippable or non skippable video ads.[7] Revenues will of course largely depend on the popularity of a video, but not only: internet users with ad blocking software will prevent an ad from being displayed, there are cases where ads won't be triggered, etc.[8]

---

* Dr., Senior Copyright Counsel, Google.

1 https://play.google.com (all links were last accessed on June 30, 2015).

2 https://www.youtube.com/musickey .

3 https://support.google.com/youtube/answer/3005054 .

4 https://support.google.com/youtube/answer/2760471 .

5 Note that creators can find many other ways to earn money through the content they post on YouTube, in particular with sponsorship or product placement, crowdfunding... See for example Rolling Stone, *Seven Ways Musicians Make Money From YouTube* (2013), www.rollingstone.com/music/news/seven-ways-musicians-make-money-off-youtube-20130919.

6 When uploading or after: https://support.google.com/youtube/answer/94522.

7 https://support.google.com/youtube/answer/2467968. For a funny presentation by a creator of how the system works, see Le Rire Jaune, *L'argent sur YouTube* (2015), https://www.youtube.com/watch?v=GREO4tBLEm8 .

8 In the case of "YouTubers" who have a contract with multi-channel networks, the monetization depends on the contract between this network and the creator, and is separate from YouTube.

YouTube offers multiple opportunities for creators to have access to a global audience, without any distribution costs.[9] Thousands of channels are making a six figure revenues annually.[10]

Creators can only get revenues when the content is entirely theirs. If it's not, there can be revenues when the rightholder decides so. YouTube has paid over one billion dollars[11] to those who have chosen to monetize their claims through Content ID, which is the focus of this short presentation.

I. Presentation of Content ID: how are rightholders remunerated?

Beginning in 2007, YouTube developed and launched the most advanced content identification system in the world, called Content ID. With this system, rightsholders are able to identify user-uploaded videos that are entirely or partially their content, and choose, in advance, what they want to happen when those videos are found. YouTube's Content ID system has developed into a pragmatic, efficient, and scalable solution to many of the difficulties that previously faced creators, rightsholders in prior existing works, remix creators and the viewing public.

More than 5,000 rightsholder partners use Content ID to manage their copyrights appearing within user generated content on the site. These partners include network broadcasters, movie studios, music publishers, songwriters, and record labels.

Briefly described, this is how it works: Rightsholders deliver to YouTube reference files (these can be audio-only or video) of content they own, metadata describing that content, and policies describing what they want YouTube to do when it finds a match. Rightsholders can choose between three policies when an upload matches their content:

1. make money from them (for monetized videos the majority of the revenue goes to rightsholders);
2. leave them up and track viewing statistics; or
3. block them from YouTube altogether. Content ID compares videos uploaded to the site against those reference files, automatically identifies the content, and applies the rightsholder's preferred policy.

---

9 See Europe Economics, Lucie Guibault, Olivia Salamanca & Stef van Gompel, *Remuneration of authors and performers for the use of their works and the fixations of their performances* (2015), study prepared for the European Commission, SMART 2015/0093.

10 See also Answers, *39 YouTube Stars Who Became Millionaires*, http://www.answers.com/article/1178976/39-youtube-stars-who-became-millionaires.

11 Music labels make more money from user-uploaded videos than from official videos.

The Content ID system is made available to rightsholders at no cost – in fact, if the rightsholder opts to monetize matches, Google effectively pays them to use it! Each day on YouTube, creators are not only engaging in an interactive, two-way relationship with their fans and subscribers,[12] but they are also developing entirely new revenue streams from viral, creative, user-generated content.[13]

Of course, while this may be simple to describe in the abstract, making it work in real-time as more than 300 hours of new video are uploaded each minute is a monumental undertaking. Content ID scans over 400 years of video every day. Development of Content ID has required an investment of more than $ 65 million as of today.

Content ID has proven to be a pivotal technology to the success of the YouTube platform. While initially perceived by rightsholders as an antipiracy solution, today the majority of partners using Content ID choose to monetize their claims, rather than block videos from appearing on YouTube. We have more than 25 million active reference files (over 1,500,000 hours of material) in the Content ID database, which have been used to "claim" more than 300 million videos on YouTube.[14]

Content ID has been a win-win-win solution for YouTube, copyright owners, and YouTube users. The system has created a new source of revenue for copyright owners, as well as for YouTube. In fact, in 2013 Content ID "claimed" videos account for more than one-third of all monetized YouTube views. Content ID benefits YouTube creators, as well. When copyright owners choose to monetize or track user-submitted videos, it allows creators to remix and upload a wide variety of new creations built on that existing content, without having to independently seek out licenses for it.

II. The limits of Content ID for remuneration

In evaluating the costs and benefits of intermediary licensing using automated identification systems like Content ID, Google urges the ALAI to keep in mind the need for mechanisms to protect remixes covered by an exception/fair use from being blocked or being "licensed" by rightsholders who have no proper claim on them.

---

12 See, e.g., Gotye, *Somebodies: A YouTube Orchestra* (2012), http://www.youtube.com/watch?v=opg4VGvyi3M .

13 See The Guardian, *Harlem Shake: Baauer cashes in on viral video's massive YouTube success* (2013), http://www.theguardian.com/technology/2013/feb/19/harlem-shake-baaueryoutube-success .

14 See Google, *How Google Fights Piracy* (2014).

While Google is proud of Content ID and the way in which it can reduce transaction costs for licensing online video (including remixes), Content ID can never address all of the copyright complexities that remix creators face. As an initial matter, Content ID will never include reference files for every copyrighted work that might be included in every remix uploaded to the site. While Content ID currently has over 25 million reference files in its database, that represents a tiny fraction of all the audio, video, and imagery that falls within the scope of copyright. In other words, no matter how comprehensive Content ID's database of reference files may one day become, there will always be an important role for fair use when it comes to remixes on YouTube.

Fortunately, Content ID is a supplement to, not a substitute for, fair use or copyright exceptions. Content ID cannot categorically separate remixes that qualify as fair uses or are covered by an exception (and thus require no licensing) from remixes that are infringing in the absence of a license. As the US Department of Commerce recognized, for example, "[u]nder current U.S. law, some remixes may qualify as a fair use of the copyrighted material they draw on."[15] While Content ID is quite adept at identifying the inclusion in an uploaded video of preexisting material for which it has a reference file, it cannot apply the case-by-case, four factor legal analysis that is required to determine whether that inclusion constitutes a fair use under US law, nor can it determine what is covered by an exception in each jurisdiction of the world.

This can potentially create two kinds of difficulties for noninfringing remixes. First, the Content ID match may result in the blocking of the video (if the rightsholder in the pre-existing content has elected to block). Second, it may result in the video being monetized in favor of someone who has no entitlement to license fees (if the rightsholder in the pre-existing content has elected to monetize). The second case can be particularly galling to a remix creator whose video is intended as a criticism or parody of the rightsholder or work in question.

In summary, the lesson that we have drawn from our experience with Content ID is that intermediary licensing can be a pragmatic, efficient, scalable solution to some of the legal uncertainties facing some remix creators with respect to some copyrighted works. These kinds of content identification and licensing systems should be viewed as a supplement to other mechanisms, such as fair use and copyright exceptions.[16]

---

15 Department of Commerce Green Paper, Copyright Policy, Creativity, and Innovation in the Digital Economy, Docket No. 130927852-3852-01 (2013).

16 See also R. Tushnet, *All of This Has Happened Before and All of This Will Happen Again: Innovation in Copyright Licensing*, Berkeley Technology Law Journal, Vol. 28, pp. 1447–1488, 2014 (illustrating why licensing can never be a substitute for transformative fair use even when licenses are routinely available).

Rafal Sikorski*

6.2 Legal Assessment

Ladies and gentlemen, thank you very much for having me here. I am very grateful for being able to speak. My comments will be relating mostly to the YouTube Content ID service. Some of these comments however will also be applicable to various other services available today over the internet. Here are the issues that I would like to cover: I will shortly talk about the parties that are involved in Content ID service. Then I will try to talk about contractual relations surrounding the YouTube service. I will also discuss the monetizing scheme adopted. This is related very much to the topic of our conference as the rightholders decide to monetize their works instead of enforcing their exclusivity by preventing use because they see that by making their work available, they are much better off than when they just exercise their exclusive rights by prohibiting use. So, monetization which was not the most favorable option at the beginning when rightholders started to work with YouTube, turned out to be a better, more profitable, solution. That change of attitude I think is very interesting. I will also talk slightly about possible uses of copyright protected content via YouTube's Content ID service. Some of them may be lawful, some may be not. This is something that the machine cannot solve, it is something which should be solved by men. YouTube offers a fantastic technology, but the technology is not capable of solving all the problems. I will have a few remarks on the YouTube's notice and take down policy. That policy complies with notice and take down policies as they are envisaged in many of our legal systems.

The Content ID service involves a number of parties. Firstly, it is YouTube, of course, the organizer of the whole service. Secondly, there are the rightholders whose content is used via the service, these are mostly movie studios, large music labels and the game developers. There are numerous commentaries on the video-games made available via the Content ID service. Also a large number of movie reviews are available by YouTube users. Then we have the third group, which is the YouTube users, that is a very particular group of people who upload their game reviews or movie reviews which incorporate parts of the movies or scenes from the games reviewed. Frequently, music is also made available.

Now, let me just briefly outline the contractual relations. We have here the relationship between YouTube and the rightholders and possibly also between YouTube and the ID Content users. I would like to have a few remarks on the YouTube and rightholder-relationship. There is no licensing here, YouTube only provides a service, it scans works and it blocks access to materials when it is asked to do so by the rightholders, that is when YouTube users use protected

* Dr. hab., Adam Mickiewicz University, Poznań, Poland.

content. YouTube may also only track the use of copyright protected content and provide information on how such content is used. Thus when the rightholder decides to monetize, YouTube simply tracks the use and provides remuneration to the rightholder for the use of its work. Remuneration is based on the amount of ads that show up. YouTube distributes the funds that come from advertisements to the rightholders. This remuneration is functionally a substitute for royalties. Rightholders have recognized that enforcing their exclusive rights by blocking content is not in their best interest. So many of them have decided to monetize as described above. Again, as I have said there is no licensing relationship. Thus, the situation of the YouTube's ID content user is very uncertain when it comes to the freedom to use copyrighted works. The decision to monetize may be changed by the rightholder any time. The rightholder may change that decision with respect to a given country or all countries; or the rightholder might simply decide to block YouTube users from using its content. Therefore it all hinges on the will of the rightholder. One can imagine however that a rightholder might not get revenues because the ads have not been shown when the viewers decide not to see them. May then the rightholders claim money from the YouTube users? These might be theoretical questions but I want to stress that the position of the YouTube users who want to use copyright protected content could be very uncertain here. Will such users be covered by exceptions or limitations or fair use provisions? Is YouTube in a position to decide that, and how fast should such a decision be made?

The expected remuneration might be gone because of the growing popularity of ad blocking software. When the viewers decide not to view the ads there is no basis for calculating remuneration from the ad providers. When that is the case, there will be no remuneration for the rightholder. This is an element built into this model, which you should also consider.

And the last thing, I wish to say a few words about the notice and take down policy. This is in fact an issue for a lot of Internet services today, such as Facebook and YouTube as well. That policy might sometimes be abused by various parties. It might be abused by rightholders who might simply say, I do not want your content because you are providing a critical review of my movie, using some scenes from it, which might result in less audience and less revenue etc. Rightholders might also claim that the use is outside the scope of exceptions or limitations or fair use provisions – a claim which may often be true and not constitute an abuse. I think when you analyze the notice and take down model adopted by YouTube, there are points where that notice and take down procedure may be subjected to abuse. For example, it might take a very long time for the disputes to be decided by YouTube. 75 days, I think, is a pretty long time. This might be a point for consideration in our later discussions whether we should intervene into the procedures of notice and take down adopted by services like YouTube on the internet. Thank you very much!

Session 2: Challenges for the legislature and courts
Défis à relever par le legislateur et la jurisprudence
Retos para el legislador y los tribunales

1. Need for regulation of such business models?

Mihály Ficsor*

1.1 Introduction

The title of our panel is „Need for regulation of such business models?" It seems that „*such* business models" is a reference to the „business models" discussed by the panels this morning under these titles: „1. Music Flatrates; 2. CCC/Rights Direct and VG Wort; 3. Micro Licensing; 4. Open Access in Science Publishing; 5. Payment-based online access to newspapers; 6. Free, advertisement-financed services".

These topics differ quite substantially. In the case of some of them – namely, "open-access" publishing and certain versions of "flatrates" – it is even questionable whether we may truly speak about *business* models (with emphasis on "business" which, in these cases, may not truly exist; at least not from the viewpoint of creators). Let us proceed in the order of the above-quoted topics.

"Music flatrates" mean – according to its broadly understood meaning – the use (more closely: online use) of a more or less unlimited number of works and objects of related rights (most typically performances of musical works recorded on phonograms) against a modest regular payment. At this congress, two kinds of such flatrate systems have been or still are about to be discussed: one – a compulsory license or a similar limitation – does not mean any "business" whatsoever, while the other is based on a "negotiated" (but in fact rather a take-it-or-leave it blanket) contract, it seems to be quite a bad business for authors and performers.

Our panellists will speak mainly about the *latter* version of flatrates and, on the basis of what they are going to say (see, in particular, the Spotify model to be presented by Pál Tomori) you will understand what I mean when I am speaking about bad business from the viewpoint of authors and performers. However, these kinds of music "flatrates" are based, at least, on contracts – just containing unfavourable "take-it-or-leave- it" conditions for the creators dictated by powerful monopolies or oligopolies.

This model is still relatively – very much only relatively – more advantageous than another one the idea of which seems to have emerged again. It consists in allowing by law free music – compulsory licenses or other limitations – no matter from what sources (and perhaps not only music) on the Internet

* Dr., Honorary President of the Hungarian ALAI Group, former Assistant Director General of WIPO in charge of copyright.

against a small amount of money paid for each internet connection (avoiding in this way what are regarded as unnecessary copyright complications). The first problem with it is that quite a big amount of optimism is needed to believe that such an idea would be welcomed by internet users. It is sufficient to recall what happened in Hungary about half-a-year ago. The Hungarian Parliament adopted a law introducing a modest payment on internet connections – cca. 3–4 euros per month – and immediately several ten thousand "netizens" began manifesting in the streets of Budapest for the "freedom of speech" and the "freedom of information" (because, it is obvious of course for everybody, is not it, that if you have to pay the amount of the price of a coffee per month, you would lose the chance to express freely what you wish and you cannot get information anymore because it would become terribly expensive).

However, hopefully for the participants in the congress, it is even more relevant that ALAI has also expressed its opinion about such an idea. The Executive Committee, at its January 2006 session held in Paris, unanimously adopted a Resolution in reaction to the then planned introduction of a statutory flatrate – called, by the nickname "global license" – in December 2005 a couple of days before Christmas, by the French National Assembly. The Resolution – available on ALAI's website (http://www.alai.org/en/assets/files/resolutions/affirmation-droit-exclusif.pdf) – recalled that "the fundamental rule of copyright, according to the international treaties, is the exclusive right of the author to decide on the principle and the manner of dissemination of the work of authorship" and that „the diminution of exclusive rights is authorized only to the extent set out by those treaties". It stated "firmly therefore that, beyond the limits expressly provided by the international instruments, any modification of copyright laws, whatever its form or its label, whose result would be to deprive authors of the effective exercise of their exclusive rights is contrary to the spirit and the letter of the international agreements." Rightholders may agree upon any kinds of rates as a part of a business model they wish to apply. This follows from the *exclusive* nature of their rights to be granted under the international treaties. A legislation under which the creators would be constrained to accept, instead of this, a dubious share from a modest "flatrate" would equal to the confiscation of their exclusive rights, on the basis of which they freely choose what they consider to be the most appropriate business model. It would not be a "business model" but the end of any possible "business models". In the eyes of the politicians and the general public, it would be regarded as a kind of cultural tax, and it would have to share the fate of taxes.

The advocates of "flatrates" try to justify the introduction of such a generalized compulsory licence, *inter alia*, by referring to the right to remuneration for private copying as an example of an already existing "flatrate" system. However, the reference to private copying "levies" is misplaced for various reasons. First, private copying takes place in a *domestic* environment and, thus, it cannot be controlled by rightholders. A modest payment on recording equipment and/or carriers is the only way to reduce the unreasonable prejudice caused to the legitimate interests of rightholders at least to a reasonable level (and, thus, to bring it into harmony with the three-step test). In contrast, music and other protected materials are made available on the Internet through *public* channels; in fact, it would be hard to imagine a larger public as the internet population. There are many actors – among them big companies – who make available, or participate in a decisive manner in making available, works and objects of related rights to this huge public. Second, it is in accordance with Article 9(2) of the Berne Convention on the three-step test to limit the exclusive right of reproduction to a right to remuneration for private copying, but such justification would be missing in the case of a "global license" with a "flatrate" since it would eliminate any chance for rightholders to choose normal ways of exploitation of their rights (getting thus in an absolute conflict with the second condition of the three-step test). Third, an obligation to ensure "fair compensation" – in fact, in the form of the limitation of the exclusive right to authorize or prohibit to a *right* to remuneration – is crystal-clearly provided under Article 5(2)(b) of the Information Society Directive, and still the issue is not settled in that way. It is not settled since we have seen in how many different manners and under what kinds of populist and anarchist slogans – propelled by the big lobbying power of the manufacturers and distributors of recording equipment and carriers – it has been attacked as an "unjustified tax" quite successfully in several countries. Is there anybody among us so naïve to believe that the internet intermediaries, with their even bigger lobbying capacity, would not do anything to eliminate such an "unjustified internet tax"?

The second and third topics discussed this morning have been "CCC/RightsDirect and VG Wort" and "Micro Licensing". These are licensing techniques that do not seem to require specific legislative regulation (which is the subject matter of our panel). Perhaps the next panel this afternoon on collective management may deal with these models.

The fourth topic this morning has been "open access in science publishing" based on Creative Commons licenses or other open-access systems. We have a panellist – Maria Frabboni – to speak on this. However, as mentioned above, it is doubtful whether, in this case, we may really speak about "business" from the viewpoint of authors (and in ALAI's activities this is the decisive viewpoint). From the viewpoint of publishers, it is another matter. Certain authors – some atypical ones who do not care for copyright remuneration because they have got other sources of income or just because this is necessary for their academic career – are ready to publish their works free of charge (at maximum, they receive a complimentary copy), but publishers have to recoup their investments with some reasonable profit margin. (It is to be noted that the open-source software licenses are different; they are truly used for business models – contrary to the original ideology-based free-software licenses introduced by Richard Stallman and his followers.)

Maria will speak about those cases where authors have to pay for the possibility of publishing. Her examples concern certain research projects financed from public funds where one of the conditions is that the research results must be published through a Creative Commons or other similar license free of charge. The problem is that, as pointed out, the publishers ask for money from the researchers to cover their costs. Maria is going to emphasize that this is not an acceptable system from the viewpoint of researchers. The conditions under which such research projects take place should be in accordance with the principle of "if you say *A*, you should also say *B*"; that is, if you want your researchers to publish freely, you should take care of the costs of free publication too. Nevertheless, these issues may rather only concern the internal regulations and contracts of such projects; they do not seem to require specific provisions in national laws (and the topic of our panel is about the questions of need for legislative measures).

The remaining two topics discussed this morning – "Payment-based online access to newspapers" and "Free, advertisement-financed services" – have been really about two basic models through which rightholders may exploit their rights in the online environment: payment-based and advertisement-based models. Three of the four members of our panel – Susy Frankel, Jørgen Blomqvist and Pál Tomori – will discuss these "business models" and/or the need for regulation . Let me repeat that we should keep in mind that this is a congress of an organization which according to its traditions – and as determined in its statutes – is supposed to deal with the issues of authors' rights (in the language of the founding fathers: *le droit d'auteur*) from the viewpoint of the rights and interests of creators. This, in the case of newspaper publishing (the fifth topic discussed this morning) means journalists, editors, illustrators, etc. and, as regards, advertisement-financed services (where "flatrates" appear as an issue again) now it concerns more or less all categories of authors and performers (but, in fact, also nearly all other categories of rightholders). And from their viewpoint, the typical online "business models" do not look like quite advantageous. In fact, they tend to be brutally disadvantageous – at least for two reasons: first, what is frequently involved is others' "business" (exercising their "fundamental right to conduct business") consisting in appropriation of the results of human creativity and investment in cultural products and services for the objective of earning (not quite well-deserved) profit; and second, certain intermediaries, due to their dominant position on the online market, impose scandalously unilateral conditions on rightholders.

If someone might say that it is an exaggeration to speak about scandalous conditions, it is sufficient to refer to the figures in Pál's presentation: A recent French survey has shown how unequally is shared the typical 9.99 € monthly subscription fee of music streaming: after 1.99 € is deducted for taxes, 6.54 €

goes to the producers and streaming service providers, leaving authors with a meagre sum of 1.00 €, followed by featured performers earning, collectively, the tiny amount of 0.46 €.

There are a number of intermediaries that, from "poor little fragile start-ups" – which everybody was supposed to protect and cherish – have grown into powerful world-level monopolies or parts of some narrow networks of oligopolies. They may afford operating a huge lobbying machinery financed, to a great extent, from their income obtained at the detriment of authors, performers and other rightholders (an income that, as Robert Levine has pointed out in his brave book, allows them also financing "public interest" (= read anti-copyright) "NGOs" and even buying the service of academics)[1]. This is strengthened by a special alliance with their customers whom they mobilize to fiercely oppose anything that might limit free access "guaranteed" to them by the generous intermediaries. As a result, these intermediaries have become so powerful that they have reached the "level of immunity"; they may even "discourage" governments from certain attempts to obligate them to better cooperate with rightholders or – *horribile dictu* – to apply some value-recognition system in favor of the creators.

The issue of the obligation of "aggregators" and "linkers" to share their income derived from the appropriation of the contents of newspapers and periodicals (with undermining the economic basis of quality journalism as a "collateral damage") is a good example. The German publishers – with due support by their government – were able to achieve an "ancillary copyright" (*Leistungschutzrecht*)[2]. However, before that, the Belgian publishers – even if the court made it clear that Google must pay for this kind of use of works[3] – gave in to the menace of Google, and accepted a settlement in the form of a modest amount of money as a price of their *not* insisting on the exercise of their rights (and rather accepting the payment just as a generous gesture). The menace was the same as to which later also the French publishers gave in (along with the government which originally intended to follow the German example): if they insist on their rights, the references to their articles will be removed[4]. In con-

1 *See* about this Robert Levine: "*Free Ride – How Digital Parasites Are Destroying the Cultural Business and How the Cultural Business Can Fight Back*", Doubleday, 2011.

2 *See* Articles 87f to 87h of Copyright Act of 1965 included by Act of 7 March 2013 to amend the Copyright Act entered into force on 1 August 2013.

3 Judgement of the Brussels Court of Appeal (9th Chamber) in *Google Inc v Copiepresse* et al (N°. 2007/AR/1730 of May 5, 2011).

4 A quotation from the article "*French Publishers Forge Deal with Google, Breaking Ranks with Europe*" published on February 17,2013, on the website of the New York Times reporting on the agreement: „Mr. Hollande had vowed to introduce similar legislation this winter if Google and the publishers did not come to terms. It appears that *Google*, which *had threatened to stop indexing French Web sites' content if it had to pay for links*, has sidelined the threat of legislation,

trast, the Spanish government was brave enough to introduce what was baptized as a "Google tax"[5] and the online giant did apply the punishment by removing links to Spanish newspapers. Should we blame Google for this? Not at all! If a company due to its frighteningly strong dominant position may constrain even governments to do or not to do something, it is just normal that it will use its power in order to maintain that position and the profit which goes with it. Perhaps the situation would be different if Europe acted together and the competition authorities did not allow the misuse of that oppressive power. The equation would be different if the *entire* European advertisement market might be undermined for those who reject the application of copyright or a sui generis *Leistungschutzrecht*-type right and the basic rules of fair competition; it might even influence the policy of such powerful companies.

Otherwise, the reaction of the big online intermediaries to the attempts of some brave governments to try to establish a better balance of interest has become nearly automatic: if you adopt legislation obligating us to share our profit with rightholders, we blackmail you by suspending our service in your country and we organize riots among our customers; they will make their "stupid politicians" understand that they should leave us in peace. After all, we have both the channels and the money for this. This worked perfectly in the US against the PIPA and SOPA bills which might have reduced a little bit the profit generated by online piracy (*inter alia*, through discouraging advertisers and credit card operators from contributing to financing illegal activity). It also worked a couple of months later in Europe against ACTA which – in its weakened form – happened to be in full accordance with the EU law but – through organizing a hysteric campaign based on demagogue slogans and a plethora or simple lies[6] – the online intermediaries frightened the European Parliament enough to adopt a resolution that led to the withdrawal of the Commission's well-based request to the CJEU to decide whether there was any conflict with the *acquis*.

---

at least for now; the agreement will be reviewed after three years, Mr. Hollande has said." (Emphasis added.) Available at www.nytimes.com/2013/02/18/technology/a-first-step-on-continent-for-google-on-use-of-content.html?-r=0.

5 *See* Article 32(2) of the Intellectual Property Code of 1996 included by Act of 4 November 2013 entered into force on 1 January 2015.

6 At that time, there was also a manifestation in Budapest, although not quite a big one. This was in spite of an enormously aggressive and expensive campaign. For example, an advertisement was read several times in the public radio prime time (when such advertisements cost a lot); it consisted in three statements which sounded in essence like this: If ACTA is adopted and you quote (sic!) an article on Facebook, you go to prison. If ACTA is adopted and you share a recipe you have learned at a cooking course with your neighbour, you will go to prison. If ACTA is adopted and you paint the symbol of Coca Cola on the hair of your cat, you go to prison. And the manifestations were organized on the basis of such weird allegations.

The dominance of the IT industry's influence on the EU's copyright policy continued for a while. Therefore, it is a long-awaited and welcome change that – with the publication of "A Digital Single Market Strategy for Europe"[7] there is now, at last, a policy paper that, even if cautiously, suggests that the role of online intermediaries may have to be reconsidered. It is high time since Europe's cultural policy (if it exists at all as such) is close to a "Munich moment". We might pay a heavy price if we tried to apply Chamberlain's know-how to buy "peace for our time" with the huge IT industry's mono- and oligopolies just by giving in and giving in and giving in.

Let us discuss all this. And let us discuss it in the light of the objectives of ALAI as stated on its website in accordance with its Statutes: "ALAI promotes creativity by endeavouring to assure the protection of the moral and economic rights of creators in general, a goal that Article 27(2) of the Universal Declaration of Human Rights also affirms." There is no problem if the fundamental freedom of intermediaries "to conduct business" is recognized, but they should only be allowed to conduct their lucrative business if they fully respect the creators' moral and economic rights.

7 COM(2015) 192 final, Communication from the Commission to the European Parliament, the Council, the European Economic and Social Committee and the Committee of the Regions of May 2, 2015.

Susy Frankel*

1.2 Do Copyright Related Business Models Need to be Regulated?

The answer to this question posed in the above title is both "yes and absolutely no".

The word "regulation", as it has been used in this congress, means to make law, including primary laws, secondary regulation, and tertiary regulation. Different jurisdictions use the term regulation in different ways.[1] Some jurisdictions use it to mean only those rules made by regulatory agencies. Here, however, it is used with its well established meaning to mean all laws that regulate behaviour of relevant actors either directly or indirectly There is another form of regulation called self-regulation, which is very important in copyright transactions. In this presentation regulation refers to law-making broadly.

Throughout this ALAI Congress several business models and a variety of approaches to regulation have been described. Some of these still seem to work in the modern copyright era, but many of them do not function adequately in the online environment. A key feature of many business models is their dependence on advertising combined with a preference for users in the digital world to pay more for the absence of advertisements. When streaming copyright content, the absence of advertisements is a selling point, but ironically advertising is the only way that many online copyright-using businesses make money. The elimination of advertising undoubtedly has appeal to customers. From the perspective of copyright that, however, is not the end of the matter. There remains the question of, if customers pay to avoid advertising, then who benefits from such payments? It does not seem to be authors.

I. What is a "business model"?

It is perhaps useful to point out that the business model is not just a payment model as many of the presentations have focused on. A business model broadly means: [2]

> The business model is simply a working description that includes the general details about the operations of a business. The components that are contained within the model will address all functions of a business, including such factors as the expenses, revenues,

---

* Professor of Law, Victoria University Wellington; Chair of the New Zealand Copyright Tribunal; President ATRIP 2015–2017. This is a summary of the presentation given at the congress.

1 See Regulatory Toolkit, "Definitions", online at www.regulatorytoolkit.ac.nz.

2 What is a business model? , see http://www.wisegeek.org/what-is-a-business-model.htm.

operating strategies, corporate structure, and sales and marketing procedures. Generally speaking, anything that has to do with the day to day functionality of the corporation can be said to be part of the business model.

This explanation illustrates the difficulty that there is neither a one-size-fits-all business model nor a one-size-fits-all approach to regulation.

In any matter to be addressed by regulation an understanding of the problem that the regulation might address is key to design and implementation of regulation. In the copyright context , if we reframe the question to ask what is the problem, we can get closer to an answer about the need or otherwise for regulation.

II. Is the business model the emerging problem?

It seems that the key issue, which has been discussed from various angles throughout the congress, is the distribution of the price a consumer pays (when she pays) for access to copyright works. Put differently, how do the actors in a copyright transaction divide the money? Unfair distribution may be a problem that has emerged from unregulated business models. However, it is important to note that there is a difference between regulating the business model or an aspect of that model and ensuring a fair distribution of price. This difference is extremely important to regulatory design because the regulation needs to target the right thing. Price is already regulated through various mechanisms, such as some laws, contracts, and institutions such as copyright boards and tribunals (although these vary among jurisdictions). Unfortunately, these mechanisms can be avoided or are undermined by other aspects of some business models. So, regulatory design that addresses what needs to change is important to overcome problems of regulatory avoidance.

III. Copyright is not business-model neutral

Copyright, however, is not regulation-neutral at present. It already regulates business models. Current copyright regulation has, however, unfortunately spawned non-infringing avoidance techniques, often provocatively described as innovative business models. Sometimes these are legitimate fair-uses, fair dealing, permitted acts, or other sorts of exceptions and limitations (the name will depend on the jurisdiction) and sometimes the uses are not legitimate. For those who are in a copyright contractual relationship, rather than the position of a third party user, how income is distributed depends on the contractual relationship, which is often the result of the dominant position that owners (such as recording or publishing companies) have over artists (for copyright purposes: authors). When discussing regulating the business model, the current position is not one of neutrality through non-regulation. Rather existing regulation has had both intended and unintended consequences.

Therefore the question really is "should the business model be re-regulated or re-weighted in some way"? If copyright and authors' rights reflect their rational purposes, then authors ought to be paid, but this should not mean that the law is misused to prop up redundant business models. The rights of authors/creators always rise and fall according to the business model. But who controls the model makes a difference as to whether authors, other rightsowners, and/or users can succeed in that model.

IV. What, if anything, needs to be changed and why?

A relatively new problem with copyright is that it enables business models that are a kind of copyright avoidance model. The technology adopted is devised or chosen to avoid the application of copyright law rather than because of the innovativeness of the technology from an industry perspective.[3] Many copyright cases turn on technical detail rather than the intentions of the alleged infringer or the purpose of copyright law. There may be good reasons for this relating to legal certainty. However, this makes copyright law the equivalent of an avoidance game rather than a regulation to support authors. This problem is exacerbated because exclusive rights are no longer (if they ever were) business model-neutral or indeed technologically neutral.[4] That lack of neutrality (even if neutrality was originally intended) has created the possibility of technical avoidance, rather than a full consideration of the objective and purposes of the

---

3 An example is where Aereo, a New York based company offering online access to television broadcasts, used hundreds of thousands of mini antennae in order that each "supply" to its customers was individualised. The reasons for this was not because many small antennae made sense as the best technology for online uses, but because that technique avoided the bite of copyright law, at least until the United States Supreme Court took a more purposeful approach to Aereo's activities. See Giblin, Rebecca and Ginsburg, Jane C., On Aereo and 'Avoision' (December 1, 2014). 32(4) Copyright Reporter 14, 2014. Available at SSRN: http://ssrn.com/abstract=2596963 .

4 An example is the public performance right in United States law and the debate over its effectiveness or other wise to comply with article 10 of the WCT. See Jane C. Ginsburg, 'U.S. Compliance With the International Right of Communication to the Public After Aereo: Who Is "the Public"?' The Media Institute, August 21, 2014, at http://www.mediainstitute.org/IPI/2014/082114.php.

defendant's activities.[5] So, how can international law fill the gaps? The incentives of the copyright system should not be to create avoidance. Rather, regulation needs to support the rationale of the law (its policy functions) and for ALAI that is of course the protection of authors in their works.

What we have heard several times and we will hear from a successful songwriter, Eddie Schwartz, in the next session, is that the non-earning position of some authors is simply not sustainable. Some business models seem to create the unusual situation where the business does not pay for all of their inputs (where the inputs are copyright works). This non-payment can arise from business models based on copyright exceptions or unfair distribution of income derived from copyright rights. The overall effect is problematic. It is basic accounting and economics that businesses have to pay for inputs and not just receive the profits from outputs.

V. Regulatory techniques, targets, goals, and implementation

Much of this ALAI congress has discussed aspects of what regulatory experts might describe as a regulatory problem statement. In order to have effective regulation a clear problem statement (i.e. what needs to change) is extremely important. In some ways, that may seem a straightforward point. But regulation happens in a political context and so the problem is often lost in translation to law. There is a large body of literature and expertise about regulatory design which cannot be done justice here. However, unless the diagnosis of what needs fixing is well articulated, regulation is difficult to frame appropriately. The above title "regulatory techniques, targets, goals, and implementation", are an overview of the stages of regulation that need careful attention.

The function of regulation is fundamentally about changing behaviour to achieve a defined outcome. Methods to change behaviour can vary. In order to achieve a desired outcome, such as authors earn a living, regulation can both directly and indirectly target actors involved in different aspects of copyright. Copyright law embodies both approaches. The existing regimes directly give authors property rights and indirectly regulate user activity as a result of those rights. Which approach (or combinations of approaches) to choose may depend on what triggers the need to regulate and why. Is the decision to regulate in order to change behaviour about copyright protection or use? As noted earlier, if

5 For a full discussion of avoidance and technological neutrality, see Susy Frankel, "The International Copyright Problem and Durable Solutions" (2015) 18(1) Vanderbilt Journal of Entertainment and Technology Law 39–75.

the market is not working because the distribution of payment is not working then this might be the regulatory trigger and consequently the distribution mechanism could be the regulatory target. Successful regulation will be designed to address its target rather than a peripheral goal, such as saving a redundant business model.

Changing contractual behavior, however, requires considerably more than a nudge. It requires more than self-regulation. Where there are presently some elements of self-regulation, such as dividing the royalty flow, they are not working in many jurisdictions.

Several times speakers in this congress have suggested that common law jurisdictions will not like regulating price because of sanctity of contract. There are degrees of truth in that, but it is not nearly that absolute or as much of a barrier as some have suggested. When a property right incumbent – and that would be someone with functioning property rights – states that they cannot change because of sanctity of contract, this is little more than a lobbying or political statement. Common law countries interfere with contracts all the time. They do so, when the lobbyists concerned have proven a need, or when even the government recognises a public interest in doing so. Obvious examples are consumer-related contracts and employment law.

The real issue is not sanctity of contract, but whether and how to overcome some of the politics when trying to achieve meaningful law reform. Regulation can come with unforeseen consequences. If regulation shifts the problem from point A to B, the problem is not necessarily solved, but reinvented. We know this from different points of view about copyright. The role of financial advances, for example, has been very important in the music industry, but advances have assumed a certain licensing trajectory. Many advances were made when people thought royalties would be greater. My understanding is that some of the streaming models, Spotify and Pandora are often cited, in some jurisdictions do not pay out all of the royalties collected because they recoup the advances. The unforeseen consequence is too much to recoup. By analogy, in another area of copyright we have seen safe harbours having unforeseen consequence. Those seeking safety are not always the ones at risk.

In conclusion, the institutions that implement and control regulation are very important. The culture that enables a detailed regulation of that kind, as we have heard exists in Germany, is very dependent on the institutions and the businesses that support it. That cultural approach does not easily transfer everywhere and in some places the flexibility of the business model is what can drive innovation and creativity. Music streaming business models seem unsustainable in their present form. It should not be the authors, creators and performers – the people who feed the raw inputs into the model – that are the ones who pay the price. Regulating a fair distribution of streaming revenue may not alone be satisfactory. Effective licensing across all parts of business models seems likely to be more sustainable and it may be that there needs to be some legislation in order to re-weight bargaining power in order to make the world of licensing work. Let us make it about licensing and not just advertising!

Jørgen Blomqvist*

1.3 The roles for intervention and for the market

Frankly, I don't care too much about copyright's historical emergence in either a utilitarian, natural law or personality rights philosophy, what matters to me is that we have not abolished copyright lately, simply because it has proven to be a legal tool which functions OK – not perfect but OK – channeling payments. It enables payments from those who use and enjoy works, performances, recordings and so on, to those who make, produce, publish and distribute them. What really matters is the economic sustainability of the culture, entertainment and information industries, and that presupposes the possibility for authors and performers to earn their livelihood.

In this respect, the main characteristic of the copyright system is that it is market driven. This is fundamentally a good thing, because that way the paying audience has a decisive say in which works, performances, recordings and so on that will receive the economic returns. This is good, in many ways it resembles democracy. Obviously, in many countries there is – and there should be – active cultural government policies and public and private endowments supporting culture, but the bread and butter of cultural economics must be market driven and thereby give the audiences a say, or at least the possibility to vote with their feet.

Even so, from time to time there may be needs for adjusting the raw market mechanisms, for example where due to a market failure the free forces of competition cannot interact and thereby find the natural levels where buyers and sellers both are willing to make deals. Market failure can be due to many different factors, but one may for example be that there are significant differences in the bargaining power of the actors in the market. After all, for the copyright system to work in the way I have just indicated, it must ensure that money flows in a reasonable way all the way from the consumers to the authors and performers. Significant distortions along the way, whether introduced by political intervention or by the various players in-between, disrupt the very *raison d'être* of the system.

This imbalance between the contracting parties is a classic problem in the field of copyright and related rights, and when we look at national law we find many different attempts and models approaching the problem. Some statutes have various provisions regulating specific contracts in various fields, such as publishing or film contracts, others have general provisions limiting the terms of transfer, establishing restrictive interpretation of broad rights assignments

* Honorary Professor at the University of Copenhagen, Faculty of Law, Denmark.

(such as the German *Zweckübertragungslehre*) or enabling judicial review of contractual clauses which eventually lead to unjustified results due to the developments taking place over the many years, such contracts are often in force.

There is probably just one thing we can state in general about all such solutions; they are politically controversial and are often results of long and difficult negotiations, because the involved stakeholders typically take very strong positions. This also means that they are difficult to amend and keep updated in step with the ongoing technological, commercial and thereby also economic developments. They are also by nature national, or regional in the EU, and may therefore create practical complications in a media picture which is increasingly global. For this reason, I not quite convinced as regards the ability of this model to solve problems of market failure in the modern media landscape. It is too slow, too inflexible and too localized, and in the end it will certainly not provide any relief in those many countries where there is no tradition for legislative solutions to such problems.

I do believe, however, that the market for creative products merits some close inspection, characterized as it is by few very big global players, albeit supplemented by a quite large independent sector, and an enormous offer of creative talent which fights for the limelight and where market entrants are typically willing to accept modest contract terms, just to get the foot in the door. At the same time, there are few standard contracts and in many cases it has been difficult or impossible for creators' and performers' associations to convince publishers and producers to engage in serious negotiations regarding minimum terms and the like. At the same time we can see that in those fields where for one or another reason collective management has become the rule, whether based on exclusive rights or non-voluntary licenses, the creators and performers tend to be much better off than in those areas where they are left to negotiate their terms individually. It is not the non-voluntary licenses in themselves that ensure that authors and performers are better off than under exclusive rights, it is the collective management of rights which is normally required to make such licenses work.

It is understandable why competition authorities have engaged so strongly in the collective management organizations. Obviously, such organizations should treat both their members and customers in a fair and transparent way and not abuse the legal or *de facto* monopoly they enjoy in many countries. But it would behoove those authorities well to also invest some of their energy into examining some of the practices of the information, culture and entertainment industries. Why, for example, are book royalties often higher than or equal to e-book royalties, despite the fact that the whole printing and distribution machinery, a legacy from the late middle ages, is no longer required? Do authors and performers get a fair share of the income from streaming services, or at least a chance to negotiate their pay, or is it a deal done behind their back by the commercial players?

When contracting and trying to take care of their interests in individual contracts, the authors and performers are in a situation which very much resembles the situation of the consumer, apart from the fact that these industries both legally and commercially are probably much more complex than what the ordinary consumer ever encounters. I think the competition authorities by and large have the legal tools and competence to make a real difference here, and if they don't, that is where I would then recommend that the necessary statutory amendments be made.

Maria Mercedes Frabboni*

1.4 Open Access and remuneration of researchers: considerations on the author's perspective

In the context of the discussion concerning remuneration systems under the law of copyright, it seems fitting to reflect on the role and challenges that a particular group of authors currently face. This group is composed of academic authors in their role of creators and contributors to research outputs traditionally published in academic journals. Following the adoption of open access policies by universities, by a large number of public and private funding institutions[1] worldwide and by international organisations,[2] academic authors have been called to comply with terms that directly affect their ability to exercise rights conferred to them by law. As discussed in this note, the remuneration derived from their creative outputs is also likely to be affected in the long run.

'Open access' is an expression characterized by many connotations but that lacks a straightforward and univocal definition. Open access policies share common justifications but, in their implementation, tend to vary from one university to another or from country to country. Significantly, the ways explored to ensure that open access to publicly funded research is granted to the general public do not venture in the field of exceptions or limitations to the exclusive rights of authors. Therefore, the question of whether an exception for the purpose of open access would trigger a system of compensation – as it does for other copyright exceptions – is not the focus of the discussion contained in this note. Conversely, open access policies are firmly based on copyright licences and related contractual practices adopted by the relevant stakeholders.

In this note, it is observed that, in the semantic confusion surrounding the open access discourse, the role of authors risks to be reduced to that of accidental extras, who have left the stage to other key actors in the negotiations, such as higher education institutions, funding bodies and academic publishers. Ultimately, however, the voice of academic authors should not be neglected. In the context of academia, the researcher is a protagonist in the creation and authorship of publishable outputs. This note offers a few observations on the understanding of incentives, of both monetary and non-monetary nature, that

---

* Dr., Sussex Law School, University of Sussex, UK.

1 Bill & Melinda Gates Foundation Open Access Policy (http://www.gatesfoundation.org/How-We-Work/General-Information/Open-Access-Policy, accessed on 20 June 2016).

2 UNESCO Open Access policy 'grants an irrevocable right of access to copy, use, distribute, transmit and make derivative works in any format within certain constraints' (www.unesco.org/new/en/openaccesspolicy, accessed on 20 June 2016).

drive academic authors, in order to fully appreciate and evaluate the impact and desirability of open access policies currently rolled out in academic institutions worldwide.

I. Justification for Open Access to scholarly publications

The focus of formal open access requirements is publicly funded research, but the approach to open access taken by funding bodies could extend beyond this scope. When research is supported by public funds, the awarding body is called to justify how those funds are spent. The main argument is that the public, as indirect contributor to research funding (e.g. via taxation), should obtain access to the relevant outputs generated by such research. In this sense, research outputs would be fully accessible as public goods, presenting non-exclusionary and non-rival characteristics. In this context, 'Free licenses attempt to draw lines to nurture and protect free culture'.[3]

Accordingly, the European Commission illustrates this approach in the following terms: 'The vision underlying the Commission's strategy on open data and knowledge circulation is that information already paid for by the public purse should not be paid for again each time it is accessed or used, and that it should benefit European companies and citizens to the full'.[4] This logic naturally encourages to associate the terms 'open' with the term 'free'. Nevertheless, these two terms have quite different meanings when addressing the matter of remuneration due to authors. While monetary and non-monetary incentives characterise the work of an academic author, it is important to emphasise that the production of publishable academic outputs is not cost-free,[5] for individual contributors, the academic institutions to which they belong, the university libraries that host their content and especially in the eyes of the funding institutions that award grants to applicants.

A disambiguation, however, ought to be highlighted here. In theory, 'free access' refers to the notion of unrestricted entry. Initially, it does not trigger issues related to the re-use of content. Conversely, the concept of 'open access' as

3 V Grassmuck, 'Towards a New Social Contract: Free-Licensing into the Knowledge Commons', in L Guibault and C Angelopoulos (eds.), *Open Content Licensing – From Theory to Practice* (Amsterdam University Press, Amsterdam, 2011), p. 48.
4 European Commission, Communication 'Towards better access to scientific information: Boosting the benefits of public investments in research', 17 July 2012, COM(2012) 401 final, p. 4.
5 For reference, see T Dreier, 'Overview of Legal Aspects in the European Union' in J M Asanu and P F Uhlir (eds.), *Open Access and the Public Domain in Digital Data and Information for Science* (The national Academies Press, Washington DC, 2004), p. 20.

currently developed, seeks to ensure that re-use is allowed in the widest and most flexible manners.

In this discourse, researchers are described, for example, as 'generators of research papers'.[6] It is possible that some authors and copyright communities feel uncomfortable with this description. Moreover, this approach does not reflect the inevitable and significant variations that exist in attitudes to academic publishing in different disciplines.[7]

To add to this picture, it is acknowledged that higher education institutions are key players in the process of adoption and implementation of open access policies. They employ a large number of academic authors. With their libraries, they are also the designated holders of large-scale repositories, which facilitate access to publicly funded research. Often, university libraries have been called to coordinate the activities necessary to ensure that authors comply with open access policies when required. Accordingly, '[l]ibraries play an essential role in open access developments by their expertise in building infrastructure, in creating user-friendly services of high quality and in securing long-term access ... Open access has ... changed the profile of academic and research libraries. National libraries are involved in developing national open access policies and supporting national research infrastructures and open access to cultural heritage. Public libraries disseminate open access content targeted for their users'.[8]

II. The rationale and implementation through 'green' and 'gold' open access

In order to fulfil the aims and objectives of open access policy, access to research outputs is not the only requisite. Funding bodies also require the possibility for users to be able to re-use freely accessible content for example by 'right to copy, distribute, search, link, crawl, and mine'.[9] On this basis, two main pub-

6 Research Councils UK, 'RCUK Policy on Open Access and Supporting Guidance', (8th April 2013), p. 2 (http://www.rcuk.ac.uk/documents/documents/rcukopenaccesspolicy-pdf/, accessed on 20 June 2016).

7 Evidence based results on this matter are discussed, for example, in T Eger, M Scheufen and D Meierrieks, 'The determinants of open access publishing: survey evidence from Germany', (2015) European Journal of Law and Economics, Volume 39, Issue 3, pp. 475–503.

8 International Federation of Library Association, 'IFLA Statement on open Access' (18 April 2011) (http://www.ifla.org/files/assets/hq/news/documents/ifla-statement-on-open-access.pdf, accessed on 20 June 2016).

9 European Commission DG for Research and Innovation, 'Guidelines on Open Access to Scientific Publications and Research Data in Horizon 2020 ' (Version 2.1) (15 February 2016), p. 2

lishing models have been elected as the preferred routes to comply with open access requirements, with slight variations that are specific to each funding body or other institutions involved in the process.

The Green route consists in self-archiving research outputs in institutional repositories, such as those set up by universities. The archived document submitted to the repository by a researcher should be the final peer-reviewed version as accepted by the publisher. An embargo period may apply but, after that period expires, the content should be freely available to everyone.[10]

Via the Gold route, a publisher offers access to the relevant research output immediately and free of charge. However, behind this system, there is a nexus of agreed terms which often entail the payment of fees known as 'article processing charges' (APCs). Effectively, APCs are sums transferred to publishers, which determine the flexible availability of content in compliance with open access policies. APCs are often a budgeted component for funded research projects, so that when the time of publication arrives, researchers will be in the position to be compliant with the open access requirements contained in the agreements they signed with the funding institution. Especially in a time of transition and adaptation of publishing business models, several university libraries, schools and departments have set aside monies to ensure that also non-funded researchers could be given the opportunity to publish outputs under open access conditions.

With the Gold route, several publishers have chosen to use Creative Commons Attribution Licences (CC-BY), which allow third parties to copy, 'distribute, remix, tweak, and build upon' the work, as long as the author is credited.[11] Significantly, this permits non-commercial and commercial re-use of the output in question. Moral rights remain unaffected under this licence.[12]

The Gold route is preferred by some funding institutions[13] for the immediate and unrestricted nature of the access guaranteed by the publisher. This aspect is noteworthy because it highlights the persistent confusion between free and open forms of access. Remuneration, in fact, remains a key factor of copyright licensing.

(http://ec.europa.eu/research/participants/data/ref/h2020/grants_manual/hi/oa_pilot/h2020-hi-oa-pilot-guide_en.pdf , accessed on 20 June 2016).

10 Research Councils UK, 'RCUK Policy on Open Access and Supporting Guidance' (fn 7), p. 6.

11 Creative Commons Attribution 4.0 International (CC BY 4.0).

12 On this aspect, see, however, C. Scollo Lavizzari, in this book, at p. 351 ff.

13 This is the case of Research Councils UK ('RCUK Policy on Open Access and Supporting Guidance' (fn 7), p. 1 and p. 6).

III. Scope

Three examples I include in this note will briefly illustrate the possible scope of open access policies.

Under the European Commission's FP7[14] Grant Agreement, which can be considered a precursor of the current Horizon 2020 model discussed below, the requirement was for beneficiaries to 'deposit an electronic copy of the published version or the final manuscript accepted for publication of a scientific publication relating to [results, including information, whether or not they can be protected, which are generated under the project] published before or after the final report in an institutional or subject-based repository at the moment of publication.'[15] Beneficiaries were required 'to make their best efforts to ensure that this electronic copy becomes freely and electronically available to anyone through this repository'[16] in line with the Green or Gold routes illustrated above.

The Horizon 2020 Model Grant Agreement sets stricter and more specific requirements: '[e]ach beneficiary must ensure open access (free of charge, online access for any user) to all peer-reviewed scientific publications relating to its results.'[17] In comparison to the FP7 Agreement, here the Commission preferred not to rely uniquely on the 'best effort' of beneficiaries. However, the requirement specifically refers to 'peer-reviewed scientific publications' relating to the results of the project,[18] and not to the wider array of results generated under a project.

Research Councils UK indicates that its 'policy covers all peer-reviewed research and review articles normally published in academic journals or conference proceedings, and which acknowledge Research Council funding. The policy does not cover monographs, books, critical editions, volumes and catalogues, or forms of non-peer-reviewed material. However, RCUK encourages authors of such material to consider making them Open Access where possible.'[19] According

---

14 The 7th Framework Programme funded European Research and Technological Development from 2007 until 2013.

15 This was the case also under the FP7 scheme (European Commission, 'FP7 Grant Agreement – List of Special Clauses' (Version 4, 14 February 2012), Clause 39 (http://ec.europa.eu/research/participants/data/ref/fp7/100308/rea-special-clauses_en.pdf , accessed on 20 June 2016).

16 *Ibid.*

17 European Commission, 'H2020 General Model Grant Agreement – Multi, Version 2.1., 1 October 2015, Article 29(2) (http://ec.europa.eu/research/participants/data/ref/h2020/mga/gga/h2020-mga-gga-multi_en.pdf , accessed on 20 June 2016).

18 *Ibid.*

19 Research Councils UK, 'RCUK Policy on Open Access and Supporting Guidance' (fn 7), p. 4. See also G Crossick, 'Monographs and Open Access', a report prepared for the Higher Education Funding Council for England (January 2105).

to this policy, an author is afforded more freedom as to the licensing conditions when he or she decides to publish a monograph or an edited book.

The Horizon 2020 Grant Agreement contains an obligation for the successful grant applicant to disseminate the results of the research funded under this scheme. The Grant Agreement reads as follows: 'Unless it goes against their legitimate interests, each beneficiary must – as soon as possible – 'disseminate' its results by disclosing them to the public by appropriate means (other than those resulting from protecting or exploiting the results), including in scientific publications (in any medium)'.[20] From an author's perspective, this note illustrates how a legitimate question can be raised as what constitutes a beneficiary's legitimate interest.

The mandatory nature of open access in H2020 marks a significant change from the FP7 scheme. The effectiveness of dissemination of research results funded by H2020 will also be enhanced by the 'Pilot Action on Open Research Data'. This affects beneficiaries in certain strands of the H2020 scheme and works accordingly to a policy of 'open access as the default mode (but including an opt-out option) and obligatory data management plans'.[21] A Data Management Plan can be considered as a further supporting tool to ensure the widest possible dissemination of results through accurate budgeting.[22]

A researcher's decisions to divulge or publish content appear to be safeguarded under grant model contracts. This point is of significance in countries where this is recognised as a moral right belonging to the author (such as France) as well as in countries where the decision falls within the realm of the economic right of distribution (such as the UK). Accordingly, 'open access requirements in no way imply an obligation to publish results. The decision on whether or not to publish lies entirely with the grantees. Open access becomes an issue only if publication is elected as a means of dissemination'.[23]

---

20 European Commission, 'H2020 General Model Grant Agreement – Multi, Version 2.1., 1 October 2015, Article 29(1) (http://ec.europa.eu/research/participants/data/ref/h2020/mga/gga/h2020-mga-gga-multi_en.pdf, accessed on 20 June 2016).

21 European Commission, Communication 'On the Response to the Report of the High Level Expert Group on the Ex Post Evaluation of the Seventh Framework Programme', 19 January 2016, COM(2016) 5 final, p. 8.

22 European Commission (Directorate-General for Research & Innovation), 'Guidelines on Data Management in Horizon 2020', (Version 2.1, 15 February 2016) (http://ec.europa.eu/research/participants/data/ref/h2020/grants_manual/hi/oa_pilot/h2020-hi-oa-data-mgt_en.pdf, accessed on 20 June 2016).

23 European Commission DG for Research and Innovation, 'Guidelines on Open Access to Scientific Publications and Research Data in Horizon 2020', (Version 2.1) (15 February 2016), p. 3 (http://ec.europa.eu/research/participants/data/ref/h2020/grants_manual/hi/oa_pilot/h2020-hi-oa-pilot-guide_en.pdf, accessed on 20 June 2016).

IV. Incentives

Authors who have been offered the opportunity to enter into an agreement with a funding institution, in accordance with the contractual conditions illustrated in this note, have also been asked to reach a compromise between the possible requests of commercial publishers and the requirements with the terms of the grant agreement. It has been argued that room for negotiations with academic publishers is often limited, with authors 'confronted – as a pre-condition to the publication of their article – with the publisher's standard form agreement, according to which the author grants the latter a transfer of the rights on his work.'[24] However, a 'take-it-or-leave-it' approach is not a practice exclusively adopted by publishers. Overall, the open access and copyright clauses of a standard form agreement by a funding institution impose precise conditions on the author. They may be seen as 'take-it-or leave-it' clauses themselves, whereby the author is asked to choose between being the beneficiary of a grant, or renouncing it.

Overall, it could be said that the academic author finds himself or herself in between two 'take-it or leave-it' scenarios. Naturally, it would be highly desirable if these two sets of conditions did not develop in opposing directions, and the market was capable of evolving in a way that facilitated the alignment of aims and incentives of publishers and funding institutions. Could authors be the key to the resolution of this riddle? A process aimed at enhancing the effectiveness of open access to published research should engage with academic authors to fully appreciate the nature of the incentives and pressure that drive their choices.

In the relationship with commercial publishers, it is not a taboo for authors in certain disciplines to negotiate terms of publishing agreements, for example with regard to moral rights and royalty rates for monographs. But it is also accepted that, in certain disciplines more than in others, remuneration based on prestige and/or prospects of promotion is closely linked to the number of peer-reviewed articles published by an author and to the destination of such articles in terms of scientific ranking of the targeted journals. Economists have argued that '[p]restige is the currency of academia. Aside from the pure enjoyment of prestige, a scholar's chances for promotion, tenure, a higher salary, etc., increase with his or her prestige. Prestige comes from doing high-quality research'.[25] Also,

---

24 L Guibault, 'Owning the Right to Open Up Access to Scientific Publications', in L Guibault and C Angelopoulos (eds.), *Open Content Licensing – From Theory to Practice* (Amsterdam University Press, Amsterdam, 2011), p. 150.
25 M J McCabe and C M Snyder, 'The best business model for scholarly journals: an economist's perspective', Nature Web Focus, 16 July 2004.

'[p]ublication would bring ... monetary benefits to academics even if academic copyright were eliminated ... That academics in fact generally obtain only insubstantial or no royalty income from publishing yet they devote great effort to writing implies that the incentives to publish that are unrelated to copyright must be strong'.[26]

The monetary incentive is often dismissed as irrelevant to academics. However, it has been argued that 'free access and accessibility are somehow linked to pricing'.[27] Overall, it would be imprudent to dismiss the impact of copyright royalties for all academics. In response to the observation that 'in the scholarly journal publishing context, authors do not typically receive royalties or other payments based on the sale of copies of their articles',[28] here it is submitted that it would be preferable to obtain reliable evidence on actual earnings by such authors from schemes set up in order to distribute remuneration earned from academic publishing (including publishing in academic journals). Collecting societies – such as ALCS in the UK[29] – could provide valuable information to discover whether earnings derived by authors from the use of outputs published in academic journals are in fact a sizable amount.

V. Concluding observations

The market of academic publishing is experiencing significant changes prompted *inter alia* by the requirements included in model agreements of funding bodies. Consultations are being held to ensure that the views of stakeholders are heard and evaluated in the process.[30] It is observed, however, that the recognition of the role of researchers as authors and beneficiaries of rights is limited, and minimal evidential consideration is given to the potential direct and indirect commercial value of academic publishing for individual research-

26 S Shavell, 'Should Copyright of Academic Works Be Abolished?', (2010) Journal of Legal Analysis, Vol. 2, Issue 1, pp. 316–317.

27 T Dreier, ‚Overview of Legal Aspects in the European Union' in J M Esanu and P F Uhlir (eds.), *Open Access and the Public Domain in Digital Data and Information Science* (The National Academies Press, Washington, D.C., 2004), p. 20.

28 http://www.authorsalliance.org/2014/10/16/open-access-faq/, accessed on 20 June 2016).

29 Authors' Licensing and Collecting Society, 'The Business of Being an Author. A Survey of Author's Earnings and Contracts' (April 2015) (https://www.alcs.co.uk/Documents/Final-Report-For-Web-Publication-(2).aspx, accessed on 20 June 2016).

30 These include the European Commission one-day public consultation on open research data (2 July 2013) (https://ec.europa.eu/digital-single-market/node/67533 , accessed on 20 June 2016). See also Higher Education Funding Council for England, 'Consultation on open access in the post-2014 Research Excellence Framework' (24 July 2013) (http://www.hefce.ac.uk/pubs/year/2013/201316/, accessed on 20 June 2016).

ers. The matter of the link between publishing attitudes and earnings is a multifaceted one, and largely unexplored.

Crucially, academic authors are individuals who work towards peer recognition through publishing. Open access policies interfere with publishing decisions and therefore have an effect on authors' decisions and incentives. It can be argued that the different treatment that is granted by model agreements set out for publications in social sciences subjects on the one hand and publications in hard sciences subjects on the other hand is partly an acknowledgement of the different market incentives that influence authors' decisions.[31] From this perspective, one can note the different embargo periods contained in the Horizon 2020 model agreement, to distinguish the requirements set for social sciences and humanities from those set for other disciplines.[32] If an embargo period applies, the Agreement establishes a maximum term of six months, which is extended to twelve months for publications in the social sciences and humanities.[33]

The issues addressed in this note lead to two main observations. The first is that it would be a drawback to achieving effective open access not to consider the fine details of the economic impact of open access policy on monetary and non-monetary remuneration of academic authors. Copyright law grants them economic and moral rights: focusing policy concerns on moral rights and neglecting the patrimonial element would be a limitation of the analysis. The second observation is that the ethos shared in different academic and research disciplines should also be duly considered and evaluated on the basis of rigorous evidence across jurisdictions, in order to ensure that embargo periods are available when necessary, and that a degree of choice is left to authors as to the best possible journal to target for the publication of their research findings.

31 T Eger, M Scheufen and D Meierrieks, 'The determinants of open access publishing: survey evidence from Germany' (fn 7), p. 500.

32 This was the case also under the FP7 scheme (European Commission, 'FP7 Grant Agreement – List of Special Clauses' (Version 4, 14 February 2012), Clause 39, p. 18, fn. 6 (http://ec.europa.eu/research/participants/data/ref/fp7/100308/rea-special-clauses_en.pdf, accessed on 20 June 2016).

33 European Commission, 'H2020 General Model Grant Agreement – Multi, Version 2.1, 1 October 2015, Article 29(2)(b)(ii) (http://ec.europa.eu/research/participants/data/ref/h2020/mga/gga/h2020-mga-gga-multi_en.pdf , accessed on 20 June 2016).

Pál Tomori*

1.5 Need and options for regulatory intervention

For the purposes of this panel, my claim is very simple: new business models should not be based on old business rules.

Earlier this week, the European Parliament's Committee on Legal Affairs voted for an amendment to the report on the implementation of the EU Copyright Directive[1], also known after its rapporteur as the "Reda Report", which calls "for improvements to the contractual position of authors and performers in relation to other rightholders and intermediaries, notably by considering a reasonable period for the use of rights transferred by authors to third parties, after which those rights would lapse, as contractual exchanges may be marked by an imbalance of power"[2]. I wish to remain non-committal at this time about the vices and virtues of the report itself. I have quoted this amendment merely to remind ourselves that when the need to regulate certain business models or industry practices is discussed, very often the weaker contractual position of authors and performers is called upon for justification; and probably rightly so.

A recent survey published in November 2014 by the French performers' collecting society ADAMI shows that at least in France the typical 9.99 € monthly subscription fee of music streaming services is shared rather unequally among the contributors, with authors and performers getting the worst end of the bargain. After 1.99 € is deducted for taxes, 6.54 € goes to the producers and streaming service providers, leaving authors with a meagre 1.00 €, followed by featured performers earning, collectively, for all their records listened to for a month, a derisory 0.46 €. (Please note the irony of how even the amount deducted for taxes is higher than aggregate share of authors and performers.)

This hardly seems fair towards authors and performers. So, making certain fairness as a fundamental principle of contractual relations prevails also in these new business models may be a justified ground for regulatory intervention – for example, by introducing an unwaivable remuneration right retained even after the transfer of exclusive rights, modelled after Art 5 of the EU Rental and

* Director of the collective management organization EJI (Society for the Protection of Performers' Rights) (Hungary).

1 Report of the Committee on Legal Affairs on the implementation of Directive 2001/29/EC of the European Parliament and of the Council of 22 May 2001 on the harmonisation of certain aspects of copyright and related rights in the information society (Ref. 2014/2256(INI)).

2 For the amendment tabled, see Amendment 187 on pages 86–87 of Amendments 1-280 (ref. AM-PE549.435v01-00) submitted to the 16 June 2015 meeting of the Committee on Legal Affairs; for the draft report adopted in the Committee, see paragraph 25 of the report dated 24 June 2015 (Ref. A8-0209/2015).

Lending Rights Directive[3]. From an industry perspective, this is perhaps a tool even better fitting performers than authors, for this would enable producers to preserve their existing business models and still obtain the exclusive making available right of performers, through individual or collective bargaining.

Imbalance in powers is also a serious obstacle to renegotiating older recording deals and to reshape them to fit the new business models. Streaming music services typically amass huge music libraries consisting of tens of millions of sound recordings, a substantial part of which was created in the pre-internet era and is covered by contracts devised for the analogue world. One does not have to be a recording industry insider to see how some of the most essential contractual terms of the pre-internet era such as, for example, "copies" or "sales" have become obsolete, or are to be construed very differently in the online environment.

In a recent decision, the Market Court of Finland[4] ordered Universal Music to stop making available to the public via the Internet – both as music files or as part of subscriber-selected online services – the performances of a Finnish band, called the Hurriganes. The records were made in 1973 and 1974, respectively, on the basis of two recording agreements entered into at about the same time. The recording agreements were lost or destroyed, so during the procedure great emphasis was put on standard or generally accepted industry practices as substitutes for explicit contractual stipulations.

The Market Court held that an agreement on the surrender of the rights specifying that the rights only apply to performances recorded on physical media, such as phonographic records or tapes, shall not automatically authorise the other party to make the performances available to the public via the Internet.

Universal has argued that irrespective of what the exact contents of agreement may have been, it should be understood, based on the generally accepted practice in the industry, that the concerned member of the band had surrendered all his rights under the recording agreement regarding whatever use of the performances in the music business in general. The Court however found that since under the Finnish Copyright Act the scope of rights transferred or assigned in an agreement must be construed by way of strict interpretation, reference to standard industry practices is just not specific enough to counterbalance the absence of an explicit provision.

---

3 Directive 2006/115/EC of the European Parliament and of the Council of 12 December 2006 on rental right and lending right and on certain rights related to copyright in the field of intellectual property.

4 MAO 191/15; issued 2015/03/18 (http://www.finlex.fi/fi/oikeus/mao/2015/20150191; retrieved on 8 June 2015. English translation provided by the Finnish Musicians' Union (Suomen Muusikkojen Liitto).

Universal has also argued that under the agreements it was compelled to sell and market the recordings as efficiently as possible. Considering the development of the music market, Universal would have been in breach of this obligation if it failed to offer the recordings as part of digital online services as well. This argument was also dismissed by the Court.

Universal has also submitted that royalties for digital sales were paid to the legal successor of the band member concerned and acceptance of such payments should be understood as tacit approval of surrendering the rights to the benefit of the payer of such royalties. The court rejected this argument, amongst others, on the basis that the payment of royalties for digital sales were a unilateral act based on a unilaterally determined percentage of the proceeds, and acceptance of payment without knowing of, and agreeing to, the terms on which payment were calculated does not constitute tacit acceptance of surrendering the right for the exploitation of which the payment was made.

Regardless of the findings of the Court, one may deem it rather peculiar that while most other contributors and interested parties of the music streaming business – producers, intermediaries, advertisers and music service providers – re-evaluated their terms and conditions, and adapted themselves to new business models over the years, most creators and performers were denied of this opportunity. They have to rely on recording deals signed, sometimes, decades ago in a totally different business environment.

Enabling contracting parties to renegotiate their deal in case the circumstances under which the deal was made changed substantially may be yet another reason for regulatory intervention. This is certainly not unheard of. Article 1(4) of the EU Term of Protection Directive[5], accompanied by Recital (16), offers this as an option by stating that Member States may provide that after 50 years certain terms in the contracts which provide for recurring payments can be renegotiated for the benefit of performers. It even invites Member States to have procedures in place to cover the eventuality that the renegotiation fails.

Another detrimental effect of using pre-internet contracts for online uses is that this chaos in terminology I was referring to, may directly and adversely affect the calculation of royalties. I am trying to decipher for over five years the algorithm by way of which the terms of a pre-internet contract originally applied to reward physical sales of records are converted to royalties for music streams but to no avail. It is perhaps time for the industry to unveil this great mystery.

Extended/improved reporting obligations to ensure that creators and performers, both reasonably considered to be laymen in matters of contract law

5 Directive 2011/77/EU of the European Parliament and of the Council of 27 September 2011 amending Directive 2006/116/EC on the term of protection of copyright and certain related rights.

and accountancy, understand how their rights are managed by an entity exploiting such rights may also be a justified ground for regulatory intervention. After all, the very same logic is applied to collective management organisations who represent their own stakeholders yet are compelled by statutory law to provide detailed information to right holders. Why asking for the same information from a record label controlling, say, over one third of the global music market or, for that matter, from any record label obtaining revenues from a global streaming music service provider would be undue interference with the contractual freedom of parties?

In recapitulation: there is a strong need and there are certain tried and tested options for regulatory intervention. These options may include:

a. Extended/improved reporting obligations
b. Certain contractual terms can be re-negotiated for the benefit of creators/performers
c. An unwaivable remuneration right retained even after the transfer of exclusive rights, paid by users (as opposed to royalties paid by producers) and managed by CMOs.

2. Role of collective administration in such business models?

Raquel Xalabarder*

2.1 Introduction

Good afternoon! Welcome to the second panel of this afternoon where we will examine the role of CMOs (collective management organizations) in managing these new digital online business models. As we have seen over these past two days, we are all aware that authors and performers do not always get too much (enough?) remuneration from these business models. So, the question that we are facing in this panel is: how can CMOs help improve this? Or, perhaps a previous question: should CMOs help in assuring them a better remuneration?

The answer to these questions may depend on whether we are dealing with exclusive rights of exploitation or simple "remuneration" rights, as well as whether these new means of exploitation are being licensed by CMOs or directly by the right owners (usually, producers). More and more often, CMOs are being left aside, to the extent that these new business models are being directly licensed by copyright owners. A good example of this tendency is found in the EU Directive 2014/26/EU on multi-territorial licensing of music online, which expressly empowers copyright owners to grant multi-territorial licenses (also by means of the "independent management entities") regardless of any CMOs established in the EU territories.

Of course, we also need to take into account the fact that what CMOs can do (as we have seen in previous panels) largely depends – on how the rights are designed in the national copyright law. As someone put it this morning, it is "the complexity of copyright" that will tell us how much CMOs can do or cannot do to help authors and performers strike a better deal. Dealing with statutory remuneration rights subject to compulsory collective management is very different from the voluntary licensing of exclusive rights, which is usually in the hands of producers. In between these extremes, better statutory contract rules could also help ensure a better deal for authors and performers when contracting out their rights with producers and publishers.

But, my role as a moderator is to keep it short and introduce the panelists of this session. We have a very attractive and diverse panel.

First, Martin Schaefer – lawyer at Boehmert & Boehmert from Germany – will offer us an overview of the current law regarding CMOs and some thoughts as to what could or should be their role regarding these new business models.

---

* Professor of law at the Universitat Oberta de Catalunya, Spain.

Then, Claude Brunet – lawyer at Norton Rose Fulbright from Canada – will look into some examples in Canadian law, as to how CMOs may help (or not) in protecting authors and performers. We will then have from Europe Romana Matánovac Vučković – professor of law at the University of Zagreb – who will tell us about the new Directive 2014/26/EU on collective management and music online and how it may affect the work that CMOs can do in favor of authors and performers. And last, but not least, Brigitte Lindner –from Serle Court Chambers in the UK – will tell us about the complexity of managing rights in audiovisual works and about the role of CMOs in securing a better remuneration for authors and performers.

So, without further delay, Martin, the floor is yours.

Martin Schaefer*

2.2 Possible roles for CMOs in new business models

In preparation of today's discussion here, all speakers have been reminded by Silke von Lewinski that our topic was to be put in context with the overall topic of the conference, "How to assure remuneration for use" and she went on to say: "How to assure remuneration **for right holders in general and for creators and performers in particular**."

I. Which role can CMOs play in that context?

The answer you receive on this question will largely depend on whom you ask.

- If you ask the "internet community" – whoever that might be and whoever provides those who speak with authority to speak on their behalf – this group will to a large part be in favor of CMO-administered statutory flatrate models that are by definition directly opposed to most of the new business models we heard of in Session One.
  Who would still subscribe to a flatrate music service such as Spotify if there was a general staturory flatrate effectively legalizing hitherto illegal offers?
- If you ask the CMOs, they will of course see an important role for themselves in administering part of or all of the new business models – and they might be sympathetic regarding ideas to create new statutory remuneration schemes (that is to say: levies) as those are increasingly regarded to be a reliable guarantee of their future existence.
- If you ask large corporate users, such as broadcasters and platforms of the kind of Youtube, you will probably hear that yes, they liked the centralized access to repertoire very much but disliked the absence of competition in this field. Their ideal would be a broad choice of CMOs to negotiate with, each representing the world repertoire, yet all of those CMO's being set in competition with each other to induce what some would call healthy competition and others – among which I count myself – a "race to the bottom".

---

* Dr. iur., Intellectual Property Lawyer at Boehmert & Boehmert, Berlin (Germany).
Member of the Board of ALAI Germany, Member of the Expert Committee on Copyright of the GRUR, Co-Chairman of the International Chapter of the Copyright Society of the USA as well as Chairman of the Advisory Council of the German Music Archive in the German National Library.

- If you ask corporate right holders that are investing in content, they will probably answer: Collecting Societies are a good thing and we will continue to employ them where it helps. But they are likely to add:

"CMOs don't invest in content. CMOs don't pay advances. CMOs don't need to recoup."

- If you ask individual creators – the individual author, the individual performing artist, they will give you a similar answer from their perspective:

"We are extremely happy with what we get paid via CMOs but unfortunately they don't invest in the production nor do they pay advances – while my publisher does and my record company does, too."

II. The technical role CMOs can play

1. Access to world repertoire ("One stop shop")

By definition CMOs are good at administering large scale uses of comprehensive repertoires. Wherever rights are needed for uses requiring access to repertoires owned by multiple right holders – such as "all protected works of music", "all sound recordings of all times", "all scientific articles existing worldwide" – this is a role they have learned to play.

Of the business models discussed in Session One, this would be especially relevant for the "Flatrate-Model" and clearly is the case for the model described in the CCC/RightsDirect cooperation with VG Wort where CMOs set up a new business model attractive for right holders and users alike.

Accordingly, whether or not CMOs can perform their task, to a large part depends on whether they can accumulate the comprehensive repertoire needed. This is no longer an easy task. Just one example from Europe:

The EU Commission's "Recommendation on the Management of Online Rights in Musical Works" of 2005 has led to a severe fragmentation of repertoire regarding certain rights needed for online exploitation of works of music.

One of the principal reasons for this problem lies in the fact that according to the Continental European collecting society tradition, CMOs are expected to operate on the basis of exclusive mandates. In contrast, copyright lawyers from outside Europe, especially the US, find it hard to believe that licensable rights could be signed away in their entirety to CMOs by means of an exclusive mandate. I can still recall the response of an US colleague: "But that cannot possibly be the case. The publishers would effectively lose their ability to license by themselves." And my answer was: "This is exactly how it works in Europe."

Indeed, the concept of an "exclusive mandate" can have unexpected consequences if practiced in the field of primary exploitation.

E.g., for traditional physical exploitation – primarily on CD – music publishers had and still have entrusted a large part of their licensable rights to CMOs (to the so called Mechanical Rights Societies and the Public Performance Societies such as GEMA) with the effect of having become almost invisible behind them. This has changed only recently due to a different practice in licensing ringtone and online uses.

But is it really true that right holders need to make a choice between administering their rights individually **or** collectively?

CMOs could play many roles in new business models if they offered their services on basis of non-exclusive mandates, leaving right holders the ability to strike deals themselves.

2. Administering large scale uses by allocating and distributing income to right holders

Administering large scale uses is no longer an issue only CMOs are qualified to deal with. It rests on usage data generated in the course of running the various business models described in Session One and on data concerning rights ownership, including repertoire meta-data. The latter are another natural domain of CMOs but this does not necessarily need to be the case in future any more.

Increasingly, not the least due to technical improvements in using existing proprietary databases of content industries (such as producers and publishers) and of various institutions (such as public library catalogs) by linking their resources – rather than by creating huge international repertoire databases – CMOs will be (or already are) challenged in their monopoly on monitoring and administering such kind of use.

Not to forget: As you will recall from the epic struggle over the Google Book Project in the US, the solution proposed by Google included the idea to establish a "semi collective" body for distributing the monies Google was willing to pay. The Content ID model of which we heard today is close to this concept.

Would this be a CMO in the first place? It is a question we might want to discuss.

III. The commercial role of CMOs

Clearly, the most natural habitat for CMOs is the administration of statutory remuneration rights or levies. Usually, at least according to the European approach, this implies direct distribution of the income generated to the respective original right holders (authors, performers, producers). But is this always the best way to deal with it? Is it necessarily in the interest of the individual author or performing artist?

In fact, it is this question what this whole conference is all about: Does it make sense to convert more licensable rights into statutory remuneration rights?

The answer to this question brings us back to my initial statement: CMOs do not pay advances, whereas one of the principal roles of the traditional content industries – such as producers and publishers – lies in providing upfront payments and advances to those who are contributing – and to invest in the production of content. If you are doing business in a risk-taking branch of the creative industries, such as the music or film industries where often economic expectations in a work or performance are not met, you will rely on cross financing throughout your catalog and throughout the lifespan of the product.

I am sure the other participants on our panel will further elaborate on this issue.

Thus, as you will of course have noticed during my presentation, I am favoring licensable rights and voluntary employment of CMO services over statutory schemes.

- As Session One has shown, micro licensing does work – it can make acquiring a license much as easy as purchasing a book on, e.g., Amazon.
- The VG Wort Digital License, as displayed at Session One, is a voluntary model employed by right holders tailored to fit the needs of a special group of prospective licensees.
- And the flatrate-model based on licenses is now firmly established in an increasingly broadening sector of the entertainment industry– again on a voluntary basis.

None of these models would be commercially viable if they were replaced by a statutory scheme. I admit that things might look different with regard to secondary and tertiary exploitation of content. Also, not all fields of exploiting protected matter do rely on advances.

IV. Conclusion

1. It might be worth spending some more thought on allowing CMOs to operate on the basis of non-exclusive mandates.
2. It is not always right to assume that direct distribution of income via CMOs to authors and performers does them well – as long as CMOs are not prepared to pay non-refundable advances.
3. Levy schemes are beneficial to users but harmful to industries investing in content – and in consequence, indirectly, to creators as well.

Romana Matanovac Vučković*

2.3 The Role of Collective Management Organisations in New Business Models – Challenges for the Legislature and Courts

I. Introduction

Collective Management Organisations (CMOs) today are confronted with serious challenges brought about by the rapid development of the digital market. While the principles of functioning of the digital market raise the question of protection of copyright within the model of exclusive territorial rights as such, by putting in the forefront the need for free circulation of goods and services of all kind, CMOs, because of their traditional common features explained *infra*, emphasise the relation of tension between copyright and the digital market. In addition, the common market of the European Union also puts a lot of challenges to the CMOs in the European Union, as it is in particular emphasised by the European Commission, which threatens the future existence of CMOs as we know them today, especially by insisting on the competition between CMOs with respect to the territories, right owners, and users.[1] Therefore, it is not easy to predict what the role of CMOs will be in the development of new business models for the exploitation of works in the digital environment and other subject matters protected by related rights. Unfortunately, right owners did not timely respond to the phenomenon of the digital market. Therefore, illegal uses of copyright works and subject matters protected by related rights still pose a serious threat to the industries based on copyright. Also, the legislators in the European Union were not very vigilant in designing the adequate legal framework for new circumstances that were arising in the digital world. Legal instruments that were intended to serve as a tool for

---

* PhD, Ass. Professor, University of Zagreb, Faculty of Law, Croatia.

1 *E.g.* the European Commission accused European CMOs of exercising concerted practices when negotiating the reciprocal representation agreements, which resulted in national territorial limitations. It also concluded that the exclusive representation clauses and membership clauses in those agreements were anti-competitive. *See* Commission Decision of 16 July 2008 relating to a proceeding under Article 81 of the EC Treaty and Article 53 of the EEA Agreement, (Case COMP/C2/38.698 – CISAC) C(2008) 3435 final (CISAC decision). The CJEU answered that there was no evidence on concerted practices and annulled this part of the Commission's decision. See CJEU case T-442/08(CISAC), [20013 ECR -2013-00000]. Nevertheless, the Commission's decision in this case had already provoked changes in collective management business and this wheel could not be turned back, even though the CJEU a couple of years later decided otherwise.

achieving an optimal balance between the copyright, the digital market and the European common market do not seem to be very successful so far.[2]

This paper presents concerns about the role of CMOs for music authors and performers in new business models of exploitation of music, as well as challenges for national legislatures and courts in the light of the legal framework and jurisprudence developed by the CJEU. Since the main purpose of existence of CMOs is, in brief, to collect and distribute the remuneration for right owners,[3] concerns regarding the amount of remuneration established in tariffs of CMOs will also be presented here.

II. CMOs for authors' rights in musical works

1. Traditional features of CMOs

Traditional CMOs in Continental Europe are built on the principle of territoriality, like copyright itself. From this follow their three important featu-

2 *See* Commission Recommendation of 18 May 2005 on collective cross-border management of copyright and related rights for legitimate online music services (2005/737/EC) OJEU L 276 of 21 October 2005 (hereinafter Commission Recommendation of 2005), which is of a non-binding nature. This Recommendation influenced the changes in collective management of musical rights by supporting pan-European licensing while abandoning all territorial restrictions and introducing new basic principles for cross-border online management such as the freedom of choice (substantive and territorial, regardless of nationality) of the CMO by the right holders, the right to withdraw online rights from any existing reciprocal representation agreement concluded, transparency of the repertoire, distribution and deductions. *See* also Guibault L./van Gompel S.: Collective Management in the European Union, in: Gervais D. (ed.), Collective Management of Copyright and Related Rights. Kluwer Law International 2nd edn., 2010, Netherlands, p. 155–158. The answer to the Commission Recommendation of 2005 was the European Parliament Resolution of 13 March 2007 on the Commission Recommendation of 18 October 2005 on collective cross-border management of copyright and related rights for legitimate online music services (2005/737/EC), P6_TA(2007) 0064, Strasbourg and European Parliament Resolution of 25 September 2008 on collective cross-border management of copyright and related rights for legitimate online music services, P6_TA(2008)0462, Brussels. *See* also Frabboni, M.M., Collective management of copyright and related rights: achievements and problems of institutional efforts towards harmonisation, in: Derclaye E. (ed), Research handbook on the future of EU copyright, Edward Elgar, 2009, Cheltenham, p. 390–391; Guibault/van Gompel, op.cit., p. 158–159. See also Directive 2014/26/EU of the European Parliament and of the Council of 26 February 2014 on collective management of copyright and related rights and multi-territorial licensing of rights in musical works for online use in the internal market, OJEU L 84 of 20 March 2014 (hereinafter Directive 2014/26/EU).

3 There are also other purposes and roles of collective management and CMOs, such as cultural and social roles. Nevertheless, those roles are called into question by the Commission Recommendation of 2005 and especially by Directive 2014/26/EU (*see* in particular its Arts. 12(1) and 15(1) and Recitals 28 and 30).

res.[4] The first of them is the monopoly position of nationally established CMOs, which is guaranteed by the law (*de jure* monopoly) or applied consistently in practice (*de facto* monopoly). In order to support the position of the CMOs, both in licensing and enforcement of rights, many among the national copyright laws provide for the presumption of the representation of the entire world repertoire or the extended licensing system. They both enable representation by CMOs also of those right owners who did not expressly empower the respective CMO, but are represented by it on the basis of the rebuttable legal presumption. If not prescribed by the law, the representation of the world repertoire is usually ensured through interpretation in national jurisprudence. And finally, the national CMOs are interconnected through a network of reciprocal representation agreements. These agreements may not be exclusive, but *de facto* usually are so in respect of rights of public performance and/or reproduction of works and other protected subject matters as regards traditional acts of exploitation. Through this network of reciprocal representation agreements the CMOs mutually empower each other to represent the respective repertoires in respective territories, while at the same time they refrain from interfering within each other's territory.

Territorial CMOs are usually supervised by state administrative authorities, that is, the national IP office or copyright authority. Very often this is an *ex ante* supervision within the system of approval whereby the CMO is allowed to manage the rights collectively only after the competent administrative state authority verifies that it meets the conditions for undertaking the activity of collective management.[5] In the European Union, there should always be *ex post* supervision of CMOs, meaning that the administrative state authority regularly supervises the performance of their duties. In the circumstances described here, the tariff-setting systems are also more or less susceptible to the control of the competent authority: a national official authority such as the intellectual property office, copyright office or competent minister or a council, board or similar body, which acts on the basis of independent experts but is directly or indirectly appointed by the state, in most cases by the competent minister or even the government.

---

4 *See* also Gyertyánfy P., Collective Management of Music Rights in Europe after the CISAC Decision. IIC 41(1), 2010, p. 66, 67, who summarises eight essential traits of the Continental European collective management societies.

5 In some European Member States, such as Great Britain, there is no *ex ante* control over CMOs. In contrast, in all Central and Eastern countries there is a system of approval for operating collective management.

2. New legal framework for CMOs for on-line cross-border licensing

It seems impossible that the traditional legal framework described *supra* and reserved until recently specifically for CMOs in Continental Europe will be able to survive in the new business environment for the exploitation of music, namely the digital environment. Directive 2014/26/EU gives directions for the new organisational and legal framework for CMOs, especially in respect of cross-border on-line licences of musical works. It does not insomuch affect the legal framework for collective management for traditional uses,[6] and it stays with tested legal figures.[7] However, in respect of collective management of rights in the digital environment, it removes the possibility of monopoly position and the presumption of the representation of the world repertoire or the application of the extended licensing systems. It is also out of the question that the reciprocal representation agreements are of an exclusive nature. Namely, the right owners are supposed, according to the idea which underlies the system introduced by the Directive, to empower different CMOs to represent them for the same territories. So the idea of competition between the CMOs is promoted also through the possibility of competition for the repertoires in the same territory. Since there is competition between CMOs in the same territory, they should not act territorially anymore and the monopoly position connected with the territory of the establishment cannot subsist. The right owners, especially major publishers, are invited to empower different CMOs for the same territories in order to promote competition between them. When answering the criticism that the competition between CMOs for the repertoire will induce a race to the bottom in relation to remuneration, the European Commission, which strongly supports this approach, insisted that this competition between CMOs will not lead to a decrease of the amount of remuneration since they should not compete over the price of the repertoire, but on the margin added to this price, that is, the management fee.[8] It is to be seen whether this prediction will come true or the value of music

---

6 In respect of all CMOs which operate in the traditional off-line environment, Directive 2014/26/EU introduces significant improvements related to transparency and government. Even though there were many CMOs which already regularly publicly presented their financial reports and other financial data, it was not harmonised in the European Union which level of transparency should be achieved among the CMOs.

7 With the exception of multi-territorial licensing in an online environment, Directive 2014/26/EU does not affect any type of extended collective licensing or similar schemes such as legal presumptions of representation (*See* its Recital 12).

8 *See* Commission Decision 2003/300/EC of 8 October 2002 relating to a proceeding under Article 81 of the EC Treaty and Article 53 of the EEA Agreement (Case No COMP/C2/38.014 – *IFPI "Simulcasting"*), OJEU L 107 of 30 April 2003. After this intervention of the European Commission into the reciprocal representation agreements among CMOs representing phonogram pro-

will decrease due to evolving competition among CMOs in digital cross-border licensing.

CMOs are, according to the provisions of Directive 2014/26/EU related to digital uses, now entitled to grant mono-repertoire licences or aggregated-repertoire licences all over Europe, but the tariff-setting procedures for the remuneration that should be paid for the mentioned licences are not regulated. As said *supra*, in the traditional off-line environment the tariff-setting procedures are generally regulated by the national copyright laws and very often some state or quasi-state authority (such as a board of experts or arbitration panel) participates in the tariff-setting procedure.[9] Consequently, within the traditional legal framework, the tariff of the country where the copyrighted work or other protected subject matter is used was always applied by the local CMO and the tariff was always proposed/issued by the local CMO. Directive 2014/26/EU does not regulate which tariff-setting procedure and which tariff should be applied in online licensing, but it does specially regulate that disputes regarding licensing conditions and tariffs related to cross-border licensing can be subjected to an independent and impartial alternative dispute-resolution procedure of the country of establishment of the CMO.[10] This provision determines the law of the country of establishment as the applicable law for the resolution of disputes, but the question remains whether this provision implicitly also regulates the applicable law for the tariff-setting procedure. Since Directive 2014/26/EU fails to regulate the applicable law, it thus remains with the solutions from Regulations Rome I[11] and Rome II,[12] which only confirm the principle of territoriality of copyright and the application of *lex loci protectionis*.[13]

Nevertheless, it is not Directive 2014/26/EU which first introduced the new paradigm of collective management. The system of cooperation between the CMOs in the European Union basically changed shortly after the issuance of

---

ducers for simulcasting (*IFPI Simulcasting Agreement*) the user was free to approach any of the CMOs party to this Agreement because competition was introduced among them on the basis of "cost and efficiency". The tariffs had to be created in a way that made it clear which part refers to the royalty and which to the administration fee.

9 Some EU Member States, such as Hungary and Romania, regulate even the procedure of negotiations for tariffs before any dispute arises whereby the negotiations are conducted through the national intellectual property/copyright office.

10 *See* Art 34(2)(a) and Recital 49 of Directive 2014/26/EU.

11 Regulation (EC) No 593/2008 of the European Parliament and of the Council of 17 June 2008 on the law applicable to contractual obligations (Rome I Regulation), OJEU L 177 of 4 July 2008.

12 Regulation (EC) No 864/2007 of the European Parliament and of the Council of 11 July 2007 on the law applicable to non-contractual obligations (Rome II), OJEU L 199 of 31 July 2007.

13 The law of the country of protection is regularly applied to so-called copyright-related issues, while contractual and tort issues fall within the law of the country towards which regular rules of international private law direct. See e.g. Fawcett J.J., Torremans P., Intellectual Property and Private International Law, Clarendon Press, Oxford, 1998, p.488.

Commission Recommendation 2005. Most major publishers and big CMOs withdrew their online rights from national CMOs, especially in Central and Eastern Europe, and started to license directly. The national CMOs, on the other hand, licensed only nationally the repertoire which remained after the withdrawal of the repertoire of major publishing companies. At the same time, national CMOs mostly continued to enjoy the presumption of the representation of the repertoire of all right owners for which the on-line rights had not been withdrawn. Consequently, they should have issued tariffs according to the national rules and procedures for the repertoire which remained. It looked like this was a combination of individual cross-border licensing and national collective licensing. Nevertheless, the situation was far from clear and transparent because the tariffs applied were not published, on the one hand, and the foreign licensors were mostly unknown to anyone but the licensees, on the other hand. It is also disputable whether such a combination was strictly legal, since the national laws regulated collective management as described above under point 2.1 and demanded that CMOs apply for approval from the national administrative authority before undertaking to manage copyright and related rights collectively.[14] In those circumstances it is very difficult to find out who represents whose rights, especially when the need for enforcement against unauthorised use comes into play. In a situation of authorised use, all involved parties declare their repertoire, and what remains, as unknown repertoire, should stay with the national CMO, which usually still enjoys the presumption of representation of the rest of the world repertoire (which was not withdrawn).

Since Directive 2014/26/EU came into force, this messy situation in an online environment has become even more complicated, because, as announced, it is not possible for the legal presumption of the representation of the repertoire which was not withdrawn to survive, and it is clear that the monopoly position of the national CMO is incompatible with the new rules. At the same time, all CMOs may (but should not) be involved in cross-border licensing in the whole European Union representing their repertoire, which they have to prove. One open question is how they are going to set the tariffs – which law is applicable for which repertoire and what is the value of the repertoire. Another one is how they are going to prove ownership in the repertoire when a need for enforcement comes into play.

Here we come to another question. Namely, until recently the amounts of remuneration set in tariffs of CMOs referred to the entire global repertoire, though the opt-out possibility was available. However, when speaking of multi-

---

14 In those circumstances foreign CMOs did not apply for approval of the competent national administrative authorities (Copyright Office or Intellectual Property Office) for undertaking the activity of collective management, namely cross-border licensing of copyright, as regulated by national copyright acts of the countries where they acted as CMOs.

territorial mono-repertoire licences, the explained mechanisms cannot subsist, even in cases where there is aggregation of several repertoires. By applying the new rules for online collective management, it turns out that the burden of proof concerning representation lies with the CMO. It should be able at any given moment to define its repertoire and to prove the chain of title from the original right owner to the CMO. At the same time, CMOs compete among themselves for the repertoire and for the users on the whole European market. Since this is a completely new legal environment for the CMOs, it is questionable how they are going to overcome the problems and to fulfil their tasks, especially if they are small and medium ones, representing the small and generally unknown repertoires from Central and Eastern Europe. It also remains to be seen how this situation will affect the size of the remunerations fixed in tariffs.

And finally, it is necessary to raise the question of criteria for setting the tariffs. Usually, the criteria for setting the amounts of remuneration in tariffs were given on the basis of examples in national copyright laws and sporadically touched upon in the jurisprudence of the CJEU.[15] According to Directive 2014/26/EU, both parties must negotiate licences in good faith and provide each other with all necessary information.[16] Licensing terms must be based on objective and non-discriminatory criteria.[17] Tariffs must be reasonable in relation to, *inter alia*, the economic value of the use of the rights in trade, taking into account the nature and scope of the use, as well as in relation to the economic value of the service provided by the CMO.[18] "The economic value of the use of the rights in trade" and "economic value of the service provided by the collective management organisation" referred to in the Directive 2014/26/EU are certainly different for the whole world repertoire on the one side, and the limited repertoire on the other side, just as there are differences between the well-known limited repertoire of Anglo-American and/or English-language music and small and less-known limited repertoires of Eastern and Central European origin. It remains to be seen how national legislatures will answer the questions and challenges posed by Directive 2014/26/EU and how the national courts, but also the CJEU, will interpret the new rules.

---

15 *See* C-395/87(*Tournier*), [1989] ECR 02521; C- 110/88, 241/88 and 242/88 (*Lucazeau*), [1989] ECR 02811; C-192/04 (*Lagardère*), [2005] ECR I-07199; C-245/00 (SENA), [2003] ECR I-01251; C-52/07 (*Kanal 5 Ltd*), [2008] ECR I-09275 and C- 351/12 (*OSA*), ECLI:EU:C:2014:110.

16 *See* Art 16(1) of Directive 2014/26/EU.

17 *See* Art 16(2) and Recital 31 of Directive 2014/26/EU.

18 *See* Art 16(2)(2) and Recital 31 of Directive 2014/26/EU.

III. Management of music performers' rights

Even from the title of Directive 2014/26/EU it is clear that it does not affect the rights of music performers. Also, the Commission Recommendation of 2005 did not pay attention to the rights of music performers. This is because the European Commission supposes that their rights are indispensably connected with the rights and interests of their publishers and phonogram producers due to specific and very intensive contractual relations among them. Therefore, it is assumed that music performers should license their rights together with the rights of phonogram producers, which means individually and directly European-wide. Nevertheless, this solution seems far from being perfect and far from being satisfactory for music performers. We are witnessing their struggle to overcome this perception.[19] It seems that they are interested in managing their rights through the CMOs because they expect more income from this side. In Croatia, for example, the national CMO for music performers has issued tariffs for online uses, declaring that the online rights of the music performers are not transferred to phonogram producers but remain with the music performers. Finally, it has brought lawsuits against *Deezer* and *Croatian Telecom* claiming that performers' rights are not acquired tacitly in contracts between the performers and phonogram producers/publishers and therefore should be administered collectively.[20]

IV. Conclusion

As stated in the title of this article, the legislatures and courts are today faced with serious challenges when speaking about the role of CMOs in new business models employed in the digital environment. The traditional principle of territoriality, which is unconditionally applied both in copyright in general and in collective management of copyright, seems to be too narrow for the new digital environment since in the online world there are no boundaries between the

---

19 Four international associations of performers are running the campaign for a better position of musicians in the digital environment called "FAIR INTERNET", *see* http://www.fair-internet.eu/. Those associations represent together over half a million performers in Europe: The Association of European Performers' Organisations (AEPO-ARTIS), The International Federation of Actors (FIA), The International Federation of Musicians (FIM) and The International Artists Organisations (IAO). *See also* http://www.fim-musicians.org/posts/musicians-denounce-industry-practices and http://www.aepo-artis.org/pages/176_1.html (last visited on 10.9.2015).

20 *See* http://www.huzip.hr/novosti/obavijest-clanovima-huzipa-i-hgua (last visited on 10.9.2015).

markets – the Internet is one single market. National boundaries only artificially partition the online market and therefore the principle of territoriality, which *de lege lata* applies also in the digital environment, should *de lege ferenda* carefully be redefined and adapted to new circumstances. It will be a great challenge for national legislatures to implement Directive 2014/26/EU in a manner which is supportive of collective management, especially in Central and Eastern Europe, where the repertoires are not so attractive to a European and worldwide audience. It is a difficult time for collective management, which needs to change its profile and promote a new paradigm in licensing and enforcement of rights of authors and performers, one that relies on the competition among CMOs for right owners, users and territories. Since Directive 2014/26/EU does not provide a complete legal solution it is for the national legislatures to find the best solution and fill the gaps. Especially since the prominent aim of collective management is to collect and distribute remuneration for right owners, it will be interesting to see whether CMOs will be in the position to meet this challenge, taking into consideration the problem of tariff-setting and applying the tariffs in licensing and especially in enforcement of rights in the digital environment. The position of CMOs for performers' rights is even more complicated than the position of CMOs for authors' rights, because there is no legal tool that would balance their position in the digital music market. Therefore, it is yet to be seen how national legislatures and in particular courts, including the CJEU, will respond to the requirements of performers for a better and what they consider fairer position regarding their rights and the remuneration derived from those rights.

Brigitte Lindner*

2.4 The role of collective administration in new business models in the audiovisual sector

This contribution to the discussions on the remuneration for the use of works at the ALAI Congress 2015 examines the question of whether collective administration could be a suitable means for securing a better pay for authors and performers where audiovisual works are used in new business models.

I. Background

From the times of Beaumarchais till today, collecting societies have embraced various technological changes. In principle, there is hence no reason why collecting societies should not play a role in securing an income for authors and performers from the new business models of this time and age.

Nevertheless, in view of the diversity of the cultural sector, which comprises a variety of differently functioning industries, one should be cautious to view collective administration as a one-size-fits-all model, particularly where new business models are concerned. For example, while collective administration has traditionally played an important role in the music business, it is less prominent in the audiovisual sector where it is used primarily in the natural habitat of collecting societies such as private copying or cable retransmission. Why is that?

Producing a film is a high risk business which involves the handling of large production budgets[1]. In order to orchestrate the funding as well as the smooth production and exploitation of a film at all stages, the producer needs to be able to take a number of vital decisions: whether to grant rights on an exclusive or non-exclusive basis, whether to limit them geographically, and whether to restrict them in time. The producer can take these decisions on the basis of the bundle of exclusive rights that he acquires from his creative contributors on the basis of a contract, by operation of law or through a combination of both. He

* Lawyer, Serle Court Chambers, Lincoln's Inn, London.

1 For example, the average film production budget in the UK stands at EUR 10.9 million whereas it is EUR 5 million in Germany and France, EUR 2.6 million in Sweden and 15 million USD in the US, Source: Communication from the Commission, European film in the digital era, 15 May 2014, Com(2014)272 final, at p. 6, accessible at: http://ec.europa.eu/culture/library/reports/com272_en.pdf (accessed on 14 June 2016).

therefore becomes a kind of 'one stop shop', which guarantees legal certainty for both the producer and his contractual partners. To keep all the rights in one hand also enables him to raise financing for films on the basis of presales agreements and to accommodate specific release patterns, which often reflect the arrangements made in the funding process and are sometimes required by law[2].

II. Collective administration as a tool for improving authors' and performers' remuneration?

While this particular system of allocation of rights to the producer keeps audiovisual productions running, there have been complaints that it may leave authors and performers empty-handed, particularly in the online world. Collective administration is seen as a recipe to redress this situation. In particular, mandatory collective administration of an unwaivable right to equitable remuneration for the making available to the public of works and performances incorporated in audiovisual works directly against the platform operator is considered by some as a means to improve the livelihoods of authors and performers and to ensure a fair return for the use of their creative contributions[3].

The proponents of this approach argue that the exclusive right of authors and performers would remain unaffected so that the film producer could still obtain the bundle of exclusive rights which is necessary to control the exploitation of the film through all stages[4]. In addition, there would be an unwaivable right to equitable remuneration subject to mandatory collective administration, which would allow authors' and performers' collecting societies to claim remuneration directly from the platform operator once authors and performers have transferred their right to the producer, and this seemingly regardless of contractual arrangements concluded by the producer with his creative contributors and with the platform operator. For the advocates of this approach mandatory collective administration appears to be the decisive factor; without mandatory collective administration, the unwaivable right to equitable remuneration would

2 Cf. for example in France: Arts. L. 231-1–234-2 Code du Cinéma et de l'image animée; Germany: § 20 FFG (Filmförderungsgesetz).

3 SAA White Paper, Audiovisual Authors' Rights and Remuneration in Europe, 2nd edition March 2015, which may be found at: http://www.saa-authors.eu/en/news/168/SAA-White-Paper-download; cf. also the initiative 'Fair internet for Performers', see http://www.fair-internet.eu (accessed on 14 June 2016).

4 SAA White Paper, ibid., p. 38/39.

lose much of its meaning[5]. They also take the view that the model would guarantee adequate remuneration for authors and performers in the online world without weakening their bargaining position and would not interfere with the role of the producer. Hence no interference with the status quo but better pay. This approach sounds promising, but can it live up to its promise?

While nobody can seriously question the principle of adequate pay for creators, the strictness of mandatory collective administration may not be palatable for everyone. Not every free-spirited author may welcome the fact of being forced into collective administration by the legislator. Film producers are also unlikely to show much sympathy for this model as they may see their bargaining power vis-à-vis internet platforms undermined by separate deals between collecting societies and platforms. Faced with additional claims from collecting societies, platform operators may well decide to pay less for the audiovisual content they acquire under the contract with the producer. This may lead to reduced upfront payments for authors and performers who would have to wait until online exploitation materialises. It may also have a negative effect on the cross-financing of works, i.e., sustaining less popular productions with more successful works, and may affect presales agreements. Mandatory collective administration may therefore have a negative impact on raising financing for films. Ultimately, the real winners would be global internet platforms.

In any event, would mandatory collective administration lead indeed to a substantial increase of remuneration? It is likely that a specific tariff for the online use of an author's and a performer's contribution to a film, whether agreed by the relevant societies with the platform operator or determined by the regulator, may increase the remuneration of lower paid creative contributors to some extent, but perhaps not significantly; at the same time, it may lead to other contributors earning considerably less. So while some may earn a little more, there is a risk that others might earn much less.

National law may also contain some surprises that could constitute an impediment to increased earnings through a mandatory collective administration scheme: one example is Article 60(2) of the Swiss Authors' Right Law, which squeezes performers as related right owners into a 3% and authors into a 10% bracket. The bracket sets an upper limit which may only be exceeded under very exceptional circumstances and thus invites to seek tariffs generally within the 10% and 3% limits[6].

Moreover, in view of the open-ended concept of the film author, particularly in continental-European legal systems, collecting societies and platform opera-

5 SAA White Paper, ibid., p. 38.

6 Swiss Federal Court, Judgment of 24 March 1994 at paras 10 and 11, SMI 1996 III p. 437 – Leerkassettenurteil and Judgment of 27 February 2014, BGE 140 II 305 (at para. 6.4) – GT S (2011–2013); cf. discussion in Barrelet/Egloff, *Das neue Urheberrecht*, 3rd edition (2008), Article 60, note 19.

tors may not find a straightforward answer to the question of who would be entitled to remuneration. While the principal director may generally be one of the authors of the film, at least in the EU[7], there may be other authors who can only be determined by looking closer at each particular film. For example, German law does not determine the film author as such with the consequence that any person who makes a sufficiently creative contribution which amalgamates in the film work and cannot be used separately may qualify as a film author[8]. The situation in France is similar: although French law provides for a rebuttable presumption for the authors of a film in Article L. 113-7 of the Intellectual Property Code, the principle in French law is nonetheless that the individuals who make a creative contribution to the film are to be considered its authors[9]. In order to support the emergence of online business models through securing legal certainty, legislators would face an uphill struggle to find a practical solution to this problem.

There are hence various reasons why mandatory collective administration may ultimately not be the ingredient one would wish for in this recipe. This does however not rule out collective administration altogether. Where collective administration is voluntary, it can be used effectively to respond to specific situations. This would however not be the case if it became a one-size-fits-all model for all unconventional business models across the different cultural industries as it could hardly accommodate the complexity and costs associated with film production.

III. Alternatives

Are there any other recipes which could help to secure a better remuneration for authors and performers in new business models in the audiovisual sector?

One route could be the creation of awareness in the creative community aiming at familiarizing authors and performers with strategies which would enable them to invoke their rights and the contents of a fair contract with more vigour. For example, with its fair contracts initiative, the American Authors' Guild intends "to create a climate of 'just say no' to egregious contractual terms"[10]. Enhancing relations between authors and performers and their contractual partners through the determination of mutually acceptable standard

7 As a result of Art 2(2) Directive 2006/115/EC and Art 2(1) Directive 2006/116/EC.

8 Cf. Schricker/Loewenheim – Katzenberger, Urheberrecht, 4th edition, 2010, Vor §§ 88 ff., notes 57, 61–64.

9 Cf. for example Cour de Cassation (First Chamber), Judgment of 5 February 2002, RIDA 2002 (193), 397 (404); Kamina, P., Film Copyright in the European Union, 2002, para 138.

10 Cf. https://www.authorsguild.org/industry-advocacy/the-authors-guild-fair-contract-initiative-a-preview/ (accessed on 14 June 2016).

contract terms would be another option worth exploring[11]. Rather than imposing collective administration by law, strengthening the voice of creators in negotiating and agreeing fair contracts might therefore be a more promising way to improving individually tailored remuneration for authors and performers.

Another route could be collective bargaining agreements, which have been successfully used in the United States where authors and performers in the audiovisual sector are remunerated on the basis of guild agreements for the uses of their works and performances in all forms of exploitation[12]. While the market realities in the US and elsewhere may differ, collective bargaining is certainly an area that is worth investigating further when searching for ways to achieve a fairer remuneration for authors and performers, as are other forms of collective agreements. Although the example of so-called joint remuneration rules under German law has had some teething problems, such initiatives, if implemented and applied properly, could be a flexible alternative to mandatory collective administration which could accommodate both the circumstances of the particular sector and the start-up environment in which new business models operate. Such agreements could incorporate a sophisticated remuneration package that reflects the particularities of the sector concerned and could also serve as guidelines for courts as to what could constitute a proper remuneration.

IV. Conclusions

In conclusion, a variety of measures could improve the remuneration of authors and performers:

- Collective administration on a voluntary basis can be a useful tool for authors and performers, as well as for other right owners, if the particular circumstances of the individual sector are taken into consideration. This being said, one should beware of turning it into a one-size-fits-all model for all unconventional business models across the different cultural sectors.

---

11 Cf. for example the ANFASA-PASA Agreement on Contract Terms between the Academic and Non-Fiction Authors' Association and the Publishers' Association of South Africa, accessible at: http://www.publishsa.co.za/downloads/APACT_document.pdf (accessed 14 June 2016).

12 Cf. for example: 2014 Theatrical and Television Basic Agreement of the Writers Guild of America, accessible at: http://wga.org/content/default.aspx?id=1610; TV/Theatrical Agreements by the Screen Actors Guild (SAG) and the American Federation of Television and Radio Artists (AFTRA) accessible at: http://www.sagaftra.org/files/sag/documents/sag-aftra_2014_tv_theatrical_contracts_referendum_booklet.pdf; Directors Guild Agreements accessible at: http://www.dga.org/Contracts/Agreements.aspx (all accessed on 14 June 2016). See also the discussion by Amit Datta, *Collective bargaining agreements in the film industry: U.S. guild agreements for Germany?*, 2 Berkeley J. Ent. & Sports L. (2013). Available at: http://scholarship.law.berkeley.edu/bjesl/vol2/iss1/10 (accessed on 14 June 2016).

- A further option is strengthening the voice of creators, particularly through the creation of awareness for fairer contracts for authors and performers.
- Collective bargaining agreements and other collective arrangements such as joint remuneration rules can also play an important role in securing an adequate remuneration for authors and performers, if implemented and applied in an appropriate manner.

Finally, one should not forget the talents of one of the great sons of the city of Bonn where the ALAI community is reunited in 2015 to discuss the remuneration for the use of works: Ludwig van Beethoven was a savvy negotiator. In the negotiations with his publishers, he used various tactics to obtain the best price for his works. This was particularly important in view of his imminent deafness which would no longer allow him to earn parts of his living from performance. Beethoven's diverse profit-making strategies included the offering of the same work to several publishers simultaneously in order to stimulate competition between them and to thus obtain optimal conditions, often with success[13]. Beethoven's negotiation tactics – perhaps an encouragement for his colleagues in the 21st century?

13 Ladenburger, M., Beethoven und seine Verleger. 'Geschäftsbeziehungen. Strategien. Honorare. Probleme' in Kämpken, N., Ladenburger, M., Biba, O., "Alle Noten bringen mich nicht aus den Nöthen!": Beethoven und das Geld: Begleitbuch zu einer Ausstellung des Beethoven-Hauses in Zusammenarbeit mit dem Archiv der Gesellschaft für Musikfreunde in Wien und der Österreichischen Nationalbank, 2005, p. 143 at p. 146; Information may also be found on the dedicated website of the Beethoven-Haus at: http://www.beethoven-haus-bonn.de/sixcms/detail.php/31559 (accessed on 14 June 2016).

3. Participation of creators and performers

Axel Metzger*

3.1 Introduction

Ladies and Gentlemen, thank you all for coming back. I still see many participants interested in this last session. Thank you very much for giving us your attention. The title of the last session is "Participation of creators and performers" and in a sense, this brings us back to the focal point of ALAI in general and of this conference, namely, the role of the authors and the performers. And as you can see from the composition of our panel – I will introduce my panelists in a moment – we will take this very serious because we have invited real authors to discuss with us and I am very happy that this is not a pure legal panel at the end. "Participation" is a concept with multiple dimensions. The first dimension is the participation in the revenues – revenues that may come from different business models. We have discussed during the last two days that it is not always easy to guarantee that authors and performers get their adequate share in the revenues in all the new business models. But participation in revenues is also something which is not trivial these days when it comes to collecting societies. We have discussed yesterday that the exact percentage of shares for publishers and authors may be a critical issue to discuss and there are more critical issues concerning the distribution of revenues. However, "participation" also has another dimension, which is the participation in the creation of legal rules and the enforcement of legal rules. Do authors and performers really participate in the political process? When law-making is taking place in Brussels, are authors and performers represented by professional stakeholders, or is this always intermingled with the interests of intermediaries? And, finally, "participation" is also something you may use as an umbrella term when it comes to participation in law enforcement: Do authors and performers have a realistic chance to enforce their rights in court, or is this something which is hampered by their weak position? These and some other questions are what we want to discuss in the next 60 minutes or so. Let me briefly introduce my panel to you: On my left hand side you see Maureen Duffy, famous British novelist and author, and very vocal on authors' rights on different international panels. We are very happy that Maureen is with us. Also to my left side, we have Eddie Schwartz, Canadian musician, song writer and producer who is also active in authors' organizations, in particular in CISAC. To my right hand side, that is the legal part of the panel if you want, you see Maria Martin-Prat, head of the Copyright Unit in the European Commission, and, at the far right, Franck Macrez, Maître de Conférences of

* LL.M. (Harvard), Professor, Humboldt-Universität zu Berlin, Germany.

CEIPI in Strasbourg. Franck will start with his presentation, then Maria will take over, and afterwards, you may say that this is symbolic, the authors will have the last word at the conference and I think we will have a nice discussion afterwards. Franck you have the floor.

Franck Macrez*

3.2 Libres propos sur le rôle du créateur dans l'évolution du Droit – Pour un droit des créateurs

Mesdames, Messieurs, c'est un grand honneur pour moi d'avoir la possibilité de m'exprimer face à l'assemblée de notre association et auprès d'un si prestigieux panel. J'en remercie donc nos hôtes, collègues et amis, de l'ALAI Allemagne et en particulier Silke von Lewinski pour la confiance dont ils me témoignent à travers cette invitation. Et je n'ose pas modérer mes remerciements en constatant la difficulté de la tâche à mener par une comparaison entre l'ampleur du sujet à traiter et les quelques minutes imparties pour ce faire.

« La participation des créateurs »... entre le législateur et le juge. La tâche est rude ... pour les créateurs. C'est un poncif que de remarquer que le créateur est en situation de faiblesse – économique, technique, juridique – face aux autres acteurs exploitant leurs créations à quelque titre que ce soit et spécialement ceux dont il a été question lors des sessions précédentes de ce Congrès. La fonction du Droit est de protéger la partie faible, celle du droit d'auteur de protéger le créateur. La question ici posée me paraît avant tout préjuridique : comment le créateur peut-il se faire entendre du législateur et du juge dans un contexte général de bouleversement des modèles économiques, d'hypercomplexité de ces modèles et de leur évolution très rapide, ainsi que de contestation des droits de propriété intellectuelle? Le peut-il, en vérité? L'organisation collective des créateurs est évidemment, et historiquement, le meilleur moyen pour eux de se faire entendre auprès du législateur, des juridictions ou encore de leurs cocontractants.

Il me faudra m'en tenir à quelques remarques générales qui pourront sembler élémentaires, mais n'en restent pas moins fondamentales: le préliminaire me semble nécessairement sémantique (I), pour constater la délicate position du créateur entre juge et législateur (II), ce qui me conduira à poser la question du rôle de la doctrine du droit d'auteur dans ce contexte proprement politique (III).

* *Maître de Conférences, Centre d'Études internationales de la propriété intellectuelle (CEIPI), Université de Strasbourg, France – franck.macrez@unistra.fr.* Le style oral de l'intervention a été volontairement conservé.

I. Sémantique (élémentaire) du droit d'auteur

Les créateurs sont des personnes de langage, tout comme les hommes de loi. Il ne fait pas de doute qu'il convient de « prendre la contrefaçon au sérieux »[1] ni que les approximations langagières ne doivent pas avoir leur place dans le discours juridique. Banalité? Et pourtant ...

1. Nommer la contrefaçon sérieusement

Le terme de « piraterie » est omniprésent dans les débats contemporains. Il semble, la majorité du temps, désigner une contrefaçon de droit d'auteur sans objectif lucratif. Force est de constater qu'en lui-même, le mot est une métaphore, c'est-à-dire une figure de rhétorique. Le vocable, qui n'a pas sa place dans un discours de science juridique,[2] conserve pourtant une place de choix dans les discours législatifs ou doctrinaux, le fait s'expliquant sans doute par un Moi collectif nous renvoyant à des héros de notre enfance, si ce n'est par une certaine attirance pour l'acteur Johnny Depp dont le charisme ne laisse, semble-t-il, pas indifférent[3] ...

Il reste que le message est biaisé, et le législateur européen l'a fort bien exprimé lorsqu'il a décidé de la création de ce qui devait être un « Observatoire de la contrefaçon et du piratage » :

> « *En este informe hemos superado, de una vez por todas, el término «piratería». Creemos que el término «piratería» es equívoco, pues no entendemos bien cuál es su relación con el abordaje de barcos en el mar ni con las míticas leyendas corsarias.* »[4]

On ne saurait mieux dire. Laissons donc la rhétorique aux rhéteurs ...

L'institution d'Alicante s'appelle finalement « Observatoire européen des atteintes aux droits de propriété intellectuelle »[5] ; voilà qui semble plus sérieux.

---

1 M. Vivant, « Prendre la contrefaçon au sérieux », *Dalloz* 2009, p. 1839.

2 F. Macrez, « De la "piraterie" – Brèves remarques sur une métaphore endormie », in C. Geiger et C. Rodà (coord.), *Le droit de la propriété intellectuelle dans un monde globalisé – Mélanges en l'honneur du Professeur Joanna Schmidt-Szalewski*, Litec, coll. du CEIPI, 2014, p.221.

3 L. Marino, « Piratage » in *C. Geiger et C. Rodà (coord.), Le droit de la propriété intellectuelle dans un monde globalisé,* Mélanges en l'honneur du Professeur Joanna Schmidt-Szalewski, LexisNexis, coll. CEIPI, 2014, p. 233.

4 M. Antonio Masip Hidalgo, débats au Parlement Européen du 13 février 2012, CRE 13/02/2012 – 15.

5 Règlement (UE) n° 386/2012 du 19 avril 2012.

2. Traduire le droit d'auteur scrupuleusement

Le « principe du créateur », exprimé dans l'un des premiers paragraphes de la loi allemande (« *Schöpferprinzip* »), est-il toujours existant en droit positif européen, tandis que la référence systématique depuis dix ans pour les autorités de l'Union est le « titulaire de droits »[6]? La plupart des créateurs français que je connais (dont des traducteurs professionnels) marquent leur incompréhension face à la traduction du syntagme « droit d'auteur » (« *Urheberrecht* », « *derecho de autor* » ...) par « *copyright* ». Bien entendu, les divergences historiques et philosophiques entre les deux systèmes se sont estompées à l'époque contemporaine. Il reste que les tenir pour strictement synonymes (à tel point qu'en français, « copyright » est fréquemment utilisé dans le débat public, souvent par des contempteurs de la propriété intellectuelle) peut paraître propre à ce que la discussion soit biaisée.

La conception du droit d'auteur européen que la Commission européenne appelle de ses vœux passe avant tout par la manière de le nommer: c'est une condition *sine qua non* de la clarté des débats. Sans naïveté ni aucune illusion, l'évolution de ce qui est aujourd'hui un *copyright* européen pourrait se discuter autour d'un « *author's rights* », ce qui remettrait le créateur au centre des échanges. Car, dans les nouveaux modèles, la conclusion du Rapport français est frappante :

> « *L'ensemble des intermédiaires se partage une valeur qui (...) échappe (aux auteurs et artistes interprètes)* .»[7]

Que la créativité figure, dans les derniers documents de la Commission, en première position de ses préoccupations ne doit pas relever de la formule de style restant lettre morte :

> « *La créativité* est *un élément essentiel de la compétitivité de l'UE sur le plan international.* »[8]

Le créateur est-il au centre des préoccupations du législateur européen? C'est la créativité qui est ici visée, ce qui peut déjà manifester un glissement sémantique, donc conceptuel : pense-t-on avant tout à l'innovation – mais on est loin

---

6 V. la contribution de S. Nérisson à cet ouvrage : « L'article 5.7 de la directive 2014/26, une introduction diabolique du droit des contrats dans le droit d'auteur européen », *supra*, p. 259 ff.

7 T. Azzi, N. Binctin, A.-C. Jeancard, V. Tabary et G. Vercken, « Questions sur les nouveaux modèles économiques et leur statut juridique » *in* Rapport français, http://alai2015.org/en/national-reports.html, p. 52.

8 Communication de la Commission européenne au Parlement, « Stratégie pour un marché unique numérique en Europe », 6 mai 2015, COM (2015) 192 final, p. 7.

du brevet – et non à l'œuvre de l'esprit ? Il convient à mon sens, et en tout état de cause de veiller à ce que le créateur demeure, ou revienne, au centre des objectifs de politique législative.

Ces « jeux de langages », relevés sans exhaustivité, sans en appeler à Wittgenstein (encore que des enseignements pourraient en être tirés et que l'étude reste, à ma connaissance, à mener), qui sont à l'œuvre ne sont en tout cas pas neutres et ne me paraissent pas anodins.

II. Les créateurs entre le législateur et le juge

La question est essentiellement sociologique: le non-sociologue que je suis s'en tiendra à une analyse descriptive des rapports complexes unissant le créateur d'œuvres de l'esprit aux créateurs de Droit.

1. Les créateurs organisés collectivement

Face au *lobbying* forcené qui est à l'œuvre auprès du législateur, la multiplication des acteurs, l'accroissement exponentiel des enjeux économiques, le créateur, individuellement, n'est évidemment pas apte à porter une action propre à se faire entendre efficacement du législateur.

L'organisation collective paraît indispensable. La constitution en syndicats en est un des modes. La société de gestion collective également, et même vraisemblablement la plus efficace. Il reste à vérifier, au cas par cas, que les intérêts sont bien convergents. Car une société de gestion collective, n'est dans les faits, qu'assez rarement une société *d'auteurs*. La divergence peut surgir, les créateurs pouvant se plaindre – à tort ou à raison – de clés de répartition qui ne seraient pas suffisamment en leur faveur, du manque de transparence de la gestion, voire d'une mauvaise gestion ou encore de frais de gestion qui seraient à leur sens trop élevés.

Ces problématiques sont traitées par le législateur, conscient de l'importance de la transparence du fonctionnement des sociétés de gestion. Et en bonne logique, la rigueur du contrôle de la bonne gestion doit se renforcer en même temps que les sommes gérées augmentent.

Si, de manière générale, on peut rester optimiste sur l'efficacité des sociétés de gestion dans la défense des intérêts des créateurs, force est de constater que le conflit est parfois inévitable et amené à être traité par les tribunaux.[9]

9 A. Lucas-Schloetter, « Les éditeurs peuvent-ils percevoir la rémunération pour copie privée ? », RIDA 2015/01, n° 243, p. 2.

2. Le créateur devant le juge

Le droit au juge, droit fondamental garanti par la Convention européenne des droits de l'homme, bénéficie évidemment à la personne du créateur, comme tout citoyen. La mise en œuvre du principe n'est pas aisée et le constat doit être dressé avec une particulière acuité en matière de droit d'auteur: la matière est technique, en perpétuel mouvement, et les affaires sont souvent complexes. Et le créateur personne physique défend rarement ses droits en justice, comme l'a relevé le Professeur Azzi dans son Rapport.

La problématique spécifique de l'aide juridictionnelle, que la Cour de Strasbourg a étendue de la matière pénale à l'ensemble du champ de l'article 6 de la Convention, et la longueur des procédures sont autant d'éléments qui sont propres à dissuader effectivement.

Je m'en tiendrai à deux exemples qui me sont proches. Dans le domaine du plagiat universitaire (généralement des thèses de doctorat, les thèses juridiques n'étant pas épargnées par le phénomène), l'on sait que le jeune docteur découvrant une contrefaçon de sa thèse (mais le plagiat peut aussi être habile et non sanctionnable sur le terrain du droit d'auteur) agit assez rarement en contrefaçon : le procès est long et coûteux. Si le contentieux en la matière semble plus fourni ces dernières années, la seule raison en est que les cas de plagiat sont plus nombreux et non que la procédure judiciaire est facilitée.[10]

Le cas de la loi française sur la « numérisation des livres indisponibles du XXe siècle » me paraît symptomatique. L'affaire est particulièrement complexe : numérisation, gestion collective, titularité des droits numériques sur des œuvres littéraires publiées au siècle précédent, rôle des éditeurs, notion de « formalité » au sens de la Convention de Berne, question de la protection constitutionnelle du droit de propriété de l'auteur et de son contenu précis... Sans compter la stylistique législative rendant le texte en cause proprement incompréhensible. Quel avocat irait plaider un tel dossier pour des écrivains qui refusent de partager avec des éditeurs des droits numériques qu'ils estiment n'avoir jamais cédés, vivent de leur plume, mais restent modérément fortunés, dans une procédure face au gouvernement français et la société de gestion collective agréée pour l'occasion, impliquant une saisine du Conseil d'État puis du Conseil constitutionnel? Je ne dis pas qu'il n'en existe aucun, qui renoncerait à une rémunération équitable de son travail, mais en l'occurrence je n'en ai pas trouvé... Et le Conseil d'État français a au final trouvé la question suffisamment sérieuse et épineuse pour transmettre le dossier au Conseil constitutionnel, puis récemment une question préjudicielle à la Cour de Justice de Luxembourg afin de sa-

10 V. J. Passa, « La contrefaçon ou le "plagiat" dans les thèses de doctorat », *in* « L'intérêt général », *Mélanges en l'honneur de Didier Truchet*, Dalloz, Paris, 2015.

voir comment définir une exception ou limitation au sens de la directive 2001/29.[11]

Il me semble que la doctrine du droit d'auteur a son rôle à jouer ; et qu'il convient de s'interroger sur ce rôle et son efficacité.

III. Existentialisme de la doctrine du droit d'auteur

Il ne s'agit pas ici de faire subir à l'auditoire, en cette fin de Congrès, une dissertation portant sur « Existentialisme et droit d'auteur », que je serais sans doute incapable de traiter. Quoiqu'il ne me semble faire aucun doute que le principe nietzschéen, selon lequel il n'existe pas de pensée « pure » et que l'on ne peut appréhender correctement une doctrine qu'en connaissant la personnalité et la biographie de son auteur, me paraît devoir s'appliquer à la doctrine juridique.

Mais en réalité, un certain nombre de situations et spécialement le dernier exemple évoqué me font me poser des questions existentielles en tant qu'universitaire ...

1. Le rôle de la doctrine dans le processus judiciaire

Il est généralement reconnu que la doctrine universitaire bénéficie d'une certaine autorité auprès des juges, et par conséquent d'un pouvoir d'influence quant à la solution à adopter. Un tel avis peut être produit auprès du juge à l'initiative d'une des parties, mais encore à l'initiative du juge lui-même. Il est d'ailleurs frappant qu'en France, le Conseil d'État ait rappelé cette possibilité de faire appel à l'expertise d'un enseignant-chercheur dans un arrêt daté du même jour que celui concernant les « livres indisponibles »[12], tandis que le rapporteur à cette dernière affaire avait liminairement remarqué que c'était la première fois que la haute juridiction administrative française avait à interpréter la Convention de Berne au contentieux ... La consultation d'un spécialiste, normalement indépendant en raison de son statut, aurait pu être salutaire en l'espèce. Mais est-ce encore le cas aujourd'hui en matière de droit d'auteur? Il est permis d'être

---

11 Conseil d'État, 10ème /9ème SSR, 6 mai 2015, n° 368208, note S. Nérisson, Dalloz 2015, p.1427.

12 Conseil d'État, 8ème /3ème SSR, 06 mai 2015, n° 375036, Publié au recueil Lebon ; article R. 625-3 du Code de justice administrative : « La formation chargée de l'instruction peut inviter toute personne, dont la compétence ou les connaissances seraient de nature à l'éclairer utilement sur la solution à donner à un litige, à produire des observations d'ordre général sur les points qu'elle détermine. (...) ».

dubitatif à l'écoute d'un haut magistrat de la Cour de cassation française qui estime désormais que les activités annexes des universitaires l'invitent à tenir compte de leurs écrits avec une grande circonspection, tout en me devant de préciser qu'il s'agit d'une personne, fort sympathique au demeurant, qui assume aisément son goût pour la provocation ...

Pourtant, si l'on estime que les créateurs doivent être défendus et qu'une certaine partie de la doctrine considère toujours que le droit d'auteur est un droit du créateur, il faut s'interroger sur son efficacité. Critiquer une décision de jurisprudence après que celle-ci a été rendue : nous sommes dans notre rôle. Ne le serions-nous pas tout autant en apportant une expertise *a priori*, lors des débats devant donner lieu à la décision en question? L'évolution du droit d'auteur aurait à y gagner en cohérence, là où bien souvent nous en sommes réduits à tenter de trouver une rationalité *a posteriori* à un mouvement jurisprudentiel.

2. Le rôle de la doctrine dans le processus législatif

La question de l'efficacité de la pensée doctrinale dans la construction du Droit se pose également quant à l'évolution législative, bien entendu nécessaire face au développement complexe et hétérogène du numérique. J'avoue ne pas avoir recensé le nombre de Livres Verts et de consultations de la Commission européenne auprès des plus éminents spécialistes européens depuis dix ans. Force est de constater que l'harmonisation européenne promise reste encore au stade de la promesse, bien qu'à ce jour la volonté politique de la Commission paraisse forte.

Les travaux européens semblent ainsi devoir s'intensifier dans les mois qui viennent et les gouvernements nationaux sont bien inspirés de s'appuyer sur l'expertise des spécialistes éminents à l'instant évoqués, qui sont nombreux dans cette salle. Pour m'en tenir à la France, et comme membre du Conseil supérieur de la propriété littéraire et artistique auprès du Ministère français de la Culture et de la Communication, je ne mentionnerai que le rapport du Doyen Sirinelli sur la révision de la directive 2001/29[13], qui sera prochainement complété par un rapport sur « une meilleure articulation entre les directives 2001/29 "société de l'information" et 2000/31 "commerce électronique" ».[14]

Peut-être, comme s'agissant des créateurs, et pour reprendre une devise chère à nos amis Belges, que « l'union fait la force »: la résurgence, ces derniè-

13 P. Sirinelli, *Rapport de la mission sur la révision de la directive 2001/29/CE sur l'harmonisation de certains aspects du droit d'auteur et des droits voisins dans la société de l'information*, CSPLA, Ministère de la culture et de la communication, décembre 2014, < http://www.culture communication.gouv.fr/>.

14 Mission du CSPLA sur une meilleure articulation entre les directives 2001/29 « société de l'information » et 2000/31 « commerce électronique » confiée le 8 avril 2015 à Pierre Sirinelli.

res années, des résolutions de l'Association Littéraire et Artistique internationale, est en ce sens salutaire et propre à défendre le plus efficacement possible la protection internationale du droit d'auteur.

Mesdames, Messieurs, je vous remercie pour votre attention.

Maria Martin-Prat*

3.3 Current discussions in Brussels

Thank you very much. Let me start by thanking ALAI Germany for having invited the Commission to be here. I must say that I was a bit surprised when I saw that I would be in the same panel as Maureen Duffy and Eddie Schwartz. Maybe, I have another career here. Maureen reminded me that there is originality in the drafting of legislation. I am not sure that I would be able to go that far so I will stay in my traditional role of someone working in the area of policy making and I will try to explain to you how the topic of this panel is currently being discussed and assessed at EU level. I will talk about the political discussions in Brussels, in the European Parliament and in the Commission. I do not believe these discussions are very different at national level.

In my intervention I would like to highlight four points that are often put forward in this debate but, in my view, are not necessarily correct.

First, in the current political debate there seems to be an increasing demand for exceptions to rights while maintaining regular calls for fair remuneration of creators. I do not deny that there are valid reasons for the ongoing debate on exceptions, some need to be updated to take into account the changes brought about by digital technologies, some may need to be considered anew. However, we cannot assume that more exceptions to the (economic) rights will not affect the remuneration of, inter alia, authors and performers. In other words, I do not agree with the presumption that creators will be better remunerated on the basis of weaker rights. This is a difficult proposition to maintain at least on the basis of the system of authors' rights and neighbouring rights that we have known until now. A completely different proposition would be, for instance, to provide that creators be remunerated on the basis of taxes or by the state budget – or by the voluntary financing of corporations that would become the new patrons of the 21st century. Such a system would not only be very far away from the essence of a system of copyright based on the concept of (intellectual) property but would also raise many other questions, from the incentives to create, produce or publish works to the principle of national treatment – questions that go well beyond our discussions today.

A second element that distorts the debate is the recurrent references to the fact that the creator ought to be remunerated – sometimes the term compensated is used – "appropriately". Often, one has the impression in these discussions that the objective should be to pay creators not too little but not too much. And that the creator should only be remunerated to the extent that this does not hinder the dissemination of his work or the development of innovative services.

* Head of the Copyright Unit in the European Commission, DG CONNECT.

The third element distorting the debate is the presumption that technology would give no option to the author but to let go his exclusive rights since, as the assumption goes, exclusive rights – i.e., the rights to authorise or prohibit – cannot be exercised in the current technological environment. This is a discussion that has been ongoing for quite some time and that, in my view, is misleading. The technology that allegedly would make it impossible to maintain copyright as a permission-based system, to maintain a link between the author and his work, is the same technology that also allows service providers not only to deliver to me any work at any time I want, but also to determine the works I may be in a mood to listen to or to choose the advertisements that should be placed in front of my eyes. Technology is neutral and thus should be used as much to disseminate content as to determine when a work is being used and to ensure compliance with the terms under which it is licenced, including – if this is the case – the remuneration for such use.

The fourth presumption is that this is a new debate. I disagree, the digital market may make the debate more complex, but it is not a new one. It is, like in the past, a debate about mostly commercial interests between rightholders and users. There has always been tension between, on the one hand, creators and those investing in creativity and, on the other hand, users and those who want to use content in a commercial (or non-commercial) manner and this is also the case in the debate today.

Even today, the basic objectives of most creators remain to be able to decide whether and how their works are disseminated and to be remunerated – and not just compensated – for the use of their works. Exclusive rights – the rights to authorise or prohibit – are not only important as economic rights; they also keep the link between the author and the work, between the performer and the performance. Of course, this does not mean that exclusive rights necessarily suffice to ensure the remuneration of authors and performers or that there are no instances in which the balance between such rights and reasons of general interest would not call for a limitation of these rights.

If we believe that the principles underlying the system of authors' rights and neighbouring rights remain valid, the question is how can we make them work in the digital environment, including to ensure as much as possible the fair remuneration of authors and performers. A number of mechanisms have been examined during today's discussions, including the role of exclusive rights, of collective management, of an unwaivable right of remuneration as well as the role of contracts and the role of unions. The European Commission is interested in these issues and we are looking into all of them. The debate is complex and, when you undertake it at the European level, it gains an extra layer of complexity. There are mechanisms that work well in some Member States but do not work in other Member States. Differences not only in legal systems and traditions but also in the functioning of collective management or the role of the unions are important. Therefore, it is difficult sometimes to establish common minimum rules. Besides, Member States have very different views as to how much intervention should take place at European level, for instance, in matters related to the regulation of contracts. Even if there are elements in that respect in some of the provisions of the existing directives – for instance in the Rental and Lending Rights Directive – this continues to be an area where Member States, or at least a number of them, are opposed to harmonization at a European level. Nevertheless, I think that fair remuneration of authors is an issue that should not be discarded in our discussions at EU level.

These considerations are applicable both to offline- and online-exploitation. So the issue of fair remuneration is not a completely new challenge. Today it might be more difficult because of the functioning of the markets but it has always been there. There is, however, a new aspect that has entered the discussions. Again, you discussed it to some extent yesterday. This is the question of the "value transfer". How value is being shared when works and other protected subject matter are exploited online, who is remunerated, who is receiving the value generated by the exploitation of those creations. This is a debate which includes elements related to both copyright policy and competition law. It is a debate that takes place in a difficult environment since, due to years of piracy, there is a widespread mentality that is characterized by the (erroneus) concept of having a "right" to free access to works. Going ahead, we will be considering to what extent we are able to address problems related to that value transfer on the basis of copyright protection.

The fair remuneration of authors and performers and the sharing of value and the value transfer issue in general are on the agenda of the Commission, and also of the European Parliament. You can see it clearly in the own initiative report that the European Parliament recently adopted on the reform of copyright. In the Commission, political discussions are ongoing and no policy choices have been made yet. I have nevertheless tried to explain to you the parameters of our discussion as well as the challenges we face.

But with this, I will finish. Thank you very much!

Eddie Schwartz*

3.4 A view from the musical field

Good afternoon, my name is Eddie Schwartz and I am a songwriter, artist and record producer from Canada. I am honored to be here speaking with you today, and especially to members of an organization founded by a creator, Victor Hugo.

Full disclosure before I go on: my mother's fondest dream was that I become a lawyer. In that regard I failed her utterly. However, as some small consolation, I have had the honor of writings songs and/or producing artists such as Joe Cocker, Pat Benatar, The Doobie Brothers, Donna Summer, Carly Simon, Robert Palmer, Rascal Flatts and others. So copyright has been fundamental to my life in the most real and concrete ways imaginable. It has allowed me to dedicate my life to the creation of music.

Currently, I am increasingly involved in the activities of organizations that represent music authors. One of them is the International Council of Authors of Music also known as CIAM, which operates under the umbrella of CISAC, the International Confederation of Authors' Societies. And I volunteer for this work, because I am deeply concerned about future generations of music creators. Their opportunities to make a living creating music as I have been able to do are quite simply being extinguished. And this ironically at a time when music is a fundamental element in a value chain that generates billions annually.

At the dawn of this century, the Internet and digital technology offered huge potential – the promise of a new "Golden Age of culture and creativity".

While now that may seem like a distant dream, I believe that promise is still within our grasp, and I'll get to more on why I believe that, in a moment.

But first a few words about the reality on the ground for music creators.

In Nashville Tennessee, also known as "Music City USA", where I have lived and worked for the last 18 years, 80% of the professional music creator community has disappeared. And given the almost 100% drop in the revenue received by creators from online sources, it's certainly not hard to understand why.

Let me take a moment to explain this catastrophic drop in creator revenue. In the latter part of the 20th century, if for example a song of mine sold a million copies, I would received about $ 45,000.00US in mechanical royalties, and I was awarded a platinum record.

Today, a major music service pays me an average of $ .000035 per stream, or about $ 35.00US for a million streams, thus reducing a reasonable middle class living, to the value of a pizza. We've heard a lot about monetization here. But that's the kind of "monetization" that creators are actually experiencing.

* Songwriter, artist, record producer (Canada).

So at current per stream rates, I would need not only every human being on Earth to stream my music, but life forms on other planets, and galaxies far, far away, creatures from other dimensions would need to stream my work before I could earn a small fraction of just the bonuses that CEOs of major streaming services pay themselves. So, yes, this is a "Golden Age" – for some.

Now indulge me while I do a quick "back of the envelope" calculation of how big this value chain that pays me .000035 per stream is.

If we take that million streams that earns me the prodigious sum of $ 35.00, and if we assume for a moment that those million streams represent a million unique internet accounts, those million accounts would generate something like $ 600 million US dollars annually in ISP access fees alone. On top of that, there are also device and mobile access fees, monthly subscriber and download fees, advertising and data mining revenues, and a whole dark portfolio of other hidden fees, advances, equity stakes etc..

So even this quick exercise exposes an undeniable truth: Music is part of a huge value chain generating billions of dollars annually and consumers, and creators alike are paying hugely. And yet some are still propagating this myth of "free". Sure, music wants to be free, but only when it serves to extract massive fortunes for CEOs and shareholders.

Despite all this, as I mentioned earlier, I for one am hopeful. I see signs that we are now at the beginning of what could be a significant turning point to a better and more balanced digital future. Here in part are my reasons for optimism.

To start with, light is beginning to shine into the dark shadows of the digital value chain. The recent revelations regarding Sony Records' 2011 agreement with Spotify are a perfect example. We now have proof that tens of millions are being paid by digital services to record labels, in a manner that appears to be designed to hide those revenues from artists and songwriters so those revenues don't have to be shared.

Non-disclosure agreements are clearly also a big part of the problem. How do you know if you are receiving 50% if you can never know what 100% is?

What we don't know will indeed hurt us, and transparency must come and is coming to the music value chain, and that is a crucial first step if creators are ever to be fairly compensated.

Also, safe harbor legislation, intended to protect the so called "dumb pipes" is today abused by "not so dumb" major multinational entities because it allows them to amass huge profits, while providing access to our creative works for virtually nothing. Creators are now calling for updates and reforms of this legislation, which in essence is currently protecting the rich and powerful from the digitally disenfranchised.

On another front, and one I am personally very excited about, CIAM is uniting music creators from Africa, Latin and South America, Europe and North

America, and more recently creators in Asia. This global creator unity has never existed before, and I wish to thank Lorenzo Ferrero, Chair of CIAM, and Gadi Oron, Director General of CISAC for their leadership and support.

Through CIAM, music creators from all over the world are developing a broadly based non-governmental initiative called Fair Trade Music. You can learn more about it at www.fairtrademusic.info. DSPs and other intermediaries would be certified as Fair Trade compliant if they worked with creators to implement best practices towards a fair, transparent and sustainable music eco system from consumer to creator and everyone in between.

Last and certainly not least, in my work with young music creators, I see a new generation coming into their own that are not as dazzled by technology as my generation may have been. They care about sustainability and ethical behavior, whether at Wal Mart, or MacDonald's or garment workers in Bangladesh, and most assuredly for the music creators whose work they love and want to support.

They are a generation that understands that our humanity and our technology can and must find a balance, and that if music is allocated a fair, transparent and sustainable share of the enormous value chain it contributes to so significantly, we will attain that "New Golden Age of Culture and Creativity" in this 21st century.

And as creators we look to you as decision makers here in Europe and everywhere around the world to help us attain this worthy goal.

Thank you

Maureen Duffy*

3.5 Will authors cease to exist? Frightening developments for writers

Good afternoon ladies and gentlemen. This is the last panel of the conference in which we have been discussing the future of authors' rights. It could be argued that as the rights under discussion are those of creators, granted or recognised by the Universal Declaration of Human Rights and codified and sanctioned by the Berne Convention and other national and international treaties and legislation, that the creators should have had the first rather than the last word. However, we are grateful to be given this chance to put our case for the continued need and support for a copyright system that does what was intended by the original Statute of Anne 1709 in the UK: make it possible for creators to continue to do what society requires of them: continue to create.

And I must warn the conference that this is under serious threat if the attempts to undermine the real basis of copyright continue – the creator's right to govern the future of her creation by contract and the exercise of primary rights being continually eroded. In 2005 ALCS, the exclusive writers' CMO in the UK, commissioned research which showed that already median earnings per annum from writing were a mere £ 4,000 per annum, less than a fifth of the median wage, on a survey of 25,000 authors. Last year ALCS initiated a further study[1] which showed that, from even that low base, writers' income had declined by 29% since the previous study.

Furthermore the imbalance between the top earners and those at the bottom has widened, with the latter 50% sharing only 7% of the total earnings between them, while the percentage of those able to make a living from their writing had fallen from 40 to a mere 11%. Recent research by A–N, the visual artists organisation, shows the same dismal result of falling income.[2]

Proposals to replace our primary rights with statutory rights to remuneration will only make creators' lives more difficult. As with Public Lending Right, the amount of compensation/remuneration will be imposed by external authority, not individual negotiation and, as we have seen in the UK in the case of private copying, governments may decide, in pursuit of their own financial policies, that 'damage is minimal' and no compensation is due.

At best statutory licensing with related rights to remuneration is better than nothing but it cannot be a substitute for the exclusive right of authors protected as a Human Right, including of course the droits moraux. Piracy is rife, and

---

* FRSL, Author & President of Honour, British Copyright Council, UK.

1 See http://www.alcs.co.uk/Resources/Research .

2 See https://www.a-n.co.uk/artists-livelihoods.

what I call the corporatisation of culture diminishes the variety of work that has a chance to find its full audience, by a concentration on returns to shareholders reflected in the huge imbalance in the art market and, in publishing, by the concentration on the best seller, all leading to the homogenisation of culture and society itself, under the guise of giving the consumer access to 'the best', and leading to the exponential growth in self/indie publishing as a counter to this.

The UK government's decision not to even grant equitable remuneration, the levy, for private copying while exempting it effectively from copyright law is a dangerous precedent, and at present a judicial review is being sought. If it fails it will be clear to creators in all fields that, as has already happened in Canada,[3] without statutory protection for creators and their work the profession of author, in whatever medium, will no longer be viable and cease to exist.

---

3 See, for ex., http://internationalauthors.org/wp-content/uploads/Canada-Case-Study.pdf and presentations by John Degen from http://internationalauthors.org/events/event/standing-committee-copyright-related-rights/.

Antoon Quaedvlieg*

Conclusions

Dear *Urheberrechtler*,
German intellectual property law has a leading position in Europe. The program of the past two days illustrates the exceptional quality of our guest country in identifying the problems and developing the debate on the issues which matter most for present and future copyright. The abundant harvest of this congress will continue to inspire us for long times ahead.

Almost come to an end, the program now promises the audience a 'Conclusion': a dessert which summarizes the opulent intellectual dishes we enjoyed. This is no easy task. If made brief, it would undervalue many individual contributions; if made more extensive it will place a burden on the exhausted audience.

I will therefore concentrate on the topic brought up by the President of German ALAI on our first day: where should copyright navigate between the traditional '*property approach*' and an alternative '*liability approach*'?

This choice between the philosophy of the traditional system of exclusive rights on the one hand or which departs from a more or less generalized philosophy of reasonable remunerations on the other hand, certainly is a fundamental question, and perhaps one of the most fundamental ones ever brought up at an ALAI congress.

A remuneration system has many advantages:

Every author receives compensation, and compensation will be reasonable. So it will serve authors.

A remuneration system can be built in a way as to encompass all those many uses which according to the present system violate the law and the property right, but which we are unable to stop. Those acts will be decriminalized, which will greatly enhance the public acceptance of copyright law and put an end to the great discrepancies between the law and social practice.

A general remuneration model will therefore guarantee accessibility and serve the interests of users. It will serve society.

But it also might have disadvantages. Let me ask two questions.

Can a generalized remuneration system stimulate innovation?

(a) The first one is whether a generalized statutory system of reasonable remunerations could optimally serve innovation. The question arises because some-

* Professor, Radboud University Nijmegen, Netherlands.

thing fundamental has changed since 1965. The remuneration system for private copies created in the then new German *Urheberrechtsgesetz* was a brilliant idea. But it concerned a private practice at the fringes of the copyright economy. Private copies were hard to make, it took time, one needed expensive devices, one could only make one copy at a time, copies would often be of a sub optimal quality, and it was not possible to easily distribute copies, let alone to share them.

These activities could hardly hurt core industrial interests. And a simple remuneration could repair the damage.

But today we talk about the *digital* private copy. This is not an activity far away from the center of economic interest. The digital reproduction, storage and distribution is the *primary* market; it is the market itself. The private individual is not an innocuous amateur anymore; he is an essential component of the production process serving this primary market, because he can reproduce, store and make available himself.

So this is one: a generalized system of fair remunerations targets the central, the basic, the standard market of the future and indeed of the present moment.

(b) A system of fair remunerations presupposes a model of negotiations between all the stakeholders. These negotiations will be supervised in some form or another by the public authorities: the state.

This means that as far as the price for the use of creative works is concerned, the free market model makes room for a fundamentally different approach, which, if promoted on a more universal scale, injects into copyright the temptations of a guided market economy.

Is that a wise move on a digital information market, where innovation is vital? Innovation results from entrepreneurial initiative in a free, competitive market. Countries striving to be a prominent information economy should create room for those initiatives. Intervention in areas as central as pricing strategy on the core market of the information industry therefore is a step which should not be taken too lightly.

Moreover, although a remuneration system may secure good payment for many authors in a weak bargaining position, it is not as obvious that it will be optimal for all authors, in particular for the best works of the best authors.

A fair remuneration system has an inherent tendency to keep remuneration fair for *users*: a fair price is a low price. Don’t let us forget that the amount of the reasonable remuneration is determined by negotiation mechanisms in which many interested parties are represented. Compromises in such bodies take the form of general political pacts instead of genuinely commercial agreements. Moreover, collective mechanisms are increasingly put under government supervision: a tendency that can be observed on the European as well as on the national level.

Depending on how loud voters will claim cheaper access to works, the already existing downward bias of the fair remuneration might be reinforced. And that would, it should be recalled, not just touch some accessory market, causing some collateral damage, but the primary market.

Could that mean that one important incentive to find and market important new authors and important new works would be weakened? It is difficult to say, because obviously, *other* incentives to offer good quality will continue to exist. It is nevertheless felt that in an information economy, *no* serious incentive to improve quality and innovation should be sacrificed without very careful consideration. In all the cases in which the investment in the quality of works is still primarily determined by the expected return on investment under free pricing mechanisms, the height of those investments may be affected if that system of free pricing is affected.

In short, the choice between either maintaining the free exercise of the exclusive right or steering copyright towards a system of supervised remunerations is so fundamental, that it ultimately compromises the very paradigm on which copyright is built. That choice opposes a free market for the copyright industry and a guided market for consumer information; and to the extent that the latter were to be given more preference, it might cause our legal perception of copyright law as a branch of commercial and economic law to be replaced by an approach based on *public* law principles.

Whether adopting remuneration systems as a more basic or general exploitation model would be viable and desirable therefore is a question which goes beyond the practical implications alone.

(c) Under present European (and national) law, the exclusive right and remuneration systems coexist within one and the same system. Apart from that, even the exercise of the 'free' exclusive right is in many ways limited by the law. That creates a balance, even if that balance is not always very logical.

However, there is a noticeable exception to that balanced system. It concerns works made available on sites protected by TPMs. Article 6 of the Copyright Directive 2001/29 allows to protect works made available to the public online on agreed contractual terms and with TPMs preventing (inter alia) private copying. Under such conditions, *all* exceptions and limitations can be contracted out.

It is surprising that the same digitization development which leads to an ever stronger call for the solution of more or less generalized remuneration systems, is also at the root of this Jurassic Park reserved for wild copyright capitalism. If this experimental rule – if it is one – were to be maintained in the law, it will be hard to explain what justifies the near-collectivization of other exploitation methods. But if it were to be abandoned, online publishing in Europe might lose much of its charm for daring entrepreneurs.

Can the 'liability' model encompass copyright as a whole?

If the statutory remuneration rights system were to be promoted as the general model, it would affect copyright *as a whole*. It would therefore not only concern digital works made available on the internet, but also the traditional printing industry. Logically, it indeed is difficult to see why traditional exploitation methods would have to be exempted from the general rule.

But existing law shows that practice can sometimes be stronger than logic, and that specific creations may in certain cases be spoilt with a more favourable regime. For instance, computer programs are exempted from the private copying exception. Is the public interest in making computer programs freely available less urgent? I guess not, but I also expect that subjecting their use to simple levies or other remuneration systems would meet with very tough resistance.

The same might happen in the domain of industrial design. The democratic movement of the digital revolution now also penetrates this dark kingdom of traditional industry. Three-dimensional copying is coming within the reach of consumers, and with it the perspective of applying the exception for private copying, which will release them from the burden of paying fancy prices for spare parts of damaged articles.

Right owners might then be inclined to vest their hopes in the rules of industrial property or unfair competition, still offering exclusivity where copyright would have abolished it. It might help, but such supplementary protection is not guaranteed. If the legislature rules[1] or if the courts were to find that the general private copying exception was based on an *overriding* public interest, creating an actual *right* for the consumer, the new copyright regime would not only put aside claims to exclusivity based on copyright but also the regimes of other IP laws.

Imagine the position of the car industry – and the numerous industries delivering to them – when millions of happy consumers start to produce those spare parts themselves, paying, for new spare parts of their expensive quality cars, no more than a reasonable remuneration under the umbrella of collectively controlled prices.

That might not happen in Germany, where a wise copyright policy of the legislature and the courts maintained a realistic threshold for copyright protection for products of industrial design, and where consequently, most spare parts fall outside the protected domain. But it will *certainly* happen in Holland, won over for an extremely liberal *unité de l'art* approach and notorious for its stingy consumers.

But more seriously: it is inherent in the public interest justifications at the basis of the remuneration systems that copyright *will* try to export them to

1 As for example in recital (16) of the Computer Program Directive 2009/24/EC of 23 April 2009.

other IP regimes, bringing civil war upon the whole system. Who would win *that* battle?

Suppose that, in view of the industrial interests concerned, the exclusive right philosophy would prevail after all in our case of the spare parts. That would create a clear contradiction, for the consumer would be prevented from making his own copies in a field where he should be entitled to do so *par excellence*: the products of industrial design he acquired for daily use.

That could strengthen apprehensions that remuneration systems are sometimes more readily applied to products of industries considered of less central importance for the core of economy, whereas the holy grail of the exclusive right remains the basis for industries considered as (more) vital. This might be perceived as a vicious thought, as it suggests that political opportunity could replace the rule of law here, and allow discriminating between branches of industry. However, in the skeptic perception that remuneration systems up to some extent inherently show this susceptibility to be arranged according to political priorities, such consequences would not really surprise. Another question is whether that makes good law.

I conclude. A remuneration rights approach may certainly offer advantages. But like the system in place, the exclusive right, it also entails certain risks. One would readily support remuneration systems if they were less susceptible to political whims reducing the amount of the remuneration to levels appreciably below market values. One would more readily support them if they could reassure us that, secondly, the market would not become less attentive at the best creative sparks and that thirdly, that they would be equally applied to all creators and not seek the weakest among them in the first place.

It still remains true, and no one could deny, that the '*liability approach*' could secure at least some equitable remuneration for many authors who otherwise would get none at all. That is an important argument in the enthralling discourse paving the way for a sustainable copyright of the future, in which ALAI has a central function.

We therefore will stay in inspired discussion!

Thank you, German ALAI, for this wonderful congress.

Victor Nabhan*

Discours de clôture – Closing Speech

On a confié à Antoon Quaedvlieg une tâche périlleuse, voire ingrate. On lui a demandé de tirer les conclusions d'un Congrès non traditionnel, et en quelque sorte éclaté: la première journée étant de facture théorique, où les approches étaient divergentes, et la deuxième vouée à l'examen des pratiques contractuelles. Il devait en quelque sorte, et particulièrement pour la première journée, marier l'eau et le feu.

C'est dire que la mission qu'on lui a confiée n'était pas exactement un cadeau, tant s'en faut! Et dans ce dernier cas, c'eût été plutôt un cadeau empoisonné. Mais Antoon avec sa gentillesse et sa modestie, nous a généreusement retourné le cadeau, poison en moins. D'abord en acceptant de relever le défi. Ensuite en le relevant avec brio, de façon élégante, brillante, convaincante. Un grand merci à Antoon pour ses belles conclusions.

A mon tour maintenant, de prononcer les mots de la fin.

J'aimerais d'abord relater un fait historique, qui s'est déroulé en Allemagne, c'était au début du 19eme siècle. Il s'agissait de Goethe. Celui-ci avait l'intention de publier à compte d'auteur ses œuvres complètes (Ausgabe Letzter Hand). Il a dû pour cela faire des demandes auprès des 39 Etats Confédérés, afin d'obtenir de chaque Etat un privilège d'imprimer. Les privilèges lui furent accordés non en tant qu'auteur, mais comme éditeur assumant les risques financiers. De ce privilège dépendait la protection de l'éditeur sur l'œuvre publiée.

Goethe ne manqua pas de s'insurger contre cette situation, et je le cite: "il serait opportun que les plus hautes autorités de l'Etat accordent **à l'auteur et à ses héritiers** un droit régulier de possession, droit justifié par son activité intellectuelle".

Goethe fait référence à un "droit de possession". De nos jours il serait plutôt question d'un droit de "propriété intellectuelle". Ce droit se déclinant en ses 3 éléments d' « usus, fructus et abusus ». En l'occurrence, ce qui importait pour Goethe, c'était bien sûr le "fructus". En d'autres termes, la rémunération.

Et bien, les choses n'ont pas fondamentalement changé depuis. Il est vrai que la Convention de Berne octroie dorénavant des droits de propriété intellectuelle aux auteurs, ab initio, du seul fait de la création. Et que la protection n'est plus sujette à l'octroi d'un privilège par l'Etat. Mais il demeure que de nos jours, comme du temps de Goethe, la question essentielle est toujours celle de savoir si et comment les auteurs vont recueillir les fruits de l'exploitation de leurs œuvres, s'ils vont être adéquatement rémunérés.

* President of ALAI; Professor at Nottingham University.

C'est dire que le thème choisi par le groupe allemand de l'ALAI pour ce Congrès s'adressait au nerf de la guerre, touchait aux préoccupations fondamentales, je dirais même vitales, des auteurs. Il faut donc savoir gré à nos amis allemands de cette heureuse initiative.

Voici donc pour le point de départ.

Mais qu'en est-il à l'arrivée?

Et bien la magie de Bonn, cette ville conviviale et ouverte, a opéré. Le Congrès de Bonn a tenu ses promesses. Tous les ingrédients étaient là pour en assurer la réussite:

Un service d'accueil aimable, courtois, souriant, efficace. Sehr Gut!

Des modérateurs qui ont dirigé les débats avec tact et doigté. Super!

De conférenciers qui nous ont enrichis de leurs connaissances. Einfach Toll!

Et des interprètes d'un grand professionnalisme. Hervorragend!

À tous, un grand merci.

Mais derrière tout cela, il y avait un travail de planification, de conception, d'organisation. Il ya ceux qui ont réuni tous ces éléments en un ensemble cohérent. Je réfère ici au professeur Hilty et à son équipe. À eux aussi, j'exprime notre reconnaissance et nos félicitations! Alles war wirklich perfekt!

Vielleicht sogar noch mehr: Plus-quam-perfekt!

Usually I offer my compliments accompanied with flowers. But this time it will be Champagne. More than amply deserved!

...

Annex 1
Questionnaire and National Reports
Questionnaire et Rapports Nationaux

I. Questionnaire

1. English version

A. Questions in relation to scope and enforcement of exclusive rights under existing law

In many areas, exclusive rights can be exercised and enforced in relation to users either on the basis of license agreements or, in cases of infringements, on the basis of enforcement rules and mechanisms. However, in particular in the internet environment, it may be difficult to identify users, who may be anonymous, so that a license agreement in the first place cannot be concluded and infringements are difficult to pursue. The first set of questions addresses these problematic areas. Since most problems arise in the digital environment, questions focus thereon.

1. How are the following acts covered by the copyright law of your country (statute and case law):
   i. Offering of hyperlinks to works
   ii. Offering of deep links to works
   iii. Framing/embedding of works
   iv. Streaming of works
   v. Download of works
   vi. Upload of works
   vii. Supply of a platform for 'user-generated content'
   viii. Other novel forms of use on the internet.
2. In cases in which there are practical obstacles to the conclusion of licensing agreements, in particular where multiple individual (end) users do not address right owners before using works (eg, users uploading protected content on platforms like Youtube), are there particular clearing mechanisms? In particular, are license agreements possible and practiced with involved third parties, such as platforms, regarding the exploitation acts done by the actual users (e.g., license agreements with the platform operator rather than with the platform users (uploaders))?
3. a) If there is infringement of copyright, in particular of exclusive rights covering the acts listed under 1. above, and the direct infringer cannot be identified or addressed, does your law (including case law) provide

for liability of intermediaries or others for infringement by third persons, namely:
- for content providers
- for host providers
- for access providers
- for others?

b) If so, under what conditions are they liable, and for what (in particular, damages, information on the direct infringer, information on the scope of infringement to estimate the amount of damage)?

4. In these cases of infringement, who has standing to sue:
   - the author
   - the exclusive licensee
   - the non-exclusive licensee
   - the employer of the author
   - the CMO that manages the exclusive right?

B. Questions regarding mechanisms to ensure adequate remuneration for creators and performers in their relationship with licensees

If authors and performers exercise their exclusive rights by licensing them to exploitation businesses, such as publishers, the question arises how they best may ensure an adequate remuneration from such licenses.

1. Does your law provide for legal rules, including by case law, on mechanisms for authors and performers to ensure an adequate remuneration in relation to exploitation businesses in the following cases:
   - as a general rule for all kinds of contracts;
   - as regards 'best-seller' situations (i.e., when parties did not presume that the work would become a best-seller);
   - in the case of oppressive contracts;
   - in other cases;

   and if so, under what conditions?
2. If your law provides for rules as addressed under B. 1. above, does the law determine the percentage of the income from exploitation to be received by authors and performers, or does it otherwise specify the amount of remuneration?
3. Please indicate also whether these mechanisms that are addressed under B. 1. and 2. above are efficient in practice.

C. Questions in relation to statutory remuneration rights

The questions below concern the question of the scope of remuneration rights and their enforcement (which usually takes place through collective management organizations (CMOs)) towards users.

1. In which cases do statutory remuneration rights exist in your country, e.g., public lending rights, resale rights, remuneration rights for private copying, or others (often, they are provided in the context with limitations of rights)?
2. Is there the possibility of obtaining compulsory licenses, and if so, under what conditions and for what categories of works?
3. i. For which statutory remuneration rights does your law provide for obligatory collective management?
   ii. For which statutory remuneration rights does your law not provide for obligatory collective management, but in practice, the right is managed by a CMO?
   iii. Who has to pay the remuneration regarding each of these statutory remuneration rights – the user, a third person (e.g., a copy shop or a manufacturer of a copying equipment and devices) or a tax payer (through money allocated from the public budget)?
   iv. How is the tariff / the remuneration for each of these remuneration rights fixed (in particular, by contract, by law, by a Commission, etc.)?
   v. Is there supervision of CMOs regarding tariffs, and if so, what are the criteria for supervision?
   vi. What problems exist when right holders assert the statutory remuneration right in relation to users or others who are obliged to pay the remuneration (e.g., a claim is rejected and results in long legal proceedings; those who are obliged to pay in the meantime go bankrupt, etc.)?
   vii. If problems to assert the remuneration exist, does your law provide for any solutions to these problems (e.g., an obligation to deposit a certain amount in a neutral account)?

D. Mechanisms to ensure adequate remuneration for creators and performers

The questions below address the issue of existing mechanisms, in particular within CMOs, to ensure that authors and performers, also in relation to exploitation businesses such as publishers and phonogram producers, receive an adequate remuneration.

1. In respect of the statutory remuneration rights under your law, does the law determine the percentage of the collected remuneration to be received by

particular groups of right owners (e.g., the allocation between authors and producers, among different kinds of authors, performers, and producers, et al.)?

2. If so, what percentages are fixed by the law? Are these percentages different for different statutory remuneration rights?
3. If there are no such legal determinations, how are the percentages or the otherwise fixed distribution keys for the different rights of remuneration determined in practice (in particular, by which decision-making procedures and by whom are these distribution keys determined inside CMOs)? Which percentages are in practice applied?
4. If owners of derived rights (such as publishers who derived the rights from their authors) transfer these derived statutory remuneration rights to a CMO, how and on the basis of which agreement is the remuneration distributed between them in this case?
5. Which mechanisms of supervision exist in your country to control the distribution keys applied by CMOs, if any?

E. Questions on new business models and their legal assessment

1. Which new business models do you know in your country in respect of the supply of works via the internet?
   Please list such business models, such as Spotify, Netflix, etc., and describe them briefly.
2. Which of these business models have raised legal problems, which are, or have been, dealt with by courts? If there have been problems, please describe them and the solutions found
3. In your country, are there offers that are based on flat rates, 'pay-per-click' or on other micro-payment models? Please indicate how popular (frequently offered or used) each of these models is.
4. Within these business models, how do authors and performers get paid?

2. Version française

A. Questions quant à l'étendue et à la mise en œuvre des droits exclusifs en droit positif

Dans beaucoup de domaines, les droits exclusifs peuvent être exercés et mis en œuvre en relation avec les utilisateurs soit sur la base de contrats de licence, soit en cas de contrefaçon sur la base de règles et de mécanismes de mise en œuvre judiciaire. Cependant, en particulier dans l'environnement d'internet, il peut être difficile d'identifier les utilisateurs, possiblement anonymes, si bien que d'abord la conclusion d'un contrat de licence est impossible, mais aussi la poursuite des contrefacteurs est rendue ardue. Le premier groupe de questions se penche sur ces problèmes. Puisque la plupart des problèmes surviennent dans l'environnement numérique, ces questions se concentrent sur ce domaine.

1. Comment les actes suivants sont-ils couverts par le droit d'auteur dans votre pays (selon la loi et la jurisprudence) ?:
   i. Offre de hyperliens à des oeuvres
   ii. Offre de *deep links* à des oeuvres
   iii. *Framing/embedding* d'oeuvres
   iv. *Streaming* d'oeuvres
   v. Téléchargement descendent (*download*) d'oeuvres
   vi. Téléchargement ascendent (*upload*) d'oeuvres
   vii. Fourniture d'une plateforme pour du *'user-generated content'*
   viii. Autres nouvelles utilisations sur internet
2. Lorsque des obstacles pratiques empêchent la conclusion de contrats de licence, en particulier quand de multiples utilisateurs individuels (et finaux) ne s'adressent pas aux ayants droit avant d'utiliser les œuvres (par exemple, les utilisateurs ont mis en ligne des oeuvres et des prestations protégées sur une plateforme comme Youtube), y-a-t-il des mécanismes particuliers pour liciter l'utilisation ("des mécanismes de clearing")? Est-ce que, en particulier, des accords de licence sont possibles et pratiqués avec des parties tierces impliquées, telles que des plateformes, à propos d'actes d'exploitation commis par les réels utilisateurs de la plateforme (tels que les téléchargeurs/*uploaders*)?
3. a) Lorsqu'il y a une contrefaçon de droit d'auteur, notamment de droits exclusifs couvrant les actes énoncés sous 1 ci-dessus, et que le contrefacteur direct ne peut pas être identifié ou contacté, votre droit (y compris la jurisprudence) prévoit il la responsabilité d'intermédiaires ou d'autres pour une contrefaçon commise par un tiers, c'est-à-dire:
   - pour les fournisseurs de contenu
   - pour l'hébergeur

  - pour le fournisseur d'accès
  - pour d'autres?

b) Dans ce cas, quelles sont les conditions de la responsabilité, et à quoi le tiers est-il tenu (notamment, à la réparation des dommages, ou à fournir des informations sur le contrefacteur direct ou des informations sur l'étendue de la violation afin d'estimer le préjudice)?

4. Dans ces cas de contrefaçon, qui peut ester en justice:
   - l'auteur
   - le titulaire d'une licence exclusive
   - le titulaire d'une licence non-exclusive
   - l'employeur de l'auteur
   - la société de gestion collective qui gère ce droit?

B. Questions à propos des mécanismes pour la rémunération appropriée des créateurs et des artistes interprètes dans leurs relations avec des licenciés

Si les auteurs et les artistes interprètes exercent leurs droits exclusifs en en donnant licence à des entreprises d'exploitation, telles que des éditeurs, la question se pose de la meilleure manière pour garantir une rémunération appropriée par ces licences.

1. Votre droit prévoit-il des règles juridiques, dont la jurisprudence, sur les mécanismes assurant une rémunération appropriée des auteurs et des artistes interprètes en relation avec les entreprises d'exploitation dans les cas suivants:
   - une règle générale concernant tout type de contrat;
   - une règle concernant les situations de *best sellers* (ie. quand les parties ne pouvaient pas prévoir le succès de l'œuvre);
   - en cas de contrats léonins;
   - en d'autres cas;

   et le cas échéant, à quelles conditions?
2. Si votre droit prévoit des règles telles que celles mentionnées au B.1 ci-dessus, la loi détermine-t-elle le pourcentage des revenus de l'exploitation à verser aux auteurs et aux artistes interprètes, ou spécifie–t-elle autrement le montant de la rémunération?
3. Indiquez si des mécanismes mentionnés au B.1 et 2 ci-dessus sont efficaces en pratique.

C. Questions à propos des droits légaux à rémunération

Les questions suivantes concernent l'étendue des droits à rémunération et leur mise en œuvre (généralement par le biais d'une société de gestion collective) à l'égard des utilisateurs.

1. Dans quels cas existe-t-il dans votre pays des droits légaux à rémunération, par exemple le droit de prêt public, le droit de suite, la rémunération pour copie privée, ou d'autres (ils sont souvent prévus dans le contexte de limitations aux droits)?
2. Est-il possible d'obtenir une licence obligatoire, et le cas échéant, à quelles conditions et pour quelles catégories d'œuvres?
3. i. Pour quels droits à rémunération votre droit prévoit-il une gestion collective obligatoire?
   ii. Pour quels droits à rémunération votre droit ne prévoit-il pas de gestion collective obligatoire, mais en pratique, le droit est géré par une société de gestion collective?
   iii. Qui doit payer la rémunération découlant de chacun de ces droits légaux à rémunération – l'utilisateur, un tiers (par exemple une officine de photocopies, un fabricant d'équipements de copie) ou le contribuable (par le biais d'un financement par le budget public)?
   iv. Comment le tarif est-il / comment la rémunération est-elle fixé(e) pour chacun de ces droits à rémunération (en particulier : contractuellement, légalement, par une commission, etc.)?
   v. Les sociétés de gestion collective sont-elles surveillées à propos des tarifs, et le cas échéant, quels sont les critères du contrôle?
   vi. Quels problèmes surviennent lorsque les ayants droit font valoir leurs droits légaux à rémunération contre des utilisateurs ou d'autres qui sont obligés de payer la rémunération (par exemple, une demande de paiement est contestée et donne lieu à une longue procédure pendant laquelle le débiteur peut faire faillite, etc.)?
   vii. Lorsque des problèmes pour recouvrer les paiements des droits légaux à rémunération existent, votre droit prévoit-il des solutions à ces problèmes (par exemple, une obligation de verser une certaine somme en garantie sur un compte neutre)?

D. Mécanismes pour garantir une rémunération des créateurs et des artistes interprètes

Les questions suivantes concernent les mécanismes existants, en particulier au sein des sociétés de gestion collective, pour garantir que les auteurs et les artistes interprètes reçoivent une rémunération appropriée, aussi à l'égard des entreprises d'exploitation telles que les éditeurs ou les producteurs de phonogrammes.

1. Concernant les droits légaux à rémunération prévus par votre droit, la loi ou des textes règlementaires déterminent-ils le pourcentage des revenus perçus à verser à un groupe particulier de titulaires de droit (par exemple, la répartition entre auteurs et producteurs, entre différents types d'auteurs, d'artistes interprètes, de producteurs etc.)?
2. Le cas échéant, quels pourcentages la loi ou des textes règlementaires fixent-ils? Ces pourcentages varient-ils selon le droit légal à rémunération concerné?
3. En l'absence de telles fixations légales, comment les pourcentages ou les clés de répartition fixées autrement sont-ils déterminés en pratique pour les différents droits à rémunération (notamment, par quels processus de décision et par qui sont déterminées ces clés de répartition au sein des sociétés de gestion collective)? Quels sont les pourcentages appliqués en pratique?
4. Si les titulaires de droits dérivés (tels que les éditeurs qui ont des droits dérivés de ceux de leurs auteurs) transfèrent ces droits légaux à rémunération à une société de gestion collective, comment et sur la base de quelle convention la rémunération leur est-elle versée dans ce cas?
5. Quels mécanismes de contrôle existent-ils dans votre pays pour superviser les clés de répartition appliquées par les sociétés de gestion collective, s'il en existe?

E. Questions sur les nouveaux modèles économiques et leur statut juridique

1. Quels nouveaux modèles économiques connaissez-vous dans votre pays pour la fourniture / l'offre d'œuvres sur internet?
   Veuillez établir une liste de ces modèles économiques, (tels que Spotify, Netflix, etc.), et les décrire brièvement.
2. Le(s)quel(s) de ces modèles économiques ont posé des problèmes juridiques, qui sont, ou ont été, traités par les juges? S'il y en a eu, veuillez décrire les problèmes et les solutions apportées.
3. Y-a-t-il dans votre pays des offres qui sont basées sur des forfaits, des paiements au clic (*pay per click*) ou d'autres modèles de micro-paiement? Veuillez indiquer la popularité de chacun de ces modèles du point de vue des offrants et des utilisateurs.
4. Dans le cadre de ces modèles économiques, comment les auteurs et les artistes-interprètes sont rémunérés ?

II. Overview of national reports/Vue d'ensemble des rapports nationaux

Le texte des rapports nationaux mentionnés ci-dessous est disponible sur le site suivant: http://alai2015.org/en/national-reports.html.

The text of the national reports mentioned below is available on the following website: http://alai2015.org/en/national-reports.html.

- Argentina – by Alejo Barrenechea and Pablo Wegbrait;
- Austria – by Michel Walter;
- Belgium – by Sebastian Witmeur ;
- Canada – by Catherine Bergeron, Gaëlle Beauregard, Jean-Philippe Paré, Ysolde Gendreau and Madeleine Lamothe-Samson;
- Croatia – by Marko Jurić, Katarina Matanovac Furić and Tihomir Katulić;
- Egypt – by Yasser Omar Amine;
- Finland – by Rainer Oesch, Petteri Günther and Taina Pihlajarinne;
- France – by Tristan Azzi, Nicolas Binctin, Anne-Charlotte Jeancard, Florence-Marie Piriou, Virginie Tabary and Gilles Vercken;
- Greece – by Dionysia Kallinikou, Sylvia Stavridou and Anna Despotidou;
- Germany – by Claudius Pflüger and Victor Struppler;
- Hungary – by Gábor Faludi, Mihály Ficsor, Péter Mezei, Alexandra Molnár, András Szinger, Pál Tomori;
- Israel – by Tony Greenman;
- Italy – by Stefania Ercolani;
- Japan – by Satoshi Watanabe;
- Mexico – by Ricardo Larrea and Luis Schmidt;
- Netherlands – by Emilie Kannekens, Saba Sluiter, Olivia Salamanca and Mireille van Eechoud;
- Norway – by Astri M. Lund;
- Portugal – by Victor Castro Rosa;
- Spain – by Ramón Casas Vallés, Raquel Evangelio Llorca, Sebastián López Maza, Patricia Riera Barsallo, Rafael Sánchez Aristi and Nerea Sanjuán Rodríguez;
- Switzerland – by Vincent Salvadé and Ivan Cherpillod
- United Kingdom – by Gillian Davies, Gaetano Dimita, Stephen Edwards, Maria Mercedes Frabboni, Florian Koempel and Uma Suthersanen;
- United States of America – by Bart M.J. Szewczyk and June M. Besek.

Annex 2
RESOLUTION FOLLOWING THE 2015 BONN CONGRESS OF ALAI
concerning proposals to base the exploitation right on a comprehensive system of remunerations

In its September 14, 2016 meeting in Rome the Executive Committee of The International Literary and Artistic Association (l'Association Litteraire et Artistique Internationale – ALAI), has unanimously adopted a resolution, following the Congress of ALAI of June 18–19, 2015 in Bonn:

The Executive Committee,

Stating

That ALAI devoted its congress of 2015 to the subject of 'the remuneration for the use of works';

That it is a basic principle of the system of copyright universally in place and laid down in the international treaties, that authors and other copyright owners are free to negotiate the best conditions for the use of works by consumers and intermediaries on the basis of licensing their exclusive rights, including the best price;

That this is only different where, within the limits allowed by the international treaties, certain statutory exceptions and limitations to the exclusive right apply, which allow the use of the work on the condition of the payment of a remuneration;

That proposals are raised to replace copyright's primary basis in the private law model of an exclusive right by a generalized system of exceptions and reasonable remunerations;

That these find their basis in a strong favour for rules which allow consumers an easy and large access to cultural production, making it possible for them to take full advantage of digital means of storage, distribution and adaptation ;

That some are also driven by a desire to arrive at effective statutory guarantees realizing the fair remuneration of authors, as it is believed that a system of remunerations would secure better rewards for most of them;

Considering

That ALAI fully supports efforts leading to an improved contractual and pecuniary situation of authors;

That ALAI welcomes the aim of helping to make authors better known with the public and their work more widely accessible;

Considering however

That, especially where it concerns the exploitation of works on primary markets, proposals to replace the exclusive right by an approach based on a global license system call for caution;

That there is no promise that remuneration systems will create a better balance between authors, exploiters and consumers, guarantee a proper reward and preserve strong incentives to foster a flourishing market for creativity and creative products;

That remuneration systems, if based on governmental tariffs instead of the rules of offer and demand, create room for lobbying and bureaucracy and make the authors and creative industry as a whole more dependent on the government; that stake holders placed relatively far from the relevant market mechanisms might be led to exert downward pressure on prices, and that an excess of administrative formalities could stifle entrepreneurial initiative;

That rate-setting by the State almost invariably leads to a depressive effect on the development of market license mechanisms and on the level of remuneration; that generalizing this solution will create a chilling effect on material and non material investments by parties who act as vital intermediaries between the author and his public, in discovering new talents, creating new content for new media, and enhancing the quality of cultural information products;

That the principle of exclusive rights has proven its eminent value as a basis for establishing and fostering a flourishing market for culture and information, and that it consequently should be retained as the indispensable principal form of right;

Recalls and reconfirms

its resolution unanimously adopted at its January 14, 2006 session, in light of the deliberations in the French legislative assembly concerning the transposition of the European Union Directive of 22 May 2001, and particularly with regard to the proposal of amendments to adopt a system of obligatory collective management under the name of a "global license" in which it was stated as follows:

> Whereas the fundamental rule of copyright, according to the international treaties, is the exclusive right of the author to decide on the principle and the manner of dissemination of the work of authorship, and
>
> Whereas the diminution of exclusive rights is authorized only to the extent set out by those treaties,
>
> Recalls firmly therefore that, beyond the limits expressly provided by the international instruments, any modification of copyright laws, whatever its form or its label, whose result would be to deprive authors of the effective exercise of their exclusive rights is contrary to the spirit and the letter of the international agreements.

Therefore, calls for

Utmost circumspection with regard to every proposal to replace copyright's primary basis in the private law model of an exclusive right by models based on statutory remunerations.

On the understanding that

Any limitation of an exclusive right to a mere right to remuneration should be in accordance with the three-step test under the international treaties and the European Union directives, in a way, however, that in the application of the test, the legitimate interests of authors as original owners of rights, should be taken into account as a decisive factor.

Annex 2
Résolution à la suite du congrès de l'ALAI tenu en 2015 à Bonn concernant certaines propositions visant à baser les droits d'exploitation sur un système global de rémunérations

Le Comité Exécutif de l'Association Littéraire et Artistique Internationale (ALAI), lors de sa réunion à Rome du 14 septembre 2016, a adopté à l'unanimité la résolution suivante qui fait suite aux résultats du congrès de Bonn de l'ALAI, tenu du 18 au 19 juin 2015 :

Le Comité Exécutif,

Constatant

Que ALAI a consacré son congrès de 2015 au sujet de « la rémunération de l'utilisation des œuvres » ;

Qu'un principe fondamental du système du droit d'auteur universellement reconnu et contenu dans les traités internationaux consiste en la liberté des auteurs et des autres ayants droit du droit d'auteur de négocier par voie de licences basées sur leurs droits exclusifs, les meilleures conditions, y compris le meilleur prix, pour l'utilisation des œuvres par les consommateurs et les intermédiaires ;

Que cette situation est différente seulement lorsque, dans les limites permises par les traités internationaux, certaines exceptions et limitations légales des droits exclusifs s'appliquent permettant l'usage des œuvres sous condition de paiement d'une rémunération ;

Que des propositions ont été avancées visant à remplacer le modèle primaire en droit privé du droit d'auteur fondé sur un droit exclusif par un système général d'exceptions et de rémunérations raisonnables ;

Que ces propositions montrent une préférence marquée pour une réglementation permettant un accès facile et large à la production culturelle aux consommateurs, qui seraient mis en mesure ainsi de tirer pleinement profit des moyens numériques de mise en mémoire, de distribution et d'adaptation ;

Que certains sont également animés par le désir d'instaurer ainsi les garanties légales nécessaires à une juste rémunération des auteurs, croyant que la majorité d'entre eux serait mieux rémunérée par un pareil système ;

Considérant

Que l'ALAI soutient pleinement tous les efforts qui pourraient mener à une meilleure situation contractuelle et pécuniaire des auteurs ;

Que l'ALAI se félicite des efforts entrepris pour promouvoir la notoriété des auteurs et la diffusion de leurs œuvres auprès du public ;

Considérant toutefois

Que, particulièrement dans le cas d'une exploitation sur un marché primaire, les propositions visant à remplacer le droit exclusif par un système de licence globale appellent la prudence ;

Qu'il n'existe point de garantie que ces systèmes de rémunération réaliseraient un meilleur équilibre entre les auteurs, les exploitants et les consommateurs, pour assurer une rémunération convenable et stimuler un marché prospère de la créativité et de ses produits ;

Que, dans la mesure où ces systèmes, quittant les règles de l'offre et de la demande, iraient s'insérer dans un ensemble de tarifications gouvernementales, risquent de favoriser le lobbying et la bureaucratie, rendant ainsi les auteurs et l'industrie culturelle dépendants des autorités ; qu'il serait à craindre que des acteurs assez éloignés du marché concerné s'emploieraient à faire baisser les prix et qu'un excès de formalités administratives irait étouffer la volonté d'entreprendre ;

Que la fixation de tarifs par l'État exerce un effet dépressif sur les mécanismes de licences sur le marché et sur le montant des rémunérations ; que la généralisation de pareille solution risque de décourager les intermédiaires qui, par leurs investissements matériels et immatériels, forment le chaînon indispensable pour la découverte de nouveaux talents et pour l'enrichissement qualitatif des produits culturels ;

Que le principe de l'exclusivité des droits a fait ses preuves dans l'instauration et le développement d'un marché performant de la culture et de l'information, faisant figure ainsi d'un outil indispensable ;

Rappelle et reconfirme

sa résolution du 14 janvier 2006 par laquelle, au vu des travaux législatifs français relatifs à la transposition de la directive communautaire du 22 mai 2001, et notamment au regard des amendements proposés en vue de l'adoption d'un système de gestion collective obligatoire sous le nom de « licence globale », elle avait adopté la résolution suivante :

Considérant que la règle fondamentale du droit d'auteur est, selon les textes internationaux, le droit exclusif de décider du principe et des modalités de diffusion de l'œuvre ; et

Considérant que l'amoindrissement du droit exclusif n'est autorisé que dans le cadre des exceptions prévues par ces textes ;

Rappelle fermement que tout aménagement légal du droit d'auteur, quels qu'en soient la forme ou l'intitulé, dont le résultat serait de priver les auteurs de l'exercice effectif de leurs droits exclusifs en dehors des limites expressément autorisées est contraire à l'esprit et à la lettre des textes internationaux.

Appelle dès lors

A la plus grande prudence vis-à-vis de toute proposition qui vise à remplacer le modèle primaire en droit privé du droit d'auteur fondé sur un droit exclusif par un système de rémunérations légales.

Étant entendu que

Toute réduction d'un droit exclusif à un simple droit à rémunération devrait être soumise au triple test issu des conventions internationales et du droit de l'Union européenne, tenant compte en tant que facteur décisif des intérêts légitimes des auteurs comme titulaires originaires de droits.

FSC
www.fsc.org
MIX
Papier | Fördert gute Waldnutzung
FSC® C083411

Kolibri 360 GmbH
Ferdinand-Jühlke-Straße 7
99095 Erfurt, Deutschland
produktsicherheit@kolibri360.de